The Mexican American

The Mexican American

CHURCH VIEWS
OF THE
MEXICAN AMERICAN

ARNO PRESS
A New York Times Company
New York — 1974

Reprint Edition 1974 by Arno Press Inc.

The Latin Immigrant in the South was
   reprinted from a copy in The Garrett
   Theological Seminary Library
From Over the Border was reprinted from
   a copy in The State Historical Society
   of Wisconsin Library
The Mexican in Chicago was reprinted from
   a copy in The University of Illinois Library
Spanish-Speaking Americans was reprinted from
   a copy in The Church Divinity School of the
   Pacific Library

THE MEXICAN AMERICAN
ISBN for complete set: 0-405-05670-2
See last pages of this volume for titles.

Manufactured in the United States of America

Library of Congress Cataloging in Publication Data
Main entry under title:

Church views of the Mexican American.

   (The Mexican American)
   CONTENTS: Clark, E. T. The Latin immigrant in the
South.—McLean, R. N. and Thomson, C. A. Spanish and
Mexican in Colorado.—McCombs, V. M. From over the
border. [etc.]
   1. Mexican Americans—Collected works. 2. Mis-
sions to Mexican Americans—Collected works. I. Series
E184.M5C48   917.3'06'6872   73-14198
ISBN 0-405-05672-9

CONTENTS

INTRODUCTION

The Mexican American has been the target of a constant interfaith struggle. Although overwhelmingly Catholic—by both historical, traditional and contemporary commitment—Chicanos have been the object of vigorous and often successful conversion efforts by other churches. One of the by-products of this process has been a revealing multi-church literature on the Mexican American.

This anthology—*Church Views of the Mexican American*—brings together selections covering thirty-five years of church writings. These selections represent the efforts of such groups as the Board of National Missions of the Presbyterian Church, the Comity Commission of the Chicago Church Federation, the Council of Women for Home Missions, the Missionary Education Movement, the Presbyterian Woman's Synodical of Texas, and the Home Missions Division of the National Council of Churches of Christ. The selections also reflect the long-term existence of missionary interest in the Mexican as a prime target for church social services, conversion efforts, and "Americanization" programs.

The various books offer sharp contrasts. Some are subtle, perceptive, and sympathetic; others are ethnocentric, paternalistic, and insensitive. Some provide a sweeping view of the Mexican American throughout the United States; others concentrate on specific locales, such as Chicago, Colorado, and Texas. Some focus on Mexicans per se; others view Mexicans within a framework of "Spanish-Speaking Americans" or "Latin Immigrants." Yet throughout this diverse collection runs a unifying thread—the complexity of the relationship between Mexican Americans and U.S. churches, a complexity which continues to defy clear understanding.

Dr. Carlos E. Cortes
University of California,
Riverside

THE LATIN IMMIGRANT IN THE SOUTH

Published under the auspices of the Home Department of the Board of Missions, Methodist Episcopal Church, South

The Homeland Series, Number Three

The Latin Immigrant in the South

By

ELMER T. CLARK

Reprinted from "Healing Ourselves, the First Task of the
Church in America"

THE COKESBURY PRESS

NASHVILLE   DALLAS   RICHMOND   SAN FRANCISCO

CONTENTS.

(5)

The Latin Immigrant in the South

I.

A NATION OF IMMIGRANTS.

MAN is a migratory animal. History is largely a record of his rovings to and fro upon the face of the earth, driven by the triple forces of economic necessity, political oppression, and religious persecution. Few lands are now controlled by descendants of the original inhabitants, so universal have been the migrations. Some peoples even to-day have no homes of their own. The Jews live everywhere under the flags of other men, and the Gypsies, leaving the Indian Peninsula about the thirteenth century, have been roving ever since.

The character of our present civilization has been largely determined by the great modern migrations, for these movements were not all in the past. Some of the most significant of them occurred in comparatively recent times, and the mightiest, perhaps, of all history is now in process. In connection with the discovery and exploration of new lands in the modern period, an era of colonization swept Europeans broadcast and brought under their dominion the vast reaches of Africa, North America, parts of Asia, and the islands of the sea. Following the era of colonization the modern immigration movement set in. Multiplied millions of people left their homes in Europe and migrated to other parts of the world, particularly to the United States, thus creating the immigrant problem.

But before entering upon a discussion of this problem we should pause and reflect upon the patent fact that all Americans, save only the Indians, are immigrants and their children. None of us, not even those who proudly trace back to the "first families," are far removed from immigrant parents who came to these shores for exactly the same reasons which impel the Italians and Mexicans who are now coming. Our forefathers possessed no more wealth when they arrived here than the immigrants to-day carry in their rude packs. If the newly arrived foreigner lives in an adobe hut or an unsightly tenement, our own parents a few generations ago lived in log cabins quite as humble. In truth, we all came from the same pit, the chief difference between us being in the chronology of the digging. When, therefore, we study the immigrant problem we are studying a human problem, one in which our own fathers were once involved. Sympathy and charity are, therefore, incumbent upon us.

The only "native American" is the Indian. We are a nation of people contributed by other nations. Three great motives drew us together: the necessity of securing economic independence or "making a living"; the desire to escape from political tyranny and secure liberty; the desire to avoid persecution on account of religious faith and to obtain freedom to worship God according to the dictates of the conscience. These are the impelling causes of all migrations, and it is our glory, shared by few other lands, that these motives have drawn and still draw multiplied millions to us, but have never driven a single individual from us.

There are 94,820,915 white people in the United States,[1] this being 89.7% of the entire population. In this number there are 13,712,754 foreign-born persons and 22,686,204 persons of foreign or mixed parentage. Thus we have in our midst 46,398,958 white persons who may properly be called immigrants, and it is rather startling to realize that this is nearly one-half of all the white people in the country.

This situation is by no means unusual; on the other hand, it is customary and has been constant for many years. In 1900 the native whites born of native parents in the United States constituted only 53.8% and in 1920 only 55.3%. Our country, then, always has nearly as many of the immigrant class as of those whose parents were native born.

A study of the nearly 14,000,000 foreign-born whites in our population shows that the Germans and Italians predominate, the Russians, Poles, and Irish following in the order named. Each of these nationalities has given us more than a million inhabitants who are now living. The largest number of immigrants are found in New York, where there are nearly three million foreign born, and in Pennsylvania, Illinois, and Massachusetts, each of which has more than a million. Yet they are scattered everywhere. Only the distinctly Southern States of Arkansas, Tennessee, North Carolina, South Carolina, Georgia, Alabama, and Mississippi have less

---

[1] All these statistics are from the 1920 census.

than 1% of foreign-born elements in their population.

New York City is a foreign city, though the metropolis of America. Of a total population of 5,620,048, only 1,164,834, or about one-fifth, are white persons born of native parents. Since there are comparatively few Negroes, less than 2% of the total, and when we consider the Asiatics, all of whom are foreigners, we find that nearly 80% of the inhabitants of New York City belong to what may be called the immigrant group. Few Americans have realized this fact, nor have they fully appreciated the potential, if not actual, menace of this situation.

The immigrant groups in our country constitute at once our greatest liability and our greatest asset. They furnish the radicals, the agitators, and the atheists. The Black Hand and the "Tong Wars" are their products. They provide a goodly proportion of our criminals, our paupers, and our diseased. They contribute to our political corruption and instability. They not infrequently injure our laboring men by serving as strike breakers and lowering wages and the standard of living.

On the other hand, the value of the contributions they have made and are making to our social life cannot be estimated. From the humble homes of immigrants have come some of our greatest and most trusted leaders. Their sons fought valiantly for our ideals in the World War. The labor of their hands, often at tasks the American shuns, is one of our greatest industrial assets.

There are more Italians in America than any

other foreign group save the Germans, the total number being 1,610,109, or 11% of all the foreign born. Since these figures represent only those actually born in Italy, and since Italian families are three time as large as American,[1] it is apparent that we have with us a much larger number who are properly in the Italian immigrant class. In 1917 it was estimated by Prof. Mangano[2] that there were in the United States 3,500,000 Italians.

While most of the Italians live in the New England, Middle Atlantic, and East North Central States, there are multitudes in the South, Southwest, and West. California has 88,502, Louisiana has 16,264, Texas has 8,024, Florida has 4,745, and Alabama has 2,732. In Missouri, which we include in our present survey, there are 14,609. Altogether, in the territory occupied by the Methodist Episcopal Church, South, there are 211,370 foreign-born Italians, to which large number should be added those who are Italians in all characteristics, though born in this country of foreign or mixed parents.

Before the enactment of the limited quota Immigration Act in 1921, Italians were coming to our shores at the rate of nearly a quarter of a million annually. The new law limited immigration from each nation to 2% of the foreign born of such nationality already in this country and provided that not more than 20% of the annual quota could be admitted in any one month. Under the statute the Italian quota was completely filled the first

---

[1] Rose, *The Italians in America*, page 68.
[2] *Religious Work among Italians in America*, page 5.

year; 42,149 were admitted during the year 1921-22 against a quota of 42,057, the number above the quota being those returning from visits to the homeland and persons admitted because their exclusion would have caused undue hardship and suffering. This number represents a decrease of about 180,000 in comparison with the figures of the previous year.

During the fiscal year of 1921-22, 63,647 Italians returned to Italy, this being a decrease in returns of 21,235. The operation of the new law, therefore, has immediately reduced the number of Italians in this country; the reduction is more apparent than real, however, because most of those leaving America soon return, and, returning, are not counted against the Italian quota.

Of the 42,149 immigrants who entered the United States from Italy only 7,777 were professional men and skilled workers; 34,372 were farm laborers, common laborers, servants, and persons, including women and children, having no occupation. Thus the vast majority of our Italians are laborers. This is due largely to the fact that skilled Italians are not needed in this country and find no demand for their services, while common laborers are eagerly sought.

II.

THE ITALIAN IN HIS HOMELAND.

In order to understand the Italian in America it is necessary to know something of the environment from which he came. It has been said that Italy leaped from the Middle Ages to the twentieth century at a single bound. This land had no unity, no real nationality, until the middle of the nineteenth century, when the armies of Garibaldi broke the temporal power of the pope and delivered the government to the people. Italy is, therefore, a backward nation, and while great strides have been made in recent years, primitive conditions still prevail in a large degree among the lower classes, especially in the southern provinces.

In studying the problem of Italian immigrants it is important to bear in mind the great difference between the Northern and Southern sections of Italy. In the north lies the great and fairly fertile valley of the Po, and here agriculture is more advanced and profitable. Here also are the great factories and industrial centers, and the industrial workers are organized and secure better wages than their brothers in the south. The climate is more healthful and productive of a vigorous type of manhood. There are better educational facilities, and the percentage of illiteracy is relatively low. From Northern Italy, therefore, comes a more intelligent, virile, and skilled worker than from any other section.

Southern Italy, including the Island of Sicily, differs materially from the north. It has always been a rural section, often devastated, and always priest-ridden. Wars ravaged the land through long ages, and the people became isolated, ignorant, and frequently barbaric. Its misgovernment became so notorious just before the unification of Italy that Gladstone referred to the rule of the Bourbons in Naples and Sicily as "the negation of God." Here the lack of rainfall in the summer months renders efficient and profitable agriculture impossible, and since there has been little industrial development, the position of the lower class is miserable.

As might be expected in such a situation, the percentage of illiteracy among the southern Italians is appallingly high. Throughout the whole of Italy 37.6% of the population above six years of age were unable to read or write in 1911. In 1917 it was estimated that Italy contained 7,000,000 illiterates. It is significant to note that in the most northern province of Piedmont only 11% of the people are illiterate, while in southern Calabria the rate is 70%. In the southern province of Abruzzi the illiterates are 58% of the whole population above six years of age, in Sicily they number 58%, and in Basilicata 65%.

The abject condition of southern Italians is important for us because it is from that section that we receive the bulk of our immigrants. During the first half of the nineteenth century immigration from the south was prohibited, but since these provinces became an integral part of United Italy they have sent their sons to our shores in mighty streams. We are now receiving six times as many immigrants from the south as from the north of Italy; of the

YOUNG MEXICAN GIRLS, STUDENTS IN VALLEY INSTITUTE, PHARR, TEX.

VALLEY INSTITUTE FOR MEXICAN GIRLS, PHARR, TEX

(15)

42,149 admitted in 1921-22, only 6,000 were from the north. From July, 1922, to May, 1923, our authorities at Ellis Island admitted 8,854 northern Italians, and 37,991 from the south.

America is thus the haven for the most needy class of Italians, driven here by the stern demands of economic necessity. From the standpoint of their contribution to us they are the least desirable of all Italians, but from the standpoint of our service to them they are the most desirable. From these humble and suffering folk we are likely to obtain an erroneous impression of Italians in general, and it is constantly necessary to remind oursleves that we are here to minister rather than be ministered unto, and that sunny Italy has not only produced these poor "dagoes," but also gave to the world the Cæsars, Raphael, Michelangelo, St. Francis of Assisi, Caruso, and a vast concourse of the world's celebrated immortals.

Christian work on the part of the Protestant forces of America for Italians is rendered peculiarly difficult by the religious environment which surrounded them in their native land. Nominally, Italy is overwhelmingly Roman Catholic. There the pope maintains the headquarters of the Catholic hierarchy of the world. There are the world's finest churches and most magnificent collections of religious art and architecture. The entire land, from Piedmont to Sicily, swarms with priests. Every Italian in his native land grows to manhood in an atmosphere crammed with priestcraft and ecclesiastical reminders; they are as familiar to him as his own home,

In the official census of 1911, 95% of all the people declared themselves Catholics, 123,253 Protestants, 874,532 avowed atheists, and 563,404 refused to acknowledge any religious preference and are claimed by all factions. Thus it will be seen that the atheists outnumber the Protestants nearly eight to one, or nearly twelve to one if the "actively indifferent" be included with the avowed opponents of religion. These figures show that there is a considerable drift from Roman Catholicism; but those who leave the fold do not become Protestants. They become nothing—or worse.

It is safe to say that large numbers of those who call themselves Catholics really despise the hierarchy of that Church. This anomalous situation roots in history. Italy became a nation only by recognizing the pope as an enemy of the country and making war upon him. To this day he claims temporal power and regards the Italian government as usurping; he calls himself the "prisoner" of the government. A small clerical party is in politics, and its representatives in Parliament keep up the papal pretenses of supremacy.

To all of this the people strenuously object. They are patriots, and to be a patriotic Italian is necessarily to be strenuously opposed to the papal claims. In every conflict they take the side of the State against the Church. In Rome itself one may hear more outspoken denunciation of the Catholic Church than in any other city of Europe.

This opposition, it is fair to say, is against the Church as an institution and the papal hierarchy rather than against the Catholic religion. The men

2

who denounce the Vatican most vehemently are often good and devout Catholics; the writer has frequently seen men rise from their knees in the churches of Rome and in conversation pronounce bitter strictures upon the Roman Church.

It is evident, however, that such an attitude toward the Church must affect individual spiritual life. Men cannot despise their religious leaders and maintain strong faith in their religion. So to-day in Italy Catholicism has lost its hold upon the affections of the people, who are lukewarm, indifferent, and often positively irreligious. It has been said that religiously the people of Italy are in three classes: devout Catholics, mostly illiterate peasants with a sprinkling of the so-called "black aristocracy"; freethinkers and atheists, whose ranks are swelled by the socialists, workers, and educated professional men; the indifferent millions who may perform the ritual of religion, but who in reality are indifferent and possess no spiritual life whatever.

"Italy is divided into unbelievers and lukewarm believers," declared Ferdinand Martini. Professor Luzzi, a distinguished Italian, says: "The hurricane of the French Revolution carried away from the mind of even the best that small remnant of religion which they no longer possessed in their hearts."

It is not a question of how much, but how little he believes in anything at all, except possibly in a Supreme Being. There are those who point to the enthusiasm of the peasants for their religious processions. The peasant will sometimes pay several francs for the honor of a prominent place in one of the processions in honor of the Madonna; and if they cannot pay in money they will pay in kind, sending to the priest chickens, grain, and wine. The very peasant who is vic-

timized does not hestitate to express the most profound
skepticism and even contempt for miraculous Madonnas,
and all the rest of the priestly myths. Occasionally, but very
rarely, I have met with a simple faith that is evidently
genuine. . . . As likely as not he (the peasant) will give
vent to language of a wholly irreligious kind when he is called
upon to contribute of his hard-earned money to the glory of
the local Madonna, and he cherishes no sort of illusion as to
where the money eventually finds its way. But he would be
roused to fury were the local Madonna to be held up to
ignominy as a painted fraud.[1]

The Italian peasant comes to America. He is
driven by hard necessity, nothing else; he comes
only to escape the abject misery and near-starvation
which he has always known at home and from which
there is no escape in southern Italy. He has heard
of America as the land at the end of the rainbow,
and herein he hopes to find prosperity. Temporal
improvement is the only motive that prompts him.

At first he is disappointed, for his dreams have
often been too rosy. The steerage of the immigrant
ship and the rigors of Ellis Island tend to disenchant
him. He is dumped unceremoniously into a land
which did not invite him and which, according
to all outward indications, does not want him.
He cannot speak the language. He is hustled away
to a tenement and crowded in with others of his
kind; there are Italian blocks in New York containing 3,500 people, or 1,100 to the acre. Unable
to get a job or negotiate with American business,
he becomes the oppressed victim of the Italian
banker and the padrone, or gang boss. As a result
of all this his instinct to get and to save becomes a

[1]Bagot, *Italians of To-Day*, pages 67, 44.

passion, while his desire to become a real part of America is likely to wane.

The newly arrived Italian is often indifferent, reticent, even supicious when approached on the subject of the Protestant religion. He perhaps has no vital religion of his own, but the Roman Catholic system is more or less a habit with him. If he ever heard of Protestantism in his native land, he was taught to hate it. He remembers the pious frauds and extortions of the priests and does not discriminate. He, who recalls the glories of St. Peter's and the cathedrals of Naples or Palermo, is invited to a dingy, dirty mission in a side street; he, who in days agone was thrilled by the solemn masses and colorful processions of Rome, is asked to sit on a hard bench through a service entirely lacking in all the details of solemnity which marked the religious services of his youth. It is small wonder that he shows little enthusiasm for the Protestant faith as it is offered to him.

The Church must reach the immigrant. Not only is it a Christian duty and opportunity, but the very future of our land depends upon it. Our Italian brothers are ignorant, suspicious, poor. They are a favorite field of propaganda for the radical, the I. W. W., and the anarchist. The Mafia and the Black Hand are distinctly Italian institutions. While their natures possess unusual spiritual depths, few of them can be said to be definitely and vitally religious. They do not understand the spirit of America and, in their poverty and exploitation, are easily inflamed against our government.

One of the first duties we owe to these people is to

educate them in Americanism, and in this the Church
may coöperate with other social agencies by maintaining classes for elementary instruction in our
Constitution, form of government, and duties of
citizenship. It is needless to point out that all such
activities should and will be thoroughly permeated
with the religious impulse. The immigrant will
never evolve into the best type of American until
he is profoundly influenced by Protestant Christianity. Roman Catholicism in Europe is largely responsible for his present ignorance, poverty, and lack
of religious sentiment, and to leave him to the tender
mercies of the Catholic Church in the United States
will not make his last state any better than the first.

In winning the Italian one of our first steps must
be to offer him à capable ministry speaking his own
language and preferably of his own nationality.
The scarcity of efficient workers, here as in the case
of activity among all other foreigners, is the most
perplexing single problem we face, even more difficult of solution than the financial problem. When
workers have been found it is highly necessary to
provide for them an adequate equipment. The
family which may have worshiped under the dome
of Michelangelo must at least be given a clean,
sightly, and well-equipped church in which to worship here. The dingy mission in a rented store will
not suffice.

Christian strategy in the winning of Italians calls
for large activity among the children. The desire
of the immigrant to educate his children is a passion,
and it is a striking fact that the school attendance
among the younger children of foreign or mixed

parentage, in both city and rural sections, is better than among those of native parents. Between the ages of five and thirteen years, at which latter age many immigrant children are forced to seek employment, 70.6% of all children of foreign or mixed parentage attend schools, while among those of native white parentage the proportion is only 66.5%. Between the ages of seven and thirteen years the percentage is 94.1 for the immigrants and 92.2 for the native whites.

In the education of Italian children lies one of the important fields of service. Here is the Church's greatest duty and service. As in the case of all our "submerged" peoples, the States cannot or will not provide proper and adequate educational facilities, and because the Christian school is an agency of evangelism as well as enlightenment, few Italian children leave the Christian school unconverted. And through the instrumentality of the school and the children access may be most readily obtained to the interests of the parents.

III.

METHODISM AND THE ITALIANS.

IN ·the territory of the Methodist Episcopal Church, South, there are, according to the census of 1920, more than 211,000 persons born in Italy; and when we add to that number the children born in this country of Italian parents we find that the Italian immigrant population of the South and Southwest is very large. In every city and large town the Italians are found as sellers of statuettes, fruit dealers, barbers, restaurant keepers, truck gardeners, peddlers, bootblacks, and teamsters. In industrial centers, on public works, and in other places where common labor is demanded they are very numerous; indeed, in many places they are indispensable as workers.

The Methodist Episcopal Church, South, has projected its work among Italians in the States of Florida, Alabama, Louisiana, Missouri, and Texas. This service is directed by the Home Departments of the Board of Missions and takes the form of the regular activity of the organized Church, with added institutional and social features when these are found desirable. No day or boarding schools for young people are as yet maintained, but in all the Italian missions vigorous and constant evangelistic efforts are made with an ever-increasing degree of success. The workers report that it is generally easier to reach the Italians with the gospel message than to influence any other immigrant group.

In Florida the Italian missionary work of the

Church centers in Tampa and its suburban "ghetto," Ybor City. More than half of all the Italians in the State are found here. The total number of foreign-born Italians in Tampa is 2,817, these constituting by far the largest foreign group save the Spanish-speaking element; the total Italian colony, including those born here, perhaps number 6,000. Among these the work of Methodism is regularly organized and is operated in the Latin District of the Florida Conference. The San Paulo Church, at Ybor City, has an actual membership of nearly two hundred Italians, with a constituency several times as large. The pastor is a native Italian, who preaches to the people in their own tongue and exercises a wide influence among them. Near at hand stands the Wolff Settlement and the Urban Bird Clinic, operated by the women of the Methodist Episcopal Church, South, and these provide day nurseries and all the forms of social settlement activity needed to supplement the evangelistic work of the pastor. In Tampa another Italian Mission was opened in 1923 and given the name of "Russell Mission," in honor of Dr. R. L. Russell, Home Secretary of the Board of Missions in charge of work for immigrants.

In Birmingham, Ala., and the industrial section surrounding it there are 2,160 Italians born in "the old country," and these, with their families, constitute a large colony. At Ensley and its suburb, Pratt City, large numbers are engaged as laborers in the steel and iron plants, and among them the Methodist Episcopal Church, South, maintains an Italian Mission. Here has been built a handsome new church for this foreign-speaking group, and the Ensley Community House adds various lines of community and social activity. Seven workers are employed in this great center, and it is one of the most useful agencies of Methodism in serving and influencing the Italian people.

Regular preaching, evangelistic, and community service is being rendered by the Church to colonies of Italians at Thurber, Erath County, Tex., and Bryan, Brazos County, Tex. At the latter place a regularly organized Italian mission is being operated by Italian preachers who have achieved a large success in conducting religious services in their native language.

Kansas City, Mo., has an Italian colony of nearly 10,000, and of these 3,318 were born abroad. Among this group the Institutional Methodist Church carries on an activity which includes not only the work of the regular Methodist congregation, but also a full range of community and social effort. Supplementing the Institutional Church is the Spofford Home for children. These two institutions employ ten permanent workers and are rendering an invaluable service in the Americanization and Christianization of the foreign population.

A most extensive work for Italians is conducted at St. Mark's Hall, in New Orleans, La. This city has the largest Italian colony found in any Southern State, a total of 7,633 foreign born. The predominance of Roman Catholicism in Louisiana makes Methodist work among Italians unusually difficult, but they respond readily when they can be reached, and large results have already been attained. St. Mark's Hall is a great Church and community center located in the foreign section of New Orleans, containing about 30,000 population. A plant has been erected at a cost of approximately $120,000. It consists of a church, a man's building, and a woman's building, and in these every form of social service is carried on by the pastor, salaried deaconesses, and volunteer workers. St. Mark's Hall has a membership of only one hundred and fifty, but its Christian constituency is very large. Its clinic alone treats nearly four thousand persons annually, while numbers attend its various classes and participate in its activities.

These distinctive centers by no means cover the range of work being furthered by the Home Department of the Board of Missions among the Italians of the South and Southwest. Great social centers like Kingdom House, in St. Louis, Mo., and the Centenary Institute, in Nashville, Tenn., while not listed as Italian work, carry on extensive Christian operations of every kind among this immigrant group. The same is true of many of the city Churches throughout the country which receive financial assistance from the Home Department or to which the Department allocates workers, while the various Wesley Houses and similar centers of the Woman's Missionary Council manifest never-failing interest in our immigrants from Italy. Indeed, it may be said that in every city where the Methodist Episcopal Church, South, is influential its hand of helpfulness is extended and its gospel is preached to this group of foreigners.

One of the greatest difficulties faced by the Home

Department is that of securing workers for the Italian field. The few that have been found in the past were for the most part untrained, and hence the results have not always been substantially conserved. To remedy this situation the Department has undertaken to discover volunteers among the Italian boys and girls and give them a thorough training for their Christian tasks. An annual appropriation of $3,000 is now being made for the education of ministerial students of foreign parentage.

IV.

FROM ACROSS THE RIO GRANDE.

FOR a straight stretch of 1,833 miles our country is joined to Mexico by an imaginary line. East of El Paso the Rio Grande flows between the two Republics, but westward there is no division save an occasional concrete post and a few uncertain stretches of wire fence. Vast distances are wholly unmarked and unguarded, and the stranger observing the life, people, and characteristics in the towns and villages along the border would not be aware that on one side lay a great civilized world power and on the other a small and backward land of revolutions, illiteracy, and superstition. For it has been truly said that human nature has ever ignored artificial barriers, and human nature on the border is no exception.

The activity of the Methodist Episcopal Church, South, among the Mexican immigrants of the Southwest is the most extensive and successful missionary work carried on by the Church in the home field. This is as it should be, since the problem of the Mexican in the United States is a distinctively Southern problem. Practically all of these immigrants are in the Southwest, from one-third to one-half of them being in Texas. Their presence in the heart of Southern Methodist territory places a special responsibility upon this Church, and the home mission agencies have governed themselves accordingly. So fruitful have been the efforts that the Mexican missionary work is to-day organized in two great missions rapidly nearing the status of Annual Conferences.

It is impossible to ascertain the exact number of Mexicans in the United States. The official census of 1920 gives the number of foreign-born Mexican immigrants as 478,383 and states that of this number 249,652 are in Texas, 86,610 in California, 60,325 in Arizona, and 19,906 in New Mexico. It is apparent, however, that these figures do not even closely approximate the total Mexican population of the country. They take no account of the vast number born on this side of the international boundary. Immigration officials frankly admit that thousands of Mexicans cross the poorly policed border clandestinely, and these might be loath to admit the fact of their foreign birth. The Mexican is a white man, and therefore the census figures do not segregate him in its figures based on color.

It has been officially estimated that 60% of the total population of New Mexico is Mexican or Spanish-American; if this be true, the State contains nearly 220,000 of these people, whereas the census figures of the foreign-born Mexicans are less than 20,000. Authoritative estimates place the number in Arizona at 100,000 and those in California at 250,000, these figures being far above those of the census.

According to a recent estimate there are now at least 1,500,000 Mexicans in the United States, 450,-000 of these being in Texas. The largest colony is at San Antonio, where there is a Mexican population of 50,000. El Paso is 55% Mexican, and Los Angeles, Calif., has 30,000.[1]

---

[1] Figures of Jay S. Stowell in *The Near Side of the Mexican Question*, pages 33, 34.

This large Mexican population is constantly and rapidly increasing. The new limitation law does not apply to Mexico. On the contrary, while the government has severely restricted immigration from other countries, a great laxity prevails with reference to Mexico; during the war the literacy test, head tax, and contract labor clauses of the law were suspended, and they have not yet been restored; hence we have for several years been receiving thousands of Mexicans ordinarily classed as inadmissible. It is true that many return to their native land, but the number of those leaving is insignificant in comparison with those entering. The report of the Bureau of Immigration for the fiscal year ending in June, 1922, reveals that in this period we admitted 18,246 Mexicans, 12,572 of these indicating Texas as their place of intended residence, and during the same year only 2,155 left Texas. It is significant that only one naturalized Mexican departed from Texas to Mexico. The rapid increase in our Mexican population is illustrated by the Bureau's supplementary report covering the period from July, 1922, to May, 1923, which shows that between these dates 54,574 Mexicans entered the United States, while only 2,319 departed.

These Mexicans who are flocking to the United States are immigrants of the humbler sort. Most of them are common laborers who come to do the work that many of our native-born citizens refuse to do. Of the 18,246 immigrants who arrived here from Mexico in 1921-22, only 1,165 were skilled workers, and but 291 were listed as professional men.

The common laborers find employment largely on

CUBAN CHURCH, WEST TAMPA, FLA., MAINTAINED BY THE HOME
DEPARTMENT OF THE BOARD OF MISSIONS.

MEXICAN CHURCH MAINTAINED BY THE HOME DEPARTMENT
OF THE BOARD OF MISSIONS AT SAN ANTONIO, TEX.

(31)

the railroads of the Southwest; it is reported that one line employs nearly 15,000 Mexicans. Large numbers are working in the mines and other industries. The most hopeful sign in the Mexican immigration situation is that many are finding their way to the farms. In Texas, where a great majority of all the foreigners are Mexicans, the census figures show that 468,722 of the immigrant class, including the foreign born and those of foreign or mixed parentage, are living in the rural sections, while only 337,181 are in the centers of population. Texas to-day ranks as one of the first agricultural States of the country, and its prosperity has been made possible by the labor of the Mexicans.

The immigrant from South of the Rio Grande is nearly always miserably poor. He comes across the line to escape starvation, and he usually brings his family with him. His entire earthly wealth consists of the few rags and articles carried in a pack. Unskilled, unlettered, unable even to speak the language, he must take the first job offered to him. He lives in an adobe hut, often with a dirt floor, subsists on beans, and ekes out a most abject existence.

In 1912 it was found that 18% of the Mexicans lived in one-room houses and 60% in two-room houses. Conditions have improved, however, and a recent study in Los Angeles revealed the fact that only 1% live in one-room shacks, while 2% have two rooms, 24% have three rooms, 30% have four rooms, and 20% have five rooms. In the same survey it was found that 28% of these habitations have no sinks, 32% no lavatories, and 79% no baths. The Housing

Commission rated more than 50% of the houses as bad and only 5% as good.[1]

Living thus in surroundings more or less unsanitary and squalid, and being ignorant concerning even the fundamentals of sanitation and feeding, disease, particularly tuberculosis, is quite prevalent among them. Infant mortality is unusually high; in Los Angeles it is 152 in 1,000 among Mexicans, but only 54 in 1,000 among the general population; the Mexican baby has one-third the chance to live that is possessed by the average baby.

Our immigrants from Mexico are illiterate; perhaps no group in the country has a higher percentage of illiteracy than our foreign-born Mexicans. In their homeland, dominated by the Roman Catholic Church, they had few educational opportunities; nine out of ten native Mexicans are to-day unable to read and write. The absence or suspension of a literacy test in our immigration laws allowed these ignorant Mexicans to cross our borders, and accordingly we have among us multiplied hundreds of thousands who are wholly illiterate.

Definite authentic statistics on the rate of illiteracy make no distinctions between white persons of foreign birth. But the situation can be realized from the fact that Texas, Arizona, and New Mexico, which have the largest percentage of Mexicans among their foreign-born population, have also the highest percentage of illiteracy among the foreign-born whites of any States in the Union. In Texas

---

[1]Reported by Stowell, *The Near Side of the Mexican Question*, page 44.

more than two-thirds of the foreign born are Mexicans, and 33.8% are illiterate, this being the highest rate in the United States. The foreign population of Arizona is three-fourths Mexican, and 27.5% are illiterate, while in New Mexico two-thirds are Mexican, and 27.1% are illiterate.

Facts arrived at on a similar basis indicate, however, that the Mexican, though ignorant himself, has an appreciation of education and is eager to secure its advantages for his children. In Texas only 9.4% of the children of foreign and mixed parentage above ten years of age are illiterate; in Arizona the percentage is only 4.6. In New Mexico the illiteracy of immigrant children is 3.7% below that of children of native parents, while in Texas and Arizona it is respectively 7.2% and 3.3% above.

Similar results are obtained from a study of school attendance. In Texas 70.6% of the immigrants' children between seven and thirteen years attend school, and among those of native parents the rate of attendance is 88%. In Arizona the figures are 83.7% for immigrants' children and 92.8% for the native whites; in New Mexico the rate is 85.7% and 90%. Such facts are indeed encouraging, especially in the light of the additional facts that nowhere are educational opportunities for the Mexican children equal to those of the boys and girls of native parentage, and everywhere the attendance of the children at school involves a much heavier sacrifice and burden upon the immigrant parents. To provide an adequate and full educational opportunity for all Mexican children is at once the duty and the opportunity of the Church.

V.

THE MEXICAN AT HOME.

OF all the lands on earth, Mexico is perhaps the most unfortunate from the social and political angle. This nation is efficient in nothing, but unstable in everything. The population is a conglomeration of various bloods and mixtures, and there is really no such thing as a distinct Mexican type. The official census in 1910 gave the total population as 15,115,-612, but this is no doubt at least a million below the correct figure at the present time. An analysis of the polyglot population in 1900 showed that of the natives only 19% were classed as whites, 38% being Indians and 43% mixed bloods. Seven classes have been listed among the Mexican people, as follows: (1) Spaniards; (2) native Creoles or mixed whites; (3) Indians; (4) mestizos or mixed whites and Indians; (5) mulattos or mixed whites and Negroes; (6) zamboos or mixed Indians and Negroes; (7) Negroes.

Mexico is a shrunken, weakened nation, no longer the proud land it once was. More than half of the territory which was hers at the middle of the nineteenth century now belongs to the United States, our nation having acquired Texas, Colorado, New Mexico, Oklahoma, Arizona, California, Nevada, Utah, and parts of Kansas and Wyoming. Thus some of the richest sections of the United States formerly belonged to Mexico.

The country, from the dawn of its history, has never been able to establish and long maintain a stable government. It has ever been a land of revolution and near-anarchy. It was annexed to the Spanish crown by conquest in 1521 and ruled by foreign and tyrannical viceroys for three hundred years. A revolt led by the priest Hidalgo secured independence in 1810. In 1822 General Augustin Iturbide declared himself emperor, but in two years he was driven out and the republic was established. In 1864 the people tired of the severity of their presidents and gave the throne to the Archduke Ferdinand Maximilian of Austria. He was shot in 1867, and Benito Juarez took the reins. His successor fled in 1876 before General Porfirio Diaz, who ruled, with the exception of four years, with a rod of iron until 1911, when he was virtually forced to resign. Francisco I. Madero followed and was murdered in 1913, when the notorious General Victoriano Huerta became president. A year later civil war broke out and Huerta was succeeded by General Carranza, who in turn was forced to flee and murdered in 1920. General Adolph de la Huerta became provisional president, and in the fall of 1920 General Alvero Obregon was elected.

In recent years the internal discord in Mexico has been an international scandal. Diplomatic relations were severed by the United States and various European states, and on more than one occasion during the past few years our government has been on the very brink of war with our southern neighbor. This discord made property rights unstable and human life unsafe; it plunged the peons still deeper into the already abject poverty and in large measure augmented the stream of immigrants pouring into Texas and California.

Mexico is not naturally a poor country. On the contrary, her natural resources represent vast wealth. But the instability of the government and the ignorance and poverty of the masses have made development impossible. The Roman Catholic Church grasped much of the land and wealth of the country, and foreign capitalists grasped much more. It is said that $2,000,000,000 of American capital is invested in Mexico, and it is to protect this that interested persons have urged American intervention in Mexico's internal affairs. Mexico has been, and is, in a pitiable plight and deserves the sympathy rather than the censure of the world in her attempts to get her resources from the grip of a foreign Church and foreign capitalists that they may be exploited and developed by and for her own people.

Mexico has always suffered from the blighting power and influence of the Roman Catholic Church, which, more than any other single force, is responsible for Mexican ignorance, superstition, and backwardness. There were, according to the 1910 census, 15,033,176 professing Catholics and only 68,839 Protestants.

The policy of Rome from 1517, when the Church entered Mexico, to 1859 was to acquire as much property as possible, and by the latter date fully one-third of all the wealth of the nation was in its possession. In such an intolerable situation the people were necessarily pauperized and burdened by oppressive taxation. For more than sixty years Mexico has been struggling to break the grip of Rome, and it is not surprising that she has at times been some-what unjust to Protestantism.

The struggle began in 1856 when the Jesuits were expelled. In 1859 the Church and state were di-vorced, and in the following year all the male re-ligious orders were driven out. By 1874 all the fe-male orders were suppressed. Since these reforms were completed the Catholic Church has not been permitted to own the buildings in which it worships, nor has its clergy been allowed to appear in public exposing to view any insignia of their calling. No con-vents for nuns or friars have been allowed. A new constitution was adopted in 1917, and an attempt has been made to prohibit the operations of all priests and preachers save those of native birth.

But the grip of Rome has never relaxed in Mexico; in spite of laws and confiscations the Catholic Church still holds the masses in virtual bondage. Since this Church has largely controlled education, il-literacy in Mexico is even now well-nigh universal; from 85% to 90% of all the people are unable to read or write. A studied attempt has been made to keep the Bible out of the hands of the people, and the burning of Bibles distributed by Protestants has been common.

The nature of the Roman Catholic religion in Mexico is degenerate, as it always is where this Church has little competition. Disgraceful stories of the conduct of the priests and the official acts of the Church abound in Mexican annals. For example, in the old days thieves could purchase immunity from the priests, although the "Bull of Composition" would allow only fifty licenses per year to one individual thief. Even as late as 1914 it was said that the priests still sold indulgences publicly. In 1865 a Roman Catholic delegate from the Vatican officially reported to the pope that Mexican Catholicism was idolatrous and that many priests lived in flagrant immorality; he declared that many pastors refused to entertain him because they did not want him to see their illegitimate children.

By thus divorcing religion from morality, the Catholic Church has wrought great havoc among the people. "To-day we see the fruitage of such a system, for observers everywhere testify to the fact that Mexicans raised under such a system may have many virtues, but they will persistently steal and lie." This fact constitutes a great problem in missionary work among Mexican immigrants and makes necessary a long educational process. To the Mexican raised under Catholic auspices religion means a hollow form, extortion, meaningless ceremonies and no morality. The attitudes of a lifetime must be uprooted and changed, and the transformation of Mexican character is necessarily a slow process. Among the older persons it is almost impossible, and the Protestant missionary agencies find their most fruitful field of effort among the children.

Therefore the educational program bulks large in all missionary work for the Mexicans.

Speaking of Mexico, the *Encyclopedia Britannica* says: "A large percentage of the natives may still be considered semipagan, the gods of their ancestors being worshiped in secret, and the forms and tenets of the dominant faith, which they but faintly comprehend, being largely adulterated with superstitions

and practices of pagan origin." Catholicism among
the Mexican peons has indeed been little better than
actual paganism, and when these peons come into
the United States they frequently and naturally bring
their superstitions with them. We accordingly find
among certain groups of Mexicans in the Southwest
ideas, customs, and practices which can only be regarded as hang-overs from paganism. A review of
some of these practices will indicate the necessity of
Protestant missionary work among these people.[1]

In our own State of New Mexico as late as 1887 a
"witch" was stoned to death for turning a man into
a woman for three months. Here also live people
who claim to be on close personal terms with the
devil and to have seen and conversed with him. In
Santa Fe many superstitions gather about the famous
De Varges Day Celebration, and grotesque legends
concerning the miraculous power of a certain sacred
picture are preserved and foisted upon the ignorant
people as truth. At Chimago, N. Mex., there is a
little adobe church building, the dirt from one room
of which is supposed to possess marvelous properties
and to heal all manner of diseases. Mexican pilgrims
come to this church from far and wide, crawling about
on their hands and knees and digging up dirt to be
applied to diseased parts or to be drunk as tea.

The most striking example of superstition and
paganism in New Mexico is the order of Penitentes,
or Flagellantes, which is said to be incorporated by
the State as "The Society of Our Father Jesus, the
Nazarene," and to have great political influence.

----

[1] Fuller accounts will be found in Stowell's book, *The Near
Side of the Mexican Question,* pages 74-79.

This order builds upon the text, "Without the shedding of blood there is no remission of sins," and its worship consists in inflicting all sorts of suffering upon its devotees. To-day "there are scores of towns where the Penitentes are the dominating political, social, and religious factor in the community."

During Holy Week some of their ceremonies, and particularly their processions, are in the open. The participants in these open processions wear a black mask over the entire head, so that even their neighbors do not know who is taking part. They wear a small lower garment, but aside from that and the mask their bodies are naked. Their backs are gashed with flint or some other sharp instrument, and they whip themselves with whips made of yucca or other harsh cactus as they proceed on their weary march. Some carry wooden crosses of great weight to a distant hill; some wheel barrels of stone through almost impassable sand, and others draw heavy loads with cords which cut into their naked bodies. Many sorts of suffering are devised, and there is little or no general supervision of the order. There is also on the part of some a desire to do sufficient penance at one time to last for the entire year. It should not be inferred, however, that these people are particularly contrite, for some of the worst characters appear to enter most zealously into the ritual and then to go out for another year of unimproved conduct.

While the Penitentes exercises are supposed to be secret, especially inside the building, what may be considered as an official description of them is found in the *Catholic Encyclopedia*.

The candidate is escorted to the *morado* (abode), the home, or the council house, by two or more Penitentes where, after a series of questions and answers consisting in the main of prayer, he is admitted. He then undergoes various humiliations. First, he washes the feet of all present, kneeling before each; then he recites a long prayer, asking pardon for any

offense he may have given. If anyone present has been offend-
ed by the candidate, he lashes the offender on the bare neck.
Then comes the last and crucial test: four or six incisions, in
the shape of a cross, are made just below the shoulders of the
candidate with a piece of flint.

VI.

METHODISM AMONG THE MEXICANS.

ENOUGH has been said to show the great need of Christian service which exists among the Mexicans and the Spanish-speaking peoples of the Southwest. Let us now sketch what is being done to meet this need by the Methodist Episcopal Church, South. Needless to say, the Church has long realized its reponsibility and opportunity and has long been active among the Mexicans on both sides of the international border. The success that has been achieved is great, though it should be measured more by the degree of service rendered than by the visible results attained and organized.

As a matter of fact, the visible results of missionary work among our immigrants is never a safe or just criterion of its value and success. The population is constantly shifting, and a congregation which is populous to-day may be bankrupt of members to-morrow as a result of the closing of public works or a new demand for laborers elsewhere. Effort has not been wasted, however, because the Mexican carries with him his new-found faith, his nobler ideals, his broader information, his better habits of living and his desire to educate his children. These things abide and bear fruit wherever he goes, though they may not be organized.

The work of Southern Methodism among the Mexicans is far-flung. It is organized in two missions— the Texas Mexican Mission and the Western Mexican Mission. The former embraces all the work for

Mexicans in Texas east of the Pecos River. This
Mission contains 19 pastoral charges, with 44 local
Churches having a total membership of approximately
2,000. Other statistics of the Mission show that
there are Sunday schools at about three-fourths of the
preaching places, with an average of one Epworth
League to each charge. Within the bounds of this
Mission the Church maintains three important boarding schools for Mexican children—the Valley Institute, at Pharr, Holding Institute, at Laredo, and
Wesleyan Institute, at San Antonio, while day schools
are conducted at Eagle Pass and Hillsboro, Tex.
Wesley Houses for social settlement work are in
operation at San Antonio and Fort Worth.

The Western Mexican Mission, in which is a
Church membership of 1,200 includes all the Mexi-
can work in Texas west of the Pecos River, New
Mexico, Arizona, California, and a strip along the
border in Mexico. In this vast territory there are two
districts, the Eastern and Western. The Eastern
District alone is four hundred and fifty miles long and
two hundred miles wide, and in this territory the
Church is reponsible for more than 20,000 Mexicans.
The Western District covers a part of Texas, the
work in Mexico, Arizona, and California. In the
Mexican section of El Paso are located the great
Mexican Community Center, the Lydia E. Patterson
Institute, and the Effie Edington Boarding School,
and, in connection with the Churches, schools for
Mexican children are in operation at Phoenix, Ariz.,
and Magdalena, Mexico.

It will thus be seen that Methodist work among the
Mexicans takes the regular connectional form of

Methodism everywhere.   Although close organization
is difficult, the Mexican Churches operate true to
Methodist form, and they are related to the Mission
exactly as others are related to the Annual Conference; and in due time these Missions will be
recognized as Conferences.

The evangelization of these people is proceeding
by means of the triple and allied agencies of preaching, social service, and education.   Great emphasis
is placed upon evangelistic preaching, and this is
carried on in open public places as well as in the
churches at the appointed hours.   Much of this
preaching is necessarily in the Spanish language by
ministers of Mexican nationality.   These native
preachers establish a vital bond of kinship and sympathy between the Church and the people, and,
though often poorly trained, they are more influential than American preachers could possibly be.
One of the most important problems to be solved is
that of developing a native leadership among the
Mexicans and securing a trained ministry for them.

Social service work is everywhere carried on in
connection with the Mexican Churches and is effectively used as an agency of evangelism.   The ignorance and poverty of the Mexicans make this form
of activity absolutely necessary.   The Woman's
Missionary Council maintains several deaconesses,
and other full-time workers are engaged, while
volunteers from the American congregations make
possible a wide range of such service.   Its nature
varies with the equipment and community needs,
the most effective and needful operations usually
being employment agencies, language and Americani-

zation classes, nurseries, visiting nurses, clinics, sewing and cooking instruction, and athletic and recreational facilities for the young people. The Mexicans can have little social and community life save as it is provided by the Church, and efforts put forth in this direction are meeting a great need.

Mexican social service work has been highly institutionalized in San Antonio, Fort Worth, Dallas, Houston, Los Angeles, and El Paso. In San Antonio and Fort Worth Wesley Houses are operated under the active direction of regularly appointed deaconesses and a full complement of volunteers from the American Churches. Three workers are employed in connection with the Mexican Church at Houston. The Homer Toberman Mission and Clinic in Los Angeles is noted for the excellence of its service. These institutions are the natural centers of Mexican society and community activity and are constantly leading the people into sympathetic relations with the gospel and the Church.

At El Paso the great Mexican Community Center is operated by the Home Department of the Board of Missions. In 1920 the Department purchased a large public school building in the heart of the Mexican section and transformed it into a modern social service plant. Salaried workers carry on its activities. These consist, in the main, of an employment bureau, domestic science classes, mothers' clubs, boys' and girls' clubs, and a Goodwill Industry. In all the Southwest there is no finer institution of its kind.

The ultimate solution of the problems raised by the presence of immigrants must be accomplished by a trained native leadership. The refusal to develop leaders among the natives has been the main cause of the failure of the Roman Catholic Church, which has deliberately kept the Mexicans in subjection to a foreign priesthood in order to increase its own power. The success of Protestant agencies depends upon the adoption of an exactly opposite policy, one which seeks to train young Mexicans for leadership and thus allows the people to develop naturally and work out their own problems until they become harmoniously blended into our social body. This is the fundamental policy of the Methodist Episcopal Church, South. Native preachers are used in the Mexican Churches in so far as they can be found, but the scarcity of adequately trained ministers has made it necessary to produce them outright. For the development of leaders and the training of young men for the Mexican ministry a number of educational institutions have been established. Some of these—Holding Institute, at Laredo, Tex., Lydia E. Patterson Institute and Effie Edington Boarding School, both at El Paso, Tex.—are supported by the Woman's Missionary Council. The Wesleyan Institute, at San Antonio, Tex., and Valley Institute, at Pharr, Tex., together with several day schools, are maintained by the Home Department of the Board of Missions.

The Wesleyan Institute is a school for Mexican boys and the recruiting ground for the Mexican ministry; many of the most successful preachers in the two Missions are its graduates, and the class of volunteers in preparation usually contains about twenty young men. It is necessary to provide the entire support of many of these young preachers, and the Home Department has adopted the policy of assigning such support as Specials. The total sum of $200 per year will keep a young Methodist preacher in training for his future tasks.

The Valley Institute renders a similar service to Mexican girls; it was established in 1921, and its entire boarding capacity was taxed the second year. The school is located at Pharr, Tex., in the Rio Grande Valley, and it specializes in training young Mexican girls of good breeding for Christian life service. Its evangelical character is attested by the fact that all of the students are usually converted to the Protestant Christian faith before its sessions close. Scholarships for girls at $200 per year are offered as Specials by the Home Department of the Board of Missions.

In addition to these boarding schools, the Church has found it necessary to maintain day schools of an elementary character at such places as Phoenix, Ariz., Magdalena, Mexico, and Hillsboro and Eagle Pass, Tex. These are for the most part small schools, operated by one, two, or three teachers, and are made necessary because of inadequate educational opportunity in the public schools. The children are taught English, the elementary subjects, and the fundamentals of the Christian religion. From these schools the children are easily led to the Sunday school and the Church, and as evangelistic agencies they render a vital service. They are maintained at an outlay of from $1,000 to $1,500 annually.

Missionary work among the Mexican children is uniquely profitable and interesting. Naturally spiritual in nature, they respond readily to a religious appeal. Some of the young ministerial students in

Wesleyan Institute serve small Churches and preach on the streets of San Antonio for experience. One such boy entered the school as a Roman Catholic and was converted to the Prostestant faith. On his return to his home for the holidays he undertook the education of his own parents in the Bible, and their conversion followed. The native intelligence of these young Mexicans is illustrated by a girl, fourteen years of age, who came from Mexico to the Valley Institute, unable to speak English and without any semblance of religious training. In five months she spoke English correctly and displayed talent as a Bible student; in one year she was converted and began training for a life of Christian service. Such instances are by no means uncommon, and they lend attractiveness to the Specials in the Mexican field being offered by the Home Department of the Board of Missions.

4

VII.

THE CUBANS OF FLORIDA.

The Methodist Episcopal Church, South, being a Southern Church, recognizes a peculiar duty to the Cuban people, whether they be at home in the "Pearl of the Antilles" or immigrants in the United States. As Cuba owes her independence to America and depends upon American friendship for her stability, so she depends upon American Protestantism for the advantages of Christianity.

The religious problem among Cuban immigrants presents the same features that are found among the Mexicans; being a kindred people, speaking the same language, and kept in ignorance by the same Church, one naturally meets similar characteristics. Social conditions, however, have never been as deplorable in Cuba as in Mexico, although never admirable.

Except for a brief period of British occupancy in 1762, Cuba was controlled by the Spanish from the date of its discovery by Columbus in 1492 until the United States intervened to stop Spanish tyranny in 1898. During this period the Roman Catholic Church had a free hand, with the usual consequence that the people were kept in superstitious ignorance and the wealth gravitated into the hands of the Church. Early in the nineteenth century the Spanish took away much of the ecclesiastical landed property, paying instead a certain sum for the support of the Church, an arrangement which, with certain modifications, has been continued. The priests in the past controlled education, the result being that in 1898, when Spanish control was broken, 84% of the people were unable to read or write. Under American occupancy a system of public schools was established, and to-day the percentage of illiteracy is only 54. The fact that the supplanting of Catholic education by a public system has in twenty-five years reduced illiteracy by 30% is eloquent with meaning.

Of the 2,898,905 people in Cuba, 74% are white, the remainder being Negroes and mixed bloods. The overwhelming majority are Roman Catholics, there being only 12,000 Protestants on the Island. Protestantism, however, is influential far beyond its numerical strength, the 65 schools of various grades maintained by the different mission boards having done much to reduce the percentage of illiteracy.

Cuba lies but one hundred miles from Florida, and passage to and fro is a simple and inexpensive proceeding; it is not strange, therefore, that Cubans should constantly seek the industrial advantages of the United States. According to the census of 1920 there are 6,613 Cubans of foreign birth in Florida, these constituting the largest foreign-born group in the State. The largest numbers are in Tampa and Key West; Tampa and Hillsborough County have 4,755, while there are 1,704 in Key West. The tide of Cubans fluctuates back and forth in greater degree than is true of any other immigrants; the number in this country is, therefore, variable, but seems to be slowly increasing. For example, during May, 1923, 169 Cubans entered and 74 departed; and between July, 1922, and May, 1923, the number coming in was 1,179 and the number going out was 699.

Socially the Cuban immigrant is of a better class

than the Mexican. Of 698 Cubans entering this country in 1921–22, all those above sixteen years of age could read and write, while all save 109 possessed at least $50 in cash; 504 gave no occupation, these being largely the women and the 203 children under sixteen years of age; but among the other 194 there were 41 professional men, 40 merchants, and 82 listed as skilled workers.

It is not to be thought, however, that these Cuban immigrants are of such a high type that they can immediately take their places in American social life. Such is far from the case. They come from the Catholic environment sketched above, and for the most part they are poor, ignorant, and superstitious; it is not to be expected that immigrants from a land wherein more than half the people are illiterate would be of the highest type. These Cubans, almost as much as the Mexicans, need the social and religious ministry of the Protestant Church.

Most of the Cubans in Florida are cigar makers, and it is said that in many cases the saturation of their bodies with nicotine has a decidedly adverse effect on their health and mentality; one missionary secretary is authority for the statement that because of the nicotine "in many cases we find it difficult to bring them to understand in fullest measure the meaning of Christianity." These people live mainly in the foreign sections of Tampa and Key West, in unsanitary quarters, and are a prey to the vices and diseases which usually beset our immigrant population.

Methodism first launched its work among the Cubans in January, 1874, when the Florida Conference appointed a mere boy, Rev. J. E. A. Van Duser, as a missionary among the Latin people at Key West. He spent the year in studying the Spanish language and in the distribution of Bibles and Christian literature. Reappointed the following year, he died of yellow fever on June 7, 1875, without witnessing the conversion of a single Cuban, and his last words form the epitaph on his simple monument at Key West: "Don't let the Church give up the Cuban Mission."

The Methodist Episcopal Church, South, confines its work for Cuban immigrants to the two largest centers of Tampa and Key West. In the former there are four Cuban congregations under Cuban pastors; these have a combined membership of about five hundred, and each Church operates with a full organization in line with connectional Methodism. There are two such Churches in Key West with a total foreign membership of about one hundred and seventy-five. The congregations in both cities are organized as the Latin District of the Florida Conference.

On account of the shifting nature of the Cuban population it is even more difficult to conserve missionary results and perfect a strong organization among them than among the other foreigners; the constant coming and going also prevents the congregations from becoming self-supporting. The Cubans contribute liberally to their Churches in proportion to their limited means, but it is still necessary for the Home Department of the Board of Missions to subsidize the Cuban work to the extent of about $8,000 annually.

Here, as elsewhere, the evangelistic method is supplemented by social service and an educational program. In Tampa the Rosa Valdes Settlement, under the control of the women of the Church, operates across the street from the San Mateo Church. Full-time workers, deaconesses, and volunteers are in this great center engaged in the full program of service customary to such institutions. In Key West the well-known Ruth Hargrove Settlement carries on a similar program of service.

On account of the relatively small number of Cubans it has not been necessary for the Church to establish boarding schools, but day schools are in operation in both Tampa and Key West. Large numbers of Cuban children flock to these schools, the curricula of which include elementary subjects and religious training. These schools not only provide educational opportunities equal in quality to those enjoyed by American children, but they also serve as recruiting grounds for the Sunday school and Church.

The Cubans eagerly welcome and take advantage of the Church's offer to train their children. In 1921 the wife of the pastor opened a school in San Mateo Church, Tampa, with four or five Cuban children. In three years the attendance grew to one hundred and fifty, and the services of four teachers were required. In response to this evident challenge the Home Department of the Board of Missions acquired a tract of land near this church and proposes to erect a building in which this school may be permanently housed.

Other racial groups found in the territory of the Methodist Episcopal Church, South, are more easily assimilated into the regular organization of the Church, and where conditions render the step advisable such assimilation is always under'aken. In Texas two groups—the Germans and Bohemians— have already been thus merged. Missionary work among the Germans was independently organized as the German Mission Conference until 1918, when it became an integral part of the West Texas Conference, its Churches becoming regular appointments in and the missionaries members of that Conference. An official organ of the Church is still published in the German language, however, and the Churches are yet subsidized by the Home Department of the Board of Missions.

Missionary work among the Czechs in Texas is undergoing an even more complete assimilation. For many years separate congregations were maintained for the Bohemian population, but their familiarity with the English language and their complete sympathy with the American spirit have caused many of them to take their places in the American Churches. By so doing two of the most efficient missionaries, Joseph Dobes and J. P. Bartak, were released for service among their brethren in Czechoslovakia. Sent to this newly resurrected nation by the Foreign Department of the Board of Missions, these American-trained Czechs have led one of the most remarkable revivals of history and have been largely instrumental in establishing Southern Methodism upon a basis of permanency there, in four years winning seven thousand converts and developing some congregations as large as any in America.

In 1921 an interesting work was started on a small scale among the Syrians and Greeks of Mississippi by Rev. Charles Assaf, a native Syrian born in Damascus, whose life story is like a romance. Leaving his native land, he spent some time in France and England before coming to America as an immigrant in 1905. Unable to speak English, he was "tagged" at Ellis Island and shipped first to New Orleans and from that place to McComb, Miss. He states that upon his arrival at McComb he possessed but ten cents and owed $500. "I used the dime to buy food and had to trust the Lord to pay my debt. The Lord blessed me, and in six months I was out of debt, although I could not speak a word of English."

Always a sincere Christian, Mr. Assaf felt called to service among his people and was licensed to preach in 1921, immediately entering upon a life of personal evangelism. Supported by the Home Department of the Board of Missions, he goes from town to town and house to house among the foreign population with his message. No definite special organization has yet been attempted. The groups are gathered in homes or in the American Churches for the services conducted by Mr. Assaf, and the people are related to these Churches upon his departure. He has had a large success in placing his converts in the regular Methodist congregations and Sunday schools, and in the first year of his labors more than one hundred definitely entered the membership.

A recent report made by this missionary reveals the interesting and varied nature of his work. In one month he preached fifteen sermons in seven different places, including the largest Church in his Conference, a Confederate Soldiers' Home, and a Negro chapel.   Among his conversions in these services he counted twenty-six Confederate veterans, eight Chinese, eight Mexicans, one Italian, one Syrian, one Negro, and one Mohammedan.

SPANISH AND MEXICAN
IN COLORADO

A SURVEY *of the*
SPANISH AMERICANS AND MEXICANS
in the STATE OF COLORADO

By
ROBERT N. McLEAN, D.D.
and
CHARLES A. THOMSON

August, 1924

Department of City, Immigrant, and Industrial Work
BOARD OF NATIONAL MISSIONS
OF THE PRESBYTERIAN CHURCH IN THE U. S. A.
156 FIFTH AVENUE, NEW YORK.

FOREWORD

In preparation for an enlarged program of National Missions in Colorado, Rev. Robert N. McLean, D.D., and Rev. C. A. Thomson, who has charge of our Spanish program in San Francisco, were asked by the Department of City, Immigrant, and Industrial Work to prepare a study of the Spanish-speaking people in Colorado. This survey was presented in part at the meeting of the Synod in Denver, October, 1924.

Mr. Thomson, who did the field work and prepared the data of the study, is one of the Fellowship men of the Board in the Sub-Department of Spanish-Speaking Work. Previous to his taking up work in the United States, he spent a year in the University at Mexico City, where he obtained the degree of M.A. in a special study of industrial economics in Mexico. Mr. Thomson has contributed articles to several well-known magazines as a result of his study, and approaches from an intelligent viewpoint the problems which attend upon the great tide of Mexican immigration.

The Rev. Robert N. McLean, D.D., who for the past seven years has given his entire time to the work of home missions among Mexicans and Spanish Americans as Superintendent of the Spanish Department under the former Board of Home Missions, has been instrumental in giving this work great prominence in the mission program of the Church. Dr. McLean is now Associate Director in the Department of City, Immigrant, and Industrial Work, with special charge of the Sub-Department of Spanish-

Speaking Work in the U. S. A., making his headquarters in Los Angeles, one of the large centers of Mexican immigrants in the Southwest. Previous to coming into this work, Dr. McLean was head of the Department of Spanish in the University of Dubuque, at Dubuque, Iowa.

Colorado, with her vast area and diversified types of community life, is still on the frontier of National Missions. The Synod of Colorado has integrated its work with the Board of National Missions and has set up a Synodical organization which makes for unity of purpose and a progressive Christian service to the State. This survey of Colorado's Spanish-speaking populations is a contribution to the thinking and planning of the Synod as with a new enthusiasm it undertakes its share in the building of a Christian Commonwealth.

CONTENTS

III

INDUSTRIAL CENTERS

Religious work
    (a) The Methodists
    (b) The Presbyterians

IV

THE MEXICAN ON THE RAILROADS

V

THE MEXICAN IN THE BEET FIELDS

    1. In the Arkansas Valley
    2. In the South Platte Valley

VI

PRESBYTERIAN SPANISH WORK IN COLORADO

VII

RECOMMENDATIONS

APPENDIX

INTRODUCTION

Traveling through the beet fields of Colorado, or across her broad grazing lands, one thinks of the state as comparatively level. But if one attempts to cross from one table-land to table-land—"parks" they call them—one is convinced of the fact that one is indeed upon the backbone of America.

Colorado is high—so high in fact that only one fourth of its area lies below 5,000 feet, while about two thirds of its surface ranges between 6,000 and 14,000 feet. Lots of potatoes are raised in Colorado, but boiled with difficulty in almost every corner of the state.

And Colorado is large. Within its borders the Plymouth fathers could have found land to make twelve states the size of Massachusetts. Although it is seventh in size among the states in the Union, its total population in 1920 was only 939,629; this means a little more than nine persons to the square mile. Still it must be remembered that some of the square miles of Colorado are too vertical for anyone even to try to stand upon them.

Colorado also is diverse in its topography, as well as in its crops. There are no less than nine clearly defined districts. Beginning with the non-irrigated prairie section in the eastern part of the state, one passes to the broad valley watered by the Arkansas in the southeastern part. Across the La Veta pass, where the road crosses the divide at an elevation of ten thousand feet, one comes to the San Luis valley, where since the early days of the Spanish adventurers, millions of sheep have grazed. Another jump over the mountains to the west, and we are in the great San Juan basin, fertile in resources, and needing only adequate transportation facilities to awaken it from slumber.   Then there is the valley of the South Platte, the valleys of the Colorado and tributary streams in the central western part, the mountainous mineral districts, and the broad upland grazing lands known as north central and south parks.   But whether it be mountain, plain, or valley it is always Colorado—whimsical, strong, resourceful—Colorado with her face set toward the days which are to be.

Colorado is diverse also in her population groups; and it is a diversity which is exemplified even among the Spanish people which this survey studies.   The earliest Americans of European blood were the Spanish Americans living principally in the counties bordering upon New Mexico.   These people have been in Colorado for fifty or sixty years; in fact they were there before the Anglo-American appeared, and so were really the first settlers. They are descended from immigrants from New Mexico, who though they passed through old Mexico on their way from Spain, did not dwell there for any considerable length of time, and so supposedly kept their blood free from any Indian tinge.   Having been born on American soil, these Spanish Americans are American citizens.   Because they are native to the United States, they are sometimes referred to by Anglo-Americans as "native Mexicans," in distinction to the Mexicans born south of the Rio Grande who are "old Mexico Mexicans."   The Spanish used by these people is in many instances extremely archaic.   There are obsolete expressions upon the lips of the Spanish Americans which cannot be found outside the pages of the writers of Spain's golden age. The isolation which distances furnished for so many years has been replaced by an isolation of language and blood; and the people have therefore perpetuated many of the characteristics of Spain during her age of gold.

The *Mexicans* are those who were born south of the Rio Grande in the Republic of Mexico, and who have emigrated to the United States, usually within the last five or ten years.   They are not American citizens, and usually do not wish to become so.

In many cases their skin is slightly darker than that of the Spanish Americans. The Spanish Americans are more phlegmatic, more taciturn than are the old Mexico Mexicans. It is harder to move them; but they "stay put" better than their neighbors from the south. Also they are very much more "Catholic" in the narrow sense of the word than are the Mexicans. The immigrant Mexicans have seen the effects of unchecked Romanism in governmental affairs. They have learned to identify church and state, and there has resulted a decided reaction against both. Hence, while Protestantism makes less apparent headway among the Spanish Americans, the results gained are more permanent.

In addition to the descendents of the early settlers there are people of Spanish blood in southern Colorado, Las Animas and Huerfano counties, in the southeastern part of the state, and also the southeastern end of the mountainous belt. In all, these districts contain about 25,000 persons. The San Luis valley has approximately 5,000 and the San Juan valley to the west between 2,000 and 3,000. For the state, a total of 35,000 is probably a fair estimate.

According to the census of 1920, *Mexicans* were found in fifty-two of the sixty-three counties of Colorado. In eighteen of these counties there was a population of 100 or more Mexicans.* Their work as section hands on the railroads probably does more to give them this wide distribution, than any other cause. Their work in the coal mines attracts them in considerable numbers to the eastern edge of the mineral belt, in Weld, Boulder, Fremont, Huerfano, and Las Animas counties. But they are found in greatest numbers in the South Platte and Arkansas valleys, drawn there by the demand for labor for the beet fields. The two industrial centers of Pueblo and Denver also possess a considerable colony of Mexicans. Pueblo has 5,000; Denver a steady population of about 2,000, which is augmented to two or three times that number during the winter, by beet workers who come there

---

*See Table I.

after the close of the beet season and remain until the spring work begins.* In 1920 the census showed that in the whole state there were 10,894 Mexicans. With regard to the situation at present, it is impossible to give anything more than an estimate. But considering all the industrial and agricultural fields in which the Mexican is now found, the figure suggested by Mr. José Esparza, the Mexican consul of Denver, of 22,000-25,000, does not appear improbable, if we understand it to include the migratory beet workers. Thus, with 25,000 Mexicans, and 35,000 Spanish Americans, we have 60,000 people of Spanish speech in the state.

And there are more to follow. Experimentation as to the adaptability of the soil of the San Luis valley for beet culture is being made. Colorado, the diverse, the gigantic Rocky Mountain state is just coming into her kingdom.

---

*The development of sugar beets on the Western Slope in the valley of the Grand is attracting the Mexican to that section. Montrose is reported to have a winter population of 1,000 Mexicans, Grand Junction of 800. The Holly Sugar Company shipped 400 into Delta also this year.

I

LAS ANIMAS AND HUERFANO COUNTIES

(A) GENERAL DESCRIPTION

Las Animas County, lying in the southeastern corner of the state, just over the New Mexico line, is Colorado's largest county, having an area of 4,809 square miles. Its population according to the 1920 census was 38,975, but it now claims with some justice 45,000. The western third of the county is clearly marked off from the remainder by the front rampart of the Rocky Mountains, which passing a little to the west of the city of Trinidad, the county seat, runs almost due north and south. To the east of this geological dividing line lie the plains, covered with sparse grass and in color a dry brown, save for the vivid green of the irrigated sections. To the west are the mountains, the grey earth staring through their scant vegetation, the slopes dotted with piñón and dwarf cedars. Many of their valleys reward cultivation, but their greatest treasure is that of coal. A long, narrow basin of about 2,000 square miles along the foot of the Rocky Mountains contains the largest and best deposits of bituminous coal west of the Missouri River. Trinidad is the largest town in the county; the 1920 census gave it a population of 10,906; it now claims 15,000 and probably has at least 12,000. It lies at an altitude of 6,000 feet. Its prosperity is based on the mines adjacent to it, and the agricultural and live-stock section of its own and surrounding counties.

Huerfano County is found to the north of the western half of Las Animas County. Its area of 1,500 square miles is largely mountainous, though the western part of the county is an elevated "park". Its population in 1920 was 16,879, but to-day it claims eighteen to twenty thousand. Its county seat and largest town is Walsenburg with approximately 4,000 people. (1920 census gave it 3,142.)

[1]

1. *In Trinidad and Las Animas County*

The evidence obtained points to a population of about 16,000 Spanish Americans in Las Animas County. There are very few Mexicans, and those few are found in the mining camps. Mr. Vigil, clerk of the County Court, stated that 35 per cent of Las Animas County (pop. 45,000) is Spanish American. His estimate is based on lists of voters, and constitutes the most objective evidence obtained. Mr. McCartney, assistant county superintendent of schools, also estimated the Spanish American population as 35 per cent. Mr. J. M. Madrid, a real estate man, a leading representative of the Spanish Americans, who has lived his whole life in the county (from 1905-1913 he was County Superintendent of Schools) stated that there are 17,000 or 18,000 Spanish Americans in the county. He estimates there are 35,000 in the entire state.

At the present time, more of the Spanish population is found up toward the mountains, that is in the western third of the county, than on the plains. Formerly the eastern part of the county was all Spanish, but within the last ten years many Americans have come in. One of the priests of the Catholic Rectory in Trinidad, who serves the churches to the west, estimates that in the agricultural valleys in that section there are seven Spanish Americans to every three Anglo-Americans or others.

The mining camps are found in the western third of the county. The mines employ about 4,500 miners, who with their families represent a population of some 14,000 or 15,000. We find that in the Colorado Fuel and Iron Company mines in this county approximately one-third of the miners are Spanish Americans or Mexicans (705 out of 2,054, see Table II). It seems likely that this same proportion would rule in the other mines of the county, since the C. F. & I. mines have made no special effort to attract Spanish or Mexican labor. If this be assumed, we may estimate a population of 5,000 Mexicans and Spanish Americans in the coal mining camps of the western third of Las Animas County.

In support of the above estimate, it may be said that in January 1923, out of a total of 14,051 miners in all the coal mines of Colorado, 3,218, or 23 per cent were Mexicans and Spanish Americans.

Mr. Felix Poliano, District Secretary of the United Mine Workers, with offices at Pueblo, states that the coal strike which occurred in the spring of 1922, cut down the number of almost all the national groups, with the exception of the Mexicans and Negroes.

The Spanish American population in the city of Trinidad was estimated by Mr. Madrid, as 2,000 or 2,500. It is not localized in any one section, but is scattered in all parts of the city. However, there is perhaps a larger proportion in the southwestern section than in others.

2. *In Huerfano County*

As we said above the total population of Huerfano County is about 18,000. Estimates place the Spanish population anywhere from 35 per cent to 60 per cent, or between 6,000 and 12,000.

Mr. J. B. Guerrero, the assistant county assessor, who for the past six years has been in the assessor's office, states that there are 1,500 Spanish tax-payers, and that sixty to sixty five per cent of the county is Spanish, or between ten and twelve thousand. Mr. Guerrero was generally recommended as the person most accurately informed on the Spanish Americans.

Mr. Atencio, the postmaster, also a Spanish American and born in the county, said that the population is usually estimated at 50 per cent Spanish, 25 per cent foreign, and 25 per cent Anglo-American.

The Secretary of the Chamber of Commerce stated that the population is usually estimated at 50 per cent Spanish.

The Catholic priest, a well-informed man, gave the lowest figure, placing the Spanish population of the county at approximately 6,000, or 35 per cent.

As for distribution, the Spanish agriculturists and ranches are found largely in the valley of the Huerfano River, which runs north and west from Walsenburg. Gardner is a center for them, though the irrigated lands near that village and La Veta are held more largely by Americans and Italians than by Spanish Americans. The country southwest of Walsenburg toward La Veta is populated principally by Americans. The Catholic priest reported 500 "Mexican" families in and around Gardner.

The coal mines of Huerfano County are found in a broad band which runs north and south across the eastern half of the county. Walsenburg lies almost in the center of this band. There are 2,491 miners in the county (1923 Report of Inspector Coal Mines, page 57). We may safely assume that between 25 per cent and 30 per cent of these are Mexicans and Spanish Americans; and 600-800 miners will give us a Mexican and Spanish American population in the mining camps of 2,500 to 3,000.

The city of Walsenburg has at present about 4,000 people. Of these probably about one third are Spanish. Mr. Guerrero estimates 35 per cent, and Father Liccioli, the priest, puts the number at 2,000. They are found in all parts of the town, though a greater number live on the west side, near the Walsen mine.

(c) ECONOMIC CONDITIONS OF THE SPANISH AMERICANS

In the cities of Trinidad and Walsenburg, the Spanish Americans are found in many occupations; there are lawyers, doctors, jewelers, masons, clerks, merchants, etc. In Walsenburg it was noted that none of the stores on the principal street was owned by Spanish Americans, though the best barber shop in town and many small groceries and refreshment and cigar stores on the side streets were their property. They also take a prominent part in politics. In Trinidad the County Clerk is Juan B. Romero, and the representative in the state legislature is Carlos Romero; Eusebio Chacón is assistant district attorney. In Walsenburg, both the assessor and assistant assessor are Spanish Americans, as is the postmaster and one of the county commissioners. One-third of the delegates to the Republican and one-half of the delegates to the Democratic County Convention in Las Animas County were Spanish Americans, and in both conventions an interpreter was employed.

[4]

However, the facts noted above concern chiefly the leaders of this group, and for the Spanish Americans as a whole it may be said that they are found in two occupations—agriculture and mining.

1. *Agriculture*

Most of the eastern part of both Las Animas and Huerfano Counties is suitable for cultivation, and where irrigation is possible, excellent crops are raised. The rainfall is generally sufficient to produce fair crops even without irrigation. The higher lands in the western sections of the counties provide good grazing territory, and the irrigated valleys furnish excellent farm land for hay and small grain crops. The principal crops are alfalfa, native hay, potatoes, small grains, beans, and vegetables. Many cattle and goats are raised, though less sheep than formerly.

With few exceptions the holdings of the Spanish Americans are small. The priest who serves the valley of the Las Animas River west of Trinidad reports that the farms are small and poor, often long and narrow strips lying along the bottom of the valleys, where hay and a little corn are grown; on the hills cattle and goats graze. As a rule, the farmers are poor. Mr. Madrid states that the farms of the Spanish Americans run from 25 to 150 acres. Mr. Atencio of Walsenburg says that the ranchers are content with 160 acres. The County Veterinary of Huerfano County reports a few large farms held by Spanish Americans, such as Mr. Martínez, who has several hundred acres of good alfalfa land. But the greater number of the holdings are very small, running oftentimes ten or fifteen acres.

The ranchers do not as a rule live in palatial quarters. An adobe hut is the common habitation, its exterior surface plastered smooth with mud. The roof is often of antique and picturesque flatness, made also of adobe, though more often to-day one sees the use of shingles or corrugated iron. Many of the huts are accompanied by the ancient outdoor ovens. Some of the more shiftless build their house by standing old railroad ties on end and daubing the interstices with mud.

These huts on the inside contain one or two rooms, with the floor of dirt. The latter is usually swept very clean, and the sweeping is sometimes extended to the ground in front for a considerable distance.

Testimony agreed that the land held by the Spanish Americans is, as a rule, so poor that no one else would want it, and so their tenure is not likely to be seriously disturbed in the future. However, both Las Animas and Huerfano Counties are anxious to attract more American agriculturists, and there are plans to stimulate dairying and the production of sugar beets.

2. *Mining*

Las Animas and Huerfano Counties together furnished more than half of Colorado's total production of coal in 1923. The total for the state was 10,336,735 tons; of this Las Animas County produced almost a third, 3,195,434 tons, and Huerfano 1,969,399 tons. The former has fifty mines, of which twenty-two employed a force of fifty men or more each. The latter operated thirty-one mines, of which nineteen employed on the average more than fifty men. The coal is bituminous, of good quality, and much of it is good coking coal.

The mines in Las Animas County last year employed 4,456 men; those of Huerfano County 2,491. But very few of them could boast of steady employment. The mines of Colorado like those in other parts of the United States are suffering from a chronic economic depression due basically to the existence of too many mines and too many miners, and accentuated by the present oil boom and high freight rates. As a consequence, the Colorado mines as a rule are working only half time, from two to four days a week. Last year the Las Animas mines worked 177.6 days during the year; the Huerfano mines 190.3 days. But production during the first six months of 1924 has not maintained even that rate. These conditions should be remembered when we consider daily wages.

The Mexicans and Spanish Americans in the mines make from $5 to $9 a day. Most of the actual mining is contract work, and the man is paid according to the number of tons produced. For day work the standard wage is $7.75, the eight hour day now being the standard; the six day week also prevails, except for a few men whose presence is required at the mine seven days a week.

The Colorado Fuel and Iron Company has an agreement with its men that the wage rates shall conform substantially with the rates of other coal companies whose products are sold in competition with the products of the C. F. & I. So that though the C. F. & I. mines are not completely unionized, the employees there profit from the standard maintained by the labor unions in other mines.

Following the "Ludlow Massacre", April 21, 1914, it will be remembered that John D. Rockefeller, Jr., made a personal inspection of the conditions prevailing in the coal mines and other properties of the Colorado Fuel and Iron Co. As a result of this visit, there was worked out the "Joint Representation Plan," providing for a certain degree of constitutional government and employee representation in the conduct of the industry. The company does not recognize any labor unions, but the Plan provides (Part III, No. 3), "There shall be no discrimination by the management or by any of the employees on account of membership or non-membership in any society, fraternity, or union."

Many of the miners, how many it was impossible to determine, are members of the United Mine Workers of America. The company officials all maintain that there is no discrimination against a man for belonging to the union. A union official, however, states that there is discrimination against at least the officials of the unions; that if a man shows too much activity in behalf of the union, he is not discharged, but his work is temporarily discontinued, he is laid off, and never taken on again. The Company does not permit the locals of the United Mine Workers to hold their meetings in the Y. M. C. A.'s or company clubs situated in the mining camps.

Other mining companies are reported even more unfriendly in their attitude toward union labor than the C. F. & I.

The Mexican and Spanish American seems to stand well in the opinion of the mine superintendents. A larger proportion is found doing skilled labor than is usually the case. In answer to the question: "Is the Mexican or Spanish American as good a worker as the Italian or Slav?" the answer generally was, "No, not quite, perhaps. He won't mine quite as much coal in a day." "Why not?" was asked. "Well, he doesn't seem to have as sturdy a constitution," said one superintendent. "He's not so greedy," said another, "the Italian is always after the money." To the same question another mine boss rejoined in the same tenor, "He's not so hoggish."

Neither Mexican or Spanish American has yet shown much capacity for leadership. As a rule the mine superintendents do not distinguish between them when it comes to working ability. However, two superintendents made the distinction, that the Mexican makes the better miner on the inside, and the Spanish American the better mule driver and company man. In Valdez, where 199 Mexicans and Spanish Americans are employed, only one man had even started on the way to become a boss. Some Spanish Americans become wagon bosses, but that is about the limit of their rise in the industrial world. In some camps, the racial line is maintained, and only Americans are considered for the responsible positions. But this is not universally the case, and in one camp visited, the superintendent is an Italian. This man, by the way, is accused by the Mexicans of partiality toward his own nationality; the Mexicans say they cannot get a square deal.

The Mexican is often accused of being a "floater", and not staying any great length of time in any one job. This accusation is hardly borne out by the results of an investigation made by Mr. Dickerson, of the Y. M. C. A., in May, 1921. He examined the service records of about five hundred Mexicans and Spanish Americans in the six camps of Cameron, Ideal, Lester, Morley, Pictou, and Walsen. The summary was as follows:

Length of Service	
Less than one year	71
One to five years	203
Five to ten years	117
Ten to fifteen years	51
Fifteen to twenty years	27
More than twenty years	19
Total	488

He says, "Length of service in this connection does not necessarily mean that the men have served the number of years indicated in any one camp. On the contrary it seems to be not unusual for miners of all nationalities to move about from camp to camp. They are, however, employed by the same employer and their cards show the total number of years in which they have been in the employ of the company in the various camps . . . In some instances, the men own farms at hand and break into the continuity of their service to work on them during the summer, or to work in the beet fields."

The housing conditions in the camps are generally quite satisfactory. Following the Rockefeller visit referred to above, the C. F. & I. company noticeably improved their arrangements. All the camps were provided with electricity, running water, and sewage facilities. In most of the camps the miners live in company houses. These are rented at the very nominal rate of $2.00 per room per month.

(D) SOCIAL CONDITIONS

1. *Education*

The Spanish American and Mexican children in the larger towns of Trinidad and Walsenburg, and in the mining camps are attending school with regularity, and are profiting from their educational advantages. As a rule they speak English with facility. In Walsenburg there is a large parochial school which has twelve grades. It enrolls 800 pupils, of which the priest estimates that 500 are Mexican or Spanish American. There is, also, a parochial school in Trinidad. Because of the absence of teachers and educational authorities during the summer vacation, this phase of the investigation was not carried through with any thoroughness.

The country districts still show much educational backwardness. Colorado has a compulsory attendance law, but it is difficult to enforce it. Funds are not provided to hire a sufficient number of truant officers, and the teachers themselves tread softly for fear of offending some power which might amputate their job. Miss Nelson, the school nurse of Huerfano County, reports that attendance is most irregular in rural districts which are largely Spanish American. Often the parents do not appreciate the value of education sufficiently to send their children to school. The latter are kept at home, even when there is no work for them to do. Where there exists an element of Anglo-Americans in the rural population, the standard is higher. In the rural sections Spanish is still the language of the natives. The younger children, up to eight or nine years of age, do not know English, and

Spanish is spoken on the play-grounds. The fathers, as a rule, speak enough English to "get by" in their daily occupations, but the mothers usually are limited to the Spanish.

Up until very recent years the language in many of these schools was Spanish. But now the educational authorities have adopted the policy of sending only American teachers into these districts, and Dr. Katherine C. Polly, the State Rural School Supervisor, announces that the state is now planning a definite campaign to send only its best teachers to these difficult districts.

2. *Health*

"Is there more illness among the Spanish American than among other population groups?" Miss Nelson, the school nurse of Huerfano County, was asked. "From my observation during the past year, I could not say that there is," she answered. "But that may be true largely because only the fittest survive infancy. During the past few months, I have gone through the rural sections of the county, registering births. The work has never been done before, and as a consequence there are many children eight and ten years old whose births have never been registered. I find that in large families, with more than five or six children, there is a high mortality rate; often more than half of the children have died. For instance, here is a family of thirteen children, of which eight have died; another of seven children, of which five have died. Here is another, however, of six, of which five are living.

"I have noticed," she continued, "that a large number of these Mexican children have eye trouble. Out of 2,000 children, of all races, examined in the county, 400 had some eye trouble, and a large proportion of these were Mexican. More than half had really serious defects. The older children often have pyorrhea. I notice that the younger children have good teeth, and I tell them it is because they have to chew their tortillas so well; that pleases them. But often children of fifteen or sixteen will be toothless."

Miss Nelson had not found a noticeably large number of tubercular cases among the Spanish Americans, but Miss Clark of the Red Cross in Las Animas County states that 80 per cent of applicants for family relief are Spanish Americans, and about 90 per cent of these applicants have tuberculosis in the family. Miss Phillips, health nurse of Las Animas County, states that the county has more on its blind list (116) than any other county in the state, though it stands fifth in population. Of these blind, 96 per cent are Spanish Americans. Both nurses testified to the fact the Mexican children often suffered from malnutrition, due to ignorance of the mothers as to feeding.

Dr. McKelvey, of the Venereal Section of the State Board of Health, states that the Mexicans and Spanish Americans have as much or more venereal disease than any other racial group with the possible exception of the Negroes.

Miss Nelson recounted some interesting cases where superstition had made her work difficult.

A. She was called in for a family (Spanish American) where the three children were ill with typhoid fever. The two older girls were delirious. The doctor had also been called in, and he advised the use of an ice-pack for the head. The older girl had a great mass of hair, but it had not been combed for days, and was heavily matted. "I asked to cut it," said Miss Nelson. "Oh, no," said the father; "if you cut off her hair she will lose all her strength and will surely die." "Nonsense," I answered, "the child will be more comfortable, and the ice pack will do much more good." So at last the father consented and thanks be, the child did not die. But where did they get the idea about the hair giving strength? Had they ever read about Samson?

B. "I visited a confinement case where the baby was about five or six days old. The mother was lying in bed, unwashed and with her hair uncombed. I asked why. "Oh," came the answer from the neighbor who was attending her, "If you bathe or care for a woman at her stage, she will surely have to have an operation later on." But I disregarded the prophecy, and so far the woman has escaped any operation.

C. In one family a child was ill with diphtheria. It was given antitoxin against the wishes of the father, who said it would kill the child. The doctor told him to keep the boy in bed, since the antitoxin causes heart weakness; but the father shrugged his shoulders at the possibility of forcing his son to stay in bed. The boy got up, walked about, and died from overexertion. A second child was taken ill with diphtheria. The father refused to permit the use of antitoxin since that was the poison which had killed his son, and as a consequence the second child died. Then the father himself fell ill with the same disease, and this time nothing would have it, but he must have the antitoxin. He vehemently insisted on it; it was given and he recovered."

3. *Recreation*

The Mexicans and Spanish Americans living in the towns of Walsenburg and Trinidad have at their disposal all of the amusements usually available in any town of from five to ten thousand population—moving pictures, good, bad, and indifferent, pool rooms, athletics, occasional dances and parties, and various school, church, lodge, and club affairs. Many families in the rural districts still live an isolated existence, in spite of the apparent ubiquity of the Ford, and their social life is quite barren, consisting of neighborhood acquaintance, an occasional visit from the priest, and the contacts which the school brings to the children.

In the mining camps, particularly those of the C. F. & I., the center of social life is the industrial Y. M. C. A. or company club. The buildings are relatively new, having been built within the last five or ten years, another of the fruits of Mr. Rockefeller's conversion. They house a satisfactory equipment including a reading room, a good-sized lobby, an auditorium with stage where moving pictures are shown once or twice a week, and also occasional dances are held, a soda fountain, pool tables, bowling alleys, a barber shop, moving picture machine, and games and magazines. In Walsen, Lester, Valdez, Primero, Morley, Berwind, and Segundo these institutions are directly under the Y. M. C. A. management, and are known as Y. M. C. A.'s. A good secretary is in charge. In the other camps of Ideal, Pictou, Tioga, Farr, and Sopris, they are company clubs, and not under the direct supervision of the "Y." Those of this second class are not staffed as well as the first. For instance, the club visited was in charge of an old barber, a man of no personality or leadership.

These buildings provide an attractive social center for the men and boys, and are extensively used. Through their movies and dances they serve also the women and girls. The Mexicans and Spanish Americans are generally reported to use these buildings extensively; and in some camps, such as Morley and Primero, they are seen about the building more than any other group.

(E) ASSIMILATION

In the contact of Anglo-American culture with the older Spanish American culture of southern Colorado, we have a unique and very interesting case of assimilation. The Spanish Americans were the pioneers and original settlers in this section. They came in during the fifties and sixties and were well-established economically and socially before the American infiltration began.

With the coming of the Americans in increasing numbers into this territory, the cultural isolation of the Spanish Americans was largely destroyed. In the more secluded rural districts they have maintained and still do, a certain degree of geographical isolation. But economically they found themselves in both mining and agriculture, the two dominant industries of the section, thrown in company with the "gringos." Politically they have also mingled, for Spanish Americans are found in both Republican and Democratic parties. They play the game of politics with great enthusiasm and interest, and often with intense feeling. Long-standing family feuds have resulted from some elections. The strongest group bonds of these people have been the Spanish language, the Catholic religion, and their heritage of Spanish culture.

It must always be kept in mind, however, that they look on themselves as real Americans, and cordially resent any accusation of lack of patriotism. Mr. J. M. Madrid, a leading Spanish American of Trinidad, told of starting out on April 17, 1917, only eleven days after the entrance of the United States into the World War, in company with two other men on a campaign of enlistment . "The first eighty-one men who enlisted," he said, "were Spanish Americans."

These people look not to Mexico or to Spain as their home land. They have been born in the United States and America is their country. But they do look with regret at the passing of their old Spanish culture. For instance, there is Mr. Atencio, the young postmaster at Walsenburg, a man of about thirty. There was no trace of the Indian in his narrow face, but his olive complexion, black hair, and large black eyes showed clearly his Spanish blood. "My family," he began, "was the second one to enter this region. First came the Leons and after them the Atencios. I can remember when a little boy hearing my grandmother tell of the early days, but now those days seem far away. A few years ago I went down into New Mexico for my vacation to some places which still conserve the old Spanish ways, where people still have the hospitality which gives all to the stranger. Here when we go away from the house, we lock up everything, so no one can get in. But there, the only thing they think about is to keep out an animal; they are willing to have a human enter their house. The doors, you remember are cut in two sections. When they go out, they may close he lower half, but the upper half is left open. And even when they go away for several days, they may close the door, but they do not lock it. People trust their neighbors. You can't help liking it. I remember my father still kept many old customs. He spoke little English, and my mother none at all. (His own English was perfect.) He taught us in meeting an elderly person on the street always to lift our hat and salute him courteously. But our young people have none of that."

It is easily seen that in the meeting of these two cultures, the Anglo-American is the dominant one. The Spanish is passing, and rapidly now, save in certain of the rural districts. Said Mr. Madrid, "Within fifty years the Spanish population will be entirely absorbed. You would be surprised at the assimilation which has taken place in the last ten years. Since 1905 or 1910 there has been a great increase in the use of English. The Spanish Americans have come to realize that it is the language of the country, and that it must be used." Mr. Madrid himself spoke English well, but with those slight idiomatic slips, which revealed that for him it was an acquired and not a native tongue. "In no school, even in the smallest place, will you now hear Spanish taught or spoken in the class room. Last Saturday, for example, we held our Republican County Convention. Of the 275 delegates, seventy to eighty were Spanish Americans, but all but three of them understood English. Previously in our conventions, we have always used an interpreter, but this time our business went along for some time, until one of those three rose and asked for a translation."

The priest at Walsenburg was of the opinion that Spanish would be spoken for a long time in Southern Colorado. Accordingly Mr. Atencio, was asked: "Do you think the Spanish language will disappear?" "It is already," he answered. "Few are trying to preserve it, though some of us teach it to our children. I have been married for seven years, and we have three children. We resolved to talk Spanish at home, and so the children learned it. But of course they talk English outside, and now the oldest boy talks Spanish only to his grandmother. He will use it with us only when we force him."

Mr. J. J. Guerrero, the assistant assessor of Huerfano County, said, "Our rule in the family is that the children speak English to me and Spanish to their mother. But now our two oldest boys are rusty in Spanish, and the baby, only three years old, has played outside so much with the other children of the neighborhood, that he won't talk Spanish, though he understands it".

Said Juan Romero, the county clerk of Las Animas County, who has held that office since 1906, a man of clear-cut speech, sturdy physique and forceful personality, "I was born in this country; at seven I began my English education; I finished the grades and since then have educated myself by hard knocks. I only had one term of Spanish in school, but I learned it at home and so can speak it well. But I trained my children to speak English at home. That is the most difficult language and also the most essential for their self-support. Then when they went to high school, they got Spanish and now they speak it well. And Spanish helps any man in business in this part of the country."

Mr. Romero emphasized the danger when transition from the Spanish to the American culture is too brusque. "When the children are in the midst of an American society from childhood, when they get American culture in the schools, they get it right. But I have noticed here in the courthouse young fellows who had come in from the country districts where all was Spanish. They would last in a job one year, perhaps two years, and then fall away. You see they had gotten away from their own environment, from the family group which is so important among the Spanish; they came to look down on their parents; they got the vices but not the virtues of the Americans and so assimilation ruined them."

The American culture is overwhelming the Spanish; but apparently the latter is making no impression, or leaving no imprint on the former. Said one of the priests at the Catholic rectory in Trinidad, "The Mexicans have contributed nothing to the Americans. They have taken on American vices, but not their virtues. Because of their contact with the Americans, they have not improved with regard to drunkenness, gambling, sex relations, or in their attitude toward property. They are said to steal; they may take some little thing when they need it, but they will return it and they will not take anything big. Now from the Americans they are learning to steal big things."

Socially, the racial line is still evident between the Spanish Americans and the Anglo-Americans. In the mining camps the "Mexicans" are reported to mix very well with the other national groups, in fact, they are not as cliquish as are the Italians. All the groups use the Y. M. C. A. or the company club, but when it comes to dances, the groups separate—Americans have their dances, the Italians theirs, the Spanish Americans theirs—with the exception that sometimes the young fellows, Spanish and Italians, will mix.

Said one of the priests of Trinidad, "The two races (Anglo- and Spanish American) do not have an antipathy for each other. It is rather mistrust, like a person you meet for the first time. The American regards the "Mexican" as inferior; the "Mexican" is rather afraid of the American; he does not known what he will do to him." The Spanish American is less energetic and more easy-going than the American, and is suspicious of what his quicker neighbor may put over on him.

The Spanish Americans of course feel the condescending attitude of the Americans and heartily resent it. Said Mr. Guerrero of Walsenburg, "The Americans think we are no good; they class us with this trash that comes over from Mexico; we are greasers and nothing more. We have suffered much from these Mexicans, for the Americans lump us all together because we speak Spanish. But we are coming to some leadership. A young Spanish American lawyer has just come here, who is fine. There is a Spanish American doctor who has all he can do. My oldest boy, who has just graduated from high school, has decided to study medicine. He has been working in a drug store, but decided to take a vacation of about four weeks around Denver.

Well, he rested five or six days and that was all he could stand. He went to work at hard labor on a rick pile. Now he has just written me that he has gone to the military training camp at Fort Logan for the summer camp."

Of course, the walls of prejudice and mistrust are breaking down gradually, and as the two groups come to know each other, there is more mutual esteem. So far there has been very little intermarriage.

In Walsenburg, the Ku Klux Klan has been active, and has done much to drive the two groups apart. Last January the sheriff and the chief prohibition officer were shot, and shortly after that the Klan held a parade. As a result, feeling has been very bitter. Said a leading Spanish American, "The Klan has made the Spanish Americans a solid group again. We were drifting apart, away from the church, away from our old friends. But this has brought us all together again. But you know this bitter feeling hurts. Here's a fellow in town whom I chummed with at school since we were kids. We sat in the same double desk, went to picnics and parties together. I was at home at his house, and he at mine. When mother made some Spanish dish that he especially liked, we had him over for a meal. He married and I did too, but our wives were friends in the same way. And now he's leader of the Klan, and ready to knife me in the back any time. Gosh darn it, it hurts to believe it. (His voice grew a little husky and a lump came in his throat.) But the Klan is wrong and it can't last."

II

SAN LUIS AND SAN JUAN VALLEYS

(A) SAN LUIS VALLEY

1. *Introduction*

The six counties of Alamosa, Conejos, Costilla, Mineral, Rio Grande, and Saguache, which comprise the San Luis Valley, together have an area slightly larger than that of the state of Massachusetts. This valley, lying at an altitude of seven and eight thousand feet, was formerly the bed of a great inland lake, and consequently the soil is very fertile. The average rainfall here is the lowest in the state, being in some localities only 6.5 inches. But the Rio Grande and its tributaries, and a large number of artesian wells supply all the water necessary for successful agriculture. The principal crops are grains, alfalfa and other hays, potatoes, field peas, and garden vegetables. Rio Grande county is a leading potato growing district in the state and in September imports many Mexicans for the harvest. Rio Grande and Conejos counties are the two leading sheep producing counties of the state—an industry which provides employment for many Spanish Americans as herders. More field peas are grown in the San Luis valley than in all other sections of the state, and are used largely as feed for hogs and lambs. Mexican laborers are also imported for this crop. The 1920 census gave the six counties of this valley a population of 31,751.

2. *Spanish Americans in the valley*

Rev. M. D. J. Sanchez, Presbyterian pastor at Alamosa, who has been in the valley all his life stated that it contains 5,000 Spanish Americans, the majority of whom are found in the two southern counties, Conejos and Costilla.

3. *Economic and social conditions*

The Spanish population of this section is maintained principally by agricultural activities. In Alamosa there are railroad shops and a newly established lumber mill, but otherwise the occupation of the people is dominantly agricultural. Many of the Spanish Americans own their farms, small holdings running 80 to 160 acres. They raise grains, potatoes and peas, and some stock, though less sheep than formerly. Many others are agricultural laborers. Housing, educational, and health conditions are largely similar to those among the rural population of Las Animas and Huerfano counties. The following selection from the report of Miss Pecover, health nurse for the Child Welfare Bureau, gives a vivid picture of certain health conditions:

"For the most part the Mexican women of this district are afraid of going to a doctor for a delivery unless they have money enough to pay the minimum "full fee" charge which is $35.00. They are afraid of being sued for the amount they are unable to pay, even though agreement is reached with the physician. That this is true was told by several reliable citizens, the Superintendent of the Del Norte Schools being one. They say that some few years ago there were a few doctors who took the attitude that there could be no good in a Mexican; two were sued and all they had was taken to pay for a supposed charity delivery. The Mexicans are having difficulty in believing that all doctors are not alike. The result is that they go to the dirty unregistered midwives even though some of them realize the necessity of having a doctor, and pay them what they can, which is usually from five to twenty dollars. Because these women are unregistered they almost never call a doctor when there is a complication of labor, seldom use prophylaxis in the eyes of the babies, and never register the births. At present most of these midwives are friendly toward us and have said that if there were some other way for them to earn a livelihood for another year or two they would be willing to stop their illegal practices, but they must live and this is all they can get to do."

(B)   SAN JUAN VALLEY

This region in the southwestern part of Colorado is largely mountainous, but possesses a considerable area of agricultural land. Its development as yet has been limited, due to lack of transportation facilities, it being served by a narrow gauge line of the Denver and Rio Grande Western system.

Inadequate transportation has long impaired the development of this very important section of the State. Because the valley is served only by a narrow guage all exports and imports must be rehandled at Alamosa. The grades also are extremely heavy, and the road runs at such a high elevation—10,015 feet at the pass—that it is frequently blocked to traffic by snow during the winter. The Santa Fe, however, is contemplating a direct line from Denver to Los Angeles through Durango—a development which will mean much to the San Juan basin. There are valuable coal deposits in both Archuleta and La Plata counties, which are entirely inaccessible to transportation, and it is said that farmers and sheep herders shovel free coal out of the hills and haul it away in their carts.

The Spanish Americans in this section are found principally in the La Plata and Archuleta counties. Little information was obtained on the latter county; the total population is 3,590, and the Spanish probably not more than 1,000, and largely rural. In La Plata County, Durango with a population of 5,000 is the principal center. The county has a total population of about 15,000 (1920, 11,200) and of these there are 5,000 registered voters. It is commonly estimated there are 700 "Mexican" voters, which would give us a population of 2,000 to 2,500. Of these 700 voters, 400 are found in Durango, which would give us a Spanish American population there of 1,200 to 1,500.

The Durango smelter, owned by the American Smelting and Refining Company is the principal economic foundation for the Spanish American colony in Durango. It employs 177 men of that group, with only 26 Austrians and 9 Italians. The men work the eight hour day and the six day week. Their wage runs from three to five dollars per day. Their work is largely semi- and unskilled; for example, there is no "Mexican" mechanic and only one "Mexican" carpenter. Mr. Reynolds, the general manager, reports them as satisfactory workmen, and that the turnover is not excessive. The older men are very steady. During the war the smelter shipped in sixty Mexicans from old

Mexico, but they have gradually drifted away and now not one of them remains.

Some of the Spanish Americans, of course, are agriculturists. Their farms are not large, running from 160 to 320 acres. They are reported as especially skillful as sheep herders; they do not do so well with cattle.

Not many of the Spanish Americans are reported in the mines of this section. Even in the coal mines, there are more Italians and Austrians.

Miss McCartney did not seem especially optimistic about the efficiency of the schools in educating or Americanizing this group. She stated that the children rarely go beyond the fourth grade. The ignorance of the people is particularly noticeable in the field of politics where they are considered a "manipulated" vote and are the tools of picturesque but corrupt bosses. A local hero is reported to be worthy of a magazine article. After the passage of the Eighteenth Amendment it is said he went to a lawyer to ask him how much he would charge to defend him *by the year*. In a recent election he is said to have provided his Mexican cohorts with dummy ballots, with slits cut in the exact places where an X should be placed. Armed with these documents, they went to the polls, laid them over the official ballots, marked their X where the slits were, and thus voted exactly for all the men desired. This same local hero appeared one time at a Durango precinct to vote. He was recognized by one of the judges, a woman. "You can't vote here," she said, "you're registered in Ignacio." "That's all right," he answered, unperturbed, "I voted at Ignacio, I voted at Perins, and I'll vote here, if you want me to."

The Spanish Americans in Durango are found in the south part of town on the eastern side of the railroad in the section known as "Mexicans Flats", and on the west in the region known as the "bottoms." These sections are marked by the usual picturesque and motley assemblage of shacks and small cottages.

III

INDUSTRIAL CENTERS

(A) PUEBLO

Pueblo, the second largest city of Colorado, is considered its principal industrial center. Its proximity to coal and iron, and its excellent railroad facilities, have occasioned the development there of the largest steel plant west of Chicago, together with almost two hundred other manufactories. The 1920 census fixed its population as 42,908, but the extensive growth of the city even outside its limits affords considerable basis for its claim to have at present 60,000 people.

All the information obtained points to an estimate of about 5,000 Mexicans in Pueblo. The steel works of the Colorado Fuel and Iron Company now employ almost 1,200 Mexicans. A proportion of these are Spanish Americans, but the percentage is not large. About fifty are employed by the U. S. Zinc Co., and small groups by the city, the contractors, and the railroads, notably the Sante Fe, D. & R. G., and the Missouri Pacific.

As was said above, the steel works dominate the industrial situation for the Mexican.

The steel works normally employ between five and six thousand men, and their figures show that the percentage of Mexicans increased from 8.1 per cent in 1912 to over 20 per cent in 1917, and has continued at that proportion or greater ever since.* In 1920 the Mexicans employed comprised 39.8 per cent of the total force, but in 1923 the figure had dropped to 20.24 per cent. Mr. Selleck, the personnel manager, stated that the Mexicans are

---

*See Table III.

satisfactory workmen, and their number is not likely to decrease and may increase in future years.

The Mexican is often accused of being a "floater" in industry, of being unwilling to remain a great length of time in any one job. On being asked about the turn-over among the Mexicans, Mr. Selleck answered: "The Mexican cannot be blamed for a large turn-over. He is a common laborer; he does the hardest work for the lowest pay, and the turn-over is always greatest in that kind of work. Naturally if a man thinks he can better himself he will quit that kind of a job for something better. The cause for the turn-over among the Mexicans is industrial rather than racial."

In the steel works, the Mexicans as a rule do the unskilled or semi-skilled work. A few are wire-drawers; one finds an occasional man working as a machinist or boiler-maker, but the great majority do common labor. The steel works now has an eight hour day instituted in 1918 in the month of November. In this connection it may be stated that this steel works was the first to institute the eight hour day. When Mr. Gary in October, 1918, announced that the policy of the United States Steel Corporation was a *basic* eight hour day, with time and a half for overtime, the manager here announced to the men, that he did not know the meaning of a "basic" eight hour day, but that the C. F. & I. stood for a real eight hour day. He offered the men eight hours and a 10 per cent wage increase and the men accepted. The six day week is now generally observed. There is a minimum of $3.98 for eight hours, and this or a little more is the average wage of the Mexicans.

Mr. A. T. Manzanares, the court interpreter, stated that on an average about fifteen cases a month of Mexicans come before the courts; about two-thirds are for petty larceny, and one-third for drunkenness.

(B) DENVER

Denver, the capital and largest city of Colorado, with a present population of about 275,000, has never had a large Mexican population. The 1920 census could find but 1,390 Mexicans. Since that date, however, the number has grown. Mr. José Esparza, the Mexican Consul with office at 402 Mercantile Building, states that Denver now has a permanent Mexican population of over two thousand, and that in the winter time, when the beet and other migratory workers come to the city, that number is doubled or tripled. The Mexicans live in all parts of the city, on the outskirts to the west and north, but are centralized somewhat west of Speer Boulevard, both north and south of Colfax Avenue.

They are engaged largely in common labor, but their economic situation is not dominated by any one industry as in Pueblo. They work for the railroads, the street car company, the city, and various manufacturing concerns. There has been considerable destitution among them, which the Mexican Blue Cross has been fairly successful in alleviating.

1. *Religious Work*

(a) **The Methodists.** The Colfax Avenue M. E. Church, situated at the corner of Ninth and Colfax, carries on some work among the Mexicans, which took its rise from a marked interest in that group shown by one of the deaconesses. About 1921 a Mexican pastor, Seneca Garcia, was called to the field, and now has a church of about 100 members. There is a Sunday school, but little social work. The Methodists have been allocated the district north of Colfax Avenue.

(b) **The Presbyterians.** The Jerome Park Mission is situated at 2004 W. Holden Place, south of the West Colfax viaduct and just east of the bed of the South Platte River. It is in a district which looks as if both God and Denver had forgotten it. Surrounded by factories, and overhung by a dusky veil of smoke, its little wooden cottages, or ancient one-story bricks, scattered among weed-grown vacant lots, make it seem the mongrel offspring of a deserted village and a city slum. The district has no paving, no side walks, no sewers. It is one of the most depressing sections ever visited.

The church itself, an old brick structure, with one room and a shallow wing, is situated at the end of the most attractive street of the district, shaded by fine old trees. There is no American pastor, and the staff consists of one woman worker, with whom is now working a Mexican pastor. He has a Sunday school and preaching service at 10:00 and 10:45 in the morning which have attracted 40 people. There is a Sunday school and preaching service in English in the afternoon.

IV

THE MEXICAN ON THE RAILROADS

In the table below will be found listed all the railroads in Colorado which have a mileage exceeding 100 miles:

Railroad	Mileage
Denver and Rio Grande Western	1,504.33
Colorado and Southern	729.15
Union Pacific	852.51
Santa Fe	505.62
Chicago, Burlington & Quincy	395.39
Denver and Salt Lake	252.00
Rio Grande Southern	171.16
Rock Island	165.83
Missouri Pacific	152.11

(From "Colorado Year Book, 1924," *page 10*).

The Mexicans work chiefly on these roads as section men. The length of a section varies, but it usually runs eight to ten miles, and four to six men care for a section. We can safely say that the Mexican on the sections and in the extra gangs represents a population of 5,000.

DENVER AND RIO GRANDE WESTERN

On this road, all the regular section men, with the exception of a few Irish between Denver and Pueblo, are Mexican. They have 3,000 men working on the sections, and of these probably two-thirds are in Colorado. Fifty per cent of these are married. There are 1,000 men on "extra gangs," in groups of about fifty men each. These "extra gangs" are shifted to different parts of the system, and they lay tracks, and roadbeds, and do all special work, for which the regular section men cannot care. In these extra gangs there are some Greeks, but eighty per cent of them are Mexicans.

In the Colorado Division, La Junta-Pueblo-Denver-Canon City, there are about forty sections, with about four Mexicans to a section, or a total of 160. The number has recently been reduced from six to a section. Eighty-five men are in extra gangs. Most of the section men have families, and about one-fifth of the extra gangs. In this division we find thirty-eight American bosses, two Mexican, and four or five Italian.

MISSOURI PACIFIC

From Pueblo east to the state line, they have about fifty Mexicans averaging two to a section. There are three to four men usually in a section, Americans working in addition to the Mexicans. In Pueblo there is a yard gang of fifteen (ten Mexicans, four Greeks, and an American boss), and an extra gang of ten Mexicans.

COLORADO AND SOUTHERN

This railroad has its division office at Trinidad, but no information was obtained.

ROCK ISLAND

Reported to have few Mexicans employed. These section men work the eight hour day, and the wage is thirty-five to thirty-eight cents an hour. The extra gangs are housed in regular box cars, with usually four bunks to a car, one in each corner. The furniture of the car includes a stove and a wash-stand.

The section men live in concrete bunk houses, portable frame bunk houses, or box cars set off their trucks and on to the ground. A family may occupy one or two rooms, size about twelve by twelve. The box cars usually have two or three windows in each side, and a door at each end.

No trace of any social work among these people initiated by the railroads was found, yet they often live lonely, isolated lives. The section men who work near the large towns usually live in or near the Mexican colony, and so have the contacts which that association affords. But those living in the smaller towns, in groups of from two to eight families, are cut off from those of their own language and race. And, of course, the extra gangs, shunted around the system from place to place, lead a nomadic kind of existence.

So far we do not have sufficient information to initiate an intelligent program for this group, but the following suggestions might be carried out:

(1)   Lay upon each one of our pastors and workers the responsibility of informing himself about and working with the section men in his territory. The distribution of literature should be especially effective with these people.

(2)   Detail one man, preferably one holding a railroad pass, to spend at least one month a year, to make a tour of the points from which the section men and extra gangs could be most effectively reached. One of the most valuable results of such a tour would be the assemblying of information on which to base a future program. If stereopticon slides and moving pictures could be used, he would be sure of a warm welcome. On such a tour, the co-operation of various social agencies, particularly those interested in health, child welfare, and education, could be enlisted, and thus a well-rounded program of social as well as religious instruction could be given to these people.

V

THE MEXICAN IN THE BEET FIELDS

(A) THE BEET SUGAR INDUSTRY

The journey of a load of beets from the field to the sugar sack is a most fascinating one. Trucks, wagons, and cars conspire in bringing the great white nuggets to the factory. And no sooner have the wheels of the cars ceased turning than the load of beets tumbles down to add itself to the immense pile waiting to take the plunge down the causeway.

Torrents of hot water bear the beets to the cutting knives. And as they are borne along, they are washed. In the factory elevators like Gargantuan corkscrews raise the beets to be cut and shredded, whence they whirl away to the various chemical and boiling vats. From the vats slowly flowing rivers of black molasses toil onward in the refining processes. The syrup drips upon the inside surfaces of great whirling cylinders, where the centrifugal motion holds it in a vertical wall. Streams of water play upon the syrup as it crystalizes, whitens into sugar—then on and on, until at last the weighing machine accurately drops one hundred pounds of warm sugar into the mouth of each waiting sack. A beet travels just twenty-seven miles during this long journey, but so rapid is the process, that the load of beets which is hauled out after luncheon, may be sugar for your coffee-cup at dinner the same evening.

The beet industry in the United States is about twenty-five years old. But though a youth, it has already become a lusty one, for in 1920, its ninety-eight factories produced more than one million tons of sugar.

There are three great areas—the middle western, of which the most important states are Michigan, Ohio, and Wisconsin;

the western mountain section comprising the states of Colorado, Utah, and Idaho; and the western section, of which California is the chief beet producing state.

Colorado, in 1920, produced more than one fourth of all the sugar refined in the United States, next comes California, Michigan, and Utah, in the order named.

Of course, this new industry has demanded new labor, and throughout the United States, the greater part of the rough work is done by Mexican hands.

"Contracts for beet growing are arranged every year between the sugar manufacturing companies and the farmers in beet-raising localities, and every acre of sugar beets is contracted for before the seed is sown. The farmer with his machinery prepares the ground for planting, seeds the crop, cultivates between the rows, and at harvest time loosens the beet roots from the soil. But the intermediate and subsequent processes are performed by an army of hand workers, for although machinery for certain of these processes is being tried, it is not as yet in general use. As the work is distinctly seasonal and also comes at a time when regular farm labor is busy with other crops, the farmer usually hires labor on contract to do the handwork. These laborers have no more to do with the regular farm work than harvest hands or fruit pickers, though in the intervals between the hand processes they sometimes hire themselves out to the farmers for other work. The amount of hand labor required for the beets is usually estimated at one adult worker for every ten acres, which means that in the United States approximately 87,238 adult laborers or an equivalent working force of adults and children were required in 1920."

The supply of contract hand laborers comes from two sources. First, there are the families resident near the beet farms. Since about 1905, a constant stream of Russian-Germans had been flowing into the beet sections of northern Colorado, and these people supplied the bulk of the hand labor. Their ancestors had emigrated from Germany to Russia in the eighteenth century, but had never intermarried to any great degree with the Russians, and had conserved their German language, customs, and religion. The World War naturally cut off this stream, and created a labor shortage. It was necessary to turn to the second and more distant source, and this was the Mexican and Spanish American labor to the south. From southern Colorado and New Mexico Spanish American labor was recruited, but this supply was not adequate to meet the demand. And so agents were sent to Texas and the border of Mexico. Now Fort Worth, El Paso, and San Antonio have become important recruiting centers for beet-field laborers, from which whole trainloads of Mexicans are shipped north, east and west to the beet fields.

"The laborer contracts to do the handwork on as many acres as he thinks he and his family group can take care of. The sugar companies or the farmer—the agreement is made directly with the latter—contracts to pay the laborer a fixed rate per acre (in 1924 this was $21 to $23 per acre), part of the amount to be paid after each operation. In addition, the railroad fares of the workers to the fields where they are to work are paid by the sugar farmer for whom the laborer is to work."

The season for hand work extends over six or seven months, from May to November. The families are usually brought to the beet fields in April and occasionally as early as March. The first operations turned over to them are "blocking" and "thinning," which usually take about five or six weeks. It has been found cheaper to be liberal with the seed and to plant more than enough than to risk a poor stand, but to obtain the most perfect beets only one plant must be allowed to mature, and the plants should be from ten to twelve inches apart. Blocking, as it is called, is usually done by adult laborers, and is followed immediately by thinning, a process performed as a rule by children. It consists in pulling out all but one beet plant and leaving one—preferably the strongest. The blocking and thinning must be done before the beet plants grow too large, and the work is usually done under pressure.

Hoeing is the operation which follows blocking and thinning, and it is spread over a period of four or five weeks. Between the last hoeing—that is, about the end of July—and the time of harvest, a period of six or seven weeks elapses in which there is no hand work in the beet fields.

The beet harvest begins about the first of October and lasts until about the middle of November, or between six and seven weeks. " The date of beginning the harvest depends upon the sugar content of the beets and is determined by the chemists in the testing stations of the sugar companies. After the beets have been loosened from the soil by a horsedrawn machine known as a lifter, they are pulled up by the hand worker and thrown in piles or rows to be "topped." For the latter operation a sharp, heavy knife about eighteen inches long, with a hook at the end, is used. The worker, with the knife grasped in the right hand, hooks up the beet and chops off the crown of leaves with a sharp, downward stroke."

As has been stated, Colorado leads all other States in the Union in beet sugar production. "The beets are grown in the irrigated basins of the Platte and the Arkansas Rivers, the Arkansas Valley covering a tract of land approximately 125 miles long from the Kansas State line to Pueblo, and the northern irrigated districts reaching north from Denver for about 75 miles, then running east and north again along the Platte River. On the Western slope of the Rockies along the Grand and the Gunnison Rivers is another irrigated beet-growing section, but the area there is small compared to that in the Eastern part of the state."

A large part of the above material, and all of that enclosed within quotation marks, was taken from Bureau Publication No. 115, of the Children's Bureau of the Department of Labor, entitled "Child Labor and the Work of Mothers in the Beet Fields of Colorado and Michigan."

In Table IV will be found a list of the counties of Colorado growing sugar beets, with the acreage and value of the crop produced in each one. Table V gives the monetary value in 1923 of the principal agricultural products of the state. From this it will be seen that the crop of sugar beets, valued at $15,001,063, exceeded the valuation of the wheat crop, and was exceeded in turn by only two products, hay and corn.

(B) NUMBER AND LOCATION OF MEXICANS

1. *In the Arkansas Valley*

The Holly Sugar Company, with their factory at Swink estimated that a population of about 800 Mexicans passed the winter of 1923 in their territory, half of them in Otero County, some on the farms but most of them at La Junta, and the balance divided between Pueblo and Prowers Counties. In 1923 they imported 540 fares, and in 1924, 800. Six hundred of these were brought in from El Paso and the balance from Albuquerque, and other parts of New Mexico. Of the 800, 500 were sent to Otero County, and most of the rest to Prowers.

Before going further, it may be well to state that all figures for the number of Mexicans imported, are for "equivalent full fares," which represent the total of full fares paid for adults plus one half the number of half fares paid for all children under twelve. So that the total number of persons brought in is always somewhat in excess of the number of "fares" quoted.

The American Beet Sugar Company, with its sugar factory at Rocky Ford in Otero County, is estimated to have brought in 1,200, of which probably 1,000 came from El Paso. Probably more than one-half of these would go to Bent County, and most of the balance to Otero.

2. *In the South Platte Valley*

The Great Western Sugar Company has as its total acreage almost nine times as large an area as the combined acreage of the Holly and American Sugar Companies. For, in addition to Colorado, it has large holdings in Utah, Montana, and Idaho.

At the beginning of the 1924 season there were 1,026 resident Mexican families within its territory. It shipped in 10,500 Mexican fares for its whole territory, of whom 7,481 were sent to Colorado. Of the 10,500, 2,500 were sent from Denver, 2,500 from New Mexico, some from Kansas City, and four or five thousand from Texas.

This company has ten factories in Colorado, four in Nebraska, one in Wyoming, and one in Montana. Its factories in Colorado are located at the following points:

Brighton	Greeley
Brush	Longmont
Baton	Loveland
Fort Collins	Sterling
Fort Morgan	Windsor

(C) THE MEXICAN AS A LABORER

The Mexicans were brought in to do the contract hand labor, and in that status they have so far remained. In no place but Fort Collins was there any report of their becoming farm tenants or owners. There the labor manager stated that ten or twelve were farming beets for themselves. He said; "I do not look for them to buy land. They are not thrifty like the German-Russians. But the farmers may come more and more to turn the beets over to them and let them farm them. This work, you know, is adapted to the Mexican temperament. They take life easily and don't mind being idle a part of the year."

Mr. Kaspar, Manager of the Holly Sugar Company, on being asked what they would do without the Mexican, threw up his hands and said, "We would be out of luck. We'd have to close up our factory and the farmers would lose the crop. You can't get white labor to do this work. We are absolutely dependent on the Mexican."

An official of the American Beet Sugar Company, said, "The Mexican is a good worker, if treated right. If not, he won't work. He is very loyal or very mean. The trouble is, we haven't known how to treat him. Too many have thought they could beat the Mexican and they would be that much ahead. If any farmer beats the Mexican now, he has to talk to us."

There is unquestionably much child labor in the beet fields, and it is more prevalent among the Russian-German and Mexicans than other groups. The redeeming feature of the situation, is that the children, with rare exceptions, work with and under the supervision of their own parents, and except where the parents are ignorant or cruel, may not suffer physically from overwork. The greatest evil seems to be that they are kept out of school, especially in the fall, and thus retarded in their advancement. An apparently careful study of child and women's labor in the beet fields was made in 1920, under the direction of the Children's Bureau of the Department of Labor, and published in the bulletin No. 115 referred to above. But this survey because of inadequate publicity and follow-up produced no tangible results. Consequently, another survey is in process this summer, supervised by Professor F. B. Coen, of the State Agricultural College at Fort Collins, co-operating with the National Committee on

Child Labor. This survey should turn up some interesting and up-to-the-minute data.

(D) COLONIZATION SCHEMES

Every Mexican fare shipped into Colorado costs the sugar companies from ten to twenty-five dollars. Further, an inexperienced man cannot do nearly so effective work as a man who knows the beets. For these reasons the companies are endeavoring to hold as many of the Mexicans as possible, especially the steadier and more dependable class, within easy distance of the beet fields, and are developing Mexican colonies of various classes and sizes.

The Holly and American companies are building the colonies at their own expense, and giving the houses rent free to the Mexicans. The houses are of adobe, either in single huts, or built together in "long houses." The rooms are about twelve by twelve, and as a rule two are allotted to a family. The floors are sometimes of dirt, sometimes of cement, sometimes of board. Ground is furnished for a garden if desired, with sufficient water for irrigation. It is planned to set out trees, and make these colonies really pleasant little communities.

The Holly Company proposes colonies at the following points:

Swink	Devine
Cheraw	Dinsmore
	Holly

The American Beet Sugar Company has colonies at the following points:

Rocky Ford
La Mar
Las Animas
Manzanola

A woman in the colony at Rocky Ford was asked how she liked the cement floor in the house. "Oh, Senor, not as well as dirt. It is too cold, and then every time you drop a dish, smash, it is gone."

La Junta in the Arkansas Valley has a considerable Mexican population of 600 to 1,000. The Baptists have work here. The

Catholics have just completed a new edifice for the Mexicans and Italians, which is a better looking church than the one the Americans ·use.

The Great Western Sugar Company, under the leadership of Mr. Maddux, is following a different policy from the two companies already mentioned. It is encouraging the Mexican to buy and own his own house and lot. In their colonies the lots run about fifty by eighty-five feet in size. The company furnishes the straw, lime, and gravel for the houses, while the Mexican furnishes the labor to make the adobe, and under supervision to lay the walls and build the house. He is given five years in which to pay for his little property. The first year he pays nothing; the next three he pays $40.00 a year, thus reimbursing the company for the $120 cost of each house. In the fifth year, he pays for his lot, which costs from $25.00 to $50.00. He then receives a deed to the property. During the five year period, the company carries the taxes on the property and also all interest charges. It also holds a contract with the individual Mexican which gives it the right to eject him from the property within thirty days, of course, on the provision that it repay him all he has invested. This is to prevent bootlegging or the establishment of a bawdy house in the colonies.

Fifteen of these houses were built in 1922, forty-two in the next year, and two hundred are projected for this year. They will be located in the following places:

West Greeley	Brush
Johnston	Morgan
Hudson	Fort Collins
Kersey	Ovid
Kingsbury	Sedgewick

In Nebraska there will be colonies at Scotts Bluff, Mitchell, Miniature, and Bayard. In Montana at Billings and Lovell.

At Fort Collins, in addition to the Mexican colony, which is situated to the north of the factory, a number of Mexicans live in the "Jungles," a collection of wooden shacks in the river bottom to the south of the factory.

Mr. Maddux stated that he hoped about 2,000 Mexican families would pass the winter of 1924 in their territory. Of these about 300 will be in the Longmont territory. The farmers themselves are beginning to give the Mexican better housing on the individual farm. Some families are given enough work to occupy them through the winter, feeding stock, etc., and if the farmer wants to hold this labor, he must provide adequate housing.

The Holly Company expects about one-fourth of the 800 they imported this year to remain over the winter.

(E) RELIGIOUS AND SOCIAL WORK

The Companies already realize that to hold the Mexicans, it is necessary to do more than to build them adobe houses; that there will be need to encourage the development of a healthful social and religious atmosphere. Mr. Kaspar spoke of the intention to build social centers or small churches in the colonies of the Holly Company. This company has already given some financial aid to the building of the Catholic Church for the Mexicans and Italians at La Junta, and that in spite of the fact that the company is reported as dominantly Jewish.

In Fort Collins, an illuminating story came to our attention. There the Presbyterian Church has just sold its old edifice to the Catholics, who were aided in the purchase and remodeling by the Great Western Sugar Company. "The company did it," explained Mr. Griffin, "not on any sectarian basis, but it wanted to establish some center that these people could call their own. It has a French priest who speaks Spanish." Mr. Maddux attended the dedication of this church, and reported an audience of over 500. "I witnessed them as they came out," he said, "and you could just see goodness shining in their faces." Mr. Maddux announces himself as interested in all religious efforts to help these people. He assumes the catholic position that all religions make for social good.

In the large colony of West Greeley, he has reserved two fine lots for a social center, which is already drawn in on the prospective blue print of the colony. As soon as thirty houses are up there, he says it will be built.

VI

PRESBYTERIAN SPANISH WORK IN COLORADO

In preparation of this survey statistics were not gathered covering the history of our Presbyterian work in Colorado. Such material should be collected before it is lost. It will include the stories of the lives of Alexander Darley, J. J. Gilchrist, the McLean brothers, Eneas and John, as well as the acts of the lives of faithful service rendered by such missionary teachers as Miss Mollie Clements. There are many interesting stories about the early hardship endured and persecutions suffered, by the first missionaries in the state.

Not far from Conejos, about three-quarters of a century ago, there was a rancher named Gómez. He had heard about the Bible, and was exceedingly eager to secure a copy. Finally a Frenchman came into the valley, who was reputed to be the owner of a copy of the Scriptures. After some bargaining, Mr. Gómez bought it for ten dollars, a fat steer, and the use of a yoke of oxen to make the trip to Santa Fe, the nearest trading point one hundred and twenty-eight miles distant over the mountains. From the time of the possession of this Bible the entire Gómez family embraced the evangelical faith, and when the first missionaries came into Colorado they found a group of Protestant people worshipping in the home of the Gómez family.

Including the wives of ministers there are six missionaries in our Presbyterian force today who are descendents of the original Gómez family.

One of the most significant and well planned policies of the early missionary program, was the development of an educational institution for the training of leaders at Del Norte. This college in its early days ministered almost entirely to the Spanish-speaking population, and when the larger plans of the synod were

[38]

taken into consideration in the development of Westminster College near Salt Lake City, Del Norte College was abandoned. The veterans of our missionary force, both in New Mexico and Colorado, are graduates of Del Norte College, and it makes one pause in his thought for the future, when he questions how these men are to be replaced when their span of service shall be ended.

The veteran workers in Colorado are the Rev. M. D. J. Sanchez, located at Alamosa, and the Rev. Refugio Jaramillo, who is pastor of the church at Walsenburg and the church at Huerfano Canyon, which is located at Tioga.

Mr. Sanchez has lived all his life in the San Luis Valley, and it is impossible to measure the influence which his ministry has had upon the Spanish-speaking people of that section. He serves also as presbyterial evangelist for the Spanish-speaking population of the Presbytery of Pueblo, and gives at least half of his time to travel, caring for a mission in Salida, which is a department of the American church, and which, therefore, does not figure in our statistical tabulation; in caring for a mission at La Jara, the organized church at Saguache; and in serving as a sort of general advisor for all of the other pastors in the area. He is looked upon as the dean of the force in Pueblo Presbytery, and his wise counsel and evangelistic aid have been of inestimable value in all of the fields.

The church at Alamosa is the second largest Spanish church in the presbytery. It has a total membership of 104, and last year 26 were received into membership, 23 of these being on confession of faith. The church has been trained to give, and last year contributed $1,800 for local expenses and $100 for benevolences. The Spanish-speaking people who attend this church, which is called the Second Presbyterian Church of Alamosa, are for the most part clerks and railroad workers living in the city. Because Alamosa is a railroad center and comes in constant contact with English-speaking people, most of the members of this church are able to speak and understand English, and except for prejudice in favor of the Spanish language, it would perhaps not be difficult to carry on most of the program of the church in the English language. The property includes a neat cement block church of two rooms, with a shingle roof, a good adobe community house, with kitchen and social hall, and a small manse, upon which the church has a debt of $1,000 to the Division of Buildings and Property. Alamosa is a strategic point in the San Luis Valley and the missions, which the church conducts through its pastor, are an important feature of the work.

There is an organized church, worshipping in an adobe building at Saguache, eighteen miles from Moffett, on the narrow gauge of the Denver & Rio Grande. Saguache has been without a pastor for years, and receives only the monthly visits of Mr. Sanchez. The field is an important one, and ours is the only evangelical work for Mexicans which is being done in the city. Our church at the present time numbers only six in membership and the work is not in good condition. The church last year contributed $150 for its own support and $15 for benevolences.

About eighteen miles from the New Mexico boundary line in the county of Costilla, is located the San Pablo church. The district is a sheep growing district, although field peas, hay and wheat, and other products are also produced in large quantities. There is an interesting collection of Spanish villages in the group. The most important of these is San Luis, the county seat. To the south are San Pedro and San Pablo, located only a mile apart. About two and one-half miles to the east of San Pablo is the little village of Chama. The two communities of San Pablo and San Pedro may be considered as one; San Pedro being the Catholic community with its large and imposing church, and San Pablo the Protestant community with its no less commodious structure. Chama and San Luis have no Protestant work of any sort, although there are members of the San Pablo church living in San Luis. The most notable of these is Mr. Valdez, who is editor of the *Heraldo Del Valle*. Mr. Valdez is a very influential man, not only in San Luis, but in the whole county of Costilla; he is also a graduate of the college at Del Norte.

There are about 4,000 Spanish-speaking people in the field which the San Pablo church ought to serve. The territory is occupied almost entirely by the Latins, there being scarcely any influx of American settlers as yet. Our San Pablo church, because of lack of funds, has been without a pastor for the past seven years and has been cared for by periodical visits made by Mr. Sanchez. Because of the intense cold during the winter months, and because of the great distance from Alamosa, these visits have not been so frequent as the needs of the church would warrant, and the work, therefore, is not in the condition in which it ought to be. Nevertheless, during the period when the church has been without a pastor, a summer student has been placed upon the field each year, and during the period of service of one of these, Mr. Primitivo Acosta, who is now located in Cuba, a new adobe building was constructed which cost about $3,500, not including the labor of the people. A very effective work could be done through the location of a permanent pastor at San Pablo, and the field ought not to be cared for in the desultory way in which it has received administration in the past seven years. A man with some vision of community service, who could put on a program which would help the agricultural people living in the district, could make himself not only the spiritual, but the material leader of the whole community. In 1923 Costilla County had 4,000 acres of spring wheat, but less than 2,000 acres in winter wheat. The climate, however, is high, being on the average about 8,000 feet above sea level, and is covered with snow for a large part of the year. Up in the San Luis Valley they have a saying that it is winter for eleven months and then one month when it is very cold. There seems to be a prejudice, however, on the part of the Spanish people to the sowing of winter wheat, and some sort of a demonstration given by adequate leadership might accomplish wonders in increasing the productive powers of the people living in the area.

South of San Pablo, and directly on the state line are located the two towns of Garcia and Costilla, Costilla being in Colorado and Garcia in New Mexico. For a number of years our two Home Mission Boards maintained both a school and a church at Costilla, the work being carried on in a building, half of which was manse and the other half church, the separation being by a community wall. In 1917, however, the work by a comity agreement was turned over to the Methodist church, and the property has been transferred to the Methodist Conference in exchange for a like transfer on their part at Llano, New Mexico, where they have turned over a field to us. An interesting thing, however, is the fact that the Christian Endeavor Society which was established at Costilla during the Presbyterian tenure, still sends delegates to the convention of the Presbyterian Christian Endeavor Society at its annual meeting in August.

At Ignacio, in La Platte County, is located a church which has served both Spanish-speaking people and Indians under the leadership of the Rev. A. J. Rodriguez for many years. The property consists of a very attractive and commodious building of cement blocks, well located. The town, however, is small, the 1920 census giving it a population of 240 and the Colorado Year Book for 1924 estimating the population at 340. At least half of these are Americans, and are served by an American Methodist church, located about three blocks from our Spanish-Indian church. The building is of wood, but commodious and attractive. Our church serves also the Ute Indians, from the nearby reservation, and yet by the most liberal estimate and counting the nearby ranchers, the two churches, Methodist and Presbyterian, cannot possibly reach more than 1,000 people, of whom half would be Americans. The wisdom of building at Ignacio with the small population which the church could serve is questionable, and wiser strategy would have dictated the policy of spending the money involved in Durango twenty miles to the west, a town of about 5,000 population. The urgent petition on the part of the presbytery for the construction of the church at Ignacio may have been due to the fact that the pastor, the Rev. A. J. Rodriguez had his residence there. It is criminal and foolish in this day and age for two Home Mission Boards to be putting money into a town like Ignacio. If the Methodist church plans to drink the cream off the community, it ought to drink the skim milk also, and plans ought to be made which would serve Americans, Indians, and Spanish-speaking people alike. This ought not to be difficult, because the Spanish-speaking people have been so long at Ignacio and hold such an important part in its social and industrial life that racial barriers are inconsequential.

Mr. Rodriguez two years ago reached the age of retirement, and because of the apparent folly of spending Home Mission money in such a field, the sub-department of Spanish-speaking work, recommended to the Board that the appropriation be discontinued and to the presbytery that Mr. Rodriguez be recommended for aid to the Board of Ministerial Relief. Both recommendations have been adopted, and Mr. Rodriguez is now upon the retired list. He is aged and infirm, and has been unable for eight or ten years to do the work of an active pastorate. He has a neat home in Ignacio, which he owns, and ever since his retirement has carried on the work of the Ignacio church exactly as he did when he was upon the active list. For some time he has been unable to do very much more than to care for the services of the church and to do such calling as cases of sickness and urgent need required. Mr. Rodriguez has for years had a small mission in Durango, holding services in the home of one of the members living there, but belonging to the Ignacio church. A wise policy for the future would divorce this plan of letting the tail wag the dog in the Ignacio-Durango field, and would locate a minister in Durango where there is an opportunity for a large and important work and would plan for the continuation of Ignacio as a mission of Durango in the future, unless the Methodists can be persuaded to take over the work there.

In spite of the lack of opportunity the Ignacio church has always been one of the best in the presbytery. They reported last year a membership of fifty and received four upon confession of faith during the year. The finances, however, have been at low ebb, the church contributing $52 for its own support and $20 for benevolences. Doubtless the fact that Mr. Rodriguez is not receiving his salary from the Board, and that the church people know that he is cared for by a pension, is largely responsible for this fact.

Another of our Spanish fields centers about Antonito, thirty miles to the south of Alamosa.

Six miles north of Antonito is the Spanish town of Mogote. Mogote is very much like San Pablo, in that it has close to it a smaller town named San Rafael, which is intensely Romanistic. Our Spanish church was first located at San Rafael and bore the name of the town. Because of intense opposition to the Presbyterians it seemed wise when it was possible to construct a building, to erect it in the neighboring town of Mogote where most of the members lived. The church has served for more than half a century in that community, and as a result Mogote is largely Protestant, while San Rafael is entirely Catholic. In Mogote Miss Mollie Clements served continuously under the Woman's Board as a teacher for twenty-seven years. Her Christian character is written into the lives of all the people of the town, most of whom·at one time were pupils of her mission school.

The Mogote field has as its out-stations the Antonito church, with fifteen members, and the Ortiz church with twenty-six members. The Mogote church this year reports a membership of 143 and received fifteen upon confession of faith. The church contributed $268 to its own support and gave $112 for benevolences.

Just at present the field is vacant, Rev. C. A. Romero having been transferred by presbytery's committee on National Missions to Las Animas, where he is to have a roving commission in caring for the beet workers in the Arkansas Valley. The removal of Mr. Romero leaves the largest Spanish church in the presbytery without pastoral care, and immediate steps must be taken to provide for it. There are elders, however, in the Mogote church who can carry on the work temporarily, and it would seem to be wise, in view of the fact that San Pablo has been without a pastor so much longer, to locate a man at San Pablo for the current year, allowing him to make periodical visits to Mogote.

Of course, the most strategic point in this field is Antonito, but as yet our work has not made very much of an impression there. In the days of Eneas McLean, who served as pastor on this field, a church was erected in Antonito for the Spanish work. Through some sort of shifting that church, however, has passed over to the Americans and is used by them to the exclusion of the Spanish people, who worship in a home.

Over the La Veta pass, in the county of Huerfano, is located the town of Walsenburg. Detailed information has already been made elsewhere in this survey about the mining industries, and the number of Spanish-speaking people employed. Our church there is of long standing, has a desirable and well located property, but the building consists only of a good-looking brick manse, in the front rooms of which services are held. A very urgent need is that of a new church building. The town is important and the church has been a decided influence in the moulding of its character. The Walsenburg church last year reported a membership of 120, receiving twenty on confession of faith and three by letter; contributed $400 to its own support and $128 to benevolences. It has an out-station in Huerfano Cañon church which is located in Tioga. This church last year reported thirty-three members, received two on confession of faith, four by letter; contributed $40 to its own support and $20 to benevolences.

One of the most important fields in the whole presbytery is the city of Trinidad. The Spanish work in this city has had a checkered career. For years services were held in an adobe structure, which was very poorly located. As the district deteriorated it came to be the red light district of the city, and it was impossible to attract any except the people who lived in the immediate vicinity to its services. In 1921 through aid given by the Board of Church Erection, an adequate and well located stone church was purchased from the Disciples denomination for the sum of $10,-000. Since that time the activities of the church have increased, and its membership has grown under the pastor in charge, Rev. Amadeo Maes. He serves not only the Trindad field, but, also, in his Dodge car a number of the mining camps located round about. As an illustration of how much a building counts in the development of a church, a comparison of statistics immediately preceeding the purchase of the new building and the last year, will be interesting in the case of the Trinidad church. In 1920 the membership was 80, in 1924 it was 115. The church in 1920 contributed for all purposes $315, in 1924, $634.

There is located also in Trinidad an Italian Presbyterian church served by the Rev. A. Sulmonetti, which reported in 1923 a membership of 36, with a Sunday school of 75. There seems to be little or no co-ordination between the American church, the Italian church, and the Spanish church; and Trinidad as well as Walsenburg and Alamosa present a fertile field for the working out of a unified Presbyterian program, especially for the industrial group which our Presbyterian work attempts to serve.

The development of the sugar beet industry in eastern Colorado has very largely changed the complexion of our work at Las Animas. The people who have come in to care for this industry have for the larger part been immigrant Mexicans from old Mexico. Las Animas for years has been cared for as a mission church from Trinidad, the pastor of the Trinidad church making monthly visits, and the work being carried on in the interim by the elders. The field has become so important, however, that the Rev. C. A. Romero located until August at Mogote, has now been transferred to Las Animas where he will have his residence, and where he will care for as many of the beet workers as he can reach in his immediate territory. Our whole program for work among such a population is in a most primitive stage. Experimentation has been made among the cotton pickers of the Salt River Valley around Phoenix, by equipping a car with a moving picture machine, Testaments, tracts, and other literature. It is probable that an adaptation of some such sort of a program will be used for reaching the beet workers in the vicinity of Las

Animas. The Las Animas church has a membership of thirty-eight and gave $249 for local support and $32 for benevolences last year.

From a denominational standpoint it is to be regretted that our Presbyterian Spanish mission in Pueblo was abandoned some ten or twelve years ago. There are no facts on file which would indicate the reason of the abandonment, but the remains of the work have been turned over to the Baptists, who are now doing a good piece of work as indicated above.

The work in Denver Presbytery is of very recent development and has been due largely to the efforts of the Rev. Paul H. Buchholz, serving under the sub-department of the Spanish Work and located at Denver in October of 1922. Mr. José Candelaria was brought from Dubuque Seminary to Iliffe Seminary in Denver, in order that he might give part time during the completion of his seminary course to the work in Jerome Center, an enterprise under the direction of the Church Extension Board at Denver. Mr. Candelaria has succeeded in getting together an interesting group of Spanish people, and while the opportunity for work in Denver is not particularly large at the present time, the movement of the beet workers will make that city a point of increasingly strategic importance.

Probably the greatest untouched fields, as this survey shows, are the great beet fields north of Denver. A beginning has been made in the locating of Miss Patricia Salazar at Brighton, and an attractive adobe building to serve as a Home of Neighborly Service has been built. It is hoped that this Home will serve as a model for other communities in which there are Mexican colonies. Miss Salazar is the product of our Home Mission work in Southern Colorado, her father being an elder in the Ignacio church. She speaks English and Spanish fluently, is of attractive personality, bright, and ought to put over a very successful program. If the first Home of Neighborly Service at Brighton can be made a success, there is no reason why the Great Western Sugar Company would not go halfway with us in the establishment of a number of such community houses in the area which they serve. Miss Salazar began her work this summer with a Daily Vacation Bible School.

One of the most interesting phases of the work in southern Colorado is the Christian Endeavor Convention which is held annually. These conventions have been held without a break for the last quarter century and are largely attended by our young people in the southern part of the state. It is the custom to meet on Thursday night in the convention church, and services are held all day Friday, Saturday, and Sunday. Much enthusiasm is shown and the young people look forward from year to year to these conventions. Great good is done the visited church, but the enthusiasm and set up ought to be used for a more educational program than has been the custom in years past.

The outstanding needs religiously in the development of our Presbyterian work seem to be the following:

First.—The development of local committees, Presbyterian unions, or Boards of Church Extension, which will vision our Presbyterian work in the larger communities as a unit, instead of along racial lines.

Second.—The extension of our program in the coal mining districts, so that it will more adequately serve the social and economical needs of the Spanish workers in the mines.

Third.—It is essential that we meet the situation among the beet workers.

Fourth.—There must be developed a more adequate program of religious education in the church than already exists.

For the past ten years the Sunday school membership has each year lagged far behind the church membership, not only in Colorado, but throughout the whole southwest, except in California. This is not as it should be, and the churches of the future will ultimately be about the same size as the Sunday schools of the present. Our Spanish people all have large families, and one is led to inquire as to the whereabouts of the children whose parents are members of our churches.*

An interesting and perhaps mitigating circumstance in this connection, however, is the fact that while our increase in church membership throughout the whole southwest would plot a continually ascending line, the Sunday school membership from year to year fluctuates. One is led to the conclusion, therefore, that the statistics on church membership, because of the necessity of balancing returns according to the blanks furnished by the stated

*See Tables VI and VII.

[47]

clerks, prompts a more accurate keeping of the records, than is the case in the Sunday schools. It is probable that the personal element of judgment enters more largely into the statistical information we have on the Sunday schools than on the churches; but the relative unimportance of the Sunday schools in the minds of the ministers, which this fact would indicate, is not encouraging.

As a matter of fact, in our Sunday schools all over the southwest, the service is made more of a preaching service for children than a school of religious education. There is too much inspiration and too little perspiration; they are exhorted too much and taught too little. Furthermore, the religious leadership is all furnished and not enough effort is being made by our pastors to develop leaders on the part of the coming generation. Much attention must be given in the religious program of our Spanish churches to the expressional side of the work. It is noted that where we have Christian Endeavor Societies, which enable the young people to develop this side of their lives, the Sunday schools are always more flourishing and prosperous, than where such societies do not exist.

A study of the growth in membership of the churches and Sunday schools of Colorado (Table VI) indicates that there has been much fluctuation year by year. The plotted curve is discouraging, for it does not seem to be getting anywhere, either up or down. There is not the regularity which is noted in growth in membership for the whole southwest.

The same fact is true in the study of the comparative giving in the Spanish-speaking churches of Colorado.* One is at a loss to explain why the years of 1916, 1921, and 1924, are so much above the general average, and the conclusion is almost forced home upon one, that the churches are inclined to give in accordance with the pressure placed upon them. Nevertheless there is an element of permanency in the Spanish-speaking churches of Colorado which is encouraging. Our churches in the southern part of the state fairly adequately cover the field, but there ought to be laid upon the consciousness of all of us that there is much ground yet to be possessed in the beet fields and in the mining camps.

*See Table VIII.

VII

RECOMMENDATIONS

1. The present and future importance of the Spanish work in Colorado, as shown by this survey, fully justifies the wisdom of placing an executive in that field. The already excellent work of Mr. Buchholz in this area is further proof of the rightness of this step. Denver because of its unexcelled railroad connections is the point from which all parts of the field may be reached most easily, and is also very accessible to the rapidly developing situation among the beet workers to the north.

2. The work among the beet workers seems the outstanding opportunity among the Spanish-speaking people in the state. Here we have a population movement of quite unique interest, where industrial needs are causing the importation of thousands of individuals of a group almost entirely new to the environment and social setting. This region is to be dotted with small Mexican settlements. The movement is still in its early, formative stages. We have now an opportunity to get in early, to do something to mold these small communities in the making, and early to arouse the American communities to their responsibility toward the new-comers.

3. The greatest opportunity in the two counties of Las Animas and Huerfano appears to lie in the coal mining camps, especially those of the C. F. & I. Company. In almost all these camps there is concentrated a considerable number of Mexicans and Spanish Americans. We have estimated that in Las Animas County there are about 5,000, in Huerfano County between 2,500 and 3,000. In all the C. F. & I. Camps there is a Y. M. C. A. or company club, which could easily be secured as a locale for our work.

As has been stated, the Y. M. C. A. is providing adequately for the social needs of the men, and also doing something for the boys. Little seems to be done for the women and girls. Accordingly it would appear advisable for us to enter the field with a woman worker, who could direct organized clubs and classes for the girls and women, help in the Sunday school, and conduct a D. V. B. S. in the summer.

4. Our two churches at Trinidad and Walsenburg are well located, and seem to be doing good work. It has been suggested that they might render their greatest service by inspiring young people to become leaders, such as health nurses, teachers, and agricultural experts.

5. The question of the extent of the assimilation of the Spanish Americans was gone into carefully, in an endeavor to learn to what extent separate churches are still needed for this group, and to what extent the Spanish language should still be employed. Investigation has established the fact, We believe, that this group is still sufficiently distinct to warrant separate churches and other organizations, except possibly in the mining camps, where they might form part of a joint program for all racial groups. With regard to the language, though Spanish is indeed rapidly passing, and all work for children can be carried on in English, it is evident that for the next ten or fifteen years, Spanish will still have to be used with the adults, and possibly longer in the rural districts. As one Catholic priest expressed it, "Most of the Spanish Americans, especially the men, understand enough English to 'get by' in their daily business and industrial life; but if you want to make sure that they understand a thing clearly, if you want to give them a talk or a lecture, you must use Spanish."

6. Care should be taken to keep our churches entirely clear from any connection with the Ku Klux Klan. Otherwise they will be the object of much greater bitterness and prejudice than they now suffer.

7. The Mexican situation of Denver is not yet crystallized. But it seems likely that Denver because of the large number of beet workers which pass through it, will, especially during the winter months, come to house a considerable population. For this reason the situation there should be watched with care during the next two years.

8. Pueblo warrants a more intensive survey, to establish the possibility of initiating work there which would not compete with the Baptist Center and the Y. M. C. A.

9. Durango with its 1,000 or 1,200 Spanish Americans is an important and virgin field as far as Protestant work is concerned. The Catholics there seem to be rendering real social service, and have a hold on the people which might make Protestant progress difficult.

APPENDIX

TABLE I

MEXICANS* IN COLORADO

1920 Census, Vol. III, page 149

A total of 10,894 Mexicans were found in the state, in 52 of its 63 counties. The 18 counties, in each of which were more than 100 Mexicans are listed below:

Adams	100	Las Animas	893
Bent	475	Mesa	152
Boulder	108	Mineral	136
Crowley	183	Morgan	132
Denver	1,390	Otero	1,153
El Paso	230	Prowers	951
Fremont	202	Pueblo	2,486
Huerfano	424	Saguache	115
Larimer	231	Weld	756
	By cities		
Boulder	1	Greeley	96
Colorado Springs	85	Pueblo	1,882
Denver	1,390	Trinidad	89

In 1920, Colorado had a total of 116,954 foreign-born white, of which 10,894 Mexicans comprised 9.3 per cent.

---

*Mexicans born in the Republic of Mexico.

TABLE II

COAL MINES OF COLORADO FUEL & IRON COMPANY

County	Mine	P. O. Address	Y. or Co.	Cath. Ch.	Mex.	Sp.	Ital.	Total (1)	Total (2)
Fremont	Coal Creek	Rockvale	Club						159
	Rockvale	Rockvale							181
	Fremont	Florence	Club		1		77	154	146
	Emerald	Canon City			25		19	78	42
Gunnison	Elk Mountain	Crested Butte	Club		11		36	174	} 85
	Crested Butte	Crested Butte							112
Huerfano	Robinson No. 1	Walsenburg	YMCA	Yes	89		85	426	302
	Robinson No. 2	Walsenburg							
	Ideal	Ideal	Club		118		56	226	M. 211
	Lester & Rouse	Lester	YMCA		41		32	218	M. 210
	Cameron	Cameron			36		16	156	174
	Pictou	Pictou	Club		3		1	38	91
	Kebler No. 2	Tioga	Club		58		13	183	64
	Farr	Farr	Club						
[Las Animas]	Frederick	Valdez	YMCA		199		89	397	344
	Primero	Primero	YMCA	Yes	149	4	49	338	306
	Morley	Morley	YMCA	Yes	98	9	72	285	
	Tabasco	Berwind	YMCA		133		176	494	} 217
	Berwind	Berwind		Yes		28			224
	Toller	Tollerburg	Y at Berwind		9		7	100	M. 261
	Segundo	Segundo	YMCA	Yes	46		27	86	157
	(coke ovens)								
	Sopris	Sopris	Club		69		185	342	371
	Engleburg (closed)				2		3	12	
	(Quarries)								
Pueblo	Line		Club		11		20	54	
Fremont	Calcite						8	25	
	Caretakers and staff at mines temporarily closed				7		44	263	
			TOTAL		1,105	41	1,015	4,049	

Americans	876	21.63%
Austrians	314	7.74%
Slavs	111	2.74%
Colored	140	3.47%
Others	447	11.04%

According to total (1)

Total in camps	4,049		
Mexicans and Spanish Americans	1,105	or	27.03%
Italians	1,015		25.07%
Spanish	41		1.01%

Total (1) and figures on the number of Mexicans (including Spanish Americans), Spanish, and Italians, were of January, 1924, and were furnished by Mr. Wakeman Business Secretary of the C. F. & I

Total (2) was taken from the 1923 report of the State Inspector of Coal Mines.

"M" Signifies a large proportion of Half Mexican...

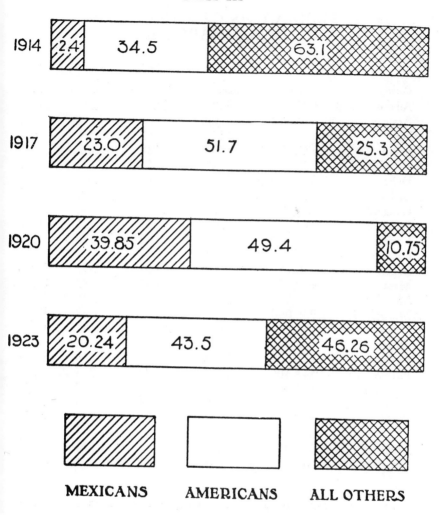

TABLE III

PERCENTAGE BY NATIONALITIES OF TOTAL
NUMBER OF EMPLOYEES 1914-1923
C.F.&I. STEEL WORKS

TABLE IV

PRODUCTION OF SUGAR BEETS
IN COLORADO, 1923

County	Value	Acreage	Per cent of cultivated land devoted to	No. of farms reporting	Total No. of farms
Adams	$ 502,975	5,396	3.26	249	1,535
Arapahoe	21,258	228	.28	8	624
Bent	347,288	2,756	3.47	94	859
Boulder	682,000	7,710	10.28	332	796
Crowley	292,600	2,526	6.84	131	531
Delta	333,300	2,710	6.01	208	1,500
El Paso	16,170	124	.10	3	1,189
Garfield	222,200	1,410	2.94	88	844
Jefferson	43,450	384	1.07	31	1,029
Larimer	320,880	13,018	12.42	575	1,088
Las Animas	12,120	98	.11	...	1,820
Logan	1,520,750	15,340	3.81	395	2,216
Mesa	479,325	3,582	5.95	182	2,662
Montrose	306,075	2,287	3.47	224	1,216
Morgan	1,936,000	22,089	11.62	462	1,432
Otero	1,144,275	10,426	14.02	457	1,187
Ouray	2,222	17	.16	3	170
Prowers	435,600	3,586	2.26	150	1,197
Pueblo	444,400	3,387	3.83	273	1,583
Sedgewick	504,900	5,181	4.44	127	534
Washington	67,375	640	.14	26	1,905
Weld	4,365,900	45,305	8.96	1,752	4,176
Total	$15,001,063	147,720		5,775	

The above data is taken from the Colorado Year Book, 1924, pages 50, 51, 73, 83, 87.

From the map on the following page it will be noted that there are three principal areas for growing sugar beets in the state:

1. The South Platte valley, including Adams, Arapahoe, Boulder, Jefferson, Larimer, Logan, Morgan, Sedgewick, Washington, and Weld counties.

2. The Arkansas valley, including Bent, Crowley, Las Animas, Otero, Prowers, and Pueblo counties; also El Paso.

3. The West Slope, including Delta, Garfield, Mesa, Montrose, and Ouray counties.

ACREAGE OF SUGAR BEETS, 1923

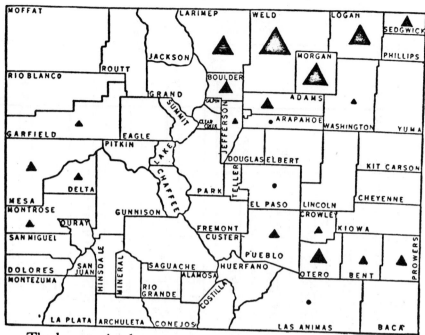

The largest triangle represents 45,305 acres. The dot represents less than 450 acres.

TABLE V

VALUE OF THE PRINCIPAL FARM CROPS OF COLORADO, 1923

(From Colorado Year Book, 1924, pp. 50, 51.)

		Acreage
Corn	$23,476,676	1,400,000
Wheat	14,182,857	1,390,000
Oats	3,309,066	
Barley	3,346,346	
Rye	639,561	
Potatoes	8,463,499	110,000
Beans	4,951,663	
Sorghums	5,917,220	
Sugar beets	15,001,063	165,453
Hay	29,615,941	1,576,000
Fruits	7,865,310	
Miscellaneous	7,037,200	
Total	$123,806,402	

TABLE VI

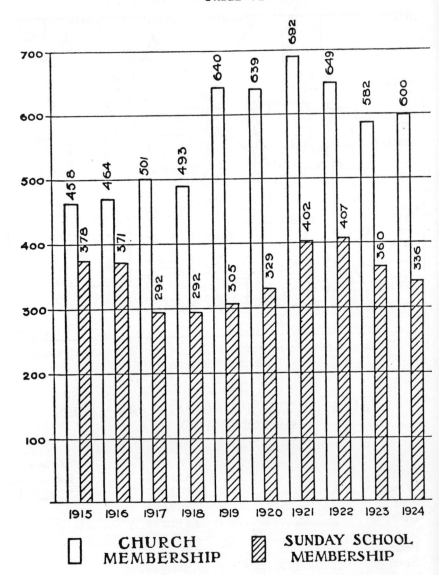

GROWTH IN MEMBERSHIP

CHURCH AND SUNDAY SCHOOL

SPANISH SPEAKING CHURCHES IN COLORADO

[58]

TABLE VII

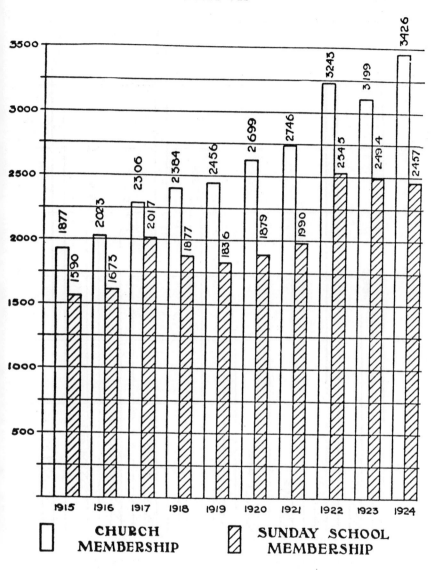

GROWTH IN MEMBERSHIP
CHURCH AND SUNDAY SCHOOL
SPANISH SPEAKING WORK IN SOUTHWEST

TABLE VIII

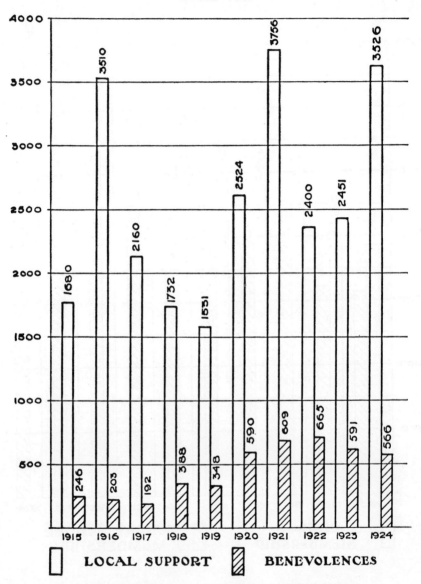

LOCAL SUPPORT   BENEVOLENCES

GIVING IN THE SPANISH SPEAKING
CHURCHES OF COLORADO

TABLE IX

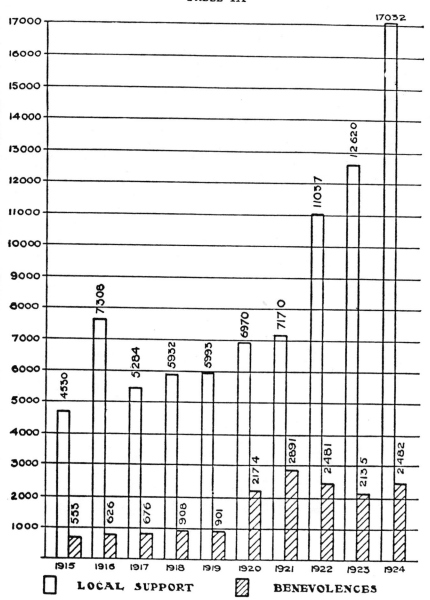

GIVING IN THE SPANISH SPEAKING
CHURCHES OF THE SOUTHWEST

FROM
OVER THE BORDER

NEW CITIZENS FROM OVER THE BORDER

The Mexican has established himself firmly in the economic life of the United States. Vast areas of the country are dependent upon his labor. His children and his children's children will live here as American citizens. They will help to elect our presidents; they will help establish our moral, political, and religious ideals and practices. Our future is bound up with theirs. We must think about them; we must come to know them; we must work with them in the constructive and worthwhile things of life.

FROM
OVER THE BORDER

A STUDY OF THE MEXICANS
IN THE UNITED STATES

By VERNON MONROE McCOMBS

COUNCIL OF WOMEN FOR HOME MISSIONS
and
MISSIONARY EDUCATION MOVEMENT
NEW YORK

The Rev. Vernon Monroe McCombs, D.D., is
Superintendent of the Latin American Mission
of the Methodist Episcopal Church with headquarters in Los Angeles. He is a graduate of
Minnesota State Teachers College, Hamline
University, Drew Theological Seminary, and
New York University. The son of frontier
missionaries, he himself served in a frontier
mission station for several years after his
graduation. He then went to the west coast
of South America under the Board of Foreign
Missions of the Methodist Episcopal Church
and was for four years Superintendent of the
North Andes Mission in Peru. A break in
health compelled his return to the United
States, and for the past fourteen years he has
been supervising the work of his Church in the
Southwest among immigrants using the Romance Languages—Mexicans, Portuguese, Italians, Filipinos, and Spaniards. He has traveled
for study in Central America and in Mexico
and has lectured in various colleges and seminaries. Dr. McCombs' work has brought him
into touch especially with the Mexicans, and
his long association with them as their trusted
friend and helper makes him one of the best
qualified interpreters in America of those who
come to us "from over the border."

TO EVA

MY FAITHFUL COMRADE
IN LABORS AMONG OUR NOBLE LATIN FRIENDS
BELOW AND ABOVE THE BORDER,
IS THIS HOME MISSION STUDY BOOK
AFFECTIONATELY DEDICATED.

CONTENTS

ILLUSTRATIONS

FOREWORD

AFTER labors in two continents and among eight races, we aver that we have never met a more responsive or delightsome people than the Mexicans from over the Border. In youth the author had been led by stories to fear and despise these same people. Thus Border prejudices (current among well-meaning Americans) clouded our vision of brotherhood toward our nearest neighbors. Laggard have been our missionary feet in going to the relief of a people we have so long given over to be the preserves of the vicious, exploiting, and adventurous. The task is delicate. We have been so near so long. We are dealing with noble souls who are the product of an age-old civilization and high ideals.

The veteran Presbyterian Superintendent, Robert McLean, D.D., declares, "I believe it to be true that we really know less of the Mexican people than of any other people on earth, and the worst of it all is that so many think they know." Doctor D. F. Howe says: "Those who scoff at a Mexican in rude clothes in the street or fields are scoffing at a mass of ignorance in the back of their own heads. Mexicans come from a great past from which they have been dragged down. Our task is to help them to rise yet higher than even in those golden years of the most perfect socialistic government probably in all history."

ix

In Mexico Calles, peaceably elected by the
processes of a true democracy, has recently succeeded Obregon, who has successfully concluded a
dignified, democratic, "impossible" labor that was
perhaps unequaled in all the history of the Mexican people. Our trade volume with Mexico now,
exceeds, not only that of the past, but also that
of Mexico with any other nation. The Mexican
people and the rest of Pan-America are now in
the spotlight of interest. Those who have been
"around the world" and others who have crossed
the Atlantic many times are beginning with surprised delight to visit and to know these people
above and below the Border. The new interpretation of the Monroe Doctrine is coming to mean
an unselfish purpose to help in the uplift of the
other Americans on both sides of the Border who
have been the victims of both a bad start and bad
contacts.

All this is climaxed by a new and pressing situation in Home Missions, brought about by the
new immigration law. For the last fifteen years
Mexicans have been coming into the United States
by multitudes. The World War rushed them as
laborers into our vacant and high pressure industries. Now comes the new immigration legislation shutting off most of our former stream of
immigration, at the same time opening wide all
gates from the twenty nations of the New World,
particularly from Mexico.

In writing this book, the author has had two

main purposes. First, to put into Home Missions
the thrill of the great adventure such as is rightly
felt in the realm of foreign missions. These
strangers within our gates are an unexplored field
awaiting the Columbus who will "Sail on, and
on" away from the comfortable ports of theories
of Americanization, City Problems, Immigration
Trends, etc., to the New World of helping these
less fortunate neighbors to help themselves. Second, to stimulate new friends to definite action.
The startling facts of this Home Missionary book
will scarcely be credited by the reader. Thousands of people will exclaim, "Is it possible?"
But the half has not yet been told, either of
conditions, or of results obtained.

Much credit is due to Jay S. Stowell for invaluable aid in collaboration and for references
to *The Near Side of the Mexican Question* and
other works by him and others who know the situation from first-hand study along the Border.
The board secretaries and superintendents have
shown invaluable courtesies in filling in questionnaires and sending photos and other aids. Dr.
Ralph E. Diffendorfer, the Joint Committee officers, and a multitude of sympathetic friends and
comrades of "God's Border Legion," all deserve
their meed of grateful mention.

Genuine love, admiration, and concern, atmosphere the purpose, if not the message, of these
chapters. Only a burning desire to aid the nobly
striving Mexicans could stir up sufficient courage

to portray herein conditions for which after all we above the Border have been largely responsible.

Paul Laurence Dunbar says, "Slow moves the pageant of a climbing race." I thoroughly believe that the Mexicans are achieving a present progress rivaled by few if any other race today. But much yet remains to be done.

On account of space limitations much of value has been omitted from this volume. For example, studies of such related peoples as the immigrant Spaniards, South Americans, Italians, Portuguese, and particularly the so-called "Indians."

Because of this limitation of space the committee has advised changing some portions of the book as originally planned. In a longer book the statistics and numbers, classifications, and the accounting for the problem we face would demand a fuller, if not a different, treatment in several cases. In fact, this volume is but a beginning in the study of the Mexicans above the Border—who should have been the first and not the last folk for us to come to know intimately, esteem highly, and help constructively.

The book goes out with a prayer that it may serve to acquaint many with our Mexican neighbors and hasten the coming of the Kingdom in the thousands of communities in which they live.

VERNON MONROE McCOMBS

"Ivycroft"
Berkeley, California
1925

From Over the Border

I

LIFE ABOVE THE BORDER

They tramp over my breast at night. It seems as though I never can be happy again.

BISHOP W. F. McDOWELL
On his return from Asia

HERE we are at the little home of Pedro Soto, the sugar-beet topper, in California. Our guide having called before, we are admitted at once. At first glance we wonder if this is an out-of-doors school—or an orphanage. Out under the spreading fig tree are ten children, the eldest but seventeen. Near the door sits a pale, listless boy. The glands of his neck are diseased and greatly swelled. Don Pedro explains that within the *señora* and two more children are very sick.

As we pass in, the once vigorous toiler from the great silver mines of central Mexico adds that he has not been able to work for five weeks because of his injured foot. The offending member is carelessly bound up in dirty rags which are soaked with blood and pus and surrounded with flies. The misfortune came from a runaway accident. We are told later that this was the result of some extra "weeskey" on pay day.

We find the poor little mother sitting on the

rude, cold floor. There are no chairs, just two boxes. Her face is drawn with pain and from long suffering. She is still young, though she says she has borne fourteen children. She is not too ill to brush away from the fevered little cheeks and lips of the two very sick children at either side of her the clouds of lazy flies which are bred by thousands in a pile of refuse from the horse stall just outside the unscreened windows. The mother tells us that the expected fifteenth child will demand another visit by the *medico* which will cost twenty dollars. We understand better why Don Pedro's injured foot is not "surgically safe" when he relates that it costs three dollars cash in advance for each visit of the doctor.

We have noted that there are only two rooms in the *casa* (hut) for a family of fourteen. There are only two beds, both in the same room. We wonder if the ivory image of the Savior on the silver-mounted ebony cross above the larger bed can save this situation. At any rate, the pain-racked face of the brave *mamacita* is lifted like a Madonna to that relic of better days down in her *patria,* Mexico.

Given courteous permission to read from *la Biblia,* our guide, an unpaid, beet-topper evangelist reads in Spanish *Psalm* 121 and part of *John* 14; then pours out his soul in prayer. Some of the family, unaccustomed to such extempore prayer in their own Spanish tongue, at first join in embarrassed repetition as they used to do with the *Padre*. At last their murmurs die away under the spell of this first direct, personal appeal to the God of the real and now that they have ever heard and the mother died when her fifteenth baby was born.

Such sad affairs as this true story of Don Pedro, though all too common, are of course impossible with many Mexicans. There are numbers of them who never touch drink, especially those who have had the gospel. But the foregoing is a typical scene from life among the unskilled Mexican laborers now living in the United States. The multitudes of humble cabins like Don Pedro's offer us a challenge.

A Christian gentleman, after visiting in the "Sonora town" of a great city of the Southwest, exclaimed, "Who would think that conditions could exist like these! We come here from the East and everything seems so delightful and prosperous, with churches and culture all about, that one would not dream that folks are in this section in such large numbers and living like this."

Let us now follow some of a group of sixty street-car track-men "home" after their heavy day's work. We observe a most interesting piece of social camouflage. No partridge ever tried harder to conceal her nest or brood than these Mexican fathers and mothers their places of abode. We Americans whirl heedlessly along by the wayside groves into which some of these men pass to their small rude huts and tents under the concealing eucalyptus trees.

A few of the mothers are on their knees grinding corn for the tortillas, though now these Mexican pancakes are mostly patted out and baked from flour. Here, just around the hill, is apparently a side-tracked train of box cars; but telltale steps lead up to the doors of this long row of houses on wheels. Mexican children pour out to greet, in musical Spanish, the returning brothers and fathers. There are red geraniums, artfully potted, on the sides of the box-car homes. Their matchless language, their love of flowers, color and music, and their love of children is royal, even if the huts are humble.

Some dozen or more of the men get off the car by a cemetery. Entering the mouth of a canyon, they climb up to a *colonia Mexicana* of huddling little *casitas*. There is no word for "home" in common use in Spanish; *casa* literally means "house." It is soon apparent that there are enough sorrows and social ills in this group of dwellings to challenge the Christian efforts, the welfare activities, and, at times, the police ingenuity of a metropolis. The majority of these families are surprisingly refined and eager for good, but there is ever a factor of ferment which causes heartaches to the more respectable element and gives an ill reputation to the whole colony.

A laughing trio of men go to a two-room "habitation." Two pretty daughters of thirteen and

MEXICANS AT WORK

Mexicans are engaged in every conceivable type of occupation. We
have become so dependent upon them in many sections of our agricultural and industrial life that were they suddenly to be with-
drawn, these enterprises would at least temporarily collapse.

MEXICAN HOMES ABOVE THE BORDER

Mexican laborers who have come to the United States live in homes of many sorts. Often they are little more than shacks, without adequate space for even a small family or sanitary provisions of any sort. Yet the rents charged these newcomers are frequently exorbitant.

fifteen and four other children run out to greet the eldest as "Papa." The two younger men "board" there! No wonder there are so many broken-hearted young Mexican girls. A baker across the street remarks to us, "It makes me shudder to think of the future of the girls from twelve to fifteen on this one street. Why, at least twenty-five folks come out of that small four-room cottage every morning."

One tall, haggard man comes in with the crew. He has sought in vain for work, and he returns to a small room where his wife and two children sit in the gloomy chill beside the form of their little son who died three days ago. No work, no friends, no doctor, no fire, no food, and now no money to bury their dead. They are paying five dollars' rent for this one germ-trap room with no bed or other furniture. They cannot speak English.

The priests long ago gave up trying to help all the flood of needy Mexicans. After visiting the houses of even that one crew of laborers we are appalled. It is all outside of our experience: some families living in shacks made of ragged burlap and under pieces of tin cut from old oil cans; huts dug into hillsides; five "families" living in one windowless cellar; some even living in old stables. Here is one mother with her twenty-sixth baby born in a hovel, with no furniture, no doctor, and few other provisions than Nature's.

As one visits the Mexican colonies and fruit

camps, he will find huts in back yards, and tents out under the picturesque walnut and orange groves. The entire families of those so fortunate as to secure this seasonal employment usually go out for several weeks each year to this tent life, to work in the apricots, raisins, oranges, nuts, sugar beets, Bermuda onions, and lima beans.

Cultured Exiles often Suffer

Suffering and need are not limited to these products of Mexican peonage. The case is oft repeated among people of high ideals and good education who have left Mexico and are suffering above the Border. All life is different here. They almost never beg or make their needs known. They simply ask for work, school, or medical aid. Their American neighbors do not know the suffering being endured by people who often appear well dressed, courteous, and uncomplaining, even though their faces daily grow more pallid, and later there is enforced "change of residence" because they can no longer pay the rent.

A former educator under Porfirio Diaz was for months compelled to walk three miles at two o'clock in the morning down to a bakery where he got a sack of stale bread for twenty-five cents. Don Antonio explained that bread was practically his only article of diet and it required but two trips a week. He also told of a relative of the President, whom he found in the market, picking up lettuce leaves and garbage to provide thin soup and bare salad for his starving family.

A former colonel from the Mexican army, and his very large family, all showed, in their emaciated faces and bodies, marked evidence of an empty cupboard. Weeks later I succeeded in discovering that this military gentleman was disposing, one by one, of the treasures of his previously luxurious social station—his diamonds, his military field glasses, etc. The prices obtained for them were ridiculously small; but he was helpless, for his family was in dire need.

The pinch of hard circumstances is felt keenly by those who strive to maintain their former station. One cultured Mexican mother strove in vain to make her meager income meet the social demands for her children in school,—who, by the way, were soon leading in the high school, not only socially but in scholarship and athletics. This required that the mother quietly take in washing. This and other unaccustomed labors, impossible even in her former younger and more vigorous years, soon left the children motherless.

The Mexicans as Laborers

The proportions of the Mexican problem loom up as we discover the varied industries in which Mexican labor is becoming increasingly a basic factor. Their accessibility, docility, and strength make them prime subjects of exploitation for labor contractors. They are the typical unskilled laborers. More than half of them in the United States would be classed usually as "common laborers." They are employed on the ranches and in cotton fields, on cantaloupe, onion, and great lima bean farms, in the walnut and orange groves, apricot, grape, and other fruit picking. They are used on the great vineyards.[1] They become expert landscape gardeners. They are excellent teamsters, and specialists as wood choppers and in clearing of land, more particularly in Texas, Colorado, and New Mexico. They are being used increasingly in the great lumber woods. Reading the classic novel, *Ramona,* one is reminded that they have long been sheep herders and sheep shearers throughout all the Southwest. One great range in New Mexico formerly had 2,000,000 sheep and employed 2,700 shepherds, mostly Mexicans.

They are fishermen like those first disciples, and carpenters like the Master himself, and they are in the crews of coastwise shipping. For every spoonful of porridge and other foods made more delectable by beet sugar, we are primarily indebted to the Mexicans, who do most of the hard work in producing the sugar beets through the central and southwestern states. From the days of the Dons, their taste and skill in leather work have led them to be clever as shoemakers and sad-

---

[1] Mexicans pick in California annually 250,000 tons of raisins, 25,000 tons of walnuts, 5,000,000 boxes of lemons, and 25,000,000 boxes of oranges.

dlers. They are being increasingly employed as
mechanics, for which they have a real aptitude.
The brick-yards, stone quarries, cement factories,
and great mines look to Mexicans for their most
satisfactory laborers. Arizona, for this reason,
is employing tens of thousands of Mexicans, and
large numbers are migrating there for work in
the mines. The great projects requiring excava-
tion and large contracts of concrete work look to
the Mexicans for much of the heavy work. The
networks of sewers in many great cities are being
constructed and repaired by Mexican *gasfiteros*.

A veteran section boss of thirty years' experience on the Santa Fé and Southern Pacific railroads said: "The Mexicans are the best laborers on earth. I have tried Italians, Negroes, Japanese, and Americans. Give me the Mexicans and
I will do the job. You cannot drive them, but
use firm kindness and they are all right—at least,
until they get drunk."

Mr. R. A. Rutledge of La Junta, Colorado, a
graduate of the University of Kansas, Chief Engineer on the Santa Fé, says: "We have let the
Greeks and Italians go; ninety per cent of all our
track-men from the Coast to Chicago are Mexicans. . . . The Mexicans were an experiment at
first. We gave them poor section shacks made
of ties piled up and plastered; but now we are
giving them good concrete or tile houses. The
Mexican cannot be driven like the Negro; but anyone who knows how to manage the Mexicans can

get more work out of them than any other class. They must be kept contented. They will not stay until they get their families from Mexico. Mexicans are not all peons.''

Walter L. Armacost, head of the greatest rose nursery on the Pacific Coast and handling millions of nearly all sorts of the finest flowers and shrubs, specializing in orchids, said: ''I employ Mexicans altogether. I have tried Hollanders, Japanese, Americans, and selected mixed labor, but I am fully persuaded that we have no laborers in the world who are better, if as good, for work like ours. The Mexican can be made to be not only contented, but in love with his work. He bestows an affectionate skill upon the delicate stock which is indispensable. I find that other leading heads of industry requiring not only unskilled labor but particular and responsible operations are coming to our conclusion that Providence is turning our way now the best labor, all considered, to be found. They must be shown, trained, directed by young lieutenants who get our idea and can speak their language. We must give vastly more attention to the long neglected and too little appreciated people from over the Border, and to those Spanish-Americans who have always been here.''

Better-class Mexicans seem particularly fitted to become mechanics, merchants, traveling men, lawyers, officers of the law, physicians, professors, printers, and collectors. Their bilingual facility and delightful courtesy along with ability to memorize and imitate quickly, combined with willingness to serve and sacrifice, adapt them peculiarly for the above professions. Scores of Latin Americans are holding places of large responsibility and influence in the state, especially in New Mexico.

From these facts it can be seen that Mexicans can and do fill a more useful place in the nation than the common conception that they are either bandits, exiles, or tourists might suggest. As a matter of fact, few Americans recognize these people as "Mexicans" unless they are dressed in blue overalls or black shawls, or appear with their stooped and emaciated forms crowned with sombreros.

Most of the Mexicans in the United States, however, are laborers. Drawn or driven out of the simplicity of Mexican peonage, what is the lot of these folks who are earning their bread by the sweat of their brow? The Mexicans generally are not working too hard. Our frontier builders worked much harder. Work is not a disgrace or a misfortune. The real hardship is that they are underpaid and uninspired.

Two traveling men on a limited train, well dressed and thoughtful, seemed to be very much in earnest. They were saying: "You see that poor devil out there lifting that heavy iron? He is as strong as an ox, but he can scarcely lift it for the reason that it is so hot in the summer sun. Right now he has to have two pairs of gloves so as not to blister his calloused hands. Those are Mexicans. They certainly do have it hard! They work when we are sleeping, mush around in the mud and water in big rains, and at that are glad to get work at small wages and board themselves and their large families. When a wreck occurs, they are the first there though it be, as it usually is, at night. If one of them happens to leave a switch open, or be drowsy at his job, we curse him as no good. They surely have my pity!''

The other rejoined: ''Yes, and what kind of a chance have they to enjoy their work? They are doing work that the average American would not and cannot think of doing. Last week at Bagdad in the desert the heat killed three Mexicans and prostrated a score more. The temperature was up to 120 degrees. I am with you in saying that those faithful boys do not have the chance they have earned.''

The work of the Mexicans is seasonal and irregular and thoughtlessly supervised. The mutual distrust renders cooperation and organization for mutual benefit almost impossible. Their only weapon is a strike. Agitators keep them restless, and they certainly have good soil and a strong case to present for their anarchistic propaganda.

Stories like those related on the preceding pages might be multiplied almost indefinitely, but those already given are sufficient to introduce us to the poorer Mexicans in the United States and

to lead us to inquire why they are here, how many
there are of them, and where they are to be found.

Recent Mexican Migration to the United States

For several centuries the history of our Southwest has been very closely tied up with Mexico
and the Mexicans. Through the long period during which President Porfirio Diaz controlled the
destinies of Mexico there was relatively little
Mexican immigration to this country. Diaz dominated Mexico from about 1875 until the year 1911,
although during a brief portion of that time he
was not the actual president of the Mexican Republic. During the period of his control he established the credit of Mexico, negotiated treaties
with foreign countries, built railroads and har-
bors, extended education, and made life in Mexico
to a large extent stable and dependable. Under
those conditions there was little incentive for the
Mexican to migrate. The fact that Diaz was more
or less of a despot did not count largely so long
as living conditions were reasonably satisfactory,
and the Mexican had learned to be satisfied with
very little.

With the overthrow of Diaz in 1911, however, a
new situation developed. Unsettled political conditions made life precarious, and unsettled business and economic conditions made the securing
of the necessities of life a difficult matter. The
result was the beginning of a new northward mi-

gration of Mexicans to the United States. Some
of these newcomers were political refugees; more
of them were poor Mexicans seeking a chance to
earn a living and to secure opportunities for their
children. Soon after this new period of unrest
arose in Mexico, the World War was begun in
Europe, and very quickly there was an unprece-
dented demand for labor in the United States.
Both of these forces tended to increase the number of Mexicans coming into this country. In
the face of the need for more laborers, the contract labor clause of our national immigration law,
was suspended and thousands of Mexicans were
brought into this country under contract.

In order, then, to discover how many Mexicans
have come into the United States during the last
decade, we must add the number of those who
have come in under temporary contracts as contract laborers and those who have crossed the
international line between Mexico and the United
States surreptitiously without the knowledge of
immigration officers. How large this latter group
is, no one can declare accurately. That it is very
large is evident. So far as the number of regular immigrants is concerned the figures are available. They are as follows:

1914	13,089	1919	28,844
1915	10,993	1920	51,042
1916	17,198	1921	29,603
1917	16,438	1922	18,246
1918	17,602	1923	62,709
	1924		87,648

It should be noted that the year 1924 witnessed the largest migration of Mexicans to this country of any year of the past decade, probably of our entire history. The cause of that migration does not lie in Mexico, but rather in the United States, where, by recent immigration legislation. all immigration from Europe has been put upon a "quota" basis, thus largely cutting off our supply of labor from that source. Immigration from countries in the Western world is not upon a "quota" basis, so that immigration from Mexico, so far as numbers are concerned, is unlimited. There is reason to believe that Mexican immigration will be an increasingly important factor in the life of the United States because of that fact, and the question of the conditions under which Mexican immigrants to this country live takes on greater significance than ever before.

The Mexicans who have migrated to the United States have come first to one of our four border states, Texas, New Mexico, Arizona, or California. As a matter of fact, by far the largest proportion have entered this country by way of Texas, and Texas has the largest number of Mexicans of any of our states. Of the Mexican immigrants admitted during the year ending June 30, 1924, 63 per cent gave Texas as their future permanent home, 17.1 per cent California, 13.9 per cent Arizona, 1.3 per cent New Mexico, and 1 per cent Illinois. The 1920 Census showed 398,174 Mexicans in Texas, 126,086 in California, 91,574 in Arizona, and 34,083 in New Mexico. Considerable numbers were also reported in Colorado, Kansas, Oklahoma, Illinois, Missouri, New York, and other states. Since the taking of the census the number has considerably increased and they have become very widely distributed throughout eastern and western states and even in Alaska where considerable numbers have been taken to help in the salmon industry. The three largest individual settlements of Mexicans in the United States are San Antonio, El Paso, and Los Angeles.

A Mexican colony estimated at more than 5,000 is reported in the neighborhood of the steel mills of Joliet, Illinois; other colonies are to be found at Gary and Indiana Harbor, Indiana, as well as at Erie and Johnstown, Pennsylvania. Last year 18,744 Mexican school children were registered in the city of Los Angeles, California.[1] A Protestant church in Chicago has been turned over to a Mexican congregation, and other such congregations have been gathered in eastern cities.

In estimating the number of Mexicans in the United States we must always make allowance for those who have been admitted as immigrants since the previous census and then estimate as best we may the number who come into this country under cover of darkness or over paths that are not guarded by immigration officers. Even this addition, however, does not tell the entire story, since

[1] There are over 93,000 Mexicans in Los Angeles, not including Spanish Americans and California Spanish.

for practical purposes we must add thousands of Spanish-speaking immigrants from Argentina and other South American countries, from Hawaii, from the Philippines, from Spain, and other Latin American countries, and then add tens of thousands of native sons of Spanish speech who easily merge with these great Spanish-language groups made up predominantly of Mexicans. The actual numbers with which we are dealing, therefore, are larger than either the census figures or the immigration statistics would suggest. It is said that there are at least a quarter of a million Spanish-speaking people in New York City alone.

For the present, however, our attention is centered upon that large group of more or less recent immigrants from Mexico who are for the most part uneducated laborers. These people who do so much of our rougher work comprise nearly four fifths of all the Mexicans in this country. We must always remember, however, that there is a smaller group of educated Mexicans in this country, many of whom are economically independent.

Their Homes

There is no race within the nation which has a greater variety of domiciles than the Mexicans. Many of the better-class political exiles, who were able to save part or all of their property in Mexico, or who have established themselves in successful business here, live in comfortable dwellings or bungalows rented in select sections or suburbs. The native sons and better-class artisans have their own neat little cottages covered with roses or vines, often with orderly though small gardens at the front or rear. The people in these inviting homes are very courteous, often cultured, and usually their young folks have fairer faces than the average American. It is to be remembered that all Mexicans are legally "white." They are so classified by marriage license bureaus and in all government statistics.

The Mexican home life is beautiful where the God-given factors are supplemented by social opportunity and a human chance. They have much of love, and abundance of beauty, and usually many babies. And yet they have no word in common use for "home."

Vice, Crime, and "Unmorality"

Much of the vice of the Mexican people is really "unmorality." They have never known better, for their feudal lords of old and their priests, too often, have been blind guides, and all three have fallen into the ditch. Ignorance, however, does not keep people out of jail, and the inmates of penal institutions in our border states are often seventy-five per cent Mexican.

The large number of persons living out of wedlock may be accounted for by improper huddling and congestion in their habitations; by the traditional attitude of the Roman Catholic Church, which winks at the marriages that are awaiting the *mañana* until the big fee can be paid; by the vital tides of unrestrained and misdirected passion; and by the constant inflaming of the baser elements of nature by unspeakably improper novels, moving pictures, and familiar dances.

A now-devoted and worthy couple lived together without marriage until they had two boys of school age. After a domestic tempest, which was stimulated by a third party, the mother left the home. At length both father and mother were converted. The mother returned to her home, and she and the father were married at an American church. The whole community participated, even to preparing wedding garments, and the couple lived happily together, both working ardently in the local Mexican mission. Such experiences, with some variations, are constantly brought to the attention of any missionary among Latin Americans. We recently married grandparents who had never been wed. A prominent young couple, just converted, came, with their baby, three hundred miles to be given Christian marriage and baptism. Yet some people ask whether Mexicans are ever genuinely converted! These unmarried couples, when converted, want to fulfil all righteousness and be lawfully married.

Health Conditions among the Mexicans

In examining the little children of the poor
Mexican families, one is usually impressed with
their attractive faces and bewitching eyes. What
can account for the grave conditions of later
years well known to doctors who visit these Mexican colonies?

An unfavorable physical inheritance accounts
for much. We noted that Don Pedro's face was
deeply pockmarked. Indeed, all through Latin
America pockmarks are very common. In Don
Pedro's boyhood it was thought that the earlier
in life he could have infectious diseases, the
lighter would be the attack. This, by nimble logic,
soon came to mean that the sooner children had
smallpox, the better. Many mothers in all Latin
America expose their children to this and other
epidemics. Little care and no quarantine are observed among the mountain people and the lower
classes. So we understand why pockmarks are
so common.

Here is some clue, also, as to why Latin America, though settled first in the New World, is so
sparsely settled. At the Panama Congress it was
stated that in a Mexican village on the Border,
by actual record kept by missionaries, seventy
per cent of the babies died before they were a
year old and ninety per cent before they were six
years old. Wrong ideas of diseases and sanitation
deeply imbedded in unlettered minds are not cor-

rected by the mere crossing of the Border, but persist to the consternation of health authorities that deal with conditions in Mexican colonies.

The Mexicans are coming increasingly from the open country or quiet villages of Mexico and are jamming into the most cramped and undesirable house-courts of our cities. They are unacquainted with city life and speedily become victims of its ills.

A beautiful Christian family, before coming from Mexico, sent to some friends a picture of their family and expressed their joy that at last they were coming to California. Six weeks after their arrival, the chubby little daughter, Flora, had died of pneumonia contracted as a result of cold, wet feet from the muddy court, and the absence of proper bedding and clothes in the dark, cold, gloomy, stoveless rooms. The number of these new Americans who die of pneumonia during the winter is out of all proportion to the population. We recently conducted the funeral of an elder sister of this same family, who died of tuberculosis soon after becoming a bride.

Undernourished

One reason for the ravages of disease among the Mexicans is their undernourished condition. Physicians say that it is not so much underfeeding as improper feeding. Small children are given tea, wine, and all sorts of indigestible food.

A three-months-old baby was given cinnamon water instead of the diet prescribed by the nurse and physician. A baby that was well in the morning, was given a piece of ham to suck, and the young parents were surprised to find the baby dead at noon. A lack of proper food is the common experience of the masses of Mexicans. An officer of the police force, on being drawn out to speak of the Mexicans, said: "There is a great deal of crime among them; most of those who are arrested are charged with drunkenness or with petty thieving, due to the fact that they are starving most of the time. At midnight, recently, I saw a Mexican pick up a rotten fruit core from the street. I remonstrated with him, but he did not understand English. I then got him a tamale at a near-by stand and in a moment he was dividing it with three other starving Mexicans." Are the folks who deliberately exploit the labor of these people, without providing for their welfare, any less culpable than those who steal because they and their families are starving?

A Bad Situation

Actual conditions revealed by careful investigation in the Plaza District of Los Angeles disclosed the fact that of the 40,000 people of that one district, 51.8 per cent are Mexicans and 30 per cent Italians. Of the children born in the whole city last year, 7.9 per cent were Mexicans;

of the children of the city who died, 12.2 per cent were Mexicans. Of cases treated at the venereal clinic, 20 per cent were Mexicans. For the entire city, 17.4 per cent of the deaths were from tuberculosis. Among the Mexicans in the Plaza District, 39.2 per cent of deaths were due to tuberculosis, 26.4 to infant diseases of the digestive tract, 13.2 to still-birth and 13 per cent to pneumonia, leaving only 8 per cent to other causes. A large proportion of these deaths might have been prevented. On the tuberculosis chart for the city there is a black cloud about the Plaza region.

The causes are clear: low wages, seasonal employment, high rent, overcrowding, and inadequate nourishment. The average family has five members and the average house two rooms, for which exorbitant rents are charged. In Los Angeles 28 per cent of these Mexican homes have no running water; 79 per cent have no bathrooms, and 68 per cent no inside toilets—in many cases six or eight families use a common toilet.

The houses of the poorer Mexican colonies are badly located, usually near some objectionable factory or institution such as a gas plant, the abattoir, or the brewery. During storms, and also in summer heat, serious situations arise. In one storm a Mexican grandmother, starving and alone, died from drowning, in her own little room almost under the shadow of the largest church in Sacramento, because of a broken sewer. Driving along the boulevards, one sees not infrequently

sick Mexicans on their cots out under the gum-
tree, amid flies, "dying alone at the close of the
day" like the Gypsy boy.

It is not the Mexicans alone who pay the price
for these unfortunate conditions, nor are they
chiefly responsible for them. Gradually we are
coming to see that the community itself is responsible, and that the conditions which exist are a
peril to everyone. A striking illustration of that
is the pneumonic plague which broke out in the
Mexican quarter of Los Angeles in the fall of
1924. The rushing of a thousand vials of serum
from Philadelphia to Los Angeles helped to check
what might have become a national scourge. The
fortunate thing is that these unwholesome conditions can be remedied when we once undertake
the task.

The Use of Drugs

The use of *marihuana* is not uncommon in the
colonies of the lower class of Mexican immigrants.
This is a native drug made from what is sometimes called the "crazy weed." The effects are
high exhilaration and intoxication, followed by
extreme depression and broken nerves. Officers
and Mexicans both ascribe many of the moral ir-
regularities of Mexicans to the effect of *marihuana*. Mexican names are frequently seen in
the lists of those arrested for smuggling opium
over the Border. Drug-stores report very large

sales of patent remedies which are taboo by most informed people. Patent remedies, both good and bad, bear directions in Spanish. Elaborate advertisements of drugs and medicines are circulating among Mexicans on both sides of the Border. Homes are sometimes broken up by the use of drugs.

Drink

Drink is the fountain of many sorrows among Mexicans. We took the picture of a murderer with his family, upon his return from the penitentiary. He, with another Mexican, killed an American while they were all drunk. He awakened the next morning to find that he had murdered a man against whom he had no hate.

In Chester, Pennsylvania, where there is usually a large colony of Mexicans, we met a respectable and thoughtful young Mexican who said that eighty Mexicans had just lost their jobs because one of them had stabbed another while under the influence of drink.

It is unnecessary to multiply cases to suggest that unskilled Mexicans who have come into the United States stand in urgent need of our friendly help. However, in our attempt to picture the needs of the vast multitude of these poorer Mexicans, we must not do an injustice to the other thousands who have already attained better things and are fitting their lives into our social, political,

and economic life. Mexicans in the United States
are on the upward climb, and they must not be
judged so much by their present achievements as
by their possibilities. The Mexican, in common
with other races, has certain faults, but he also
has some very pronounced virtues. We, too, have
some very pronounced faults, and, let us hope,
some virtues. We can demonstrate the latter by
assuming a brotherly attitude toward the Mexican and by helping him in every way possible to
make the most of himself in the new home to which
he has come.

A Far-reaching Problem

The "Mexican Problem" as we like to call it,
although in the eyes of the Mexican it is the
"United States Problem," is one from which we
cannot run away. The border line between
Mexico and the United States stretches 1,833
miles. It is a political boundary rather than a
natural barrier, and, as such, is artificial and
easily crossed. Our border relationships with
Mexico are most intimate. Thousands of Americans are continually crossing the line into Mexico,
some of them being our criminals and other undesirable citizens who go as a curse to our sister
republic. It is hardly fitting that we should assume a "holier than thou" attitude toward
Mexico until we have taken into account what is
going on on both sides of the Border. Our trade

across the Border is enormous and growing. We have many things that Mexico wants and Mexico is rich in resources which we can use to advantage. Economically our interests are one.

Nor can we afford to forget that long before our Southwest was a part of the United States, the Mexican had struck his roots deep down into the country. When he comes to us, he is coming to a section of country which was once a part of Mexico. Of this we shall have more to say later.

More than half a century ago Daniel Webster, speaking in a hotel lobby in Washington, said, "No, gentlemen, if we ever have any international difficulties, it will not be in the Northeast or in the Northwest, but down in the Southwest where a great and noble nation is in the throes of mortal conflict, and none of us seems willing to lend a hand." We have largely ignored Mexico as far as constructive help is concerned, but we cannot permanently ignore the hundreds of thousands of Mexicans who have dug their way with pick and shovel into the life of our country. Over vast areas in the Southwest we are entirely dependent upon the Mexican. His children and his children's children will live there as American citizens. They will help to elect our presidents; they will help to establish our moral, political, and religious ideals and practises. Our future is bound up with theirs. We must think about them; we must come to know them; we must work with them in the constructive and worth-while things of life.

Fortunately they are by nature a delightful people with many personal charms and graces. We must not judge them by the unfortunate conditions under which we are forcing many of them to live; rather we should judge ourselves. We have offered the inducements to bring them into the United States and we could not well get along without them, yet we have neglected to provide for them now that they are here. It is to help us to understand better and to stimulate us to plan and work more wisely that this book is written.

> Every night and every morn
> Some to misery are born;
> Every morn and every night,
> Some are born to sweet delight . . .
> I will not cease from mental fight,
>   Nor shall my sword sleep in my hand
> Till we have built Jerusalem,
>   In England's green and pleasant land.
>
> WILLIAM BLAKE
> *Souls in Action*

II

BACKGROUNDS

No railing accusation is to be brought against a
whole nation nor even against a whole class in
a nation.

G. B. Winton

THE present immigration of Mexicans into
the United States cannot be fully understood unless we also take into consideration
some important facts in the history of Mexico and
of our own Southwest.

The Spaniards were the first Europeans to
come into Mexico, and they succeeded in impres-
sing not only their customs but also their language upon the new country. Long before they
arrived, however, a fascinating panorama of life
was being enacted there and throughout the territory which now comprises our own southwestern
states. The migrations, conquests, and other
movements of those prehistoric peoples are
wrapped in impenetrable mystery, except as the
story is suggested by the hieroglyphics, picture
writings, sculptures, ruins, mounds, and other remains of those early days.

It is believed that about the year 754 A.D. the
people known as the Toltecs settled in the Valley
of Mexico close to the present site of Mexico City.
There they lived and presumably prospered un-

til about 1064, when their power was overthrown
by the Chichimecas. About 1325 the Chichimecas
were, in turn, conquered by a group of peoples
from the north, of whom the Aztecs were the most
powerful. It is believed that the Aztecs came into
Mexico from what is now the region of Arizona
and New Mexico. The first authentic date in
Mexican history is the year 1376, when the election of an Aztec war chief is recorded. Other
Aztec rulers followed, and the Aztecs, in turn,
prospered and developed a civilization of their
own. In 1502 Montezuma II was elected to the
chief position in the tribe.

It was seventeen years later, in 1519, that the
first Spaniards made their appearance under the
leadership of Cortes. These energetic Spaniards, representing the mingled blood of the
Moors, the Romans, and the Iberian *conquistadores,* very quickly gained control of the country,
and the long period of Spanish domination was
begun. Large tribute was demanded and much
attention given to the complete subjugation of the
native groups. Injustice and oppression of many
sorts abounded. Spain transplanted the decaying
feudalism of Europe to the New World, and its
influence still prevails. All of this was before the
coming of the Pilgrim band to New England. Several of the Spanish missions yet standing were
built before the Boston Tea Party and the Revolutionary War.

Exploring the Southwest

Soon after the arrival of the Spaniards in Mexico, they began to hear of a "fair land" to the north, but they were so busy at the moment in winning control of the south that they paid slight attention to the stories. In 1527, however, Panfilo de Narvaez, a Spanish soldier, was given a grant authorizing him to explore and govern all of that part of New Spain which extended from Florida westward through our present gulf states and on to and including the present states of New Mexico, Texas, and part of northern Mexico. The same year he organized an expedition, sailed from Spain, and landed on the coast of Florida. From there he started westward. It was an ill-fated expedition, and those who took part in it suffered almost every kind of hardship. They were misled, attacked by natives, lost in the swamps, and often on the verge of starvation. The final calamity was that of shipwreck on boats which they had hastily constructed with the hope of escape. The expedition collapsed, and Narvaez died. Nine years later a few stragglers who had worked their way down through Texas and Mexico arrived at Mexico City on July 24, 1536.

In 1539 Friar Marcos de Niza started out from Mexico City to explore the region to the north— now Arizona and New Mexico. When the party reached the pueblos of the Zuni Indians, Marcos returned to Mexico City with glowing accounts of the things he had seen in this new country.

The following year Francisco Vasquez Coronado was appointed governor of this northern country, which was known as the "Province of New Galicia." He organized an expedition and started out to find the "Seven Cities of Cibola," of which many stories had been told. When he reached the Zuni country, he divided his large group and sent one section toward the west and another toward the east. The western expedition traveled as far as the Grand Canyon, and the eastern group got over into New Mexico. The Zunis, who were eager to get rid of Coronado, told him wonderful tales of a rich land farther toward the east. The party wandered many weary miles over a barren country and finally hanged the guide who had deliberately misled them. The expedition returned to Mexico, where Coronado was permitted to resign as governor of New Galicia. He had not proved to be much of a success as a governor, although he brought back considerable information about the country.

First Settlement and the Indian Revolt

In 1598 Don Juan de Onate with seven hundred men and one hundred and thirty families succeeded in establishing a settlement at Chamita in New Mexico. Seven years later this settlement was moved to Santa Fé, New Mexico. Here again the Spaniard began the subjugation and enslavement of the natives, who, in this case, chanced to be the Pueblo Indians. With the forced aid of the Indians they began to develop the mining, agricultural, and grazing interests of the country, and continued to do so for three quarters of a century. Then the Indians succeeded in organizing a successful revolt. They burned ranch houses and finally besieged the governor in the old Governor's Palace in Santa Fé, and he was forced to flee with as many of his people as he could assemble.

This revolt cost four hundred and one lives, including seventy-eight soldiers and twenty priests. Nor did the Indians stop there. They set about removing every possible trace of their former conquerors. They destroyed the mines; they prohibited the use of the Spanish language; they burned the seeds which the Spaniards had brought into the country; and they destroyed all the Spanish records.

For twelve years, or until 1692, the Pueblos once more controlled the country and did their best to restore their former life and customs. But their triumph did not last long, for in 1692 De Vargas was appointed governor of the "lost province," and he succeeded in subjugating it once more. To this day he is the great Spanish hero of the Southwest, and no celebration in all the region equals the splendor of the annual De Vargas Day celebration in the city of Santa Fé, the capital of New Mexico.

Mexican Control

From the time of the coming of De Vargas, in 1692, until 1821 Spain was in control of New Mexico, and in fact she was the dominating influence throughout our entire Southwest. In 1821 Mexico succeeded in throwing off the political control of Spain and three years later, on October 4, 1824, the first constitution of the Republic of Mexico was declared to be in effect.

The internal affairs of Mexico did not quiet down at once with the withdrawal of the Spaniards. For half a century following the winning of Mexican independence there was much of turmoil and many changes occurred in the centralized authority. In 1876 Porfirio Diaz assumed control, and from that date until 1911 he was the dominating figure in Mexico. Then came the revolution under the idealist, Francisco Madero. He was quickly succeeded by the despot, Huerta, and he in turn by the erratic, self-seeking Carranza. In 1920 the Carranza government was overthrown and Adolfo de la Huerta became temporary president of Mexico. A little later General Alvaro Obregon, a farmer-soldier hero, was duly elected president. Although facing many complications and genuine difficulties, he succeeded in quieting much of the unsettled life of Mexico, and on December 1, 1924, General Plutarcho Elias Calles was peacefully inaugurated as the newly elected president of Mexico.

The long story from Cortes (1519) to Calles (1924) is full of many dramatic features. In this book we have not space even to hint of them, but they are well worth studying if we are to understand fully the life and thought of our neighbors, the Mexicans.

While all of these events were taking place in Mexico, even more amazing things were going on in the great region east of the Mississippi River. Explorers had covered the country; settlements had been established; the thirteen colonies had grown up; the Revolutionary War had been fought; American independence had been established; the United States of America had become a reality, and a throbbing agricultural and industrial life was seeking a westward expansion.

Approach from the East

Until the beginning of the nineteenth century, explorers from the East had paid little or no attention to the region of New Mexico and Arizona. In 1804 a peddler from St. Louis wandered down into Mexico and there, in Santa Fé, sold his wares. He then decided to remain in the country rather than to go back and make settlement with his employers. The following year a hunter named James Pursley became lost in the Rocky Mountains and finally found himself in New Mexico. In 1806 Lieutenant Zebulon Montgomery Pike, after whom Pike's Peak is named, entered this country by mistake and built a fort. He was arrested and taken to Santa Fé and later to Mexico City. These were the forerunners from the East.

By the year 1812 enterprising merchants from St. Louis had opened the now famous Santa Fé trail and within a few years this was a permanent pathway over which large trading caravans passed. One such caravan is recorded which included 230 wagons and 350 men and which carried half a million dollars' worth of goods. In 1826 Kit Carson went down into Santa Fé, and from that time until his death it was the center of many of his famous exploits.

During all of this time, following the overthrow of Spanish control in 1821, this southwestern region was a part of Mexico. Mexico, however, was having her troubles with Texas, and in 1836 Texas won her independence and established herself as the Republic of Texas. Nine years later Texas was received as one of the states of the United States. The question of the Texas border line was still in dispute and out of that grew the Mexican War during which, in 1846, General S. W. Kearney marched into the city of Santa Fé, raised the United States flag, and declared that the entire region was the possession of the United States. Not a shot was fired or a drop of blood spilled. Two years later, February 2, 1848, by an agreement with Mexico—the Treaty of Guadalupe Hidalgo—this territory through to California was known as a part of the United States.

A SPANISH-SPEAKING CONGREGATION IN NEW YORK CITY

There are also several distinctly Mexican congregations in Chicago, as well as in other cities in Illinois, and in Pennsylvania and other eastern states.

A BORDER TOWN, SHOWING THE INTERNATIONAL FENCE

The traveler along the Border cannot fail to be impressed with the way the life of Old Mexico mingles with that of the United States. A wire fence is not a very potent separation, and for most of the 1,833 miles there is not even so much as a fence to separate the two countries.

Effects of Spanish Rule

Throughout our four border states, Texas, New Mexico, Arizona, and California, the Spanish and Mexican control of more than three centuries has left a marked impress. The old Spanish missions are but outward symbols of that important period. The blood of the Spanish *conquistadores* was freely mingled with the native stock, and the social and religious life of medieval Spain was impressed upon the country. The surging life of Texas, Arizona, and California has, however, largely submerged the older Spanish inheritance, and one must search if he would find it. Not so in New Mexico! There, doubtless because of the isolation of the people, the old medieval life of Spain has remained largely unchanged down until recent years.

When this territory was taken over by the United States the residents of the region were made citizens of the United States. The treaty also provided that the validity of the old Spanish land-grants should be recognized. These provisions have brought about many strange conditions. Thus we have a state of the Union in which more than half of the people speak the Spanish language, and where interpreters are continually necessary in the transaction of the business of the state. This grows out of the fact that much of the life of New Mexico is rural and the scattered hamlets, many miles from the railroad, are almost

entirely shut off from the English-speaking life
of the state. In these places the language of the
home and the street is Spanish, and the difficulty
of any effective teaching of English, even in the
public schools, becomes very great. It was not
until 1878 that the first railroad entered the state,
and it was two more years before it was completed
through to Santa Fé.

The difficulties over the old land-grants in New
Mexico have been very great, leading at times even
to a sort of civil war within the state. Congress
took what seemed to be a long time to find a way
out of the complexity in which the treaty had left
the situation. Finally a Court of Private Claims
was established and most of the questions of land-
titles have now been so adjusted that an individual may secure land in New Mexico with as valid
a title as in any other state.

New Mexico was an ancient land long before
the Spaniards found it, and it is today one of the
strangest parts of the United States. It has been
called the "Holy Land of America" because the
social customs of the people suggest so strongly
the life of Palestine in the time of Jesus. To
visit the many plaza towns far from the railroad,
one would hardly imagine that this country has
been a part of the United States for three quarters of a century.

When we acquired this region there were no
public schools, almost no Bibles or books of any
sort, and practically no roads worthy of the name.

Even today hundreds of Spanish-speaking settlements are reached only by roads which follow the beds of streams, with the result that in times of high water they are entirely cut off from outside communication. All of this has tended to give the people in New Mexico a separate and distinct life.

Spanish-speaking Americans

In speaking of "Mexicans" in the United States it has not been easy to find a nomenclature which would cover with exactness the two groups of Spanish-speaking people in the Southwest. We have large numbers of Mexicans in the United States who have come here as immigrants in recent years. They, too, are rearing their families in this country, and their children are citizens of the United States. The children of these immigrants grow up largely in communities which are predominantly English-speaking. This is not true of the young people in many New Mexican villages. Because these people in New Mexico have such a distinct life of their own, we have come to think of them commonly as Spanish-speaking Americans. That seems more accurate than to call them "Mexicans" since they are native sons and since, for the most part, their fathers and their grandfathers, sometimes for several generations, have been citizens of the United States. They predominate only in the one state, New Mexico, and they have not been greatly affected by the recent immigration of Mexicans, since only a little more than one per cent of the Mexicans now coming into the United States have New Mexico as their destination, in spite of the fact that New Mexico is one of our four border states.

Early Missionary Work

Almost as soon as this region became a part of the United States, home missionaries found their way to these people. Their coming was not welcomed. There was serious opposition and at least one or two of those early workers were killed. The lives of others were placed in jeopardy. In spite of opposition, the churches have stayed at the task, and they have some very definite results to show for their labors. We shall have more to say of this work later.

The veteran Presbyterian missionary superintendent, Doctor Robert McLean, from his rich experience in South America and along the Border has written a remarkably interesting chapter upon these heroic annals of the Southwest.[1] In the first chapter he notes the effects of the blood mixture, and the reasons for the failure of Spain in America. Among the latter he lists the following: the defeat of the Spanish Armada by England; Spain's neglect of colonization; the refusal

1 *Old Spain in New America*, page 8 ff.

of her sons to toil; their lust for gold and adventure; her iron grip upon her colonies; in general, Spain's negligence of the ideals of progress, love, hope, education, and the higher life. It is interesting right here to note that Mexico's new president, General Plutarcho Elias Calles, has two hobbies—prohibition and the public school. Mexico has progressed considerably from Cortez to Calles!

Social and Economic Backgrounds

"The rich becoming richer and the poor becoming poorer" is the apt phrase to characterize Mexico's past social and economic order. The amassing of wealth by a favored class, which included the Roman Catholic Church, had progressed to an intolerable degree. It was said that the Roman Church alone controlled one third of the national wealth. The revolutionary spirit in Mexico in recent years has been directed particularly toward the land-barons. Many noble, innocent, and thrifty victims, such as merchants and small land-holders, were caught in the upheaval. Many of these lost all of their property and are now exiles above the Border, trying to get started once more. Despite these unfortunate by-products, the chief ends sought by the revolutionists have been accomplished or are in process of being achieved. The government has become more genuinely responsible to the people than ever before, and special laws against exploitation and abuses have been enacted. The closed confessional, the wearing of religious garbs, the holding of religious processions, and all owning of property by churches are now prohibited. This legislation is aimed directly at the Roman Catholic Church, which had carried its abuses to such lengths that it had become intolerable to the people.[1] It carries one step further the process of throwing off the Spanish influence, the political aspects of which were ended at the time of the overthrow of Spanish control in the year 1821.

The various recent revolutions in Mexico have had at their root a common cause. Pancho Villa, the famous bandit-leader of Mexico, was an untutored, plebeian, popular leader. On the other hand, Francisco Madero, who overthrew the power of Diaz, was a very wealthy, refined, and cultured gentleman and idealist. Yet Villa and Madero led the same folk.

One of our brightest young Mexican friends was an officer under Villa for many months. The Mexican federals had despoiled his father of horses, cattle, and merchandise. To "get even" with the robbers and assassins of his father, he joined the "revolutionaries." Finally he came across the Border, as so many of his fellows have

[1] In March, 1925, dispatches from Mexico reported that no member of the Knights of Columbus might hold a government position. Reports also indicate that the Catholic Church of Mexico is succeeding the Roman Catholic Church in that republic.

done. He talks of returning, but he will never do so, unless, perchance, he should go back as a missionary. He has been in school for several years and is now serving a fine congregation of his own people in California as pastor.

Along with his other experiences the Mexican has tasted the true depths of poverty. Few Americans realize just what is involved in "eking out an existence." The Mexican knows, for he has lived through the experience, and his previous economic helplessness persists when he reaches this land of plenty. A young Mexican widower represented a vast number of his people when he said once to the writer: "In my *patria* I got little pay, about fourteen cents a day. *Señor, muy poco* (very little). When later I got my woman, it was impossible. So we come to this country for *major pago* (better pay). But in three years we had three children. My young woman died when the last little girl was born. Now what can I do?"

Who Are the Mexicans?

Not long ago a man in New York became acquainted with a Mexican youth employed in a business office. It chanced that this Mexican was of fairer complexion than his Anglo-Saxon friend. One day the Anglo-Saxon said, "You're not a real Mexican, are you? You're Spanish."

"What are you talking about!" exclaimed the

Mexican youth. "A Mexican? Of course I am a Mexican."

The incident introduces us to one of the common misconceptions as to just what a Mexican is. One hears many strange words in conversation about Mexicans such as "mestizo," "cholo," "Creole," and "peon." Many of these words are used loosely, and it would be hard to give a scientific definition of them which would meet the approval of all who use them. In general, however, the descendants of the original infusion of some Spanish blood with the aborigines during the "days of the Dons" and of the *conquistadores* in the sixteenth century are the true Latin Americans, or "pure" Mexicans, Cubans, Spanish Californians, etc.

Those who mixed blood later on, who have not been able by wealth, fair countenance, education, or great public service to break through into this upper class of four hundred years of family history, are really the Creoles, the *mestizos,* or the *cholos.* Usually the real facts are courteously ignored concerning this point and people are only referred to as Creoles or *mestizos* when occasion demands it,—in literature, history, or social explanations. It is a delicate subject.

Cholos and peons form really more of a social than a hereditary class, including both the *mestizos* or mixed, and Indians. It refers to a humble class condition of servitude and dependence rather than to race or even color. The *cholo* or peon is a large, unconsciously wretched, though potentially mighty, ultimate factor to reckon with in Latin American society.

What was the original stock into which the Latin European white blood was infused? A volume would be required to show the vast difference between the average conception of the North American Indian—"The red men of the forest" —and the stock into which Cortez and Pizarro succeeded in planting the strain that formed the first Latin Americans. Putting it abruptly: when some cultured pilgrims intermarried with belles of the original red men, they usually lifted those savage lives, but the white men who came were not all "cultured pilgrims"—far from it. Let us look at this native trunk of the Latin American racial tree.

The pure Indians of Mexico speak at least one hundred and eighty dialects. Benito Juarez was a full-blooded Mixtec Indian. Hidalgo and other great Mexican deliverers were pure Indians; Porfirio Diaz was of nearly pure Indian blood. It is interesting to speculate on whether we might not have today a different Mexico had Diaz likewise been of pure aboriginal stock. Recent estimates that have been made after careful investigation reveal the fact that there are approximately eighteen million aboriginal Indians in Latin America. Wandering Mexicans constantly mix with the

Indians on both sides of the Border. The Ysleta
Indians speak Spanish well. Indians and *cholos*
pass interchangeably. Pure Mexicans are found
at such Indian schools as Sherman Institute.

Those who say Mexicans are Indians are surprised to have Mexicans frankly admit that most
of them are largely of Indian blood, if we perpetuate Columbus' colossal ethnological blunder, but
they point out that the aborigines of Mexico were
a striking contrast to the fighting nomads known
to American pioneers as the "red-skins." Yet,
these savage red-skins have scions now in the
government of the United States occupying posts
of honor and prominence. The Mexicans are seeing all this and feeling the stirring of a new race
consciousness. Such a race consciousness bodes
well for the future of this New World. The lure
of a new fraternity, a new comity, a new liberty
in religious life, and economic opportunity is back
of it. There is a new sense in Pan-America of
mutual appreciation and mutual interdependence.
Every small or large Latin American mission in
the Southwest or farther east is helping to build
the life of this entire Western Hemisphere.

What the Mexican Thinks of Himself

The inborn pride of all Latin peoples leads
them to counter in self-defense when referred to
slightingly.

They take the following lines of defense: (1)

There is a difference in racial and national ideals.
They canonize kindness, courtesy, affection, art,
love of beauty, generosity. We revere efficiency,
truthfulness, frankness, firmness, thrift, practicality, enterprise. Our religion, they say, has
taught us our ideals, while theirs has taught them
their ideals. They do not ask which code is better. They simply seek thus for an accounting.
(2) They frankly admit the presence of caste in
their social system, and recognize a negligible
lower class. Certain people "count," others do
not "have importance." (3) Though not satisfactory to us, it appears to satisfy masses of in-
dulgent politicians, parents, and priests simply
to apologize naïvely for the weaknesses and foi-
bles of their people. Here is a real reason for
those belated millions who have never, until recently, begun seriously to improve their community conditions. Few of those in places of influence and authority in the past have expected
them to do so. A peon agitator once sought to
account for his people by saying: "We are no
good. We are food for powder. Yes, we are just
good to stand up against the wall and be shot."

All this has resulted in a state of strain for
the Mexican. This accounts for the apparent air
of self-sufficiency about many of them, even when
they feel very unable to cope with their problems
and to measure up to the keen competition above
the Border. The other horn of the dilemma seems
to be to renounce and forsake their race. It is not

uncommon to meet Mexicans who disclaim their
racial stock and say, "Me no espeakee Espan-
ishe." One youth said, after we had angled with
him on the matter for several minutes, "Yes, I
am Spanish, but I don't like to tell people."

So much for what the Latin American thinks
of himself. There is bright hope in the fact that
at last he is beginning "to stand off and watch
himself go by," indicating the dawn of a better
day of efficiency and of good-natured give and
take.

The Problems of Adjustment

A true judgment of Mexicans requires a study
of them in their own element. They are out of
their element in the United States. They are un-
adjusted—unassimilated. One bright lawyer of
Spanish blood said, "I am a man without a country, and so are my people." They do not feel natural here. They are suspicious and on their guard.
No rooting down is possible to an organism in
such a relation to life. In making their approach,
too often they are subjected to a romantic mollycoddling by the Americans. Most harmful to
character and progress is this silly sort of
"Americanization." People will exclaim in public over the Mexican "eyes of midnight," dim-
pled smiles, poetic phrases, and musical talents,
and at the same time ride rough-shod over brothers of these same people—often those who have

more strength of character, but who do not possess these charms. Many a Spanish girl has been pushed over the precipice to her ruin by this foolish and sinister approach. They should be treated like other people. Then we learn that they are fascinating candidates for fine friendship, useful service, and good citizenship. This world needs more heart, and the Latins have it.

All who work sympathetically with Mexicans discover qualities of nobility which are quite surprising to us. In addition to those mentioned above, other traits are characteristic of them. They are self-forgetful and generous beyond all measure—or even common sense. They share their last crust with each other. Sacrifices of life itself are not uncommon. One of our young Mexican Epworth League members, when he saw his boss in peril, quickly climbed down the ladder into the deadly gas-tank, helped his employer out, and was himself fatally overcome. A train carrying passengers and dynamite was standing at a station along the Border. Suddenly fire was discovered in the car next to the tons of explosives. Instantly the Mexican engineer rushed his fireman back to warn the passengers and crew, while he threw open the throttle and pulled the train out away from the town, where the frightful explosion left only memories of the brave hero, the savior of many lives. These are typical cases, and they might be multiplied. Of the fifteen thousand Spanish-American soldiers in the World

War, it is notable that a large proportion chose machine gun companies, which they well knew represented serious business.

There is marked talent among these people for diplomacy and adaptability to delicate situations. With minds accustomed to drawing the most courtly and fine shades of meaning in spoken or written speech, they possess winning powers which are the despair of the average American. Here they resemble the Oriental, to whom many regard them as ethnically related.

They are versatile and dignified. They seem so deferential and complimentary that our slow wits surrender for want of anything else that we can do. They wear us out, and force seems to be our only recourse unless we can win them over. It should be noted that in events reaching back several years Mexico has moved each time toward Uncle Sam's "King Row" in our international game of checkers. They did *not* salute the flag, nor did they *surrender* Villa. Turned to useful purposes, such powers of diplomacy are invaluable in this world where peace-makers are at high premium.

Foes of the Mexican Home and Community

A police officer of San Francisco said: "Not less than ten thousand Mexicans, Spaniards, Filipinos, and Porto Ricans crowd in here each winter from the fruit ranches, and I tell you the

sharks are waiting for them on every corner.''
The Mexicans everywhere fall easy prey to clever
exploiters, usually of foreign or mixed blood.
The sad story begins with the exorbitant rents
charged for cramped and dirty habitations. In
one case, the rent charged for a house paid the
entire cost of its construction in seven months.

Another social bandit preying on the Mexicans
is the employment agency. There seems to be
some double-action railroading being done by a
collusion between *oficinas de empleo* and the
mayordomos (bosses) of the construction gangs.
The Mexicans pay advance charges of from one
to five dollars and then mysteriously lose their
jobs after three days or a week, for no apparent
reason. If there is a company commissary, they
are required to buy their clothing, food, and other
supplies there at a price often from fifty to one
hundred per cent more than they would cost in
the near-by town. And any Mexican who
''squeals'' is promptly laid off.

The next shark is the loan shark or pawn-
broker, who grows fat on his easy prey. Hopes
of soon getting work bring to the pawn shop thousands of fine and rare treasures, which are never
seen again, and which were parted with for the
convenience of a loan. The chronic emergency of
the optimistic victims, who are products of Mexican peonage, has absorbed all funds and more
when at last the hoped-for work is secured.

Life insurance, which is usually a blessing to

society, is forced upon Mexican laborers by un-
scrupulous agents in a fashion reminding one of
how the early *conquistadores* forced the aborigines to buy spectacles of window-glass for eyes
which could see like the eagle, and razors for
beards which never grew.

It is significant that halls and all sorts of shops
and stores are usually maintained in, or near to,
the Mexican colonies by Japanese, Chinese,
Greeks, Italians, and some—usually American-
born—Spanish Americans. The Mexicans seem
to know how to run blind pigs successfully, as
tools of the bilingual merchant-rogues of other
races.

Among the most prolific exploiters of unheed-
ing Mexicans are the shyster lawyers. Going to
the jails with their daily grist of Mexican un-
fortunates, these vampires study the case of each
and proceed to extort money under the plea of advance fees, somewhat after the fashion of the
priests asking for money to get loved ones out of
purgatory.

One Mexican father had not drunk for years.
He lived in a tent house with a large and happy
family. His pride was his new bicycle which became the envy of some young neighbors. On a
holiday they came with whiskey bottles which may
have contained something else besides. The se-
quel was that the drunken owner of the bicycle,
while being pressed to sell the bicycle below its
cost, at last lost consciousness and awakened in

MEXICANS? NO! THEY ARE AMERICANS IN THE MAKING!

People frequently talk about "the Mexicans in the United States," forgetful of the fact that "Mexican" children are really American children. Above is a group in a Home for Mexican Orphans in California. Below is a club of boys gathered from the streets of San Antonio.

SCHOLARSHIP GIRLS AT THE UNIVERSITY OF SOUTHERN CALIFORNIA

These four girls were all born in Mexico. Two of them are "pure" Mexicans.
Perhaps you can tell which these two are.

the city jail. One of the young men was in the county hospital with a leg shattered by a bullet from Don Juan's revolver.

The usual nimble-tongued bilingual lawyer brought the promise of speedy liberty to this man who had never had experience with courts or jail before, if the family could raise forty dollars. Toll was levied upon the heart-broken wife's meager savings and those of all well-disposed friends of whom Mexicans in trouble always have a wealth, in number at least. It was a pathetic sight to see the faithful father reach out his strong, useful arms through the bars of the prison cell to embrace his beloved and really beautiful children.

Other and larger sums were demanded by the so-called "lawyer." But Don Juan never got his liberty. Who knows what immoral and anarchistic impressions stained his soul during those first months of life in a congested prison—all brought to pass through the crime of having taken a glass or two of doped whiskey.

Agents, merchants, and all sorts of dealers ply their nefarious traffic among these "new Americans." A newsboy on a train will often be seen to pass by forty people in the time he will devote to one or two Mexicans. Frequently he will sit down with them, for he is pretty sure to make a sale. It is to be noted that those who succeed in luring away the meager pay of the Mexicans have gone to the trouble to learn Spanish.

The Value of Money

Puritanic, thrifty, bargain-driving Yankees are disgusted with the incongruity of purse and purchase and the foolish luxuries indulged in by the Mexicans. Families in need of public aid, who have been pauperized by unscientific American charity, will be seen buying ice-cream cones, candy, and gay attire, all to the disgust of friends at first inclined to help. Hasty judgment suggests that they are either mentally deficient or lacking in common sense and plain honesty. The fact is, they have never discovered the value of money, as they have never discovered the value of time. Savings accounts and wonderful feats of economy in dress and living are important by-products of our mission work. In matters of money, as in morals, they swing far over when converted. It is from citizens of the most prodigal nation on earth, our United States, that these Mexicans take lessons in buying luxuries and making other injudicious purchases. They are like the poor country boy making unwise expenditures of his first earnings in a great city, particularly if he has not had Christian restraints and wise business counsels before he left home.

Early Marriages

The early marriages contracted by many beautiful Mexican girls rob them of their young womanhood and in the end create genuine social problems. Just after opening the clinic door one morning at half-past eight, a tall Mexican woman with a very pretty face followed me back to the examination room and asked if we had some baby clothes. Seeing the lines of sorrow and care on her face, I asked her if I could be of any further service to her. She seemed to appreciate immediately the sympathetic touch, and unburdened her heart by giving a bit of her life's story. "I was married one month before I was thirteen years old; before I was fourteen I was a mother. I never had any girlhood; I am now twenty-six years old, and the mother of eleven children, six of whom are dead. Three of my children could not walk; yes, it was a blessing when they died. I suffer much from my husband at times. Men do not care for their wives. Oh, I am so sorry these babies came. I am so sorry I was married so young; but it is too late now!" Her eyes brightened when she was asked to bring her children to Sunday school, to join our Mothers' Club, and to learn to sew and to speak better English.

A Challenge

Perhaps, however, no menace to the welfare of the Mexican is greater than our own indifference to him. Several years ago this remark fell on our ears: " 'Taint American, I tell ye. We don't treat any other foreigners the way we treat these

Mexicans.'' The speaker was an Irish Catholic. We were seeking a youth, a relative of President Diaz, who had been found by a Christian woman along the roadside, very near to death. After convalescence, we lost sight of him and found him again in a roadhouse of bad repute, where he had found refuge and light work. It was here that he told us the story of his attempted suicide. Chafing under the caste of Mexico, he had fled over the Border where his lot was a hard one, for his hands and mind were unaccustomed to heavy toil on ranch and railroad. His peon fellow-toilers bantered him. In his loneliness and chagrin, he sent a bullet through his head, severing one optic nerve. In a letter found beside his wounded body, he had written that his burden had become too heavy to endure, and requested the officers not to accuse his fellows, especially naming the one who had gaffed him the most and who had stolen his guitar. The first moment of conversation with this young Mexican nobleman disclosed his culture and high ideals. Later correspondence with the young man emphasized the observation of our Irish friend who helped us to locate him and who had gone on to say as we parted: ''Juan is a foine fellow, pure as sunlight, even in this place. I tell ye, 'taint American the way we treat the Mexicans!'' And Patrick's words have haunted us these five years. Perhaps here is a hint of why Mexican immigrants rarely of themselves become American citizens.

While we remain indifferent, however, other forces are playing upon the Mexican within our borders. Inflammatory speeches are constantly being delivered in Mexican colonies, and a radical literature distributed among Mexicans.

In the plaza we heard a vicious-appearing but witty demagogue haranguing two hundred Mexicans. Among other blasphemous things, we heard him say: "Religion is false and dangerous. It unbalances the lobes of the brain. The Bible is a lie and a deception. That church over there in front of you (the Catholic Plaza Church) is a den of rogues and graft. All other churches are like it. The great Nazarene himself said, 'Those who injure and wrong you are rogues and deceivers.'" This superficial and shocking freethought is more or less accepted by at least half of the Latins of Pan-America, who have come in contact with the doctrines.

> Sin works; let me work, too.
> Sin undoes; let me do.
> Busy as Sin, my work I ply,
> Till I rest in the rest of eternity.

III

MAKING CONTACTS WITH THE
MEXICANS

The Kingdom of God consists of the brotherly
sons of God using their powers in a friendly
fashion.

BOSWORTH

SINCE the real "Border" is more racial
than geographical, it is the line of racial
contact rather than the Rio Grande which
must be crossed in order to reach the Mexicans.
Workers among Mexicans and other Latins come
to understand and to love them. And Latins know
how to reciprocate promptly and cordially the efforts to open a way for mutual understanding.
The avenue of interracial approach is clearly
marked. It is along the way of friendliness and
common sense. But there are many obstacles.

A college girl, seeking a position in "Spanish
missions," was invited to an excellent position,
with an apartment, in a new, fine, institutional
Mexican church. It was a fascinating opportunity in a cultured, progressive American city. But
the girl and her parents recoiled in terror at the
thought of her "serving on the Border." Their
ideas were distorted.

This misconception is a common one. What do
you suppose the Mexicans *think of us?* Evi-

dently we all need to think again on certain points. We are *too near* to be neighborly in a constructive, interracial Christian way. We are interested in poor, ignorant folk on the other side of the globe, but when we get into actual contact with people of different races, we bring out a social steam-roller instead of the Bible, a handshake, and a generous missionary offering. The Japanese question illustrates the point. It is easier to get a thousand dollars for Japan than a dollar for local Japanese. They are too near. It is not merely because "distance lends enchantment"; it is more the close-up revelation of racial antipathies that exist in un-Christian and selfish individuals. Isolated cases and exceptional incidents become highly colored in the heated imagination of interested and provincial individuals until all Mexicans become "sheep-killing dogs." The first obstacle is that of nearness. Familiarity, rather than "breeding contempt," must be made to result in awakening genuine interest and action.

Then again the very vastness of the task appalls rather than invites. Yet here is a lure of the baffling—a call of the impossible. A border that cannot be sealed can be healed. A people who are not provident can be made socially efficient. A Latin American life on either side of the Border, though nominally Roman Catholic and very illiterate, passionate, and prejudiced, can and does respond promptly to the right approach. Yet the size of the task strikes terror to the heart and is a severe obstacle to be overcome by faith and experience.

The fact that the task is inevitable makes people shrink from it. It is one American task that is not optional. Providence clearly beckons us to the Latin Americans now as never before. We must come to sense an obligation and an opportunity in every house-court, railroad section, fruit camp, and, most of all, in each individual Mexican above the Border. Most of our native pastors were reached by the approach of some friendly Americans who saw in them possibilities of leadership among their own people. Mexicans are not "in our back yard" but they are coming to our front door.

Some vain and vicious theories and prejudices must be removed in our approach to Latin Americans. A fever of "intervention" frequently seizes the press and, through it, reaches the people of our country. People tell us that "in helping the Mexicans, we are helping our future foes. They will use their education and independence to fight us later on."

As with the Negroes, there are ever present individuals who propose deportation or a forced exodus of Mexicans back across the Border "where they belong," with the suggestion that the "Border be walled up and you missionaries to the Mexicans be sent down there to keep order.'' Such an attitude is not helpful in the uplift of a supersensitive and wronged people. Somebody should be around to remind such detractors that if there are interlopers to be pushed back or expelled from other people's lands, we are perhaps the ones who should be so pushed back.

The most common fling taken at the Mexicans is to say that they are ''just Indians'' and are therefore, like all savages, doomed to extinction. The fact is, as we have seen, they are not savages— nor were they ever; and the numerous families and very high birth-rate does not look like ''race suicide'' or the ''end of the trail'' of the Latin Americans. Such specious slanders of a people we are to help must be answered by facts and a more friendly approach.

Another obstacle to right approach is the mutual recoil of comfortable, better-dressed people from the toiling and needy poor. A Mexican pastor, after seeing his new parsonage for the first time, said, ''Oh, my brothers, you are too kind to give us so fine a home. When my wife and I saw it, our hearts ached, because our Mexican people are all so poor. They have no place to sleep. They are hungry and have poor clothes. Many of my young men have no place except bad resorts to lodge. My Mexicans have very poor houses. Oh, brothers, this, my lovely pastor's home, is too fine! The *señora* and I went home and could not sleep for three nights thinking about what our people will say when we live so comfortably.''

This pastor is a spiritual magnet. He draws his people, for he recoils from comfort and elegance when his people cannot share it all. On the other hand, no finer contribution can be made to the Mexican colony than to plant in it a neat, attractive, happy, model community home. Half of the Mexicans will never enter a Protestant chapel, but they will come to this "pastor's house" and get incentives and ideas about neat homes.

The pastor referred to above is a former educator in Mexico and finely cultured. He is a first-class tailor and always dresses neatly and well. His children are leading students and athletes in the university and high school. But he feels no recoil from the poorly dressed and suffering Mexicans.

The Color Line

Besides the matter of dress and environment, another external which bars immediate approach is the matter of reference to color. Mexicans are of the "white race"; but their past or present occupation and manner of life may have given them a trigeño (dark) complexion, as is usually the case with Indian types. The approach to Mexicans is blocked when reference is made to "white folks" in contrast to the Mexicans. Even if Latin Americans did have color, it is an external which any tactful, experienced servant of God who deals with "foreigners" learns to forget.

Other external and inevitable occasions for failure to make immediate approach are the following. The socially independent, possessed of thrift, initiative, and the mystic, price-reducing power of "cash to buy," usually feel a condescension or even scornful impatience with those who "live from hand to mouth." Here is a main barrier between the average Yankee and the Mexican. There is an arrogance that goes with better fortune. It is seen among the "get rich quick" of any race. We Americans are all rich compared with the Mexicans, and most of us have become rich quickly, not only in the comforts of life, but also in education, opportunity, and the removing of external barriers. There is a recoil of light from darkness in matters of culture—an arrogance of enlightenment when dealing with the benighted. The problem of approach is to remove not only from self-sufficient Americans this sense of superiority, but also from the better-class Mexicans and other Latins the spirit which stiffly, coldly responds to the challenge to approach the "proletariat" of their own people. A major portion of the prejudice, barring a sincere, immediate approach, is lodged in the minds of the people needing help. They say: "They are above us. They have plenty to eat and to wear, and they do not care for us. We do not want their charity." Here is suggested the leading approach which socialism is enabled to make to these masses. For, listening to the better-class Mexicans, one hears often remarks like the following: "They are just peons." "They ought to know better." "They are really no good." "They just travel from place to place and are useful only to stir up trouble for society." Fortunately, a far different spirit between classes is being reflected above the Border. Both classes are learning.

Two unique obstacles to be overcome are: first, the Mexican sensitiveness about the taking of their territory in 1847, and second, their recent real and fancied exploitation by the "gringos" (Americans). We are paying the price now for America's record in Mexican affairs which has often been inconsistent with the spirit of Christian missions. Mexicans are prompt to respond to things of the heart. In the approach, if it be genuinely sincere and unaffected, they will go the last two thirds of the way. But usually the first approach brings one into contact with the sentiment, "We don't want the Yankee religion. You are just trying to get a hold on us."

The second unique obstacle is the remoteness of the Border from the East with its stubborn prejudices as to "what you can do with the Mexicans." Between the Eastern lack of sympathy with the real problem and its solution, and the Western spirit of the Border and of the Forty-niners, the task of laying deep foundations for mutual understanding with Latin Americans in the Southwest is retarded. It is more than a matter of mere missionary appropriation and equip-

ment; it is more a matter of sympathetic cooperation between the Mexicans themselves and those
who know them best. One of the bilingual workers says, ''Unless people have Latin Americans
really upon their hearts, they can have ever so
much training and missionary zeal, but they will
not approach the Mexican work from the right
point of view.'' Plans which are apparently ideal
for the East, and even methods which have
worked with other foreign-speaking groups and
in other sections, do not always work with the
people from over the Border.

Most human problems are personal and arise
from misunderstandings. For Americans the
problem of understanding the Mexicans is simply
a matter of study and attention.

Asking the Mexican admiral to salute the
United States flag was a capital blunder. Asking
Mexico to cooperate in capturing Francisco Villa,
the bandit chieftain, was just as stupid a misunderstanding of the Mexican personal equation.
It overlooked ''Spanish pride.'' Racial incom-
patibility crops out when American practicality is
pitted against Latin honor.

Scars of the Past

In accounting for the Latin American personality certain scars of their past, suggested in a previous chapter, must be sympathetically kept in
mind.

(1) The Mexicans have been an *isolated* people, and isolated peoples are likely to be innocent, sensitive, naïve, provincial, and possessed of traits which may be classified as adolescent if not puerile. They are not faults: they are traits or stages of development.

(2) There is the scar of *oppression*. This is due to Spanish viceroys, land owners, despotic governments, and an exploiting Church.

(3) Latin Americans *have been or are Roman Catholics,* socially if not devotedly. Their faith, as compellingly taught by the character of the saints they worship, is one of worshiping the recluse, the unnatural, the inversion rather than the development of nature's charms and talents.

(4) In the approach we feel the venom of much *propaganda of hate.* It is a virus that works most mischief in Mexico. Down there things said are more easily believed, especially if backed by the parochial priest and press. Multitudes in Mexico have been taught that "American plows are bewitched," and similar superstitions.

(5) The anachronism of *peonage and virtual serfdom* in this twentieth century and in this New World raises a barrier to natural approach and frank understanding. The deep scars of this social cancer are observed in dealing with the laboring class of Mexicans. That is why they can be treated by large employers of labor as if they were cattle and regarded as of little more worth to society and the kingdom of God.

Unwelcome Clients and Patients

The difficulty of linking the Mexican immigrants with our social life, even in the great cities where civic organizations with skilled specialists have facilities for all manner of relief work, is a perplexing one.

It should be realized that, poorly dressed and uncouth as many of the needy Mexicans are, these suffering people cannot be admitted to the offices of doctors and professional men. They would prejudice respectable patronage. Physicians and specialists, however, show wonderful interest in the founding of special clinics where the best of skill may be administered to the worst of physical needs.

Dr. W. Curtis Brigham writes:

It has been my lot to work among the poor Spanish and Mexican people of southern California to some extent for about eleven years. In this work I have observed several things. First, the Spanish people, no matter how poor or illiterate, are proud, and one's influence is soon destroyed if their poverty or ignorance is apparently noticed. Second, their homes are impossible from a surgical standpoint. Sanitary, dietetic, and hygienic measures for the prevention and relief of disease are very difficult in their homes. Third, they have a great fear of the institutions supported by the public moneys, largely, I think, because institutions so supported do not and cannot take the time to explain their methods. Fourth, they become greatly attached to those who give them relief in their sufferings; in fact, they almost deify their benefactors.

The Latin Americans are extremely grateful to friends who show them a better way of living than theirs of suffering, grief, and the all-too-common drugs. One mother, aided at a critical time at Angel Island, San Francisco, named her twin babies "Los Angeles" and "San Francisco." A little boy, who had suffered long with infantile paralysis, vigorously resisted the first attentions at the clinic, but later cried when compelled to leave the bath, and went away in his little wagon affectionately grasping his new crutches.

Dr. Robert McLean, Superintendent of Presbyterian Mexican work in the United States, after years of labor in at least three foreign fields, says, "No field at home or abroad is in greater need of doctors and nurses than this southwest region." [1]

Mexicans are sometimes accused of being proud, lazy, and improvident. As a matter of fact, they stand destitute and helpless in the stream of American life and industrial competition. They are ignorant of the customs and ideals of the country. They do not know how to "take the Americans." They become prejudiced against us in their own country, and come only to improve conditions for themselves and their families. They believe that all Americans are Protestants and that their churches are either portals to hell or institutions of graft, depending on whether the prejudices were instilled by Romanist or socialist.

[1] *Old Spain in New America,* page 140.

They read little, but talk and listen much. Rumors abound throughout Latin America that Americans are hard taskmasters and are "insolently indifferent" when it comes to a disagreement in closing a bargain or in making payment for services rendered.

What Prevents Social Amalgamation?

(1) *Distrust.* Mexicans live in distrust of each other to a large extent. As this ceases to be true, Mexico promises to become a united and strong nation. Mexicans will unite for social clubs, but not for ventures requiring practical confidence such as contracts. Though utterly gracious, generous, and hospitable to strangers, they have learned to live in distrust of strangers. They are especially suspicious of any sort of new propaganda which does not quite fit into their way of thinking.

(2) *Fear.* A whole chapter might be written concerning the fears of the Mexicans. In their own country they have lived from infancy in terror of revolution, exploitation, and domestic disaster. With them every day has been an experience of living but a step from death.

A well-educated Mexican, in his address before a young people's convention, said: "You young people even in infancy have looked up from your cradles into parental eyes which reflected peace, confidence, hope, and joy. You have had nothing to fear. Most of us Mexicans from our cradles, if we were so fortunate as to have cradles, have looked up into the faces of parents in whose eyes were not reflected the contentment, hopes, and Christian faith that you have always known.''

The poorer Mexicans rarely have a stove to warm their chilly rooms; they are afraid of warm air and of warm water. They are afraid to start a new thing lest they fail. They are afraid to attempt a new thing lest something happen. They are afraid to begin learning English, as other foreigners do, lest somebody will hear them make a mistake and laugh at them. Most of all, they are afraid of social ostracism or persecution. Castilian pride cannot endure being laughed at. Bold and valorous in battle and heroic in adventure, the Mexicans are still a people who live largely in a chronic state of fear. They brood over somebody who is sick, or the last misfortune, or the lost job. The strange thing is that this state of fear is not revealed on first acquaintance, but it is none the less a fact.

(3) *Prejudice.* Mexican immigrants have been so long despised and made the objects of unkind reference in literature and jest that they have come to meet prejudice with prejudice. One American criticism can create a ferment in a whole crew. It is probable that if less were said in criticism of the Mexicans' refusal to become American citizens, they themselves would much more quickly join our other new Americans who

are eager for citizenship. Ignorance is not the only reason for the Mexicans' distaste for American citizenship. Other reasons are: his residence is so close to Mexico; the Border friction; and the persistent bitterness over the treaties of Guadalupe Hidalgo and Cahuenga. All these considerations in a subconscious way, combined with ignorance of American ideals and of the English language, contribute to retard the Americanization of the Mexicans.

A further complication in recent years comes from the agitation by so-called socialists who are seeking to form an international republic. These agitators constantly harangue the Mexicans in the plazas and Mexican quarters, and publish in Spanish scurrilous tracts and editorials to the effect that America is a nation of oppressors, dupes, and grafters. This constantly prejudices the Mexicans, particularly the ignorant and suffering ones, against the American Government and the securing of their citizenship therein.

These agitators boast that they are the only true friends of the masses and that the revolutions in France, Russia, and Mexico must sweep over the entire world. They slyly insinuate that should the Mexicans become American citizens, they might some day be compelled to fight against their own country, Mexico. The average Mexican mind of all classes drops into the *"mañana"* philosophy, saying, "Well, we will probably go back to Mexico sometime, so what is the use of becom-

ing American citizens?'' There is a still further
factor involved here, for the Mexican soon learns
that as a citizen of Mexico he can, in time of trouble, turn to the Mexican consul in the United
States. If he becomes a citizen of the United
States, there is no one upon whom he can call in
time of need.

(4) *A false philosophy of life.* With the average Mexican, his philosophy—and he always has
one—is that of seeking the line of least resistance
to a fancied personal gain. Such philosophy
among any culturally handicapped people usually
results in a search for objectives that are immediate, easy, and free from unpleasant contacts with
others. They believe that what happens had to
happen. Reading few, if any, great books to lift
up ideals of active soul adventure, their existence
is largely one of uninspired toil and lonely striving, or, more commonly, a resigned existence of
unawakened living for personal pleasure. The
Mexicans, as a people, on both sides of the Border
are like a sleeping giant.

But the doings in Mexico today indicate that
the giant is awaking. The new constitution of
Mexico is unique among the nations in most respects. Its efforts for a new and much more general public education indicate an intellectual
awakening below the Border. It is very important to determine who shall awaken these strong
men to the South.

The Mexicans and Play

"Oh, come on, let's have another picnic!" "Señor, fix us up a handball court." "Why can't we come in like those girls and have a good time? We boys can sew, too." So our workers are greeted.

The play instinct is a part of Mexican life as is the case in every other country. The trouble is lack of direction. Much of Mexican play is of the "bleacher" sort. As a nation they have for generations watched cock-fights and *los toros* (bull-fights), and sat around playing the guitar or bantering each other with quips and superficial jokes and, in maturer years, playing cards. "Thrumming a guitar and cheering on a cock-fight or a bull-fight do not exhaust life's possibilities," wisely observes Ralph Welles Keeler.

Among the diversions of the Mexicans, music is very prominent. Guitar, piano, orchestra, and band are delightful features of their life. The Mexican bands and orchestras are a remarkable aggregation of artists. They often include several mere boys, sometimes as young as nine years of age. Dressed in the bright colors of the Mexican Military Band, with much red in evidence, and helmets with white cockades, they impress one greatly even before they render, in their remarkably fine form, classic selections, many of which are composed by the directors themselves.

Vice is the threshold between play and sin. All too frequently the witchery of music and easy flow of merry words and laughter degenerates into vice. The dancing girl and the wine-cup are star attractions in every Mexican colony. The Santa Rosa Club, the Independence Day balls, and the *Benavides* pool hall form an altogether disproportionate and unwholesome attraction for the social and physical welfare of these pleasure-loving Latins. They are coming to have a perfect mania for moving pictures. Stereopticon lectures given to Mexicans are popular and usually draw out some "operators" who have had experience running the *cinematografo*. The famous San Gabriel Mission Play, like the Passion Play at Oberammergau, has such a hold through its spectacular and local material interests that it is very popular. Mexican and Portuguese names are becoming very common on Sunday baseball teams and in boxing bouts. At a New Year's Day navy tournament, the program showed that five of the boxers were men with Latin American names. Mexican boys and men are becoming increasingly popular as caddies on the golf links. One often sees these caddies picking up the cigarettes laid down or thrown away by the players.

Unfortunate Press Comments

In the *Fresno Republican,* probably the most thoughtful daily west of Kansas City, one reads:

The Mexican is an habitual indigent. His presence in my community is destructive to American ideals. . . . There are certain respects in which the Mexican presents a less serious race problem than any other form of imported servile labor. Temporarily, Orientals are better. Japanese, Chinese, and Hindus are clean, intelligent, and enterprisingly able to take care of themselves. Mexican peons are dirty, diseased, stupid, and helpless. . . . If imported, then we must recognize that we are bringing in the *most helpless people on earth,* for whom somebody must care, if we do not, after we are through with them in this industrial crisis.

The Relief and Employment Commission of the same city (a city in which, at the time, there was no Mexican mission) gives out the following as the sentiment of the Commission.

We are constantly called upon to administer relief to local Mexican residents. The Commission finds that the presence of Mexican laborers, whose standards of living are much lower than those of the community at large, is a continual menace to the health and welfare of the community. It is informed by other relief agencies of the state that a similar problem exists wherever there is a Mexican settlement. Most of these Mexican laborers have been brought here by large employers of labor who have made a practise of leaving them on the community when the season of employment is at an end.

Such a situation in the community tends to aggravate the race problem.

How a Judge Made Contact

A judge was present at an illustrated address delivered in an American church. At its close he said: "You have shown me two things tonight: first, the remarkable possibilities of Mexicans when given a chance; and second, the possibility of employing the stereopticon among the Mexicans themselves for their own uplift. I am getting tired of sentencing Mexicans to jail and to the pen by scores. I want to help them. Would you come and give some of these views of sacred art and happy, temperate Mexican home-life to a crowd of Mexicans in my court-room if I could get them together?" We gladly consented. Invitations in Spanish were sent out to all the Mexican colonies round about. A tremendous crowd of Mexicans of all classes jammed the court-room; even the judge himself had to stand. They packed the aisles and the crowd reached outside the doors. After the lecture and when the last footfall had died away, the bailiff observed: "Say, Judge, I saw something tonight I have never seen before: hundreds of Mexicans going away from a public gathering without one of them lighting a cigarette. I guess those tobacco views hit the mark."

In the afternoon, in company with the judge, we had visited the many sick Mexicans in the near-by hospital and the soul-sick in the jail. One of them was a one-armed, quiet youth, who later did a marvelous drawing, by minute pen points in ink, of the judge who had taken this interest in his people. This young man was called to our attention by the discovery of a drawing of the

Savior's face on a board in his cell. We wrote to him and sent him a copy of the Bible. His letter of acknowledgment, written from the penitentiary, runs as follows:

Such stimulating words and their influence are very strengthening. There are times when my thoughts seem to wander in lanes that are dark and dangerous to my welfare, except through the exercise of the will and determination which I am gradually acquiring through the reading of His Book and power of prayer. You cannot possibly realize, I think, what an influence for happiness and good there is for one who will try to find help within the pages of His written words. . . . I shall persistently strive in the searching for the light from the truth and pray that I may be used for the good of my countrymen, with His help. I remain, with thanks and prayer.

This story is not yet finished. While writing these pages, there appeared in a secular daily the following heading on the front page:

DRAWS SAVIOR'S FACE IN CELL. IS FREED.

Two judges make affidavit that the drawing left in the cell led to the reformation of four other Mexicans.

The kind judge wrote us, "Our friend . . . is on the way to your Plaza Community Center to see you." The end is not yet! We are only beginning to look for talents that lie dormant in lives darkened and enslaved by sin and ignorance!

It is becoming increasingly true in the great cities that the Mexican immigrants, as they them-

selves say, are not wanted in any place that is respectable—hotels, coaches, or even pool halls.
There is no place for them except low "Spanish
hotels" and the worst saloons. What is their social opportunity now when the saloons are closed?
Their cheerless hovels are usually a far cry from
the quiet comfort enjoyed by the average American in his evening hours at home.

Why the Mexican Quits His Job

The universal complaint against the Mexican is
the difficulty of holding him to his job. For some
reason he frequently appears singularly indifferent to permanent employment. There is a reason
for everything, and a cure. Conduct flows from
ideas. The Mexican has not grasped any idea of
the meaning and the *value of time*. Again, it must
be remembered that he is, as a race, arising like
a drowsy giant lifting himself out of the mire.
His peon existence has its very lax industrial and
social standards. It is like Grandmother's recipe
for doughnuts: "Put in some flour, some milk,
and some sugar, salt," etc. The masses of Latin
America have been accustomed to put into life
some time, *some* thought, *some* sense of responsibility, all according to their taste and free desire.
They have had no needs but for today and no clock
but the sun. Mexicans more often come too early
than too late to their work. Shrewd, impatient
Saxon bosses pay no attention if they are early,

but cannot forgive them if they are late.   The
Mexican finds it hard to hold a job which involves
the elements of punctuality and steady employment—especially when it requires his presence
early Monday morning after "pay-day."   He will
hunt another job rather than receive a reprimand
or a punishment.   He prefers to starve rather
than let his Castilian pride suffer.   This is now
changing most remarkably as the United States
has gone dry.

Lessons that Must Be Learned

In order to blend into American life, the Mexican must learn the following lessons:

1. *The value of cooperation and the sacredness
of contract.*   He must learn these lessons both for
his personal profit and for the industrial betterment of his race, whose welfare is to his own advantage.   The Spanish word *"socio,"* which is
the root of "social," means "partner."   "Social
service" literally says "partner service" to the
Mexican mind.   It expresses just what he needs
to learn—social partnership, confidence, and a
spirit of give and take.

2. *Loyalty to the Government.*   The War has
taught all Latin America the high principles of
the United States.   The Mexican must learn that
in the States he is an American whether a citizen
of the United States or not.

3. *Submission when in the wrong.*   He must

learn to apologize rather than leave his job. Americans have been reputed to be hard taskmasters—gruff, abrupt, and unreasonable. The Mexican is coming to see that frank, fair conduct on his part transforms this taskmaster into a delightful friend, who expects him to be prompt, orderly, and a hearty sharer in the enterprise.

4. *The value of "getting past the dead points."* He must cultivate a sense of responsibility and dependableness, even though unpleasant incidents arise, and a continuity of purpose which will be stronger than race sensitiveness.

5. *The cultivation of high ideals and incentives in life.* Chief of these is a happy home, and living on property that belongs to him and is beautified by him.

6. *A wiser recourse to law.* He must learn when suffering injustice how to obtain the benefits of the law. He is beginning to see that pettifogging lawyers are simply vampires. He is beginning to seek out trustworthy and experienced Mexicans, or responsible American friends, to help adjust his legal difficulties. Our pastors spend a considerable proportion of their time visiting and helping those who are in court, jail, or hospital.

A drunken section boss came to the section on a Sunday afternoon, and finding one Mexican asleep, kicked him. Through natural pride, the Mexican remonstrated, but the drunken boss struck him down and then had him sent to the county jail for assault and battery, where he remained two weeks *without trial!* The intervention of the Mexican pastor speedily resulted in his release.

7. *The meaning of real business responsibility.* Mexicans as a rule shy from either entering into or negotiating business contracts. They are good pay. Most of the bad Mexican accounts complained of by houses of business really arise from lax business methods. Mexicans are sometimes slow to pay, but in following up the account, if consideration is paid to their own way of thinking and doing, the Mexicans are anxious to pay so as to be well thought of. Pages might be quoted of hearty testimonies to the fidelity of Mexicans in ultimately paying accounts despaired of and almost forgotten. They will usually bring the money due, though it cost in travel an amount almost equal to the consideration itself.

8. *The wisdom of learning English.* Steiner says, "Blood is thicker than water, but language is thicker than blood."

Business Catastrophies

Running into debt is one form of borrowing. Peonage and pawn-shops are not dissimilar in the character of their transactions or in their effects. This explains incidents like the following. A contract for wood-cutting is taken by an enterprising and leading Mexican in the colony. He forms his

crew; he is sure of his pay; he runs accounts at
the stores and buys horses and wagons, all well
within the amount of the contract. Later a wagon
breaks down and then a horse dies. Sickness
compels unexpected expenditures. Some of the
crew have to run accounts. Before the wood is
hauled, the creditors compare notes and secure a
lien on the piles of eucalyptus cord-wood. The discharged and helpless Mexican contractor, rather
than face a situation horrible to his pride as a
leader in the community, flees and, possibly, gets
drunk, adding still more to his shame. Later
he repents and returns, asks forgiveness and begins to pay his accounts. But no more Mexican
contracts for his creditors or for the men of his
crew! This is why the latter usually prefer to
work under contracts with people of other races;
their own contracts end in *molestia* (bother) and
loss.

Americans and Mexicans

In a Christmas offering for the Mexicans, we
received the following note: "My contribution to
the Mexicans at this Christmas time is the suggestion that we ship them all across the Border
where they belong, and build a wall so high that
they can never get back, and send Doctor ——
down to be their general. They are crowding out
the white man." That there are a great many
things wrong with this doubtless sincere sugges-

tion, is evident. First, the Mexicans are also *white* people. Second, if anybody is to be pushed back, who should it be? They were here first! Then, although the suggestion reflects an attitude that is altogether too common, it is not the solution.

In spite of difficulties, however, we are making progress in our attempt to understand the Mexicans. The difficulty of the task must not discourage us. During the War an English officer starting on a perilous charge upon a redoubt was told, "That cannot be taken." He replied: "Yes, it can. I have the orders here in my pocket." So is it in making our approach to these myriads of Mexicans and other Latin Americans who are standing ready for Christian America to Christianize and help them. Providence has given us the orders; it will be done. Mexican colonies from one coast to the other will soon experience the friendly interest of awakened Americans who recognize their clear duty.

God is notably leading in these labors. In the year 1920 a company of some forty Mexican editors and publicists visited the entire United States, and enjoyed, among other things, an extended conference with President Wilson. They left, saying, "The relations between the United States and Mexico can never be the same again after this intimate approach and better understanding of our good neighbors to the North." The missionaries and church press of both nations are spreading facts of better understanding, thereby developing friendship. The War drew us nearer together. Even the unfortunate "punitive expedition" did serve to lead us to a better understanding of "what Mexico and the United States are up against" in the Border problem.

Large delegations of members of Chambers of Commerce and Trade Associations are going in formal fashion to Mexico City and are bringing back a new conception of the Mexican people. This is awakening new interest in the Mexicans employed above the Border.

Perhaps no influence is more significant than that of the numbers of Latin Americans now attending colleges of the United States. These charming, versatile, talented young men and women are showing Americans a new side to the Mexican question. They are attending conventions, social occasions, and are taking part in college and community work along with other students, native and foreign. Many of these Latin students are working their way through college. Of course, they are studying in a language foreign to them, with methods of study still more foreign to their habits of thought, but they are returning to their countrymen with a better understanding of America.

The whole problem is a matter of social and interracial atmosphere. Bishop McConnell at the Panama Congress of Missions illustrated the situation by telling how this country was once deni-

A SUNDAY-SCHOOL AND YOUNG PEOPLE'S CONVENTION FOR SOUTHERN CALIFORNIA

A movement that can draw together Mexican young people from a number of different denominations for an annual convention must have an inherent vitality that is hopeful for the church life of today. The Sunday-school and Young People's Convention shown above assembled at Gardena, California, June 10, 1924.

A GRADUATING CLASS IN A GIRLS' BOARDING SCHOOL

Boarding schools conducted by Protestant agencies for Mexican girls in the United States differ considerably, but most of them, in addition to the usual studies, give special attention to domestic science and household arts. Some provide a regular normal training, and others, technical and secretarial training for those who plan to enter the business world.

zened by monsters, vast and awful. The Great
Father might have exterminated them by creating
a race of giants with enormous weapons and thus
have killed off the mammoths and dinosaurs. But
the Almighty did not do it that way. He simply
changed the climate and they all died. When the
fraternal, social, and Christian climate along the
Border, and where these races meet us within our
borders, has been tempered with kindly sympathy
and earnest endeavor, the evils which are now of
major proportions will disappear altogether.

> These clumsy feet, still in the mire,
> Go crushing blossoms without end.
> These hard, well-meaning hands we thrust
> Among the heart-strings of a friend.
>
> *The Fool's Prayer*

IV

EDUCATION

Ignorance and evil, even in full flight, deal terribly back-handed strokes at their pursuers.

CHARLES KINGSLEY

THREE Mexican boys were seen sitting on the doorstep of the ruins of the adobe headquarters building of General Frémont, on the Plaza at Los Angeles. One boy had an old magazine and was reading aloud; the other two were looking at the pictures and eagerly listening—one little torch held aloft for light. This scene, which incidentally deeply touched and won a friend to the educational need of Mexico, is being enacted over and over among Mexican youth.

Problems for Public Schools

The problem which the large influx of Mexicans into the United States has raised for the public schools in our four border states is a very complex one. The Mexican immigrant brings his family with him to this country, and thousands of boys and girls of school age, who have never been in school a day in their lives and who do not understand the English language, have been crowded into our border communities. In 1915 a school superintendent in one of these large border towns said: "Of those entering the first grade in school, ninety-two per cent are unable to understand one word of English, much less to speak it. Those of you who have three or four such children in your classes can have no idea of what it means to have the numbers reversed and to have three or four English-speaking children among a class of non-English-speaking ones." In all border communities, however, the percentage is, of course, not so high.

In some respects it is an advantage to the Mexican child when there are many of his kind in the school. It tends to make him feel at home and to keep him from getting discouraged, for among the tragedies in the lives of Mexican boys and girls in the United States is that of dropping out of school at an early age. There are many reasons for this tendency. The poverty in the home which makes it important for the children to begin to earn money is one factor. Then, too, there is often a lack of home cooperation; many parents do not appreciate the advantages of an education and particularly of a training which goes beyond the mere rudiments of reading and writing. On the other hand, there are many Mexican parents who will sacrifice their own comfort and welfare to buy text-books for their children and to give them an opportunity to go on with their school work. Perhaps there is no more serious obstacle, however, to the continuance of the school work than embarrassment on the part of the Mexican pupil himself and prejudice on the part of the

American pupil in the same school. In some places this is much worse than in others, but the problem is serious enough to cause us genuine concern.

Of course, there are many Americans who think that it is not worth while to attempt to educate Mexicans, and there are altogether too many Mexicans who are inclined to agree with them or who will accept their judgment without vocal protest. There are also some snap judgments as to Mexican ignorance and illiteracy. The kindest perhaps is this: "They are just like our pioneer grandparents; they simply have not had schools. They need teachers, books, clubs, and debating societies as we used to have in the little country school." Others blame Mexican ignorance upon Mexican indolence. That is, however, hardly a fair judgment.

The fact is that the Mexican comes to the United States from a country where most of the people are still illiterate and where popular education has been only gradually gaining ground. Introduced into Mexico by Porfirio Diaz, public education was extended far enough by him to dethrone him. The new government now in control in Mexico is pledged to a far greater extension of public education than Mexico has ever before known. We on this side of the Border are really working at the same task as is President Calles and his assistants in Mexico. We are having here the opportunity to help train native leaders and reformers who will lead the Mexicans out into a great future. President Madero, the leader of the 1911 revolution, said: "My people are a great and noble people; all they need is *ilustracion* (enlightenment). It will be my supreme effort to give this to them." The Madero family, educated in the best colleges of America, appreciated education. Madero himself was wealthy as well as cultured, but he left his comfortable life for the rough life of the bivouac and the fate of a martyr in order that his people might be enlightened.

Our Mexican immigrants who have had any training have come from an educational system which has been difficult, impracticable, exclusive, and uninviting. Even if schools had been open to all the masses, the Mexican peons and many of the middle-class group would not have availed themselves of the opportunity for higher education. Mexican education has not been made attractive to the masses. Yet when given a chance in our schools, or in any schools with modern, inviting methods, the Mexicans are eager pupils. Teachers in the public schools frequently comment upon the eagerness and precocity of Mexican children. They say that their bright minds, when awakened by a sympathetic attitude on the part of teachers, are a delight to real educators.

The illiterate Mexican in the United States is

continually handicapped in the struggle for existence by his ignorance. A young Mexican in the Los Angeles post-office, wishing to send eighty dollars to his poor mother in Mexico, asked an American standing near by to make out the money order for him, since he could neither read nor write. The money never arrived. Investigation showed that the friendly-looking American had made the order out to himself. Naturally when this fact became widely known, it did not tend to develop confidence on the part of Mexicans in the character of the United States and her people.

Segregation

One by-product of the influx of Mexicans into our schools has been a tendency toward segregation of Mexican pupils. Some insist that segregation is better for the Mexican children themselves, and that it is the easiest way to avoid race bitterness. Others believe in segregation because the Mexican children may bring dirt, disease, and vermin into the schools and for this reason they should not be permitted to mingle with other children. All these matters raise very delicate problems. At present the tide seems to be turning towards a policy of segregation for pupils up to a certain age who do not speak English. As soon as they have learned to speak English and are qualified therefor, they are permitted to enter the regular schools. So long as segregation is a matter of condition, rather than of race, there is probably little peril in it.

The opportunity offered to the teachers in the public schools who are assigned to Mexican pupils is very great. Many of these teachers are devoted to their work and are enthusiastic in their praises of the Mexican pupils in their charge.

The Problem of Transiency

The seasonable character of much of the work done by Mexicans indirectly creates an educational problem. As the workers themselves are of necessity migratory in their habits, the children are not long enough in any one place to establish a residence and to make satisfactory connection with the public schools. The state of California has recognized that fact and has taken some steps toward providing educational opportunities for these migrating families.

Truancy and deception about age are common. The vicious circle, which is started by taking promising students out of school at a time when they ought to go on with their school work, leads ultimately to the breaking down of ideals, health, hope, and of the new homes which are formed. Ignorance, poverty, and disease are the causes of this difficulty. It is a matter of fact that there are very few Mexican students in our high schools, and almost none in the universities and colleges of the United States, who have come from our poorer

Mexican immigrants to this country. Most of the
young people of this class who ought to have gone
on to college went out to work instead. If later
they discover their need of education there are
few public or state institutions to which they can
turn. There are several Indian schools into which
some Mexicans have found their way, but for the
most part the opportunities offered by public institutions to these handicapped young people are
conspicuous by their absence.

In New Mexico

The educational problems among our Spanish-
speaking peoples are not, however, limited to
those which have to do with our newly-arrived
Mexicans. The educational situation among our
native-born, Spanish-speaking Americans in New
Mexico has long been distressing. When the region now known as New Mexico became a part of
the United States, there were no public schools in
the territory, and only a few persons were attending schools of any sort; nor did matters improve with any great rapidity when this territory
was acquired by the United States. The federal
government tried in a feeble way to promote education, and, in fact, the territorial legislature of
New Mexico passed a bill at its 1855-56 session
establishing a common school system to be supported by public taxation. There was a provision, however, that the measure be submitted to

the people for vote and when so submitted it was defeated by a vote of 5,016 to 37. When Dr. Thomas Harwood arrived in New Mexico in 1870, he declared that not a schoolhouse could be found anywhere.

Since the establishment of the public school system in New Mexico in 1891, education has moved more rapidly, but it has had many impediments. The fact that the language of the country was predominantly Spanish made it difficult to secure public school teachers who had anything approaching an adequate command of the English language. Even when the teachers knew English, the situation of the pupil was not an easy one. In their homes, boys and girls learned to speak the Spanish language. They came to a poorly-equipped, poorly-taught school where some English was used but where the teacher, in order to be understood by the pupils, must, during most of the school hours, speak Spanish. As soon as school was dismissed, Spanish was, of course, the language used both on the playground and at home. The result was that many boys and girls educated in the public schools grew up with no real knowledge of the English language. Gradually these conditions have been changing, but even today in many communities Spanish is the only current language. The present state law provides that books used and instruction given in the public schools in New Mexico shall be in the English language, but that Spanish may be used to explain the meaning of English words to Spanish-speaking pupils who do not understand our language.

Possibly we do not need to go into further detail in regard to the need for education among Mexican and Spanish-speaking youth in our Southwest to suggest why the Church at an early stage in its work became concerned with the matter of education, and why throughout the years it has expended considerable sums of money upon the maintenance of so-called ''mission schools'' in our four border states.

Protestant Mission Schools

From the very beginning of Protestant mission work in the Southwest the need for educational work under the direction of the Church was clearly recognized. As early as 1865 Miss Melinda Rankin, a worker under the Baptist Board, organized a school for Mexicans at Brownsville, Texas, and two years later another school in Monterrey, Mexico. From that time on the educational work has grown steadily. The women's boards of missions have been particularly active in school work. The general home mission boards of the various denominations have also appropriated money for the educational work, and have organized numerous schools throughout the four border states. At present, missionary agencies are conducting approximately forty mission

schools in these states with a total enrolment of
nearly four thousand pupils and a teaching staff
of approximately two hundred. More than a million dollars is invested in school property and an
annual expenditure of about two hundred thousand dollars is involved in the upkeep of these institutions. The foregoing figures do not include
several hundred Mexican pupils who are enrolled
in English or other special educational classes in
connection with local churches, Y.W.C.A. and
Y.M.C.A. organizations, and similar agencies.

The mission schools fall into two general
groups—the day school and the boarding school.
The plaza day schools have attained their highest development in New Mexico, where for many
years (until 1891) no public school system existed.
Within a few decades a public school system has
been developed in New Mexico, however, and it
has been the general policy of mission boards at
work in New Mexico to discontinue the mission
day schools as rapidly as the public schools in the
various communities become able to care for the
educational needs of the boys and girls. Acting
on this policy, a number of schools have already
been discontinued, and others will ultimately be
closed. The closing of the plaza mission day
schools does not mean the discontinuance of missionary work in the communities involved, but
rather an increased emphasis upon the social and
distinctly religious activities of the mission. It is
a welcome relief when the mission boards are

freed from the responsibility of carrying on day school education, so that their attention may be turned to other matters. It must be recognized, however, that although the providing of day school education has been a genuine tax upon missionary funds, the schools themselves have furnished the very finest opportunity for inculcating Christian ideas and ideals in the hearts and lives of the boys and girls growing up in New Mexico. What better opportunity could any mission board desire than to have a group of from thirty to sixty pupils under the daily influence of a consecrated Christian teacher with high ideals? It should be remembered also that these teachers have, for the most part, remained in their respective communities throughout the entire year, and that they have carried on Sunday-school work and maintained religious services throughout the year. They have also given much time to visitation in the homes.

Not all of the day schools have, however, been limited to New Mexico. In some of the border towns large day schools have recently grown up. These are attended by Mexican boys and girls who live in Mexico but who come across the boundary each school day to attend a school conducted under missionary auspices. This type of day school, just as in the case of the plaza day schools in New Mexico, furnishes a unique opportunity for influencing in a very vital way the life of the Mexicans of the future.

The Presbyterian Church in the U. S. A., the Congregational Church, and the United Brethren have been most active in the conduct of the plaza day schools in New Mexico; while the Southern Baptist Convention, the Presbyterian Church in the U. S., and the Methodist Episcopal Church, South, have been chiefly responsible for the day schools conducted in border towns.

While the day schools have played an important part in the task and are continuing to do so at present, it is in the boarding schools that the churches are making perhaps the largest contribution to Mexican youth in the United States. In these schools, of which there are nearly twenty, thousands of Mexican young people are not only receiving regular educational training under missionary auspices, but they are continually under the direct influence of consecrated Christian workers, who by their lives and by their words are steadily interpreting Christianity to their pupils. From these schools have gone some of the finest Mexican leaders whom the church has yet produced. A bright and successful Spanish-speaking American, who is now an influential and very successful state attorney general, got his start as a poor country boy in one of these schools. He later attended a public high school, and in a great Christian university finished his course with honors and won a gold medal in forensic oratory. He then went on to the study of law at Harvard, and received his diploma, *cum laude*. After spending several years in Y.M.C.A. work in Mexico City, his health failed, and he was compelled to return to the United States. His wife is the daughter of an American pastor, and they maintain an ideal Christian home for their growing daughter. Illustrations might be multiplied of cultured pastors and other professional and pioneer men who have received their start in these mission schools, but this one is sufficient to answer the question, "Can it be done?" with the statement, "It has been done." There is no question but that the difference between such leaders and the multitudes of other Mexican and Spanish-American boys lies chiefly in the impressions which they receive at an early age in a Protestant mission school, the results of modern, thought-provoking education and the Christian character which is developed at the same time. This man sometimes says that the curse of his people is that so many of them are named "Moreno," so that everyone thinks one Moreno is just like another, and that there is no hope for any of them.

Sometimes a tragedy is enacted when vacation time comes, and the pupils from the boarding schools must return to their home influences or go out to work in the camps, where they must fight during the vacation season to maintain the ideals which have been implanted during the school year. Most of these pupils stand firm, morally, although they often return to the schools with cheeks thin

from improper diet or some other marks of the
vacation upon their habits of living. Usually they
are extremely eager to get back to the schools.

The worker among the Mexicans quickly recognizes the need for the training of these racial
leaders, if the work of Christianizing them is to
move forward. They must be helped to help themselves. They must be made conscious that they
are delivering their own people. It was Moses
who led the children of Israel out of bondage, and
it was Booker T. Washington who led the Negroes
out into a larger life. Possibly the forms of religious and community life worked out by racial
leaders are better adapted to their own races than
any which might be devised for them by an outsider. These trained racial leaders of indis-
courageable convictions must, for the most part,
be developed in special Christian schools and
colleges.

Often their awakening comes by simple and surprising means. One Mexican, now a preacher,
was converted by reading *Uncle Tom's Cabin.*
Pilgrim's Progress, translated into Spanish, is
also doing great things for the Kingdom among
Spanish-speaking folk. Good books are the "silent messengers" which mean even more to Latin
Americans than to us. An education is the key
that opens the door to such books.

We do not need to call the roll of all the schools
conducted by missionary agencies along the Border, but Christians of all denominations might

well take time to get acquainted with such outstanding institutions as the Lydia Patterson Institute, and the Effie Eddington School, both at El
Paso, Texas, the Methodist Mexican Institute at
San Antonio, Texas, and Holding Institute at
Laredo, Texas, conducted by the Methodist Epis-
copal Church, South; the Rio Grande Institute at
Albuquerque, New Mexico, conducted by the Congregational churches; the Allison-James School,
at Santa Fé, New Mexico, the Menaul School
at Albuquerque, New Mexico, and the Forsythe
School at Los Angeles, California, conducted
by the Presbyterian Church in the U. S. A.; the
Harwood Girls' School and the Harwood Boys'
School at Albuquerque, New Mexico, the Mary J.
Platt School at Tucson, Arizona, the Frances M.
De Pauw Industrial School, Los Angeles, California, and the Spanish American Institute, Gardena, California, conducted by the Methodist
Episcopal Church. The influence of these schools,
and others, can hardly be overestimated. They
are playing a most important part in the molding
of the Mexican life in the United States, and they
are worthy of most generous support. Not only
are the schools crowded, but each year they are
forced to turn away literally hundreds of boys
and girls who are seeking admission to them.
Some of these pupils come even from Mexico,
from homes of high government officials. A Cuban
millionaire wrote recently asking admission for
his son into one of these border mission schools.

SOME PRACTICAL ASPECTS OF MISSION SCHOOL WORK

The training at mission schools is not altogether confined to books.
Many a boy acquires, by the time of his graduation, sufficient skill
in some one trade to command a job and earn a livelihood.

LEADERS IN TRAINING

The future of the work among Mexicans in the United States depends upon the leaders whom we can train. The young men pictured above with their teachers are studying at San Antonio, Texas, for the Christian ministry.

Tuition is charged where parents are able to pay for the schooling of the children, but some of the schools are fairly generous in providing scholarships to pupils who are not able to pay their own way. Into these schools come boys and girls, who, because of age or lack of a knowledge of the English language, feel out of place in the public school and, in fact, cannot make a place for themselves there. These same young people after some years of training in the mission schools go out into the business and social life of their respective communities, not only with high ideals of personal conduct, but with a training which makes them valuable helpers in the local churches which are ministering to their people. These schools are proving to the satisfaction of the most slow of heart that something worth while can be done with Mexican youth.

Up to the present time few of these boarding schools have been co-educational in character. Holding Institute situated at Laredo, Texas, and the Rio Grande Institute at Albuquerque, New Mexico, are notable exceptions. Fortunately, however, some of the schools for boys alone and the schools exclusively for girls are located so close to each other that social relationships can be established, and some of the definitely religious activities are carried on together. This is as it should be in that it provides a very greatly needed opportunity for the making of wholesome acquaintanceships.

A number of the schools maintain industrial departments so that printers and skilled workers in other crafts, including dressmaking, millinery, stenography, and the like, are produced. In these institutions Mexican young people learn to organize themselves for Christian service, and the Christian Endeavor societies and Epworth League groups existing in the schools play an important part in the life and training of these Mexican youths. A Christian Endeavor member at a young people's convention said: "The Young People's Society is a great college. It awakens talents and develops them; creates a taste for books, good associations, wholesome habits of mind, and unselfish service to the world." Through these schools Mexican youths are brought from almost abject illiteracy and from ideas of the world which are cramped and untrue out into the brighter and truer world of the normal American youth. Then, too, they acquire facility in the use of two languages at least, and the schools are looked upon as sources of supply for bilingual teachers, clerks, attorneys, and Christian workers. The supply is never equal to the demand.

However, the chief characteristics of graduates of these schools, which make them indispensable in public life and business, are their American ideals, their wholesome enthusiasm, and a pleasant spirit of service which they have developed during their course. These students are being taught that they belong to God, and that their strength and ability belongs to Him and should be used in service for the world. Stewardship and life service follow normally in the lives of many of these ambitious Latin American youth, and they are receiving a training which many other American youths might desire and profitably be afforded.

In all these schools there is definite, daily education in religion. The pupils learn for the first time the meaning of the Protestant Reformation, and they receive courses in the history, content, and teachings of the Bible. They are also trained to develop religious themes, and they learn many things about the lives of church and missionary heroes. Instruction in the matter of the Christian life, of prayer, of God's goodness, and the meaning of salvation is given.

The eagerness of these young people for new ideas which come to them is sometimes pathetic. When they come to the schools they hardly know the meaning of prayer, but it is not long before they have learned not only to pray but even to lead their own religious meetings. They memorize masterpieces of speech by American heroes, —Lincoln being the favorite,—poems, hymns, and the great passages of Christian literature (in both languages), the Lord's Prayer, the Creed, the Ten Commandments, and choice portions of Scripture. It is wonderful to hear the prompt and glad response with verses from the Bible when opportunity is given in chapel.

Rev. Jay S. Stowell, who visited all these institutions, was delighted with the work that is being done, but suggests more careful selection of potential candidates for Christian leadership, a still more carefully worked out religious training curriculum to carry all boarding pupils to the twelfth grade and to give more definite and extensive training in racial leadership, such as, teaching in Sunday schools and organizing classes, schools, and missions; some knowledge of child psychology and practise in story-telling, speaking, and actual community work, making the locality of the school an observation ground if not a laboratory. He also suggests the need of coordinating all mission school work into a unified system.

The principal of Lasell Seminary, a great school in the East, was approached for funds to build a dormitory for a Spanish American mission school. Before the committee had said ten sentences he exclaimed: "Do not go any further. I can see that thing. I will give you $1,000." He gave more! When asked to state his reasons as an educator for so prompt a response, he wrote:

WHY I SUBSCRIBED

I believe in training youth. We are what we are by training. In youth one accepts training easily. So I liked the idea of a school.

Boys and girls like to see things grow. They enjoy doing

things with their own hands. They do best what they enjoy. So I liked the idea of an Industrial School.

Why should I send more money to the non-Christians abroad than to the non-Christians who are my neighbors?

Why may I not have the privilege of helping the faithful men and women who are helping to build up my own country?

Cut out the Mexicans and you cut out a large factor in our industries. Educate them and you add a sound and useful aid to our country's development, especially here in the Southwest.

Money in schools goes further than money in prisons for the idle and vicious—usually vicious because idle, and idle because untrained.

So I was glad to have a chance to help build the Spanish American Institute where it was most needed. Besides, we want trained boys for our trained girls.

C. C. BRAGDON, D.D.

Normal and Advanced Training

The importance of normal training in connection with these schools for Spanish-speaking youth, particularly in the girls' boarding schools, is not likely to be overestimated. Some progress has already been made in this field and a limited provision for using graduates from the schools as teachers of Mexican children in the lower grades has been made, but there is still need for the extension of normal training and the opportunity for practise teaching. A thoroughgoing normal course in a Christian boarding school makes it possible for the school automatically to extend its influence very widely. The teachers thus trained go out as genuine missionaries without tax upon missionary funds. The need for such teachers in New Mexico and in the other border states where large numbers of Mexican children are found in the public schools is greater than the supply. The meeting of this need is a real opportunity for the missionary boarding school.

None of the boarding schools for Mexican youth in the United States offer college training. The culmination of the training for native leaders comes when these young men and women come out from the boarding schools to enter the regular colleges and theological seminaries in departments and courses adapted to their previous training and life requirements. These Latin American departments in colleges are at present in a hopeful pioneer stage. We may expect important results from them. Mexican youths are particularly eager to acquire an education which will give them familiarity with correct usage of both the English and the Spanish languages. The importance of thorough training in the Spanish language and literature is clear; only through it can the pupils command the respect and the position of leadership which should be theirs among their own people.

The need for trained leadership among the Mexicans, especially for trained gospel workers, is felt by all denominations now at work. Various attempts have been and are being made to meet this need, and to train pastors and preachers. The Northern Baptists have a seminary of good grade at Los Angeles, with eighteen Mexican young men preparing themselves for the Christian ministry. The Methodist Episcopal Plaza Center Christian Training School in Los Angeles has twelve student pastors enrolled. There are also as many in the Wesleyan Institute of the Methodist Episcopal Church, South, at San Antonio. Some of them have already proved the effectiveness of the training received by giving splendid proofs of the increased efficiency in the conduct of all church work. Other denominations are attempting to meet a similar need.

The School and the Community

The relation of the mission school to the community in which it is located is of importance both to the pupils themselves and to the community. The best results are secured when this relationship is a vital and mutually helpful one. The community itself plays an important part in introducing the students to some of the finer things in our life. The churches in these school communities have unusual opportunity to make a large contribution to the life of these young people. Unfortunately, not all such churches have recognized either their opportunity or their obligation in this particular. In other cases, however, the relationship has been a most delightful and helpful one. The communities furnish an opportunity for many of the students to earn money to pay their way through school, and where there are Mexican colonies, either in the community or close at hand, a most important field of training in missionary service is provided.

A number of the boarding schools have organized "gospel teams" with great effectiveness. The members of these teams go out to Mexican colonies, hold religious services, and in the spirit of Jesus Christ interpret his way of life to their own people. Fortunately, most communities in which Mexican mission schools are located soon become ardent enthusiasts for the school and active cooperators in its work. The attractive students and their amazing progress draws out unbounded praise, and volunteer workers are often enlisted to aid in the recreational and religious programs for the students. A community pride in the school enterprise is thus developed. Where schools are located in the vicinity of colleges or universities, still further opportunities are offered. An address by an eloquent, trained Christian Mexican may be a revolutionary event in the life of a growing youth. When the schools are located in educational centers, such opportunities are therefore greatly multiplied.

Adult Education

For the education of adult Mexicans in the United States no adequate and well-organized program of training corresponding to the "Moonlight Schools" in the southern mountains has, as yet, been worked out. However, through the local churches and Christian associations a large number of classes for Mexican men and women have been organized. Some of these classes are conducted for the purpose of teaching the English language, citizenship, and similar subjects. Mothers are trained in the care of children and in various branches of home-making. Thousands of Mexicans are being reached by this informal educational work through churches and community agencies.

Despite all this, there is still too much indifference on the part of American communities toward the need for education among these adult Mexicans. In some cases it is to be feared that there is a genuine prejudice against such education, the feeling being that these Mexican immigrants will be more useful as laborers when left in contented ignorance. Such an attitude is to be deprecated by all benevolently-minded Christians.

Roman Catholic Schools

Although the Roman Catholic Church was very slow to recognize the importance of education for Mexicans, yet much good work is now being done by devoted teachers in Roman Catholic schools. The sisters in these schools are often greatly beloved. It is, however, much to be regretted that bigotry and lax moral and educational standards have tended to mar what otherwise might have been a very great force in the improvement of the conditions of Mexicans in the United States. When the mother of a Catholic family dies, the father naturally turns to the church schools to care for his half-orphans, but many Mexicans who have placed their children in these Catholic schools are very emphatic in saying that they do not like them. "They just learn *'misas y un catecismo'* (masses and catechism). We want them to learn *'cosas practicas y un oficio'* (practical things and a trade)."

An Opportunity and a Responsibility

Just as millions of acres of the great American desert have been transformed into a paradise by water, cultivation, and patience, so can these potentially brilliant, passionate Mexican young people be transformed into the flower of human culture. Thus he who says, "It cannot be done," is already being interrupted by people saying, "It is being done." Some day it will be said of the products of our mission schools for Mexicans, "Ye are God's tilled land." Sympathetic trained American teachers in these schools are leaving the impress of their lives upon their plastic students by giving practical training amid surroundings where all possible racial and hereditary handicaps have been removed.

A Mexican pastor pleading for his people and picturing their needs for education, tells this story: "A king became desperate over the misery, crime, and wars of his people. His wise men were unable to advise him. At length he heard of a strange, practical sage and called him to the royal court. In reply to the king's request for advice, the sage replied, 'Grant me, O king, one year to make answer.'

"At the end of the year the king called a great gathering of his people to witness the wise man's reply. A dog and a rabbit were brought out. The rabbit was released first and he ran swiftly away. The dog was then set loose and soon overtook and killed the rabbit. Another rabbit and dog were brought in. When they were set free, they fondled each other and began playing together. The first pair was wild, but the second pair had been educated."

Don Antonio eloquently concludes his story by saying, "*Amigos* (friends), ignorance is the fountain of all the ills of our Mexican people."

This man himself is an illustration of what education can accomplish. He was once an actor. Ten years ago he and his family were destitute and suffering. They chose the path of God and of education, and they are now cultured and happy. Two of the children are among the brightest students and the best athletes in the high schools and universities of California. The father and son have just taken out naturalization papers, and the father is freely giving his life in service to the people of his own race above the Border.

When Benjamin Franklin wished to sell his newly-discovered commercial fertilizer, he sprinkled the barren hillsides in such a way that when the crop came up the incredulous farmers could read in gigantic verdant letters these words: THIS HAS BEEN PLASTERED. Most of the best racial leaders among Mexicans in the United States have been "plastered" by the influence of Christian training. One can always recognize former students from any one of these Christian schools. Their children, their homes, their meals, and their personality all show the result of this Christian culture.

The Interchurch Survey declared that the weakest spot in Protestantism in America is the fact that two thirds of our children and youth never attend a religious school or receive religious training. These millions unreached by the church include an overwhelming proportion of our Mexican and Spanish-speaking American young people. In the World War no group appeared more pitiful than these thousands of young people. Many of these native sons were pathetically eager students of English, their very lives even depending upon their ability to understand orders. They thronged the Y.M.C.A. huts and meetings, and listened to the gospel songs on the phonograph— fertile soil for culture that has long remained fallow ground.

From ignorance and narrowness flow race hatred. Christian education can drive out prejudice and lead our Mexican youth into a finer, richer life. It has been said that fifty thousand teachers would be fifty thousand times better than fifty thousand American soldiers in Mexico, and what is true of the Mexican below the international line is equally true of the Mexican above the Border. In our work in Christian education we are putting into operation forces whose influence cannot be calculated.

One of our students, Ambrosio C. Gonzales, expected to become a bartender, but in a mission school he was converted and went out to become a Christian minister. He has recently laid down his life, but during his years of service he led hundreds of Mexicans into the Christian way of life and was the means of enlisting approximately fifty young people in definite Christian service. One of these is a young man who was formerly an officer under the bandit, Villa. Mrs. Gonzales is also a graduate of a mission school; she is a direct descendant of De la Vaca, one of the early explorers in New Mexico. She has reached thousands of her people through the power of her addresses and through poems which she has written. Who can calculate the influence of such people as these and the hundreds of others who have gone out to lives of service from the mission schools?

President Francisco Madero was one of the

thousands of Mexicans educated above the Border. He was a cultured Christian idealist. We may yet train other presidents and leaders in every walk of life for our sister republic, and we may do this within our own United States. Surely the racial leaders for the many Mexicans now within our borders must be educated here, and ours is the responsibility for providing the opportunity for their training.

Browning expresses what is happening above the Border through the magic of Christian education when he says in "Pippa Passes":

> Day: faster and more fast.
> O'er night's brim, day boils at last;
> Boils, pure gold, o'er the cloud cup's brim
> Where spurting and suppressed it lay,
> For not a froth-flake touched the rim
> Of yonder gap in the solid gray
> Of the eastern cloud, an hour away;
> But forth one wavelet, then another, curled,
> Till, the whole sunrise, not to be suppressed,
> Rose, reddened, and its seething breast
> Flickered in bounds, grew gold, then overflowed the world.
>
> *Pippa's song from the silk mills.*

V

WHAT MEXICANS BELIEVE

The most potent habit in life is the every-day
treatment of Jesus Christ.

JAMES A. FRANCIS

"PANCHO" Villa while at his Canutillo Ranch once met a clean, winsome Protestant Mexican who caught the bandit chieftain's fancy. One day he said, "What is your religion, *amigo?*"

"*Evangélico,* General Villa," was the reply.

"How many of you *evangélicos* are there in Mexico?"

"About thirty thousand, señor."

"Thirty thousand of you! Why don't you do something?" The great chieftain had begun to believe.

"The Mexicans are a Roman Catholic people without a religion," said a Catholic priest who had just come from Mexico.

What lies back of such statements? And what is to be our religious contact with these Latin Americans with whom we must prepare to live on spiritual, social, and commercial planes of increasing intimacy? To sympathize with them and to help them effectively, we must know what our long misunderstood and neglected neighbors really do believe.

Religious Classes

There are five classes, religiously speaking, among the Mexicans: the Roman Catholics, the positivists or freethinkers, the evangelicals or Protestants, the modern fanatics, and the atheistic *socialistas*. There are many persons of clean, sincere, and earnest lives in all five. Each class with its beliefs, tinctures all the rest, one shading into the other. Experience would lead us to apportion the Latin Americans above the Border among these five religious classes approximately as follows, allowing for variations due to their locality, length of residence, and privileges in this country.

(1) Roman Catholics claim about sixty per cent, made up for the most part of the women, the aged, the ignorant peons, and the old patrician families who have thought they had much to gain in business and in social standing by at least nominal adherence to the old established church. The adherence is largely nominal, and the church attendance occasional. A very prominent Mexican official of thoughtful integrity said, "Those who are ignorant are superstitious and attend the Catholic Church. In the mountains where there are few or no schools perhaps most of the women and half the men at some time attend mass. But in the towns where there is education, half of the women and almost no men attend the Catholic Church."

(2) The positivists, or freethinkers, number about ten per cent, made up of the men who have read or listened to the ubiquitous French philosophy. Many of these have come to America with a shrug of the shoulders as their reaction to the appeal of this country of myriad faiths and sects. There are many thoughtful younger women who have studied in the schools who are practically positivists or agnostics. But women soon suffer too much and bear too great a load of moral responsibility for their families for them to accept generally and finally this cold, inert attitude of the soul toward life.

(3) The *Evangélicos,* or Protestants, make up some ten per cent. They are hand-picked, awakened people, most of them from the middle class and many of them young people. They form a gallant array of leaders who are products of missions and mission schools. Many of these have received the gospel in Mexico.

(4) Various fanatical, divisive sects number about ten per cent. These reflect the social bigotry of their Roman Catholic traditions and the various superficial religious philosophies of the day. They usually exceed the bounds of their respective sects in extravagances and bigotry. They include Pentecostal groups, New Thought followers, Mormons, Spiritualists, Russellites, Christian Scientists, Holy Rollers, some "Faith Missions" members, *Independientes,* and some extreme Protestant groups as difficult to

combat as to classify. They often unscrupu-
lously honeycomb and disintegrate the evangelical groups temporarily. At times the Seventh
Day Adventists and even some of the other evangelical groups yield to the temptation to assume
this divisive, proselyting rôle. Whoever does so
perpetrates a crime which results in the creation
of the embittered, unfraternal adherents found
everywhere above the Border.

(5) The socialists, atheists, and anarchists
number about ten per cent. They are also hand-
picked and leavened people who have no easier
lot than the Protestants. They are almost exclusively adult men of the middle and lower class.
This group has grown up as a logical result of
the abuses of a state church, the neglect of evangelical Christian missions, the sufferings caused
by the present industrial system, and the interpretation of these ills by active, enthusiastic agents
of the doctrine of a Republic of the World.

Religious Life in the Home

It is quite impossible to picture fairly the religious aspects of a Mexican Catholic home without giving the wrong features of the picture. It
is not so much the materials as materialism that
stultifies souls. Saddest of all is the fact that
when the material image disappears, the supposed
reality goes with it. This is too often the concomitant of migration to our country. But in

some cases Rachel's images are brought with
their baggage.

Let us visit one little house where these so-
called "aids to devotion" form part of the fur-
nishing of this refuge in a strange land. The
walls have pictures of the newly-weds, the national heroes, and several original drawings by
Manuel, the artist of the family. Here in the corner opposite the door into the "visitors' room" is
a crucifix, supposedly of silver. It represents the
Lord in agony upon the cross. Before it are two
candles which are lighted on certain occasions.
Back of the crucifix is a felt cloth upon which are
some medals and ribbons, reminders of special
feast days and dispensations. About the room
hang framed chromos of Maria of the Sacred
Heart, picturing the sweet-faced "Queen of
Heaven," wearing on her bosom a red heart upon
which is a flame of fire. It is to be noted that
there is a great disparity between the repellent
features of the agonized Savior and the attractive
woman-deity, Mary, as objects of adoration and
helps to God. About the room are images of
favorite saints, selected by the experiences and
occupations of the family.

The guardian angel of all these objects of worship is the dear old grandmother who never wears
a hat anywhere but always dons her black *reboso*
since it is not proper to wear a hat in church.
One associates this dear little shawl-clad, thin-
faced Mexican devotee with all the images and

shrines and, also, with the religious activities of
the whole family. She is its spiritual monitor.
Not one of the family would remove a single object of her veneration because they all love her
too much to cause her pain. And nothing could
cause her more pain than some neglect or indig-
nity shown these treasures of her heart.

One interesting class of these material objects
of worship is not apparent to the casual visitor:
the *medallos* worn under the clothing on the
breasts of the faithful and the superstitious.
These little metal or felt tokens are supposed to
protect the wearer. Since they cause no incon-
venience from persecution by heretics and unbelievers, and since they cost little, and since there
are many perils to Mexicans due to their occupations, it is easy to understand why the Catholic
bookstores sell thousands of these "Christian
charms." One young Mexican, so drunk that he
could not get on a trolley car without help, said
as he was being helped aboard, "You do not believe I should drink whiskey! Maria will keep me
from *desgracia* (accident). See, here I wear under my shirt this 'Maria' and she will keep me
safe. I think, Señor, that you do not believe in
Maria?" He was an illiterate young track-man
who confessed that he had drunk ten whiskeys
since he left work that evening. It would require
a good many "queens of heaven" to protect a
wilful sinner like that in the traffic and tempta-
tions of a great city.

This sketch is a typical picture of what one finds in many Mexican homes. Bare, rude shacks are often the homes which have the largest number of these images. It is in such places that the greatest ignorance and superstition exists. The images of our Lord are usually, to us, of a very horrible sort—red paint on his wounds, pallor and terrible distress marking his features—all so unreal and harrowing. There are horrible, life-size images of Christ represented with the forehead slit and a thorn thrust thus under the flesh. Of course there is a locked collection box in front of such images, as is true of practically all these gruesome *Cristos*. This does not blend with the spirit of free, glad America. Here people cannot be frightened into duty and sacrifice—at least, not for long. The crass and spectacular do not form a wholesome basis for permanent devotion, or for real spiritual worship. The Latin Americans desire increasingly these blessings, as well as an escape from the morbid, costly, and burdensome worship of their past.

The Modern Inquisition

We soon see that the atmosphere of a Mexican colony is far different from that of even an average English-speaking Catholic community in America. Years of diligently-inculcated prejudice among them have done their work well. They have awakened a general fear and hatred of all non-Catho-

lics. · They have produced a fanaticism which has
very often proved fatal to the objects of Catholic
prejudice. This persecution takes the form more
commonly now of social persecution, with occasional acts of violence against preachers who are
too frank and propagators of unwelcome revela-
tions of the abuses of the church.

All of this tends, especially among the men and
the student class, either towards open ridicule
against all religion, or a truly typical Latin
American indifference to the scandal and bother,
expressed with a shrug of the shoulders. They
have come almost *en masse* to regard religion as a
foe to liberty and progress. This is illustrated by
the waves of successful striving to secure religious liberty in all Latin American countries. Old
Spain is practically the only bigoted, enslaved
Roman Catholic country in the world today. A
short time ago a Spanish American, a former officer in the American army in France, volunteered
the following: "The trouble with Spain is too
much religion. The priests are the most powerful persons in the country. They tell the king
what to do and he does not dare do anything
else. They even elect the government officers and
the members of the *cortes*. When France drove
out the Catholic Church, then the priests all went
to Spain, the United States, and Latin America.
Since then France, like Italy, has progressed, but
Spain has been left behind."

Prejudice

"Esos Protestantes!" (Ah, those Protestants!)
is the up-to-date form of the rack and screw.
The Protestant mission halls are said to "smell
of brimstone." In Mexico the people are taught
to prefer a saloon to a gospel hall. Two Mexicans
have frankly stated that their priests have told
them to rent or sell their property for a saloon
rather than for a Protestant mission. Of course,
with education and wholesome contact with Protestant Americans these prejudices disappear.

The priests are commonly reported to be, with
few exceptions, cold, grasping, exigent, and unreasonable, and often immoral. Any convert who
has lived long amid the conditions of his *patria*
will tell startling facts as to these and other
points in comparison with which this chapter is
mild indeed. We have seen the peons above the
Border kneel before the priests and kiss their
hands. And we note that the Latin American
children either giggle at or stand in terror of the
church and priests. One girl of good family
seemed in great mental distress one Sunday. At
length she was persuaded to tell what troubled
her. A priest in town had declared a "mass for
the dead" for all who attended the Protestant
baptism of the children of a prominent family in
the town. The same priest pronounced anathe-
mas against the Bible, but this brought results
contrary to his expectation. The young men or-

ganized a Bible club and the priest, a former
schoolmate of some of them, to their infinite delight, had to change his tactics. He was soon competing with the leader of the Bible club in teaching from the formerly despised Book.

Thus, it is not surprising that there are frequent exhibitions of a disintegration in the faith
which Latin Americans have for centuries subscribed to and subsidized, though with lessening
loyalty. They mark with impatience the frequent
efforts made to checkmate a new Protestant mission by building close to it a Catholic church in
a community that has been neglected for half a
century. These abortive competing missions usually do not last long. Their "Sunday schools"
do not continue, and neither do their clubs. We
welcome every effort on the part of the Roman
Catholic Church which is for the good of the
people, but, with the people, we wonder why they
do not rather go to unoccupied points. Nothing
could be a greater crown to our gospel efforts
than to have our efforts work like a leaven toward
the reformation of the abuses of the Roman Catholic Church itself. In the fine volume, *The Work
of the Roman Catholic Church in the World,* published by the Roman Catholics, frequent references are made to the winning methods of Protestant denominations, commending such methods as
the Laymen's Missionary Movement, the "every
member canvass," etc. In the same volume we
mark with pleasure the fact that neither is there

a spirit of bitterness nor are there acrimonious references to Protestant work.

What the Latin Americans Do not Believe

Fully seventy-five per cent of the Mexican men do not believe in anything. We recall that "in a Y.M.C.A. canvass in Buenos Aires only four out of five thousand students expressed any faith or belief in God whatsoever." That was in the most enlightened city in all Latin America, and among a class which is usually the most Christian—the student class. Latin Americans are beginning to consult their growing doubts and prejudices on religious subjects. These intellectual and spiritual warps are increasing with education and unfettered experience. There has grown up among the Mexicans a monotheistic faith called the Masonic Scottish Rite which permits naturalism and even pantheism but prohibits the confessional. It is a grave matter that these evolutions and these prejudices are developing, for the most part, outside and apart from direct Bible influence, save for those limited portions made available in the splendid Masonic ritual, and the limited operations of Protestant missions.

At the Panama Congress on Protestant missions in 1916, Honorable Sr. del Toro, a Catholic, said that his countrymen in Porto Rico were in consternation when the Americans came, lest their missions would destroy the Roman Catholic faith. But, on the contrary, it is notable that the effect of the coming of the Presbyterians, Methodists, Baptists, and others has caused a resurrection of Romanism and brought new life, morality, and efficiency to all the religious life.

(1) The fact of the matter is that the Latin Americans do not want any more religion which enslaves the mind and wrecks the social order. They believe in a religion which serves and helps them win in their personal and national struggles. They regard the old religion of their forefathers as an unnecessary and arbitrary burden. They are impatient with its round of fees, *fiestas,* and state taxation to support that which hinders their progress as a people and which serves to prolong the days of their ignorance and the consequent power of their social and political overlords. They rebel at the arrogance of the priests in their un-American methods of church administration.

(2) The Mexicans very decidedly do not believe in the celibacy of the priests. Moral conditions with them demand spiritual leaders who may be examples and sincere teachers of normal home life. Scandals, fancied and all too often real, destroy domestic felicity and confidence. This, with the confessional, has raised a hue and cry that will in the end bring about a reform in the Catholic Church.

(3) They do not believe in the protection of the priests and the glossing over of their immorality.

A tremendous battle has been waged over all Latin America against special exemptions and trials by ecclesiastical courts of sinning priests.

(4) They do not believe in a religion based on fear. They have had "wolf" cried to them so often in the threat of purgatory and excommunication that it has ceased to have much terror for them, but it is still a positive annoyance.

(5) They do not believe in a priestly interference in domestic and political matters which destroys fraternity and confidence in social relationships. They have never been trained in establishing relations of mutual trust in home, in business, and in matters of state. They fear to be frank even with best friends lest some secret proceeding be breathed out into the priest's ear to the too-confiding person's sorrow. This distrust honeycombs every relationship in the life of the Latin Americans.

(6) They do not believe in having even their religious life dominated by a foreign potentate in Rome. The present swing to nationalism increases this growing repugnance against a religion dominated by foreigners.

What we note in the foregoing should suggest that even to the Roman Catholic of Anglo-Saxon origin the religious attitudes of Latin America are startling; still more is it amazing to the average American Protestant. There is so little left of any sort of positive faith or religion. What is left is very meager and cold and unsatisfying.

Many a Mexican's negative creed would read very nearly as follows:

"I do not believe in the traditional God who is distant, partial, and cruel.

"I do not believe in the traditional Christ. If Jesus of Nazareth ever existed, He was too weak to command my worship, and too impractical to merit my respect.

"I do not know whether there is a Holy Spirit.

"I do not know whether the world came into existence by evolution or by chance.

"I do not know whether there is a future existence.

"I do not believe in eternal punishment."

One Mexican's Testimony

"Well, what you are saying is good. It is all true. But when you write about our people, do not say much about religion. We do not like to think about that subject." This was the comment of a cultured Mexican fellow traveler after reading several pages of this chapter, and then he offered to interview several Mexicans with whom we were traveling on the matter of religion. He returned, verifying the facts we have already stated. One illiterate Mexican said to him, "I used to go to church and also to believe in God because my father told me to. I rarely go to church now." It pretty well sums up "the law and the prophets" of Latin Americans to say that they believe in service, with emphasis upon courtesy; in such truth as may be demonstrated by science or logic; and in brotherhood developed from the ideals of generosity and concord in family and community.

Words Lose Their Meaning

One real difficulty in dealing with the matter of religion with Mexicans is that the familiar words and phrases which are vehicles of thought for the most sacred and vital of subjects have been prostituted by the established church to cheap and misleading uses, until they have lost their thought-bearing value. "Spiritual" does not mean the mystic energy of the eternal world, but it means the *power of the Pope* and of the Roman Catholic Church. The term that most nearly expresses in Spanish our idea of spiritual is "moral." The parents of the children in our mission schools, noting with satisfaction the improvement in their conduct, came to us urging us to teach their children *mas moralidad* (more spirituality). The last adult we baptized was *Jesus Maria* Ochoa. There is a saint for each day in the year and a large number over.

Profanity is practised in a unique way among Mexicans. The women do most of the swearing in Spanish, the men, apparently avoiding even this appearance of being religious, exclaim only "Carramba!" which merely means "Pshaw!" The

men, however, all too commonly make up with
English oaths used in Spanish conversation what
they may lack in Spanish expletives. It seems
that they remember these oaths better than anything else, due probably to the emphasis employed
in their expression. The use of "Aye Dios!" and
"Oh, Jesus!" especially by the women, does not
really correspond to our idea of profanity. They
are more or less innocent expressions of surprise,
anxiety, or grief. They really savor of prayer,
and yet are mere form rather than petition.

Participation in religious services in Mexico
has consisted largely of soul agony and some
form of works. Our vital experience of invisible,
glad realities, looking toward victory rather than
the anticipation of moral failure to be atoned for
by penance at the next mass, is so utterly new
and intangible and withal so joyful that it seems
too good to be true! There is a helplessness of
soul in the first steps into this new life for Latin
Americans that is very pathetic.

In Mexico Christianity became a "paganized
Romanism." Latin American Catholics may
have almost any sort of heyday they wish, even
on Sunday, if only they attend mass in the morning. Bandits and plotting murderers often attend mass before their nefarious deeds. Stating
in a simple way a monstrous fact, we have indis-
putable evidence that the code of morals employed
by father confessors permits stealing, gambling,
lying, and even the blackest crimes under certain

conditions. The conditions permitting stealing, for example, are that it must be from one who has more treasure than the robber and the amount that may be stolen is determined by the amount possessed by the party robbed. It is thus seen that there may be, and in Latin American life practically is, a divorce between religion and morality.

One of our young Mexicans wrote a fellow toiler, urging him to read the Great Book. He replied as follows:

"I refer to your good letter dated the 9th of last month. The Bible is not a Holy Book. The Bible is not a book written by men inspired.

"The Old Testament is a book written by savages in a complete state of barbarism. The New Testament, even when it possesses something of good, demonstrates in each page intolerance, credulity, and ignorance. There are passages in the Old Testament worthy of an Apache or harlot half civilized. There are passages in the New Testament worthy of an inquisitor or a benighted Mexican savage (*desilustre chichimeca*).

"This book offends science and outrages reason. This book has caused misery, slavery, war, ignorance, torment, famines, and tears. This book is one of the greatest calamities that weigh upon the unredeemed pilgrims (*irredento*) of earth.

"Christ (?)—I want justice before all else in

this world! Christ (?)—I want knowledge and tolerance! Christ (?)—I want civilization!''

Since this letter was written, however, the young man has taken a stand for Christ. Now the Bible is to him *an inspired Book.*

Religious Substitutes Prevalent

We turn now to the straws and broken *chatties* [1] which millions of Latin Americans clasp and grasp in their moral and spiritual struggles.

1. *Fatalism.* The annual *Almanaque* of a leading Mexican daily paper is full of horoscopes of days of the month, influence of names on character, the key to dreams, and popular superstitions. Gambling and the lottery flourish upon the main trunk-line of popular fatalism. This is more than determinism. Fatalism holds the belief that the issue of all events is so fixed by fate or divine decree that man is powerless to change it. Practically this means that all that happens had to happen, and that *nothing will happen except what has to happen!* This is what undermines moral character and destroys morals.

On the trunk-line of fatalism, along with gambling and superstition, will also be found flourishing neglect of health, moral license, procrastination, dishonesty, and the degeneration of the will and judgment. Light of mind and soul alone

---

[1] A clay globe used to float swimmers in the Orient. When it breaks, the hapless one drowns.

A MOTHERS' CLASS IN ENGLISH

It is often the Mexican mother who has least opportunity to learn the English language. The churches along the Border are trying to make up for this lack by providing special classes for mothers.

IN RURAL NEW MEXICO

The two buildings shown above stand for ideals that are quite different. One is a Protestant mission school hidden away in the mountains many miles from the railroad; the other is a Penitente house or *morada*, representing the survival of some of the most unenlightened ideas and crudest superstitions of the Middle Ages. The Penitente organization thrives only in northeastern New Mexico.

will restore faith in God and self and in the laws of nature.

Santiago, a slim, pale youth, a new member of our mission, came to the *Liga Epworth* smoking a cigarette. Carlos challenged him with, "Dost thou not know that thou art digging thy grave by smoking? Thy brothers have died, and why dost thou use those things which the Yankees call coffin-nails?" Santiago languidly replied, "Ah, *amigo* (friend), have no care; twelve of my brothers and sisters have died. I will not die unless it is my fate." So reason myriads of Latin Americans, especially in the hour of temptation to indulge some forbidden appetite or lust.

Latin American reformers often refer to the lax family discipline of their people. Fathers and mothers spoil their children and indulge them with improper foods, especially when they display a caprice or a tantrum. They do not duly weigh the certain sad results since fatalism again whispers, "It will not result badly unless it had to be." Later they say, "It was the will of God."

Where did the famous (or infamous) *"mañana"* habit come from, if not from the subtle and seductive philosophy of fatalism? Nothing bad will result—unless it had to—from tardiness, procrastination, and improvidence.

2. *The Independientes.* All Christian work among Mexicans is embarrassed and imperiled by the sect of *Independientes* (Independent Mexican Church) founded by a fanatic. Even the founder

himself has repented the step now as he sees the
mischief his movement is doing. It decries salaried pastors, theology, sects, and any dependence
upon American or other "foreign" aid or direction. This propaganda is infecting many a formerly prosperous mission above the Border. The
idea works better here than in Mexico itself because the back-sliders who, for the most part,
head these movements get daily wages to support them and glory in it, and they can carpet-bag
their way into almost any mission by anti-American sentiment growing out of the "Border question." This movement is chiefly confined to the
laboring class.

3. *The Intellectuals.* There are hundreds of
thousands of intellectually awakened Latin
Americans in our country. They do not form *In-
dependiente* missions. Instead they form liberal
clubs, free thought circles, new thought societies,
and the like. Of course these various wings of
the intellectual and religious campaign of liberation are not labeled as above. They are ofttimes
known as *"Tertulias,"* "Social Clubs," "Pan-
American Societies," "Pro-patria Clubs." They
are the legitimate harvest of the intellectual and
religious past of these people gone to seed.

4. *Socialism.* The word "socialism" has become synonymous among Latin Americans with
atheism. Its protest is against the traditional
church. Its chief tenet, supposedly, among the
average Mexican group of any class, is the doing

away with all religion as the "chief cause of misery in human society." This social bigotry becomes a substitute for religion. This extreme and unchristian form of socialism often walks arm in arm through the Latin American colonies with an extreme and violent form of I.W.W. and sovietism, both being practically vicious substitutes for all organized religion. The leaders of both of these movements harangue the plaza mobs of a Sunday afternoon with the propaganda that established religion of all kinds sides with wealth against labor and the masses. It is startling to know that just as Leon Trotsky obtained his Bolshevik infection in the Russian quarters of New York, so are many Mexican "Trotskys" developing similar social virus in colonies above the Border and then moving southward to inoculate their countrymen.

5. *Freemasonry.* The Masonic Order has figured largely in Latin American life, especially among the free and independent, educated, or politically powerful classes. An astonishing majority of the deliverers of Mexico and South America have been high-degree Masons. In many parts the most common synonym for *Protestantes* is "Masons." Juarez, Porfirio Diaz, and Madero are among the large number of statesmen who were Masons. This, combined with the profoundly scriptural, fraternal, and noble ritual of Masonry, has produced a Masonic fraternity throughout all Pan-America which has become a

substitute for Romanism. Masonry is growing very rapidly among the Mexicans above the Border. Many a strained interracial situation has been bridged by the introductory remark of the peace-maker, *"Somos tres Masones. Ahora, primero oremos!"* (We are three Masons. First let us pray.) It is a well-recognized fact that in the halls of the Masons more than in any other place in all the Latin world the spark of liberty was kept aglow when there was nowhere else in which leading spirits could trust each other.

6. *Mormonism.* Mormonism seems strangely attractive to the Mexicans. One preacher and several members in one mission have been baptized as Mormons. This sect is strongly entrenched among the Mexicans in Arizona, California, and in Mexico itself. In view of the loose marital relations resulting from the attitude toward matrimony held by many nominal Roman Catholics in the Southwest, the menace of Mormonism casts a dark shadow along the Rio Grande.

7. *Spiritualism.* Spiritualism is getting quite a foothold with the better-class Latin Americans. In talking with a prominent Spanish lawyer the question of religion was brought up. The lawyer quickly sought my opinion of "spiritism, occult science, mental transfer, mesmerism, and suggestion." It was painful to recognize that he considered these things religion. A brilliant teacher recently arrived from Mexico, when asked to give a testimonial in the Mexican church, scandalized

the pastor by her evident saturation with spiritualism. Latin personality lends ready ear and credence to "teachers of the occult." Every Gypsy fortune-teller seems to speak Spanish.

8. *Other Groups.* Russellism, Christian Science, and "divine healers" in their crass and exploiting forms, prey upon the faith and the flat purses of our friends from over the Border. These groups cause situations like the following, to which we now are seeking some solution.

We have word that a poor Mexican laborer in Kansas has a wife in the last stages of tuberculosis. He heard of a divine healer in Los Angeles who promised healing for the patient upon payment of $100. The deaconess writes that this faithful worker in the mission has sent $25 and has promised to send the balance when his wife is able to come, meaning when he has $75 in addition to the money needed for her railroad fare and her lodging in some hovel here. Even if she should reach Los Angeles, she will soon die, far from her loved ones, after having infected scores of other Mexicans. The money could have been used to much better advantage for the sick woman, and could have helped to save her children. Yet this swindler is reaping the benefit of this money instead. He is widely advertised in all the Spanish papers above the Border with a picture of his handsome face and many testimonials. It seems at present impossible either to prosecute or dislodge him.

9. *Holy Rollers.* Without doubt some moral good is done by the "Holy Rollers." Their effect in general, however, is the drawing from the various missions of hundreds of enthusiastic people, including pastors and their entire congregations. After they have tried this form of religion for a while, the disgusted ones come back, but rarely do they have their former spirit of harmony and unity. Instead, they are ever seeking in the missions to unsettle the peace and faith of the most devout, and all on the basis of physical extravagances. They make much of the "gift of tongues."

10. *The Penitentes.* In northeastern New Mexico we find a peculiar group of people known as *Penitentes.* They seem to be spiritual descendants of the Third Order of St. Francis, which in the early days of Spanish control was widely extended over New Mexico. The order is a secret one and the *Penitente* houses, or *moradas,* where their meetings are held are familiar sights in scores of New Mexico villages. Because of the secret character of the organization little is known of the activities of this order during the greater part of the year, but at Easter time an annual procession is held in the open. During this march the members inflict keen and sometimes extravagant torture upon themselves. They have been known to whip themselves with yucca or other cactus whips until blood has been drawn. It was supposed that this order was dying out, but more

recently it seems to be taking on renewed life. It is now said by those who are well informed concerning the matter that in many communities the *Penitente* organization is the controlling factor in politics, and that politicians are therefore encouraging the maintenance of the organization so that they may use it for political ends. The *Penitente* groups are not confined to the older members of the community. Young men are continually joining the organization and taking part in its ceremonies.

Protestant Difficulties

Many of our Latin brothers do not believe that the "Anglo-Saxon religion" is possible for their temperament. We have too little of art, reverence, and loving-kindness for those who fall. Our religion is too exacting and impatient. It is too "practical" to be immediately possible or even desirable.

Many believe that most of us do not really care whether they are ever "saved" or even given a chance to become Christian Americans. Mexicans, Italians, Portuguese, and Filipinos are all too frequently told plainly that they are not wanted in American churches. If they come, they are just as clearly informed—usually without words, of course, though not always in so kind a way—that they are inferior and curious specimens, not quite safe to have about. In one community a nice mission had been started in an American church, out of hours. A few "brethren" objected, and it had to stop. Another community refused them an unused church because it did not want to encourage "those people." One trustee said, "The whole country will be turned over to Japs and 'Blackbirds' (Mexicans) if we do not watch out."

Poor, wretched "Gospel Halls" and churches, bare of aids to worship and facilities for a community program, are bad forms of missionary strategy among the Yaquis of Mexico or in the Amazon Valley. But to have these excuses for places of worship maintained for years by the side of one or several palatial churches in the United States where we and our children worship God, all the while neglecting these ostracized neighbors and hard-working servants of our industrial system—all this does not help to open doors into Latin hearts for the Americans' religion. Terrible "architectural tragedies" might be described here. We have many buildings which are tragedies, and only a few of the better sort. Our Mexican pastors cry out in despair over the effect of neglect and discrimination.

The Value of Tracts

It may be noted incidentally that one very effective means of combating errors and under-

standing Mexican hearts is the Christian tract. A
Mexican student with joy told how she handed a
tract to a well-dressed Mexican lady just as she
left the train. A few days later a maid called
upon the student, who was studying to become a
deaconess, inviting her to call at the home of her
mistress, who was the wife of a merchant. On
calling, she was met affectionately by the lady,
who said: "I read those words in that *tratado*
you gave me at the train. It has changed my life.
I am a Christian and I want to thank you and to
have you come often to our house."

The pastor of a great Mexican church, when he
was a senior in the University of Mexico, was one
of the millions of freethinkers in Latin America. He would not touch the Bible for he did not
believe in it. But he chanced upon a tract which
referred to matters that required him to verify or
challenge after consulting the despised Book. As
a result of his investigation, he became a believer.
For several years this man was general secretary
of the International Sunday School Association
for the Republic of Mexico. He has visited all
parts of the nation, as well as Cuba, Panama, and
the United States. His eloquent and convincing
addresses in church and plaza were made possible
by the entrance of the Light by means of a gospel
tract. This preacher is a constant distributor,
personally and through his assistants, of appropriate tracts.

Great care must be taken in selecting safe

tracts. While the missionary boards are sending
out pastors and building churches, various sects
and propagandists are busy adding to some excellent matter conclusions of their own. These
are often mischievous. They soon honeycomb the
missions with the bigotry and fanaticism of dis-
affected and critical schismatics. Of course the
cure is to produce a wealth of helpful literature
for use in the work. At present there is a pathetic
lack of this mighty agency for reaching into the
very depths of the task, especially above the Border where it is easy to ''sow knee-deep'' the unprepared new converts with tracts very harmful
in their results. These propagandists cannot easily reach unconverted Mexicans with their narrow
and dogmatic appeals, but they can disturb awakened souls who are conscientiously seeking for the
whole truth, and who are made to think that these
new ideas, such as Russellism, ''unsalaried pastors,'' Mormonism, ''keeping the real Sabbath,''
New Thought, and the various other divisive
teachings are the truth. Tracts which are in part
excellent are tinctured with some partisan bias
which does damage to peace, comity, and real
progress in organizing a stable church. The sects
responsible usually have little conscience in their
methods, and their tactics are often highly dishonest. Fortunately such a program is not ultimately welcome among Latin Americans; they
have had enough of that sort of thing. But inspiring, frank, and unsectarian gospel tracts in

brief form, and particularly incidents and illustrations, are greatly needed.

Multitudes of Mexicans are within our borders. We may ignore or evade our duty here, but we cannot escape it. We believe God has sent them to us for a purpose. The church which has pretended to serve them through four centuries has woefully failed. The Panama Congress declared, "The Latin Church is unable to do for these people what they need to see accomplished." Shall we despise and neglect these newly-arrived friends or shall we give them our hands and our hearts and lead them to Jesus Christ and his way of life? His call is clear. What shall be the response?

The crest and crowning of all good, life's final star is brotherhood;
For it will bring again to earth her long-lost Poesy and Mirth;
Will send new light on every face, a kingly Power upon the race.
And till it come, we men are slaves, and travel downward to dust of graves.
Come, clear the way, then, clear the way; blind creeds and kings have had their day.
Break the dead branches from the path; our hope is in the aftermath.
Our hope is in heroic men, star-led to build the world again.
To this event the ages ran; make way for Brotherhood—make way for man.

                                        EDWIN MARKHAM

VI

RELIGIOUS WORK

What the world has been waiting for through
the centuries is a sample Christian nation. America has the best chance of being that sample.

EDWARD LAIRD MILLS

TWO questions are constantly being asked:
Are Mexicans ever really converted? How
do you start a mission among them? One
of many answers that come from actual experience is the following.

"Suppose, my brothers, that you had to pay the
Lord for all the light which he sends down to you
from his great electric light plant. How much
would your bill be? Suppose you had to pay for
all his irrigation from the skies. That would be a
big water bill—*mucho dinero, hermanos mios*
(much money, brothers mine!)" The vigorous
speaker, a Mexican blacksmith, was addressing
(through an interpreter) a large audience in
Orange County, California. He captivated the
formerly prejudiced audience. That started the
good work. Within a week the old Mormon
church in the community had been bought, and a
Mexican mission "started" which now, after
eight years, has eight missions as off-shoots.

Five years later the pastor of the church in
which this Mexican spoke wanted, in the church

he was then serving, a Mexican speaker for a special service. He said: "Bring to my Hollywood church that same Mexican. Señor Valencia, he's the boy! He will stir my exclusive people. And let him tell them about their bills for God's electric light and irrigation!"

Twenty-eight years before, this same José Valencia was out shooting birds one Sunday morning with a new .22 rifle. A Christian American foreman on his way to church greeted the Mexican boy with, "Oye, José, if you are going to shoot birds, you ought not to shoot them on Sunday; this is God's day." José liked the kind stranger, hunted out his church, attended it, and was soon on the way to becoming a Christian. He sold his prized rifle and, with the money, bought a Bible. It was a four-volume Douay version, a Catholic version bought to please his Catholic parents and relatives.

In this great soul-winner, now superintendent of one of the most important Sunday schools above the Border and a local preacher with a beautiful Christian family, we have an answer to the frequent question, "Are Mexicans ever really converted?" This heroic Christian layman sells many Bibles. He often has polemic conferences with priests, to which he goes on Sunday afternoons armed with his beloved Word of God affectionately wrapped up and carried in his hand. He talks with poor laborers and with proud but

unfortunate Mexican exiles whom he meets in the
street or plaza, always emphasizing Christ as a
friend. He takes especial interest in every member of his own circle of relatives. This man, whom
anyone may visit in his neat, happy home—his
own property—in Los Angeles, could fill a book if
he were to tell what God is doing through him,
"an unworthy and humble servant."

The story of the missionary *Camino Real* in the
Southwest records many thrilling annals. It
tells how Roman Catholic priests came first. They
began their formal missionary work in 1595 when
the Southwest became a territory of Spain. Probably no typical Protestant pioneer has made so
much material relating to this time available for
our study as has the Rev. Thomas Harwood, D.D.,
one of the pioneer missionaries to New Mexico.
He writes:

Roman Catholics had the right of way in New Mexico for
almost three hundred years. They had the entire religious
control of New Mexico, unmolested by Protestants or Americans for nearly ten generations. What a golden opportunity
was this for Romanism. The so-called infallible Pope at their
head, the crowned heads of Spain and her civil and military
officials and soldiery, for most of the time, at their back, and
a conquered territory at their feet; with no Protestant Bible
or Protestant press or Protestant preacher or public school in
the way, the priests could sow the gospel seed, water it with
their tears, bask in papal benedictions, and reap the golden
harvest!

Ten generations of sowing and reaping and what is the
harvest? . . . In 1850 it was, intellectually, morally, and religiously, one of the darkest corners in Christendom. While

the march of civilization had taken grand strides almost everywhere else, New Mexico had fallen behind. . . . In 1870 not a public schoolhouse could be found, hardly a Bible in one family in a thousand, and only a few other books; hardly a public road or a bridge, only those that had been built by the government or the Protestant pioneer; hardly an American plow, wagon, or buggy could be found. . . . Some fruits were growing here, but chiefly grapes for wine.

But feeble efforts were made to open the gates of civilization compared with our Protestant eastern states. The priests and church preferred to go on gathering tithes of flocks, fleeces, and grain, administering sacraments at high prices, baptisms, marriages, extreme unction, and prayers for the dead at extortionate prices; all of which could be practised only among an ignorant and superstitious people. If such was the condition in 1869 when I came, it must have been so when the first pioneers came in 1850.

In 1870, when the first census was taken, every citizen felt ashamed of the illiteracy of the territory. Seventy-three and a half per cent of the people over ten years of age could not read and five per cent more were unable to write. And yet we are told: "These are our people. Protestant missionaries have no business here."

It may surprise some to learn that the first evangelical Spanish sermon in the New World, and probably in the entire world, was preached by Padre Benigno Cardenas, at Santa Fé, November 20, 1853; and he then became the first licensed Spanish Protestant preacher in the world.

The first denomination to enter New Mexico seems to have been the Baptists. Samuel Gorman, the first missionary to the Pueblo Indians, in 1854 erected in Santa Fé the first Protestant church in New Mexico.

The first Presbyterian missionary was W. J. Kephart, who entered the field in 1850. He was followed soon afterward by Rev. John A. Annin, the "Father of Mexican Work" under the same board. In 1869 Mr. Annin went to Vegas where he was welcomed by a young Mexican in the following characteristic way: "I have been praying for a missionary. You can depend upon me for anything I can do."

The Congregational, United Brethren, Episcopal, and some other denominations, including all of the distinctly southern denominations, have work in this field. The Y.M.C.A. and the Y.W.C.A. are also rendering an important service. The first Methodist missionaries sent out with the purpose of ministering only in English, turned home because of illness and discouragement and resolved to give up the mission. But the altruistic work of "Father" John L. Dyer and the later efforts of E. G. Nicholson, Walter Hansen—who spoke Spanish—and others, was accomplished by Providence bringing them into touch with an eloquent, influential, and well-educated but dissatisfied Roman Catholic priest of Santa Fé, Benigno Cardenas.

This priest made bitter reference to the bishop and the church which caused the controversy to seem like a personal quarrel, and he was not encouraged. He went to Rome with his cause, and this visit only served to open his eyes completely. After ten weeks of affectionate and intensive

A MEXICAN FRIENDLY CENTER

This $4,000 chapel and community center for Mexicans was made possible by an interdenominational Bible class in Orange, California. It is a step forward when local communities take a friendly interest in the Mexicans within their borders.

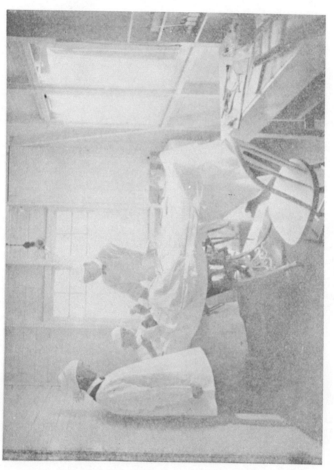

A CLINIC FOR MEXICANS

The pathetic conditions under which many Mexicans are forced to live in this country, and the improper feeding they endure account largely for their many diseases and abnormally high death-rate. Clinics are important adjuncts of many border missions.

Christian training in the family of a Mr. Rule in London, he brought letters to the New York Board of Missions (Methodist) and was appointed to the Spanish work under Superintendent Nicholson. With his ministry the real work began among the Mexicans in the great Southwest. He was alone in the territory for a year, and the records show that up to that time his was "the only productive Protestant ministry in the territory," and that he really laid the foundations of a living evangelical church among his people.

This racial pioneer had his trials. When one of his first meetings was advertised in the plaza, the notices were torn down. On the day this meeting was to be held, the bishop denounced Cardenas in the extended mass, saying that the people must not even look at him because he was an apostate and his very looks might contaminate them. When the mass could be prolonged no further, the bells kept up a great din until the priests and nuns had all retired. Then, at the appointed hour, close in front of the Governor's palace, thus gaining the protection of the United States, Cardenas spoke. His subject was "Repentance and Justification of Man." The address was delivered with great force and clearness. The talk was appropriate in sentiment, illustration, and spirit. Then, after introducing Superintendent Nicholson, Cardenas unfolded and explained his parchment and letters of ordination and character as a presbyter and priest of the Church of Rome, and as an apostolic missionary to New Mexico. These he placed, one by one, in the hands of Superintendent Nicholson, expressing as he did so a desire to be connected with his mission and to be authorized to officiate as a minister. The plaza seats were filled, and many sat on the ground. Everyone listened with unbroken attention as Cardenas in a touching manner uttered his reasons for renouncing the dogmas and legends of Rome and embracing the faith and worship of Protestants.

The first Mexican convert to follow Benigno Cardenas seems to have been Ambrosio Gonzales at Peralta. His story is as follows:

"One evening in 1853 Superintendent Nicholson left a Bible with me. It was the first Bible of any kind that I had ever seen. The Book had a charm for me. When the rest retired, I sat up and continued to read. I read nearly the whole book of Genesis. I then turned to the New Testament and read several chapters in St. John—one of which was the fourteenth, beginning, 'Let not your heart be troubled.' It was to me a new book. I read until the chickens were crowing for day. I lay down on a lounge in the same room and soon fell asleep. When I awoke, the sun was shining through the window into my face, and the Son of Righteousness was shining brightly in my soul. I have been a Christian and a Protestant ever since."

When this first convert lay dying, years afterward, he placed his hand on the head of his little nine-year-old grandson, who was named for him, and said, "Ambrosio, as you have borne my name, I trust that some day you will also fill my place as a minister of the gospel." This grandson became a most successful and outstanding preacher. But it required the encouragement of those "prophets of the long trails," traveling with saddle-bags or buckboard, in those days of adobe huts and fanaticism, to lead him and others like him to decide for Christ and his ministry.

Persecution

The first to lay down his life as a martyr for the redemption of Latin Americans within our borders was Rev. F. J. Tolby. Two years after leaving his home in northwest Indiana for labors in the Spanish Southwest, he was shot and killed. On the 14th of September, 1875, he was returning on horseback from the out-station of Elizabethtown, New Mexico, when he was fired at from ambush. A lonely but honored grave marks the holy ground where this bold, promising missionary laid down his life.

On Christmas Eve, 1880, a Presbyterian editor and preacher at Socorro was shot and killed at the church door as he was entering for a Christmas gathering. In the same year a Mexican preacher was shot and badly wounded while on his circuit. A lead bullet can still be seen in the door of the church at Peralta where Rev. John

Steele was shot at while working at a carpenter's bench, helping to build the church. Two later attempts were made to take his life.

Dr. T. M. Harwood and E. Barela were stoned while serving as Protestant ministers; and Bishop McCabe tells that after he had laid the cornerstone at El Paso for the new Spanish Church, it was removed and defaced during the night. Many others have been threatened, stoned, and mobbed, thus sharing the sufferings of Christ and of the sixty-four evangelical martyrs in Old Mexico, and the many others throughout all Latin America. A most hopeful sign is the present recognition by friends and foes that such methods only work harm to the persecutors and promote the work of the gospel.

Dr. Thomas Harwood died in 1918 at Albuquerque, New Mexico. Little would one believe, looking into those blue eyes always set in a bright, kindly smile, that this old Civil War chaplain had spent four decades of untiring labor as circuit-rider, teacher, and administrator, using constantly both English and Spanish, sleeping and eating under impossible conditions and bearing burdens and the rigors of climate impossible for most of us to conceive. He had a keen sense of sympathy for the people he served, and, like the Emancipator he admired, he had a sense of humor as a saving grace. In his "History of New Mexico Missions" he quaintly tells the following story.

"Mr. Johnson at Cherry Valley in 1869 turned his chickens out in the sage-brush so that the adobe hen-house with its dirt floor might be used, after it had been neatly white-washed and fixed up, for the day-school; and, two days after, for Sunday School and preaching services. Years after this the question arose as to who had the first Sunday School in the territory. I stated the time and the place, and that if nobody else could show that he had a school earlier than we, I should claim that we were first. At any rate, we think that we had reason to *crow* as ours was opened in a *hen house!*"

Eager Workers

It is evident from the foregoing and from the memories of anyone reared on the frontier that most efficient work is done by the Mexican local preachers, colporteurs, Sunday School superintendents and teachers, and by women missionaries. Years of experience with the Latin Americans and other foreign-speaking people deepen the conviction that such workers are the real advance guard and frontline fighters in this work. Their lowly estate is often an advantage to them, though they may seem to us greatly handicapped in limitations as to education, dress, and conveniences of life, and, even, in clear or correct convictions as to ecclesiastical and theological dictums. They seem best able to make the personal contact needed.

The most effective workers, especially among the most needy about the Border, are those trained or untrained, whose hearts are on fire with concern for their fellows. I think of one now who cannot read or write, but he can win souls and lead meetings. He reaches many whom cultured, correct, ordained pastors could not touch. The more that our best-trained workers can preserve this spirit of true Christian democracy, the more valuable they are. They are like the early reformers who set the world on fire, who were accustomed simply to say, "Is thy heart right, give me thy hand."

Our most successful trained pastors are those who can raise up, as staff members and as candidates for Christian work, the largest corps of this type of workers to work under careful supervision. From these colporteurs, lay workers, and "women helpers" will be recruited some of the best pastors and women missionaries. This does not do away with the absolute necessity of well-trained, ten-talent leaders to organize, train, and direct the increasingly complicated life of a really efficient and adequate church and community plant for Spanish-speaking people. But God keep these greater leaders free from the snares which might lead them to neglect the mass of lowly Mexicans which forms the major portion of all Mexican colonies. Success in this group will not fail to win the loyalty and cooperation of important racial leaders of the more fortunate class.

The Bible at Work

Throughout Latin America the Bible is the "Silent Missionary." The pastor of a city church early one Sunday morning had a caller. At the door he found a typical Mexican, from *sombrero* to *zapatos*, with courtesy and amiability just radiating from his tanned face and brawny figure. Every token showed him to be a "Mexican pure."

"Hagame el favor, Señor, de venderme una Biblia." (Do me the favor, Sir, to sell me a Bible.) Though long a resident in the Southwest, Doctor McClish confesses his amazement in having a real Mexican seeking a Bible. "For," said he, "are they not all Catholics?" His surprise grew during the several weeks which passed until the precious volume in Spanish could be secured from the American Bible Society in New York. His Mexican friend walked eight miles into town, through intense heat, every Sunday for about two months, until at last *la Biblia* came. There was no Mexican mission in that region in those days, so this seeker was left to the ministry of the "Silent Missionary."

We know a Christian Mexican layman who is accustomed to seek out and visit with his expatriated countrymen on the streets after his day's work. He found one who was evidently of better class, but who seemed ill. A brief conversation led him to visit the sick man's cottage. The family accepted the gospel, and the father found

comfort from the new-found Word of God until
he died. His wife, to ease his intense suffering,
read to him from the New Testament through the
long night hours. He kept the "Silent Missionary" under his pillow when his cultured wife was
not reading it to him aloud. It became known at
last that his family is related to the Madero
family in Mexico. They asked that the funeral
be conducted in the Protestant chapel—a dark, sin-
gle-room hall. After the pastor and superintendent had delivered tactful messages appropriate
to the occasion, because supposedly all were high-
class Catholics, it was thought a courtesy due the
Christian brother who found him on the street at
the first to let him "speak briefly." But consternation fell upon the pastor and superintendent when Señor V——, after heartfelt words of
sympathy, began to preach to the large circle of
relatives the appeal of God to their lives: "You
who sit here in sorrow today know what joy and
peace the Word of the Lord brought to your loved
one. You will all some day come to this parting
and you will need the same Light. Most of you
sons and daughters are no longer thoughtless
children; you are married and have children and
this day should see you possessing the faith of
your father. Your lives are an open book before
God. Give your hearts to Him."

At the cemetery it was decided not to permit
the zealous layman to embarrass further the progress of the gospel by a second inappropriate ad-

dress. We had finished the ritual and were about to give the signal for the casket to be lowered, when the most prominent of the sons-in-law stepped out quickly, saying, "The friends of the deceased would like to have Señor V—— speak again." And this time it was an evangelistic appeal of the first rank, with no apology or hesitation. On the way back this godly lay Mexican said to me, "We must have a better chapel. These sons and daughters have children whom they wish us to baptize, but that gospel hall is not respectable for this class of Mexicans." It was all due to work of the "Silent Missionary" and a humble spokesman to form the contact.

Old "Hundred Fires"

Let *Cienfuegos* ("Hundred Fires") give his testimony. Speaking among a group of Mexicans and local Americans who knew him well, he said: "I've been a bad Mexican. Everybody in the saloons knows me from Santa Barbara to Los Angeles. Cards have been my god. I laughed in their faces when these friends here first asked me to come to this little mission. But now I am a new man. I feel a great change since I found the Lord Jesus." This man immediately began finding and bringing in new people to the mission and getting the workers to visit or write to the acquaintances of his days when "cards were his god." If he—past middle life—fail of God's highest, yet the little children at least whom he is bringing in will be more perfect fruits of his conversion.

An Incident

Around a rude table out of doors under the live-oaks we found Perez with the members of his large family eating their noon-day meal. With thanks we declined the invitation to join them, and proceeded to have gospel songs and a message. Right promptly at its close the brawny father said: "Why may not I and my family enjoy this religion? I have been a bad man. These brothers with you know I have been a drunkard because the first time they came here there was a jug of wine here on this table. I want to be a Christian like you tell us about." This man and his family drove several miles on a following Sunday through a chilly rain to present themselves to the Mexican pastor for baptism and membership in the church.

Starting a Mission

Years of observation and experience with Latin Americans have developed outlines of principles which seem fundamental to success in organizing missions among them.

(1) *Locating the mission plant is half the battle.* Mexicans by nature or heritage are a plaza peo-

ple. This is inevitable with an illiterate people who have to gather at the plaza to get the news, meet friends, and secure employment. The old dominant church has always occupied one side of the public square, just as the *palacio del gobierno* has occupied the adjoining side. They want their church to be central and commanding. It is wise to expend, if necessary, half the funds available to secure a central and ample location—none is too good, and rarely is it large enough. As in catching trout, one must go where they are!

(2) *Get their view-point and work from that angle.* One of the most valuable lessons one learns in Normal School is: When you have a "bad boy" do not ask what you are thinking about him, but *what he is thinking about you?* It will soon become apparent that a spirit of condescension in workers among Latin Americans is as obnoxious as is a spirit of coercion. Both traits are native to the efficient and lordly Saxons, and both are abhorrent to the long oppressed Latins.

(3) *Become familiar with their racial traits and beautiful language.* It is essential to know these well. They love color, adore music. They think with their hearts, rarely with their heads, in matters of policy and quick decision. They are born orators. Their feats of memorizing amaze the average Saxon. They are very gregarious, affable, imaginative, generous, obliging,—and they expect the same in return. Of sanguine racial

moods, they are naturally passionate and often pessimistic, jealous, and fearful of meeting and adopting "Americanisms." Truly this personality is a Joseph's coat of many colors. One must appreciate it to win these folks.

(4) *Daringly lead them right out to full-orbed activity in Christian work.* They will testify and pray, when they have reason for doing so, because of their grateful recognition of how much God has done for them in their personal experience. Their gratitude and eloquence helps them to do it in a fashion that astonishes most Christian workers unacquainted with Latin Christians. New converts and little children "take part" like veterans, and with earnestness and sincerity. They should also be just as immediately and daringly introduced to the highest ideals and moral standards, true social viewpoints, and to the soul exercise of active service. They enjoy it.

(5) *Do not weary them.* Their "attention is short." We often see successful workers intersperse a happy hymn in the midst of a sermon. Have lots of singing of a joyous sort. They like good music; it lifts their burdens and bears them on their upward way. But plan things brief and varied. Remembering this, there may be arranged the long programs, of which they are fond. But keep in mind the varied and spectacular character of their hereditary religious services, and do not weary them. Make them hungry to come again.

(6) *"Talk to the heart."* Francisco Penzotti, veteran Bible Society worker in all Latin America, in reply to the request for advice as to how to reach the people in such large numbers and so effectively, said, *"Habla al corazon."* They are simple, trustful, and withal great philosophers. Truth is of the heart as truly as of the head, and the solutions of life's problems arise in the intuitions and sentiments as often as in the reason and the logical or mathematical formula. At any rate, the Latin Americans are best reached by direct, sincere appeal to their better selves.

(7) *Make up sermons which are bona-fide, urgent appeals and deliver them in a real and direct fashion.* They are sick and tired of the all too often superficial, exaggerated, and fulsome sentences of the stereotyped old Spanish form of *discurso;* they are groping for reality and the truth. Make the message such that the folks, always there!—who hear the gospel message for the first time in their lives and who may never hear it again, may find Christ and his way of life. Put Jesus Christ in every sermon. Make them eager to buy a Bible!

(8) *Formulate a cheerful, natural, cultural order of church service.* Feature the cooperative character of the service. Bring in the living and the beautiful. One of our pastors wanted to have pots of flowers and singing canaries in his church auditorium. At any rate, here is a situation where it is a sin to be dry and uninteresting. The

order of church service may well be dignified and formal, but still very happy and helpful in tone.

(9) *Lead the pastors and people out into a well-defined and unselfish Christian program for the community.* Here is difficulty and dismay, for it is a new thing for a folk weak in initiative; but it can and must be done. They must learn as a community to help themselves. A community and a racial consciousness must be awakened. This is being done increasingly in many centers. Needless to say, the real problem is to train and lead the pastors to organize such community programs. And back of the Mexican pastor's vision must be that of his superintendent. Americans should allow the Mexican people themselves to have a voice in the conduct of the mission. The English-speaking friends should be, like the Lord, near at hand and helpful, but in administration as much as possible out of sight.

(10) *Prayerfully strive to play up the racial spirit and excellencies in terms of American and Christian ideals.* Plan as you would for the reconstruction of any oppressed, war-torn, and awakening people. Tie up to worthy Christian movements familiar to them in their own *patrias.* Regard them as citizens of that Kingdom which includes all the world, and sees them as promising candidates for character, faith and service in the molds of *their own racial past* and *personality.* They must not be expected to become Anglo-Saxon Christians any more than we should ex-

pect ten-year-old Tommy to become on the spot
the sort of saint that his dear Aunt Eliza is.

(11) *Temper the message, program and administration with due consideration of the people's
past.* Avoid controversy. Do not discuss
Romanism, socialism, or even specific vices except
in a fine spirit of love and patience. Keep them
coming. "Weep sore for him that goeth away."
Publish their virtues and moral victories and
soft-pedal on their lapses and vices which have
not yet dropped off. Insist on their getting the
heart right and they will usually make fully as
quick time in their moral house-cleaning as the
Anglo-Saxon Christian world has made since the
Reformation. They have never had the Reformation. That great movement did not penetrate
Spain or Portugal, nor has it ever leavened those
countries nor Latin America except as it is now
slowly filtering in as our missionaries are beginning to go out in larger numbers to those lands.
Latin Americans above the Border are really a
part with those peoples to the South.

Interdenominational Cooperation

There is a growing interdenominational attempt to avoid overlapping and to promote amity
and cooperation in all Mexican work. The Interdenominational Home Missions Council on Spanish-Speaking Work meets annually. Each society is entitled to two field members and one

Board member. The sessions continue two or three days. The findings are printed. There is a growing desire to standardize the whole work, to discover and do away with friction, to provide a vernacular and bilingual literature, to assemble and make available all the language materials now published by the various boards, and to bring the supporting missionary boards and the fields together in a vital and intelligent program of service. Much progress has been made, but "there remaineth yet much land to be possessed" in this interdenominational realm.

Organizing the Work

A Mexican mission is like a baby in that it is born, needs help and direction until able to walk alone, may be made a deformed cripple, a helpless dependent, and, worst of all, it may die. The latter is a common occurrence, and it is a tragedy.

It is easy to "start" a Mexican mission. Hundreds have been started, and then have lapsed and have thus become a joke to our many foes and a "scandal" to valiant Mexican believers who have found that they stood forth in vain in their new faith, suffering the mental agony of persecution and temptation at the hands of their fellows. There are all too few successful Latin American missions.

Among suggestions that have proved helpful are the following:

(1) Have a mothering, local association organized before the mission is opened. Let the dominant principle be a firm purpose that the mission shall never die. This will require careful planning and a far look. Insist upon all members being favorable to the enterprise. Develop a spiritual, sympathetic and sacrificial spirit. Regard the enterprise as a very real and large missionary labor. Do not permit mere social service to absorb the attention until the objectives of developing character and faith are forgotten. A young people's society in a great industrial town in Pennsylvania put its foreign missionary work under the missionary department of the society, and the missionary work in its midst *under the social service department!* The heart of the work must be religion.

(2) Organize the local association, with constitution, by-laws and officers, and regular meetings monthly. Have the following three committees at least: (1) Program and Organization Committee to develop and push the mothering association; to arrange interesting programs and social features; to secure members and monthly attendance. Let that be their job, and hold them responsible for it and nothing else. Work them. (2) Finance and Property Committee to handle the budget and to execute the financial plans for the building and equipment. Let the budget be respectable and adequate and expect this committee to carry it through. (3) Employment and Welfare Commit-

tee whose motto shall be, "There is no help which helps people like the help which helps them to help themselves." Cases of need and relief and constructive plans will be referred to this committee and through it to the local board. Scientific charity is their art and neighborliness and Americanization their passion.

(3) Secure a safe and successful language pastor, preferably of the same race. This racial leadership is essential to growth and permanency. The pastor should be under supervision of a sympathetic American superintendent to whom alone he will be responsible. Hold the superintendent responsible and trust him to manage the pastor. Let him pay the salary upon receipt of the monthly report. At all points in the mission program let Americans seem to keep out of sight, but be none the less active. There will be many places where American workers will be needed; let them be on hand, but not to "boss."

(4) Inspire the community and workers by having full and definite reports at the regular meetings both written and verbal, by pastor, committees and cooperators in the work. Let them be brief and real reports with concrete facts and incidents.

(5) Have much publicity given the work in the local papers and through the American services. Get materials from the reports of workers and minutes of the monthly meeting.

(6) Several starts may have to be made, but

when once begun never give up nor let anybody mention the idea of failure.

(7) Do not try to understand all that the native pastor does. Try love and trust upon the situation. Give it time. You are growing oaks out of slime beds. Do not insist upon quick, sectarian and faultless products.

(8) Undertake the adequate. The adequate is divinely possible, ultimately. It is strategically easier and in the end the quicker method. The apologetic efforts and contented helplessness of most Mexican missions are no compliment to God nor the people we serve. They do not challenge the strenuous cooperation and prayer of the whole community, particularly the business men upon whom much dependence must be placed.

(9) Make a definite goal of raising up racial leadership. Keep your eye out for possible workers. Get them on the King's Highway and keep them going. This is the big business. Raise up and train leaders—and do not spoil them by mollycoddling. Surely, these leaders must be found in just such missions as we are talking about; that is just where they are always found.

A Plaza Community Center in Action

Let us visit a Mexican Mission of the present and future in a great city. We find a good property which has cost much money, but its commanding location led friends to give generously

to it. We are met at a business-like office desk by
a young woman who seems to be "Big Sister"
incarnate. She excuses herself in Spanish from
the Mexican family with whom she was dealing
earnestly as we entered, and after greeting us and
securing our signatures in the guest book, she
takes us to the superintendent, telling him our
home addresses and our special interest in the
work. We find ourselves in the presence of a man
who is kindly, direct, uplifting in his very presence. We would like him as a friend; so do the
Mexicans! We are told the plan and purpose of
the plant. He explains that everyone in the
Plaza Community Center is a missionary—the
young lady who welcomed us, aside from her
steady ministry to the needy and the ones who
come to the center, goes to the jails and sings,
plays the harp, and speaks in two languages in
those fearful institutions where bad men and
often innocent Mexican youth are herded together.
We are told that one young Mexican, converted in
one of these jails before he went to the penitentiary, has just sent back from the "Pen" another
Mexican whom he led to Christ before the latter
was paroled. This paroled convict came straight
to the Plaza Center and there got employment and
further inspiration and help in the Christian way
of life.

The superintendent takes us to another woman
worker in charge of the Christian social service
department. She says, "We never give anything

away here. We help folks to help themselves. The Mexicans are noble folks. They never beg. We have a hard time to find out their needs because they will not let us know of their sufferings. There are no Mexican tramps. More Americans come here to this Plaza Center asking for charity than Mexicans, and the Mexicans have infinitely more need. The problem is to let the American community know the facts and to get them to believe in the Mexicans and then constructively to help them.''

The next hour passes quickly while we look and listen. Here are sick folks waiting for clinical service and operations. The most serious cases are taken to kind-hearted specialists in the city hospitals. Here are all kinds of folks seeking employment and thousands of them finding it and being introduced properly to it. Here is the day nursery for little folks whose mothers are at work. The Plaza Center Bank teaches saving and finances itself. In fact, everything finances itself and more, excepting equipment and heads of departments. This cultured Mexican nurse is a graduate of the finest hospital in the city. Here it was she found a faith and a field of which she little dreamed when she came as an exiled, upper-class, ambitious student seeking training and a career four years ago.

Throughout the plant one thing is often impressed upon the visitor; a careful file system is kept of every individual who comes in touch with the institution—even of the visitor, not to say the many givers. Every sick person, all folks seeking work, students in the "Opportunity School" and in the Christian racial Bible Training Department, young people in the social and religious clubs and activities, are all listed in the very systematically kept files. Their country, age, occupation, family, address and their relation to the Plaza Center are progressively recorded. Touching incidents a-plenty are noted. One day's history would thrill a nation could the people know these "border conditions" and what is being done to meet them by providing wholesome race contacts and scientific help.

We find that there is a regularly organized Mexican Church. The pastor is a man of broad culture and eloquence. He speaks English and fraternizes with Americans. His young people mingle freely in the religious life of the city, but with their own racial group spirit.

We hear of the architectural dream of the cathedral-like church soon to be built with very modern facilities, equipment and program. There is to be a tower with chimes and large clock to serve the illiterate Plaza community. The elegant and worshipful auditorium will seat great audiences on special occasions and yet be cozy. Its pipe organ will be the delight of several Latin American players and thousands of listeners. The Church school departments are to equal the church in appropriateness and accommodations. Already four afternoons and four nights in the week there are Bible school classes. There is also a vacation Bible school growing in favor and attendance. There is to be a racial pastor for each larger group and an American religious director, who likewise radiates big brotherhood and enthusiasm. Into this church all the language branches feed. The talent of the American churches of the city serve here and it is becoming an outstanding city church. There is an affiliated membership in the Plaza Church which permits folks of any faith or no church membership to subscribe to a simple creed and thus to be related to the membership.

The working force includes both races. Much visiting is done in the humble homes and also among the better class. Community prayer meetings in the various "quarters" of which the Plaza Center is the colony center, are popular. It is evident that it is a community clearing house for all classes and conditions of folks—a small idealized America.

It is evident to the visitor that there is something like a Niagara in operation. The large, well-lighted basement which serves as a social hall and forum with its reading and lounging room and its café, is thronged by folks. The clinic, day nursery, employment office, the church, the Opportunity School, and, in fact, the whole plant is a beehive of activity. In the industrial classes the day opens with a bilingual religious service of thirty minutes devoted to song, Scripture, and occasionally to testimony. It is voluntary, but few of the toilers fail to secure this morning blessing of peace and good will. The former fiddler for the red-light dances has been converted and plays for these services. He has brought in a Mexican photographer who plays the rich-toned cello. The workers ask for more of this religious opportunity and want to be taught to memorize the beautiful Spanish hymns, for they cannot read any language. Several of them are coming to the night classes to learn to read so that they can read the Bible and the hymns. A young Mexican woman worked here a half day for seventy-five cents at first. It turned out that she had been stenographer for Francisco Madero, the martyred president of Mexico. Now her old mother works all day and the girl is giving her life in full-time service to her people, though she was, like Madero, a spiritualist when she came into this realm of the King's Highway. One visitor of wide experience said jokingly after attending one of the morning workers' meetings, "I believe I could keep my religion if I could attend these meetings once in a while. It is the real thing."

Much of the success of an enterprise consists in getting the attention and confidence of a kindly public and of the church. This great Center thronged with needy and grateful people stands

> Where cross the crowded ways of life,
> Where sound the cries of race and clan,

and folks soon see the great work that is being
done for the entire community. Racial leaders
are raised up. Industrial leaders are impressed.
The influence reaches into the local colleges and
the great university. The city officials and officers of the law are impressed. Leading racial
representatives are moved to study and commend
the work. It is *practico* they say. One vigorous, brilliant attorney, an ex-governor of the
Mexican state, and now a prominent official of the
Government said:

"The passions of my people must be restrained
and educated. You folks there at the Plaza Community Center are laying down just such a moral
and social program as our people need. It is just
what the Mexicans want. I am deeply interested
in it and I will look further into your great work.
I congratulate you upon it."

A volume might be written of incidents which
take place in centers like the one just described.
Social agencies in desperation are seeking the aid
which the church plainly is able to give. One secretary said, "We have an avalanche of Mexican
girls and crime. What shall we do?" A young
banker, a Spaniard, said he was not much interested in religion, but this sort of program ap-
pealed to him, especially the open-air conference
held by the Mexican pastor and his young people
in the Plaza, and the other social activities of the
Spanish-speaking youth.

If such a great city plant cannot always be

built at once and its staff and program fully
achieved, still the elemental factors can be
wrought out in every mission. A well-equipped
Mexican mission, however small, should at least
be provided with: (1) A three or more roomed
plant with good bell to call the people. Many of
them cannot read the time by clocks if they had
clocks. (2) Supplies in both Spanish and English
—wherever possible bilingual in character so that
children from the schools can read to the
parents, and the whole family have this aid to the
learning of English. There should be hymnals,
Bibles, tracts, library, stereopticon, and funds for
renting temperance, citizenship, and gospel slides.
There should be an adequate though adapted
Sunday-school equipment. (3) There should be
money and talent for regular concerts and socials.
We know of one old Mexican bootlegger who was
converted at an Epworth League social, and of
three ex-priests who were won by the larger program and the general spirit of big brotherhood
and uplift evident in one single mission above the
Border. Young men who give up cigarettes,
liquor, gambling and wrong relations with young
women must be given a wholesome and absorbing
social program.

The Lure of Latin American Missions

The impression made upon the hearts of every
open-minded investigator who comes in contact

with missions among the Mexicans or other Latin Americans is a pleasant one. Mexicans are usually responsive to efforts in their behalf. They are passionate in message, fervent in achievement, and charmingly grateful. They impart to our calculating, sober Anglo-Saxon moods and methods much of their fire, love and courtesy. There is also a strong and growing conviction that there is no better chance to help this neighboring people than that offered above the Border.

The outreach of this work has directly touched Mexico, Cuba, Spain, Portugal, Porto Rico, Greece, Hawaii, Philippines, Africa, Madeira Islands, Peru, Chile, and Brazil.

Still more significant is the outreach into the various strata of society, the sections of the community, and the departments of civic life. Think of having vital relations with the official departments of education, health, charity, justice, labor; the chamber of commerce, women's clubs; great ranches, packing companies, mining, sugar, railroad, cotton and other corporations. The most godless of them exclaim, "Sure, we want to help a work like that. It is better for you to cheer and convert the Mexicans than for them to be neglected and cut themselves to pieces in our camps. If you folks are willing to brave disease, squalor, strange tongue and stranger folks, all at little salary, we ought to give the easier part of money and property."

What a people even the most lowly Mexicans

are, when won! Below that Border during a recent revolution an Aztec preacher went his circuit as usual and was captured by fanatics and tortured. He preached Jesus to them. They cut out his tongue, sawed his body nearly in two with American (!) barbed-wire, and then burned his heroic body in the Plaza. The next Sunday members of his flock fearlessly carried the gospel message around the mountain circuit of their martyred pastor. This is typical of their spirit. What a tug is the challenge of a people like these, *waiting at our front door* for the Bread of Life.

When big vessels meet, they say,
They salute and sail away;
Just the same as you and me,
Lonely ships upon the sea,
Each one sailing his own jog
For a port beyond the fog;
Let your speaking trumpet blow;
Lift your horn and cry "Hullo";

Say "Hullo"; and "How d'ye do?"
Other folks are good as you,
When you leave your house of clay,
Wandering in the far away,
When you travel through the strange
Country far beyond the range,
Then the souls you've cheered will know
Who you be, and say "Hullo."

SAM WALTER FOSS

BIBLIOGRAPHY

El Gringo, or New Mexico and Her People. WILLIAM W. H.
DAVIS. Harper and Brothers, New York. 1857. o. p.[1]
This book contains much graphic information about the
early days of New Mexico.

History of New Mexico. THOMAS HARWOOD. El Abogado
Press, Albuquerque, New Mexico. Two volumes. Spanish
and English missions, a story of forty years in New
Mexico. o. p.

Intervention in Mexico. SAMUEL GUY INMAN. George H.
Doran Co., New York. 1919. $1.50.
A plea for a Christian attitude in our international rela-
tions with Mexico.

Land of Poco Tiempo, The. CHARLES F. LUMMIS. Charles
Scribner's Sons, New York. $2.50. 1893.
A fascinating account of New Mexico and New Mexican
life.

Methodism's New Frontier. JAY S. STOWELL. Methodist
Book Concern, New York. 1924. Cloth, 75 cents; paper,
50 cents.
This book describes the foreign-language work of the
Methodist Episcopal Church in the United States. One
entire chapter is given over to the Spanish work.

Mexican Nation, The. H. PRIESTLEY. The Macmillan Co.,
New York. 1923. $4.00.
A recent and helpful history of Mexico.

Mexican People, The; Their Struggle for Freedom. L.
GUTIERREZ DE LARA and EDGCUMB PINCHON. Doubleday,
Page and Co., Garden City, New York. 1914. $1.50.
An exhaustive, narrative volume full of evidence and ap-
peal from the heart of this liberal young Mexican seeking
for friends to view Mexico's struggles fairly.

Mexico on the Verge. E. J. DILLON. George H. Doran Co.,
New York. 1921. $3.00.
A critical analysis of recent events in Mexican history.

[1] Books marked "o. p." are out of print but may be found in
many missionary and public libraries.

Mexico Today. GEORGE B. WINTON. Missionary Education Movement, New York. o. p.

Mexico has had no more sincere and daring advocate than the editor and missionary leader who wrote this mission study book.

Mexico: Today and Tomorrow. E. D. TROWBRIDGE. The Macmillan Co., New York. 1919. $2.00.

This tells the story of Mexico from the time of the Aztecs through the period of the World War.

Near Side of the Mexican Question, The. JAY S. STOWELL. George H. Doran Co., New York. 1921. $1.00.

This book is good for reference in study classes and for evidence in discussions; and as an authority on Border conditions and relations it is unexcelled.

Old Spain in New America. ROBERT MCLEAN and GRACE WILLIAMS. Council of Women for Home Missions, 156 Fifth Avenue, New York. 1916. Cloth, 50 cents; paper, 35 cents. A most valuable reference book for getting at the root of the problem.

Seen in a Mexican Plaza. GEORGE F. WEEKS. Fleming H. Revell Co., New York. 1918. $1.00.

A summer's idyll of an idle summer. This work gives a graphic picture of Mexican life and customs as witnessed by the author.

Social Revolution in Mexico, The. E. A. ROSS. Century Co., New York. 1923. $1.75.

A valuable interpretation of recent Mexican history by one who is a keen student, a trained observer, and a remarkably interesting writer.

Spanish Institutions of the Southwest. F. W. BLACKMAR. Johns Hopkins Press, Homewood, Baltimore. $2.00.

This book has been highly recommended as a study of Spanish customs in the United States.

Spanish Pioneers, The. CHARLES F. LUMMIS. A. C. McClurg and Co., Chicago. 1914. $1.50.

This story is one of the best of the Southwest.

BIBLIOGRAPHY 191

Handbook Bibliography on Foreign Language Groups in the United States and Canada. Compiled by AMY BLANCHE GREENE and FREDERICK A. GOULD. Council of Women for Home Missions and Missionary Education Movement, New York. 1925. Cloth, $1.50; paper, $1.25.
Compact information about all race groups in the United States.

PERIODICAL ARTICLES

"A Remarkable Chinese Colony in Mexico." JAY S. STOWELL. *Missionary Review of the World.* February, 1924.

"Exchanging Educational Facilities with Mexico." *Literary Digest.* February 26, 1921.

"Getting God Counted among the Mexicans." ROBERT N. McLEAN. *Missionary Review of the World.* May, 1923.

"Immigrant from Mexico." S. I. ESQUIVEL. *Outlook.* May 19, 1920.

"Immigration along our Southern Border." J. B. GWIN. *Annals of the American Academy.* January, 1921.

"In What Position Does the Mexican Revolt Place American Interests?" EDSON READE. *Financial World.* January 26, 1924.

"Little Melting-Pot on the Plains, The." C. E. COULTER. *Normal Instructor and Primary Plans.* May, 1923.

"Little Mexico in Northern Cities." *World's Work.* September, 1924.

"Mexican-American Amity Conference, The." *Southwestern Political and Social Science Quarterly.* September, 1923.

"Mexican-American Friendship." *Pan-American Magazine.* August, 1919.

"Mexican as He Is, The." C. BEALS. *North American Review.* October, 1921.

"Mexican Immigration to the United States." E. M. ALVARADO. *National Conference of Social Work.* 1920.

"Mexicans in Los Angeles, The." *Survey.* September 15, 1920.

"Mexicans in Los Angeles, The." *Los Angeles City Survey,*

prepared by the Interchurch World Movement. June, 1920.

"Mexicans in Los Angeles from the Standpoint of the Religious Forces of the City, The." G. B. OXNAM. *Annals of the American Academy.* January, 1921.

"Mexican in Our Midst, The." R. W. ROUNDY. *Missionary Review of the World.* May, 1921.

"Mexicans in the Southwest, The." J. H. HEALD. *Missionary Review of the World.* November, 1919.

"Mexican Invaders Relieving Our Farm Labor Shortage." *Literary Digest.* July 17, 1920.

"Mexican Peon in Texas, The." F. CALLCOTT. *Survey.* June 26, 1920.

"Mexican Problem Solved, The: Settlement of Claims." G. C. THORPE. *North American Review.* September, 1924.

"Mexican Rights in the United States." *Nation.* July 12, 1922.

"Mexican Traits." H. D. MARSTON. *Survey.* August 2, 1920.

"Mexico and the United States." F. BOHN. *Current History Magazine of the New York Times.* September, 1921.

"New International Movement, The." C. S. WILLIAMS. *Bulletin of the Pan American Union.* May, 1924.

"Our Southern Neighbors." *Nation.* August 27, 1924.

"Progress of Adjustment in Mexico and United States Life, The." V. L. STURGES. *National Conference of Social Work.* 1920.

"Results of Admission of Mexican Laborers, under Departmental Orders for Employment in Agricultural Pursuits, The." *Monthly Labor Review.* November, 1920.

"Rubbing Shoulders on the Border." R. N. MCLEAN. *Survey.* May 1, 1924.

"Settlement of Outstanding Claims between Mexico and the United States, The." J. B. SCOTT. *American Journal of International Law.* April, 1924.

"Some Observations of Mexican Immigration." J. L. SLAYDEN. *Annals of the American Academy.* January, 1921.

"Without Quota." *Survey.* May 15, 1924.

MEXICANS

IN THE

UNITED STATES

A Report of a Brief Survey

Conducted by

LINNA E. BRESETTE

of the Staff

of the Social Action Department

NATIONAL CATHOLIC WELFARE CONFERENCE

1312 MASSACHUSETTS AVENUE, N. W.

WASHINGTON, D. C.

THE BELVEDERE PRESS, INC.
BALTIMORE MARYLAND

TABLE OF CONTENTS

Mexicans in the United States

INTRODUCTION

Data and information used in this Survey were gathered from many sources during the spring, summer and fall of 1928. Owing to the limitation of time, it was possible to visit only a selected number of places. Altogether, ten weeks were spent in the field, the time used in each place ranging from two days at Tucson, Arizona, to nine days at Los Angeles. The field investigation was supplemented by correspondence.

Eight states were visited, the work being done in the following centers: Chicago, Illinois; St. Louis and Kansas City, Missouri; Kansas City, Topeka and Hutchinson, Kansas; El Paso and San Antonio, Texas; Tucson and Phoenix, Arizona; Albuquerque and Santa Fe, New Mexico; Los Angeles, San Francisco and Bakersfield, California; Denver, Pueblo, Longmont, Greely, Brighton and Fort Lupton, Colorado.

The greater part of the time was spent in the border states where the largest part of Mexicans and Spanish-speaking people are centered. Second in the amount of time spent was Colorado. Middle west Mexican centers were visited for a briefer time. The survey necessarily deals only with certain outstanding and important facts and observations. The subject is much too large to be exhausted in a brief study.

SOURCES OF INFORMATION

Whenever it was possible the Bishop or the Archbishop of the diocese was first consulted. Interviews were held with priests and missionaries, teachers, social workers, employers, labor leaders, superintendents of schools, special students and with Mexicans themselves. Visits were made to churches, community houses, day nurseries, libraries, associated charities, outdoor relief groups, schools, Catholic Charities, Chambers of Commerce, Knights of Columbus, members of the Society of St. Vincent de Paul and diocesan and local councils of Catholic Women. Wherever possible, the person in charge was interviewed.

5

TWO GROUPS

The Survey concerns itself with two groups of Spanish-speaking people in the United States, the Mexican immigrant and the native and poor Spanish-American. The greater part of the Mexican immigrants have come here for economic reasons, attracted largely by the promises of labor agents who contract with large employers of labor to furnish the necessary "hands."

It is claimed by employers that the number of European immigrants now being admitted by the quota system is not sufficient to meet their demands for unskilled labor. Industry is constantly inviting Mexicans. The cotton fields, mines, railroads, fruit companies and beet fields seek them. During the World War a great impetus was given to immigration from Mexico. At that time laborers were exempt from paying the head tax or passing the literacy test, exceptions which no longer prevail. With the increased acreage in the beet fields and other agriculture and with the restricted immigration imposed by the Quota Law of May, 1921, and the later law of 1924 imposing the Visa Fee, Mexican laborers are more in demand than ever.

The second group, the Spanish-Americans, are descendents of the Spaniards who were living in the border territory before it was acquired by the United States. They are native-born Americans, their parents and their parents' parents having been born in the United States. Many of them are very poor and the districts in which most of them live are poor in resources and are undeveloped.

While both groups may be found throughout the Southwest, the Mexican immigrants are found in the largest numbers in Texas, Arizona, California and Colorado and the Spanish-Americans in New Mexico. Less than one per cent of the Mexican immigration gives New Mexico as its destination. The poor among the Spanish-Americans and Mexicans live under much the same conditions.

Needless to say this study is cursory and as will be noted is based in part on second hand evidence. Since much of this information was given in confidence, the identity in such cases is concealed in this report.

I

NUMBER AND LOCATION

In 1900 there were only 100,000 Mexican immigrants in the United States. In 1920 the number, according to the United States census, was 725,332. This number has been steadily increasing until it is now variously estimated at from two to two and one-half millions. Accurate figures will not be available before the next Census. By far the most of them are within the boundaries of the four border states and Colorado. Within these limits can be found a population of probably two million Mexicans and Spanish-Americans.

The Annual Report of the Commissioner General of Immigration of the United States Department of Labor for the year ending June, 1927, shows that nearly one-half of the immigrants come from countries in the Western Hemisphere, particularly Canada and Mexico, and that Mexico is far in the lead. In addition to those who come in legally, account must be taken of those who come in illegally. The smuggling of Mexicans across the border, it is said, is an easy process, as much of the southern boundary is unguarded and the Rio Grande, which forms the greater part of it, is easily crossed. The Secretary of Labor says, "We estimate that more than one million Mexicans are illegally in this country." Some of those working with Mexicans say that for every one who enters legally there are three who enter illegally.

From figures available by the United States Department of Labor, the five Southwestern states visited have a Mexican population estimated as follows: Texas, 555,000; California, 350,000; New Mexico, 180,000; Colorado, 70,000; Arizona, 60,000. No longer, however, can it be said that the Mexicans are confined to the Southwest. They are found in Oklahoma, Arkansas, Kansas, Missouri, Iowa, Nebraska, Illinois, Michigan, Wisconsin, Indiana, Pennsylvania and even New York. They are in Wyoming, Montana and North Dakota. They are found in the South in Georgia, Tennessee, Alabama, and ˙Mississippi. There is hardly a state where they have not penetrated. Even a considerable number are in Alaska.

The border towns are filled with them. The three largest individual settlements of Mexicans are in San Antonio, El Paso and Los Angeles. El Paso, a city of 100,000 population, is estimated to be 61¾% Mexican, with a floating population of perhaps 10,000 more. Los Angeles has the largest Mexican population of any city in the United States. The closest estimate is that there are 250,000 in the city and county of Los Angeles. San Antonio officially estimates its Mexican population at about 60,000. The Archbishop and the Catholic clergy say that there are probably 80,000. Corpus Christi and Laredo, Texas, follow closely in proportionate numbers.

The Mexican population for certain selected cities is given as shown by the United States Census for 1920 and the estimated population for 1928, so that the rapid growth may be noticed.

Town	1920	1928
Chicago	1,310	75,000
Dallas	2,902	15,000
Gary	....	10,000
St. Louis	526	8,000
Toledo	233	8,000
Pueblo	....	6,000
Kansas City	2,105	6,000
Denver	1,783	50,000
Los Angeles*	31,173	75,000
Detroit	733	8,000
San Antonio	42,437	80,000

Nor is it only in congested groups in the larger cities that Mexicans are found. One authority states that they are living in 1417 American communities of less than 25,000 population. The study shows that they are scattered over the rural districts doing much of the seasonal farm labor, working in the mining and railroad camps and serving the railroads along the right-of-way. They are found tending sheep and doing countless other tasks in out of the way places on ranches miles from any railroad.

THE MEXICAN HERE TO STAY

Those who have worked with the Mexicans and those who have studied the situation say that the Mexican is here to stay. They point to Texas, Los Angeles, St. Louis, Denver, Topeka and many other places where Mexicans are known to have permanent residences and to have been in the country for several years. Of 32,000 who entered

---

*It is estimated that there are at present 250,000 Mexicans in Los Angeles city and county including 100 refugee Mexican priests.

in six months of 1928, 20,000 were men, more than half of whom were married. Over 6,000 were children under 16 years of age. Dr. Emory Bogardus of the University of Southern California says that while practically none of the Mexicans come expecting to stay, yet in a large group studied in Southern California many of them were found to own their own homes. The number of Mexican children regularly enrolled in the schools in many of the cities of the Southwest points to their permanency of residence and to their increasing number. In El Paso the school population is 70% Mexican. "In 1920," according to the City Statistician of El Paso, "55 more Americans were born in the city than Mexicans. In 1927 almost three times as many Mexicans were born as Americans. In July, 1928, there were 465 Americans born and 1047 Mexicans."

II

EMPLOYMENT

Mexican labor is becoming an increasingly basic factor in certain lines of industry. Most of the Mexicans who come to the United States work at unskilled labor. They are much in demand for the reason, expressed by many employers, that they are "not radical," "easily controlled by those in authority" and "willing to take orders." In the North, East, South and West the Mexican is being used. Lumbering, agriculture, mining, grazing, railroad construction, all demand his labor. They furnish the great supply of transient labor for the perishable crops of the Southwest. Much of their work is seasonal and they drift from one occupation to another, from state to state, and between seasons are often idle and unemployed.

It is reported that in the Imperial Valley in California each year Mexican labor picks "25 tons of raisins, 25 tons of walnuts, 5 million boxes of lemons and 25 million boxes of oranges." In Texas thousands of acres of Bermuda onions are cared for by the Mexicans. Families are to be found in large numbers in the beet areas of California, Utah, Colorado, Montana, Wyoming, North Dakota, Michigan and Ohio. In three counties of Colorado 18,000 cared for 110,000 acres of beets, more than two thirds of its entire beet acreage.

They travel with the crops and the jobs. Whole families of them may be seen loaded in old and half broken-down Fords going from the oranges to the cantaloupes, then to the grape picking, and then to the walnuts. From the beet fields they go to whatever work is offered them. In the Southwest they are the principal highway builders and almost exclusively the railroad section hands. They pick much of the cotton in Texas and Arizona, they tend vineyards, citrus orchards, walnut groves and melon fields in California, they care for the sugar beets in Colorado, Wyoming, Montana, and California, they are in the copper mines of Arizona and New Mexico.

Women, too, are numbered among the workers. Though women have not migrated as much as the men, they are being used throughout the Southwest in industry. Their entrance into industry has been gradual, but they are there in considerable number. In the agricultural districts they are engaged in many tasks, weeding, chopping and hoeing beets, picking and packing fruits.

10

Mexican labor is found in the construction and maintenance-of-way gangs as soon as the weather opens up in the Spring and as late as it will permit in the Fall. The vice-president of one western railroad states that his road has a steady employment of about 1,036 Mexicans, and "during the summer when construction work is in progress" an employment of as many as 1,476. The engineer of maintenance-of-way of another railroad states that his road employs approximately 9,000 Mexicans. Only 4% of these, he states, are employed in "other than maintenance-of-way forces." Practically all of the Western railroads employ Mexican labor. One road reports "normally 1,800, the number increasing to about 2,900 during the peak season in track work, and to some extent they are employed in the store departments." Another road reports employment of as many as 2,600 in 1926, mostly used as track men all over the system. According to an official of another railroad, his railway employs 500 to 1,000 Mexicans in track work in Iowa, Illinois and Wisconsin.

Kansas furnishes a good example of their employment on the railroads. Here two or three energetic priests have made a survey of the number of Mexicans in many towns in the State. No less than two or three families are to be found on every section of certain of its roads. The Mexican population by families in a number of the towns is as follows: Manhattan, 12; Salina, 60; Harrington, 40; Kanopolis, 35; Belleville, 15; Norton, 3; Ellsworth, 5; Kansas City, 1,000; Topeka, 600; Hutchinson, 60; Lyons, 35; Newton, 48; Wichita, 125; Chanute, 80; Parsons, 50; Coffeyville, 25; Arkansas City, 20; Independence, 40; Abeline, 15; Ottawa, 12; Junction, 12; Lawrence, 10; Horton, 200.

Many of the great industrial centres claim their quota of Mexican workers. They are to be found in the steel mills of Gary, the slaughter and meat packing houses of Chicago, Kansas City and Omaha, the mines of Arizona, New Mexico and Colorado, and railroad construction work and maintenance-of-way. In Chicago the 1925 Report of the Department of Public Welfare lists 1,042 in the steel mills, 606 in the foundries, and a considerable but uncomputed number in the railroads and packing houses.

In one large cotton mill in a southwestern city the entire force of 400 is made up of Mexican women and girls. Many of the girls appear under the age limit set by the Child Labor laws. In a cigar factory 600 women are employed in one city of the Southwest. Mexican women are also found in the garment factories making overalls and jumpers.

Being good needle workers, they are used also on finer work, such as
infants' and women's wear.

FAMILY LABOR

The practice of contracting for family labor is not uncommon especially in the cotton, fruit and beet fields, where whole families are
hired to care for a certain acreage. In the early morning at the market
places in some of the cities of the Southwest where labor agents hold
forth, whole truckloads of workingmen and their families are seen being
taken to the fields where jobs have been secured for them.

CHILD LABOR

Family labor brings its quota of child labor. Child labor is used to
a great extent in the beet fields and in the cotton fields. In a personal
visit to the beet fields, many children were found to work "from sunrise
to sunset." A 1926 study in Colorado made by the National Child
Labor Committee listed 650 Mexican children doing some kind of farm
labor; 292 of these assisted those growing beets. The children work
long hours in the sun doing the topping and weeding. Especially in
the beet industry of Colorado it is claimed that the labor of children
is needed. Except among a few, local sentiment seems to be with the
industry and a general opinion prevails that the work of the children in
the beet fields "doesn't hurt them." The Knights of Columbus Mexican Welfare Committee of Colorado holds a contrary view. It insists
that "the welfare of the child should be superior to the needs of the
industry," and that if Child Labor laws are enforced, "the industry will
quickly find out how to adapt itself to the new condition . . . and
be the better for it."

WAGES

The wages of the Mexican workers are very low. Priests and Bishops
speak often of the poverty. The Committee on Mexican Immigration
for the Federation of Labor in one state declares the Mexicans in the
agricultural district in the Southwest are working for as low as $1.50
a day. It was stated by an official of the Chamber of Commerce that
they receive as much as "white labor" especially in the Imperial Valley.
There is discrimination in the wages paid Mexican and American labor.
In certain railroad maintenance-of-way gangs Mexican labor receives
twenty-eight to thirty-two cents an hour while at the same work
American labor receives forty-two cents.

The beet money attracts the Mexicans. Twenty-three dollars an acre is paid; the whole family works and the contract usually provides for 25 acres. This brings the actual earnings of the Mexican and his family to $575.00 for the beet season. According to a study of the National Child Labor Committee, the average estimated income for all families *from all sources* was $743.00 a year. In the steel mills and factories the wage paid, local reports declare, averages $2.50 to $3.00 for an eight-hour day.

The wages of women are very low. For domestic service and general housework, they can be had in any number in some of the Southwestern states for four or five dollars a week. In one large factory the information was locally given that the wages paid the women would not average ten dollars a week. In another factory where house aprons were made, it was reported that the women are receiving ten cents for making house aprons that retail for $1.89. On several occasions factories were pointed out and the comment was that they had "moved in from New York in order to have the cheap labor of women and girls."

ATTITUDES TOWARD MEXICANS AS WORKERS

A controversy is on between employers and workers and others about the employment of Mexicans. Opposition to Mexican labor is one motive behind the attempt to pass the Harris-Box bill to restrict Mexican immigration and place it on the quota basis.

The Chief Statistician of the International Brotherhood of Maintenance of Way Workers says: "Mexicans are driving American citizens out of jobs, the reason being that they (employers) can impose any kind of working conditions upon the Mexican peon, work him long hours and pay any miserable wage they like." A prominent labor official says the Mexican is "nothing better than a slave. . . . and accepts any condition without protest."

According to the Secretary of the Federation of Labor in one state visited, about 13% of the workers were Mexicans in a chain of sugar companies in 1913 while in 1926, 50%. He charges the chain of sugar companies with compelling the coal company to hire the Mexicans after it is through with them.

Labor leaders in that particular state are convinced of a combination between the coal operators, the sugar companies and others and say the situation is against the public welfare. Interlocking ownership is accused of controlling costs, shifting cheap Mexican labor back and

forth and keeping wages down.   The American Federation of Labor
has taken a definite stand against unrestricted Mexican immigration.

One man in a semi-official position with one of the great railroads,
and unsympathetic with the employment of Mexican labor, declares:
"The Mexicans are schooled to meet the plans of the railroads.   They
are first set to digging or working on the tracks.   Then they take the
smartest of them and promote them to cleaning around the yards and
depots; then they promote them to labor in shops, next, to helping
mechanics, and then, in case of a strike they have their own 'scabs' to
carry on."

On the other hand, there is the contention that conditions in the
Southwest and other places unquestionably demand Mexican labor and
that the withdrawal of Mexican labor from the Southwest would para-
lyze the industries of those states.   The vice-president of one western
railroad wrote in reply to a request for a statement on the subject:
"We use Mexican labor only when we cannot secure American labor.
We do not feel American labor is being displaced."   Another railroad
official similarly writes: "Native laborers are getting scarce in this work.
Mexicans make good track labor. . . .   The employment of Mexican
labor is essential in the Maintenance of Way Department. . . .   The
employment of Mexicans is caused by the scarcity of Americans for
this class of work due to the non-stability of track forces and higher
wages paid for other kinds of work which Americans prefer and follow.
Americans are not displaced by Mexicans so far as our track work is
concerned."

A California railroad official writes: "We do not see how agricultural, industrial, and railroad interests can get along without the Mexican.   He is a very good laborer and we consider him quite essential in
the successful operation of the railroad."   Other qualifications he cites
are, "not radical, easily controlled by those in authority, takes orders
cheerfully."   A Los Angeles Chamber of Commerce official writes:
"We are totally dependent at the present time upon Mexico for agricultural, common or casual labor.   It is our only source of supply."

Members of the Chamber of Commerce in California claim that for
much of the work with the crops Mexican labor is all that is available.
They say the Mexican will work in temperatures American labor will
not tolerate.

As has already been noted much of the employment the Mexican
secures is seasonal and when his seasonal job is finished he is out of
employment.   He drifts to the city and when his money is gone, he be-

comes a public charge. Social agencies repeatedly declare that "the dependency among Mexicans is due to starvation wages and lack of steady employment."

On the whole the Mexican laborer in this country has had little help in bettering his economic conditions. Some of the members of the American Federation of Labor complain that the Mexican refuses to organize. Others say that he is capable of organization and as proof they point to the strength of labor unions in Mexico and charge that there has been no real effort on the part of the standard labor organizations in America to organize him.

The matter was discussed during the convention of the American Federation of Labor in Los Angeles in 1927 and an agreement was drawn up between the American Federation of Labor and the Mexican Federation of Labor that they would recommend to their respective organizations the establishment of emigration and immigration bureaus to which workers and trade unions of the respective countries might apply for information on all economic, social and industrial conditions. It was also agreed that these bureaus would serve as a useful organizing medium for both countries. The Mexican Federation of Labor agreed to send representatives to the United States to impress upon Mexican workers in this country the necessity of joining the trade union of their calling. This agreement has not been lived up to. The present decline in influence of the Mexican Confederation of Labor practically nullifies for the time the possibility of relying upon this agreement.

Outstanding members of the American Federation of Labor declare that efforts have been made to organize Mexican labor and, that while the response has not been what they would like, they have met with some success, particularly in the mining industry, and in some agricultural districts of the Southwest.

A prominent Catholic layman working in the interest of the Mexicans declares that it is very necessary that Mexicans be encouraged to organize. A priest recalls that one reason for the bitterness against the United States felt by Mexicans is caused by the belief that the Mexicans here are exploited, and a prominent Bishop says: "Hatred for us does not bode for future good."

The Knights of Columbus Mexican Welfare Committee of Colorado in its Fourth Annual Report states: "It behooves the people of this state to see to it that existing abuses are done away with and fair and decent treatment accorded to these people (the Mexicans). . . . This is one of the most serious problems facing the Catholic Church in the

state. The movement for the religious and social welfare of these Mexican people should have the loyal support of every member of the
Order in Colorado. They are our people—they are fellow Catholics.
As such they have a right to look to us confidently for help. . . . We
must not fail them!''

The General Secretary of the I. W. W. claims that "a large number
of Mexican workers have joined and are joining the I. W. W., mainly
Colorado miners and beet workers of Colorado and other Western
states." The Knights of Columbus Welfare Committee of one state
denies that the I. W. W. has made much progress, but adds, that "when
representatives of the I. W. W. and other radical groups go into the
fields and talk with the Mexicans, who are already conscious of the
discrimination against them, about labor unionism, exploitation, in-
equality and injustice, they have used the existing bad conditions
effectively to attract and secure followers." The chairman of this Committee says a deplorable economic exploitation of the Mexicans and
Spanish-speaking people is taking place under the very noses of the
Catholics, who ought to be the first to raise their voices in protest and
to help introduce reforms for better working conditions. The Knights
of Columbus Welfare Committee in Colorado and representatives of
the Knights of Columbus, particularly in New Mexico and Texas, and
a number of the Bishops have on many occasions spoken against their
bad working conditions.

EXPLOITATION

Exploitation of the Mexicans is practiced in many ways. The
Mexican Consuls visited complained of companies that take up the immigration papers of Mexicans and refuse to return them if a worker
wants to leave before his employer is through with him. The assistant
to the Mexican Consul in one city permitted the reading of the letters
on file in his office which told of high fees paid by Mexicans for jobs.
Another Consul told of Mexicans who had worked for three months and
had been dismissed without pay and had been threatened, if complaint were made, with deportation for illegally entering the country.
An official of the Chamber of Commerce in Los Angeles says that illegal
entrants are used by exploiting employers who when they wish to
"jump the contract or cheat the laborer" threaten to send him back
over the border.

The story is common of high prices charged by the commissary cars
that some of the railroads send out to supply the men in the camps.

A comparison of the price list of one car with the prevailing rates in the local market shows a great disparity. Soap, ordinarily five cents, is priced at ten cents; coffee at thirty cents is sold for almost double the price.

Labor agencies seize upon the Mexicans for private gain. A certain type of employment agency gets the Mexican a relatively good job for which he pays an exorbitant fee. During an interview with a railroad general official, he gave the information that his road was the only one in his railroad center that did not support its own employment office from the fees charged for jobs. He added that these railroad employment agencies maintain a system of hiring, firing and rehiring in order to keep the coffers of the agency filled, sometimes even sending out a "disturber" to roust the men off their jobs so that they (or others) can be rehired.

It is not unusual for Mexicans to be exploited by their own countrymen. In a middle western city comment was made upon the arrest of so many Mexicans. Investigation showed that a Mexican policeman entrusted with the charge of Mexicans was arresting many, imposing upon them a five dollar fee on the pretext that they had to pay so much to the "law," and was then letting them go.

The Mexican Consul in a middle western city produced letters to show that bus drivers frequently negotiate to carry Mexican laborers from one place to another at dishonest rates. In one case cited, the driver collected thirty dollars for the trip, taking the laborers part way and then stopping in a small town presumably for them to have something to eat. He drove off while they were eating and left them stranded

A Savings Association on the western coast was reported as encouraging the Mexicans to deposit money with the promise of high interest for short term deposits and then charging heavy fees for withdrawal. Cases of inhuman treatment of the Mexicans are not infrequent. In one of the middle western states, there is a law on the statute books which prohibits the use of public funds to pay the burial expenses of the poor. Where families are too poor to pay the funeral expenses, the body must be turned over in twenty-four hours to a medical college for dissection. This law operates against the poor Mexican, who, because of low wages, has no funds to carry him through the periods of unemployment, sickness and death. Low wages and bad working and living conditions are blamed by many for the dependency and for the apparent lack of interest in citizenship.

RELIEF

In many cities with a large Mexican population, the Mexican is a great burden on the charities and social agencies of the city and state. His labor is seasonal, when his job is finished he is out of employment; his wages are insufficient to carry him and his family over this period of unemployment, and he becomes a public charge.

In El Paso the Secretary of the Board of Managers of the County Hospital reports that from September, 1927, to September, 1928, there were 1,172 Mexicans, three times the number of Americans, served at the county hospital. One hundred and twenty-six Americans went through the general clinic and 9,890 Mexicans. Forty per cent of the cases cared for by the Associated Charities were Mexican.

In 1926, one County in California, paid for the hospital care of its Mexicans $328,075.90. Forty-four per cent of the cases of tuberculosis treated by the Charities Departmental Clinic were Mexicans and the Mexicans made up a large number of other case loads. The Executive Secretary of a County Welfare Committee reports that 30% of the total budget was spent on the Mexicans. Its maternity department spent 73% of its budget. The Catholic Charities in the same city use 50% of its budget in serving the Mexican population. Out of 3,241 homeless men from thirty-one nationalities served during one winter month in 1928, it was said 250 of them were Mexican. The same story of relief work is told everywhere. Out of 538 Mexican families in another community, 71 were receiving relief.

DELINQUENCY

The pastor of one of the large Mexican parishes in Texas said, in commenting on delinquency of the Mexicans: "We need community houses, social centers and trained workers. We have little to offer." There are many cheap pool halls and cheap moving picture houses always ready to attract them. One city with a large Mexican population has thirty second-class moving picture houses.

One very dependable man doing immigration work says that he has known "children to be given money for smuggling liquor across the line." He adds that the Mexican delinquent is often the tool of the higher-ups and that because of his ignorance of our laws not all the blame can be placed upon him. Those who work among the Mexicans affirm that the Mexican goes to jail as often for ignorance of the law as for other causes, and that new conditions and new customs handicap him.

A Southern paper in commenting on its Mexican citizens, said: "They obey the laws, respect authority, and prosper according to their capacities."

The chaplain of a Western prison made the statement to the Knights of Columbus Welfare Committee of Colorado that of 4,139 prisoners within its walls, 542 were from old Mexico and a number of others were of Mexican descent, but that lacking money, their legal defense had been inadequate. The Knights of Columbus Committee also states that as a result of the fee system of paying public officials for convictions some innocent Mexicans must at least occasionally be convicted.

The different view-points are summed up in the following incident. In one of the industries employing Mexican labor a Labor Commissioner discussing delinquency among Mexicans said in public: "We need more jails for them." A Catholic priest who works with the Mexicans responded: "Give us churches and good working conditions and we'll need no jails."

HOUSING

The Mexicans are found living in the most crowded and unsanitary quarters under conditions much below the recognized minimum of decency measured in American standards. The condition of living among many, especially in the Southwest, is appalling. There are ten, twelve, and as many as seventeen sleeping in one or two rooms with no ventilation other than the door. The rents vary from $1.00 a month to the railroads for box cars to $5.00 and $7.50 for one or two room adobe huts, and $20.00 to $25.00 in other districts.

In districts visited in the beet fields the living conditions are very bad. Here shacks have been built by the farmers for the workers. Many families visited lived in board shacks of one or two rooms, unplastered and unpapered. Part of the guarantee made to contract workers is safe drinking water. The contract is violated in some places, and the laborers drink from irrigating ditches and unclean cisterns.

One of the largest Mexican colonies is referred to as the "corrals." Here the Mexicans, about 50,000 of them, are herded. They live usually in one or two rooms. Outside toilet and water facilities are used in common with the neighbors in the "corral."

The Department of Public Welfare in Chicago made a study of the housing of Mexicans in Chicago in 1925. The report states that they found "much overcrowding, with as many as four or five individuals in each bedroom in nine Mexican homes. In 28% of the homes visited there was an average of four or more in each bedroom and 40% of the one family households contained lodgers." In homes of beet workers visited in Denver, it was frequently found that seven or eight people occupied one room.

The Chief Statistician for the Brotherhood of Maintenance of Way says: "The general housing practice for workers on the railroad right of way is to put old box cars in the railroad yards and let people use them, sometimes with as many as two or three families in the same box car."

Very little has been done, on the whole, to improve the living conditions of the Mexican workers. The poverty of the people and their poor housing and bad sanitation result in lowered vitality and they become easy victims to disease.

It is commonly said that if the Mexican can have a steady job, even though the wages are poor, he will buy a home. In one district in Texas about 800 families own their own homes. These homes are empty during the cotton season but the Mexican returns with his family in the Fall when the season closes. In another city where wages for Mexicans are the highest, the majority of the Mexicans are home builders and owners. According to a survey made there, 63% of them own their own homes and 50% of these have their homes paid for.

CITIZENSHIP AND ASSIMABILITY

The 1910 Census of the United States gives 182,193 Mexicans as naturalized citizens. The number has increased somewhat since then, but the Mexican so far has manifested no marked desire for citizenship. The Mexican resents "Americanization," as such, but he responds quickly to kindly offers of friendship and help, which result sometimes in citizenship. An immigration worker in El Paso says that out of the large population of Spanish-speaking people in El Paso only 1,800 are on the poll tax record. There could be many more, he said, "if an organization would take the responsibility of educating those old enough for citizenship." "With good conscientious work," he added, "several thousand citizens could be developed with little trouble." He says that while seven Mexicans took out their final papers and five their first papers in 1927, forty Mexicans have taken out their first papers in 1928 as a result of special work among them.

Professor Jensen, speaking before the National Conference of Social Work in 1928 at Memphis, said: "The people most readily assimilated are the people against whom the American people do not discriminate. The surest way to bring about assimilation is to break down race prejudice."

There appears to be little chance for the assimilation of the Mexican as long as the status of the Mexican remains as it is. He belongs to a minority whose rights are denied. He is at the bottom of the ladder. There are many towns where he is not served an ice cream cone over the counter and where he is not admitted to moving picture houses which others attend. Many congregations do not welcome him and in places where there is no Spanish-speaking priest the Mexican stays away. In some towns visited in a western state are to be found such signs in the stores as these: "No Mexican Trade Wanted, White Trade Only." A university professor, writing on the subject, says: "There is no reason why the Mexican should not become a citizen of the United States. He is theoretically limited neither in his capabilities nor his occupational field, nor is he disfranchised."

Prejudice against the Mexicans as a race is very strong and it is shown on all sides. Many people go on the theory that "anything is good enough for a Mexican." A Mexican very prominent in civic affairs in one of the Southwestern border towns said: "It is very difficult for even a well educated Mexican to get recognition among the American people." "The Mexicans, however," he continued, "are very sensitive of these feelings against them, and they are thinking a lot and looking to discover who are their friends in America."

CATHOLIC ACTIVITY

Many phases of Catholic activity are being carried on throughout the Southwest among the Mexican and Spanish-speaking peoples. The Catholic Directory tells a part but only a part of the work that is done. Catholic churches and schools have been built, Catholic centers have been established, and still the work is only started. On the whole, wherever Catholic action has been possible even to a small degree it has met with quick response from the Mexicans and Spanish-speaking peoples. Most of the work for the Mexican people has centered around individual parishes.

One outstanding piece of work organized on a diocesan basis is to be found in one of the Southwestern states where, under the direction of the Bishop, the Bureau of Catholic Charities has organized seven community houses and numerous social centers from which Catholic educational and social activities are being carried on. Each of these houses has its full time worker and some have a full time assistant and part time workers. A report of the Charities Bureau in this Diocese shows that through them 159,330 individuals were served in one year. The great majority served were Mexicans. One hundred and twenty-eight Masses were said in these centers. Under the direction of the Bureau the Diocesan Confraternity of Christian Doctrine is pushing a vigorous program. Its aim is to have a "center at the door of every public school and every child not attending a Catholic school in a Catechism class."

CATECHETICAL CENTERS

With approximately 48,000 Mexican children in the diocese, the undertaking is huge but a good beginning has been made. The report of the Confraternity for one month showed 181 catechetical centers reaching approximately 14,415 children. The Bureau of Catholic Charities reports that they have had to counteract Protestant effort, but that, notwithstanding, the Catholic church in that district "is doing more for the Mexican children than the Protestants are doing for the education of their own." A number of the Catholic centers are open on week days for private religious instruction.

MISSIONARY CATECHISTS

Another outstanding piece of work on a diocesan basis is the work done by the Missionary Catechists, who have been invited by the Bishops into three Southwestern dioceses. They now have thirty-five centers. Members of the clergy speak of their work in high praise. These catechists are in isolated places and have already given instruction to many thousands of children and prepared them for their first Holy Communion.

Under great hardships and adverse circumstances many of the priests are doing heroic work. In one Catholic church visited over 20,000 people hear Mass on Sunday morning. There are eight Masses, with from 2,500 to 3,000 people at each Mass. Unable to build a new church and the present church being too small to accomodate them, the balcony has been extended close to the front of the church. Both floors are crowded at the Sunday Masses.

One priest in New Mexico has established two schools taught by the Dominican Sisters. They have an enrollment of about 700 children. Since the establishment of these schools the enrollment in a near-by Protestant school previously established has dropped off to almost nothing. In this parish covering 2,000 square miles, there are more than 800 families of Mexicans and more than 1,200 children. There are no railroads. Travel in this parish is mostly by mountain trails. All are poor.

One parish of seven thousand souls in a city of approximately 80,000 is conducting night and day schools and is giving religious instruction three times a week to children in the public schools. Another church in the same city has a parish school with 450 Mexican children enrolled and is giving religious instruction to 400 children attending the public schools.

A young Redemptorist priest in the Southwest built a church next door to the public school. He has won the highest cooperation from the public school, and the teachers announce his instruction hours. He is also reaching the young people through organized recreational and community work on the principle that social life is intimately related to religious life.

In a district with a Mexican population about 50,000 when extensive Catholic activity began there were four Protestant centers. Three priests have built a very good church and, aided by the work of Sisters, have been able to hold the Mexican people. A generous gift from an interested layman helped to make this work possible.

One priest in California, who built his church and school in a colony of at least 10,000 Mexicans, combatted at first the efforts of fourteen Protestant churches in the district, all of which were trying to attract the Mexicans. Two years ago when the church was built not more than 200 went to Mass, now 2,000 go regularly. There are now only seven Protestant churches in the district with not more than 1,000 in attendance.

In a diocese where the Spanish Americans predominate the distances are so great and the people so poor that there has been little opportunity for Catholic training and education. There were no public schools until 1891 and today the public school system is undeveloped. The children in many places have little opportunity for education except that offered by the Protestant mission schools. In the whole diocese, comprising 104,168 square miles and a Catholic population of 131,579, there are thirty-five Catholic schools. The diocese has cooperated with the public authorities and in more than ten centers schools have been built by Catholic effort in which Sisters teach and are paid from public funds.

A new school and community house have been built for the Mexicans by one religious order. The small school which they had before could accommodate only sixty children. Since the new school was opened 213 children have enrolled and "more are coming every day." At the beginning of the year when the families return from picking cotton the enrollment increases greatly. The school cost $30,000 and the community house $75,000. Most of the work in constructing the buildings was done freely by the Mexicans.

Community houses are commonly looked upon as filling the need for a meeting place and recreation. One community house, established in a border city by the National Catholic War Council and continued for a time under the auspices of the National Catholic Welfare Conference, is now the property of the Diocese. The Council of Catholic Women directs its activities. The entire community considers it an excellent piece of religious and civic work. Four nights a week instruction for citizenship is given for young and old alike. Baseball and other athletic teams have been organized for the boys, home classes for the mothers, and sewing classes and picnics for the girls. Clinics are held.

Vacation schools are being conducted at a number of centers. These are sometimes taught by lay teachers, members usually of the Confraternity of Christian Doctrine, and sometimes by Sisters. One vacation school in the Southwest, taught by the Mexican Sisters of the Company of Mary, has 100 children enrolled. Another taught by four lay teachers has sixty-eight children enrolled. A group of public school teachers in one center is conducting a vacation school in a Mexican rural colony.

Many Mexican children are being cared for and instructed in day nurseries. The Mexican mothers have been forced into industry and the day nurseries are helping them greatly. One of those visited was established by refugee nuns from Mexico. They are caring for 150 Mexican children through the day while the mothers work, and they give full time care to thirty Mexican orphans.

In dioceses where Councils of Catholic Women are organized, they are carrying on a number of activities. In three cities they are operating clinics for the Mexicans. In other cities they are doing "follow up work" for Mexican immigrants and looking after their spiritual and material welfare. Through their efforts, children have been baptized and children of school age given catechetical instruction. In one place they conduct a "rummage store."

The Knights of Columbus in the Southwest and especially in Colorado has been active in educating public opinion and especially Catholic opinion as to the condition of the Mexicans in the United States. Knights of Columbus Welfare Committees in three of these states have published reports of their activities. These reports have had a wide distribution. With the Chairman of one Mexican Committee of the Knights of Columbus, a drive through the beet fields was made to obtain a first-hand view of conditions. Many Mexican families were visited. Every place visited, as soon as he became known, remarks would be made to this effect. "Oh, yes! We are glad to meet you. You are a great friend of our people." Several times they spoke of "The Book," the term by which they refer to the Spanish edition of the *Civics Catechism* of the National Catholic Welfare Conference. This handbook has a wide distribution among the Mexicans. One of the leaders among the Mexican men stated that this book on the rights and duties of citizens has done much to educate the Mexican to the consciousness that he has rights in America.

In various places, books, pamphlets and leaflets published by the "Revista Catolica" of El Paso, a Spanish international magazine, were favorably commented on. Its weekly leaflet "La Propagandista," is distributed gratis at every Mexican Catholic Church in El Paso and in many churches throughout the United States wherever Spanish is spoken.   Both publications are being successfully used in counter-acting widespread propaganda against the Church.

Catholic fraternal and religious societies have been organized by many pastors who are convinced that these help to hold the Mexican people together and arouse them to more zealous cooperation.   In districts in one state the Mexican people gather at each others' homes for prayer and instruction.   One old Mexican man has prepared 30 children for Holy Communion.   Even some of the very young girls are teaching the smaller ones their catechism.

The National Catholic Welfare Conference immigration officer at the largest port of entry in the Southwest is very active among the Mexicans and the Bureau in his charge performs many services for them other than on immigration cases.   It has promoted their interests in many ways and has represented them in civic matters.

The activities are carried on sometimes at great sacrifice.   More than one priest speaks of the long distances covered to reach the people in his charge, and then of the fields still untouched and the steady migration of countless thousands who have little or no contact with the Church, not alone because of the size of the parishes and the limited number of priests, but because of the lack of funds to support the parishes.

In one diocese there is an estimated Mexican population of 80,000 souls in scattered groups.   Only 2,696 children in that diocese are in Catholic schools.   One priest in this missionary diocese, forced to give up his work because of ill health and old age, in writing to his Bishop, told how he regretted leaving, saying: "The limits of my parish are like the horizon; the farther I go, the farther they recede."

In one state where nearly every sugar-beet community has a Protestant mission, Catholic workers are greatly needed.   The head of one of the largest industries in the state, which employs Mexicans in twelve centers, in numbers ranging from 800 to 1,800, says that these people are nearly all Catholics, and he deplored the lack of adequate religious care.

There are forty-six proselytizing agencies in one border city where there are nine Catholic churches and no Catholic recreational centers.   The Bishop says the need is great, but that with the limited means at his disposal it is impossible to meet the need.   According to the Superintendent of schools in that city, 60% of the enrollment in the public schools is Mexican.

The Bishop of one diocese writes that the Mexicans are scattered over 72,000 square miles of his diocese with only twenty-five priests to work in this vast territory; that there is one block of ten counties where many Mexicans live which is not only without a church or parish, but is unattended by a priest; that one priest exploring for Catholics found them widely scattered; and that one block of eighteen counties is without church, chapel, or priest.

Another diocese in the group of states studied has 50,000 Mexicans. Many homes of Mexicans in this diocese were visited. In many of the homes the families gather together for the recitation of the Rosary and a local priest said: "These people are not lost yet, even though they do not have the Church. As long as a nation knows how to pray it is not lost." He added, "It is family prayer that has kept alive the faith of many of them." The Bishop of this diocese said: "It is useless even to talk of caring for the situation. The Mexicans are scattered all over. Our only hope is to retain our hold through missionary resources. The missionary priest must be given the minimum of support, a place where he can live in decency and a place in which to hold services. This cannot be done without funds."

In the *Missionary Catechist* (May, 1928), a prominent churchman in Southern California makes a strong plea to bring the Church to "90,000 churchless Catholics." In the article he says, "physically, morally and spiritually the conditions of Mexicans in the Joaquin Valley are deplorable." He speaks of the missionary catechists as "the one agency alone" which has helped them.

"That the whole Southwest is a missionary problem" was the sentiment expressed before the Catholic Charities Conference in Los Angeles in 1927 by a Catholic authority on the Mexican problem. He says, "The greatest missionary problem that we have is the problem of the incoming hordes of our Mexican brothers." He referred to the "tremendous opportunity not alone for the Church but for the State" in looking after the Mexicans. He urged the work also as a "patriotic duty."

The distances in the rural regions of some of the states are limitless and the priests scarce. In one diocese of the Southwest of 158,000 souls there are but fifteen parish schools accommodating a total of 3,706 children. One church authority there said: "The faithful of the Southwest are too poor to make any large contribution to the Church." The priests travel far, he said, and work hard and faithfully.

The same story is heard every place, that money and workers are needed to make possible the work necessary to help thousands remain faithful to the Church and to counteract the effect of the many proselytizing agencies that are seeking to deprive the Mexicans of their Faith.

Effort has been made to use some of the refugee priests and nuns in promoting work among the Mexican people. Refugee nuns were found engaged in various tasks, teaching school, teaching special classes in Spanish, operating day nurseries, etc. One order of Sisters in a Southwestern city support themselves by operating a bakery. Refugee priests are acting as assistants to pastors of Mexican parishes and as pastors.

Several excellent pieces of work are under the direction of refugee priests or nuns. Nine vacations schools were visited in which the Sisters were teaching children catechism, basket weaving, clay modeling and sewing. One particularly outstanding piece of parish work was organized and directed by one of the refugee priests who has a large parish and with the help of other regufee priests has kept in close contact with his parishioners. In that place the proseletyzers have almost completely failed.

IV

PROTESTANT ACTIVITY

The work undertaken by Protestantism among the Mexicans and the Spanish-speaking peoples in this country is far reaching in its effect. Protestant work among the Mexicans and Spanish Americans in the Southwest according to one authority, is carried on in 391 different centers. The distribution of these centers is as follows: California, 144; Texas, 110, New Mexico, 62; Arizona, 26; Colorado, 28; Kansas, 10; and the remaining centers scattered through Florida, Illinois and Michigan.

By denominations, the Presbyterians are in the lead in the number of points reached. They are followed by the Methodists, Baptists, and Congregationalists in the order named. The field is not limited to them however, and other sects actively at work, it is stated, are the Friends, Mormons, Nazarenes and United Brethren.

The united and organized action of the various Protestant denominations makes the work of the Church much more difficult. Protestant organizations have carried on an active campaign of proselytizing through their various centers and their efforts have been backed by generous funds. It is not uncommon to read of gifts generously given by "zealous friends." While the investigator was in San Antonio a gift of $50,000 to the Wesleyan Institute by a prominent lawyer of the Southwest was announced in the daily press.

Protestants promoting missionary activity in the Southwest recognize that they are working with a Catholic population and they make capital of it. One of their prominent workers makes the following statement in a book of which he is the author: "The future of the Spanish Americans would seem to lie in the hands of the Catholic Church, if she would take advantage of her opportunity." But he adds: "It is needless to talk about the rights of the Protestant Church to work in the field. . . . There has been a challenge of great need to which the Protestant Church could do no less than respond." He makes it appear that because the Catholic Church gives little material aid to the Mexicans, it is neglecting them.

Professor M. D. Handman of the University of Texas, speaking before the National Conference of Social Work at Cleveland, said that Protestant denominations are making inroads into the traditional

29

Faith of the Mexican people. He referred to a partial survey made of Dallas, Texas, where of three hundred families visited nearly fifty families were Protestant.

In California, a worker in the Plaza Community Church claimed that 800 families are actually identified with the Protestant Church, some of them over a period of eight years. Numerous Protestant Spanish and Mexican churches are much in evidence today. Visits to some of them show a moderately large congregation seemingly interested.

PROTESTANT MISSION SCHOOLS

The greatest danger to the Faith of the Mexicans and Spanish American Catholics has come from the well-organized, well-staffed, and well-financed Protestant Mission schools. One state in particular seems to have been selected as the center for their educational and proselytizing activities. In this state alone there are six mission schools five of which are in cities or towns visited during this investigation. These Protestant mission schools give a practical education. Thousands of boys and girls seeking an education find the mission schools ready to supply it either at a very small cost, if they can pay, or for nothing when they cannot. Clergy and prominent lay Catholics living in cities where mission schools are located report that workers for the schools go to the rural districts and even into Mexico to recruit students. Their catalogues show that hand in hand with the education goes a well-organized program of proselytizing. These schools have much in a material way to offer and they present many inducements to the parents to send their children to them to be educated.

School A, one of the most active, has for its ultimate purpose the training of Mexican young men for the Protestant ministry. Nearly the entire enrollment at this school is locally reported to be Catholic. The students are not permitted to attend Catholic services. The catalogue contains the following statement: "All pupils are required to attend church services, either at the Presbyterian Church at ————— or at the Spanish Presbyterian Church at ————— every Sunday morning, Sunday School at the school on Sunday and one of the Christian Endeavor meetings in the evening and all other religious exercises of the school." One of the local Catholic priests and some of the prominent laymen declared that the Superintendent was asked to permit the Catholic students to come to the Catholic Church and denied the request. This school has some two hundred acres of land which the students are required to work. They raise fruit and vegetables, and feed for the Holstein herd and hogs. The boys are taught farming. The catalogue reads that the school hopes to foster "a greater desire on the part of the boys for farm work."

School B, a secondary boarding school for girls and boys, five miles out of the city is under the care of the American Missionary Society. It too, recruits its students from the rural communities. It is an industrial training school. A maximum enrollment of 135 pupils is reported to be two-thirds Spanish American. Forty were refused admission on account of lack of room. A scholarship is one hundred dollars a year, with two hours service daily on the part of the pupil. A new administration building has just been made possible through an appropriation of $35,000 from the American Missionary Society and $10,000 secured through the labor of pupils and teachers. The students here, too, it was locally charged, are not permitted to attend Catholic services.

School C is one of the outstanding schools in the Southwest for Spanish American girls. A leaflet sent out from this school contains the following paragraph regarding persons educated in the missionary schools: "It is nothing short of miraculous how these boys and girls who have lived such a primitive, simple life under the domination of such a spiritually poor type of religion as Roman Catholicism, absorb the ideals and teaching of these schools and become loyal Christians. A typical case of a student is that of a boy who was first denied a place for lack of room. He refused to give up and applied again and was accepted. For two years he did not take part in Christian work of any kind. Finally, however, he felt the call and joined the Protestant Church, for which he was disinherited by his uncle. He was for three years one of the leaders in the school, graduating last May, and is now a Young Men's Christian Association Secretary for Mexican boys in a border city."

School D is a select school for Mexican boys and girls where they may go from the grammar grades through high school. More than 300 students were enrolled last year. It works in close cooperation with the Methodist Church nearby.

School E, an endowed school, is under the auspices of the Board of Missions of the Methodist Episcopal Church, South. The initial investment was said to be $53,000, a gift from a prominent attorney of the Southwest. The purpose of the school is to provide for the preparation of Mexican boys and young men for the ministry among their own countrymen. Most of them being without means, friends provide scholarships. "We know no better way," their advertising literature says, "for Christian people to aid in the cause of the missions than by assisting worthy young men. They are the hope of the church in Mexico." This school specializes in theological and industrial training, both in day school and night school. Board, room and laundry is $175.00 a year and the school offers opportunities for students to earn their way through. It has a fine dormitory and in the industrial department, an auto repair shop, a tailor shop and a carpenter shop which enjoy a patronage among Protestants of the city near by who are interested in the school.

School F, with twenty-three teachers on the staff, provides complete grade and high school work and industrial training. Its main purpose also is to train for missionary work. It is under the direction of the Women's Missionary Council of the Methodist Episcopal Church, South. The catalogue says: "All students are required to attend church and Sunday school on Sunday." Asking for an explanation of this clause, and if Catholic students were free to attend the Catholic Church, the written answer from the Superintendent is here given: "We maintain a Sunday School in the Institute and boarders must attend the same. Our preaching service is held Wednesday evening. All students on the campus are required to attend. However, denominationalism is not in evidence. Fully 90% of our children are members of the Catholic Church. No effort is made to proselytize." The expense for attendance at this school is $15.00 a month.

School G, for the education of young Mexican men for the ministry, is operated by the Board of Missions of the Methodist Episcopal Church, South. When a survey was made several years ago, around thirty students were reported. It now numbers 140 boarding students, 80% of whom are from Mexico. The school has recently acquired fifteen acres of land adjoining the original five acres. A three story brick administration and classroom building has been built and a $50,000 gift was recently made to help pay for a new dining hall and dormitory; the dining hall will seat 175 students.

School H is an institution for girls under the direction and control of the Women's Home Missionary Society of the Methodist Episcopal Church. According to the catalogue, this school "affords excellent opportunities for a good education according to Christian principles and sane morals." Girls from 12 years and up are admitted. They enter as resident students and the cost for room and board is $12.00 monthly. The parents of the girls may visit them any day save Sunday, which is set aside for religious observance.   The girls must attend the Protestant service.

School I (Presbyterian) gives attention to the Protestant religious education of the Mexican children.

School J requires "all students to be in weekly Bible study classes and to attend Sunday morning services in the ———————— Methodist Church."   The tuition, including board and room, is $180.00 a year.

In addition to these Protestant mission schools offering higher education and industrial training to the boys and girls, there are numerous Protestant parochial or mission schools dotting the whole Southwest, particularly New Mexico, California and Colorado.

PROTESTANT COMMUNITY CENTERS

Often priests speak of the part community centers play in the program of proselytizing.   These centers give well directed physical education which appeals especially to the Mexican boy.   In many places the community houses offer the only recreation.   One of the priests said: "If only they would give recreation without trying to make them hate the Church!"   "Why," he said, "right here in this Catholic state with its Catholic heritage, the second generation after their training with Protestants will boo at a priest as he goes by."

On calling at a community center in one city, the first thing which attracted my attention was a large cross on the wall.   At the point of intersection was tacked a large red paper heart, which was readily interpreted as providing the appeal of the Sacred Heart to the Mexicans. One room in this center was set aside for the chapel and in one corner of the chapel was a baptistry.   The remark, "Oh you go the whole way here," brought the answer from my attendant, "Yes, our minister feels that his job is not finished until he has baptized these people into the church."   In reply to the question, "But don't you find them already identified with a Church?" the answer was: "Oh, yes, they are all Catholics and we find it very hard to get them."   A second worker, who had previously been silent, said: "That is our bone of contention here. I insist it is not good social work to proselytize, but our minister thinks we must get them away from Catholicism.   Our present minister is not so bad as his predecessor who spent all of his time ranting against Catholicism."

At the Mexican Christian Institute in another city, Mexican young women were active.   The day nursery, which houses forty-five babies was airy and clean. The Mexican woman in charge opened a cupboard to exhibit the clothing which the children had worn at the nursery. The babies are bathed by the Mexican women attendants, their clothing changed to clean dresses or suits provided by the Institute.

A community center in one large Mexican center is conducted by the Methodist Episcopal Church and is situated a block from the old Catholic Mission, until recently the center of Catholic Mexican activity. It describes itself as a "Philanthropic, non-profit, non-industrial institution, placing emphasis on moral and spiritual values in all its contacts." A circular given me on my visit sets forth that its program is four-fold: Religious, Educational, Clinical and General Aid. Important features of these departments are a well-organized church, Sunday School, Epworth League, Junior League, Ladies' Aid Society and a Men's Brotherhood, a Training School for student-pastors and other Christian workers, and a Children's Home for Mexican orphans and half-orphans. Its support comes largely from the Board of Home Missions.

A Methodist community center in one city does most of its work with young men. It is educational and recreational. It has a library, gymnasium and full-time physical director. It boasts the champion basket ball team of the city, the members of which it was locally said, are all Catholics. The initial investment here was about $35,000.

A Methodist settlement house in the same city has an investment of about $40,000. It maintains five workers on the staff. It has a clinic, a full time nurse, a visiting nurse and five doctors on the staff. Domestic science and sewing are taught to the girls and women. Boy Scout and Girl Scout troops have both been organized. A party is held every Friday evening for all Mexican children of the community.

A Baptist Institute visited was found to be largely recreational. Its aim is to attract the children. Many are enrolled in the Baptist Sunday School classes, notwithstanding the fact that the patronage of this Institute is said to be 100% Catholic.

An Episcopal center was one of the most attractive visited in the Southwest. It is built around a patio, at the back of which is an altar built of Spanish tile. In the center is inlaid a rose colored cross. Surmounting the altar is an iron cross and at each side are beautiful candle sticks. Because of its Catholic appearance it attracts many Mexicans. It is a beautiful Spanish building rearing its two stories in the midst of the adobe huts of the neighborhood.

A Methodist community house in another city has a clinic which serves more than 3,000 Mexican children a year. It has also a day nursery, a kindergarten in which sixty children are enrolled, a mothers' group and a vocational training class with many mothers in attendance. A gymnasium for the young men attracts large numbers. Each person served through the community house must attend religious instructions.

A Methodist maternity home in one city is an exception. It was spoken of in friendly terms by both Catholics and Protestants as one place where there is no proselytizing.

Both the Y. W. C. A. and the Y. M. C. A. are carrying on extensive programs of education. The Y. W. C. A. works chiefly through its International Institute at San Antonio, Los Angeles, Austin, Fresno, Oakland and San Francisco. One of its community centers is in charge of a specialist in Mexican work, a woman who has had training in settlement work and who speaks Spanish fluently. In all departments it is using Mexican women. It has a Mexican Catholic Girls' Club at this Institute because, the director said, it wishes to have Catholic interest and appeal.

One Y. W. C. A. worker assured me they never proselytized, but she added that "they took up work only where the Catholics left off on account of the rules of the Church." When asked for an explanation, she cited the case of a young Mexican woman, married by the priest, who lived with her husband until after three children were born, when, because of "non-support and cruelty," she had to leave him. She then found a man who was good to her and would marry her. "Of course," said the Y. W. worker, "the Church could not take care of this matter so we took up the case, showed her how to get a divorce and arranged for a second marriage. You see we just help out."

Sunday picnics are frequent. The girls are told to go to Mass first, but usually do not do so because of the early hour set for the picnic. The Y. W. C. A. worker said, "We always tell them they must go to some service in the evening to make up for it." She took me to call on some of her Mexican friends. It was noticeable that they knew and liked her.

The Y. W. C. A. has much activity at its centers and a sufficient number of trained workers. It has sent one Mexican young woman to New York for training. It is distributing literature, well prepared, instructive and attractive, on the care of the home and the baby, how to buy, etc. But evidence that it is proselytizing is not lacking.

A Southern Baptist social center in the Mexican part of one city was visited. It operates a day nursery and clinic. As a reward for Mexican children coming to Sunday School, they are taken to the "big church," the name given the Baptist Church downtown.

LITERATURE

A publishing house in a Southern city publishes a magazine and many pamphlets and books. This company is locally held to be responsible for certain very anti-Catholic sheets distributed monthly among the Mexicans in that city.

Proselytizing agencies criticise the Catholic Church in books and speeches and tell the Mexicans that "the Catholic Church fails to take care of them and that the Protestants must enter the field." They use every means to attract the young people and even to deceive them in a number of places, distributing medals, holy pictures and rosaries. One of the Missionaries told me of the threat made to Mexican children to deprive them of their Christmas baskets if they continued to go to the Catholic Church.

The pastor of a Mexican church in Los Angeles reported some of the Protestants' methods. One denomination distributes pictures of our Lady of Guadeloupe. Some of the agencies say to the Mexicans: "We are not Protestants, we are Catholics." Children are taken to the summer camps with all their expenses paid. In one town visited a number of Mexican children were following the Salvation Army. Seven under ten years old proudly stood with the Army on the corner playing ukeleles. One Mexican boy said, "The Mexican loves music. They give them the ukeleles and the Army Captain always has nickels and dimes to give away."

"We are all Catholics," said another minister, "We can pray in any church." Mexican women were reported saying the rosary in one Protestant Church. When the action was commented on, the minister said: "We can't take everything away from them at once."

At one Protestant social center the boys were trained to sing and were given a dollar each to sing at one of the Protestant churches on Sunday evening. This was the first step; the second step takes them into Sunday morning services. A wealthy business man, whose church is referred to by his name because of his generous contributions to it, holds out a standing offer of a shining quarter to every Mexican boy or girl who will attend his (the Protestant) Sunday School.

The *Missionary Magazine* not long since told the story of a little mission in the basement of a Baptist Church which counts evangelism its greatest means of victory. The minister is quoted as saying, "We have baptized more than 700 Mexican converts, chiefly adults. The Mexican Christians, pulling away from the Roman Catholic Church, are missionary in spirit." Here and there Mexicans are visited by the Baptist and Methodist ministers in their endowed chapel cars.

A priest in one of the western states tells of one Baptist church located in the heart of the Mexican colony that has fifty Mexican children in attendance each day. The teacher, when asked if any of these children were Catholics, and if so, were they encouraged to change their religion and attend the Baptist Sunday School, answered promptly, "Oh, of course, that is the point of all our work." At this same church there are 125 Mexican children and adults in attendance Sunday morning.

In another district the Methodists are conducting a daily vacation school. A large number of the 365 children registered in this school are Mexicans. One of the teachers in charge stated that, "It is rather hard to change the Mexican children after they have been instructed in the Catholic faith for the first ten years of their life, but we are trying to enlighten them, as the priests have kept them in darkness in Mexico." Each child who brings five other children to this vacation Bible School is rewarded with a box of candy.

The religious program is paramount in these vacation schools. The first part of the session is devoted to chapel services and Bible stories; afterwards the children are given some form of handwork to attract them. Many of these Catholic children go to the Protestant recreational centers in order to learn to sew or make attractive articles of various kinds. Almost without exception the Protestant activities are supported by national funds or missionary offerings.

V

OTHER FORMS OF ANTI-CATHOLIC ACTIVITY

Anti-Catholic activity is evident throughout the Southwest. Protestant proselytizing agencies in the United States and representatives of the Mexican government take advantage of the situation of the Catholic Church in Mexico to spread false propaganda about the Church. One of the priests in a western state where there has been much of such activity says, "Lies about the ignorance of the Mexicans and the condition of the Catholic Church in Mexico have been told the Mexicans."

The Mexican pastor of a Presbyterian church in the West has publicly stated: "The Catholic Church is the greatest enemy Mexico has ever had. Our real guns must be made in the schools and colleges!

An excerpt from a book having wide distribution follows: "Mexico has two enemies in the hour of her Reconstruction—the Yankees and the Priests, the Pope and the United States. The Capitol at Washington and the Vatican Palace have hurled threatening bolts against the Capitol of Mexico. Why? Because the work of Liberation of the Radical Party of Mexico has tried to reconquer the soil of the country, which an obstinate despotism sold to Americans, and to reconquer her National Soul which an obstinate despotism sold to the Vatican. Business was in the hands of the General Headquarters of the Mercenaries of Washington; the Churches in the hands of the General Headquarters of the mercenaries of Rome."

In three cities quite remote from each other in the district visited, samples of literature denouncing the priest or Bishop were distributed.

Proselytizing agencies seem to have means to travel where they wish and to promote many types of activities. They tell the people that they are neglected by the Catholic Church which wants only their money. In the beet fields where economic conditions have not been good, there has been much agitation against the Church. Many thousands of copies of the *Solidaridad*, an I. W. W. publication, have also been distributed among the beet workers. The Chairman of the Knights of Columbus Mexican Welfare Committee in Colorado thinks that the effect has been very bad. He says that, with anti-Catholic and communistic doctrine being dinned constantly into their ears, some of them become victims and begin to believe the Church is wrong. Nothing will counteract it, he said, but united, well financed effort on the part of the Catholics of America.

VI

EFFECTS OF PROSELYTIZING AND ANTI-CATHOLIC ACTIVITIES

"It depends upon Catholic action whether or not the future of the great Southwest is to be Catholic or non-Catholic," was a thought expressed many times during the course of this study. When a certain eminent Catholic prelate was asked about the truth of this stateemnt, he said: "It depends upon Catholic action, organized and directed, whether the future population is to be Catholic or *anti*-Catholic."

A Protestant writes that although their missionaries entered the field in the Southwest as early as 1850, their activities have netted them an affiliation of only 30,000 souls. The number who are becoming Protestants is not large, but the work of the Protestant agencies is far reaching.

On occasions one hears such statements as these: "Don't worry about the Mexicans. You can't make Protestants of them." "A Mexican is always a Catholic at heart." "They always come home to die." "They follow the Protestants only for material gain."

One Bishop said: "The pity of it is that one soul should be lost to the Catholic faith, when, with their inherent love for the Church, they would respond so quickly to Catholic effort."

A young priest, working for the Mexicans, said: "How we are fooling ourselves! 'Always a Catholic?' 'Come home to die?' What satisfaction is there in that, perhaps after a life of sin, lacking all reverence for the Church?" Another said: "In all my experience I have never yet been called to the deathbed of an apostate, and there have been a considerable number of them made by the mission schools." As a matter of fact, many of those who actually join the Protestant churches are very fervent and exert great influence with the other Mexicans.

A Mexican young man who seemed to be in charge of a Baptist Mission church visited, when asked the question, "Are you a Catholic?" answered, "No." The remark then was made, "Oh, your parents were Baptist, too?" The answer, with a sheepish look, was, "No, Catolica."

A Catholic teacher in one of the most densely populated counties of one State said that the majority of the county staff of teachers of Span-

40

ish descent received their education in the mission schools. All of them had Catholic parents but are themselves Protestant.

Lack of sufficient religious training and education, and in some places none at all, combined with the work of Protestant preaching and anti-Catholic attacks, is having its effect on the attitude of the Mexican toward the Church. Many of them are indifferent. Talk is common about the lack of understanding of Catholic doctrine. A Bishop of the Southwest says they are a strange combination of "piety and folly." "The attitude of the Mexicans toward the Church," he continued, "is one which needs study in order to be understood."

Even those who have become very indifferent usually, though, have their children baptized. Priests say even that some of those who have joined Protestant churches and appear fervent come to the padre for baptism of the children.

In one parish of 1,200 families the priest told me 221 families had left the Church and become apostates. These he said, have great hatred for the Church and hold it in great suspicion. Another missionary among the Mexicans said the young Mexicans are growing up in many places without religion." Eighty per cent of the Mexican young men in my district are almost unreachable even by club work. They have no religious sense, not even the most elementary Christian sense or teaching." In one parish of great size a missionary reports that he found 200 families that had fallen from the Church. In all cases Protestant activity is blamed. The missionaries say the people are aided by Protestant missions, which are accused of frequently paying parents for allowing their children to go to the mission schools for training.

Many parishes complain that the Mexican will not support the Church, but one missionary father who has worked with them many years declares he has no patience with such accusations. He says they will, according to their means, but that it must be remembered their training has been different. He insists that it is all a matter of training, that the Mexicans, unlike Americans, have not been accustomed to contribute regularly, that they have been raised on a system of fees and that it will take time and a change in their economic status to bring them to the American system of supporting the Church.

It was also stated by some that many of these people think the Church in the United States is unfriendly to them. They do not understand national parochial lines. The priest who has charge of them may be many miles away, and when a priest near at hand does no work among them, they think he is indifferent and they blame the Church for his seeming indifference.

While talking with some of the Mexican people about conditions, one devout Mexican Catholic man said, "The Americans do not understand. If my people could only have instruction in their own language. The Mexicans and Spanish Americans here are very poor. The men wear their overalls to Church. The Americans do not welcome them."

A young Spanish American girl of good education told me that she and a number of her friends had organized a branch of a large Catholic fraternal organization in her community. She said, "If the Americans had organized first we would not have been received." There are even many of the Catholic Churches in which a Mexican cannot feel that he has a right to worship. In one Church attended by the English speaking people were two signs bearing the words, "Mexicans Prohibited." In another Church a sign hung on the very last pew in the Church reads, "Mexicano" interpreted by them to mean "Mexicans, sit here." This pew could accommodate at the most six persons. A missionary, who visited that same place, told me that the sign is keeping the Mexicans away, that when he went there to give a Mission, hunted out the Mexicans in the community and urged their attendance, the Church was completely filled even to the choir loft.

VII

INCREASING NUMBER OF MEXICANS

The ever increasing number of Mexicans in this country presents a social, economic and religious problem of increasing importance to the Catholic Church, not alone in the United States but also to the future of the Church in Mexico.

The Mexican has a deeply imbedded Catholic faith and he clings to Catholic traditions. He responds quickly to Catholic effort, but the great amount of activity being carried on among them by Protestant groups is having its effect.

The Catholic Church has been handicapped in the various dioceses where the Mexicans live in large numbers by the scarcity of priests, trained workers, buildings, and funds. When Mexicans become interested in Protestantism or turn Protestant, it is usually the "outgrowth of a Protestant dispensary, kindergarten, social center, or mission school."

INTEREST IN THE MEXICANS

The problems arising from the increased Mexican population in this country have called forth from many sources interest in the Mexicans. Many are advocating a close and thoroughly scientific study of the situation so that proper remedies may be applied. Educators and churchmen especially say there is need of a better understanding of the various problems connected with the Mexicans in the United States. A number of organized groups are concentrating on this matter, writing about it, holding conferences for discussion and promoting surveys.

The Social Science Research Council has appropriated funds for two studies being made at this time. One of these, a study which Professor Paul Taylor of the University of California is making, is on "Mexican Labor in the United States." Publication of this will be made in a series of monographs issued by the University. The other study, directed also from the University of California, is on the "Antecedents of Mexican Immigration," which has just been completed by Professor Manuel Gamio of Mexico City.

The "Friends of Mexicans" hold conferences each year at Pomona College, Claremont, California, under the joint auspices of the "Friends of Mexicans" and the State Board of Public Instruction of California.

Resolutions were passed at their last conference asking for a close study of the subject before any change is made in the immigration law.

A Committee on World Friendship Among Children has been formed. It has begun the distribution of friendship bags from American children to Mexican children.

Many articles have found their way to the pages of magazines and numerous books have been written. The authors in the main have been members of the Protestant Missionary Boards. Their books have had a wide distribution. One of the latest, "That Mexican," by Robert McLean of the Plaza Community Church (in Los Angeles) and head of the Methodist missionary movement, is at the present time having wide distribution. These writers are encouraged by the Home Missions for the purposes as expressed by the writer of one of the most widely read books: "First, to put into the home missions the thrill of great adventure, such as is rightly felt in the realm of foreign missions; secondly, to stimulate new friends to definite action." The Protestant missionaries are writing of the virtues of the Mexicans and saying nothing about their vices, which they seem to consider a good attitude to take in preparing their workers.

A seminar, organized by Dr. Hubert C. Herring, is held each summer in Mexico City. Professors and students from great Universities are going into Mexico City for study.

The El Paso Conference of the Council of Home Missions is probably the largest of the conferences yet held. Reports were presented on social, educational and religious activities carried on by Protestant groups. Comparisons were made with Catholic work, and plans were made to allocate territory so as to avoid what is considered duplication of money and effort.

The Knights of Columbus in two states have been especially active in bringing the subject up for discussion among their members. Splendid reports have been made to their Councils and they are being educated to a sense of responsibility toward the whole subject.

Bishops, members of religious orders, secular priests and laymen declare the need for more united Catholic action. The following are comments made:

"We need a clergy that is not dependent for sole support upon its parishioners. A priest cannot live on fees he does not get."

"We need more priests." "We need more schools." "We need workers."

"The great need is for community centers, because through these we can show the Mexican people that we are their friends and reach a large number of children through supervised recreation."

"The principle of National churches should be applied to the Mexicans. Priests should not be bound by parochial lines in their work with Mexicans."

"Sometimes there is a large group of Mexicans near at hand and the priest who attends them is fifty miles away."

"Establishment of an employment agency with 'Centers' at each port of entry."

"We need a conference on the subject similar to the El Paso Conference held by the Protestants." "An exchange of ideas on the subject would stimulate interest." "Hearing the experiences of religious orders in the field would be helpful."

"The chief concern of the Church should be the young people. The young people are at the parting of the ways. I am much afraid that the next generation is going to witness heavy losses among the Mexicans. Their whole standard of life is changing rapidly," said a priest who has given close study to the subject. Many priests say the great need is schools, not only primary schools but high schools.

Another said, "we need a Maryknoll for our home missions. If American boys will go to China, that same zeal will bring them to the Southwest." "We need trained workers. The success of Protestant organizations working among the Mexicans is that they send among foreign groups workers who are trained and know the language. They secure first hand information and the confidence of the immigrant."

"The Y. W. C. A. and the Y. M. C. A. send their executives to all important social conventions and meetings."

"There is lack among Catholic workers of real professional training."

"The Y. W. C. A. engages trained workers and pays them well and it is able to do constructive and permanent work."

These and similar statements were made in the Southwest by interested priests who were not offering recommendations but merely expressing their ideas regarding the situation. The remarks are submitted here for whatever value they may have.

The Mexican in Chicago

By

Robert C. Jones

and

Louis R. Wilson

Published for the Comity Commission
of the Chicago Church Federation
Chicago, Illinois
1931

INTRODUCTION

This pamphlet is based upon information gathered by Robert C. Jones in a survey of the Mexicans in Chicago during the years 1928-1931. The survey was carried out under the direction of the United Religious Survey of Protestantism in Chicago and presented to a Sub-Committee of the Comity Commission of the Chicago Church Federation. This Committee recommended the publication of a pamphlet based on the findings of this survey and appointed an Editorial Committee to assume charge of the publication, consisting of M. N. English, R. H. Elliot, S. C. Kincheloe, Victor E. Marriott.

It is hoped that this pamphlet may be used by various denominations in their constituencies to stimulate an interest in the Mexican and promote a better understanding of his problems as he seeks for a place in our great city's life. It can be studied by Young People's groups, Church School classes, Women's Missionary Societies and Men's Clubs. Trips might be planned to some of the Mexican Centers, thus supplementing the reading of the pamphlet with first-hand contacts.

The authors make acknowledgment for additional information to Miss Anita Edgar Jones, who conducted a survey in 1928, under the joint auspices of the Immigrants' Protective League and the School of Social Service of the University of Chicago. They are under obligations to Rev. Lacy Simms, who prepared very helpful material on the Protestant Work in Chicago and to Dr. Robert N. McLean, whose book "That Mexican" has contributed largely to the total picture here drawn.

The linoleum cuts which illustrate this pamphlet are made by Mr. William L. Ortiz, a young Mexican artist, who does his work in the studios of Hull House. Mr. Ortiz is a native of Mexico and has made his home in Chicago for some years past. The cover design is intended to portray the Mexican Yesterday and To-day. Yesterday, a peon in the fields of Mexico, to-day a worker in the steel mills of Chicago.

THE MEXICAN IN CHICAGO

BY

ROBERT C. JONES AND LOUIS R. WILSON

THE NEW HOME

Through the open windows of a second-story room opposite Hull House on a midsummer Saturday evening come the jazz strains of a gospel hymn being lustily sung in Spanish. If we were to trace this music to its source it would lead us into the midst of a revival meeting of the Pentecostals. There in a crowded room we would find a Mexican evangelist, eyes shining and face flushed by his enthusiasm, leading the singing, while an orchestra made up of a cornet, two drums, three triangles, and a piano beats out the rhythm with a will. But we do not wish to loiter long within doors. There are other interesting things to be seen along South Halsted during this twilight hour. The strange Spanish signs upon the shop windows put us in the mood for exploration, and we turn our steps southward along the Mexican Boulevard.

First we pass a restaurant whose brilliantly painted walls are covered by designs reminiscent of that Indian culture which Cortez and his followers so ruthlessly destroyed in their conquest of Mexico.

In the next block we pause before the window of a music store and glance at the display of ukeleles, guitars, violins, and wind instruments. This little shop makes phonographic records of music as played and as sung by Chicago's finest Spanish-speaking artists. And from here the records may find their way to the portable phonographs in the box-car homes of Mexican railroad workers all over the United States, or even in the little far-away shacks which house the migratory laborers in the sugar-beet fields.

Across the street a Mexican woman of middle age, straight black hair caught up in a knot at the back of her head, modestly garbed in a long brown skirt and green silk waist, stands beside her husband. They are looking at the primitive *metates* in the window of a grocery store—those crude, stone ironing boards with their stone rollers for crushing the water soaked kernels of corn into the paste from which the Mexican bakes his thin cakes of unleavened bread, his *tortillas*. The woman is evidently considering a purchase. A well dressed young Mexican man

7

passes by, escorting a Mexican girl who is smartly attired in the most modern fashion. They are probably on their way to a dance of the Azteca Club in Bowen Hall at Hull House. The older woman gazes after them in stern disapproval. Then she shakes her head. Such an immodest dress for a girl to wear in public! And to think of any young girl being out on the streets alone with her lover! Such things are never done in Mexico!

The Mexican Boulevard
(Halsted Street)

The young man and woman are passing on up the street. As they go by a pool hall several other young Mexicans watch them enviously. Rubio always was a lucky dog! And to get such a pretty girl! The largest part of the Mexican immigration has been made up of single men or of men who have left their families in Mexico. This makes competition for the women very keen among the young men. However, the Mexican is such

8

a graceful dancer that he can often overcome the barriers of racial difference and secure a partner from among other nation-alities. Miss Anita Edgar Jones has even found some Mexicans taking wives among the Norwegian, the Polish and the German girls. Out on the street the fortunate Rubio and his companion are pausing before the window of a Jewish clothing merchant to admire the splendidly attired wax figures of a bride and groom. The Mexican temperament loves the color and gayety of any festive occasion—especially of a wedding. And these two are young and in love. But this is not the story of Rubio. Let us return and step inside the pool hall.

The Mexican pool hall, of which there are more than fifty in Chicago, is quite as much patronized as a social center, news dispensing agency, and mutual aid society as for its more obvious purposes. And although the Mexican is growing to do more and more business with the banks which are located in the immediate neighborhood of the colony, the proprietor of the pool hall remains one of his most trusted bankers. Here the newcomer to Chicago can most easily fraternize with his fellow country-men; be informed of the ways of the city; secure such small, friendly loans as he may at first need; inquire about the best way to find work; and later leave with the proprietor for safe-keeping such amounts from his weekly wages as he may be fear-ful of carrying upon his person or of leaving in his room in the cheap lodging house where he stays.

But let us end our leisurely walk down Halsted now and complete our survey of this largest of Chicago's Mexican col-onies by the swifter method of general description. The colony centers around Halsted between Harrison and 15th. That is to say, it is located in the Near West Side, a locality which has been receiving newly-arrived immigrants for the past half-century and also, though scarcely by accident, a community which has some of the poorest housing in the city. Here, where rents are cheap, where employment agencies are near at hand, and where numerous industrial plants are within easy reach, is a natural place for the immigrant to begin his life in Chicago. As the successive waves of immigrants have come into the city they have always settled in such communities and then pushed outward to occupy better residential districts as their economic status has improved. As the newest arrival in the immigrant flood the Mexicans are found living in the poorest quarters in the city. The Mexicans of this colony, however, though number-ing between seven and eight thousand, do not wholly fill the district. Between Harrison and Polk Streets and especially on Halsted and Blue Island, the Mexicans are in the midst of a Greek settlement. Between Polk and Roosevelt Road there is a heavy concentration of Italians west of Halsted and of Poles to the east. North of Roosevelt Road a great many Jews and Russians are to be found.

Along Halsted Street the north and south traffic jostles and bumps and clangs its way. Maxwell resounds with the din made by the vendors on the curb market as they scream their strangely assorted wares and haggle over a difference of a few pennies on a sale. Up and down the treeless back streets dilapidated two and three-story houses elbow each other for room and struggle to give shelter to the many families who overcrowd their interiors.

On week days the Old Town Boys' Club on Newberry Avenue reaches out to serve more than two hundred Mexican boys. Firman House on Gilpin Place has its clubs for Mexican mothers and their little daughters. The Infant Welfare Society with quarters at Hull·House labors to teach the mothers of the neighborhood how to overcome the rickets-producing effects of the smoke-dimmed daylight. And Hull House itself opens its classes to hundreds of Mexican students. There they are to be found in the pottery shop, the studio, the musical organizations, the dramatic association, the English classes, and the social groups.

The members of St. Mark's Presbyterian-Congregational Church hold their Sunday School and worship at 1213 Gilpin Place. The Methodists have a church at Polk and Sholto and the Baptists at Monroe and Morgan. In addition there are a number of other missions of the Seventh Day Adventists, Pentecostal and other sects. But at the Church of St. Francis on Roosevelt Road the predominant Catholic background of these immigrants reveals itself. There at the special Mass conducted for the Mexicans nearly a thousand worshippers often kneel and are comforted by the beauty and upreach of the prayers offered in the universal language of the Church of Rome. There at a shrine at one side of the church their own national patron saint, Our Lady of Guadelupe, gazes upon them. From there they go out after the miracle of the Mass has been consummated, assured once more of their souls' salvation.

Such, in brief outward view, is the picture of Chicago's largest and perhaps oldest Mexican colony. It is, however, by no means the only such colony in the city.

Reference to the map on the opposite page will reveal at a glance where the chief Mexican colonies are located. The two most important areas in addition to the one already described, are the Stock Yards district and the South Chicago area. In the Stock Yards district there are three distinct colonies, the largest of which is concentrated around Ashland Avenue and

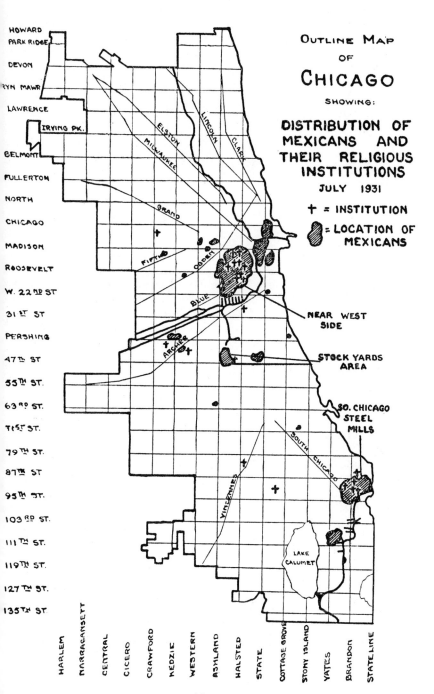

HOWARD
PARK RIDGE
DEVON
RYN MAWR
LAWRENCE
IRVING PK.
BELMONT
FULLERTON
NORTH
CHICAGO
MADISON
ROOSEVELT
W. 22ND ST
31ST ST
PERSHING
47TH ST
55TH ST.
63RD ST.
71ST ST.
79TH ST.
87TH ST
95TH ST.
103RD ST.
111TH ST.
119TH ST.
127TH ST.
135TH ST.

HARLEM
NARRAGANSETT
CENTRAL
CICERO
CRAWFORD
KEDZIE
WESTERN
ASHLAND
HALSTED
STATE
COTTAGE GROVE
STONY ISLAND
YATES
BRANDON
STATE LINE

OUTLINE MAP
OF
CHICAGO
SHOWING:
DISTRIBUTION OF
MEXICANS AND
THEIR RELIGIOUS
INSTITUTIONS
JULY 1931
✝ = INSTITUTION
◖ = LOCATION OF
MEXICANS

ELSTON
LINCOLN
CLARK
MILWAUKEE
GRAND
FIFTH
OGDEN
BLUE
ARCHER
VINCENNES
SOUTH CHICAGO

NEAR WEST
SIDE
STOCK YARDS
AREA
SO. CHICAGO
STEEL
MILLS
LAKE
CALUMET

11

Forty-sixth Street. The University of Chicago Settlement has served as a center for the Mexicans in this community for a number of years. The Settlement has employed a part-time Spanish-speaking worker and several Mexican Societies have had headquarters there. This group is employed mainly in the Stock Yards. The smaller groups to the south and east of the Yards find employment with the several packing houses, the American Can Company and the railroads.

In South Chicago, the various settlements are grouped about the industries. The main colony resides in the area bounded by the Illinois Steel Company Mills on the east, Commercial Avenue on the west, the railway tracks just below Eighty-seventh Street on the north and Ninety-second Street on the south. It is estimated that there are about five thousand Mexicans in this colony which constitutes the second largest settlement in Chicago. Previous to the financial depression beginning in 1929 the Mexicans were fairly well established here with Mexican-owned shops catering to their own people. A number of social and recreational societies are actively functioning and both Protestant and Catholic churches with a Mexican constituency are to be found. These include Our Lady of Guadalupe Roman Catholic Church; the First Mexican Baptist Church of South Chicago; the Baptist Mission of Our Savior and the United Mexican Evangelical Church (Congregational). The great majority of the men are employed by the Illinois Steel Company.

About three hundred Mexicans are living near one of the north gates of the Illinois Steel Company in what is called "The Bush", north of the *Belt Line* tracks between Eighty-seventh and Eighty-sixth Streets.

Another group is located on Torrence Avenue between One Hundred Fourth and One Hundred Seventh Streets just to the west of the Wisconsin Steel Company Mills. Most of the men are employed by the Wisconsin Steel Company. There are a number of Mexican stores in this community but the settlement is really dependent upon the main South Chicago colony for most of its organized social and religious life.

In addition to these main colonies already described, there is a small colony in Brighton Park, mostly employees of the Santa Fe Railroad, the Crane Company Plant and the McCormick Works. On West Madison Street between Clinton and Halsted with its cheap hotels and its employment agencies are to be found the highly mobile population of Mexican men, transients who have just arrived or who are seeking employment on the railroads and outside the city. Between three and six hundred Mexicans are to be found here at any one time, varying according to economic conditions. There are several thousand Mexicans located in railway camps in and about Chicago— camps of varying size and condition. In some the workers live in tumble-down shacks, while in one or two the majority live in cottages having no immediate relationship to the camp. These are the most isolated groups of Mexicans in Chicago but a ministry is carried on for these men by Rev. Lacy Simms, head of the Presbyterian-Congregational work for Mexicans.

There are a number of smaller clusters of Mexicans living in the city who in general are more Americanized than the others. These are to be found for the most part in the rooming house and cheaper apartment house areas and are made up of single men and families occupying a position of relative economic advantage. Examples of such groups are to be found among those who live in the neighborhood of the Wilson Avenue Elevated Station and in Woodlawn.

THE OLD HOME IN MEXICO

But we cannot hope to understand the Mexican in Chicago by merely knowing where he lives, or even how he lives. We need to know something of his hopes and disappointments, his dreams and his bewilderments. If we are really to discover these things we must see him as he once lived in Mexico, and know the forces which impelled him to enter the United States.

Most of the Mexicans in Chicago come from small rural communities of two or three hundred inhabitants each in the thickly populated west-central states of Jalisco, Michoacan, Guanajuato and Zacatecas. The western portions of Jalisco, and Michoacan slope down over the coastal range to the Pacific and have a tropical climate, but the larger portion of this territory lies upon the temperate central plateau in a land of perpetual springtime. It is a region of blue skies, snow-capped mountains, fertile valleys, and swift-running rivers. By the aid of irrigation the soil produces abundant crops. There are valuable timbers and rich deposits of minerals. Many flocks of sheep and goats are pastured.

Yet in the midst of this richness the Mexican has lived in grinding poverty and in ignorance for hundreds of years. In the four states mentioned, according to the 1910 census, less than four per cent of the heads of families owned any property, and less than twenty per cent could read and write. Before the revolution the common wage for peon labor was twenty-five cents

Mexican Basket-Weaver

per day. The coming of the Spaniards under Cortez in 1519 spelled doom for the earlier civilization of the Indians. Between the secular conquerers on the one hand who, when their gold hunting had ended, settled down as large landed proprietors on their richly dowered *haciendas,* and the Church on the other hand with its land and its tithes, the Indian was completely dispossessed. More, he was soon effectively bound to the land by a vicious system of starvation wages and debt slavery known as peonage. Ninety per cent of the people came to exist in slavery, ten per cent to own the land. The present government of Mexico, beginning with Obregon, has made a heroic struggle to give back to the peon his rightful heritage of land and of educational opportunities, yet the long period of revolution was in itself another severe trial to the common people. Marauding bands of soldiers continually robbed them of what little they had.

The villages themselves are made up of little, one-to-three-room adobe houses with hard-packed earthen floors and the crudest of furnishings. Yet they are not unlovely after their own fashion. The soft color tones of the adobe walls take on life beneath the same sun that flashes from their red-tiled roofs. Flowers grow in abundance. And no village is so poor that it does not boast the terra cotta walls and yellow-tiled towers of an ornate church. On Sunday the villagers will all attend mass within that church. And they will linger there to buy votive candles and set them burning before the shrine of the patron saint of the village. Of necessity, life for these people is hard and is lived upon a very primitive level. However, it is lived in the midst of natural beauty; it is held firm and sure by the unquestioned operation of social customs centuries old; and it is fortified by a simple faith centering about the village saint. Occasionally, as at Christmas or Easter or the Saint's Day, it is brightened by colorful festivals with their music and dancing and feasting.

The simple folk Catholicism of these village residents is well brought out in the following fragment taken from the life history of a Chicago resident.

> "In Mexico it was the custom for there to be a little church or chapel in each barrio or community. Each one has its patron saint and all the people living there worship that saint. On the large haciendas there is a little chapel also and the saint there generally has the name of the owner. The hacienda where we lived was owned by Don Miguel de Zepeda so that the saint in the little chapel was San Miguel. It was a large image and all of the people were very fond of it. At certain times of the year festivals were held in honor of the saint. It was very pretty. There were flowers, fireworks, and colored paper decorations.
>
> "After a while Don Miguel sold the hacienda to another man whose name was not Miguel and moved to Saltillo. Since the saint belonged to the Zepeda family, after they got settled in Saltillo they wanted to take it away from the hacienda, and

have it in Saltillo. The peons on the hacienda, however, didn't want their saint taken away. They said that it was San Miguel who made the crops grow. It was San Miguel who had cured them when they were sick. He couldn't be taken away."

To make a long story short, the outcome was that Don Miguel had the image spirited away at night and set up on his new hacienda at Saltillo. When this was discovered by the peons their faith was not wrecked but rather increased because it was believed that San Miguel by his miraculous power had transferred the image to the new location.

It must not be taken too readily for granted, however, that all Mexicans in Chicago have one common background of quiet village life, or that they share one common cultural level, or religious faith. Within the limits of a pamphlet it is not possible to paint the complete picture. It will be sufficient to remark that there are in Mexico many gradations of racial strains from the pure Indian type, through the predominating Spanish and Indian mixed blood or mestizo types, to the negligible percentage of pure white stock. There are numerous Indian tongues and dialects spoken, even to the exclusion of Spanish in some sections. According to Robert McLean there are between 50,000 and 90,000 Protestants in this Catholic country. And while the majority of Chicago immigrants have come from the small villages of the west-central states many have had more widely traveled experiences through following various trading occupations or through life in the army. A small group comes from the cities. The Chicago colonies count within their numbers Mexican "artistes", teachers, and former middle-class business men from the large centers.

THE CALL OF THE NORTH

In 1911 Porfirio Diaz, the dictator-president of Mexico, was overthrown in the first of a long series of revolutions. In the years which followed, the country was swept by one band of rebels after another—often little better than bandits. Peon and trader alike suffered under their raids. In 1914 the outbreak of the World War inaugurated a period of unparalleled prosperity for American industry and of great demand for labor. The entrance of the United States into that war drained thousands of men from industry and made the labor shortage acute. All of this resulted in an open welcome for the Mexican laborer, especially in the Southwest where he came to pick cotton, to tend sugar beets, to work in the fruit and vegetable industry of the

Imperial Valley and the California coast, and to man the railroad section crews. The war-time stimulation of industry had scarcely died away when limitation of immigration from all countries save those of the western hemisphere caused United States industries to make new demands for laborers from south of the Rio Grande. The automobile industry of the north now joined in the welcome to the Mexican. In 1923 the Illinois Steel Mills imported a group of Mexican laborers from Fort Worth, Texas. Meanwhile there had been going on in Mexico a steady increase in the building of railroads and the construction of highways. There was a new freedom in the travel both of news and of men.

Under such conditions the slow trickle of Mexican labor across the border in 1911 rapidly enlarged to the proportions first of a river, then a flood. Letters began to make their way back into the homes of those families whose relatives or friends had gone to the United States. Those letters told of a land of peace and plenty where men were paid three to six dollars a day in wages. Such sums were hard to comprehend. Often the marvelous character of the story grew as it was repeated. The more adventurous, and especially the footloose, began to make their way toward the border in increasing numbers. The single men, naturally, made up the greater part of this movement, followed by those family men who could make arrangements to leave their families behind until growing wealth would justify bringing them into the new home. Lastly came the family groups who moved north as units. This immigrant flood was checked during the depression of 1921 but renewed in 1922 and 1923. Writing in 1928 Robert McLean estimated that at least one-eighth of Mexico's total population was then living in the United States. Today, with a severe industrial depression upon us and quota laws threatening against the Mexican, the stream has dwindled to a trickle once more. Thousands of Mexicans are returning to Mexico to escape starvation in the United States. Yet even so it is doubtful if the actual number of Mexicans in the United States is being materially reduced—the birth rate being taken into consideration.

It would be both interesting and highly worth while, albeit a pain to our conscience, to track the paths of this Mexican immigration out through the fruit and vegetable fields of California and the beet fields of Colorado and other states. That record of a seasonal employment, low wages, poor housing, child labor, interrupted school life, and impaired health has much to tell us. We are primarily interested in how the Mexican got to Chicago. In brief, the roads he traveled were these: 1. As a worker in the maintenance gangs of those railroads piercing the Southwest he was transferred from point to point until he reached the railroad workers' camps in the outlying sections of Chicago. 2. Employment agents of the steel industry hired him in the Southwest and brought him here directly. 3. He came directly to Chicago to find work on the representations of friends who were already working here and reported wages to be good. 4. At the close of the beet season in Michigan and Minnesota he came to the city to seek employment rather than return south.

AND NOW HE IS HERE

And now that the Mexican is in Chicago we wonder how he has been welcomed, and what he is thinking. As we have already seen, we find him living in the shabbiest quarters in the city—not from choice but from economic necessity. When the Mexican first arrives he has but scant wealth and must take what he can afford. Moreover, he must live close to his work. And, so far as that is concerned, it is only in such disorganized sections of the city as exist in these manufacturing, commercial quarters that the Mexican is made welcome. The landlords of our prouder residential districts have not wished to rent to Mexicans. Once started within a given neighborhood the colony grows by the ties of race. The bewildered newcomer naturally seeks out a place to live among his fellows.

Here within the colony the Mexican at first finds a strong spirit of group cohesion. Later he may cross dividing lines which will separate him from some of his fellows by binding him more closely to others in some of the numerous social, mutual aid, patriotic, and religious organizations which come into being as the colony establishes a permanent character. Always, however, there is a strong element of group consciousness exercising a general governing control over the entire colony through the force of public opinion. And for the needy newcomer there is the utmost hospitality and readiness to share with his need. The Mexican is very charitable and hospitable where the barriers of suspicion are not raised. But be his welcome within the colony as friendly as it may, the newcomer is not relieved of the painful necessity of making difficult adjustments to a bewildering new world.

In the field of industry the Mexican soon finds that he is welcomed only as an unskilled laborer at jobs which are the dirtiest and most uncomfortable. At such jobs he is wanted when labor is in demand, but in time of depression he is apt to be among the first to be laid off. Then, too, as he comes into competition with other labor, his distinct racial characteristics

18

set him off as a person to be sneered at and hated. In Chicago the feuds between Mexicans and Poles are well known among all social workers.

The crowded conditions of housing in smoke-filled neighborhoods together with the low economic level result in ill health among many, especially among the babies.

But there is a strain upon the moral health also. This is due to the great proportion of single men and the small number of women in the colonies. The thwarted sex life of the men is all too apt to break across the normal social restraints, and these dangers are aggravated by the fact that many married couples, struggling to make a living, fill their houses with roomers and boarders. There is another phase of this same peril. The Mexican girl finds an entirely different standard of women's dress prevailing in this country. There is a freedom which in Mexico would have constituted an open invitation to male advances. Often enough economic necessity itself demands of the girl that she dress in modern fashion if she would win a job. Once persuaded of this she is apt to go to extremes in her modernity. The men do not understand.

THE MEXICAN IMMIGRANT'S REACTION TO THE PROTESTANT MESSAGE

Although accurate statistics as to the number of Protestants in Mexico are not available a good estimate would be that not more than one out of every two hundred of the entire population claimed that faith. In Chicago, however, one Mexican out of about every thirty is a member of a Protestant denomination or sect. What accounts for this difference? First of all, a much larger number of Protestant Mexicans have migrated from Mexico than their percentage of the total population there would indicate. Then from the time they leave Mexico the Mexicans are constantly being ministered to both materially and spiritually by the Protestant missionaries—in the cotton and beet fields, on the railroads and in the larger industrial centers. Many are won to the new faith.

A great protest has risen on the part of the Roman Church against what they call a proselyting movement. It has been said that the Protestants have disorganized the religious life of the Mexicans by showing them supposed weaknesses in the Catholic Church and have offered them nothing in return; that they have "bought" members through their social service and relief work and that since "the Mexicans are one hundred per cent Catholic they are not subjects of missionary endeavor."

It should be remembered, however, that there are very few Catholics in Mexico whose faith has been developed and shaped by systematic instruction and enlightened teaching. The Catholicism of the Mexican is principally a folk Catholicism developed through tradition and which has incorporated within itself a great deal of Indian and Spanish superstition. However beautiful it may be, however blind the devotion, such a faith is inadequate when the individual moves to a new and more complex environment where a multitude of new problems must be met. In Chicago, at least, in spite of occasional prejudice, some blindness and ignorance and at times overzealousness, the service of the Protestant Mexican missions has been to gather up the bewildered, those who are lost and those who are actively striving to find a better way of living. Very few persons whose lives were strongly organized about the Catholic Church have been taken from that church although many have been given a broader view of their faith and a new appreciation of others.

The Protestant Mexican Churches in Chicago have made four outstanding contributions to the religious life of the people they are striving to serve. (1) They have furnished a church home for those Mexicans who claim the Protestant faith. (2) They have provided groups where individuals who are seeking a "better life" mutually stimulate each other. (3) They have furnished an organization and standards about which many disorganized individuals have been able to orient their lives. (4) Through competition they have stimulated the Roman Church to action in serving its people, moving it to give greater attention than formerly to the intellectual development of its members and to furnish them with more adequate social life through the Catholic Societies.

But let us see what the Mexican himself thinks of the churches and missions with which he comes in contact. Of course, the variety of reactions is as great as the variety of individuals. Many are indifferent.

Epimenio Gonzales is an artist whose life is largely centered around his art and the social settlement in which he has his studio. He is quite indifferent to all forms of organized religion, although he still says that he is a Catholic. He says:

> "My impression is that a comparatively small number of Mexicans go to church. That is probably due to a number of reasons. I don't go because I don't care much about it, and I work so that I stay in bed Sunday morning. I also go to parties and dances Saturday night and stay up late. I think a lot of Mexicans see that the Americans do not go to church so they follow their example. There are a lot more things to do here than in Mexico."

Most of the members of the Mexican Protestant Churches in Chicago belong to the lower middle class. It is difficult for a person of different standards and ideas to find a place in them.

Dario Orozco is a student who has had educational opportunities which place him on an intellectual level superior to that of most of his fellows. He was born and raised a Protestant. On being asked why he was one of the few educated Mexicans who regularly attended a Mexican Mission Church, he answered:

> "The reason why I go to the Mexican Church instead of to an American is because I was brought up to believe that I had an obligation to help my countrymen, especially those who have not had as much opportunity as I have had. I know a number of young Mexicans here who are Protestants but who either go to American churches or don't go to any church. They all have had a better education than the average and some of them are students here. The real reason they don't come is because they don't fit in with the other members of the church."

Dario has learned the often difficult way of getting along with his less privileged countrymen on a basis of equality and without condescension. There are no widely differing Mexican Protestant churches in Chicago, so that those belonging to different social classes must work together in close communion with one another or not at all.

Jose Mendoza is a quiet, sensitive, mystical man who likes to dream. Although he has been attending the Protestant Church for two years, the beautiful ritual of the Roman Church still has a strong appeal and he sends his children to a Parochial School.

> "When I came to Chicago five years ago I don't know what went wrong with me. At times I thought that I must be crazy. I was very unhappy and at times I even wanted to take my life. My wife knew that I wasn't happy and told me to go to the Catholic Church and confess myself. I would go but I wasn't satisfied. When I heard the church bells ringing, I felt glad but after I had gone to Mass I felt sad again. No one seemed to care about me. Everything was strange and there didn't seem to be anything which would satisfy me. Finally one day when I was crossing the street one of my little boys ran ahead of me. As he was crossing, a taxi-cab rounded the corner at full speed. It swept my boy off the curb and killed him. It was a terrible blow. * * * It was at the time of the loss of this child that I found the Protestant Church. It was just about then that I heard it rumored where I could find a Protestant Church. I knew that they had the Bible there, and that was what I wanted. I felt that if I could find that book I could find some satisfaction for my disturbed mind."

21

Unemployment, death and sickness are times of extraordinary crisis to the Mexican immigrant. Not only does he often lack the supporting help of relatives and friends but the traditional ways in which these problems have been met are no longer adequate.

Jose goes on to tell how he found the Protestant Church at this time of need.

"One Sunday morning I told my wife that I was going to condemn myself; I was going to a Protestant Church. I asked her whether I should go alone or not and she said, 'You know that I would go anywhere with you. We will both go together.' So we started out. It happened that the pastor met us. He saw that we were lost so he asked us what we were looking for. We told him we were looking for a Bible. He then told us that the church service was going to begin very soon and that we should go in and wait. When we saw the good people that were there we said to ourselves, 'We have found more than we were looking for.' We also enjoyed the sermons. I was happy again and found satisfaction.

I might say here that although Americans have never mistreated or abused me they have rarely been friendly to me. I have been more or less of a fixture in a house, a useful tool but of no particular concern to anyone. When the pastor showed himself to be so friendly, I was anxious to find out why it was that this American was so much interested in me.

I am very happy in the Church. I have not only learned and grown spiritually, but I have also been helped in my problems. After God, it has been the pastor who has helped me most."

Pedro Hermandez has a back-ground which is strongly Indian. He has never had any schooling but has greatly improved himself intellectually in the church through his efforts to take an active part and his desire to find opportunities for self-expression leading a Sunday School Class or a Christian Endeavor Meeting. His standards of living have been greatly raised since he joined the church. In Spanish which clearly tells of his Indian origin he tells the following story.

"When I was working on the railroad in Harvey, Illinois, an American who was working there invited me to go to church and I went several times although I could understand hardly any English. They offered to give me clothes and a lot of things and asked me if I needed anything. It made me wonder why those people were so good to me.

Two years ago I was out of work for about five months. I was getting in a pretty desperate condition. People kept telling me that if I went to the pastor of the church or joined the church I would get a job. I didn't want to do that though. It seemed to me that if a person joined the church he should do so with a willing heart. I stuck to my principles to the last and didn't go to the church for help. Finally once when I was at my rope's end I sat down and prayed. I didn't know how to pray then like I do now but I prayed **anyway.** It seemed to me as though it were the thing to do. I promised Christ that I would accept Him and join the Church if I got a job. I got a job so I joined the church.

My relations to my family have changed since I joined the Church. My entire life has taken on new meanings. Before I joined the Church I wouldn't last any time at all at my work. I would quit for no reason at all and I would get angry at the boss and ask for my check if any little thing happened wrong. That doesn't happen any more. I used to drink and dissipate. After I joined the church it seemed perfectly easy to quit. It was in the church I came to understand the harm drinking does. I used to throw away as much as fifty or a hundred dollars on a spree, but now I am in the Church I save all that, and I am more careful in the way I spend my money."

Mathew Concha has a rather keen and analytical mind. Although he has left his original church to join the Protestant he sees many points of strength in the Roman church and conceives of the Protestant Church among the Mexicans at least as very largely a liberalizing influence. He is of almost pure white ancestry, and this has opened ways into American life which are closed to most of his countrymen. He has a strong character, and is one of the main pillars of the church. He is one of the few Mexicans who has become an American citizen.

Tomas Echaverria, a mason, was once a very ardent Catholic. He aspired to be a priest. Then came the Mexican revolution and its liberal ideas and along with them came doubt. With this doubt came a desire to completely reshape his life. First he read Schopenhauer and Nietzche, and after going through the agony of having all of his past ideas torn and shaken he began to reconstruct his life following the philosophy of William James. Although only a grammer school graduate he is quite widely read, has a library of a hundred volumes or more and likes to study. He finds the Mexican Protestant Mission too orthodox and too far removed from the scientific and philosophical world with which he has come in contact for it to appeal very much to him.

"I have never been especially attracted by the Protestant Church. Its teaching does not agree with what I learned in physiology and natural science. I would like to find some group which was thoroughly modern to which I could belong, some philosophy of life which I could follow, something which would unify my thinking."

He enjoyed a visit to one of the liberal American Churches in Hyde Park, but did not feel at home there because his background and work were so different from that of most of the members who were business and professional people.

David Alvarado, still a Catholic, has come to appreciate the good in the Protestant Church and no longer considers those who claim that faith as followers of the devil. He has seen the good which it has worked in the lives of his friends, but feels that he is best satisfied to remain in the church in which he was born and raised.

These statements indicate the influences as well as the problems of the Protestant Churches among the Mexicans.

The members of these Mexican Churches, like most church members, are not perfect. Yet the power of the church has been proved in the helping of some to hard-fought moral victories. There is the case of Pablo Rodriguez. Pablo was both a drunkard and a gambler. When labor was scarce he was hired in spite of these habits. Now, in a time of depression, he has been retained in his factory, so he believes, because his church helped him to become a Christian.

Juan Lema has become a sober man, his marital troubles have disappeared, and he testifies to greater satisfaction in life since Christ gives him daily victory—greater satisfaction now even without a job than when he had work but didn't know Christ.

Jose Donato has learned self-control since joining the church. He can now cooperate with others because he now trusts others.

Growth in initiative, ability to cooperate according to parliamentary procedure, increasing interest and ability in self-expression, together with a steady development of character—this is the story of the Mexican as he has taken part in Protestant church life.

The Mexican Protestant churches with their present active resident membership of some four hundred persons have had a history of more than seventeen years. The oldest organized church, however, is only four years old.

During these seventeen years of Protestant work several times more than the present membership have felt the influence of these churches. The aid which these churches have provided in matters of health, the finding of employment, material relief, personal problems, educational classes, etc., is deeply appreciated by the Mexican colony, so that the real influence of Protestantism is far greater than that indicated by any mere numerical test. A great number of persons who have made a contact with the church, and received help have now moved on.

The Mexican Protestant churches in Chicago, with full-time pastors, all have approximately the same number of active members each, sixty to eighty adults. The number of children seems to depend upon the amount of time which the workers can give to them. The only occasions on which the attendance rises above the number indicated above are when special public programs are given. The Pentecostal Church during its 1929 revival increased to more than three hundred, but only for a very limited time.

This suggests the importance of the Protestant Mission Church as a social group which stabilizes the life of its members. The Mexican, accustomed as he is to living in close and intimate relations with his neighbors, feels the need of associating himself with his fellow countrymen in groups where he can find opportunities for self-expression and standards which he can apply to the changing situation in which he finds himself. On migration, practically all of the Mexican's old associations are broken and unless he is already more or less accustomed to the atomized life of the city he feels lost and bewildered. The church group, with the personal and intimate contacts which it furnishes, gives him the controls which he needs.

In spite of the good work which has been done, the Mexican Protestant Churches have certain problems which call for the co-operation of the American Churches.

The Mexican Protestant Church has come into being far too often as a mere adaptation of the problem of an older, dying neighborhood church and has not been given the trained leadership necessary to fit it adequately for coping with the many needs peculiar to the Mexican immigrant. The pastor of an immigrant church has generally a difficult position. The lack of trained lay leadership in the church places an unusually heavy burden upon him. He must not only be responsible for the preaching and set an example by his moral conduct, but he is also expected to attend to the financial administration of the church and to take a lead in practically all the church activities. He is often the sole intermediary between the Mexican Church and the American Churches which help support the work. In order to meet the problems of the church he must be able to interpret American life to the congregation and Mexican life to those Americans who are interested in the work. He must understand two cultures and be the master of both. In addition he must deal with an unusual number of personality problems.

The Mexican has been made exceedingly sensitive by his immigration experiences. His feelings are easily hurt. Moreover, his position as a newcomer, divorced from his old ways and thoughts and as yet but imperfectly wedded to the new, results in a highly unstable personality pattern. He is apt to be caught up in one enthusiasm today only to have tomorrow bring a compelling new idea with a new loyalty. This is but the inevitable result of the cultural shock to which he is being subjected.

The great mobility of the Mexicans, who are forced to move from one place to another in looking for a job, makes difficult the development of permanent lay leadership and the churches must instantly reach out after new members to even maintain themselves. This tends to make a repetition of the educational work necesary and makes it difficult for the church as a whole to progress as fast as its individual members of long standing. They are often brought in contact with a great variety of new ideas through the movies, newspapers and radio which it is impossible for the church as a whole to assimilate at once. This is discouraging not only to the pastor but also to those members who have been in the church for some time and who feel that an unfair burden is being placed upon them. Their interest lags as lessons are repeated. And although these difficulties would seem to be sufficient without wilfully adding more, the work has often been additionally handicapped by denominational competition.

MAJOR DENOMINATIONS REPRESENTED

The major denominations carrying on work among the Mexicans are the Baptist, Congregational, Lutheran, Methodist and Presbyterian.

The Baptists have two churches, The first Mexican Baptist Church of South Chicago, located at Ninetieth and Houston, and the Central Mexican Baptist Church at Monroe and Morgan. They also have two missions, one near Forty-seventh and Ashland, the other at 9021 Mackinaw Avenue, South Chicago. South Chicago Neighborhood House at Eighty-fourth and Mackinaw is a Baptist institution where there is a Mexican Sunday School. This denomination employs one full-time Mexican pastor and one part-time Spanish-speaking pastor in its Mexican work.

The Congregationalists and Presbyterians are united in the work of St. Mark's Church and its associated agency for social service, Firman House at 1213 Gilpin Place. Through the missionary activities of St. Mark's these two co-operating denominations also reach out to serve the box-car camps. The staff consists of a full-time Spanish-speaking American pastor, a Cuban ministerial student helper, a full-time children's worker and home visitor, and a part-time medical worker. The Congregationalists also maintain a Mexican church in South Chicago in connection with the work of Bird Memorial Church at 9135 Brandon Avenue. The North Shore Congregational Church maintains an Italian and Mexican Mission on Taylor Street near Halsted.

The Missouri Synod of the Lutheran Church carries on a work for Mexicans at 4309 South Mozart Street, where they employ a full-time Spanish pastor.

The Methodist Episcopal Church maintains the Church of the Good Shepherd at Polk and Sholto Streets as well as the welfare work of Marcy Center at Maxwell and Newberry. They employ a full-time Porto Rican pastor and a woman visitor.

THE MEXICAN—HIS PLACE AMONG US

The question is, what place will we make for the Mexican in our American life? Undoubtedly he has a contribution to make.

The Mexican brings to us a large capacity for useful citizenship. Already he has made his labor almost indispensable during prosperous times in three major fields: in the cultivation of sugar beets and the truck farming and fruit raising industries; in the upkeep of the railroads; and in the foundries and automobile factories. Moreover, he has been found possessed of a mechanical aptitude fitting him for entrance into the skilled trades were he to be given the opportunity. But in addition to these things we find, where it has not been repressed by ill treatment and social disapproval, a native courtesy and hospitality. There is a deep mystical strain in his temperament which inclines him to religious expression. He brings a rich emotional life and a keen appreciation of color and of form capable of adding greatly to our store of artistic beauty.

Hubert Herring, Executive Director of the Committee on Cultural Relations with Latin America, who has made a careful study of the Mexican situation, says in a recent article, "Relations between Americans and Mexicans in the United States," Religious Education, February, 1931:

> "The Mexican is an Indian in his thinking and in his gifts. He has that native feeling for beauty of line and color and tone which is today making Mexico a Mecca for lovers of art. Arriving in the United States he finds himself in the midst of a people who are intensely practical and he finds it difficult to adjust himself. In his zeal to fit into the American scene, he often forgets his own cultural heritage and seeks to do as other Americans do. The result is not happy. The drabness of the average Mexican colony in our American cities is not pleasant. * * * The United States would gain immeasurably if the Mexican could bring us something of the beauty of his own land that we might have it and make it our own."

The Mexican is not inclined to seek citizenship. He has a strong feeling for his native land and a sense of racial solidarity which it is not easy to abandon. He, too, is an American and proud of that fact. Unlike the European immigrant the Mexican knows that he is not far removed from the border of his own land. Always he believes that some day he will return. Nor has he observed any warmth of welcome to United States citizenship being extended to him. He feels that his labor at unpleasant tasks has been all too gladly accepted, but that his society is not wanted. Robert McLean, recording his studies in 1928, tells us that over the entire country the number of Mexicans naturalized averages less than one hundred per year.

To quote once more from the article on ''Relations between Americans and Mexicans in the United States'':

> "The Mexican is here and in considerable numbers. He is here to stay. We have welcomed him because he works well and cheaply. We have used him to do the tasks which Anglo-Saxons do not care to do. We have used little or no intelligence in helping him to a decent housing situation. We have given him the back alleys of our cities. We have called him 'greaser' and left him to fight his own way as best he can. We have wondered that he does not show more enthusiasm for becoming Americanized."

In view of this situation what can our Protestant Churches do to help? The Protestant Church has assisted the Mexican in his adjustment to a different civilization by its friendliness and its social service. It has also helped the more intellectual individuals, who in the new situation have largely lost their faith, to find a thought readjustment and a re-establishment of a religious faith on a new basis.

On the other hand, as has been indicated, our Protestant work has touched only a small minority of Mexicans and not always in the wisest and most effective manner.

There is more that we can do. In the first place we can study more into the history and background of the Mexican. We would then learn that the country south of the Rio Grande is something more than a place of bull-fights and revolutions; that the Mexican has a heritage not to be despised. Basically Indian, with only an overcoating of Spanish speech and customs, he represents an indigenous civilization, in many respects superior to the European system which conquered it.

We could also better provide for receiving the Mexican into our land and making a place for him. Take our Chicago situation for example, if our work were properly set up and organized, lines of communication could be established with the immigration centers in the Southwest. Advice in regard to labor conditions could be forwarded to leaders in these centers so that workingmen would not come to Chicago under false hopes of employment. Some connections could be established for those who do come so that they would not need to wander around aimlessly looking for a job. More protection against exploitation could be furnished the newcomer.

In regard to these services and what is more narrowly considered the religious field, a more adequate program could be worked out if the various denominations could unite and establish a program for metropolitan Chicago. With pooled resources the general services already indicated could be better performed. In addition a more mobile leadership could be provided so as to follow a shifting population. More beauty could be put into the places of worship for Mexicans and many educational facilities could be provided which at present are not available. In all this the Protestant Church would not seek to proselyte. Neither would it favor Americanization in the sense of reducing the Mexican variant to a dull drab monotone but rather to provide a friendly atmosphere in which the Mexican can more happily adjust himself to a new world and make his own cultural contribution to the inclusive American pattern that will some day be realized.

"E pluribus unum". So reads the legend upon the United States silver dollar, "Out of many, one." To us who are citizens of Chicago those words are an ever-present command, a call to study and to labor. With our great blocks of foreign population we are not one city but many. If tomorrow's metropolis would rise beautiful, clean, healthful, law abiding, brotherly, we must make out of these many, one. This, however, can only be done if we take the trouble to understand. It is toward the understanding of one of the newest of our immigrant groups that this pamphlet is dedicated—the 20,000 Mexicans in Chicago.

A BOOK LIST

Beals, Carleton: *Mexican Maze.* Lippincott, 1931. A newspaper correspondent who has been in and out of Mexico for thirteen years writes a book full of good stories.

Chase, Stuart: *Mexico;* A Study of Two Americas. Macmillan, 1931. A good survey of Mexican history, a description of Tepoztlan, as a symbol of Mexico of today, a community of machineless men contrasted with our machine-made civilization. Sketches by Diego Rivera.

Encyclopedia Britannica (Article on *Mexico*).

Gamio, Manuel: *Mexican Immigration to the United States.* University of Chicago Press, 1930.

Gamio, Manuel: *The Mexican Immigrant; His Life Story.* University of Chicago Press, 1931.

Garcia, Manuel: *A Son's Error* (a play in ms. form.) Apply to Rev. Lacy Simms, 1213 W. Gilpin Place, Chicago, Illinois.

Gruening, Ernest: *Mexico and Its Heritage.* Century, 1928. The most scholarly modern book on Mexico, with detailed accounts of the revolution, a full bibliography.

Herring, Hubert and Katharine Terrill, editors: *The Genius of Mexico.* Committee on Cultural Relations with Latin America, 1931. Lectures delivered before the annual summer seminar which Mr. Herring conducts in Mexico.

Jones, Edgar Anita: *Mexican Colonies in Chicago.* Social Service Review, Vol. II, No. 4, December, 1928.

Jones, Robert C: *Manuscripts.* (1) A Study of the Distribution of Mexican Immigrants in Chicago and outlying areas and a description of their life and institutions; (2) A History of Mexican religious groups in Chicago; (3) A case study of a church; (4) Life histories of Mexican immigrants. (In the files of the Department of Social Ethics of the Chicago Theological Seminary, 5757 University Avenue, Chicago, Illinois.)

Redfield, Robert: *Tepoztlan, A Mexican Village.* University of Chicago, 1930. A trained anthropologist's study of a free Aztec village.

Saenz, Moises and Herbert I. Priestley: *Some Mexican Problems.* University of Chicago, 1926.

Smith, Susan: *Made in Mexico.* Knopf, 1930. An excellent book for children about Mexican handicrafts and popular arts.

Survey Graphic, May, 1931. (Number devoted to *Mexicans in the United States.*)

Tannenbaum, Frank: *The Mexican Agrarian Revolution.* Macmillan, 1929. A study of revolutionary land reforms.

Taylor, Paul S: *A Series of Studies of Labor Conditions Among the Mexican Immigrants in the United States.* University of California Press.

Vasconcelos, Jose and Manuel Gamio: *Aspects of Mexican Civilization.* University of Chicago, 1926. Discusses international relations.

In addition to the list of books given above there are a number of books and pamphlets published by the various denominational boards. Many of these are for children's reading. Just a few are given below:

McLean, Robert N.: *Jumping Beans.* (Stories and Studies about Mexicans in the United States for Junior Boys and Girls.) Friendship Press, 1929.

McLean, Robert N.: *That Mexican.* Revell, 1928.

McCombs, Vernon: *From Over the Border.* Missionary Education Movement, 1925.

Means, Florence C.: *Pepita's Adventure in Friendship.* Friendship Press, 1929. (A Play for Juniors about Mexicans in the United States.) Price twenty-five cents.

Means, Florence C. and Fullen, Harriet L.: *Rafael and Consuelo.* (Stories and Studies about Mexicans in the United States for Primary Children.) Friendship Press, 1929.

Stowell, Jay: *Methodism's New Frontier.* Methodist Book Concern, 1924.

Thompson, Charles A.: *Enter the Mexican.* (Bears the imprint of several denominations.)

Write to the following headquarters for other material:

Commission on Missions of the Congregational and Christian Churches, 19 South La Salle Street, Chicago, Illinois.

Central Distributing Agency for the Presbyterian Church, U. S. A., 77 W. Washington Street, Chicago, Illinois.

The Board of Home Missions and Church Extension of the Methodist Episcopal Church, 1701 Arch Street, Philadelphia, Pa., and to The Woman's Home Missionary Society, Methodist Episcopal Church, 420 Plum Street, Cincinnati, Ohio.

A HISTORY

OF THE

Mexican Mission Work

CONDUCTED BY

The Presbyterian Church in the United States of America

IN

THE SYNOD OF TEXAS

BY

B. A. HODGES

PUBLISHED BY

THE WOMAN'S SYNODICAL OF TEXAS

1931

EXPLANATORY

For sometime there has been a desire for a history of our Mexican Mission work in the Synod of Texas. The Executive Committee of the Synodical of Texas, at its meeting in New Orleans, asked that this history be written and published. The President was appointed to secure some one to write it. Rev. B. A. Hodges, who for twenty years had been Chairman of the Committee on Home Missions, and for five years Acting Superintendent of Home Missions, in the Synod of Texas, was asked to write the history, for it was during this period that the missions were established, and he was the only one having access to the entire correspondence in connection with this work. Miss Bessie V. Sneed, Superintendent of the Home of Neighborly Service from the beginning, was asked to furnish the "High Points" in connection with the Home.

Mrs. B. A. Hodges,

Synodical President.

Waxahachie, Texas, March, 1931.

FOREWORD

Usually our attention is so fixed upon the road ahead that we forget the way by which we have come; often we are so concerned with the tasks to be accomplished that the story of work well done grows dim with the passing of the years. Then some day we find that it is impossible to solve the problem which lies just ahead without certain definite knowledge about the problems solved in other years.

It is gratifying that all the facts about the founding and development of the three Mexican Missions of the Presbyterian Church, U. S. A., in Texas have been gathered together and preserved. The pamphlet presenting the story will serve as a ready source of reference for the questions which are usually asked so easily and answered with such difficulty.

And I for one am glad that it was Dr. Hodges who has written the story; for it was his clear eye of faith which first saw the opportunity, and his contagious personality which fired others to an appreciation of the task.

Only of late years have we learned one of the sources of his inspiration; for when Mrs. Hodges was freed from the responsibilities of a pastor's wife and became President of the Woman's Synodical, she threw a tireless energy and a dauntless courage into the work of raising funds for the new building at San Antonio. Doubtless Mrs. Hodges would not let her husband say it, but he knows, as we all know, that without the efforts of his good wife, the building in San Antonio would still be a dream.

A score of years ago we were talking of two hundred thousand, and then three hundred thousand Mexicans in Texas. Today there are three-quarters of a million.

Do three small missions represent the share of our church in the evangelization of this great population?

"What are these among so many?"

ROBERT N. McLEAN,
Superintendent of Mexican Work.

Los Angeles, Cal.

INTRODUCTION

TEXAS was originally part of Mexico. It is no part of this story to recount the early settlement and final independence of Texas. Naturally, there is a large Mexican population in Texas, many of them native to the soil, but many of them immigrants. There is a large transient population, coming and going with the seasons and the need for laborers. San Antonio and El Paso are the largest centers of this Mexican population, and they scatter out, in many towns and villages, on farms and ranches, all over the state.

The Mexican is ever with us. There will always be a large Mexican element in our population in Texas. The Mexican will be the kind of citizen we help him to become. The great agencies for making the Mexican a safe and valuable citizen are the public schools, the churches, and the attitude of the Americans with whom he comes in contact. We are concerned here with the work of the church, and particularly with that of the Presbyterian Church in the United States of America. The Presbyterian Church in the U. S. A. is one of the latest churches to undertake work for the Mexicans in Texas. And even now we have only three missions among this interesting people: San Angelo, El Paso and San Antonio.

Our aim is to tell briefly the story of these missions.

SAN ANGELO

THE Committee on Home Missions for the Synod of Texas had for several years studied the Mexican situation and faced the problem of our duty in relation to it. Repeatedly the committee had called the attention of the Synod and the Board of Home Missions to this great field for Christian work, and we were always instructed to go ahead as soon as the way was open. But there was always a shortage of funds. And so we waited.

In 1908 the Synod of Texas approved the following: "Texas was once Mexican territory. There are now in Texas more than two hundred thousands Mexicans, and their number is rapidly increasing. The Methodist, Baptist, Disciples, and Southern Presbyterian Churches are doing some work among them, but there are fewer than four thousand Mexican Protestants in the state. Our own church is doing nothing to evangelize this people. We believe this work ought to be undertaken at once. The best results can be obtained only by supplementing evangelistic work with school work. This latter is the work of the Woman's Board, and their experience among the Mexicans elsewhere prepares them for this work. We call the attention of the Presbyterian women of Texas to this Macedonian call." (Minutes, 1908, p. 23.)

The following recommendation was adopted at that time: "That you call the attention of the Board and the Woman's Board to the need of our Bohemian and Mexican population." (Minutes, p. 23.)

In 1909 the Synod was reminded that "nothing is being done for the 300,000 Mexicans."

In 1911 the Synod met in San Antonio, and made the following statement: "Meeting in San Antonio, we could not forget the 300,000 Mexicans in the state." And the. following recommendation was approved: "That you urge Presbyteries having a large Mexican population, after consultation with the Board, to undertake work among the Mexicans." (Minutes, 1911, p. 16.)

Again, in 1912, the Synod meeting in Amarillo, Oct. 9-14, adopted the following statement: "Last year you urged Presbyteries having a large Mexican population, after consultation with the Board, to undertake work among the Mexicans. As yet nothing definite has been done. But the situation calls for immediate action on our part if we are to share in the evangelization of this large and increasing part of our population." (Minutes, p. 19.)

In May of this year, 1912, Dr. B. P. Fullerton wrote to me, as Chairman of the Committee on Home Missions: "Now I want you to gather all the facts you possibly can about the Mexican situation in Texas, their number, where distributed, and what Romanism and Protestanism both are doing for them, as far as you possibly can ascertain." There was a double purpose in this request. These facts were needed for a study of the whole Mexican situation to be presented at the Conference on Work among Spanish Speaking People, to meet at Albuquerque early in the summer, June 11-13. But there was also the deepening purpose of establishing work among the Mexicans in Texas.

October the 18th I wrote to Dr. Fullerton: "We are going to start something for Mexicans soon. I do not just now see how, but feel it in my heart that we will, and at no distant day."

Finally, in October, 1912, Rev. R. E. Joiner, D. D., then pastor of Harris Avenue Presbyterian Church, San Angelo, and a member of Synod's Committee on Home Missions, wrote me a letter saying that the way was open to start our work for the Mexicans—the situation, the opportunity, and the worker were ready in San Angelo.

It seems that the public school authorities of San Angelo had excluded the Mexicans from the public schools of the city, and segregated them in a separate building, with inadequate equipment and teaching force. The Mexicans resented this. The Roman Catholic Church, with the increase of the American membership, more and more discriminated against the Mexicans. This was the situation. There was the need of providing educational and religious privileges for the children and adults of the Mexicans in San Angelo. There were between 1000 and 1500 of them. About this time there came to San Angelo a woman who had been reared in the Roman Catholic Church, who was closely related to some of the high dignitaries of that church. But she had become dissatisfied with that church and had united with the Presbyterian Church, San Angelo. This was Mrs. Jennie Suter, so long and so closely identified with the development of the San Angelo Mission. Mrs. Suter had Spanish blood in her veins and loved the Mexican children and people devotedly. She was active and influential in winning the Mexicans to the church. She was available for work among the Mexicans in connection with the Presbyterian Church.

On the invitation of Dr. Joiner, I went to San Angelo, and we surveyed the situation, found a building in which to open the school, secured the services of Mrs. Suter, and thus began our first work in Texas for the Mexicans.

Mrs. Suter began her work Nov. 1, 1912, in an old building located on Twohig Street. For this building we were to pay $4.00 a month rent. The building was in need of repairs, and furnishings and equipment must be provided. Then there was the salary of Mrs. Suter, $40.00 per month, and incidental expenses, to be provided. Where was this money to come from? We did not know. But convinced that the work ought to be undertaken, and believing that the need and the opportunity constituted a call of God, we agreed to launch out on a "venture of faith." We directed that the work go on, and guaranteed the necessary funds.

Such school work would properly come under the work of the Woman's Board of Home Missions, but the Woman's Board declined to undertake the work at San Angelo, because of a lack of funds for new work. We tried to find some unused funds appropriated to the Presbyteries, but failed. The Home Board could not find the money for the new work. The work went on, and the expenses accumulated. Mrs. Suter's salary had not been paid. Something had to be done. We borrowed the money, giving our personal note for it, and kept up the search for funds.

Dr. Joiner writes several letters about the development of the work. Dec. 12, 1912, he writes: "We fitted the old house up with new floor, paper, etc. We were able to find second-hand school desks. Mrs. Rust supplied them with a good organ; so things are going fine. The Sunday School will be organized next Sunday morning. On account of the activity of the priest, we are undertaking the religious side carefully. Mrs. Suter is a wise worker; knowing the Catholics so well, she can do the real work and keep on speaking terms with them."

Jan. 6, 1913, he writes: "I am happy to tell you that our Mexican work is booming. Mrs. Suter and Mother Rust pulled off a Christmas tree, etc., and it made a wonderful impression on the Mexican people. There are twenty-odd scholars in the school this week, with promise of others at an early date. Mrs. Suter is mastering the situation and getting hold of the Mexican population."

Feb. 3, he writes: "There is a present enrollment of 34 in the school, with prospects for more. If the school continues, it will require at least two teachers. The Catholics are greatly agitated and have offered Mrs. Suter more than twice what we are paying her to teach in their school. Her work among the Mexicans has been a revelation of the wonderful tact she has to handle the Catholics. The priests and the sisters have made a house-to-house canvass, using persuasion, offer of rewards, threats, etc., to change the children back to their school. The priest told Mrs. Suter that they were going to erect a $40,000.00 building, and wanted her at any cost. Mrs. Suter has promised me that she will continue if we will furnish her a helper who can speak Spanish, and pay her $50.00 a month, beginning at the end of this term. She is worth twice the amount."

Meantime expenses kept accumulating. Two things were done to keep the work going. Grace Presbyterian Church, Temple, Texas, directed that $200.00 of its Home Mission offering should be given to the Mexican work at San Angelo, with the understanding that in case the Home Board took over this work this money should revert to the Board and the church receive credit for it. Otherwise, it should be a donation to the Mexican work. The Harris Avenue Presbyterian Church, San Angelo, agreed to use part of its Home Mission offering for this work. Mrs. W. B. Preston, then President of the Synodical, promised to help in the work, and the Synodical gave $30.00 per month to this new work. This money was made available because of a change in the Bohemian work, releasing this amount.

April 8, 1913, Dr. C. L. Thompson wrote: "We have appointed Dr. Robert McLean, of Grant Pass, Oregon, Superintendent of our Mexican Department. As there are three to four hundred thousand Mexicans in your state, we have thought it wise to call his early attention to the great opportunity there, and have asked him to get in touch with you as early as possible in order that you and he may have a conference on the situation, the more so as Dr. Dickey of the Southern Church has written Dr. McLean a letter expressing a desire for co-operation in that state."

The coming of Dr. McLean was the beginning of real interest in the work among the Mexicans of Texas. Strong in his convictions, clear in his understanding of the situation, warm in his sympathies with the Mexican people, and an earnest Christian gentleman, he threw his whole soul into this work. It was a joy to work with him. He was a prince and a mighty man of God. The joy of his fellowship abides to this day.

One of the bright spots in the history of this mission was the ministry of Rev. Narciso Lafuerza. He was of Spanish birth and was a student in Dubuque Seminary. He was available for summer work, and we were fortunate in securing him for the San Angelo Mission. He came to San Angelo July 1, 1913, and remained till October. Above the average in intelligence, affable in manners, and deeply and genuinely interested in the work, he became popular at once. Dr. Joiner described him as "immense among the Mexicans."

It became necessary to secure a new location, and a well-built skating rink of sufficient size and well located on Washington Drive was secured. The rent on this property would be $100.00 a year, more than double that of the old location. Ultimately this property was purchased and is now used for services, but an attractive brick house has taken the place of the old skating rink.

Mrs. Suter thought it wise to have an evangelistic campaign, and then organize the church. So Mr. Lafuerza began his work with a series of evangelistic services. But the church was not organized.

It was hoped that Mr. Lafuerza would continue his work, at least for a year, but he decided it was best to go back to school.

In the meantime some important things transpired, that had a big influence upon the work. The Woman's Synodical agreed to give to this work $600.00 a year. Mrs. W. B. Preston was ever deeply interested in this work and co-operated heartily, and the women of Texas were more than glad to raise this extra amount, so that their offerings for the Home Board were not affected. Then, Nov. 17, Dr. John Dixon writes: "I am glad to report to you that the Board took favorable action on the application for a grant to Mrs. Suter. As I was in a very penitent as well as sympathetic mood, I urged that the full grant of $600.00 be made to date from the first of April last, running to the 31st of March next. The sum was voted."

That was like a benediction after prayer. The Home Board thus assumed the support of Mrs. Suter from April 1, 1913, and the money from Grace Church, Temple, was returned to the Board, thus relieving an embarrassing situation.

There was the problem of finding another minister for this work. Oct. 17, 1913, Dr. C. L. Thompson writes: "I write to suggest to you the Rev. Hubert G. Smith, for several years one of our workers in Cuba. He and his wife are familiar with the Spanish language, and we have counted them among our excellent missionary workers. Both Mr. and Mrs. Smith suffered from the tropical climate and they have been in the States for more than a year." Mr. and Mrs. Smith accepted the work and arrived at San Angelo the last of November, 1913.

Mr. Smith continued with the mission for nearly a year. He made several visits to other Mexican settlements, hoping to find a field where other work could be opened. In September, 1914, they were happy to return to Cuba, where their hearts had ever been.

In June of 1914 Mr. Lafuerza came back to take up the work in San Angelo again. Mr. Lafuerza served the church in all about seven years. It was hard for him to decide definitely and finally about his life work. He hesitated about the ministry, and delayed his ordination. But his loyalty to Mrs. Suter and the work there kept him at San Angelo. Finally he decided to be ordained, and at the meeting of Brownwood Presbytery in April, 1916, he was ordained. He was happy in this decision. During part of the year 1917 he was in Trinity University, studying, and teaching Spanish, and preaching at San Angelo part of the time. In 1918 he became an American citizen, and thought he ought to enter the war. His letters are full of the spirit of patriotism and his eagerness to do his part in the war. Sept. 17, 1918, he received his call to service and entered the U. S. navy. In December he got a ten days' furlough and spent the time in San Angelo. When the war was over he came back to San Angelo and took up the work again. Early in 1919, Mr. Lafuerza made a visit to his old home in Spain to see his parents, returning in September of that year. The last of January, 1920, he resigned and spent some time at Douglass, Arizona. He did not like Douglass, and later wanted to return to San Angelo. But at that time another man was on the field. Later Mr. Lafuerza accepted work with the Melba Perfume Company and went to Cuba and Porto Rico, and later to South America.

In the summer of 1920 Rev. Ben H. Moore, a student in Lane Theological Seminary, now pastor at Brady, Texas, supplied the church at San Angelo. He also made an extensive survey of the Big Bend country for the Board of Home Missions.

Friday, May 21, 1915, the First Mexican Presbyterian Church was organized at San Angelo. Rev. T. W. Davidson and Rev.

R. R. Rives and Elders Glover and Joiner represented the Presbytery of Brownwood in the organization. Rev. Gordon Lang, Rev. Narcisco Lafuerza and Mrs. Jennie Suter were present and took part on the program. Mr. Lafuerza acted as interpreter.

In June, 1921, Rev. Carlos Prieto became pastor, but served less than a year. Since then the church has been served by Rev. Samuel Adame, a fine Christian gentleman and whose untimely death on March 18, 1927, was sincerely mourned. Rev. Bulmaro Alvidrez and Elder Alfredo Velez served as ministers. Rev. Gabino Rendon became pastor in July, 1930, and it is expected that the church will take on new life.

During the history of the misson, at various times, Miss Bertha Vinson, Miss Blanche Ratliff, Miss Lois Snow, Miss Weimer Wiggs, and Miss Steuhenger assisted in the school work.

In the fall of 1925 Mrs. Suter resigned. But she has continued to live in San Angelo and retains the love of her old pupils. One of these students, Charlie Rodriguez, became a candidate for the ministry, and went to Dubuque Seminary for his education. He has been pastor in several fields.

The part played by the pastors of Harris Avenue Presbyterian Church should not be forgotten. Ever sympathetic and ready to help, their services were indispensable, and the work could not have gone on without them. Following Dr. Joiner, Rev. Gordon Lang, Rev. W. O. Woestermeyer, Rev. L. D. Grafton, and Rev. M. S. Epperson have been pastors and gave of their time and influence to the work of the Mission.

At one time Rev. T. W. Davidson of Santa Anna served the church.

Mrs. Suter bought the property used by the Mission, and declared her purpose to finally give it to the Mexican Church. But it was thought best for the Board of Home Missions to purchase the property. This was done in 1921. Not long after this the building was destroyed by fire. Soon the erection of a new building was begun. But the $3,000.00 received for insurance would not erect the kind of building desired. Dr. B. Wrenn Webb, who was then Superintendent of Home Missions for the Synod of Texas, went to San Angelo and led in a campaign for funds to finish and furnish the new building. Dr. Webb reports: "The Mission and workers are in high favor among the citizens; and, considering the financial situation of the town, the response was exceedingly liberal, amounting to between $1,200.00 and

First Mexican Presbyterian Church, San Angelo

$1,500.00." A handsome brick building now occupies the lot and it meets the needs of the church.

The First Presbyterian Church (U. S.), San Angelo, owned a piece of land, 50x60 feet, adjoining our property, and in the summer of 1924 graciously voted to transfer that property to our Mexican Church. This was done, and the church now owns a fine piece of property.

EL PASO

EL PASO is the second largest Mexican center in Texas. While many live there permanently, many are transient. It is easy to pass back and forth across the international boundary. Practically all denominations working among Mexicans in Texas have work in El Paso, and some that have work nowhere else have a mission there. And yet only a small per cent. of the population is being served. In December, 1913, Dr. Robert McLean made a survey of the Mexican situation in the Southwest and, speaking of El Paso, he says: "There are several denominations working there, but only the border of the population is being reached by these agencies. An official of the police force of El Paso recently told me that the Mexican population of that city was not less than 30,000, and from our survey of the city we know that not more than one out of thirty is brought within the influence of the gospel. Four of the principal churches for the Spanish work are within three blocks of each other, leaving a great mass towards the river and towards Juarez, and on the Mexican side, without any gospel agency whatever."

El Paso is a strategic center for the Presbyterian Church in the U. S. A. During the revolution many Mexicans came to El Paso from Old Mexico. Our missions in Old Mexico, before the rearrangement of the work among the denominations, furnished a goodly number of them. Dr. McLean says, June 20, 1914, "One of the members of our church in Torreon told me that nearly half of the Torreon Church is now in El Paso and Juarez." They had not connected themselves with the small and struggling mission church in El Paso supported by the Southern Presbyterian Church. Numbers from our churches in New Mexico, Arizona and California were constantly coming to El Paso. It seemed imperative that we undertake work in El Paso.

The Presbyterian Church in the U. S. had a well-organized Mexican work in Texas, with a Presbytery, the Texas-Mexican Presbytery. One of their missions was in El Paso, under the direction of Rev. C. R. Womeldorf. It was our hope to work in harmony with the Southern Presbyterian Church. Dr. Brooks I. Dickey, Chairman of the Committee on Home Missions, and of the Committee on Comity, for the Synod of Texas, U. S.; Dr.

Robert McLean, Superintendent of the Mexican Work of the Presbyterian Church in the U. S. A., and B. A. Hodges, Chairmon of the Committee on Home Missions and of the Committee on Comity, for the Synod of Texas, U. S. A., had a conference in San Antonio, May 10, 1913. Two other workers of the Southern Presbyterian Church were present at the conference—Rev. W. S. Scott and Rev. R. D. Campbell. The spirit of the conference was fine, and out of it came a general plan of work, to avoid competition and encourage co-operation.

The plan provided for such a division of the Mexican population of Texas as to leave the present work of the U. S. Church free to develop, and assigned to the U. S. A. Church a large Mexican population not then touched by any Presbyterian Church. El Paso was the only exception. The Presbyterian Church in the U. S. would transfer their work in El Paso to the Presbyterian Church in the U. S. A., proper compensation for property to be provided. The U. S. A. Church would not open work in San Antonio. It seemed that the way was clear for action. But not so.

But the failure to keep the spirit and purpose of this agreement was not on the part of the leaders in Texas. Their attitude was fine and cordial. The two General Assemblies were soon to meet in Atlanta, Ga., and this proposed plan of co-operation was submitted to the Home Mission authorities of both denominations. June 5, 1913, Dr. Charles L. Thompson writes: "I placed before our Board at its meeting last week the messages which you sent, and have pleasure in reporting the Board's approval of the plans outlined, and also the fact that it has committed the details and developments of the plan to you and Dr. McLean and Dr. Dickey in such further conferences as shall seem best." But the agreement failed to secure the approval of the Committee on Home Missions of the Presbyteran Church in the U. S. But there came from Dr. Dickey the assurance of the most cordial feelings for our work and the desire that we might co-operate in every way possible.

We decided to go ahead with plans for work in El Paso.

The Synod met in El Paso in October, 1914, and approved the following report from the Committee on Home Missions: "At a meeting of the Executiye Committee, B. A. Hodges, A. F. Bishop and R. Thomsen, in El Paso Aug. 4, with Rev. Robert McLean, D. D:, the whole Mexican work was discussed, and the Board was asked for a grant sufficient to enable us to open work in El Paso. A minister has been secured and work will begin immediately in El Paso. This is the consummation of several years planning. El Paso has the largest Mexican population of any city in Texas. About eighteen months ago Rev. Kenneth Brown was asked to make a survey of the city, and he prepared a careful study of the field, revealing an open door for aggressive work for our church. As a result of this survey and a further study of the field by Dr. McLean, the Board was asked for a grant of $50,000.00 for work in El Paso. A year ago the Synod again approved the policy of our sharing in the evangelization of the Mexicans in Texas, and asked for two new missionaries at once, one of whom was to be located in El Paso. At the meeting of the Committee on Home Missions, in February of this year, it was definitely decided to open work in El Paso, and the appeal was made for a grant for this purpose.

We rejoice that we are permitted to share in this important work. We recognize the good work being done by other churches, and shall endeavor to conduct our work so as not to hinder, but help, in the evangelization of the Mexican people in El Paso."

The following recommendation was approved: "In view of the strategic importance of El Paso in its relation to the Mexican work, your committee, at its meeting in February, 1914, recommended to the Board of Home Missions that the sum of $50,-000.00 be appropriated for the Mexican work in that city. This appropriation is intended to cover the purchase of land, the construction of buildings necessary for complete educational and religious work, and salaries of instructors and ministers for the first year. The urgency of the work is becoming more and more apparent as the days pass, and we would recommend: That the work among the Mexicans in El Paso be begun at the earliest possible date." (Minutes, 1914, pp. 21, 22, 25.)

Since September, 1913, Dr. Robert McLean had been making more or less regular visits to El Paso. Now he devoted considerable time to this field, with a view to opening the work there.

Rev. Jose Venecia came to El Paso the first of December, 1914, and began his active and fruitful ministry. Mr. Venecia was a good preacher, a virile personality, and untiring in his labors. As a result of his work, a church was organized April 25, 1915, with forty members. Dr. Robert McLean, assisted by Rev. Kenneth Brown and Rev. Jose Venecia, organized the new church. The minutes of Synod are in error as to the date of organization. By the time Synod met in October the membership

[14]

had grown to 92, with 32 candidates for membership, 130 in Sunday School, 36 in C. E. Society, 20 in the women's society, and ministers to 102 families. This was our first Mexican Presbyterian Church organized in Texas.

The work grew. The church became a great influence among the Mexicans of El Paso.

The great drawback was lack of an adequate building.

The story of the present location and the splendid building that stands on it is a long and interesting one. The great mass of the Mexican population is concentrated within a limited area, with outlying centers here and there. Naturally a location must be found accessible to the people to be served. Inevitably the churches working among the Mexicans will be close together. A report of the Joint Committee on Work Among Spanish Speaking People, submitted to the Home Missions Council, says: "Among the many outstanding facts of interest are, that in El Paso, including the Catholic Church, there are ten centers where religious work of some kind is going forward within five minutes' walk of each other."

Property is at a premium in such localities, and when you find what you want, you cannot get what you find. What you can get, sometimes, you do not want. Several locations were found and rejected.

The most interesting situation developed about the Douglass School property. The School Board had decided to sell this property and locate the school elsewhere. The building could easily and economically have been remodeled for church purposes. This fine property seemed almost within our grasp, and plans were being drawn for transforming it into a church. We could occupy it at once. But at the last moment the School Board, for some unexplained reason, decided not to sell.

Another location must be found. Dr. Robert N. McLean and Dr. Andrew Montgomery found the present location, Fourth and Ochoa Streets, and purchased it. After we had secured this desirable property, the School Board offered to trade the Douglass School property at a reasonable figure. The explanation of their action seems to be that our present location was the one they wanted for the school. But we did not trade, and everyone seems happy over the situation. Today a magnificent church building, costing, including furnishings, nearly $40,000.00, stands on that lot. But the building was not erected that year. The World War was on, and the State Council of Defense denied our

The Church of the Divine Savior, El Paso

request for permission to build. We had to wait. Such delays made the heart sick.

But the war ended Nov. 11, 1918, and that changed our prospects. In April, 1919, Dr. Robert N. McLean had an architect working on plans for the new church building. But the money had not been secured for the building. Another delay. But there was no let-up in efforts to secure the money. Finally, in November of that year, Dr. John A. Marquis writes: "The Board is willing to back El Paso with its credit when the Finance Committee has approved plans and specifications. Please forward them." Dr. McLean writes: "Praise the Lord," and adds eight exclamation points. The situation deserved them.

Immediately work was begun on the building. Quoting from "NEWS LETTER" of Feb. 13, 1920, by Dr. McLean: "Sunday, Feb. 8, was a great day in the history of our work in El Paso, Texas. The work was begun five years ago under great difficulties, and the congregation has been shuffled about until it is a marvel that the church did not fall in pieces. Yet it now has an enrollment of five hundred members, and on Sunday, with songs and prayers of thanksgiving to God, they laid the corner stone of what will be the finest edifice for Mexican work in all the Southwest. The first unit, costing approximately $40,000.00 is well under way. The whole, when complete, will cost nearly $100,000.00 and will meet the physical, moral and spiritual needs of our Mission to the Mexicans at this gateway to the heart of Mexico. A band played, the members sang their songs of gladness, the Acting Mayor of El Paso, Dr. B. Wren Webb, Dr. Floyd Poe, the Rev. Jose Venecia, and Dr. Robert McLean, who organized the church five years ago, delivered addresses. Visiting pastors took parts assigned them, and Dr. Robert N. McLean, Secretary for Mexican Work, offered prayer. It will be a beautiful and imposing structure, the visible dwelling place of the Most High among His people, and a beacon light to the Mexicans across the Rio Grande. The interest shown by the First Presbyterian Church (American) in our El Paso work is a great encouragement to the Superintendent and to the pastor. We congratulate Brother Venecia on his great work."

Then came the great day, June 13, 1930, when the building was dedicated. It was a great day. Mr. Venecia and his people were happy. And so were we all.

Back of the enterprise was the man. More than one man was back of this enterprise, mainly the McLean's, father and son. Dr. B. P. Fullerton was ever ready to lend a hand and help. The Board of Home Missions was always sympathetic, and finally saw to it that the money was secured. Synod's Committee on Home Missions gave much time and thought to the work. But this splendid enterprise was rooted and grounded in the life and labors of Rev. Jose Venecia. Dr. McLean writes, March 11, 1920: "Mr. Venecia has done a piece of work in El Paso which is of national significance. It is a wonderful piece of work to build up a church of five hundred members in five years; to do that when the material with which one must work is made up entirely of Roman Catholic people, is phenomenal."

No attempt has been made to name all the helpers who made the success of this work possible. Each one did his part, and his influence went into the final victory.

Mrs. McNary established and maintained for some time a kindergarten in connection with the church.

Miss Sophie Gilchrist labored faithfully and effectively in connection with the educational, social and financial activities of the church.

Dr. Wm. M. Orr was connected with the Mission for some time, seeking to develop the educational and social program of the church.

When Synod was to meet in El Paso, October, 1914, Dr. Robert McLean wrote that his son, Dr. Robert N. McLean, a professor in Dubuque Seminary, would be at that meeting, and he wanted him to have a part on the program, if possible. The earnest desire of the father, of which he spoke earnestly several times, was that his son might succeed him as Superintendent of Mexican Work. Dr. Robert N. McLean was present at that meeting of Synod, and had a part on the program. Later, Oct. 1, 1918, he succeeded his father as Superintendent of Mexican Work. He has put his whole soul into the work, and to him is due much of the credit for the success of our Mexican work in Texas.

Another change was made in El Paso. Dr. Charles L. Overstreet, every inch a Christian gentleman, had given his earnest support to this developing work. Dr. Overstreet became Director of the New Era Movement for the Synod of Texas. Dr. Floyd Poe became pastor of the First Presbyterian Church of El Paso. Dr. Poe gave the Mexican Mission his close attention and hearty support. Without his help the work could not have gone forward as it did. Under his leadership the First Presbyterian Church gave liberally to the support of the Mission. Miss Gilchrist and Dr. Orr were largely supported by this church.

The church passed through some severe trials. Economic conditions forced many Mexicans to leave El Paso. Many of the members of this church had to leave. At one time the entire session of the church went away. Dr. McLean says that preaching in several places in California was like a meeting of the El Paso Church. Mr. Venecia resigned early in 1924.

Rev. Carlos Cordova became pastor April 1, 1924. Under his wise and faithful leadership the church has grown. It is a busy, working lot of loyal members, and Mr. Cordova is leading them in every good work. He is building upon solid foundations, seeking to develop a high type of Christian manhood and womanhood. His work will abide. He is doing a splendid work with boys and young people. "He has equipped a playground on a very small piece of property and, because of the lack of adequate playgrounds in the community, this place is crowded every night until the lights are turned off. He has always had a splendid basket ball team in the City League, and one year entered his team in the Catholic League and won first place."

The church at El Paso is one of the outstanding Mexican churches in the United States.

SAN ANTONIO

S AN ANTONIO is one of the earliest settlements in Texas. The old Missions, still standing and some of them still in use, an evidence of the activity of the Roman Catholic Church, indicate the strategic location of San Antonio. More Mexicans of culture and wealth, probably, live in San Antonio than in any other city of Texas. San Antonio is the headquarters of most of the political activities of Mexican refugees. It is the largest center of Mexican population.

Naturally the Presbyterian Church in the U. S. A. desired to do its part in the evangelization of the Mexicans in this important center. The proposed plan of agreement with the Presbyterian Church in the U. S. gave San Antonio to the Presbyterian Church in the U. S. and El Paso to the Presbyterian Church in the U. S. A. But the failure to ratify the "agreement" left the doors wide open for us to open work in San Antonio. The attitude of the workers of the "U. S." Church was cordial and co-operative. Rev. R. D. Campbell writes (Feb. 19, 1914), in regard to our entering San Antonio, that he believes that, "even granting that there may be some small conflicts occasionally, they would be practically nothing in comparison with the benefits." In the beginning there was considerable co-operation. Several of our Foreign Missionaries, while waiting to return to Mexico, worked along with their missions, and some of the early converts of our missions united with their mission churches. When we actually began work Mr. Campbell's church loaned us seats and an organ.

We made up our minds to open work in San Antonio. But how? The Board of Home Missions had no money for extra work, and no worker seemed to be available. But Providence works in mysterious ways. The Lord made the wrath of man to work out for His own glory. The revolution broke out in Mexico, and our missionaries had to come home. As Acting Superintendent of Home Missions for the Synod of Texas, I wrote the Board of Foreign Missions, asking that some of these returned missionaries be sent to Texas for work among the Mexicans here. Rev. J. T. Molloy was visiting in Corsicana and I took up the proposition with him. Mr. Molloy declared his willingness to be used in any way to help. Oct. 23, 1913, Dr. A. W. Halsey wrote Mr. Molloy: "Look around and see what can be done in Texas. Miss Turner and Miss Spencer both agree that there is a large work to be done among the Mexicans in Texas. What would you think of our sending our newly appointed missionaries to some point in Texas where they could learn the language and even be brought into contact with Mexicans while studying the language; learning something of the manners and customs? What place would you recommend? Let me hear from you."

Mr. Molloy was asked to investigate promising fields. He made an extensive survey of Mexican communities in Texas. But he preferred to keep near the border, hoping any day he might be able to return to his work in Mexico. But conditions made it impossible for him to return. In one of his letters he writes: "There is no end to the golden opportunities for Mexican work in Texas, and if for any reason I should have to leave Mexico, I would be delighted to take the frontier of Texas and work it for all it is worth. Do your best to stir up interest in behalf of the Mexicans in Texas."

Without any warning a letter came, dated Jan. 1, 1914, saying that he is about to sail for Merida, Yucatan. But he did not stay long. He had to return to Texas. Recently the Presbytery of Austin had passed a resolution asking the Board of Foreign Missions to send some of its returned missionaries to work in Texas. Mr. Molloy was working in Laredo and along the border when he received word from the Board of Foreign Missions to respond to any call of the Board of Home Missions for work in Texas. In the meantime Miss Mary Turner and Miss Kate Spencer had been in San Antonio, doing such work among the Mexicans as they were able, mainly in co-operation with the missions of the Presbyterian Church in the U. S.

In September, 1914, Rev. J. T. Molloy and Rev. H. A. Phillips went to San Antonio and began a study of the situation. In this study they were greatly aided by Rev. W. S. Scott, a missionary of the "U. S." Church.

The location finally selected for our work was an old building near the "Sunset Shops," now the Southern Pacific, on Austin Street. In this old building, Nov. 15, 1914, at 3:30 p. m., Rev. H. A. Phillips organized the Sunday School. The school began with two officers, four teachers and twenty-two pupils. Before the close of the year fifty pupils were enrolled. Miss Kate Spencer was one of the teachers and also did work among women.

Where Work Was Started—on Austin Street

Mr. Phillips also conducted preaching services here.

Mrs. Ostrom, a devout Christian woman, was conducting an independent mission among the Mexicans on Tobin Hill. Mr. Molloy gave some of his time to helping in this Mission, and hoped to lead Mrs. Ostrom to co-operate with the Presbyterian Church. But she was proud of its interdenominational character and not inclined to make it a denominational work.

By the close of 1914 conditions in Mexico were such that most of the missionaries returned. Mr. Molloy sailed for Yucatan early in January, 1915. In his farewell letter, dated Jan. 9, 1915, on board ship, he points out what he considers the best field for our work—north of Commerce Street and west of N. Flores Street. He urges that we do not neglect the Mexicans in San Antonio. He says: "If anything should ever throw me out of Mexico I would be glad to resume work in San Antonio. It is one of the greatest fields I have ever seen. I really hated to leave San Antonio. There is such a fine opportunity for work among the Mexican people, and there is no such fanaticism as we have to contend with in Mexico."

Rev. H. A. Phillips had carried on the work on Austin Street, and continued a short time after Mr. Molloy left. Mr. Phillips was very much concerned about the permanency of the work in San Antonio and repeatedly urged that a church be organized to conserve the fruits of our labors. Early in 1915 Mr. Phillips returned to Mexico. But Rev. R. R. Gregory came soon and took up the work. He builded well on the foundation laid by Mr. Molloy and Mr. Phillips. He was both a Foreign Missionary and a Home Missionary, with organizing and executive ability. He could not stay long.

Finally the way was clear and all the missionaries went back to Mexico. But the Board of Home Missions was now ready to take up this work in earnest, and the Rev. Adalaro Marquez was secured as temporary supply. He continued about three months, from June 20 to Sept. 30, 1915.

Rev. Saul V. Gallegas was supply for a time. During this time the Church was organized, Nov. 28, 1915. Dr. Robert McLean, assisted by Dr. J. M. Todd, pastor of Madison Square Presbyterian Church, and Rev. W. S. Scott, of the Presbyterian Church, U. S., organized the church with seventeen members. Mr. Gallegos was to return to Mexico April 1, 1916.

Earnest efforts were being made to find a pastor for this church. Rev. Ramon L. Lopez, pastor of a Methodist Mexican Church at San Marcos, had spoken several times to Rev. W. B. Preston, then pastor of our church at San Marcos, about work in the Presbyterian Church, indicating his desire to enter the Presbyterian Church. We gave Mr. Lopez clearly to understand that we could not offer him work in our church while he was a member of the Methodist Church. Mr. Lopez finally resigned his work at San Marcos and applied for admission into the Presbyterian ministry. We did our best to clear this with Rev. F. S. Onderdonk, D. D., Superintendent of Mexican Work for the Methodist Episcopal Church, South.

Mr. Lopez was not without some connection with Presbyterian influences. He was born and reared in Spain; educated for the priesthood, attending the University of Madrid thirteen years. "After completing his studies in the University he became a teacher in a Catholic school in Havana, Cuba. Here he came in contact with Dr. Green, missionary of the Presbyterian Church. Dr. Green urged him to read the Bible and gave him a copy. Mr. Lopez read it and decided to become a Protestant. The first work offered him was a professorship in a girls' school in Mexico, under the direction of the Methodist Church. After a short period with this school, he came to San Antonio, and then to San Marcos. Here he married Miss Julia Rios, a Christian Mexican girl. Here he studied English under Rev. W. B. Preston, whom he has looked upon during all these years as his ideal Christian gentleman and scholar."

The Old Saloon—Second Meeting Place

Mr. Lopez began his work in San Antonio April 1, 1916, and continued until October, 1925. During these years Mr. Lopez was active and zealous in the work of the Master. In addition to his regular work as a minister he frequently taught Spanish. He did a good work for the church. He began his ministry in the old building on Austin Street, but in November, 1917, the mission was moved to the location on Moreles and Las Moras Streets.

Immediately after Mr. Lopez resigned, Rev. Earl C. Welliver, of San Diego, Cal., began his active ministry of four years. During the ministry of Mr. Lopez services were held at several points, and some members lived at each of these, and some had moved away. Mr. Welliver devoted himself, first of all, to the important task of locating these members and clearing up the roll of the church. He organized the men into a Brotherhood and trained them to help in the work of the church. An organized Sunday School class for the women gave them a larger share in the work of the Church. He and Mrs. Welliver were also very active in developing the Christian Endeavor Society.

The first of September, 1929, Rev. C. Harry Sarles and wife began their work with the Church of the Divine Redeemer. Mr. and Mrs. Sarles were native Texans, graduates of Trinity University, and Mr. Sarles of McCormick Theological Seminary. Mr. and Mrs. Sarles were no strangers to Mexican work. They had had experience in this work in Chicago. Miss Sneed says: "For the first time the Mexican church extended the call to the pastor, and he was installed. The Brotherhood was reorganized, the

Woman's Auxiliary had its beginning, pledging their support to the church; a choir, with a volunteer pianist, gave young and old a real feeling of service, and a reverent, worshipful, carefully planned order of service gave that secure feeling of a pastor indeed who is the shepherd of his flock. Mrs. Sarles, as sponsor of the Christian Endeavor Society, as teacher of an Intermediate Sunday School class, and as a talented violinist, has a large place of usefulness."

THE KINDERGARTEN

The women of Texas made another contribution to the Mexican work in San Antonio. In the summer of 1914 Miss Mary Turner and Miss Kate Spencer sent to San Antonio a fine young Mexican girl, Tabita Mireles, from Agua Calientes, to be trained as a kindergarten teacher. The women of Texas Synodical undertook the support of Tabita. Mrs. O. M. Fitzhugh cared for her in her home and guided her work. Tabita assisted in the Sunday School on Austin Street, and when the mission was moved to Moreles Street, Mr. Lopez started a kindergarten and Tabita was the first teacher. The women of the Synodical supported the kindergarten. Tabita became so strongly attached to Texas and her work that it was difficult to induce her to return to Mexico and take up the work there for which she had been trained. Tabita Mireles is one of the happy memories of this mission work.

Mrs. James Tafolla was the next teacher, during the school year of 1917 and 1918.

During part of the year 1919 Mrs. M. T. Mendez worked with the mission, assisting in the Sunday School, visiting in the homes and caring for the sick and the poor.

Miss Frances Burrett, a graduate kindergarten teacher, came to San Antonio, and taught in the kindergarten from March, 1920, till June, 1921.

Miss Lela Weatherby, of Fort Davis, Texas, taught from September, 1921, until the close of 1922. Then she went to finish her college work at Trinity University. Miss Izeyl Phelps came in January, 1923, and remained until January, 1925. Miss Fannie Stone came next, and gave more than a year to the work, faithful and efficient. The next teacher came from Madison Square Presbyterian Church, San Antonio. This was Miss Lillie Mae

Hagner. She taught a year and went away to New York City to study. During that year Miss Lois Sory, who had had considerable experience with the Mexicans on the famous Borden Ranch, near Mackey, Texas, taught in the school.

But in September, 1928, Miss Hagner was back with the kindergarten.

In 1921, Mrs. E. R. Polk volunteered her services for the Mexican work, and gave more than two years to the work. Then in 1928 she became a regular worker in the school, and she and Miss Hagner have worked together with efficiency and consecration.

A Vacation Church School became a regular feature of the work.

THE HOME OF NEIGHBORLY SERVICE

Soon after Dr. B. Wrenn Webb became Superintendent of Home Missions for the Synod of Texas, Dr. Robert McLean suggested the idea of a Home of Neighborly Service for the San Antonio Mission. Dr. Webb immediately acted on the suggestion. The success of the venture depended largely on the one selected to direct its activities. Dr. Webb was sure he had found the right person in Miss Bessie V. Sneed. Miss Sneed was a Texas young woman, a graduate of the College of Industrial Arts, Denton, Texas. She had had special training in the Mission School Department of Vanderbilt University, and the Educational Department of Peabody Normal and the University at Knoxville, Tennessee; had taught six years in the public schools of Texas, and spent three years as a missionary in Utah. The years have proved the wisdom of the choice. Wise, patient, understanding, sympathetic, a hard worker, deeply spiritual, she has given of her best to this great work. The lights and the shadows have fallen across her way, but she has gone on. Today she looks back over these years with a heart full of golden memories of service and fellowship.

A cottage at 1515 Lakeview Avenue was rented by the Texas Synodical, and here Miss Sneed began her work as Supervisor of the Home of Neighborly Service Sept. 14, 1920. Soon the kindergarten was moved to this location, and Miss Sneed and her co-workers carried on a varied program of educational, social and religious activities. The Vacation Church School soon be-

Where the Home of Neighborly Service Began

came an established part of the program. In the days when the
public schools were crowded, the workers in the Home of Neighborly Service taught certain grades for the public school. They
did not confine their ministry to the Lakeview cottage, but extended it into the homes of the people, teaching the Word of
Life, ministering to the sick and needy, comforting those in
sorrow, and in every way bearing the burdens of those in need.
The Home of Neighborly Service has become the synonym of
helpfulness and friendliness, Christlikeness.

It soon became evident that Miss Sneed could not carry all
this work alone. Dr. Webb undertook to find a competent helper. Dr. McLean joined in the search. Miss Sophie Theiler had
been active as a Junior Christian Endeavor worker in Galveston.
She had spent a year in the home of Dr. Fred Eastman, New York
City, studying for Christian service. Miss Theiler was secured
for the Home of Neighborly Service as Physical Director. Because she is devoted, conscientious, industrious, and is full of
the spirit of her Master and of human kindness, she has done a
great work. Miss Sneed, with whom she has worked in closest
sympathy, says: "While Miss Theiler does not speak Spanish,
her greatest service has been through visitation in the homes.
Her name is heralded the length and breadth of the community.
The people speak of Miss Thieler's kindergarten, mothers' club,
week-day Bible school, church, telephone, car, etc. In return
for all this confidence, there is seldom a bare, cold foot that she
cannot find a shoe to fit; a shivering body she speedily covers

with a dress hurriedly made over, and while cleansing an infected toe she can make them believe it does not hurt."

HIGH POINTS OF THE HOME OF NEIGHBORLY SERVICE

Miss Sneed was asked to indicate some of the high points in this ministry, and the following is her contribution, as are some other quotations in this narrative:

"Ten years ago when I came to this community Miss Frances Scott, Superintendent of the International Institute, said in her frank and friendly way: 'Miss Sneed, you surely have gone into one of the most corrupt vicinities of Mexican life. Do you think you will ever get anywhere in such a shifting group?'

Last year a woman from Dallas who was stopping in another Mexican center, said: 'Do you limit your membership to those who own homes, have painted houses, or how does it happen that this community is so much better housed than in other sections?' Only a proof that the building of Christian character builds better homes. In counting our blessings in the Mother's Club at Thanksgiving season we found that sixteen out of twenty owned their homes, and that not one owned a home ten years ago. The newly elected President of the Woman's Auxiliary, a widow with four girls, has steadily climbed from a tiny two-room house, where she sewed all day and far into the night, to head inspector in the factory and to a modern four-room cottage, with electric lights and gas. The oldest girl, now working in the factory, continues her high school studies at night school. She is Vice-President of the Christian Endeavor Society. The second one, Vice-President and pianist of the Intermediate Sunday School class, is in the Junior High School Glee Club and President of the Girl Reserves. The third one is ever-dependable in program and sports, and the last one, a midget of a junior, did the telling work on the poster that won first prize in the Texas Synodical Poster Contest. How did the Community House help? English for the mother; lending influence to get work; teaching the girls English, so they could go on with their grades; encouraging them in Sunday School, Christian Endeavor, Week-Day Bible School, giving music lessons to the pianist; teaching them Christian principles, etc.

"An honest man is the noblest work of God," is as true

among the Spanish speaking race as in the English speaking race. The Superintendent of the Sunday School, Elder, Clerk of the Session, and President of the Brotherhood, has never cared especially for the Community House phase of the work, being strictly evangelistic in his attitudes, is one of the most thoroughly Christian men of his race. Simple in manner, gentle in nature, and sincere in purpose, he is respected by all classes of his people, and in the Presbytery, and in other church gatherings. He commands the respect of the church at large. He has suffered much persecution in his family to remain constant to his faith. But his wife had Christian training even as a child in Mexico, and has been a stay for him in religious thought and reading. The three children are receiving genuine Christian training in the home, as well as in church and community house. Linda, the oldest child, now ten years old, a healthy, intelligent child, received her food formula in the Home of Neighborly Service the first six months of her life. Today there is in kindergarten an attractive little brown-eyed boy, active, happy and free in all the play-instruction of his gleeful days. I doubt that Dr. Burnham herself would recognize the tiny, undernourished baby she so gravely tended for several weeks in those beginning days of a dispensary conducted in the cottage, with such meager equipment. But the truth remains. Now a hearty five-year-old skips and plays and sings, and in gentle tones whispers the Thanksgiving prayer.

The Junior Endeavorers look forward each year to the Sunday before Thanksgiving, when the big basket is placed in the middle of the room, where each Junior is privileged to place a Thanksgiving token for Sister Estefinita, the dear old lady who does not know how old she is. For once there is perfect attention as they sing to her their songs, say their Bible memory verses to her, and then pass in line by her chair to feel the gentle touch of her handshake, or perchance be favored by the benediction of her hand upon the head.

The co-operative spirit has been the Jonah in the past, and likely there will be many problems for the futre. But there is a silver lining to all dark clouds. Sarah, C. E. President, Secretary of the City Union, Junior Sunday School teacher, and President of the Business Girls' Club, is a leavening lump. Last spring at the Mexican Young People's Conference she learned to carol, in spirit and in truth, that striking consecration verse:

"Come into my heart, come into my heart, come into my heart,
    Lord Jesus;
Come in today, come in to stay, come into my heart, Lord Jesus."

Every Friday night, concluding the devotional period, you
will hear Sarah, in all the grace of her Christian character, softly
singing into the hearts of the twenty-five club members this, her
own heart's desire.

A few years ago a high school girl determined that she would
find work after school hours, that she might be able to finish her
work. She wanted to be a trained nurse. Objections at home and
their financial distress sent her out to help support the family
for a year. Then the father found work. She sold her one luxury,
the victrola, and was off for training school. Only a few weeks
now and she will be a graduate nurse.

For the past four weeks there has been an exhibit of the work
of the two best artists in our Junior High School. When Arthur
was drawing a pattern of a rocking chair, and the draft did not
suit him, and he tried again, we began to wonder if there was not
far more than we had discovered working in his brain. In the
club he was always making something better. Now we find him
receiving free art lessons from one of San Antonio's best artists.

Reuben is going on at Menaul School, and Lupe is at Allison
James. This year the conference experience fixed the purpose in
Margaret's heart to go to Holden Institute. She is there and is
making good.

I realize that we cannot give out to others what we have experienced during the last ten years. Through frailties, mistakes and
misunderstandings, not a few have we passed. But there is also
the realization that for many a more abundant life has been
given, to the physical being, the moral being, and the spiritual
being, and that the way has been opened for the wooing of the
Spirit into the life eternal. We cannot but see and know that
a divine hand has led us all the way. Our hearts cry out the
more, LEAD ON, OH, KING ETERNAL."

CONSUELA MEDINA

Some years ago there came to San Antonio a family from
Old Mexico. That was nothing new. Families were continually
coming to San Antonio from Mexico. But important consequences grew out of this event. A little girl with large, hungry

eyes and eager spirit quietly slipped into one of the services of the Home of Neighborly Service. Those who heard her tell of this first experience in a Protestant service can never forget it. It seemed such an awful sin to attend a Protestant service. Consuela Medina went to the priest and made confession. But she came again. Her mind was eager to learn and her heart was hungry for fellowship. In this strange new land she was lonely. Then her tonsils had to be removed. She did not have the money for the hospital. This Home of Neighborly Service took her in and cared for her—this Protestant organization. She was deeply and essentially religious, and she must find a way to satisfy her longing soul. In the fellowship of this mission she found satisfaction for her head and heart. Soon she was identified with all the activities of the Home of Neighborly Service, and easily became a leader. Her influence extended far. As one result of a visit to Smithville the women of that church gave the drinking fountain at the Home of Neighborly Service.

Miss Sneed says: "How I am tempted to stop here long enough to write all I know of the life of that much-loved little bundle of bubbling intellectual and spiritual energy, Consuela Medina! She stopped with us for a season only, but how much she lived in those few short years! In November of 1925 arrangements had been completed, and Consuelo, with face radiating with the keenest delight, began at last the work her heart so longed for. With Bible in hand, she somehow managed to read it in homes of all classes and faiths. How her heart bled for her people, when she interpreted for me when we sought out the suffering ones, or were called to ask the city to lay to rest in the far-off corner those who were destitute. In the Young People's Union she could match wits with any one, in address, study, or social function. With the spirited temper equal to any of her race, she could denounce that which she believed to be wrong, and also with gentleness and love unbounded she could as graciously accept the favor of a little child. The second year she was with Miss Hagner until March, striving to do more as she felt her strength slipping, but brave and joyous in her departure. She was indeed our 'Laughing Allegra.' Even yet, in the stillness of memory, we sometimes hear her hearty peals of laughter ring out. Then comes the grave reality—she is gone, and the work must be carried on. With us for such a short time, but with her last ounce of strength she called out, 'Read the Book. Follow the gleam!'

Consuela Medina! Her beautiful, wonderful life goes on. It was the hope of the women of Texas that the clinic dedicated to her memory would continue to minister in His name to the Mexican people."

THE PLACES OF WORSHIP

The first place of worship, selected by Rev. H. A. Phillips, as the best location for us to begin our work was on Austin Street, near the Sunset (Southern Pacific) shops. Here the work was begun, and here the church was organized. The building was old, dilapidated, unattractive, condemned. Tabita Mireles writes of it as follows: "The hall which we use for both Sunday School and church is dangerous, for it is in such a bad condition these last few days. The second floor gallery is falling down, and it leaks so much it seems to rain inside as much as outside."

How they ever induced the Mexican people to attend worship services there is hard to explain—a people accustomed to worship in cathedrals and churches presenting every possible attraction. It must have been the drawing power of the gospel presented by the attractive personalities of J. T. Molloy, H. A. Phillips and R. R. Gregory. The building was old and the surroundings were not attractive. But within burned the warm fires of the gospel and the sympathy of those who loved their fellow-man. Here was begun that work of grace that has continued through the years.

The next place of worship was an old saloon building on the corner of Moreles and Los Moras Streets. On the same lot was a dwelling occupied by the pastor. This place was rented while the search for a suitable location was continued. Finally, the decision was made to purchase this property. Mr. Lopez began services here Nov. 19, 1917. The old saloon was an improvement over the first location, but it lacked much of being ideal. But here the work of grace went on, and the church grew. Here Mr. Lopez did his splendid work. And here Mr. Welliver began his constructive labors.

All this time it was evident that the right location had not been found. Conditions were changing in this neighborhood. A school for colored children had been erected in that neighborhood, and the community began to fill up with colored people. Evidently, a permanent work could not be established there.

The Home of Neighborly Service

The search for a location began **again.**

In one of the best sections of San Antonio, in the heart of a large Mexican population, in the 400 block of North Calaveras Street, a location was found. Here the present work is established, and it seems we may say, "This is our permanent location." At any rate, here has been erected a splendid building, well equipped for the work we are trying to do at present. Some day, however, a church building must be erected — a building that can speak in architecture the call to worship, and bear witness to the presence of God in His holy place, and lead men to say, "This is none other than the house of God, and this is the gate of heaven."

Ground was broken for the new building Sunday afternoon at 3 o'clock, April 10, 1927. Miss Bessie V. Sneed, so long in charge of the Home of Neighborly Service, dug up the first shovelful of earth. "The Mexican church members, young and old, then formed in a long line, each digging up a shovelful of earth. The small Mexican children took handfuls of the earth and scattered it about the lot."

Rev. I. T. Jones, D. D., pastor of Madison Square Presbyterian Church, was the principal speaker, his subject being "Beginning and Completing a Task." Rev. Earl C. Welliver translated the address into Spanish. Mrs. W. B. Preston spoke on "How the Woman's Synodical Helped." Rev. W. B. Preston brought a message from the Synod of **Texas.**

Nov. 29, 1929, the completed building was formally dedicated to the glory of God and the service of man. We thank God and take courage. Rev. Harry Sarles presided at the dedication services. A great audience of both Mexican and American people were present to express their joy in the success of the enterprise. In addition to the local people, Dr. Geo. W. Fender, representing the Synod of Texas, and Mrs. B. A. Hodges, representing the Texas Synodical, were present and had parts on the program.

Many contributed to the success of the enterprise. It is not possible to name them all. The foundations are laid in the wisdom and labors of Dr. Robert McLean, Superintendent of Mexican Work for the Board of Home Missions. San Antonio was ever on his heart and mind, and his spirit enters into the whole enterprise. To Dr. Robert N. McLean, who succeeded his father in this work, is due a large measure of praise for the final outcome, his wise counsels, his statesman-like grasp of the whole situation, his patience and sympathy, and his willingness to help in time of need, contributed largely to the success of the work. Dr. B. P. Fullerton, of the Board of National Missions, was largely responsible for the aid granted first and last to the Mission. His warm heart and genial optimism in times of distress and doubt, when the income of the Board ran low, encouraged all the workers never to despair. In the early days Mrs. W. B. Preston, President of Woman's Synodical, not only helped to enlist the Synodical in the work, but gave of her time and labors to the work. Rev. W. B. Preston found Mr. Lopez and sent him into the work. In 1919 Rev. B. Wrenn Webb, D. D., became Superintendent of Home Missions for the Synod of Texas, and at once gave the Mexican work his untiring attention. The establishment of the Home of Neighborly Service, the enlistment of Miss Bessie V. Sneed in the service, and securing Miss Sophie Thieler were his contributions to the Mission. When in the early part of 1925 Rev. Geo. W. Fender, D. D., became Executive Secretary of the Board of National Missions, in the Synod of Texas, the Mission found another able helper. So faithful and constant has been Dr. Fender's interest in the work that it is difficult to point out the high points of his administration. But the present strategic location is due to his insight and understanding. "The present location of the San Antonio Mission was the result of an intensive survey made by the Rev. Charles A. Greenway of the Board of National Missions. This step was taken in connection with Dr. Fender's forward-looking plan and definitely fixed the center of the Mexican population which we serve within a block or two of the site which we finally secured."

Dr. Fender was the leader in the organization of the Synodical Extension Fund, approved by Synod's Committee on National Missions Jan. 9, 1925, and approved by Synod the following October. The aim was to raise a sum of $25,000.00 in three years, and the use of it was to "include the erection of the new building already voted upon by the Synod for the Mexican work at San Antonio." Out of this fund a considerable sum was contributed to the new building. Of course all who have labored here must be recognized as sharers in the success, and this includes Miss Bessie V. Sneed and Miss Sophie Theiler. The Building Committee was composed at first of Mr. Geo. E. Bell, Mrs. O. N. Johnson and Mr. C. K. Schafer. Later Mr. Bell resigned and Mr. C. M. Stone took his place. Mr. Harvey P. Smith was the architect, and Mr. James Aiken was the contractor and builder. Mr. Aiken deserves high praise for his interest, patience and co-operation in the difficult task. The co-operation of Rev. Edgar Hubbard, Chairman of the Committee on National Missions for Austin Presbytery; of Rev. J. M. Todd, D. D., Rev. A. H. Brand, D. D., and Rev. I. T. Jones, D. D., pastors of Madison Square Presbyterian Church, and the women of that church, were essential factors in the work. We could not forget the able and valuable assistance of Hon. O. M. Fitzhugh. Mr. Fitzhugh gave freely of his time and talents in all business and legal matters connected with the property interests. Miss Sneed is proud of the fact the Home of Neighborly Service gave the first payment on the new property, $500.00, out of the savings of the Home for that purpose, and also that $400.00 from the same source was the first money paid to Mr. Aiken after the building was started.

THE WOMAN'S SYNODICAL OF TEXAS had a large share in this work from the beginning. The Synodical sponsored Tabita Mireles, and it was Tabita who started the kindergarten. They furnished $500.00 for the purchase of the first property. When the present property was purchased the Synodical contributed $450.00. Then in the spring of 1926 Mrs. B. A. Hodges, Synodical President, with the hearty co-operation of the Synodical, launched a campaign to secure from every Presbyterian woman in the Synod of Texas at least one dollar for the building fund. It was understood that in some way the fund thus raised was to be dedicated to Texas Synodical. The money was raised, and it was possible to continue work on the building. It is but fair to say that without this help the building could not so soon have been finished. Later, another campaign was launched to secure funds to furnish and equip two rooms in the new building, to be dedicated, one to Miss Sneed, whose faith and devotion had made the whole enterprise blessed, and the clinic room to Consuela Medina, whose beautiful life is one of the treasured memories of the Home of Neighborly Service and the Church of the Divine Redeemer. This campaign secured the money and the rooms are furnished and dedicated as designed.

This is the story of the past. We rejoice in what has been done by the Presbyterian Church in the U. S. A. for the evangelization of the Mexican people of Texas in these three centers. We thank God and take courage. May the future be full of noble service, and may the reward of labors in His name be rich and blessed.

SPANISH-SPEAKING AMERICANS

Mexicans and Puerto Ricans
in the United States

By

Bertha Blair

Anne O. Lively

Glen W. Trimble
Director, Home Missions Research

A Study Conducted by the Home Missions Research
Unit of the Bureau of Research and Survey
for the Home Missions Division
of the National Council of
Churches of Christ in
the United States
of America
1959

TABLE OF CONTENTS

PREFACE

"Spanish-speaking americans," the present volume, represents two of three parts of a study authorized May 24, 1957 by the Committee on Spanish American Work of the Home Missions Division of the National Council of Churches of Christ in the United States of America. This committee consists of Protestant denominational executives responsible for and cooperating in work with Spanish Americans in the United States. The responsibility for the entire study was assigned to the Home Missions Research unit of the Bureau of Research and Survey of the N.C.C.C.

The third part of the project which as a whole has carried a working label of "Missionary Opportunity Among Spanish Americans" is a survey of the actual present program of work in this field by these denominations. This phase will be reported separately.

The present content is a preliminary survey of the existing literature for light it may give on "quantity" and especially "quality" of the peoples of Spanish American background in the continental United States. The original prospectus declared that "Our deepest concern is for real penetration and basic understanding of the several culture systems which are blanketed under the term 'Spanish Americans.' At what points do they contrast and conflict with U.S. 'Anglo' culture and its regional and class sub-cultures?"

The committee regards this study as a beginning, a first step in a process of discovering areas of needed basic research and of encouraging the accomplishment of original work in the field.

[v]

INTRODUCTION

THE RELATIONSHIP of Spanish American people to American Protestantism is not a new problem. Actually it has been present as long as there have been Protestant groups in this country. However, such factors as the dynamic characteristic of Puerto Rican migration, changing patterns in Hispanic culture in the Southwest and a sincere desire on the part of the Home Mission agencies of the churches to re-think their responsibilities have led to this study. The present report, a major part of the total assignment, is designed to draw from the existing literature some of the findings and conclusions which are both of general value and, particularly, can help the program and policy makers in the churches.

For the purposes of this study, two major groups of Spanish Americans are considered. They are the Puerto Ricans and the Spanish American people of the Southwest, who have come up from Mexico over a span of four centuries. There are other Spanish American groups in the United States and even these two groups upon whom attention is focused are really made up of many sub-groups and sub-cultures. However, they are by far the largest groups and they are still growing. They therefore seem to represent a logical basis for concentrating concern.

Opportunity For What?

At the very outset the researchers' understanding of the total assignment should be set forth. What is meant by "Missionary Opportunity Among Spanish Americans," the working title assigned by the sponsoring committee?

For the purposes of this study "missionary opportunity" is considered to be the opportunity and responsibility of the churches to fulfill their basic goals. It is the "church-at-work" in the total community situation.

This seems to be perfectly consistent with the thinking now

going on in Home Missions circles. The tendency to separate the missionary task of the church into a special compartment, a tendency which has long been obvious in most mission work, is rapidly disappearing. The Home Mission task is not thought to be "doing the things the local church can't do." It is, rather, the extension of the basic task of the church into the total community, the total culture. Thus missionary opportunity means the outreach of the churches to the Spanish American people, not "to do something for them," but to draw them into the Christian fellowship with all the rights and privileges which this involves.

It should not be necessary to point out the fact that this definition provides a different setting for this study from what might be the setting if a more traditional concept had been adopted. It is well known that for a long time, and for that matter even today, the question which the churches have asked is "What can we do for these people who are different from us?" Policy has been approved and programs developed in this context. With sincere motivation, the churches have "gone out" to help and their accomplishments have been significant, at times even spectacular.

A New Dimension

However, a new dimension is added in the approach to this subject. The questions are related to inclusiveness, not to exclusiveness, not to service to an "out-group" but to building the kind of cohesive fellowship in which Christianity can do its work.

Implicit in this concept is a theological definition of the task of the church. What is it that the church is trying to do? What is it that must become the common task of American Protestants and Spanish Americans? Richard Niebuhr has defined the task of the church as "increasing the love of God and neighbors" and this seems to be an inclusive and satisfactory definition for us as a basis for the present exploration.

In terms of the definitions which have been given in the preceding paragraphs, the basic task of this project becomes an analysis of the opportunity for the churches to carry out this responsibility for increasing the love of God and neighbors in fellowship with Spanish American people. This analysis involves consideration of the need for helping these people as they seek to find their way in a new cultural environment but its main focus will be upon the problem areas in which are located the obstacles to the development of fellowship and to the fulfillment of the church's mission.

The Majority's Role

One additional statement should be made about the approach to this project. It has been characteristic in the past to deal with problems involving human relations in terms of minority group factors. Much of the research which has been done has been on this basis. What are the factors in the minority group which retard integration or impede acculturation? Recently a shift has been taking place with increasing emphasis upon majority group problems. The questions become, "What are the conditions in the majority group which create resistance to the acceptance of the minority group?" and "What are the barriers which the majority group erects against the minority?"

It has been the intention of the study to keep these two dimensions in balance and to relate the various social and cultural problems to this majority-minority polarity. Obviously this is not an attempt to dichotomize. Many factors are present in both groups—majority and minority, American Protestant and Spanish American. It is, however, an attempt to underline the fact, which emerges clearly in available data, that many of the issues confronting the churches in the involvement of Spanish Americans, probably even the major problems, are within the existing church community.

Methodology

By original definition the scope of this report is limited to secondary research, to an exploration of the existing literature in the field. There are many hundreds of research reports, books and articles on Spanish Americans. These represent work in a number of disciplines, among them, and of special concern in this enterprise, sociology, anthropology and history.

What follows is in no sense an effort to add another bit of limited primary research but, rather an effort to discover the contributions which exist within available sources which can serve as guides to church leaders and others as they evaluate present program and plan for the future. To this end, many books and articles have been studied and hundreds of pages of notes have been accumulated for analysis. The selected bibliography following the main body of the text gives some indication of the range of relevant literature. It is this material that has provided the foundation for the present report.

Obviously the nature of the concerns, the angles of attack, and the qualities of insight vary widely among writers in the field. There is little, almost no, overlapping of intensive research on Puerto Ricans and on Mexicans either in their homelands or in the United States. The "teams" in the two fields are largely separate. While there are brief descriptive treatments of both groups as instances of U.S. minorities as in Carey McWilliams *Brothers Under The Skin* and John Burma's recent work, serious cross-cultural study, comparison and contrast remains to be done.

Another generalization seems justified. There has been far more, and far more substantial, investigation along sociological and cultural anthropological lines of the Spanish-speaking peoples of the Southwest, on both sides of the border than has been done for Puerto Ricans. This is especially true of Puerto Ricans on the continental mainland and, no doubt, is explained in large part by the comparative recency of their arrival in large numbers on the mainland.

The methodological problem involved is that the available data falls far short of being parallel. To a significant extent the present treatment is governed by both the varying emphases and the varying gaps in the scientific study of the two groups with which we are concerned.

Selection

Inevitably certain selective processes have been at work, determined partly by the limitations and partly by the very definitions which were accepted for the project. The report itself will develop the arguments for points of greater or lesser emphasis, but it is appropriate here to lift up some major points. Positively, there is special concern for exploring whenever possible (1) the background culture pattern and the dynamics of its internal historic development and (2) the impact of our "American" majority culture on these particular minorities and the responsibilities *for the majority* which this entails. Negatively, there has not been special concern for (1) exhaustive and indiscriminate description of all aspects of Spanish American life in the continental United States, (2) stress on the "peculiar ways" of these minorities or their subgroups, or (3) extensive analysis of the social problems with which they are confronted in the new setting. It was felt that point one leads everywhere and nowhere, point two often simply supplies ammunition for the pre-prejudiced and point three tends to confuse effect with cause. The literature abounds with readily available supplementary material on all three points and this seemed a secondary justification for not stressing them in the present work.

There has not been an intention to exclude significant data or matter contradictory to the main thesis presented. Whether or not the explicit selective biases stated have actually worked in this way is a matter to be decided by the content that follows and the reader's judgment.

One further element of selectivity—and of broader methodological problems—the report has three authors. The consequences in variety of form and style and in shading of emphasis will doubtless be apparent.

Order of Presentation

Since the interaction of the majority and minorities, and the dominant controls of the former, are a basic concern and framework of this analysis, this is considered first. There follows in Chapters II and III a survey of the statistical knowledge of the groups especially under consideration. Although it was decided early in the project that quantitative analysis was not to be the sole or the major focus, their delineation in these terms is a preliminary aid for the cultural material that follows.

The succeeding chapters deal with what is intended as the

"meat" of the document, the effort to penetrate into the life pattern of the Spanish Americans of the Southwest and the Puerto Ricans. Here, especially, the divergencies of the data available influence the respective treatments of the two groups. The summary and conclusion seeks to point up some of the major implications of the study for Protestant strategic planning.

After a process of regretful elimination two appendices are included. Their place at the end is not a measure of their value. The discussion of "cultural democracy" is vitally and importantly related to decision making for American's minorities and, especially, for the majority and for any and all of the institutions that that majority has responsibility for. The report by Dr. Barry for the New York City Mission Society is a concrete example of an active and imaginative program of work with Puerto Ricans in the contemporary scene.

The Time Factor

Much of the information in Chapter II and III is based on the 1950 census, now almost ten years old. Similarly, all of the authors quoted throughout are "dated" by the time that they wrote. Meanwhile the ferment of change, phenomenal in Puerto Rico, rapid and accelerating in Mexico and substantial in most of the areas of settlement for both groups in the United States, never stops. Truth does not have to be very ancient to become uncouth—to lag behind the emerging situation. This qualification needs continual recognition in evaluating what follows. It is to be hoped that at least present and perhaps future trend is foreshadowed.

Acknowledgments

Within the staff the primary responsibility for research, and the longest hours of hard work belong to Mrs. Anne O. Lively and Miss Bertha Blair. Mrs. Lively had primary assignment for the Spanish-speaking peoples of the Southwest; Miss Blair for the Puerto Ricans. In terms of final authorship, although there was a continuing collaborative process, major credit belongs to Mrs. Lively for Chapters II and V and Appendix I and to Miss Blair for Chapters I, III, and VI. Glen Trimble is primarily responsible for this Introduction, Chapters IV and VII. Mrs. Margaret Mills worked skillfully and unstintingly in the preparation of the final manuscript. Dr. Lauris Whitman, Director of the Bureau of Research and Survey shared in early drafts of the Introduction and Chapter I and in many conferences and consultations as the project progressed.

The Committee on Spanish American Work of the Home Missions Division headed by Lillian Windham, the special study committee headed by Paul Warnshuis and Meryl Ruoss of the Divisional staff have all shared in the travail of the birth and development of this project.

It should be clear even at this early stage that the study is overwhelmingly indebted to the students, workers and writers in these fields. Frequent recognition of this fact appears in the text and the footnotes. Special mention should be made of the contribution of Dr. Lyle Saunders on Mexican Americans and of Clarence Senior on Puerto Ricans. They have made the task infinitely easier and, paradoxically, somewhat more difficult. The assignment was one of synthesizing and analyzing, with a special cultural concern, the existing research in the field. Saunders and Senior, each in his own field, have been doing this brilliantly for years with the immense advantage of direct, active working experience with the peoples about whom they talk and write. The men and their writings are strongly recommended to all who seek increasing understanding of Spanish-speaking Americans.

To make a distinct contribution in these circumstances was a difficulty which may or may not have been overcome. The present effort, while drawing heavily on these rich resources, has sought to steer an independent and, hopefully, an original course.

Chapter I

MAJORITY-MINORITY RELATIONSHIPS

In recent years more attention than ever before has been given to majority-minority relationships. This is true not only for the United States but for most of the world. In the United States, there has been a growing recognition that improvement in majority-minority relations is not only a serious internal problem to be solved but also that it is a matter of deep concern in connection with relations between the United States and its world neighbors.

Our research indicates that for several decades the internal problem of majority-minority relations in American society has been a major concern of social scientists in the United States. Research also reveals how widely present-day social scientists differ from the social scientists of the first twenty-five years of this century in their thinking on this matter.

There are many groups that have a minority status in American society but some have much more acute problems of majority-minority relations than others, and it is with these groups that the social scientists in recent years have been most concerned. All comprehensive studies in this field include not only the American Indians and the American Negroes but also the Spanish American groups—Hispanos, Mexicans, and Puerto Ricans.

A New Focus

In going over the available scientific and other literature in connection with this report, it has become clear that social scientific thinking today with respect to minority problems represents considerable revision over the thought of only a few years ago. For all groups concerned with this problem, and especially for the churches, this would seem to have genuine significance.

[1]

Among the most significant of the most recent changes indicated in an examination of the literature is the change in focus from emphasis on the peculiarities of the minority to the problem of the majority. While recognizing that the majority group in American society plays an important role in majority-minority relationships, the emphasis in the past was on the minority. The earlier studies of minority problems in the United States by social scientists were focused almost exclusively on the peculiarities of minority groups, particularly the ways in which the culture patterns and value systems of minority groups differed from American culture patterns and values. This emphasis has tended to place the responsibility for minority status in the United States almost entirely on the minority groups themselves.

Majority Responsibility

More recently, however, social scientific groups—sociologists, anthropologists, and psychologists—have begun to concentrate their attention on the majority group in American society. Some of them actually are now placing the principal responsibility for the persistence of minority status of such groups as American Indians, American Negroes, Mexicans, Catholics, Jews and others on the dominant majority group. A few American social scientists had made the point earlier but Myrdal in his monumental work, *An American Dilemma*, brought this point of view to the attention of Americans as it had not been brought before. Though Myrdal's research was directed to the American Negro problem, his findings have equal significance for an understanding of all minority group problems including Spanish American minority problems. The following is from his Introduction:[1]

> . . . When the present investigator started his inquiry, his preconception was that it had to be focused on the Negro people and their peculiarities. This is understandable since, from a superficial view, Negro Americans, not only in physical appearance, but also in thoughts, feelings, and in manner of life, seemed stranger to him than did white Americans. Furthermore, most of the literature on the Negro problem dealt with the

---

1 Gunnar, Myrdal, *An American Dilemma* (AAD), li.

Negroes: their racial and cultural characteristics, their living standards and occupational pursuits, their stratification in social classes, their migration, their family organization, their religion, their illiteracy, delinquency and disease, and so on. But as he proceeded in his studies into the Negro problem, it became increasingly evident that little, if anything, could be scientifically explained in terms of the peculiarities of the Negroes themselves . . . practically all the economic, social, and political power is held by whites. . . .

It is thus the white majority group that naturally determines the Negro's "place." All our attempts to reach scientific explanations of why the Negroes are what they are and why they live as they do have regularly led to determinants on the white side of the race line. In the practical and political struggles of effecting changes, the views and attitudes of the white Americans are likewise strategic. The Negro's entire life, and consequently, also his opinions on the Negro problem, are, in the main, to be considered as secondary reactions to more primary pressures from the side of the dominant white majority.

The Majority Group

Authorities tend to agree that the composition of the majority group in the United States is basically Anglo-Saxon, Protestant, and white. Stewart and Mildred Cole define "majority" in general terms and specifically for the United States as follows:[2]

> That group of people which by reason of its historic, political, social, and economic advantage enjoys privileges and influence not shared equally by other groups is the dominant culture group in the community. In the United States this group is chiefly of Anglo-Saxon extraction, belongs to the Caucasian racial stock, holds to the Protestant faith, and is numerically strongest. . . . Their culture predominates in the langauge, the laws, the religion, and the folkways in most communities in the nation, as well as in the national cultural pattern.

The federal Committee on Civil Rights described the "majority group" in the United States in the following terms in 1947:[3]

> The dominant majority in the United States is Caucasian, English-speaking, Protestant, and of comparatively distant Anglo-Saxon or European background. This majority outnum-

2 Stewart and Mildred Cole, *Minorities and the American Promise* (MAP), 46.
3 President's Committee on Civil Rights, *To Secure These Rights* (TSTR), 14.

[3]

bers any particular minority group, although its dominant position is less apparent when the minorities are added together.

The Coles proceed to define the "majority" in even sharper terms saying that the Anglo tradition[4]

> . . . stressed the priority of white persons over non-white peoples, of Protestantism over the Roman Catholic and other faiths, and of the English social-class system over others. . . . It became popular for Anglos to believe that non-Anglos transplanted inferior modes of living, perpetuated lower class folkways, and yielded easily to the corruptive influence of political machines. Consequently the favored group attempted to condition the behavior of the non-light-skinned, non-English-speaking, non-Protestants, so that they would conform to the will of the majority.

In defining the majority, authorities point out that in the acculturation process, minority groups sometimes assume majority attitudes toward each other; that minority lines in the United States often cut across one another. The Committee on Civil Rights has explained it as follows:[5]

> For example, south European immigrant groups are minority groups in relation to older, English-speaking immigrants. But they are part of the white majority in relation to the Negro minority. Members of religious minorities may belong either to minorities or majorities, based on race or national origin.

The point is usually made also that the majority has tended finally to accept some who at first occupied a distinctly minority status, so that some of these earlier minorities have almost disappeared in the larger population.

Many sources describing the attitudes, ideas and actions of the American majority toward minority groups are available, particularly historical treatments. A thoroughly documented historical study recently published under the title, *Ancestors and Immigrants*,[6] describes the Anglo-Saxon majority of New England in terms of its attitudes and ideas toward the Irish, Italian and other southern European minorities and its activities in support of immigration restriction.

---

4 Cole, MAP, 48.
5 TSTR, 14.
6 Barbara M. Solomon, Author.

[4]

Scientific inquiry into the problems of majority attitudes is relatively recent and most scientists would agree that only a bare beginning has been made in this field. However, such sources as *The Nature of Prejudice* by Allport and *The Social Psychology of Prejudice* by Saenger open up new avenues of thinking in this major area.

The Minority Groups

Minority groups are not peculiarly American and minority problems of one sort or another "are as old as civilization and as universal as the social organization of mankind."[7] But the term "minority" has come to have a special connotation in the United States.

The term "minority" used to describe population groups came into common usage after World War I when the peace treaty was being drawn up. In Europe, it referred to such people as the Ukrainians in Poland or the Germans in Czecho-slovakia, but in the transfer to the New World context the term acquired a significantly different connotation. Discussing this point Dr. Oscar Handlin says:[8]

> In Czechoslovakia or Poland it had been assumed that the preponderant majority of the population shared common traits of national origin, and, standing apart from the homogeneous majority of Czechs or Poles, there remained minority clumps of Germans or Ukrainians. The same meaning did not hold across the Atlantic. In the United States there was no majority in that sense; all the groups which considered themselves minorities after 1918, added together, were more than a majority of the total population. Furthermore, such people as the Catholics, the Germans, or the Negroes, who applied the term to themselves, by no means acknowledged thereby that they were less American in nationality than anyone else.

In a very general way, it may be said that all those population groups that do not fall within the definition of the majority as commonly defined make up the minority population of American society. As will be seen in analyzing the definitions quoted below, the term "minority" as used in the United States

---

7 Francis J. Brown and Joseph S. Roucek, *Our Racial and National Minorities* (ORNM), 3.
8 Oscar Handlin, *Race and Nationality in American Life* (RNAL), 170.

to identify population groups carries with it the connotation of inferior status as related to the majority. Moreover the definitions most often found in the literature usually define the term "minority" in terms of majority attitudes and ideas.

Definitions

Dr. Handlin defines minority status in the United States as the condition forced upon nationality and racial groups in the population by the dominant majority. Arnold and Caroline Rose in *America Divided* define "minority" in terms of the majority also but they attribute it to a deep-seated mental block in the majority as the following quotation indicates:[9]

> There are so many different kinds of people in the United States that no one kind is a majority. In terms of numbers, everyone is in a minority. Certain groups, however, are hated by most other people, and we concentrate our attention on them and label them "minorities" . . .
>
> Putting the definition in terms of "hatred" may raise some eyebrows because it is not customary, but it is probably more understandable and useful than other definitions. In the first place, it makes explicit the fact that the *problem* of the minority—that is, the hate—lies in the majority and not in the minority. Until recently it was commonly believed that the minority group had some obnoxious trait that inevitably caused it to be a problem. Well meaning people studied, and thought, and asked: "What can we do for these minority people so they won't be a problem?" Now we know that this point of view itself is a mild manifestation of the cause of the minority problem—it is a mild form of hatred. We now know that minority problems exist in the minds of the majority: the Negro problem is really a white man's problem, and the Jewish problem is really a Gentile problem. This does not mean, of course, that their is nothing wrong with the minorities themselves. It means that the singling out of certain kinds of people and considering them as "problems" because of their different race, nationality, or religion represents a distortion in the minds of the majority.

The President's Committee on Civil Rights put the definition in somewhat broader terms as follows:[10]

---

9 Arnold and Caroline Rose, *America Divided* (AD), 3-4.
10 TSTR, 14.

[6]

A minority, broadly defined, is a group which is treated or which regards itself as a people apart. It is distinguished by cultural or physical characteristics, or both. The extent to which it can be distinguished usually indicates its degree of apartness.

But none of these definitions place the emphasis entirely on cultural and racial differences in and of themselves as William G. Sumner, the most influential of the earlier scientists, did. Brown and Roucek in *Our Racial and National Minorities* have the following to say:[11]

The definition must be drawn primarily from a sociological approach. Our attitudes are determined less by numerical ratios or legalistic conceptions than by the constellation of social processes, and their expression in terms of subtle discrimination or overt behavior. We are thus dealing with intangibles impossible of exact definition. However, we shall use the term in the sociological sense: the individuals and groups which differ or are assumed to differ from their dominant social groups and have developed, in varying degree, an attitude of mind which gives them a feeling of greater social security within their own group than in their relation to the dominant group. The differences, although varying in degree, are distinguishing characteristics not only in terms of race, religion, nationality, and state allegiance but also in the composite pattern. However, such differences in and of themselves are not sufficient to make a group a minority without the accompanying attitude of dominance and subservience, consciously accepted or tacitly assumed.

It may be that the current tendency is to overemphasize the significance of mental attitudes and to underemphasize the economic basis of much of the prejudice exhibited by the majority. The same authors point out "that in times of economic stress there is a definite tendency to accentuate differences between groups and resentment against certain minorities."[12]

Distance and Color

In defining "minority," the majority generally recognizes and employs criteria to establish degrees of minority status with respect to various population groups. Emory S. Bogardus was

---

11 Brown and Roucek, ORNM, 5-6.
12 Brown and Roucek, ORNM, 6.

[7]

among the first to apply this hypothesis in developing a methodology for the measurement of prejudice or "social distance" which was the term he adopted. More recently the Anti-Defamation League has brought this point to public attention. These studies seem to indicate that color is the basic majority determinant of social distance; that the darker the color of one's skin, the more complete the isolation from the majority.

On the basis of color, then, some Spanish Americans probably do not suffer the same degree of isolation from the majority as do Negroes or American Indians. On the other hand, the darker Puerto Ricans do suffer a similar degree of isolation to that experienced by Negroes and Indians, and the social distance between Mexicans and the majority group in many areas of the Southwest is about equal to the social distance between Negroes and whites.

Numbers

The word "minority" as commonly used generally connotes a state of being less or smaller than something else. For the most part, the word has this meaning when used with reference to population groups in the United States, but there are local situations where the term actually is a misnomer. Brown and Roucek in discussing the meaning of minorities in the United States say:[13]

> . . . The most obvious division, and the one implied in the literal use of the terms, is that based upon a numerical ratio. However, one may cite many illustrations in which this ratio is reversed and the larger group is dominated by the lesser. . . . In many communities the Negro dominates numerically, and hence represents the majority dominated by the minority. An immigrant can live in a Czechoslovak settlement in Texas, wherein he is of the majority group and even the officials are his countrymen, yet, in relation to the total population of the United States, the immigrant represents a minority. Frequently, then, the problem of a "minority" is not that of a numerical minority at all but actually that of a majority. We must go beyond mere statistics to formulate our definition.

Taken separately, each of the "minority groups" in the United States are numerical minorities with respect to the

---

13 Brown and Roucek, ORNM, 4-5.

total population. For Spanish Americans, the situation in local communities varies. In so far as is known, there are no states, counties, or cities in which Puerto Ricans constitute a majority of the population. Most Puerto Ricans have settled in the larger cities and the great majority are concentrated in New York City alone where it is estimated they now constitute 8.4 per cent of the population.[14]

In the Southwest, however, there are many border communities and major areas of one entire state, New Mexico, where people of Spanish-speaking origin out-number or closely approximate the totals of the rest of the population.

Origin

Frequently the explanation for the majority's attitude toward minority groups is that they are foreigners. But this clearly is not the basic determinant of minority status. A large proportion of those that now comprise minority groups as well as several generations of their ancestors actually were born in the United States or in territory that is now part of the United States, whereas the majority includes a large proportion of foreign-born and first generation Americans.

The Indians were the original inhabitants and yet they are one of our most persistent minority groups. Most Negroes now living here were born here as were several generations of their ancestors. Hispanos of the Southwest probably are as thoroughly rooted on this continent as are the northern Europeans that colonized the eastern part of the United States. Most Puerto Ricans now living have never known any sovereignty other than the United States which took over the island from Spain in 1898. Most of the migration to the continent has occurred since that time, largely in the last twenty years. Of all present day minority groups, the Mexican American group, as distinguished from the Hispanos, probably includes the largest number of foreign-born or first generation Mexican Americans. Although some were here earlier, migration from Mexico as an independent nation to the United States did not assume large proportions until about 1900.

---

14 *Facts and Figures*, (FAF), January, 1959 edition, 17.

The majority culture group, on the other hand, is made up almost totally of people who came as immigrants themselves or whose ancestors did. Except for those with some American Indian blood there are none who may call themselves native inhabitants.

Of the Spanish American groups with whom we are here concerned, both the Hispanos and some Mexican Americans had very early connections with what is now the United States. Also, to a large extent they may properly claim actually to have been original inhabitants because of the extent to which they intermarried with Indians. Though there was some inter-marriage between Spaniards and the native Indians of Puerto Rico, there is probably much less of native Indian strain in the population than is true either of the Hispanos or the Mexican Americans. The common theory is that the Spaniards had wiped out or caused to move to other islands all but a relatively few of the members of the two Indian tribes that inhabited the island when Columbus set foot there in 1493. But even though the Puerto Ricans may not claim a large strain of native ancestry, the islanders had been there for many generations before Spain lost it to the United States in 1898.

On the other hand, very recent immigrants from Northern European countries who constitute the bulk of today's quota from Europe to the United States are readily accepted by the majority.

Economic Status

It is generally true that minority status and low economic position go hand in hand, but it does not follow that higher economic or social position afford immediate acceptance by the dominant culture group. For example, Negro and Jewish minorities as well as southern Europeans and Spanish Americans have in the past been and still are bound by various types of restrictions irrespective of personal income. Restrictive covenants have for years been used in middle or upper income neighborhoods to keep these minority groups out. Although the restrictive covenant regulating the purchase of property has been outlawed, finding a house or apartment to rent is still very difficult for members of minority groups no matter what price they are prepared to pay.

[10]

An Integrated Approach

The approach to minority problems from the perspective of majority responsibility has led social scientists also to consider minority problems as a whole. This point of view, usually referred to as the "integrated approach" to minority groups, was first introduced by Donald R. Young in 1932 in his *American Minority Peoples*. Myrdal quotes from Young as follows:[15]

> The view here presented is that the problems and principles of race relations are remarkably similar, regardless of what groups are involved; and that only by an integrated study of all minority peoples in the United States can a real understanding and sociological analysis of the involved social phenomena be achieved.

> It is . . . to be expected that dominating majorities in various regions, when faced with the problem of what to think and do about minorities, will fail to be sufficiently inventive to create unique schemes of relationships and action. Variations in intensity of restriction and oppression, special techniques in maintaining superior status and other adaptations to the local scene will always be found, but the choice of fundamental patterns of dominance in majority-minority relations is limited by the nature of man and his circumstances.

The literature is full of data that verify this point of view. The treatment that has been dealt out by the Anglo-Saxon majority has been much the same whether the difference be in nationality, race or religion. Italians, Jews, Irish, Negroes, American Indians, Chinese, Japanese, Filipinos, Mexicans, Hispanos, and Puerto Ricans all have been faced with the same forms of prejudice and discrimination, economic as well as social, and this majority attitude revealed itself very early in our history. One recent study reveals that[16]

> Horace Bushnell, as early as 1837, had cautioned the Americans to protect their noble Saxon blood against the miscellaneous tide of immigration, and in the 1850's there were occasional suggestions that a Celtic flood might swamp America's distinctive Anglo-Saxon traits. But on the whole, racial nationalists proclaimed an unqualified confidence in the American destiny. Sometimes they explicitly averred that the Anglo-Saxon would always retain predominance over all comers.

---

15 Myrdal, AAD, 1185-1186.
16 John Higham, *Strangers in the Land, Patterns of American Nativism, 1860-1925* (SIL), 10-11.

[11]

The first large group of newcomers that experienced this native Americanism were the Irish Catholics and the German Catholics that came in such large numbers in the 1850's as a result of the potato famine in Ireland and the revolution in Germany. The first large anti-foreign movement, was led by the American Know-Nothing Party, a party composed mainly of Protestants. As to the treatment of the Chinese later on, Higham says:[17]

> No variety of anti-European sentiment has ever approached the violent extremes to which anti-Chinese agitation went in the 1870's and 1880's. Lynchings, boycotts, and mass expulsions still harassed the Chinese after the federal government yielded to the clamor for their exclusion in 1882.

About the treatment of the Japanese, the same author says: "Anti-Japanese sentiment, gathering strength slowly after 1900 as immigration from Nippon increased, burst forth in a raging flood in 1905." And about the situation in the coal mines of Pennsylvania, he says:[18]

> From the outset the Slavic and Italian immigrants ran a gamut of indignities and ostracisms. They were abused in public and isolated in private, cuffed in the works and pelted on the streets, fined and imprisoned on the smallest pretext, cheated of their wages, and crowded by the score into converted barns and tumble-down shanties that served as boarding houses. . . .

This majority attitude exists today not only in individual members of the majority but it was written into the law of the land in the act of 1924 and has been continued and even extended by the McCarran-Walter Act of 1952.[19]

As has been indicated, it is the contention of those who adhere to the "integrated" approach that because so many minority problems are the same there can be no satisfactory independent solution for one or two minorities. This approach would seem to have considerable relevance for the solution of intergroup relationships where Mexicans and Puerto Ricans are concerned.

---

17 Higham, SIL, 25.
18 Higham, SIL, 47-48.
19 For a discussion of the history of the movement that led to this legislation, see "The 'Scientific' Basis of Our Immigration Policy" in the July 1955 issue of *Commentary* and *Ancestors and Immigrants* by Barbara Miller Solomon, Harvard University Press, 1956.

An All-American Problem

Social scientists are beginning not only to adopt the "integrated approach" to minority groups but they also are beginning to look at the problems of minorities in their relation to the problems of American society as a whole. This was Myrdal's approach and it would seem to have significance for an understanding of Spanish American problems. To quote Myrdal and substituting the term "Spanish American" for "Negro":[20]

> The Spanish American problem is an integral part of, or a special phase of, the whole complex of problems in the larger American civilization. It cannot be treated in isolation. There is no single side of the Spanish American problem—whether it be the Spanish American's political status, the education he gets, his place in the labor market, his cultural and personality traits, or anything else—which is not predominantly determined by its total American setting.

Again quoting Myrdal but substituting the term "minority" for the term "Negro":[21]

> The relationship between American society and the minority problem is not one-sided. The entire structure of American society is itself greatly conditioned by the presence of the minorities. American politics, the labor market, education, religious life, civic ideals, art, and recreation are as they are partly because of the important conditioning factor working throughout the history of the nation. New impulses from minority people are constantly affecting the American way of life, bending in some degree all American institutions and bringing changes in every aspect of the American's complex world view. . . .

The influence of America's large Negro population on the entire structure of American society about which Myrdal speaks holds for Spanish Americans as well, but particularly for those areas of the country in which the Spanish American minorities are concentrated. We look next at some significant facts and figures about the distribution and composition of the Mexican and Puerto Rican populations in the continental United States.

---

20 Myrdal, AAD, liii.
21 Myrdal, AAD, liii.

Chapter II

SPANISH-SPEAKING PEOPLE
OF THE SOUTHWEST[1]

THE TRANSFORMATION of the Southwest, hitherto relatively undeveloped and unpopulated, in the last fifty years has been
largely possible through the use of immigrant Mexican labor.
With Oriental immigration barred and European immigration
placed on a rigid quota basis, railroad and agricultural interests, in their search for plentiful and cheap labor, turned
south to Mexico for their supply.

The greatest number of Spanish-speaking persons in the
United States derive from this migration which had its peak
between 1910 and 1930, but the majority are now native-born.
Each year there is new migration but the numbers are less
significant and represent a considerable number of contract
workers who return to Mexico. An undetermined number of
illegal entrants, "wetbacks," continue to enter but the extent
of this group has been greatly curtailed in the last few years
by stricter enforcement of immigration controls.

Even before the Mexican immigration in the first half of
1900 there was a substantial Spanish-speaking population in
the Southwest, the bulk of which dates back to the days of
Spanish colonization and represents the progeny of early Spanish settlers. Persons of Spanish and Indian stock, they lived in
isolation for almost three hundred years and experienced little
interruption or change in their community life. Usually referred to as Hispanos or Spanish-Colonials, they are now largely concentrated in New Mexico and Southern Colorado and
while having certain characteristics in common with Mexican

---

1 In this section the term "Spanish-speaking of the Southwest" will include naturalized immigrants from Mexico, native-born persons with parents or grandparents
born in Mexico, alien Mexicans in the United States either on a temporary or permanent basis, and Spanish Colonials largely concentrated in New Mexico and
southern Colorado.

Americans—notably in their relations with Anglos—they differ in that they never really left Mexico to live in the United States but became residents through annexation. Their village-centered life, however, had many of the same qualities as Mexican villages and the problems they experience as they migrate to urban centers involve most of the same adjustments faced by Mexican Americans.

One might ask why such divergent groups—*Spanish Colonials* who have been in this country since colonial days and have lived in an agricultural economy largely isolated from modern living; *Mexican Americans*, some of them third and fourth generation, many of whom live in large urban centers; and *Mexicans*, persons recently arrived from Mexico—should be discussed as a single group? Perhaps they should not, for to so handily lump them into a single group suggests a homogeneity that does not exist. Schermerhorn, McWilliams, Saunders and Sanchez, among others, have stressed the variety within the Mexican and Hispano communities. Saunders, a leading authority on the Spanish-speaking people of this region, makes this comment:[2]

> The Spanish-speaking people of the Southwest are not now, and never have been, a homogeneous people in any narrow meaning of that term. Both biologically and culturally—and perhaps also psychologically—they differ from one part of the region to another. They came into the Southwest from different places and at different times. They settled in areas that are geographically and culturally dissimilar. They developed or adopted differing basic economies. They had somewhat different experiences with the social groups among whom they settled and who settled among them.

With such admonitions to recognize its heterogeneous nature, on what basis can the Spanish-speaking population be discussed as a unified minority group? In another context, Saunders explains:[3]

> Although it is difficult to find a set of criteria for precisely defining them, the Spanish-speaking people, viewed as a group, do have characteristics that distinguish them from the Anglo

2 Lyle Saunders, *The Spanish Speaking People in Cultural Transition*, (SSPC), mimeographed paper prepared for Council on Spanish-American Work (Protestant) of the Southwest, 1.
3 Lyle Saunders, *Cultural Difference and Medical Care*, (CDMC), 42.

population. Physically, they are easily identifiable because of their common, but by no means uniform, genetic inheritance from the populations of sixteenth- and seventeenth-century Spain and various North American Indian tribal groups. Socially, they possess a variety of combinations of cultural traits that can be traced to Spain or Mexico and that are not generally shared by Anglos. Psychologically, they tend to identify themselves as members of a distinct group and to be so identified by Anglos.

McWilliams considers the group identity which comes primarily from their relationship with the Anglo community as an especially significant factor in defining distinctiveness.[4]

The dichotomy implied in the terms "Anglo" and "Hispano," however, is real enough, no matter how vague either term may be as descriptive of the heterogeneous elements making up the two categories. The reality of this cleavage is to be found in the social history of the Southwest (much of which has been forgotten); and in the nature of the region. No matter how sharply the Spanish-speaking may differ among themselves over the question of nomenclature, the sense of cleavage from or opposition to the Anglos has always been an important factor in their lives and it is this feeling which gives cohesion to the group. The sense of group identity also arises from the fact that the Spanish-speaking have had a similar history and experience and have been influenced by a similar relationship to a sharply differentiated environment.

Thus it might be said that the "Spanish-speaking" designation that is used throughout this section is important and meaningful mainly in its relationship to a counterpart: the "English-speaking," or more accurately, the "Anglo" population, and that the cultural, social and physical heterogeneity within the Spanish-speaking group, though not discussed at any length, is to be recognized as one of its most important characteristics.

Definition

In collecting demographic data for a particular group, a delineation of the group under consideration is essential. In the case of the Spanish American population of the Southwest, however, the task of delineation and definition is exceedingly difficult as demonstrated by the United States Census Bureau's

---

4 Carey McWilliams, *North From Mexico* (NFM), 8.

efforts during the past three censuses. In 1930 the Bureau defined Mexicans as a "race," instructing their census takers to collect information on Mexicans in the same fashion as they collected data about Negroes, Japanese, Indians, etc. Following this census, there was active protest from both the Spanish-speaking groups in the United States and Latin American countries over the classification of Mexicans as "non-white." In 1940, therefore, the Bureau collected data on the basis of Spanish as the "mother tongue" or the "language other than English spoken in the home in earliest childhood." This, too, drew criticism because it did not include families in which English was generally used but which from a sociological stand-point remained part of the ethnic group. In 1950 still another criterion for counting was employed, i.e., "white persons of Spanish surname." Even though this definition also has its weaknesses, it is generally regarded as the best yet used. In all counts, there remains the problem of the undercounting of illegal wetbacks who tend to shun all official contacts in order to avoid detection and possible deportation.

Numbers and Distribution

With these limitations, what is the best estimate of the total number of Spanish-speaking persons in the Southwest?[5] Most informed authorities cite a general estimate from two and a half million to three million. The 1950 U. S. Census—which includes figures for all "white persons of Spanish surname" in five Southwestern states (Arizona, California, Colorado, New Mexico, and Texas) and persons born in Mexico or with one or both parents from Mexico for states outside the Southwest—provides the totals on the following page.

As can be seen in these figures, most (97.3%) of the Spanish-speaking persons reside in the southwestern states of Arizona, California, Colorado, New Mexico, and Texas. The next table shows their distribution in these five states.

The greatest concentrations outside of the Southwestern states are given in the third table on the next page. The stated

---

5 Most of the persons here considered are in the Southwest; however, persons, either immigrants or first generation children of immigrants from Mexico, residing in other states, are also included in the totals given.

WHITE PERSONS OF SPANISH SURNAME IN FIVE SOUTHWESTERN STATES AND PERSONS IN OTHER STATES BORN IN MEXICO OR WITH ONE OR BOTH PARENTS BORN IN MEXICO, 1950

	Native-born	Mexico-born	Total, native-born and Mexico-born
Total United States	1,998,415	450,562	2,448,977
5 Southwestern States	1,897,190	398,244	2,295,434
Other States	101,225	52,318	153,543

Source: U.S. Census of Population 1950: *Persons of Spanish Surname*, Table 1, and *Nativity and Parentage*, Table 13.

WHITE PERSONS OF SPANISH SURNAME OF FIVE SOUTHWESTERN STATES: NUMBER AND PROPORTION OF TOTAL POPULATION, 1950

State	Total Population	White population of Spanish Surname	
		Number	Per cent of total
Arizona	749,587	128,318	17.1
California	10,586,223	760,453	7.2
Colorado	1,325,089	118,131	8.9
New Mexico	681,187	248,880	36.5
Texas	7,711,194	1,033,768	13.4
Total	21,053,280	2,289,550	10.9
Per Cent Increase, 1940-1950	36.0	45.8	—

Source: U.S. Census of Population 1950: *Persons of Spanish Surname*, Table 1 and *U. S. Summary, General Characteristics*, Table 58.

PERSONS EITHER BORN IN MEXICO OR WITH ONE OR BOTH PARENTS BORN IN MEXICO, OUTSIDE THE SOUTHWEST, 1950

State	Total	Born in Mexico	Native-born of foreign or mixed parents
Illinois	34,538	22,075	12,463
Michigan	16,540	5,235	11,305
Kansas	13,429	4,204	9,225
New York	8,233	4,138	4,095
Indiana	8,677	3,222	5,455
Nebraska	6,023	1,673	4,350
Ohio	5,959	1,824	4,135
Washington	5,946	1,546	4,400
Missouri	5,862	2,057	3,805
Utah	5,321	1,396	3,925
Iowa	3,973	1,253	2,720
Pennsylvania	3,574	1,374	2,200
Wyoming	3,539	1,049	2,490
Wisconsin	3,272	1,067	2,205
Minnesota	3,305	950	2,355
Oklahoma	3,501	1,196	2,305
All other States	23,851		

Source: U.S. Census of Population 1950: *Nativity and Parentage*, Table 13.

figures include only persons born in Mexico or native-born persons with one or both parents born in Mexico; they do not include native-born Spanish-speaking persons of native-born parents.

That the current pattern of distribution continues is indicated by the annual reports of the Immigration Service. Of Mexican immigrant aliens interviewed in 1957, 85% stated they intended to go to either Arizona, California, Colorado, New Mexico, or Texas. Another 8.8% intended to locate in Illinois and the remainder in other areas.[6]

Since 1950 there have been several changes in the immigration situation that might affect the current accuracy of the census figures. 1) In 1954 the United States Immigration and Naturalization Service, in a program labeled "Operation Wetback," made a concerted effort to apprehend and deport illegal Mexican aliens. This drive resulted in the departure, primarily voluntarily, of thousands of Mexican workers. 2) With the deportation of wetbacks and stricter border control, there has been an expansion of the contract labor program, a program in which the U. S. Department of Labor and the Mexican government negotiate for the temporary entry of Mexican labor into the U. S. for seasonal work.

Future Trends

The future size of the Spanish-speaking population stemming from Mexico and the Southwest will largely depend on the following factors. Calculation of the extent to which deportation has affected the total picture will be made more feasible by the 1960 Census provided the count is conducted on the same basis as in 1950.

1. *Natural Increase.* Natural increase, calculated from vital statistics on the number of births over deaths, assumes special importance in estimating future size of the Spanish-speaking population inasmuch as the bulk of the group is now native-born. Although little documentation was encountered in the literature survey, it has been stated by several sources that the Spanish-speaking population is growing as a consequence of

---

6 Immigration and Naturalization Service, *Annual Report, 1957* (AR 57), 33.

[19]

natural increase at a more rapid rate than the Anglo population.

2. *Legal Immigration.* Immigration figures show that the greatest number of immigrants entered the United States from Mexico between 1920-1930. This period was followed by a sharp decrease due to the depression in the United States. The war years saw another increase, but in the first six years of the present decade *over three times* as many immigrants entered as in the previous ten-year period. The total number entering for the single year of 1957 was 49,154 persons.[7] 1958 saw a drop to 26,712.[8]

IMMIGRATION FROM MEXICO, 1920-1957

Total 1820-1957	1820-1910	1911-1920	1921-1930	1931-1940	1941-1950	1951-1957
1,056,247	77,645*	219,004	459,287	22,319	60,589	217,403

* No record of Mexican immigration for the years 1886-1893.
Source: *Information Please, Almanac 1959* (IPA), 406.

Under immigration regulations, Mexico is a non-quota country as are all countries of the Western Hemisphere. Free immigration from Mexico was threatened in the late '20's when an attempt was made by domestic organized labor to push through legislation to make Mexico a quota country. The proposed Harris and Box Bills, which aimed at restricting Mexican immigration to less than 2,000 immigrants a year, were opposed by a variety of groups: by persons who said it would be an affront to our southern neighbor to single her out for special restrictive treatment, by business and farm interests who wanted to assure themselves of an open and cheap labor market, and by persons who pointed out that present laws, if enforced, negated the need for quotas. With this opposition, the bills were never passed.[9]

The only legal restrictions to Mexican immigration are those which apply to any immigrant entering the country: all must meet certain standards of health, morals, literacy, and eco-

---

[7] Immigration & Naturalization Service, AR 57, 20.

[8] Immigration & Naturalization Service, AR 58, 32.

[9] Hubert C. Herring and Katherine Terrill, *The Genius of Mexico* (GOM) 221-251, and John Burma, *Spanish-Speaking Groups in the United States* (SSG), 42.

nomics. However, these requirements can be tightened or relaxed, depending on the desire for more or fewer entrants. It has been pointed out that, due to misinformation and a lack of public interest, agricultural lobbies largely control the number of Mexicans that are allowed to enter, whether through legal or illegal means.[10]

The same freedom to enter the United States applies in re-entering Mexico should an immigrant desire to return home. However, it is assumed that if conditions are favorable to the Mexican immigrant he will, in most, cases, remain in this country. The table below provides figures on the total number of foreign born persons in the U. S. by decade 1870-1950. The decrease in the 1940 figures reflects the migration back to Mexico during the depression years.

PERSONS IN THE U.S. WHO WERE BORN IN MEXICO—1870-1950

	Increase or Decrease
1870 — 42,435	—
1880 — 68,399	61.2
1890 — 77,853	13.8
1900 — 103,393	32.8
1910 — 219,802	112.6
1920 — 478,383	117.6
1930 — 639,017	33.6
1940 — 377,433	—40.9
1950 — 450,562	19.4

Source: U.S. Census of Population 1950: *U.S. Summary General Characteristics*, Table 49.

3. *Illegal Immigration.* Illegal or "wetback" immigration has, in the past, been one of the important factors in the growth of the Spanish-speaking population, perhaps responsible for the greatest numbers in the country at various times. Described as a "real caricature of the Valley 'Mexican' stereotype,"[11] the wetback is always subject to deportation and holds no legal rights in the United States.

Although this source of population continues to some extent, the tightening up of controls by the Immigration Service has both decreased the number of illegal aliens in the United States through deportation and lessened the number who at-

10 Lyle Saunders and Olen E. Leonard, *The Wetback in the Lower Rio Grande Valley of Texas* (WLRG), 82.
11 Saunders, WLRG, 88.

tempt to enter. If the Immigration Service has not eased its recent stricter control, the following figures on apprehensions would suggest that the number of wetbacks both in the country and entering the country has decreased. The total number of apprehensions in the first five months of 1958 was only 18,547.[12]

APPREHENSIONS OF MEXICAN ALIENS, BY REGIONS
1955-1957

	Total	Northeast	Northwest	Southeast	Southwest
1957	44,451	37	1,013	138	43,263
1956	72,442	74	1,451	427	70,490
1955	242,608	108	5,992	138	236,090

Source: Immigration and Naturalization Service, *I and N Reporter* (IN 58), 3.

In 1954, the year in which "Operation Wetback" went into full swing, there were, according to the Immigration Service, over 1,000,000 apprehensions of illegal entries in the Southwest.[13] These apprehensions were immigrants who had entered illegally over a period of years. The interpretation of these startlingly high figures is restricted by the fact that when the aliens were dropped on the Mexican side of the border virtually all crossed back. "Some had been arrested as much as three times daily."[14] To eliminate this problem, deported aliens are now transported by plane to the inland city of Leon, Guanajuato, which lies on the central plateau hundreds of miles from the border.[15] This method of deportation, the expansion of the bracero or contract labor program, and stricter watch at the border would all tend to decrease the entrance of illegal aliens.

4. *Contract Labor.* The contract labor program has expanded steadily since 1950. This program, which involves agreement between the Mexican and the United States Governments, grew out of World War II agreements to import temporary foreign labor during the severe domestic labor shortage. Railroad and agricultural employment were the two major industries which obtained Mexican labor through these agree-

---

12 *The New York Times,* July 26, 1958.
13 Immigration and Naturalization Service, AR 57, 11.
14 *The New York Times,* July 6, 1958.
15 *The New York Times,* July 6, 1958.

ments. After 1945, importation of Mexican nationals for railroad employment was ended; the importation of farm labor, on the other hand, has increased and 1957 figures show the admittance of the largest number up to this time. Last year the bill was extended through 1961 and unofficial reports set the number admitted in 1958 as about the same as in 1957.[16]

AGRICULTURAL LABORERS ADMITTED TO THE UNITED STATES FROM MEXICO:
Years Ended June 30, 1950-1957

1950	1951	1952	1953	1954	1955	1956	1957
116,052*	115,742*	223,541	178,606	213,763	337,996	416,843	450,422

* 1950 figures includes 96,239 illegal entrants contracted; 1951 figures include 3,626 illegal entrants contracted.
Source: Immigration and Naturalization Service, AR 57, 42.

The literature gives two different sides of the contract labor program. On the positive side it is pointed out that contract labor is the best method of providing seasonal labor because 1) the numbers permitted to enter can be related to the actual need at any particular time, 2) direct contact provides a check on the personal characteristics of the worker before he is allowed to enter, and 3) governmental supervision of the program means higher labor standards. These arguments for the program are based primarily on comparing wetback labor with contract laborers. Approval of the program has also come from analysts of the Mexican economy who see contract laborers, as they return to Mexico, carrying progressive agricultural methods back to Mexican agriculture. It is also a channel through which American dollars find their way into Mexico.

Criticism of the contract labor program is directed at its implementation. Although the legislation which covers contract labor specifies that there shall be no importation of foreign labor if domestic labor is available, it has been suggested that state employment services charged with the responsibility of determining need of labor are often "susceptible to grower influence."[17] The President's Commission on Migratory Labor in 1951 provided data showing that in areas where contract labor had been expanded since the war, wages had been lowered. This Commission stated: "It is our conclusion that

16 *The New York Times,* August 29, 1958.
17 *The Reporter,* January, 1959.

the evidence demonstrates that the agencies of Government responsible for importing and contracting foreign labor have not been successful in protecting domestic farm labor from detrimental effects of imported contract alien labor. We find alien labor has depressed farm wages, and therefore, has been detrimental to domestic labor."[18]

It is also charged that because immigration regulations do not apply to temporary braceros, the workers who enter may not meet the minimum restrictions imposed on other legal entrants. Furthermore, the maintenance of high standards of working conditions depend upon how well the treaty between the United States and Mexico is enforced. A report on migrant labor in the January, 1959 issue of the *Reporter* points out that there are not sufficient enforcement officers in the U. S. Department of Labor and that the Mexican Consulates, which are responsible for handling complaints have not adequately performed this function.

The above-mentioned types of population change, other than natural increase, depend on the "push" and "pull" of the two countries. The main factors affecting immigration, it is generally agreed, are the economic conditions in the United States which determines the demand for labor and unemployment in Mexico. The differential in the standard of living between Mexico and the United States and the difference in wage levels between the two countries is still so great that when labor is needed in the U. S., it is likely to be available from the south.

It is perhaps necessary to re-state that, although there continues to be some flow of migrants across the Southwestern borders, the major part of the Spanish-speaking group in the United States is now native-born. These are persons who have probably never been in Mexico, perhaps even their parents have not, but who are still "Mexican" in Anglo eyes. "Most of their ways are ours, just as most of the ways of the Italian Americans, the Nisei, and the Negro are ours. Adjustment to life in Mexico would be almost as difficult for an American of

---

[18] *Migratory Labor in American Agriculture,* Report of the President's Commission on Migratory Labor (MLAA), 59. This report recommended that the program not be expanded after 1950 and that an effort be made to use domestic labor to fill labor demands. (p. 35).

Mexican descent as it would be for an American of Polish descent, or Irish, or Scandinavian."[19]

Urban-Rural Distribution

The origins of the Spanish-speaking in the United States were rural. The Mexican immigration came primarily from rural, folk[20] communities in Central Mexico[21] and the Hispano communities of New Mexico and Colorado have been of the same tradition. Accounts of both areas emphasize their isolation and geographical protection from modern industrial influences.

Today, contrary to popular notions, a majority of the Spanish-speaking people in the United States live in urban places and each decennial census indicates that the trend of the group is toward increased urbanization. While this migration from rural areas to cities is not confined to Spanish groups but characterizes the whole of our society, the rural roots of both Mexican immigrants and Hispanos have been much more folk in nature than those of the rural migrant from Iowa or Arkansas. The necessary adjustments, therefore, to urban life are probably much more dramatic for the Spanish-speaking.[22]

> The significance of urban residence for the Spanish group lies mainly in the fact of a predominantly rural heritage. The change from rural to urban socio-cultural conditions of living is something of a crisis for most people, but for the recent immigrants from Mexico, coming as they did from rural and village folk societies, the problems of adjustment have been at least three-fold: to an urban-industrial society, to strange cultural forms, and to some degree of discrimination. The generally low economic status has merely aggravated the problems of adjustment.

A further complication is that a number of the Spanish-speaking urban residents are not urban-employed but are mi-

---

19 Ruth Tuck, *Not With the Fist* (NWF), Introduction.

20 See page 77 for discussion and definition of "folk" society.

21 The states which yielded most immigrants to the U.S. and from which recent wetbacks also come (Michoacan, Jalisco, Guanajuato) are still predominantly rural. In Michoacan, 71% live in communities 2,500 or under and 76% of the employed are engaged in agriculture; in Jalisco, 59% live in rural areas, 64% are employed in agriculture; in Guanajuato, 65% have rural residence, and 71% are engaged in agriculture.

22 Talbert, *Spanish Name People in the Southwest and the West* (SNP), 24.

gratory agricultural workers who work out from the city or who settle there temporarily during off-periods.

The total number of Spanish surname "urban" dwellers[23] in the five Southwestern states is over a million and a half persons (1,519,812 or 66% of the total) as compared with a total of 769,738 in rural or rural non-farm residence. The states with the largest total of Spanish persons (Texas and California) also have the highest proportion of persons in urban residence. The table below, in addition to showing the urban-rural distribution of Spanish persons in the Southwest, provides a comparison between Anglos and Spanish in the area.

DISTRIBUTION BY RURAL OR URBAN RESIDENCE, WHITE SPANISH-SURNAME POPULATION AND ANGLO POPULATION OF FIVE SOUTHWESTERN STATES, 1950

Population group and residence category	Arizona	California	Colorado	New Mexico	Texas	Total
	Number of persons					
Spanish-surname						
Total	128,318	760,453	118,131	248,880	1,033,768	2,289,550
Urban	78,723	576,334	58,704	101,939	704,112	1,519,812
Rural nonfarm	40,595	126,534	40,760	89,240	194,741	491,870
Rural farm	9,000	57,585	18,667	57,701	134,915	277,868
Anglo[a]						
Total	621,269	9,825,770	1,206,958	432,307	6,677,426	18,763,730
Urban	337,277	7,963,086	772,614	239,950	4,133,948	13,446,875
Rural nonfarm	216,078	1,352,038	254,830	118,235	1,386,126	3,327,307
Rural farm	67,914	510,646	179,514	74,122	1,157,352	1,989,548
	Percentage distribution					
Spanish-surname						
Total	100.0	100.0	100.0	100.0	100.0	100.0
Urban	61.3	75.8	49.7	41.0	68.1	66.4
Rural nonfarm	31.6	16.6	34.5	35.8	18.8	21.5
Rural farm	7.0	7.6	15.8	23.2	13.1	12.1
Anglo[a]						
Total	100.0	100.0	100.0	100.0	100.0	100.0
Urban	54.3	81.0	64.0	55.5	61.9	71.7
Rural nonfarm	34.8	13.8	21.1	27.3	20.8	17.7
Rural farm	10.9	5.2	14.9	17.1	17.3	10.6

a Residual group, obtained by subtracting Spanish-surname population from the total population.
Source; Saunders (CDMC), 293.

The tendency to concentrate in the more populous and economically attractive areas is, as Talbert has pointed out,

23 As defined by the U.S. Census Bureau, persons living in places of 2,500 population or more.

"understandable in light of the recent increased commercial and industrial activity in the Southwest, the increased mechanization of agriculture, and the resultant decreased need for agricultural labor."[24]

The standard metropolitan areas[25] and urban places of 10,000 or more where Spanish-speaking people have settled in substantial numbers can be seen in the table on the next page.

The proportion of the total population which is Spanish-speaking within a city affects the nature of the experiences the Spanish-speaking group may have. Laredo, Texas, for example, is 86% Spanish-speaking, making it virtually a non-Anglo town. Other cities with a sizeable number of Spanish-speaking but where the group represents a numerical minority (e.g., Denver whose 29,261 Spanish-speaking is but 5% of the total metropolitan population) present the probability of "either voluntary or forced segregation."[26] Persons in areas in which the number of Spanish-speaking is not only a minority but is also numerically small, face a still different kind of adjustment; the number of Spanish contacts is limited and *colonias* cannot be easily formed as a buffer.

Talbert's analysis showed that the native-born of native parentage are more likely to live in urban areas than persons born in Mexico. The step from the rural communities of Mexico to highly industrialized cities of the United States is thus sometimes buffered by an intermediate step in rural areas.

Age Distribution

The Spanish-speaking of the Southwest are a younger population than the Anglos of the region. The percentage of persons under twenty years among Spanish-speaking is 48.8%, among Anglos, 32.0%.

Spanish Americans whose antecedents date back to colonial times are represented in every age group but they also have a relatively higher proportion of young children than Anglos.

---

24 Talbert, SNP, 20.

25 *Standard Metropolitan Areas.* Defined by U.S. Census Bureau as "a county or group of contiguous counties which contains at least one city of 50,000 inhabitants or more" and other contiguous counties "if according to certain criteria . . . are essentially metropolitan in character and socially and economically integrated with the central city.

26 Talbert, SNP, 27.

TOTAL POPULATION AND NUMBER OF WHITE PERSONS OF SPANISH SURNAME IN SELECTED URBAN PLACES, 1950

	Total Population	Persons of Spanish Surname
*Phoenix, Arizona	331,770	42,560
*Tucson, Arizona	45,454	10,964
*Fresno, California	276,515	32,678
*Los Angeles, California	4,367,911	311,294
*Sacramento, California	277,140	14,883
*San Bernardino, California	281,642	35,330
*San Diego, California	556,808	28,926
*San Francisco-Oakland, Calif.	2,240,767	94,683
*San Jose, California	290,547	35,306
*Stockton, California	200,750	19,739
*Denver, Colorado	563,832	29,261
*Pueblo, Colorado	90,188	11,250
*Albuquerque, N. M.	145,673	43,729
Santa Fe, N. M.	27,998	16,492
*Austin, Texas	160,980	15,365
Brownsville, Texas	36,066	25,036
*Corpus Christi, Texas	165,471	58,939
*Dallas, Texas	614,799	14,430
*El Paso, Texas	194,968	89,555
Harlingen, Texas	23,229	11,080
*Houston, Texas	806,701	39,171
*Laredo, Texas	56,141	47,525
*McAllen, Texas	20,067	11,462
*San Antonio, Texas	500,460	176,877
*Chicago, Illinois	5,495,511	35,215a

Other standard metropolitan areas or urban places with 5,000-10,000 persons of Spanish surname include the following: **California:** Brawley, East Bakersfield, Oxnard, Riverside, Santa Ana, Santa Barbara; **New Mexico:** Las Cruces; **Texas:** Alice, Del Rio, Edinburg, Ft. Worth, Galveston, Kingsville, Lubbock, Mercedes, Mission, San Angelo, San Benito.

* Standard Metropolitan areas. (See footnote on preceding page for definition.)
a Total for Chicago includes only foreign-born persons and native-born persons of one or both parents born in Mexico.
Sources: U.S. Census of Population 1950; *Persons of Spanish Surname*, Table 8, *County and City Data Book* (CCDB) Table 1 and A3, and *Nativity and Parentage*, Table 7.

The bulk of the foreign-born, coming as they did from Mexico between 1910 and 1930, are primarily in the 40 years and over groups. The native-born are largely represented in the younger age groups and are numerically the most significant.

The following table provides the age distribution within the five southwestern states included in the census special report.

**AGE DISTRIBUTION OF ANGLOS,* WHITE PERSONS OF SPANISH SURNAME,
AND FOREIGN-BORN FROM MEXICO, 1950**

	Anglos	White Persons of Spanish Surname	Foreign-born[a] from Mexico
Under 5 years	10.5	15.9	1.3
5-9 years	8.3	12.7	2.6
10-19 years	13.2	20.2	2.3
20-29 years	16.0	18.0	3.0
30-39 years	16.1	12.3	13.1
40-49 years	13.4	9.5	18.1
50-59 years	10.2	5.9	25.4
Over 60 years	12.1	5.4	16.6
Total Numbers	18,763,730	2,289,550	451,490

* Represents Total Population less Persons of Spanish Surname.

a The figure for the foreign-born from Mexico includes persons in all states of the U.S.; only 5 Southwestern states are represented in the other two columns.
Source: Saunders, CDMC, 89 and U.S. Census of Population 1950: *Nativity and Parentage,* Table 14.

**PERCENTAGE DISTRIBUTION OF THE WHITE SPANISH-SURNAME POPULATION
AND ANGLO POPULATION OF FIVE SOUTHWESTERN STATES, BY AGE, 1950**

State and Population Group	Age					
	Under 5 years	5-14 years	15-24 years	25-44 years	45-64 years	Over 65 years
The 5 States						
Spanish-surname	15.9	23.3	19.1	25.8	12.4	3.4
Anglo	10.5	15.0	14.0	31.8	20.4	8.1
Arizona						
Spanish-surname	15.7	24.9	18.9	24.9	11.3	3.7
Anglo	11.7	18.4	14.5	30.4	18.4	6.3
California						
Spanish-surname	14.3	20.9	19.5	28.2	13.5	3.3
Anglo	10.1	13.6	12.8	32.8	21.8	8.8
Colorado						
Spanish-surname	17.1	26.4	18.5	23.0	11.6	3.4
Anglo	10.6	15.3	14.7	29.9	20.1	9.2
New Mexico						
Spanish-surname	16.6	25.5	18.4	23.2	12.6	4.1
Anglo	12.6	18.2	18.0	31.6	16.2	5.2
Texas						
Spanish-surname	16.9	24.1	19.0	25.1	11.5	3.4
Anglo	10.0	16.4	15.5	30.8	19.1	7.1

Source: Saunders, CDMC, 294.

Although the different states represent slightly different patterns, in all cases the proportion of Spanish-speaking (when compared with Anglos) is disproportionately high in the

[29]

younger age categories and disproportionately low in those over 45 years of age.

The tendency for immigrants to be primarily of young adult age is demonstrated by the following distribution of the immigrants coming from Mexico in 1957. The high proportion of children also reflects considerable moving of whole families.

AGE DISTRIBUTION OF IMMIGRANTS FROM MEXICO, 1957

Under 10 years:	19.7
10-20 years:	16.2
20-29 years:	31.3
30-39 years:	18.7
40-49 years:	8.6
50-59 years:	3.8
Over 60 years:	1.7

Source: INR 58, 27.

Sex Distribution

With the exception of the state of California where men predominate in all areas, one finds among Spanish Americans more women than men in urban centers and more men than women in rural places.

SEX DISTRIBUTION OF WHITE PERSONS OF SPANISH SURNAME 1950, BY PLACE OF RESIDENCE

	Urban	Rural, Non-Farm	Rural
Arizona			
Male	38,350	21,185	5,055
Female	40,325	19,630	4,035
Number of men per 100 women	95.0	107.9	125.3
California			
Male	289,225	69,425	33,060
Female	285,430	56,920	24,340
Number of men per 100 women	101.3	122.0	135.8
Colorado			
Male	29,105	20,960	9,965
Female	29,730	20,135	8,820
Number of men per 100 women	97.9	104.1	113.0
New Mexico			
Male	50,270	45,140	30,670
Female	51,105	44,630	26,745
Number of men per 100 women	98.4	101.1	114.7
Texas			
Male	346,730	101,065	74,610
Female	351,585	93,165	60,300
Number of men per 100 women	98.6	108.5	123.7

Source: U.S. Census of Population, *Persons of Spanish Surname,* Table 5.

There are no legal barriers in any state to intermarriage between Anglo whites and Spanish-speaking persons since the
latter are also officially classified as whites, but the social barriers which prohibit frequent contact between the two groups
and the tendency to consider Spanish Americans as a non-
white racial group regardless of legal definition limits extensive intermarriage.

The greatest disparity between the numbers of males and
females is present among the foreign-born. Contract workers
are primarily single young men or men who have families in
Mexico to which they return when their work contracts are
terminated. There is also a preponderance of males among
wetbacks.[27]

**SEX DISTRIBUTION OF WHITE PERSONS OF SPANISH SURNAME,
BY STATE AND NATIVITY, 1950**

	Native-born		
	Of Native Parents	Of Foreign or Mixed Parents	Foreign-born
Arizona			
Male	26,875	25,665	12,050
Female	26,505	26,300	11,185
Number of men per 100 women	101.4	97.6	107.7
California			
Male	131,600	165,795	94,315
Female	135,235	158,910	72,545
Number of men per 100 women	97.3	104.3	130.0
Colorado			
Male	49,470	7,530	3,030
Female	49,280	7,470	1,935
Number of men per 100 women	100.4	100.8	156.6
New Mexico			
Male	109,250	11,010	5,820
Female	107,555	10,225	4,700
Number of men per 100 women	101.6	107.7	123.8
Texas			
Male	239,735	182,175	100,495
Female	238,175	180,450	86,425
Number of men per 100 women	100.6	101.0	116.3

Source: U.S. Census of Population 1950: *Persons of Spanish Surname*, Table 5.

Marital Status

Almost two-thirds of the Spanish-speaking population fourteen years of age and over in this country is married. The 1950

---

27 Saunders, WLRG, 84.

census shows an excess of males in the "single" category, undoubtedly a result of the predominance of males among immigrants, a slight excess of married males over married females, suggesting the male separated from his family in Mexico, and a substantial excess of women in the "widowed or divorced" group.

MARITAL STATUS OF WHITE PERSONS OF SPANISH SURNAME, 14 YEARS OF AGE AND OVER, 1950

	Males		Females	
	Number	Percent	Number	Percent
All Types	736,837	100.0	700,078	100.0
Single	255,503	34.7	185,504	26.5
Married	442,560	60.1	431,139	61.6
Widowed or divorced	38,774	5.3	83,435	11.9

Source: U.S. Census of Population 1950: *Persons of Spanish Surname*, Table 3.

In all cases the proportion of single men and women is considerably higher among the Spanish-speaking population than among Anglos and the proportion of widowed or divorced is lower than among Anglos. The latter fact in itself does not mean too much, however, since the age distribution of Spanish-speaking is not a "normal" one in the upper age groups due to their late immigration. "Divorce and desertion are more rare than among Anglo families," Burma has stated,[28] pointing to the strength of family ties. However, he also cites statistics for the city of San Antonio where 31% of the Mexican American families were "broken" units which raises questions about the current stability of, at least, urban families.[29]

Racial Classification

In the United States, Spanish-speaking persons are legally defined as "white" and the Census Bureau so classifies them in their enumerations. In reality, however, most Spanish Americans are *mestizo*, i.e., of mixed Spanish and Indian stock. They vary in the proportion of Spanish or Indian admixture, but the Indian strain predominates inasmuch as only about 300,000 Spaniards entered a country of 3,000,000 Indians and inter-

---

28 Burma, SSG, 84.
29 *Idem.*

[32]

marriage was a common practice. There are still significant numbers of "pure" Indians in Mexico[30] but the states from which most immigrants have come are those where *mestizos* predominate.

Considerable variety is found within the general description of mestizo (mixed) stock. One of the explanations for variety is that in the isolated Hispano communities of New Mexico and Colorado, after they became better organized and more self-sufficient, there was a tendency to no longer choose Indian partners but to select someone from within the villages at the time of marriage. In Mexico, however, intermarriage between Indians and mestizos has continued, strengthening the Indian strain. Further variations have been produced by the physical differences among the Indian tribes with whom the Spaniards mixed in the period of exploration and conquest.

Most authorities mention physical appearance as a factor in the adjustment pattern of Spanish in the United States: As Paul Walter, Jr., has written in *Race and Cultural Relations,* "The racial background of the great majority of the Spanish-speaking people of the country gives them a social visibility which has been sufficient to set them apart in general thinking as a distinct racial group and to bring into play a racial factor in most intergroup contacts in which they have been involved."[31]

Use of Spanish

In 1940, on the basis of a five percent sample, the U. S. Census found 1,570,740 persons in the Southwest whose "mother tongue" or "language spoken in the home in earliest childhood" was Spanish.[32] No similar count was made in the Census of 1950.

On the basis of the 1940 data, Spanish seems to persist in the United States longer than any other foreign language. Among persons using a language other than English in the home, only 13% were 3rd generation families or beyond but

---

30 Today in Mexico a racial classification is no longer included in census counts but current estimates give the following breakdown: Mestizo, 55%; Indian, 29%; White, 15%; and others, 1%. *Information Please, 1959 Almanac,* 761.

31 Cited in Saunders, CDMC, 254.

32 U.S. Census of Population 1940: *Mother Tongue.* For the entire United States, the number naming Spanish as their mother tongue was 1,861,400.

among those using Spanish, the percent was 39%. The persistence of Spanish is further demonstrated by the extent to which English becomes the language used in the homes of immigrant families. Only 7% of second generation Mexican-American families replied that English was the language of the home, as compared with 66% of those whose parents were born in Denmark or 63% of those born in France. (See table below.)

PERSONS OF ENGLISH MOTHER TONGUE IN THE NATIVE WHITE POPULATION OF FOREIGN OR MIXED PARENTAGE, FOR SELECTED COUNTRIES OF ORIGIN, FOR THE U. S., 1940

Country of Parent's Birth	Percent Whose Mother Tongue Was English
Denmark	66.1
France	62.5
Sweden	56.2
Germany	49.7
Austria	41.8
Greece	40.2
Lithuania	28.4
Czechoslovakia	26.2
Finland	24.5
Poland	22.7
Mexico	7.0

Source: U.S. Census of Population 1940: *Mother Tongue.*

Of the literally Spanish-speaking population in 1940, the majority were living in urban places; fifty-six percent had urban residence, 23% rural non-farm, and 20%, rural.

Education

Saunders has summarized the educational situation among the Spanish-speaking by stating: "The educational level, as measured by number of school years completed, averages lower than that of the community as a whole. It is particularly low for persons forty years of age or older. The schools lose more children by drop-outs. Attendance is less regular. A smaller proportion of the children finish elementary school and enter junior and senior high schools."[33]

Census data for 1950 verify Saunders' statement. (See the following tables.) Among the Spanish-speaking, in 1950, 18% of the persons over 25 years of age had had no schooling what-

---

33 Saunders, CDMC, 68-69.

PERCENTAGE DISTRIBUTION BY SCHOOL YEARS COMPLETED, WHITE SPANISH-SURNAME, POPULATION AND ANGLO POPULATION TWENTY-FIVE YEARS OF AGE AND OVER OF FIVE SOUTHWESTERN STATES, 1950

School Years Completed	Arizona		California		Colorado		N. Mexico		Texas		Total	
	Sp. Sur-name	Anglo	Sp. Sur-name	Anglo	Sp. Sur-name	Anglo	Sp. Sur-name	Anglo	Sp. Sur-name	Anglo	Sp. Sur-name	Anglo
Total	100.0	100.0	100.0	100.0	100.0	100.0	100.0	100.0	100.0	100.0	100.0	100.0
None	13.4	4.2	10.7	1.3	10.1	1.1	12.5	3.1	27.0	1.8	18.0	1.6
Elementary												
1 to 4	26.1	6.0	18.6	4.3	24.8	4.2	27.1	5.4	34.8	8.9	27.2	5.9
5 to 7	24.4	11.6	20.5	9.7	26.6	10.1	23.7	11.5	19.2	19.9	20.8	13.2
8	13.1	16.2	13.7	16.2	14.4	20.8	12.3	14.0	4.3	12.1	9.4	15.1
High School												
1 to 4	16.1	39.9	28.2	45.6	17.7	41.3	16.9	40.8	9.6	39.4	17.8	43.0
College												
1 to 4	2.8	19.2	4.9	28.1	3.0	19.9	4.0	21.2	1.9	15.5	3.3	18.6
Not Reported	3.9	2.8	3.4	2.9	3.5	2.6	3.5	3.7	3.0	2.3	3.3	2.7

Source: Saunders, CDMC, 299.

DISTRIBUTION BY SCHOOL YEARS COMPLETED, WHITE MALES 14 YEARS AND OVER OF SPANISH SURNAME, BORN IN MEXICO, IN FIVE SOUTHWESTERN STATES, 1950

Yrs. of School Completed	PERSONS BORN IN MEXICO				
	Arizona	California	Colorado	New Mexico	Texas
None	21.3	18.8	25.6	27.5	34.0
Elementary					
1-4 yrs.	34.2	29.0	31.1	33.7	36.7
5-7 yrs.	20.2	20.7	19.5	14.8	14.8
8 yrs.	7.5	9.6	7.6	4.3	2.6
High School					
1-4 yrs.	7.9	13.4	8.8	7.2	5.5
College					
1-4 yrs.	1.8	3.3	2.4	7.4	1.8
No Report	7.1	5.1	4.9	5.1	4.6
Total Number Males					
14 yrs. or over	11,475	91,345	2,945	5,460	92,385
Median school years completed—					
Males—14 yrs. and over	3.9	4.9	3.8	3.4	2.5
Median school years completed—					
Females—14 yrs. and over	4.3	5.3	3.2	4.0	2.4

Source: U.S. Census of Population 1950: *Persons of Spanish Surname,* Table 6.

soever (as compared to 2% among Anglos) and three-fifths had not gone beyond the 5th grade. Only 3% had had college work (as compared with 18% of the Anglo population). Texas reflects the highest proportion of persons with no formal schooling and also has the highest proportion of early drop-outs (76% with less than seven years completed). Although

[35]

California has a higher proportion of foreign-born Mexican Americans, that state has a lower rate of illiteracy and early drop-outs than the other four states.

Native-born persons of Spanish surname have more formal education than those born in Mexico. Here again, state differences exist. Among native-born persons in California, for example, only 2.9% of those 14 years of age and over have had no schooling but in Texas, 14% have had none.

DISTRIBUTION BY SCHOOL YEARS COMPLETED, WHITE MALES 14 YEARS AND OVER OF SPANISH SURNAME, NATIVE BORN OF NATIVE PARENTS, OF FIVE SOUTHWESTERN STATES, 1950

Yrs. of School Completed	NATIVE BORN OF NATIVE PARENTAGE				
	Arizona	California	Colorado	New Mexico	Texas
None	5.6	2.9	5.1	6.9	14.0
Elementary					
1-4 yrs.	13.7	7.3	19.0	20.9	31.0
5-7 yrs.	27.7	17.0	28.9	27.4	26.4
8 yrs.	19.1	16.7	17.7	15.1	6.9
High School					
1-4 yrs.	24.7	41.9	21.8	22.6	14.8
College					
1-4 yrs.	4.1	7.2	2.6	3.7	2.6
No Report	5.1	6.9	5.0	3.4	4.4
Total Number Males 14 yrs. or over	12,150	61,505	27,915	63,600	110,965
Median school years completed— Males—14 yrs. and over	8.0	9.3	7.4	7.3	5.3
Median school years completed— Females—14 yrs. and over	8.0	9.9	7.7	7.5	5.3

Source: U.S. Census of Population 1950: *Persons of Spanish Surname*, Table 6.

Occupation

"Spearheaded by the completion of the rail lines, the westward movement of cotton, the spread of 'winter garden' fruit and vegetable production, and the phenomenally rapid economic expansion of the Southwest after 1900 created an enormous demand for unskilled labor."[34] These were the areas of the economy which drew the majority of the Mexican immigrants to the United States.

"The depression of 1930-1939 cut the Mexican migrants to the quick. For lack of markets fruit dropped off trees, vege-

---

34 McWilliams, NFM, 186.

tables rotted or were not planted. Railroad section gangs shrank down to a foreman and a couple of 'white' laborers. And having lived from hand to mouth even in so-called good times, the majority of Mexicans had no reserves; so now they went either on relief or back to Mexico."[35] "But the disaster also brought with it opportunities which many eagerly grasped. Entering the CCC camps, thousands of teenagers got their first chance to associate with other American youths, to learn English and develop working skills. Younger children—again for the first time—were able to attend classes throughout the full school year. Thus, by 1940, the maturing American-born generation was no longer bound, as its parents had been, to the treadmill of the 'big swing.'"[36]

"With World War II still another chapter in the long history of Mexican labor in the Southwest was started."[37] "During the manpower shortage of war days, many Mexicans were admitted to industries from which they had been barred in the past, and this took them away from the farms and filling stations and ranches of Southwest Texas. Others who went to war refused to work again for the low wages paid in the border area, and moved north."[38] "Long troubled by an excess of labor, employers suddenly found disconcerting shortages of manpower. . . . The first expedient was the regular use of migrants from the Western Hemisphere. . . . In the Southwest, politically powerful farm, railroad, and mining interests had earlier worked out schemes for the import of Mexicans under annual contract. Now, under agreements negotiated by the two governments, the flow of such laborers back and forth across the border increased rapidly."[39] "In pre-war days, so rare were the Mexican-Americans who could muster enough capital to start a business that even in neighborhoods where only Mexican families lived, almost all shops were owned by outsiders. But thousands of veterans returned to civil life determined to strike out on their own . . . today, with a few years of experience under their belts, many are competing

---

35 Louis Adamic, *A Nation of Nations* (NN), 65.
36 Albert Q. Maisel, *They All Chose America* (TACA), 179.
37 Carey McWilliams, *Brothers Under the Skin* (BUS) 128.
38 Hart Stilwell, "The Wetback Tide," (WT), *Common Ground*, Vol. IX, #4, 6.
39 Oscar Handlin, *Americans in the Twentieth Century* (ATC), 208-210.

successfully with old established 'Anglo' firms: running cab companies, produce houses, bakery chains, drive-ins, machine shops and trucking outfits throughout the Southwest."[40]

In the Hispano communities of New Mexico and southern Colorado where the traditional means of earning a living has been a combination of stock raising and subsistence agriculture, significant and far-reaching changes have also been occurring. "The first type of change evident in the gradual shift from an agrarian economy to wage-work, which began over 75 years ago, was the development of migrant labor."[41] "Economic conditions for Spanish-American villagers improved considerably in the late 1930's and throughout the 1940's largely as the result of income derived from non-village sources. . . . Since the end of the war, the economic gains of the 1940's have been continued. High prices for agricultural products and a somewhat decreased pressure of population on land resources have enabled those who remained in the villages to improve their economic condition. The atomic energy installation at Los Alamos, the atomic project at Sandia Base in Albuquerque, and extensive government activities at the White Sands Proving Grounds near Alamagordo, New Mexico, in Denver, and elsewhere in the Southwest have provided employment for villagers living within a 40 to 50 mile radius of any of these projects and have made it possible for many to have a higher level of living than was possible at any time in the past."[42]

But in spite of the increased involvement in business and industrial enterprises, Spanish-speaking persons still form the greater part of the seasonal agricultural workers of the Southwest and in certain Midwest areas. There seems little doubt that most contemporary migrant agricultural workers in this country are of Spanish background. The report of the President's Commission on Migratory Labor in 1951 states that "Texas-Mexicans, the term commonly applied to those Texans of Mexican or other Latin American origin, have emerged in the past decade as the largest group in our Nation's domestic migratory work force. In previous years, this group was mi-

---

40 Maisel, TACA, 181.
41 Margaret Mead, editor, *Cultural Patterns & Technical Change* (CPTC), 168.
42 Saunders, CDMC, 70-71.

gratory within Texas and from Texas into the Mountain and Great Lake States. But recently its migrancy has increased both in scale and in the area through which it moves. The primary reason for this increase of migrancy is pressure from the great influx of illegal Mexican aliens which has made it increasingly necessary for Texas-Mexicans to leave their homes annually in search of better wages and greater employment opportunity elsewhere."[43]

The same report states that in the postwar years, migratory labor "has grown again to a million. However, of this total number, domestic migrants represents only about one-half. The other half is made up of approximately 100,000 Mexicans legally under contract, a relatively small number of British East Indians and Puerto Ricans, and, by far the most important, illegal Mexican workers who in recent years have amounted to an estimated 400,000."[44] These figures tend to confirm the statement of Dean Collins in 1953 that "of the one million migrant workers—2,500,000 with their families—more than one-half are of Spanish background."[45]

The United States Census provides data about the distribution of persons of Spanish surname in various occupational

PERCENTAGE DISTRIBUTION BY OCCUPATION AND SEX, EMPLOYED WHITE SPANISH-SURNAME POPULATION FOURTEEN YEARS OF AGE AND OVER OF FIVE SOUTHWESTERN STATES, 1950

Occupation Group	Males	Females
Professional, technical, and kindred workers	2.1	4.6
Farmers and farm managers	4.9	0.3
Managers, officials, and proprietors, except farm	4.4	3.9
Clerical, sales, and kindred workers	6.4	24.0
Craftsmen, foremen, and kindred workers	12.9	1.4
Operatives and kindred workers	18.8	1.4
Private household workers	0.2	13.1
Service workers, except private household	6.1	14.7
Farm laborers, unpaid family workers	1.0	0.9
Farm laborers, except unpaid, and family foremen	23.3	5.2
Laborers, except farm and mine	18.5	1.4
Occupation not reported	1.1	2.4

Source: Saunders, CDMC, 296.

43 President's Commission on Migratory Labor, MLAA, 2.
44 President's Commission on Migratory Labor, MLAA, 3.
45 Mary Hurley Ashworth (editor), *Who?*, 12.

categories. The preceding table shows the distribution for the five Southwestern states selected for special study.

The tables below reveal considerable differences between the total white population and persons of Spanish surname in occupational distribution. Furthermore, the total white population is inclusive, *i.e.*, it includes the Spanish surname population as well as Anglos, and the differences which can be observed, especially in states where the proportion of Spanish Americans is high, would be even sharper if the two groups were separately presented.

DISTRIBUTION ON MAJOR OCCUPATIONAL GROUPS OF EMPLOYED PERSONS 14 YEARS AND OVER, OF TOTAL POPULATION AND PERSONS OF SPANISH SURNAME IN FIVE SOUTHWESTERN STATES, 1950

ARIZONA	Male		Female	
Occupation Group	Total Pop.	S.S.	Total Pop.	S.S.
Professional, technical & kindred workers	7.7	1.6	15.4	4.3
Farmers & farm managers	6.7	1.8	1.4	0.2
Managers, officials & proprietors, except farm	12.5	3.7	7.3	4.6
Clerical, sales & kindred workers	11.7	6.1	33.2	28.4
Craftsmen, foremen & kindred workers	18.1	13.1	0.8	0.6
Operatives & kindred workers	16.8	25.5	9.7	14.6
Private household workers	0.2	0.1	9.2	15.6
Service workers, except private household	6.1	5.5	17.1	22.1
Farm laborers, unpaid family workers	1.3	0.3	1.7	0.3
Farm laborers, except unpaid, and farm foremen	9.1	23.9	1.4	6.1
Laborers, except farm & mine	8.8	17.2	0.4	0.5
Occupation not reported	1.0	1.0	2.4	2.5

Sources: U.S. Census of Population 1950: *Arizona, General Characteristics,* Table 28 and Saunders, CDMC, 296.

CALIFORNIA	Male		Female	
Occupation Group	Total Pop.	S.S.	Total Pop.	S.S.
Professional, technical & kindred workers	9.8	2.6	14.1	4.6
Farmers & farm managers	3.8	2.8	0.6	0.2
Managers, officials & proprietors, except farm	13.4	4.6	6.3	3.5
Clerical, sales & kindred workers	14.9	6.4	41.3	23.7
Craftsmen, foremen & kindred workers	21.0	14.0	1.4	1.8
Operatives & kindred workers	16.3	21.6	13.1	41.2
Private household workers	0.2	0.1	6.7	5.4
Service workers, except private household	7.0	5.6	13.3	11.5
Farm laborers, unpaid family workers	0.2	0.3	0.5	0.5
Farm laborers, except unpaid & farm foremen	4.8	23.4	0.8	4.6
Laborers, except farm and mine	7.7	17.8	0.6	1.6
Occupation not reported	0.8	0.9	1.3	1.3

Sources: U.S. Census of Population 1950: *California, General Characteristics,* Table 28, and Saunders, CDMC, 296.

COLORADO	Male			Female		
Occupation Group	Total White	S.S.		Total White	S.S.	
Professional, technical & kindred workers	8.7	1.9		15.3	5.6	
Farmers & farm managers	12.0	7.6		0.8	0.6	
Managers, officials & proprietors, except farm	12.1	3.0		6.0	2.9	
Clerical, sales & kindred workers	13.1	4.4		39.4	19.5	
Craftsmen, foremen & kindred workers	17.7	9.1		1.3	1.3	
Operatives & kindred workers	14.9	22.1		8.6	20.0	
Private household workers	0.1	0.1		6.0	17.0	
Service workers, except private household	5.8	5.4		16.6	22.3	
Farm laborers, unpaid family workers	1.4	1.9		2.8	1.3	
Farm laborers, except unpaid & farm foremen	5.3	20.8		0.7	4.4	
Laborers, except farm & mine	7.8	22.2		0.7	2.1	
Occupation not reported	1.1	1.4		1.8	3.0	

Sources: U.S. Census of Population: *Colorado, General Characteristics,* Table 28 and Saunders, CDMC, 296.

NEW MEXICO	Male			Female		
Occupation Group	Total White	S.S.		Total White	S.S.	
Professional, technical & kindred workers	8.2	3.0		16.3	8.8	
Farmers & farm managers	12.9	13.1		1.3	0.8	
Managers, officials & proprietors, except farm	11.0	4.4		7.3	3.6	
Clerical, sales & kindred workers	9.3	6.5		34.4	27.5	
Craftsmen, foremen & kindred workers	17.4	13.0		1.0	0.8	
Operatives & kindred workers	15.0	14.8		6.9	9.0	
Private household workers	0.1	0.1		9.5	18.1	
Service workers, except private household	5.2	6.9		16.4	21.9	
Farmer laborers, unpaid family workers	'2.1	2.5		2.1	0.9	
Farm laborers, except unpaid & farm foremen	7.2	14.3		0.6	0.8	
Laborers, except farm & mine	9.6	19.0		0.5	0.6	
Occupation not reported	1.8	2.3		3.8	7.0	

Sources: U.S. Census of Population 1950: *New Mexico, General Characteristics,* Table 28, and Saunders, CDMC, 296.

TEXAS	Male			Female		
Occupation Group	Total White	S.S.		Total White	S.S.	
Professional, technical & kindred workers	6.8	1.6		12.2	3.8	
Farmers & farm managers	12.0	5.2		1.0	0.4	
Managers, officials & proprietors, except farm	11.5	4.4		5.5	4.3	
Clerical, sales & kindred workers	12.0	6.6		35.9	23.5	
Craftsmen, foremen & kindred workers	17.8	12.4		1.2	1.2	
Operatives & kindred workers	16.6	16.4		10.4	21.5	
Private household workers	0.2	0.2		13.1	18.7	
Service workers, except private household	5.4	6.5		15.0	14.8	
Farm laborers, unpaid family workers	1.2	1.3		2.1	1.4	
Farm laborers, except unpaid & farm foremen	6.2	25.4		1.2	6.6	
Laborers, except farm & mine	9.2	18.8		0.6	1.4	
Occupation not reported	1.2	1.1		1.8	2.4	

Sources: U.S. Census of Population 1950: *Texas, General Characteristics,* Table 28, and Saunders, CDMC, 296.

Income

"No especially good studies have been made of the incomes of the Spanish-speaking urban population," Saunders has noted, "but in general it can be said that there are proportionately more persons in unskilled, low-paying jobs among them than is true of the Anglos. Lack of skills, poor educational background, unfamiliarity with Anglo ways, and, at times, discrimination by Anglos, all operate to keep many urban Spanish-speaking persons at the bottom of the economic ladder."[46]

The Census Bureau provides the following data which show that the annual income of Spanish-surname persons in 1950 was low; eighty percent of the employed persons in the five states earned less than $2,500.

PERCENTAGE DISTRIBUTION BY ANNUAL INCOME, AND MEDIAN INCOME BY RURAL-URBAN RESIDENCE, WHITE SPANISH-SURNAME POPULATION FOURTEEN YEARS OF AGE AND OVER OF FIVE SOUTHWESTERN STATES, 1950

Annual income	Arizona	California	Colorado	New Mexico	Texas	Total
	Percentage distribution					
Total	100.0	100.0	100.0	100.0	100.0	100.0
Less than $500	19.6	17.7	24.9	25.5	26.6	22.7
$500 to $999	18.7	16.4	23.6	19.8	24.3	20.5
$1,000 to $1,499	14.3	13.0	14.1	15.1	17.5	15.2
$1,500 to $1,999	11.7	11.4	10.9	11.0	12.1	11.7
$2,000 to $2,499	10.6	13.1	10.7	10.8	8.8	10.8
$2,500 to $2,999	7.4	9.3	7.2	6.6	4.1	6.6
$3,000 to $3,999	13.1	12.5	6.2	7.3	4.0	8.2
$4,000 to $4,999	2.5	3.7	1.3	2.0	1.2	2.3
$5,000 to $5,999	0.7	1.3	0.5	0.6	0.5	0.8
$6,000 and over	1.3	1.6	0.6	1.2	0.8	1.2

Sources: Saunders, CDMC, 297.

The income of Spanish-Americans generally falls in between the median income of other white persons and Negroes. The table on the next page compares these three groups, giving figures for both rural and non-farm residents.

A factor which may affect the total median income is the percentage of employed persons within a group that are women. In Texas, for example, the median income for all per-

46 Saunders, CDMC, 72.

MEDIAN INCOMES OF TOTAL WHITE POPULATION, WHITE POPULATION OF SPANISH SURNAME AND NEGRO POPULATION, 14 YEARS AND OVER BY RURAL-URBAN RESIDENCE, IN FIVE SOUTHWESTERN STATES, 1950

		All white persons	Persons of Span. Surname	Negroes
Arizona:	Total:	$1881	$1408	$1040
	Urban	1912	1406	1089
	Rural Non-Farm } *		1497	
	Rural Farm	1572	1174	803
California:	Total:	$2234	$1628	$1575
	Urban	2260	1783	1589
	Rural Non-Farm }		1244	
	Rural Farm	1733	1174	853
Colorado:	Total:	$1759	$1052	$1328
	Urban	1802	1316	1329
	Rural Non-Farm }		899	
	Rural Farm	1500	869	—
New Mexico:	Total:	$1766	$1156	$1096
	Urban	1887	1400	1001
	Rural Non-Farm }		1066	
	Rural Farm	1239	897	—
Texas:	Total:	$1754	$ 980	$ 815
	Urban	1879	1134	896
	Rural Non-Farm }		1280	
	Rural Farm	1183	739	450

* Except for Spanish-speaking persons, the median for urban and rural non-farm is a combined figure.

Sources: U.S. Census of Population 1950: *Arizona, Detailed Characteristics, California Detailed Characteristics, Colorado, Detailed Characteristics, New Mexico, Detailed Characteristics, Texas, Detailed Characteristics,* (Tables 87) and *Persons of Spanish Surname,* Table 6.

sons of Spanish surname is $980 and for all Negroes is $815. But among Negro males in Texas (comparable figures are not available for the Spanish-speaking) the median income is $1,202. The median for Negro males and females combined is pulled down by the large number (42%) of employed persons which is female and which has an annual median income of $460. In the Spanish American community a smaller proportion—(21%)—of the women are employed and it can be expected that, if it were possible to compare medians of Negro males and Spanish males separately, the difference between the two would be substantially reduced, conceivably so much that Negro males would have a higher median income in Texas than males with Spanish surname.

Nativity and Alien Status

Census figures show that a considerably higher proportion of Mexican immigrants remain aliens than immigrants from other countries. Sixty-five percent of the 450,000 foreign-born Mexican Americans in this country have not gone through the naturalization process which would make them voting citizens of the United States.

PERCENTAGE OF IMMIGRANTS FROM SELECTED COUNTRIES WHICH HAS REMAINED ALIEN, 1950

Country of Birth	Percent Remaining Alien
England and Wales	18.3
Ireland	11.7
Norway	11.1
Sweden	9.0
Germany	13.7
Poland	22.4
Czechoslovakia	14.2
Austria	14.1
U.S.S.R.	12.6
Italy	15.5
Canada—French	20.4
Canada—Other	18.4
Mexico	64.9
Other	21.7

Source: U.S. Census of Population 1950: *Nativity and Parentage*, Table 17.

Burma has summarized the reasons why he believes Mexican immigrants show a reluctance to become naturalized citizens.[47]

> Probably the most common reason for not changing allegiance is that Mexico is easily accessible, and the *emigres* are attached to it and intend some day to return. Others are poor, and the cost and trouble of naturalization more than counterbalance any benefits which might accrue, for Anglos rarely distinguish between aliens and nonaliens. Some even feel that they are safer not to be citizens, for they can appeal for aid to the Mexican consul if they get into difficulty. Still others cannot show proof of legal entry. . . . Probably an even greater number fail to become citizens because of the trouble involved. . . . This whole process is difficult, and doubly so if the alien is a migratory agricultural worker without fixed residence.

The first reason cited by Burma and mentioned as particu-

---

47 Burma, SSG, 130.

larly significant by others, *i.e.*, the accessibility of Mexico, loses some of its strength upon scrutiny of the table above. Canadians, coming from an equally "accessible" country, tend to follow the pattern of European immigrants rather than that of persons from Mexico. While it may be an important contributing factor in the hesitancy to become citizens, therefore, the closeness of Mexico in itself does not seem too helpful in explaining the high proportion of Mexican-born persons who remain aliens in their adopted country.

NATIVITY OF THE WHITE SPANISH-SURNAME POPULATION IN FIVE SOUTHWESTERN STATES, 1950

	Arizona	California	Colorado	New Mex.	Texas	Total
		NUMBER	OF PERSONS			
Native	105,310	594,448	113,057	239,154	845,221	1,897,190
Foreign-born	23,008	166,005	5,074	9,726	188,547	392,360
		PERCENTAGE	DISTRIBUTION			
Native	82.1	78.2	95.7	96.1	81.8	82.9
Foreign-born	18.0	21.8	4.3	3.9	18.2	17.2

Source: U.S. Census of Population 1950: *Persons of Spanish Surname,* Table 1.

With immigration from Mexico now slowed down, each year the number of "native-born" increases in proportion to the foreign-born. This group, it has already been noted, includes persons who may never have been nearer Mexico than the *colonias* of Los Angeles, San Antonio, etc. It represents more clearly a "marginal" group between two cultures, not truly a part of either.

Housing and Health

"Whether Spanish-speaking southwesterners live in city or country, their housing is likely to be poor."[48] This statement by Saunders succinctly defines the housing conditions of the *colonia* and also suggests the attendant health problems that poor housing usually carries with it. The census statistics report that for the five southwestern states in which a sample was made, 27.2% of the dwelling units inhabited by people of Spanish surname were dilapidated.

The pattern of residence among Spanish Americans usually

---

48 Saunders, CDMC, 73.

involves a *colonia, i.e.,* a community, largely Spanish-speaking, which is apart from the Anglo community. Not all Spanish-speaking people find themselves confined to the *colonia,* but, in general, the combined conditions—discrimination, the desire to live near other Spanish-speaking people, a low economic status—contribute to a pressure which leads to the establishment and persistence of "Little Mexicos."

Not only are the *colonias* isolated from the Anglo community, but they are usually of substandard quality and their concomitant low level of health presents serious problems.[49]

> The relation between the quality of housing of many of the Spanish-speaking people and their needs for health services is easy to see. Overcrowding, uncertain or unsafe water supplies, lack of sewer connections, screens, and refrigeration, and many of the other conditions that are included in the concept "poor housing" contribute to the maintenance of health. Any population living under the circumstances of many of the Spanish-speaking people would be expected to have health problems; it is, therefore, not surprising to find that the Spanish-speaking group have many.

"Undernourishment, a high infant mortality rate, and a greater prevalence of some infections and contagious diseases, notably tuberculosis, and dysentery, are conditions frequently reported among the Spanish-speaking populations that have been studied. Age-specific birth and death rates are both somewhat higher for the Spanish-speaking than for the population as a whole, although the death rates have been coming down rather rapidly in recent years and the birth rates are beginning to reflect the increasing urbanization of the Spanish-speaking population."[50]

49 Saunders, CDMC, 74. See also Pauline Kibbe, *Latin Americans in Texas* (LAT). She has written a long chapter on the health and diet problems of Texas Spanish Americans in 1946. She also includes illustrations of improvement in the health of families when better housing and health facilities were made available. Chapter 9, 123-156.

50 Saunders, CDMC, 76.

Chapter III

THE PUERTO RICANS

THERE is great need for closer understanding between the people of the United States and all the Spanish-speaking people of the western hemisphere but there is a special need for this closer relationship with the people of Puerto Rico, for Puerto Ricans are United States citizens whether they live on the island or on the mainland. This is emphasized because mainland Americans and especially those of the majority group have tended to think of them as "foreigners" and to treat them as such.

Puerto Ricans never have come to the United States in such numbers as some immigrant groups in the past, in part because there aren't so many of them to come. It is only since the end of World War II that Puerto Ricans have come in sufficiently large numbers to draw widespread attention. Their reasons for coming, however, have been the same as those that brought many earlier groups—to improve their living standards. And like the earlier groups after getting here they have had to struggle against great odds.

An Old Pattern

Mills and Senior in their *Puerto Rican Journey*, in common with many other authorities, draw a close comparison between the experiences of Puerto Rican migrants to the mainland and the experiences of European immigrant groups.[1]

> . . . Most of the newcomers are poor, and hence forced into the least desirable sections of the city, from two to ten families often living in accommodations built for one. They are un-educated; the ways of the new city are strange and complex; the ways of yet another culture add to their strangeness and complexity; they are exploited by native landlords and sharks, and by some of their own countrymen who already "know the

---

1 C. Wright Mills and Clarence Senior, *Puerto Rican Journey* (PRJ), 82.

ropes." Entering the labor market, unlearned, unskilled, they seem at the mercy of economic forces. If the business cycle is on the upturn, they are welcomed; if it is on the way down, or in the middle of one of its periodic breakdowns, there is a savage struggle for even the low wage jobs between the new immigrants and the earlier ones who feel they have a prior claim.

Prior to 1890, most immigrants came from Northwestern Europe, including the Irish who came in such large numbers during the potato famine and who found such widespread antagonism among native Americans. Mills and Senior compare the attitudes of native Americans toward the Puerto Ricans today with the attitudes of the native Americans toward Irish immigrants of the last century. The contemporary "native" description was:[2]

> The conditions under which they had been born and brought up were generally of the most squalid and degrading character. Their wretched hovels, thatched with rotting straw, scantily furnished with light, hardly ventilated at all, frequently with no floor but the clay on which they were built, were crowded beyond the bounds of comfort, health, or, as it would seem to us, of simple social decency; their beds were heaps of straw or rags; their food consisted mainly of buttermilk and potatoes, often of the worst, and commonly inadequate in amount; their clothing was scanty and shabby.

After 1890 the largest numbers of immigrants came from southeastern Europe. It was the majority reaction to these southeastern Europeans that sparked the white superiority agitation of that period that resulted in the adoption in 1924 of a series of immigration laws drastically limiting the number of incoming people and favoring persons of British, German and Scandinavian ancestries. Discussing these developments, Dr. Oscar Handlin in his *Race and Nationality in American Life* says:[3]

> By the end of the century the pattern of racist practices and ideas seemed fully developed: the Orientals were to be totally excluded; the Negroes were to live in a segregated enclave; the Indians were to be confined to reservations as permanent wards of the nation; and all whites were expected to assimilate as

2 Mills and Senior, PRJ, 73.
3 Handlin, RNAL, 38.

rapidly as possible to a common standard. . . . And as the volume of immigration went up, speculation increased as to whether there were not among whites equally important racial distinctions that set the newcomers off from the native Americans.

It was in the midst of this agitation that Puerto Rico was taken over from Spain by the United States. The fact that these racist ideas were so widespread no doubt partly explains why Puerto Ricans were not granted citizenship in 1900. It also partly explains the federal government's policies in administering the island which caused so much resentment and unrest and resulted in the widespread movement for independence that was carried on for so many years.

In the early 1940's, there was a change in attitude toward Puerto Rico on the part of the Washington administration and of Puerto Rico toward the United States which greatly affected the size of the migration to the mainland as soon as the war was over.

Numbers and Distribution

The Migration Division of the Department of Labor of the Commonwealth of Puerto Rico estimates the Puerto Rican population on the mainland as of December 31, 1958 as 849,000, of which 77 percent were living in New York City. Of the total on the mainland, 71.6 percent were estimated to have been born on the island; and of the Puerto Rican population of New York City, 70.8 percent.[4] The population of the island as of July 1, 1958 was estimated as 2,317,000.[5]

For the years prior to 1950, figures are available for only the Puerto Rican-born population of the mainland. However, as may be seen below, they indicate that the substantial migration began after 1940.

Date	Population of Puerto Rico	Total P-R-Born Population of the mainland	P-R-Born Population of N.Y.C.
1950	2,210,703	226,110	187,420
1940	1,869,255	69,967	61,463
1930	1,543,913	52,774	44,908
1920	1,299,809	11,811	7,364
1910	1,118,012	1,513	554

4 FAF, 16 and 17.   5 FAF, 2.

The most recent actual count of Puerto Ricans on the mainland was made by the Bureau of the Census in a 20 percent sample of the returns obtained in the 1950 Census of Population. The projection of this sample indicated 75,265 persons of Puerto Rican parentage living on the mainland as of April 1, 1950 in addition to 226,110 persons of Puerto Rican birth. All those born on the continent who had at least one parent whose birthplace was Puerto Rico were reported by the Census in its tabulations as "Puerto Ricans of Puerto Rican parentage." The Puerto Rico-born figure includes everyone who gave Puerto Rico as his place of birth, among which was an unknown number of children of missionaries, government employees, army people, and so forth, whose parents originally were of continental origin.

For the years since 1950, the Migration Division of the Department of Labor of Puerto Rico has prepared estimates based on net migration figures and vital statistics. These estimates indicate a steady increase of Puerto Rican population both in and outside New York City and of Puerto Rico-born as well as mainland-born Puerto Ricans of Puerto Rican parentage. According to these estimates, the Puerto Rican population on the mainland in 1958 was over two and a half times what it had been in 1950. However, the rate of increase in New York City was somewhat less than in the rest of the mainland combined, as may be seen from the figures below for both Puerto Rican-born and persons of Puerto Rican parentage.

NEW YORK CITY

Year	Total P.R. Population Number	Total P.R. Population % Increase	Puerto Rican-Born Number	Puerto Rican-Born % Increase	P.R. Parents Number	P.R. Parents % Increase
Dec. 31, 1958	654,000	5.7	463,000	3.3	191,000	11.7
" 1957	619,000	7.3	448,000	5.4	171,000	13.2
" 1956	577,000	9.5	426,000	8.1	151,000	13.5
" 1955	527,000	10.0	394,000	8.5	133,000	14.7
" 1954	479,000	6.9	363,000	4.3	116,000	16.0
" 1953	448,000	17.0	348,000	17.2	100,000	16.3
" 1952	383,000	16.8	297,000	17.3	86,000	14.7
" 1951	328,000	18.8	253,000	19.9	75,000	15.6
" 1950	276,000*	—	211,000*	—	65,000*	—

Source: *Facts and Figures,* January 1959 edition, 17.

* Figure represents estimated increase as of Dec. 31, 1950 over Census figure for April 1, 1950.

Year	Total P.R. Population Number	% Increase	Puerto Rican-Born Number	% Increase	P.R. Parents Number	% Increase
Dec. 31, 1958	195,000	10.2	145,000	8.2	50,000	16.3
" 1957	177,000	11.4	134,000	10.7	43,000	13.2
" 1956	159,000	17.8	121,000	18.6	38,000	15.2
" 1955	135,000	14.4	102,000	14.6	33,000	13.8
" 1954	118,000	8.3	89,000	6.0	29,000	16.0
" 1953	109,000	22.5	84,000	25.4	25,000	13.6
" 1952	89,000	23.6	67,000	26.4	22,000	15.8
" 1951	72,000	18.0	53,000	23.2	19,000	137.5
" 1950	61,000*	—	43,000*	—	8,000*	—

Source: *Facts and Figures,* January 1959 edition, 16 and 17.
* Figure represents estimated increase as of Dec. 31, 1950 over Census figure for April 1, 1950.

New York City still has by far the greatest concentration of persons of Puerto Rican birth as well as of persons of Puerto Rican parentage, though the proportion has been declining since 1952 as is indicated in the figures below:

NEW YORK CITY AS PERCENT OF TOTAL

Year	Puerto Rican Birth	Puerto Rican Parentage
1958	76.2	79.3
1957	77.0	79.9
1956	77.9	79.8
1955	79.4	80.1
1954	80.3	80.0
1953	80.6	80.0
1952	81.6	79.6
1951	82.6	79.8
1950	—	—

Migration figures indicate a still more marked tendency toward dispersion throughout the mainland. According to the Migration Division of the Puerto Rico Department of Labor, only 60 per cent of the new arrivals came to New York City in 1957 whereas in 1950 the figure was 85 percent.[6] See table on the next page.

Total figures are not available by state but those reported by the Migration Division of the Puerto Rico Department of Labor indicate that about 151,000 of the 195,000 Puerto Ricans

---

6 FAF, 16.

Year	Estimated Migration to New York City	Percent of Total Migration
1958	17,000*	60
1957	22,600	60
1956	34,000	65
1955	31,800	70
1954	16,100	75
1953	51,800	75
1952	45,500	77
1951	42,300	80
1950	29,500	85

* Preliminary estimate.

on the mainland outside of New York in 1958 were dispersed among the 11 states listed below.[7]

State	Puerto Rican Population	
California	6,100	(L.A. and S.F.)
Connecticut	19,500	(Bridgeport, Hartford, New Haven and Waterbury)
Florida	5,000	(Miami)
Illinois	25,000	(Chicago)
Indiana	5,000	(East Chicago and Gary)
Massachusetts	3,500	(Springfield)
Michigan	1,600	(Detroit)
New Jersey	40,000	(Entire state)
New York	12,000	(Buffalo, Bayshore, L.I. and Rochester)
Ohio	11,000	(Cleveland, Lorain, Youngstown)
Pennsylvania	22,000	(Bethlehem, Philadelphia, Reading)
Total	150,700	

Urban-Rural Distribution

As has already been indicated, the great majority of Puerto Ricans that come to the mainland settle in New York City. Those that do not live in New York City for the most part live in other urban centers. The 1950 Census had no information on Puerto Rican population by city but according to the estimates of the Puerto Rico Department of Labor, there were 195,000 Puerto Ricans of Puerto Rican birth and parentage living elsewhere on the mainland than in New York City as of December 31, 1958. Twenty-nine cities accounted for 122,600 of these or 62.9 percent. The Puerto Rican population

---

7 FAF, 18.

of each of the 29 cities ranked according to the size of the
Puerto Rican population is as follows:[8]

City	Population*	City	Population*
Chicago (1957)	25,000	Hartford	3,000
Philadelphia	13,000	Milwaukee (1956)	3,000
Bridgeport	7,000	New Haven	3,000
Miami (1956)	5,000	Trenton (1957)	3,000
Camden (1955)	5,000	Youngstown (1957)	3,000
Paterson (1957)	5,000	Los Angeles (1956)	2,500
Perth Amboy (1955)	4,000	East Chicago (1956)	2,500
Rochester	4,000	Gary (1956)	2,500
Cleveland (1956)	4,000	Jersey City (1955)	2,500
Lorain (1956)	4,000	Waterbury	2,000
San Francisco (1956)	3,600	Detroit (1955)	1,600
Springfield (1956)	3,500	Bay Shore, L. I.	1,500
Newark	3,200	Washington, D. C. (1956)	1,200
Buffalo	3,000	Bethlehem, Pa. (1956)	1,000
		Reading (1954)	1,000

* The figures are for 1958 except where otherwise indicated.

According to the Puerto Rico Department of Labor, the
above list includes only about one-fifth of the towns and
cities on the mainland known to have Puerto Rican residents,
though they are the largest communities. This is very different
from the urban-rural distribution on the island. In 1950, the
population living in rural territory constituted 59.5 percent of
the total population of the island and "it is in the rural areas
that a majority of the more than two and one-quarter million
Puerto Ricans continue to live."[9]

However, there still seems to be fairly general agreement
that most of the migrants to the mainland come from the urban
areas of the island. Dr. Clarence Senior estimates that 91
percent that come to New York have urban backgrounds, most
of them have been actual long time residents of San Juan or
Ponce. An earlier (1948) study of the Puerto Rican labor force
in New York City indicated that only 5 percent had ever had
agricultural experience.

Sex Distribution

Among the differences which social scientists point to in
their comparisons between the Puerto Ricans who migrate to

8 FAF, 18.
9 Theodore Brameld, *The Remaking of a Cultural* (ROC), 5.

the mainland and the European immigrants of earlier years, is the higher proportion of women among the Puerto Ricans. There was a greater tendency among European immigrants for the husband to come to the United States first in order to get established, whereas Puerto Rican families tend more to come together, or, even, for the wife to be the original migrant.

In the summary table below, the sex distribution of the Puerto Rican population both on the island and on the mainland is compared with that of the total population. In New York City, the proportion is very similar to that of the total population as well as to the urban population of the island. Outside New York City the proportion of Puerto Rican men is noticeably more than for the total population.

TOTAL AND PUERTO RICAN POPULATION OF NEW YORK CITY AND OUTSIDE OF NEW YORK CITY BY SEX, AND POPULATION OF PUERTO RICO, URBAN AND RURAL, BY SEX—1950

Sex	New York City		Outside N. Y.		Island	
	Total	P.R.	Total	P.R.	Urban	Rural
Total —Number	7,891,957	245,880	142,805,404	55,495	894,813	1,315,890
Percent	100.0	100.0	100.0	100.0	100.0	100.0
Men —Number	3,821,788	114,300	71,011,451	32,290	429,578	681,368
Percent	48.4	46.5	49.7	58.2	48.0	51.8
Women—Number	4,070,169	131,580	71,793,953	23,205	465,235	634,522
Percent	51.6	53.5	50.3	41.8	52.0	48.2

Sources: U.S. Census of Population 1950: *U.S. Summary General Statistics, New York General Statistics, Puerto Ricans in Continental United States,* and *Puerto Rico General Statistics.*

Age Distribution

Among other signs of the social progress brought about in Puerto Rico in the last fifteen to twenty years is the remarkable increase in life expectancy of the Puerto Rican people. Whereas life expectancy on the island was only 46 years in 1940, in 1957 it was 68 years, very close to the life expectancy pattern of the mainland. Nevertheless, Puerto Ricans are still a much younger people than mainland Americans. This was reflected in the 1950 Census figures according to which 57.3 percent of the urban population of Puerto Rico was under 25 years of age as compared with 34.4 percent of the total population of New York City and 41.9 percent of the total population outside New York City.

[54]

TOTAL AND PUERTO RICAN POPULATION OF NEW YORK CITY AND OUTSIDE OF NEW YORK CITY BY AGE GROUPS AND POPULATION OF PUERTO RICO, URBAN AND RURAL, BY AGE GROUPS—1950

Age Group		New York City Total	New York City P.R.	Outside N.Y.C. Total	Outside N.Y.C. P.R.	Island Urban	Island Rural
All Age Groups	—Number	7,891,957	245,880	142,805,404	55,495	894,813	1,315,890
	Percent	100.0	100.0	100.0	100.0	100.0	100.0
Under 15	—Number	1,645,527	73,325	38,836,997	16,385	337,356	617,920
	Percent	20.9	29.8	27.2	29.5	37.7	47.0
15 to 24	—Number	1,064,783	52,855	21,033,643	13,545	175,344	237,817
	Percent	13.5	21.5	14.7	24.4	19.6	18.1
25 to 34	—Number	1,303,494	50,080	22,455,773	11,525	135,220	154,509
	Percent	16.5	20.3	15.7	20.8	15.1	11.7
35 to 44	—Number	1,310,910	36,650	20,139,449	6,770	99,761	124,585
	Percent	16.6	15.0	14.1	12.2	11.1	9.5
45 & over	—Number	2,567,243	32,970	40,339,542	7,270	147,132	181,059
	Percent	32.5	13.5	28.2	13.2	16.4	13.8

Sources: U.S. Census of Population 1950: *New York General Characteristics,* Tables 15 and 33; *Puerto Ricans in Continental United States,* Tables 2 and 3; and *Puerto Rico General Characteristics,* Table 12.

The median age of the total mainland population in 1950 was 30.2 years; for the white population it was 30.8 years and for the non-white population 26.1 years. In the summary table below the median ages of Puerto Ricans on the Island and on the mainland are compared with those of other population groups. The very low Island medians are especially striking.

Population Group	Median Age
Total U. S.	30.2
White	30.8
Non-white	26.1
Total New York City	34.4
Native white	28.2
Foreign-born white	53.7
Negro	29.8
Puerto Rican	24.5
Total Puerto Rico (Island)	18.4
White	18.8
Non-white	16.9

Sources: U.S. Census of Population 1950: *U.S. General Characteristics,* Table 38; *New York State Detailed Characteristics,* Table 53; *Puerto Ricans in Continental U.S.,* Table 3; and *Puerto Rico General Characteristics,* Table 12.

As in the United States, the rural population of Puerto Rico is considerably younger than the urban population. On the mainland the median ages for the total rural non-farm and

[55]

rural farm populations were 27.9 and 26.3 years respectively, whereas the median for the rural population of the island was only 16.5 years. Median age, the mid-point with half the population older and half younger, is of course a combination of factors. The very low figure for Puerto Ricans in all categories probably indicates both high proportions of young children and of young married couples.

Marital Status

The 1950 Census of Population showed similar proportions of single, married, and widowed or divorced persons among Puerto Ricans on the mainland and in Puerto Rico. In New York City, however, there was a considerably smaller proportion of single men than on the island and a somewhat larger proportion of married men. This was true also for the women but the differences in the proportions were not so great. The principal difference between men and women on the mainland as well as on the island was in the widowed or divorced category, as may be seen in the figures below.

NUMBER AND PERCENT OF PUERTO RICANS 14 YEARS OF AGE AND OLDER ON THE ISLAND AND ON THE MAINLAND, BY SEX AND MARITAL STATUS—1950

Sex and Marital Status	Puerto Rican Population on Mainland U.S.						Population of Puerto Rico	
	Total		N. Y. City		Outside N.Y.C.			
	Number	Percent	Number	Percent	Number	Percent	Number	Percent
Men	103,630	100.0	79,505	100.0	24,125	100.0	649,414	100.0
Single	36,290	35.0	26,450	33.3	9,840	40.8	264,854	40.8
Married	63,335	61.1	50,595	63.6	12,740	52.8	357,029*	55.0
W or D	4,005	3.9	2,460	3.1	1,545	6.4	27,531	4.2
Women	113,200	100.0	96,895	100.0	16,305	100.0	651,716	100.0
Single	28,500	25.2	24,470	25.3	4,030	24.7	193,897	29.8
Married	69,985	61.8	59,395	61.3	10,590	64.9	374,069*	57.4
W or D	14,715	13.0	13,030	13.4	1,685	10.3	83,750	12.8

* Includes consensually married persons.
Source: U.S. Census of Population 1950: *Puerto Ricans in Continental United States,* Tables 4 and 5; *Puerto Rico General Characteristics,* Table 18.

As compared with the total population, the proportion of single men as well as single women among the Puerto Ricans was greater both in New York City and the entire mainland as shown in the table below, whereas the number of married Puerto Rican men and women was somewhat less.

NUMBER AND PERCENT OF PERSONS 14 YEARS OF AGE AND OLDER IN THE UNITED
STATES AND IN NEW YORK CITY, BY SEX AND MARITAL STATUS, TOTAL
POPULATION AND PUERTO RICAN POPULATION—1950

Sex and Marital Status	Total United States				New York City			
	Total Population		P.R. Population		Total Population		P.R. Population	
	Number	Percent	Number	Percent	Number	Percent	Number	Percent
Men	53,311,617	100.0	103,630	100.0	3,013,675	100.0	79,505	100.0
Single	14,518,079	26.2	36,290	35.0	845,625	28.1	26,450	33.3
Married	37,399,617	67.6	63,335	61.1	2,004,570	66.5	50,595*	63.6
W or D	3,393,921	6.1	4,005	3.9	163,480	5.5	2,460	3.1
Women	57,042,417	100.0	113,200	100.0	3,308,440	100.0	96,895	100.0
Single	11,454,266	20.1	28,500	25.2	787,715	23.8	24,470	25.3
Married	37,503,836	65.7	69,985	61.8	2,042,210	61.7	59,395*	61.3
W or D	8,084,315	14.2	14,715	13.0	478,515	14.4	13,030	13.4

* Includes consensually married persons.
Sources: U.S. Census of Population 1950: *U.S. Summary General Characteristics*, Table 68; *New York Detailed Characteristics*, Table 57; *Puerto Ricans in Continental United States*, Tables 4 and 5.

Racial Classification

The term "race" as it is used today to differentiate population groups is frequently a simple and crude classification according to skin color and this was the basis of the classification "white" and "nonwhite" used by the Census Bureau in the 1950 Census of Population. The Census explains its use of the term as follows:[10]

> The concept of race as it has been used by the Bureau of the Census is derived from that which is commonly accepted by the general public. It does not, therefore, reflect clear-cut definitions of biological stock, and several categories obviously refer to nationalities. The information on race is ordinarily not based on a reply to questions asked by the enumerator but rather is obtained by observation. . . .
> . . . The group designated as "nonwhite" consists of Negroes, Indians, Japanese, Chinese, Filipinos, and other nonwhite races. Persons of Mexican birth or ancestry who were not definitely Indian or of other nonwhite race were classified as white in 1950 and 1940.
> Other races.—This category includes Koreans, Asiatic Indians, Indonesians, Polynesians, and so forth, similarly identified largely in terms of area of origin. . . .

It is clear from the above definition that the term "white" as used by the Census Bureau is a broad category that includes

---

10 U.S. Census of Population, 1950, *Nonwhite Population by Race*, 3B-4.

most nationality groups except persons of African or Asian extraction. Most Puerto Ricans are characterized by the Census as "white." The table below compares the "racial" distribution of Puerto Ricans living on the mainland and in Puerto Rico in 1950 with the total population of the mainland.

NUMBER AND PERCENT OF WHITE AND NON-WHITE POPULATION FOR TOTAL U.S. POPULATION AND PUERTO RICAN POPULATION ON THE MAINLAND AND IN P.R., BY AREA—1950

Area	Total Population	White		Non-White	
		Number	Percent	Number	Percent
Total U.S.	150,697,361	134,942,028	89.5	15,755,333	10.5
N.Y.C.	7,891,957	7,116,441	91.2	775,516	9.8
Outside N.Y.C.	142,805,404	127,825,587	89.5	14,979,817	10.5
Puerto Ricans	301,375	277,275	92.0	24,100	8.0
N.Y.C.	245,880	226,380	92.1	19,500	7.9
Outside N.Y.C.	55,495	50,895	91.7	4,600	8.3
Puerto Rico	2,210,703	1,762,411	79.7	448,292	20.3
Urban	894,813	704,140	78.7	190,673	21.3
Rural	1,315,890	1,058,271	80.4	257,619	19.6

Sources: U.S. Census of Population 1950: *U.S. Summary General Characteristics*, Table 59; *New York State General Characteristics*, Table 33; *Puerto Rico General Characteristics*, Table 12; *and Puerto Ricans in Continental U.S.*, Tables 2 and 3.

The above figures indicate that whereas "nonwhites" constituted a fifth of the population on the Island in 1950, "nonwhite" Puerto Ricans constituted only 8 percent of all the Puerto Ricans on the mainland. In New York City, the "nonwhite" Puerto Ricans constituted only 7.9 percent of all Puerto Ricans in the city as compared with the 9.8 percent which "nonwhites" constituted of the total population.

Estimates prepared by the Puerto Rico Department of Labor as of the end of 1958 show that 92.3 percent of persons of Puerto Rican birth living on the mainland were "white" as compared with only 79.7 percent on the island.[11]

Education

If more recent data on years of school completed were available for Puerto Rico than the 1950 Census data, there probably would be less disparity between the island and the mainland situations in view of the emphasis that the Puerto Rico government has placed on school attendance on the last ten years. No

---

11 FAF, 19.

doubt the average number of school years completed is higher today in the island than it was in 1950.

The 1950 Census data on years of school completed by people living on the island was reported for those 25 years of age and over only. For comparative purposes, the figures used for New York City in the table below also represent persons 25 years of age and over only.

Probably the most significant comparison presented in the

YEARS OF SCHOOL COMPLETED BY PERSONS 25 YEARS OF AGE AND OVER REPORTING, IN NEW YORK CITY AND ON THE ISLAND, 1950

Years of School Completed	New York City			Puerto Rico		
	Total Pop.	P.R. Parents	P.R. Birth	Total Pop.	Urban	Rural
MEN						
Total men reporting	2,357,645	2,010	50,475	424,661	180,700	243,961
No school	105,565	80	2,980	120,340	33,469	86,871
1 to 4 years	166,290	230	10,445	140,332	48,534	91,798
5 to 7 years	315,025	360	14,095	74,187	36,444	37,743
8 years	557,130	395	10,995	32,315	20,986	11,329
9 to 12 years	832,240	740	10,530	42,082	28,394	13,688
College (1 yr. or more)	381,395	205	1,430	15,405	12,873	2,532
No school	4.5	3.7	5.9	28.3	18.5	35.6
1 to 4 years	7.1	11.4	20.7	33.0	26.9	37.6
5 to 7 years	13.4	17.9	27.9	17.5	20.2	15.5
8 years	23.6	19.7	21.8	7.6	11.6	4.6
9 to 12 years	35.3	36.8	20.9	9.9	15.7	5.6
College (1 yr. or more)	16.2	10.2	2.8	3.6	7.1	1.0
WOMEN						
Total women reporting	2,608,015	2,310	61,100	415,297	200,024	215,273
No school	140,035	110	6,660	160,345	59,418	100,927
1 to 4 years	189,795	265	14,375	125,439	52,320	73,119
5 to 7 years	351,190	395	16,540	62,757	35,905	26,852
8 years	630,335	395	12,030	25,801	18,871	6,930
9 to 12 years	1,035,755	1,005	10,175	27,757	22,391	5,366
College (1 yr. or more)	260,905	140	1,320	13,198	11,119	2,079
No School	5.4	4.8	10.9	38.6	29.7	46.9
1 to 4 years	7.3	11.5	23.5	30.2	26.2	34.0
5 to 7 years	13.5	17.1	27.1	15.1	18.0	12.5
8 years	24.2	17.1	19.7	6.2	9.4	3.2
9 to 12 years	39.7	43.5	16.7	6.7	11.2	2.5
College (1 yr. or more)	10.0	6.1	2.2	3.2	5.6	1.0

Sources: U.S. Census of Population 1950: *New York Detailed Characteristics*, Table 65; *Puerto Ricans in Continental U.S.*, Table 5; and *Puerto Rico General Characteristics*, Table 16.

table is the comparison of New York City Puerto Ricans of Puerto Rican birth with the urban population of the island. This comparison bears out the statement frequently made that the migrants tend to be better educated than the population of the island in general, except that in the urban population of the island there is a larger proportion of both men and women that had had one year or more of college.

The other significant comparison is that of New York City figures for Puerto Ricans of Puerto Rican birth with the figures for the total population of the City. Though there are some marked differences between the two groups, the differences are less, particularly for the men, than might have been expected. Though the proportion of Puerto Rico-born men that had had only one to four years of school was much greater than for the total male population, there was not a great difference in the proportions that had had no school and the proportions were very similar for those that had had eight years of school.

NUMBER OF SCHOOL YEARS COMPLETED BY NUMBER OF PERSONS 14 YEARS OF AGE AND OVER REPORTING IN NEW YORK CITY, TOTAL POPULATION AND PUERTO RICAN POPULATION, BY SEX AND AGE GROUP, 1950

Years of School Completed	14 to 24 Yrs. of Age			25 Yrs. and Over		
	Total Pop.	P. R. Parents	P. R. Birth	Total Pop.	P. R. Parents	P. R. Birth
MEN						
Total reporting	525,160	6,545	17,745	2,357,645	2,010	50,475
No school	4,085	50	500	105,565	80	2,980
1 to 4 years	13,375	275	2,095	166,290	230	10,445
5 to 7 years	40,165	940	4,875	315,025	360	14,095
8 years	60,256	1,300	4,005	557,130	395	10,995
9 to 12 years	323,025	3,730	5,920	832,240	740	10,530
College (1 or more years)	84,255	250	350	381,395	205	1,430
WOMEN						
Total reporting	584,035	7,165	23,785	2,608,015	2,310	61,100
No school	4,705	85	850	140,035	110	6,660
1 to 4 years	15,425	335	3,525	189,795	265	14,375
5 to 7 years	37,985	800	6,155	351,190	395	16,540
8 years	59,590	1,120	4,845	630,335	395	12,030
9 to 12 years	397,375	4,630	7,990	1,035,755	1,005	10,175
College (1 or more years)	68,955	195	420	260,905	140	1,320

Sources: U.S. Census of Population 1950: *New York Detailed Characteristics,* Table 64; and *Puerto Ricans in Continental U.S.,* Table 65.

There were more differences between Puerto Rico-born women and the total female population, however. The proportion of Puerto Rico-born women that had not been in school was twice as large as for the total female population and there were similar differences in the other categories except that for the women, too, there was not so much difference between those that had had eight years of school.

In the tables on this and the following page, figures for persons of Puerto Rican birth and Puerto Rican parentage in New York are compared with the total population 14 years of age and over. As can be seen in the percentage table, there was a fairly close correlation between the years of school completed by the total population and by persons of Puerto Rican parentage whether in the age group 14 to 24 or 25 years of age and over. The strong inference is that the city's school requirements are effective in compelling attendance for all.

NUMBER OF SCHOOL YEARS COMPLETED BY PERCENT OF PERSONS 14 YEARS OF AGE AND OVER REPORTING IN NEW YORK CITY, TOTAL POPULATION AND PUERTO RICAN POPULATION, BY SEX AND AGE GROUP, 1950

Years of School Completed	14 to 24 Yrs. of Age			25 Yrs. and Over		
	Total Pop.	P. R. Parents	P. R. Birth	Total Pop.	P. R. Parents	P. R. Birth
MEN						
Total reporting	100.0	100.0	100.0	100.0	100.0	100.0
No school	0.8	0.8	2.8	4.5	3.7	5.9
1 to 4 years	2.5	4.2	11.8	7.1	11.4	20.7
5 to 7 years	7.6	14.4	27.5	13.4	17.9	27.9
8 years	11.5	19.9	22.6	23.6	19.7	21.8
9 to 12 years	61.5	57.0	33.4	35.3	36.8	20.9
College (1 or more years)	16.0	3.8	2.0	16.2	10.2	2.8
WOMEN						
Total reporting	100.0	100.0	100.0	100.0	100.0	100.0
No school	0.8	1.2	3.6	5.4	4.8	10.9
1 to 4 years	2.6	4.7	14.8	7.3	11.5	23.5
5 to 7 years	6.5	11.4	25.9	13.5	17.1	27.1
8 years	10.2	15.6	20.4	24.2	17.1	19.7
9 to 12 years	68.0	64.6	33.6	39.7	43.5	16.7
College (1 or more years)	11.8	2.7	1.8	10.0	6.1	2.2

Source: Percentages derived from sources of previous table.

Language

One of the most shortsighted policies followed by the Federal Government in administering Puerto Rican education apparently was its insistence on the use of English instead of Spanish in the schools. Except for a short period, this policy was followed right up to 1948 and resulted in a greatly increased Puerto Rican determination to nurture their own language and in a real antipathy toward the use of English.

As the following table shows, far less than half of the people of Puerto Rico spoke English in 1950 even in the urban areas where the schools were much better than they were in the rural areas.

NUMBER AND PERCENT OF URBAN AND RURAL PUERTO RICAN POPULATION 10 YEARS OF AGE AND OVER, BY ABILITY TO SPEAK ENGLISH, 1950

Ability to Speak English	Total Population of Puerto Rico		Urban Population		Rural Population	
	Number	Percent	Number	Percent	Number	Percent
Population 10 years of age and over						
Total	1,526,154	100.0	652,999	100.0	873,155	100.0
Men	764,564	100.0	307,652	100.0	456,912	100.0
Women	761,590	100.0	345,347	100.0	416,243	100.0
Population able to speak English						
Total	398,293	26.1	238,523	36.5	159,770	18.3
Men	214,238	28.0	122,743	39.9	91,495	20.0
Women	184,055	24.2	115,780	33.5	68,275	16.4
Population unable to speak English						
Total	1,127,861	73.9	414,476	63.5	713,385	81.7
Men	550,326	72.0	184,909	60.1	365,417	80.0
Women	577,535	75.8	229,569	66.5	347,968	83.6

Source: Census of Population 1950: *Puerto Rico General Characteristics*, Table 17.

Occupation

Since the restriction of European immigration early in the twenties, American industry has had to look to other sources of supply for the type of labor that southern Europeans and other immigrants who came in such large numbers prior to World War I had provided. Puerto Ricans have been a very important source since that time. In the nineteen twenties, the industries that needed cheap labor moved *to* the island. A study of the island by The Brookings Institution in 1930 reported that "cheap labor—or the anticipation of profiting by a cheap labor supply—accounts very largely, if not entirely, for the movement to the Island within the past few years of the cotton embroidery and clothing manufacture and of the pivot jewel and diamond cutting business."[12]

The migrations *from* the island that began in the nineteen forties have brought much-needed labor to the mainland. The New York needle trades particularly were greatly in need of labor at the end of World War II.

When the 1950 Census was taken, Puerto Ricans were concentrated in two major occupational groups—operatives and service workers. Fify-eight percent of the Puerto Rican men on the mainland were in these two occupational groups and 79 percent of the employed Puerto Rican women. In New York City, the concentration in these two groups was still greater— 65.6 percent for the men and 83.4 percent for the women. In the table following, the occupational distribution of Puerto Rican men and women on the mainland is compared with the distribution of the total white population, the Negro population, and the population of racial groups other than Negro and white.

The table on the following page shows that in 1950 a much larger proportion of Puerto Rican men were classified as "operatives" and as "service workers" than any of the other groups with which they are compared. The proportion of Puerto Rican women classified as "operatives" is still greater in comparison with the other groups but a smaller proportion of them are "service workers" than any of the other groups. The proportion of Puerto Ricans classified as "laborers" is noticeably less than any of the other groups.

Both Puerto Rican men and women are employed in the needle trades in large numbers but they are widely dispersed in a large number of other manufacturing industries as well. In the metals and machinery industry they work on welding equipment, steel containers, diesel engines, tractors, farm

---

12 Victor S. Clark and others, *Porto Rico and Its Problems* (PRIP), 462.

NUMBER AND PERCENT OF POPULATION 14 YEARS AND OVER, BY MAJOR OCCUPATIONAL GROUPS IN CONTINENTAL UNITED STATES, BY RACE OR ETHNIC GROUP, 1950

Occupation Group	Total White Number	%	Negro Number	%	Other Races Number	%	Puerto Ricans Number	%
			Men					
Total reporting	36,425,456	100.0	3,448,992	100.0	177,499	100.0	63,895	100.0
Prof., tech., etc.*	2,886,870	7.9	75,436	2.2	7,950	4.5	3,355	5.2
Mgrs., off., etc.	7,956,630	21.8	531,932	15.4	42,007	23.7	3,615	5.7
Clerical & kind.	2,490,112	6.8	106,765	3.1	5,733	3.2	6,160	9.6
Sales workers	2,552,077	7.0	38,694	1.1	6,015	3.4	—	—
Craftsmen	7,256,143	19.9	269,373	7.8	11,500	6.5	7,125	11.2
Operatives	7,368,376	20.2	738,362	21.4	20,695	11.6	21,115	33.0
Priv. household	34,270	0.1	36,069	1.0	2,817	1.6	105	0.2
Service workers	1,882,822	5.2	464,075	13.5	26,513	14.9	16,040	25.1
Laborers (farm)	1,556,279	4.3	360,086	10.4	34,093	19.2	1,710	2.7
Other laborers	2,441,877	6.7	828,200	24.0	20,176	11.4	4,670	7.3
Occ. not reported	404,731	—	50,705	—	2,793	—	1,085	—
			Women					
Total reporting	13,545,238	100.0	1,839,127	100.0	48,506	100.0	38,930	100.0
Prof., tech., etc.	1,830,440	13.5	104,728	5.7	3,817	7.9	1,320	3.4
Mgrs., off., etc.	734,118	5.4	55,506	3.0	3,505	7.2	505	1.3
Clerical & kind.	4,208,510	31.1	74,255	4.0	8,999	18.6	4,280	11.0
Sales workers	1,302,089	9.6	25,492	1.4	2,143	4.4	—	—
Craftsmen	223,496	1.6	11,629	0.6	419	0.9	665	1.7
Operatives	2,734,283	20.2	274,000	14.9	10,504	21.6	28,225	72.5
Priv. household	554,859	4.1	773,590	42.1	5,861	12.1	905	2.3
Service workers	1,556,458	11.5	351,856	19.1	5,979	12.3	2,530	6.5
Laborers (farm)	302,893	2.2	139,657	7.6	6,787	14.0	115	0.3
Other laborers	98,073	0.7	28,414	1.5	492	1.0	385	1.0
Occ. not reported	249,694	—	30,829	—	1,770	—	415	—

Sources: U.S. Census of Population 1950: *U.S. Summary Detailed Characteristics,* Table 128 and *Puerto Ricans in Continental U.S.,* Table 4.

equipment, mining machinery and many other products. In the electronics industry, they work on radio and radar equipment, TV components, electromagnetic relays, rectifiers, crystal ovens, pulse generators, fluorescent lights, electric shavers and scientific equipment. In the plastics industry where many of them are found they make dinnerware, tool handles, frames for eyeglasses, sprayers, tiles, buttons, cameras, toys, food containers, and fountain pens. Other industries where they are employed in considerable numbers are leather, automobiles, paper products, and furniture.

In the metals and machinery industry, Puerto Ricans are on the assembly line; they are grinders, punch press operators, spot welders, and foundry workers; and they are in the packaging and painting departments also. In the garment industry, Puerto Ricans are cutters as well as machine operators.

American agriculture also relies heavily on labor from Puerto Rico but this is largely seasonal labor which does not begin to arrive until about May 1 and so was not included in the 1950 Census figures which were reported as of April 1. The peak agricultural employment seasons in Puerto Rico and the mainland complement each other. The sugar cane cutting season in Puerto Rico as well as the citrus fruit picking is from January to July, the tobacco harvest from October to April, and the coffee harvest from September to March so that the Puerto Rican economy can begin to release farm labor for the mainland about May of each year.

Estimates differ as to the number of seasonal workers coming to the mainland each year. According to a report of the Puerto Rican Department of Labor in 1956 there were about 30,000 coming each year to work on farms and in canneries along the Eastern Seaboard from New Hampshire to Delaware and as far west as the State of Washington—working such crops as asparagus, tomatoes, potatoes, sweet corn, strawberries, cherries, mushrooms, and shade tobacco. About 15,000 of these "workers come under a contract arranged between the U. S. Employment Service and the affiliated Employment Service of Puerto Rico. The contract is designed to protect both the worker and the farmer, guaranteeing prevailing wages and work for a stated period, providing for medical insurance and compensation. The program is administered on the mainland by the Migration Division of the Puerto Rico Department of Labor. The remaining 15,000 come on their own and are known as 'walk-ins.' Often they are workers who have come under contract in previous years and have subsequently made individual arrangements with farmers for whom they worked. Most of the agricultural workers return to Puerto Rico when the season ends. However, some are offered year-round jobs in agriculture or industry, send for their families, and settle permanently in the States."[13]

---

13 *Puerto Rico and the Puerto Ricans* (PRPR), compiled by Herbert Sternau, 22-23.

Income

As has been true of earlier newcomers to this country, the great majority of the Puerto Rican migrants to the mainland have found employment at relatively low wages and some of them under very bad working conditions. However, the opinion has been expressed by officials of the Puerto Rico Department of Labor that Puerto Rican migrants have been able to make relatively better progress than some of the early European immigrant groups because of the better organization of labor, the existence and enforcement of labor laws, better social welfare administration, and so forth.

As for other types of data, the 1950 income figures are the most recent relatively complete figures on income that are available. They would be more interesting if they were available by industry and occupation but the comparison on an ethnic basis has some value.

The table below shows a relatively close correspondence between the incomes of Puerto Ricans and Negroes in New York City. In the two lowest income groups the correspondence was closest. There were somewhat larger proportions of Puerto Ricans than Negroes in the $1,000-$1,499 group and the $1,500-$1,999 group. But in the $2,000-$2,499 group and the $2,500 and over group, the proportion of Negroes was somewhat larger.

There was a great deal of difference, as the table shows, in the amount of income received in 1949 between island and mainland Puerto Ricans especially in the lowest income category. Most migrants to the mainland come from the urban centers of Puerto Rico where most of them have been employed before coming to the mainland. But the difference in wage standards between the island and the mainland shows up in these figures. Almost 44 percent of the Puerto Ricans living in urban areas had incomes of less than $500 in 1949 as compared with 9.6 percent of the Puerto Ricans living in New York City. There is great difference in the medians also. Whether there would be quite so much difference today is not known but in discussing the subject Rand says, "one often hears that Puerto Ricans can earn twice as much in New York as on their island, and that living costs in the two places differ little except for the item of fuel and warm clothes in the New York winter. This is probably an exaggeration, yet by and large more pay *can* be made in New York (in good times)—and more can be saved, too, or spent on TV sets or washing machines."[14]

NUMBER AND PERCENT OF PERSONS 14 YEARS OLD AND OVER OF WHITE, NEGRO AND PUERTO RICAN EXTRACTION IN NEW YORK CITY AND OF THE TOTAL PUERTO RICAN POPULATION OF THE ISLAND IN 1950 ACCORDING TO AMOUNT OF INCOME RECEIVED IN 1949

Income	New York City			The Island	
	White	Negro	Puerto Rican	Urban	Rural
Total—14 years & over	5,719,290	579,410	162,735	574,982	726,148
Persons without income	1,948,715	167,475	58,245	274,248	367,260
Persons with income—Total	3,338,095	358,375	94,475	289,670	348,803
	100.0	100.0	100.0	100.0	100.0
Less than $500	256,400	35,015	9,075	126,769	258,712
	7.7	9.8	9.6	43.8	74.2
$500 to $999	291,415	55,505	14,225	66,092	52,007
	8.7	15.5	15.1	22.8	14.9
$1,000 to $1,499	290,955	60,215	17,305	44,396	22,495
	8.7	16.8	18.3	15.3	6.4
$1,500 to $1,999	352,155	68,810	21,125	20,688	7,020
	10.5	19.2	22.4	7.1	2.0
$2,000 to $2,499	464,935	65,205	16,910	10,251	3,082
	13.9	18.2	17.9	3.5	1.0
$2,500 and over	1,682,235	73,625	15,835	21,474	5,487
	50.4	20.5	16.8	7.4	1.6
Income not reported	432,480	53,560	10,015	11,064	10,085
Median income	$2,517	$1,707	$1,657	$617	$275

Source: Census of Population 1950: *New York State Detailed Characteristics*, Table 87; *Puerto Ricans in Continental United States*, Table 5; and *Puerto Rico Detailed Characteristics*, Table 75.

Housing

For Puerto Ricans in New York, housing probably is the most immediate problem as it is in the many other areas of the mainland to which Puerto Ricans have migrated. Adequate housing, and particular low-cost housing, has been a problem all over the United States for a good many years but particularly in the urban centers where the Puerto Rican population has tended to concentrate since the war, for these were the centers where work was available. There had been prac-

---

14 Christopher Rand, *The Puerto Ricans* (PR), 52.

tically no residential building during the 1940's and relatively little during the 1930's. So, with the natural increase in population and the movement of the mainland as well as the Puerto Rican population to the cities, living accommodations became scarce and rents high. The Puerto Ricans as well as other minorities have had to take the brunt of this situation much as the non-English-speaking immigrants did in the years when European immigration was most extensive.

Whether the latest newcomers to the cities are worse or better off in the matter of housing than the earlier groups would be difficult to determine and not a fruitful expenditure of time and energy. Nor would it seem particularly pertinent if it were true that the housing conditions on the mainland are no worse or perhaps even better than the housing conditions on the island.

There probably is no disagreement that housing is a problem that has not yet been solved. It is also true that it is not an isolated problem but it is one of those problems that as Myrdal says is related to many aspects of our economic, political and social life. Neither is it a problem that affects only the Puerto Ricans. Since other minorities and, to an extent, all Americans are affected it is probable that a solution to the housing problem as it affects Puerto Ricans probably calls for the "integrated" approach advocated by Myrdal and Young and referred to earlier.

Health Characteristics

The idea frequently expressed in the past that Puerto Ricans are innately more subject to certain types of disease than mainland Americans has been found to be without foundation in fact. Certain types of disease were widespread in the island when the United States took over in 1898 and remained prevalent for several decades but as a result of the work done by the U. S. Public Health Service in the early days and particularly that of the island's Department of Health more recently these diseases have been practically eliminated as causes of death.

Professor Hanson points out that this has come about largely as a result of the recognition that the causes of tropical illnesses are not so much the natural climate as "the man-made social and economic climate" that prevails in so many tropical areas. Prof. Hanson says:[15]

> . . . it is futile to blame the natural climate for observed differences between the health of many tropical peoples and that of residents in the so-called temperate regions. . . . It is a good working principle which says, in effect, that public health is a function of an intangible called standards of living. Modern Puerto Rico is among the several societies (Australia's Queensland is another) which have shown that a tropical society which tackles its health problems by improving the man-made social climate which in its entirety is called the standard of living, instead of trying to change the natural climate, is likely to achieve notable results.

Before the improvement in public health, the predominant diseases of the island were diarrhea and enteritis, tuberculosis, and malaria. The changes that have taken place are indicated in the following statistical summary of deaths per 100,000 in 1957 as compared with 1940.

Cause of Death	Rate per 100,000	
	1940	1957
Diarrhea and enteritis	405.2	60.1
Tuberculosis	260.2	33.2
Malaria	96.8	0.0

Source: *Facts and Figures,* January 1959 edition, 4.

The same source shows that the infant mortality rate has declined almost steadily since 1941 when there were 116.2 deaths of children under one year of age per 1,000 live births as compared with 55.5 in 1956; and that life expectancy was 68 years in 1955, practically the same as the mainland, as compared with only 46 years in 1940.

This improvement in the health of the population of the island is reflected in the general health of Puerto Rican migrants to the mainland. The consensus of opinion seems to be that given the same economic and social opportunities on the mainland, the health problems of Puerto Rican migrants are not greatly different from those of the people of the main-

---

15 Earl Parker Hanson, *Transformation, The Story of Puerto Rico* (TSPR), 301.

land. A study by the New Jersey Division Against Discrimination revealed that reports of the high incidence of tuberculosis among Puerto Ricans in the state were often unfounded. The report states:[16]

> Information was given by one health officer that the Puerto Ricans were "taking over the County Tuberculosis Sanitorium." The writer visited the county hospital in question and talked to the Superintendent. He revealed that the hospital had received only 20 Puerto Rican cases in the last four years. The Superintendent stated that the Puerto Ricans are very cooperative in following directions and taking their treatments. The biggest difficulty he found was that so many of the European immigrants have T.B. These same thoughts about European immigrants were verified in a conversation with a director of the County T.B. office. . . . Additional information received from still another County T.B. office indicated that there was no higher incidence of T.B. among Puerto Ricans than any other group of people.

With regard to the use of public clinics by the Puerto Ricans, the same report states:[17]

> In Camden, Jersey City, Newark, Paterson, Perth Amboy, and Trenton, hospital officials reported that Puerto Ricans frequently used their prenatal and post-natal clinics. It was revealed that these clinics were more frequently used by them than any other clinics.
> Hospital officials revealed that Puerto Ricans generally came to the hospital on their own initiative instead of being referred by their personal physician. On some occasions when Puerto Ricans report for medical attention they need immediate hospitalization. In his own country, the Puerto Rican receives free medical care and attention. . . .

In a paper prepared for the conference of the New York Area chapter of the American Statistical Association in October 1953, Louis Weiner of the New York City Department of Health compared death rates for the Puerto Rico born population of New York City and other groups. About this he says:[18]

---

16 Isham B. Jones, *The Puerto Rican in New Jersey, His Present Status* (PRNJ), July 1955, New Jersey State Department of Education, Division against Discrimination, 26.

17 Jones, PRNJ, 27.

18 A. J. Jaffe (Editor), *Puerto Rican Population of New York City* (PRNY), 35 and 37.

During 1949-1951 the crude death rate from all causes for the entire population of the City of New York was 10.0 per 1,000 population. For whites it was slightly above 10.0 per 1,000, for non-whites 9.6, and for the Puerto Rican born population it was 4.2. The differences in the age distribution of the three groups account for much of the differences in the crude rate.

As will be recalled from previous discussion, there were very few persons in the Puerto Rican born population over the age of 45. Only 17% of the Puerto Rican born were in these older ages as compared with 34% of the total white population and 22% of the non-white population. The great bulk of the deaths occurred among the older ages; perhaps five-sixths of all the deaths in New York are to persons 45 years of age and over. Since the Puerto Rican population contained relatively fewer of these older persons, the numbers of deaths and crude death rates should be relatively smaller in this group.

Puerto Rican born males had higher death rates than white males up to 34. From 35 years and upwards, the rates in the Puerto Rican group were lower than in whites.

Among females, the death rates in the Puerto Rican group were higher than in the white group up to age 54. At the older ages the Puerto Rican rates were lower.

At practically all ages, for both sexes, the Puerto Rican rates were lower than those for non-whites.

Since the Puerto Rican population was of poorer economic status, their lower death rate at the higher ages may seem a little unusual. Without considering the possibilities of error inherent in the data and without analyzing the age-specific rates for other years, it is difficult to explain these lower rates. One possible explanation which comes to mind at this moment is that the migrants may constitute a physically select group. The sick and weak are perhaps more likely to remain in Puerto Rico and contribute to the death rate in the Island rather than to the death rate in New York City.

Chapter IV

SOME ASPECTS OF THE CULTURE OF PEOPLES OF SPANISH-SPEAKING BACKGROUND IN THE SOUTHWEST

SAUNDERS tells us that the Spanish-speaking people "constitute the largest culturally distinct population group within the larger population of the United States."[1] The key phrase here is "culturally distinct" and the definition and approach of this outstanding authority to the concepts involved is important.

As crucial definitions of culture the author cites Paul A. Walter, Jr.: "Culture is the learned ways of acting and thinking which are transmitted by group members to other group members and which provide for each individual ready-made and tested solutions for vital life problems. Every human culture is a historical growth and only as such can it be explained or understood. Since the very essence of culture is its transmission through generations, a culture may be thought of as the experience of the past entering as a determinant of thought and action in the present, and carrying, of course, important relation to the future of a group."[2] Redfield[3] is cited as identifying culture "with the extent to which the conventionalized behavior of members of the society is for all the same." The third definition is drawn from Margaret Mead and her associates and is re-quoted in full:[4]

> Culture . . . is an abstraction from the body of learned behaviour which a group of people, who share the same tradition, transmit entire to their children, and, in part, to adult immigrants who become members of the society. It covers not only

---

1 Saunders, CDMC, 12.
2 Paul A. Walter, *Race and Cultural Relations* (RCR), 17-18.
3 Robert Redfield, *The Folk Culture of Yucatan* (FCY), 132-133.
4 Margaret Mead, CPTC, 9-10.

the arts and sciences, religions and philosophies to which the word culture has historically applied, but also the system of technology, the political practices, the small intimate habits of daily life, such as the way of preparing or eating food, or of hushing a child to sleep, as well as the method of electing a prime minister or changing the constitution.

Within these definitions Saunders cites six attributes of culture as especially relevant to the point of view of his treatment of problems of medical care and cultural difference. Because they also closely relate and are vital to understanding of missionary opportunity and cultural difference, they are quoted below:[5]

1. Culture is a complex whole, the several parts of which are functionally interrelated.
2. Culture has historical continuity transcending the time span of any given generation. It is thus coercive for the individual, who, being born into it, has no choice but to accept it.
3. Culture exercises a strong determining influence in the way individuals come to perceive themselves and their relations to other people and to the nonhuman environment.
4. It provides ready-made guides to behavior, including ways of thinking and feeling as well as the more overt types of acting.
5. It changes, and it can be changed.
6. Since culture is very complex and the processes by which it is transmitted somewhat inefficient, no individual ever acquires the whole of a culture. It is thus possible to distinguish within cultural groups, subgroups made up of persons who share traits that are not common to other members of the larger group.

While all of these points are crucially important, even greater stress in this treatment is given to the first and fifth. Culture is a whole, a "pattern," a "web." It is intertwined and interdependent. Aspects such as family structure, religion, language, education, economic life, and so on and on are not in the last analysis isolatable. Nor are their "problems" solvable except as the relation of the part to the whole is recognized and taken into account. Culture, like the church, has many members but one body.

---

5 Saunders, CDMC, 248.

Culture changes and can be changed. The fatalistic "Social Darwinism" of William Graham Sumner's "mores" is widely discredited.[6] Under certain circumstances change can be startlingly rapid for whole groups as well as for individuals. In fact, an essential way of seeing culture is as a moving, sometimes kaleidoscopic *process* of constant change. As an "historical growth" it has a changing past, a changing present, and a changing future. One danger of descriptive analysis is that it is a sort of dissection which converts the subject into an immobile cadaver, "takes the life out of it." In a real sense Spanish-speaking culture in the Southwest has "life," growth, development. A major section of this survey will attempt to consider the culture as both a whole and as a whole in complex-compound process of change.

Distinct Culture

The phrase with which this section began was "culturally distinct." Culture as a concept has been dealt with but not "distinction." It is Saunders' contention that, by contrast with the much larger Negro population of the United States, "a considerable part of the distinctive culture of the Spanish-speaking people still survives."[7] While there are many shadings of opinion and emphasis among the authorities (and among Spanish Americans), this conclusion is upheld by a very wide consensus.

Broadly and historically this distinction stems from what Beals calls "a more or less self-conscious and coherent set of values and perceptions which, in the larger sense, sets off countries with a Latin Catholic tradition from countries with an Anglo-Saxon Protestant tradition."[8] Narrowing the focus slightly, it flows from the contrast between the ways of life in the geographic territory which is now Mexico, and from which over a span of four centuries the Spanish-speaking people have come, and the ways of life in the United States.

"No two other countries which are adjacent, and separated

---

6 See Myrdal, AAD, 1027-1064 for extended treatment of this and related issues of valuation and "objectivity" in social science.

7 Saunders, CDMC, 248.

8 Ralph Beals, *No Frontier to Learning* (NFL), 110.

[74]

by a boundary which is in large part artificial, differ so much in blood and tradition," says Robert Redfield. He continues, "In contributing to this difference, the contrast between Anglo-Saxon and Spanish heritage is an important factor, but even more striking is the contrast between a country in which the Indian element is insignificant and one in which it is very great, in some respects paramount. . . . It is probably safe to say, that, biologically speaking, Mexico is 300 times as Indian as the United States. The same contrast appears with respect to custom and tradition."[9]

But, says Redfield, custom and tradition are less Indian or Spanish than they are essentially primitive, non-literate, village-centered "folkways" as contrasted to the characteristics of modern urban life. He summarizes as follows:[10]

> Many, if not most, of the elements of culture of rural Mexicans are European in origin, not Indian; but Indian and Spanish elements alike and together contribute in these Mexican villages to form a round of life, a pattern for living, cut out by the cultures of non-literate peoples everywhere, and that is in these same respects different from the modes of life to be found in cities everywhere, especially in our modern western cities. To include under one term peasant and tribal natives, the Melanesian, the African, and the Mexican and Chinese villager, they and their mode of life may be denoted "folk"— for all these people have abundant folklore, folktales, and often folk songs. The essential contrast is, then, between folk and city, between folkways and city ways. Mexico's characteristics arise not so much because her rural life is specifically Indian, as from the fact that her people are still "folk."

The detailed content of "folk life" and its sharp differences from modern city life is our next major area of concern, but it should first be noted that the small, isolated, self-contained village is actually characteristic both of Mexico and of the states from which modern migration, legal and illegal, originates. The following evidence is offered by Frank Tannenbaum.[11]

> Mexico is an isolated country. Geographic obstacles have impeded communication and fostered a local, inward view and

---

9 Robert Redfield, *Folkways & City Ways* (FCW), 10.
10 Robert Redfield, FCW, 36.
11 Frank Tannenbaum, *Mexico, the Struggle for Peace & Bread* (MSPB), 3, 10.

an aloofness from the outside that has proved not merely physical, but political and spiritual as well. Mexico is unlike any other country in the world, and almost every Mexican community enjoys its own quality of uniqueness. The physical geography could not have been better designed to isolate Mexico from the world and Mexicans from one another.

Mexico is preponderantly a country of little villages. Instead of living stretched along the countryside in separate farm-steads, the people are grouped together in thousands of little hamlets, villages, and towns. In 1940 there were 105,185 communities in Mexico, of which 75,876, or 72 percent, were hamlets of one hundred people or less. Even more striking is the fact that 98,967 inhabited places in Mexico, or 94 percent of all, have under 500 people each.

Immigration to the United States stems, overwhelmingly, from these rural villages clustered on the central and northern plateaus of Mexico. The 1930 study of Manuel Gamio[12] found that more than half came from the states of Michoacan, Guanajuato and Jalisco. A 1950 study[13] of wetbacks (illegal entrants to the U. S.) confirmed Gamio's general findings. More than 70 percent of the group studied were from the three states already named, Nuevo Leon and San Luis Potosi. Only one of these states has a common boundary with the United States; all are dominantly rural and village-centered.

There is a close parallel between the typical village life in Mexico and that of the isolated village life of the Hispanos in what is now New Mexico. The fan of settlement now within the United States was an extension of village culture "north from Mexico" and itself centered and is epitomized by the more than three century history of the lonely villages in north-central New Mexico. This was the "heart of the borderlands" and according to McWilliams the "anchor" of Spanish-Indian-Mexican elements and "the rock upon which Spanish culture rests" in the whole area.[14] In a real sense the discussion of "folk-life" background applies to the Spanish-speaking settlers who preceded the "Anglos" in the Southwest as well as to later migration to this area from Mexico.

---

12 Gamio, *Mexican Immigration to the United States* (MIUS), 13-29.

13 Saunders and Leonard, WLRG, 28-32.

14 McWilliams, NFM, 80. His whole treatment of the history of the "fan" of settlement is relevant, especially Chapter IV.

The Starting Point

Understanding of the difficulties of the Spanish-speaking population in finding a place in "modern" life in the Southwest depends in considerable part on appreciation of the extreme difference of their historic and, in many cases, their personal origin. Many authorities have described and discussed the "folk"-modern industrial contrast as it applies to Mexico and the Southwestern United States. Obviously the generalizations do not apply equally to all immigrants, all Spanish-speaking "natives" of the U. S., all communities. For some persons this background may never have existed, for others it may be generations in the past, for still others it may be last week's life pattern. Yet since "every human culture is a historical growth" the generalized perception of background is essential to understanding.

The present discussion will be drawn entirely from other's research but will avoid detailed reference. The endless points of contrast between the village and modern industrial poles are here grouped under five major headings. Typically life in the Mexican folk-village was

- A. Familiar
- B. Slow
- C. Stable
- D. Simple
- E. Secure

The modern industrial extreme would be the antonyms—strange, fast, changing, complex, insecure or threatening. While these headings are not air-tight, exclusive categories, they may prove helpful. Using them, let us look at the folk-village pattern of life.

A. Life is familiar

As has already been seen, the typical village in Mexico (and in the borderland) is very small. It is also likely to be so isolated and travel so difficult that many will be born, live and die without ever leaving the environs of the village. Isolation means also that visitors fom outside are rare and new settlers rarer still. The combination of smallness and isolation

[77]

tend to create familiarity in the root sense of the word. Over a course of generations almost everyone will be related to everyone else. In the Mexican culture, the recognition of the extended family and the inclusion of god-parents in that extended circle, accelerate the process of making many villages kinship groups.

This, then, is a primary group with inter-personal relations which are face-to-face and intimate. Each resident is known in all his "social roles." "In all aspects of living—good times and bad, transition and crisis and every day routine, playing and working and worshiping—the same people were together. Uniformity of knowledge, belief and behavior was the rule, and had there been any social scientist present to observe or measure the range of any culture trait, he would have found little deviation and much clustering around the norm."[15] The "familiar" is the known and the common sharing of group experience makes for a common body of knowledge.

There is relatively little to learn and the boundaries of the single community and its needs are, in the main, the boundaries of needed learning. Its lore, its language, its beliefs and values, its rudimentary division of labor are familiar to all.

For the individual in folk-village life, the expectations of his fellows are simple and clearly understood—again "familiar." There tend to be universal tasks common to all of a particular age and sex and the transition to tasks at a higher age level is made easy by the intimacy of the whole group life and the shared initiation to new responsibility. Finally, as an element of "familiarity" for the individual, group expectation and individual experience tend to be consistent not only from day to day, but from year to year and even from generation to generation.

B. Life is slow

In the typical village there is rarely anyone in a hurry because there is seldom anything to hurry for. Life is geared to a subsistence rather than a commercial agriculture. What is not done today can usually wait until tomorrow. Scheduling is less a matter of the hours of the day or even of the days of

---

15 Saunders, SSTC, 3.

the calendar than of the times for planting, cultivation and harvest. An almost total dependence on weather, uncontrollable yet liable to drastic and sudden change, tends to generate a fatalistic acceptance of what may come and a recognition of the narrow limits and the relative unimportance of human effort.

Socially the community, whether communal or feudal, offers little or no prospect for change in social station. There is no social ladder to climb; no visible examples of what the sociologists call "vertical mobility." As we have seen, horizonal mobility, the opportunity or the practice of moving from place to place, is too difficult and costly to happen frequently or to many persons. To the degree that the village is self sufficient, money loses significance and there is little or none of it to be earned, nor is there a market for its use. "Pushing for financial success" holds no meaning. In sum, there is little or nothing to hurry to—or for.

The description would apply to villages before Cortez, to centuries of village life in New Mexico and to isolated villages in Mexico today. Slowness, then, in social change is so great that a man may live out his life without perceiving any change in the customary relationships and folk ways. The same lack of innovation would apply to tools and techniques. Here, too, change would be so slow as to be almost imperceptible.

Louis Adamic described Hispano culture in the border area in terms largely applicable to "folk-culture" anywhere:[16]

> Life had a slow, even rhythmic roll, geared to routine labor, to nature, in a sense to eternity punctuated by the seasons of the year with their church festivals. It was "backward," "primitive" in today's view, but gracious, an echo of Spain (via Mexico). Those living it did not aspire to anything different. The conquistador type of person had almost nothing to do with its unfolding through the centuries. A humble and meager civilization of the common people, created by themselves in their highland isolation, having something of grace and contentment, but leaving out the element of change, it could not last undisturbed indefinitely. . . . But much of it lasted for decades after the region became part of the United States. It is not entirely gone yet.

---

16 Adamic, NN, 47.

C. Life is stable

Dr. Whetten has said that "much of Mexico's agrarian history revolves around the struggle between the landholding village and the large, privately owned, semi-feudal, landed estate, commonly referred to as the 'hacienda.'"[17] This is an important fact, crucial in the understanding of rural Mexican, and border, history, but the present emphasis is on the degree to which both major types of agrarian organization share the common characteristics of familiarity, slow pace, stability, simplicity and security.

Certainly this is true in terms of stability. Both types have survived in Mexico over a span of more than 400 years and, in fact, both were well established in pre-conquest Spain and pre-conquest Mexico. "The Spanish conquerors," says Whetten,[18] "were familiar with both the landholding village and the individual landed estate. They had seen these two types of land tenure existing side by side in Spain, and measures were taken which were designed to foster and protect both types in the New World."

As for pre-conquest Mexico, Whetten "briefly summarizes" by emphasizing two points.[19]

> 1. The landholding village was the dominant unit in the agrarian economy at the time of the Conquest. Certain fundamental aspects of this village have survived throughout Mexico's history and are still in existence in isolated areas. From this village many of the specifications for the modern *ejido* have been derived, as we shall see later.
> 2. Although the landholding village was dominant, certain developments had taken place which were giving rise to the large, individual land estate, which was tilled by serfs bound to the soil. Thus the seeds for both the *hacienda* and the modern *ejido* had germinated among the aborigines before the Spaniards arrived.

Both systems aimed at self-sufficiency and at self-perpetuation and the long history of both is the overwhelming testimony to their success in this aim. The feudal land pattern began for the conquerors in the New World with the *encomi-*

---

17 Whetten, *Rural Mexico* (RM), 75.
18 Whetten, RM, 80.
19 Whetten, RM, 79.

enda system of rewards to Cortez and his lieutenants and soldiers. Cortez himself received a royal grant of 25,000 square miles of rich farmland, 23,000 outright serfs and "complete civil and criminal jurisdiction" over 115,000 inhabitants. By entailment, an effective device for stability, the estate was largely intact in 1800.[20]

The *encomienda* system shaded into the more modern *hacienda* system, which was still largely feudal and self-contained. In the system the owner, the *haciendado*, offered subsistence and protection from outsiders in exchange for almost unrestricted rights of exploitation.

Carey McWilliams describes a variation of the essentially feudal pattern in Spanish California which still retains the fixed social relations and resistance to change—the stability stressed here.[21]

> In many respects, the social structure of Spanish California resembled that of the Deep South: the *gente de razon* were the plantation-owners; the Indians were the slaves; and the Mexicans were the California equivalent of "poor white trash." These sharply differentiated groups reflected a division of labor which had become traditional. The Mexicans were the artisans, vaqueros, and major-domos of the ranchos; the craftsmen and *pobladores* of the pueblos. The *gente de razon* held all the government positions, made up the officer class of the military, and controlled the great ranchos. While showing a lively interest in cattle and' horses (the care of which they feared to entrust to the Indians), they were never interested in farming so that the agriculture of the province remained largely undeveloped and primitive. At the base of the pyramid were the Indians, upon whose unpaid labor the entire economy was based.

The second system, that of the largely communal, landholding village, fought tenaciously for its own perpetuation and stability over the centuries. At least in the more isolated areas it survived almost intact. Frank Tannenbaum cites a striking illustration of self-conscious resistance to "cultural invasion."[22]

> I remember that on a visit a president of Mexico offered to build the Yaquis a school. They said: "If you wish to build

---

20 Whetten, RM, 9.
21 McWilliams, NFM, 90.
22 Tannenbaum, MSPB, 13.

us a school down here near the railroad tracks, we reserve the right to burn it at any time, so please build it out of wood, for a school will attract the settlers of other 'nations' (meaning mestizos), and they will soon begin claiming our lands and we will be forced to drive them out. But if you will build a school for us up there in the mountains, it will be safe, for no strangers will disturb us there." They beat their little drum that called the nine villages from the mountains together for the occasion—for the drum can be heard far and wide and they use it to communicate among themselves.

Internally the pattern of life in the early *encomiendas* and the later *haciendas* was more Indian than Spanish or, more accurately, more primitive "folk culture" ways than those of individualistic, emergent modern man. Tannenbaum, using a slightly different frame of reference, nevertheless confirms the persistence of the old ways and their continuing dominance in the rural scene.[23]

> The fundamental difficulty lay in the incompatibility of an individualist culture and a communal culture. The Indian could never accept the ethical implications of the Spaniard's extreme individualism. The Indian was communal, impersonal, submissive, mystical, and self-denying. He wanted little for himself and aimed merely to live out his round of days in an unperturbed universe, following an ancient pattern and living by old rules. He was parochial in his vision and, after the Conquest, remained broken in spirit and oblivious of outside stimulus. He mainly wished to be left alone. The Spaniard, on the other hand, was arrogant, self-assertive, and ambitious. He had a sense of direction. He wanted to get on in the world, acquire land, silver, houses, servants, and honors. He could assume individual responsibility and was a man in his own right. The individual incentives of the European made no appeal to the Indian. The white man found that he could not bribe the Indian to labor for him by the payment of a wage, and so resorted to one or another form of compulsory service.
>
> This recalcitrance of the Indian to European incentives was symbolic of a subtler incompatibility, and the two races were doomed to suffer each other in contempt and fear, in assertive arrogance and passive but stubborn self-withdrawal. The mingling of the races and their culture took the form of attrition, a long process of wearing each other down that has now lasted for four and a half centuries and whose end is not yet in sight. In this process the Indians had the advantage of num-

---

23 Tannenbaum, MSPB, 32-33.

bers, pertinacity, and physical adaptability to the climate, the soil, and the altitude. They persisted in their ways, their languages, their manners, food, customs, superstitions, and way of being. The Spaniard could escape the Indian impact only by taking refuge in the large city. Only there could he live like a Spaniard. Even there, however, the overwhelming weight in numbers, customs, and ancient habit was on the side of the Indian. In time the Indian accepted some of the things the white man had to offer, but chiefly in the cities. It was mainly through the mestizo that Spanish culture found an increasing role in Mexico. But the process required centuries.

It is just these centuries of persistent rural stability and resistance to change which are an essential element of the "historical growth" of the culture background of the Spanish-speaking people of the Southwest.

In summary both land holding village and *hacienda* tended to be self-sufficient, closed social systems, strongly resistant to internal or external change, valuing the old, fearing and opposing innovation. Stability was both a conscious goal and, in large measure, an accomplished fact.

D. Life is simple

In a sense each of these summarizing descriptions is simply another way of looking at the same set of facts, yet each angle of vision should help to round out the picture. The familiar is easier to understand than the unfamiliar, the slow than the fast, the stable than the changing. Ease of understanding makes for simplicity as against complexity in life.

Perhaps the most essential contributor to simplicity is that in the small, homogeneous, isolated community the total knowledge, the "lore" of the group can be comprehended by all of its members. It can be passed on by parents to children, by peers to peers in the ordinary and constant contacts of living. It is complexity that gives rise to the need for writing and written records, for formalized institutional education, for division of labor, for specializations because no one person can learn all that needs to be known.

The individual's "life adjustment" is to one place, one familiar and limited group of persons, one quite uncomplicated social organization in which both the components and the structure tend to "stay put," one agricultural occupation at

[83]

elementary subsistence levels, and one religion that pervades and interprets the common life. Tools and tasks share the same rudimentary simplicity. While there are individual personal differences, persons of the same age and sex will share far more of likeness than they will represent a range of difference. The round of life is predictable both in its standard events and its usual uneventfulness. It will not differ greatly from generation to generation.

Description of isolated villages throughout Mexico and the borderland tend to reflect closely parallel patterns. Take, as instance, a summarizing description of the New Mexican Hispano life.[24]

> No new currents of life moved in this remote colony of Spain for nearly three hundred years. Education had little meaning in a society in which there was literally nothing to learn. Competition and change, initiative and innovation were, for similar reasons, mostly non-existent. The life of any today was the same as the most remote yesterday that anyone could remember; and tasks were performed as they had always been performed. Aside from the Indian influence, the society was, in Haniel Long's phrase, "a huge room in the Southwest hermetically sealed so far as any vital touch went with the life they had left behind in Mexico and Spain." Over the mystery of the slow growth of New Mexico, writes Ross Calvin, "there really is very little mystery after all": poverty and isolation explain whatever was mysterious.

E. Life is secure

A vital function of village life is security in the literal sense, self-preservation in the war with a grudging nature and mutual protection against hostile outsiders. The feudal pattern was dominant in pre-conquest Spain and developing in pre-conquest Mexico.[25] The feudal pattern is one of acceptance of one warrior overlord as protection against the marauding raids of countless others. Local power is a substitute for undeveloped national power. In the communal village self-protection might begin as the responsibility of all adult males, but frequently a special group of warriors would emerge. From

---

24 McWilliams, NFM, 71.
25 See Whetten, RM, Chapter IV.

this to special privilege and feudal organization is a short step.

In pre-conquest Mexico the external threat was the rivalry of Indian tribes; from the conquest the major marauder was the conquistador and his descendants. In areas of the border, particularly in Arizona and New Mexican territory, the marauders were the Apaches and the Navajos. "Rarely attacking a hacienda, the Navajo relentlessly pursued the poor New Mexican villagers and drove the peons 'under the shadow of the great houses.' Indeed," says McWilliams,[26] "most of the other factors . . . pale into insignificance when compared with the influence of Indians in the production of an inbred, isolated, homogeneous culture in New Mexico."

The turbulent history of Mexico since independence has contained long stretches when the direct function of armed protection was necessary for either the communal village or the *hacienda* against roving guerrillas and banditti.

Another dimension of security lies in the fact that the village or the *hacienda* tended to be a self-contained world of its own. "Each *hacienda* aspired to be self-sustaining. . . . It usually contained the essential supply of services characteristic of an independent community—a store, a church, a post office, a burying ground, a jail and occasionally a school. The houses and farm buildings, including granaries, sheds and corrals, were all constructed of local materials by local personnel, and workshops were maintained for the making of tools, implements and other essentials."[27]

This rounded full-working system means that all of the essential elements for group security and continuing livelihood are close, known and familiar. The group has control over the round of life. It is independent of all outside the group but, by the same token, completely dependent upon the group itself. The intimacy of this local interdependence is in itself a strong factor making for a strong sense of group and individual security.

It is little wonder that the tendency is to desire no interference with this enclosed world. The desire is to be "left alone,"

26 McWilliams, NFM, 67.
27 Whetten, RM, 99-100.

to preserve an "unperturbed universe, following an ancient pattern and living by old rules."

From the individual standpoint the crucial aspect of this self-contained world is a genuine sense of belonging. Life may be meager, uneventful, hand-to-mouth, with few material rewards, but it is life in a world in which the individual has a clear role, a place, a feeling of being at home. The importance of this kind of security can hardly be overstated. One authority states the general case in these terms:[28]

> Cultural security is contingent upon one's identification with or feeling of belonging to a cultural group. Belongingness is the assurance of being inwardly at home as well as outwardly accepted by a group. There is no fear of isolation or ostracism as long as one identifies with a group and conforms to its norms. The feeling of belonging gives a sense of linkage with the past and a hope of continuity through the transmission of one's culture to future generations. Not belonging, on the contrary, produces an individual shaky in his relationships, prone to anxiety and indecision—like a child reared without the security of parental love.

The general cooperative, communal pattern of life in the Mexican village, and for the vast majority of the inhabitants even in the *hacienda*, tends to increase this sense of sharing, of meaningful belonging. The whole community shares the same fate and in the awareness of the sharing, and the mutual effort to control their fate, there is a security largely lost in the individualistic "freedom" of modern industrial society.

Consequences

It is this historic-cultural background which explains the "cultural chasm" which separates many Spanish-speaking people in the Southwest from the Anglos in the same area. Lyle Saunders' excellent chapter on the "chasm"[29] analyzes in detail major differences in (1) language, (2) orientation to time, (3) attitude to change, (4) attitudes toward work and efficiency, (5) attitudes of acceptance and resignation, (6) attitudes toward personal dependency and (7) attitudes toward

---

[28] Sister Frances Jerome Woods, *Cultural Values of American Ethnic Groups* (CVA), 351-352.

[29] Saunders, CDMC, 104-140.

[86]

formal organization. Since the main concern of the present treatment is with the crucial role of the "Anglo" majority in creating a Spanish-speaking "problem," the reader is referred to this chapter and to Saunders' entire book for extended treatment of cultural difference itself.

This is not to say that difference in itself is unimportant nor that the almost universal fallacy of ethnocentrism is not a substantial factor in the generation of prejudice and discrimination. "Ethnocentrism," Saunders says,[30] "is simply the universal tendency of human beings to think that their ways of thinking, acting and believing are the only right, proper and natural ones and to regard the beliefs and practices of other people, particularly if they differ greatly, as strange, bizarre, or unenlightened."

The ethnocentric distortion can be very great and operate from two directions. This is illustrated by an abstracted illustration, again from Saunders.[31]

> Unless they are careful, medical personnel may find themselves making invidious judgments about people who impress them as being dirty, lazy, unambitious, promiscuous, ignorant, superstitious, and backward, while those being served by the program may have occasion to talk among themselves about the crazy foreigners who make a fetish of time, wear outlandish clothes, are compulsive about bathing, do women's work, and know nothing of the real causes of illness and disease. In such situations only limited cooperation . . . can be expected.

Transition at Home

The little communal and feudal worlds of rural old Mexico and the border area could not hope to survive intact. Over the span of the last hundred years and, in Mexico, especially in the last fifty years, there has been a telescoping of all the social and economic revolutions that trace the path from agrarian feudalism to the modern industrial society. The revolution of commerce and travel, of industrialization and urbanization, the fall of the old aristocracy and the rise to dominance of the urban middle-class, the population explosion and the rise of

---

30 Saunders, CDMC, 237.
31 Saunders, CDMC, 237-238.

commercial agriculture, even a semi-socialist revolution in land tenure all have been telescoped and jumbled in a brief span of years. The social disorganization and personal disorientation in these rapid and complex invasions and upheavals can scarcely be exaggerated.

Revolution in the literal military-political sense has been prominent in Mexican history. The *Encyclopedia Britannica* summarizes as follows:[32]

> Mexico has had a turbulent existence since independence. . . . Furthermore, the last 100 years have witnessed approximately that number of revolutions. Most of these, however, have been political or personal in character. In fact, since 1810 there have been only three general upheavals in Mexico, each of which has been socio-economic in character. . . . The first, begun in 1810, by Hidalgo, substituted the creoles for the gachupines and resulted in greater power and wealth for the church. . . . The second, begun in 1854, disendowed and disestablished the church, but worked to the advantage of the great landowners. The third, begun in 1910 and continuing down to the present time, was directed chiefly against the landed aristocracy and is strongly nationalistic. . . .

The Juarez revolution of 1854 was genuinely nationalistic and Juarez, himself an Indian and a champion of the people, not only disestablished the church and confiscated its lands but also abolished communal land holdings and "the indigenous peasants received individual title to lands that they had previously held in common; but since they were not accustomed to, or prepared for, individual proprietorship, they were soon dispossessed of them."[33]

This dispossession was accomplished largely during the long and reactionary rule of Porfirio Diaz from 1877 to 1910. So thorough was it that at the end of the era "a total of 96.9 of the rural heads of families owned no real property. . . . Furthermore, approximately 10,000,000 Indians (probably three-fifths of the population), in addition to losing their communal lands, had become serfs."[34] Here lay the seeds of social revolution and it began in November under Francisco Madero. While the

---

32 *Encyclopedia Britannica,* Vol. 15, 389.
33 Gamio, Manuel—in Whetten, RM, xvii.
34 *Encyclopedia Britannica,* Vol. 15, 393.

leader's aims were vague and limited, the wide popular response shaped the course of events:

> What time was to reveal, and that quickly, was an upsurge of the rural folk and a breaking down of the system of habit, law, and tradition that had for so long defined the social structure in Mexico. What was at hand was a social revolution. It had no intellectual leadership and no great name. No new philosopher, prophet, or poet was on hand to stir the folk. Their restlessness responded to something less formalized, but perhaps more real. They were hungry for land. They had been hungry for land for a long time and had striven for it in isolated instances, each village by itself.

Since the overwhelming majority of the migration north from Mexico has been of "peasants," *paisanos*, rural farm workers, it would be well to look at the Mexican transition explicitly as it has affected them. This is the central concern of Dr. Whetten's *Rural Mexico* and his analysis is summarized in the following statement:[35]

> Much of Mexico's agrarian history revolves around the struggle for supremacy between the landholding village and the large, privately owned, semifeudal, landed estate, commonly referred to as the "hacienda." For nearly four hundred years, with but minor reverses, the hacienda gradually gained the ascendancy and slowly but steadily devoured the village lands and even the villagers themselves. This process continued until 1910, at which time the landholding village had almost disappeared, its lands having been incorporated into the hacienda and its inhabitants essentially converted into serfs. Since that date, however, the tables have been reversed, and the pendulum has been swinging back toward the landholding village, slowly at first but rapidly since 1930—so rapidly that at the present time nearly half the crop land in Mexico is held by a modified form of the landholding village (ejido), while the hacienda has been fighting vigorously for survival.

The great surge of emigration to the United States parallels the most turbulent portion of Mexican history, from 1900 to 1930, or perhaps more accurately from 1909 to 1929. In this period of twenty or thirty years probably more than a million Mexicans, "nearly ten percent of the total population of Mexico"[36] entered the United States and nine-tenths settled in the border area.

---

35 Whetten, RM, 75.
36 McWilliams, NFM, 163.

The ten percent migration is striking evidence of the extent and violence of the breakup of the old culture, the uprooting of fixed village life. Many factors contributed. Testimony has been cited on the concentration of land in few hands and the extension of serfdom. This process of "depriving them of their lands that were already inadequate to provide the necessary food for their families"[37] was accompanied by wage control by the monopolistic landowners that kept "agricultural wages comparatively stable for more than fifty years at the same time that the cost of living was steadily rising. This could mean only increasing misery and degradation."[38] Out of this degradation came both revolution and emigration.

Two even more fundamental and persistent reasons for the emigration are cited by Gamio.[39] The first is geographic and climatic, the amounts of usable land are severely limited in quantity and quality. The second is the fact that the world wide population explosion has reached Mexico and in a setting of limited resources has forced out migration in search of bread and a job.

Finally, no small contemporary factor in the break-up of the old isolated village culture is the migration from these villages to the United States and then back to these same villages. In the less than two years from September 1, 1942 to May 3, 1944, over 137,000 persons migrated to the United States but over the same period nearly 54,000 returned to Mexico, 51,000 of these to the Central Plains area.

Contrast in the United States

All that has been said about the folk-culture historic roots of the Spanish-speaking people of the Southwest can be set against the opposite pole contrasts of the booming modern industrial culture of the contemporary southwestern United States.

The struggle between the two cultures is not a matter of today or of a few decades in the Southwest. It began with the Santa Fe Trail and the beginnings of the commercial invasion.

---

37 Whetten, RM, 99.
38 Whetten, RM, 106.
39 Gamio in Whetten, RM, xv-xix.

In Texas there was war and the scars of that war survive both for Anglos and the Spanish-speaking, but especially for the defeated minority, much as is true in the once Confederate South. The sheepherder-cattleman conflict through wide areas was in large part a running war between invading Anglos and Hispano sheepmen. All the devices of land grabbing from brute force to intricate "legalities" employed against the peon in Mexico were paralleled in the border area from Texas to California by the Anglo invaders.

McWilliams, in his *North From Mexico*, has stressed two facts as of basic importance. The first is that the Spanish-speaking are an indigenous people, "there first" in relation to the Anglos, with deep and fixed roots in their native soil. The second is that the long history of Anglo violence against the Spanish-speaking is not easily erased or forgotten. This fact has serious consequence:[40]

> Above all it is important to remember that Mexicans are a "conquered" people in the Southwest, a people whose culture has been under incessant attack for many years and whose character and achievements, as a people, have been consistently disparaged. Apart from physical violence, conquered and conqueror have continued to be competitors for land and jobs and power, parties to a constant economic conflict which has found expression in litigation, dispossessions, hotly contested elections, and the mutual disparagement which inevitably accompanies a situation of this kind. Throughout this struggle, the Anglo-Americans have possessed every advantage: in numbers and wealth, arms and machines. Having been subjected, first to a brutal physical attack, and then to a long process of economic attrition, it is not surprising that so many Mexicans should show evidences of the spiritual defeatism which so often arises when a cultural minority is annexed to an alien culture and way of life. More is involved, in situations of this kind, then the defeat of individual ambitions, for the victims also suffer from the defeat of their culture and of the society of which they are a part.

While the Spanish-speaking population has increased tremendously in the past fifty years the areas of original, and for most, continuing settlement have been the border areas and the Spanish-speaking colonies. The long history of the border,

---

40 McWilliams, NFM, 132.

once Spanish, then Mexican, now annexed to the United States, becomes, therefore, as much a part of the heritage of the Spanish-speaking as the life in Mexico itself.

The reader of the sections on folk-culture has doubtless set over against details of that description his own knowledge of the contrasting "American ways." The detail of this contrast is less the concern of the present paper than is the role of the majority in forcing a minority "place," but some summary is indicated. Lyle Saunders' lifetime of experience and study give him outstanding qualification for painting the contrast. This is how he stated it at the January 21-23, 1958 Council on Spanish-American Work in Phoenix, Arizona:[41]

> The situation today—if I may be permitted again to over-simplify—presents a considerable contrast. Some Spanish-speaking people still live in small communities, but more and more they are tending to concentrate in cities where the life is much different from that of the isolated village of a century ago. The rhythms of living are now regulated by the clock, not by the calendar. Economic self-sufficiency is not common. Most of the Spanish-speaking, like most of the Anglos, are dependent on a job and the wages or salary it brings. The handy man who could do anything is being replaced by the specialist who can do one thing well. Nearly everyone can read and write— a little at least—and everyone everywhere is constantly exposed to examples of the written word. The lore of the group expanded now to the point where no one can comprehend all of it, is transmitted to the children through written symbols and in formally organized situations. For every copy of a newspaper or book that was read a hundred years ago there are now a thousand that bring their readers into contact with a wide, complex, and bewildering world. The songs and sayings and superstitions of the folk are remembered only by los viejos; the common heritage of the new generation is Mickey Mouse and Superman and Sputnik and the endless procession of villains and heroes who pursue each other on the movie and TV screens and blast each other through the radio sets. The muscles of men and animals have been supplemented by the tremendous power of internal combustion and steam engines, electric motors, and atomic generators. Four legs have given way to eight cylinders and wings. Travel is rapid, easy, and fairly inexpensive, and among the Spanish-speaking as among everyone else in the United States there is a great coming and go-

---

41 Saunders, SSPC, 3.

ing. Social movement, too, is comparatively easy. No person need stay in the social class into which he was born. The acquisition of wealth or education or a new occupational or professional skill or a new set of social graces is enough to move one up the social ladder, and the ladder itself has more rungs and a greater distance between top and bottom than was true a hundred years ago. Social change is rapid—almost too rapid to keep pace with. New materials, new fuels, new machines, new amusements, new medicines, new frontiers—new styles in clothes, reading materials, architecture, furniture, religion, parent-child relations appear almost faster than any of us can adapt to them. In the larger cities, and to a considerable extent elsewhere as well, relations between people are increasingly impersonal, and one has opportunity to know other people, not as whole personalities, not in their full-blown wholeness, but only in single roles or in formal situations—as teacher or pupil, merchant or customer, doctor or patient, employer or employee, official or citizen, vendor or buyer of gasoline, newspapers, food, shelter, clothing, entertainment. Diversity of knowledge, belief, and behavior is the rule, so that the social scientist who attempts today to measure the range of any cultural characteristic will find so many variations, so wide a range, that even the concept of a norm is almost meaningless.

The principal points of difference between the lives of the Spanish-speaking people of a century ago and those of today can be summed up perhaps in the statement that the former lived mainly in communities in which the family was the major social unit, relations were personal, techniques were simple and no type of activity (except perhaps religion) was more important than any other, whereas the latter lives in a society in which the individual is the center of emphasis, relations are largely impersonal, techniques are complex, and economic activity seems to be more important than any other.

As Dr. Saunders went on to say, many of these changes are affecting all kinds of people all over the United States and, to an extent, all over the world. But there are great differences in the time span in which change occurs and in the degree of conflict or reconcilability with traditional values and customs. Clearly the conflict is extreme with the traditional Spanish culture of the Southwest. The bearer of that traditional culture will resist at every point he can, try to evade, to retreat into isolation, escape in any and every way he can.

The Majority Responsibility

The overwhelming numbers in the Anglo majority on the other hand, have few or none of these reservations. They are the bearers of this culture, proud of it, convinced of its eternal rightness, scornful of all deviance. They make the rules and laws, structure the institutions and the economic life. It is they that *compel* the minorities to "do things our way." The compulsion contributes directly to resistance and it is a problem of the majority's not the minority's creation.

There are innumerable facets of majority responsibility which tend to be lost from view when the focus is exclusively on the minority group. The majority dominance and controls are lost sight of in detailed description of the quaint ways of the minority. In point of fact, few of these ways in the shadow of the majority are entirely voluntary. Even those that are chosen are selected in the limited range allowed by the majority and in reaction to its pressures. It is important, then, to point up at least some of the crucial responsibilities of the majority for the situation of the Spanish-speaking people of the Southwest.

1. The responsibility for conquest

Annexation to the United States was not a choice of the Spanish-speaking settlers in the borderland. It was the direct and indirect consequence of the "Texas revolution" of 1836 and the Mexican-American War of 1846-48. All Mexicans, as well as many U. S. historians, regarded this sequence of events as a deliberate scheme of conquest. The wars and the cross border raiding for years afterward were marked by an unusual degree of barbarity and of flagrant atrocities, even though these are standard accompaniments of war itself. The fact that both sides shared responsibility only served to fan the flames of mutual hatred.

2. Responsibility for contempt of the conquered

The wars themselves were followed by years of border banditry and guerilla fighting in which the Mexicans constantly lost and retreated. To the victors this seemed a mandate of destiny. An army Major writing in 1859 "said that the 'white race' was 'exterminating or crushing out the inferior race' and an American soldier wrote home that 'the Mexican, like the poor Indian, is doomed to retire before the more enterprising Anglo-Americans.' "[42]

The arrogance of the conquerors has a long persistance. To quote again from McWilliams, whose treatment and emphasis on this phase of relevant history is outstanding:[43]

> When asked how many notches he had on his gun, King Fisher, the famous Texas gunman, once replied: "Thirty-seven —not counting Mexicans." This casual phrase, with its drawling understatement, epitomizes a large chapter in Anglo-Hispano relations in the Southwest. People fail to count the nonessential, the things and persons that exist only on sufferance; whose life tenure is easily revocable. The notion that Mexicans are interlopers who are never to be counted in any reckoning dies but slowly in the Southwest. To this day Mexicans do not figure in the social calculations of those who rule the border states. As I write these lines, the Mexican consul-general in Los Angeles has just entered a vigorous protest against the insulting behavior of custom inspectors at the municipal airport.

3. Responsibility for separation from the land

The conquest mentality flowed over into the long, often violent process of invading and preempting the land rights of the Spanish-speaking people along the border. Carey McWilliams deals with this unsavory history in considerable detail in his *North from Mexico,* and cites many instances of dispossession ranging from gun-point theft to massive corruption and "legalized" expropriation. Saunders' summary is, typically, more polite but covers essentially the same process.[44]

> . . . The acquisition of the Southwest by the United States brought powerful forces to bear upon the isolated and stabilized villages of the Spanish-Americans. Economic competition of a nature and scope far beyond the experience of the villagers was introduced. New concepts, new values, and a new language appeared. Money taxes were instituted; business relationships changed in nature and became more pervasive. Sharp practices and legal technicalities, based on an entirely new

---

42 McWilliams, NFM, 105.
43 McWilliams, NFM, 98.
44 Saunders, CDMC, 52-53.

system of law that was perplexing to the villagers, began to take their toll of the economic resources. One after another of the land grants was lost and village resources consequently were reduced. Grazing lands passed into the hands of the Anglos and were fenced. Forest lands were placed on a restricted use basis. The free public range disappeared. Unfortunately, these changes came at a time when the Spanish-American population was expanding and more rather than fewer resources were needed. Faced with a declining resource base and a growing need for money, the villagers were forced into wage work to supplement the income from their land. In increasing numbers the men left their villages to become sheep-herders in Utah and Wyoming, beet workers and miners in Colorado, railroad laborers wherever they could be used.

As we have seen, this continuing up-rooting was paralleled in Mexico by continual encroachment of the hacienda system on the village lands under Diaz and in the subsequent years of chaos. The forced evacuation led directly to the migration to the United States. On both sides of the border the choice and the responsibility were not the villagers'. He clung to his roots in the land until they were pulled out by others.

More recently there have been pulls as well as pushes. The last world war had a double influence. The draft compelled thousands to leave both isolated villages and urban *colonias*. At the same time labor shortages opened up opportunities for better pay and a wider range of work than had ever before obtained. Whatever the long-range consequences, a very large portion of the Spanish-speaking population were drawn closer to the complex-compound vortex of modern industrial life. The social forces both pushing and pulling, were of the majority's not the minority's making.

4. Responsibility for importation

It is perhaps most inappropriate and ironic to blame the Spanish-speaking people of the Southwest for their presence within our borders. The original settlers were annexed by conquest or purchase and had little or no choice in the matter. The "Anglo" responsibility for the subsequent immigration goes far beyond the simple fact of available employment at wage rates which, however outrageously low, are higher than those for like work in Mexico.

The commercial vegetable and fruit enterprise from the Rio Grande border through Arizona to the Imperial and San Joaquin Valleys of California has been built and structured on the assumption of the availability of a plentiful supply of cheap, seasonal labor, employable on demand, dismissable the instant demand slackens. Except for the low ebb of the depression '30's only the Mexican of recent import has met these specifications. Even somewhat "acculturated" Americans of Mexican background rebelled at these terms so the grower quest has been for an ever-new supply of "unspoiled" Mexicans. Bluntly, the flow across the border was stimulated, encouraged, organized, recruited by "Anglo" grower interests. The use of contract *braceros* instead of Mexican Americans, of "wetback" illegal immigrants instead of *braceros* is a step-by-step pursuit of the cheapest and most docile possible labor.

Broadly, this is a key and major thread in the whole history of American immigration. The demand for cheap labor and the deliberate recruitment of such labor abroad when it cannot be found at home, bears a major responsibility for one "minority" immigration wave after another. It is not at all accidental that the arrival of Mexicans (and, later, Puerto Ricans) in great numbers followed the closing of the gates to Europeans and Asian immigration. Nor is it accidental that the same stereotype group description ("lazy, ignorant, wouldn't know how to use money," etc., etc.) has been applied to each succeeding wave as a transparent device for justification of exploitation.

Majority special interests "made it their business" to achieve and continue a plentiful supply of Mexican labor. The responsibility rests in "our" group, not in "theirs." As Simmons has said in his excellent analysis of a particular Texas border agricultural town, "the Anglo motivation to subordinate the Mexican worker stems—from the desire to maintain a fluid and plentiful supply of cheap labor that is always available when needed."[45] For the Anglo economy this is the "function," the proper "place," of the Mexican.

---

[45] Ozzie G. Simmons, *Anglo-Americans and Mexican Americans in South Texas* (AAMA), 267.

5. Responsibility for assignment to hard and dirty work

In the Anglo stereotype the Mexican is "lazy." In the flatly contradictory illogic that goes with stereotypical thinking it is also taken for granted that he is naturally and ideally fitted for the hardest physical labor. From the Conquest on, the hard and menial tasks have been assigned to the conquered and to later migrants north from Mexico. In the later years theirs have been the "lands" undergirding the basic development of whole sections of the south-western economy. In McWilliams' summary "the story of the invasion of the border lands can be told in terms of railroads, cotton, sugar beets and truck or produce farming."[46]

"Since 1880 Mexicans have made up seventy percent of the section crews and ninety percent of the extra gangs on the principal western lines which regularly employ between 35,000 and 50,000 workmen in these categories."[47] McWilliams goes on to point out that the pattern has been one of recruitment by labor agents and commissary companies, a wage over many years of a dollar a day, and life on box cars shunted from place to place where work is needed.

Mexican labor from both sides of the Rio Grande was following the cotton harvest on foot in East Texas, as early as 1890. As "king cotton" invaded middle and west Texas, Arizona and the California valleys the "efficient," i.e., cheap, available and disposable, Mexican labor was brought with it. "By 1940 nearly four hundred thousand workers, two-thirds of whom were Mexican, were following 'the big swing' through the cotton growing regions of Texas."[48]

The development of large scale irrigation in the present century "has had more to do with the economic growth of the Southwest than any single factor."[49] The factors have been irrigation, refrigeration and Mexican labor competent to do the work, endure the climate of these desert and semi-desert areas and, as always, work cheaply, when, as, and if needed. Discussing the development McWilliams concludes that "it was not

---

46 McWilliams, NFM, 164.
47 McWilliams, NFM, 168.
48 McWilliams, NFM, 172.
49 McWilliams, NFM, 175.

easy to find in these years a large supply of labor that would brave the desert heat and perform the monotonous, stoop-labor, hand labor tasks which the agriculture of the Southwest demanded. Under the circumstances, the use of Mexican labor was largely non-competitive and nearly indispensable."[50]

A parallel use of Mexican labor for the hard, poorly paid and temporary work, could be traced in mining, sugar beet cultivation and several lesser fields. What is essential is the recognition that the exploiters not the exploited bear the responsibility for exploitation.

6. Responsibility for migrancy

This point follows the last. Each of the major industries cited above as using large numbers of Mexican workers is a highly seasonal one necessitating constant mobility to "follow the work." In both agriculture and railroading this is not a matter of a calendar schedule but of the unpredictabilities of the weather. The box car mobility of railroad section crews and extra gangs already mentioned, is coupled with a seasonal pattern in the work itself. While the railroads were the principal large scale importers of Mexican labor, they "constantly fed workers to other industries, since so much railroad labor is seasonal in character. Forever losing labor, the railroads kept recruiting additional workers in Mexico."[51]

The consequences of migrancy for family life, for education, for relations with the "American way" are very great. Migrancy, also, stands at the opposite pole from the rooted, stable life that is the historic background of the Spanish-speaking people of the Southwest. Once more, the responsibility for the fact and the consequences rests with "our" group not "theirs."

7. Responsibility for low status

As this list is extended, it becomes increasingly cumulative. All of the points above contribute to the proposition that the people of Mexican origin, whatever their place of birth, are assigned by the Anglo majority a place at the bottom of the

---

50 McWilliams, NFM, 178.
51 McWilliams, NFM, 168.

economic ladder. Because our social standards are in Veblen's term, so essentially "pecuniary," low economic status and low social status go hand-in-hand. We have seen in an earlier section that Bogardus' measures of social distance found Anglo ratings of Mexicans extremely low.

There are "Mexican jobs" throughout the Southwest just as there are "Negro jobs" throughout the South. These arbitrary racial-ethnic majority ascriptions of "place" tend to be contagious in majority circles and to fan out over the whole country. This kind of ascription is not simply an abstract theory, its concrete consequence is a majority "standard operating procedure" of enforcing low status by offering *only* low status employment.

The rigidity of this pattern is frequently almost total. Simmons' study of McAllen in the lower Rio Grande valley, concludes flatly that "Anglo Americans are always placed in positions which require even slight skill and responsibility."[52] He goes on to point out that this applies to "all the checkers and counters of incoming harvest loads, all supervisors, all grocery store cashiers, and so on." The use of the words "always" and "all" underline the proposition that this is majority policy for which the majority must recognize full responsibility. Simmons cites three essential factors that keep the Mexican in low status, "low remuneration, irregular employment and lack of vertical mobility."[53]

8. The responsibility for exclusion

"Lack of vertical mobility" imposed and enforced by the employer representatives of the majority is itself a major component of the Anglo majority's exclusion of the Spanish-speaking from equal opportunity. There is, of course, a great deal of what the sociologists and the social psychologists call the "self fulfilling prophecy" in a pattern of low wages, partial employment and rigid "job ceilings." These conditions imposed and enforced by employers are then used as "proof" that the victims are pretty worthless, undependable and incapable of rising in the world.

From this to geographic, housing, and the whole gamut of

---

52 Simmons, AAMA, 205.
53 Simmons, AAMA, 242.

social exclusions is an almost automatic progression. Both the poverty and the exclusion enforced by the majority have contributed to the development of isolated shacktowns, pockets of settlement, colonies "across the tracks" or "down the road." By majority preference the *colonia* or *barrio* tends to be off the beaten track; less visible and therefore less on the majority conscience. It is apt to receive a bare minimum of community services or be conveniently located outside the boundary with no services at all.

The California situation is described and analyzed by McWilliams in the following extract.[54]

> The physical isolation of the colonias has naturally bred a social and psychological isolation. As more and more barriers were erected, the walls began to grow higher, to thicken, and finally to coalesce on all sides. The building of the walls, as Mr. Ross puts it, "went on concomitantly from without and from within the colonia, layer by layer, tier by tier." While the walls may have the appearance of being natural growths, they are really man-made. For the relationship that finally emerged between parent and satellite community is the civic counterpart of the relationship between the California Fruit Growers Exchange and its Mexican employees.
>
> Living in ramshackle homes in cluttered-up, run-down shacktowns, set apart from their neighbors, denied even the minimum civic services, the residents of the colonia have come to resent the fenced-in character of their existence. They are perfectly well aware of the fact that they are not wanted, for their segregation is enforced by law as well as by custom and opinion. That the colonias lack swimming pools might be explained in terms of the ignorance or indifference of the Anglo-Americans were it not for the revealing circumstance that Mexicans are also denied access to municipal plunges in the parent community. Hence the ostracism of the Mexicans cannot be accounted for in the facile terms in which it is ordinarily rationalized.

Another analysis of factors and consequences of exclusion may be drawn from the following.[55]

> A number of factors have converged to retard acculturation of Mexicans in the United States. The pattern of mass em-

---

54 McWilliams, NFM, 219.

55 Leonard Broom and Eshref Shevky, "Mexicans in the United States: a Problem in Differentiation" (MUS), *Sociology and Social Research,* Jan.-Feb., 1952, 154.

ployment in which Mexicans worked in homogeneous gangs tended to isolate them from contacts with other ethnic groups. . . . Their position as casual laborers, linked with instability of employment and frequent migration, resulted in residential and institutional isolation. Both in rural and urban areas the ethnic enclaves were marginal neighborhoods detached from the life and economy of the large community, although dependent upon it for jobs and services. . . . Under these circumstances the language barrier which initially was an obstacle to relations between the group and American society became a persistent symbol and instrument of isolation. . . .

Exclusions may be exceedingly crude as in Burma's listing of common (but for Mexicans not universal) discriminations, "refusing service in barber shops, soda fountains, cafes, drive-ins, beauty parlors, hotel, bars, and recreation centers; segregation in housing, movies, schools, churches, and cemeteries, as well as in public buildings and public toilets; reluctant service in hospitals, colleges, social welfare offices, and courts; and even refusing to permit Mexican-American hostesses in U.S.O.'s"[56] Exclusion needs no written policy or regulation to be inexorably effective. Although "there are 1,300,000 citizens of Mexican descent in Texas—more than 20% of the total white population—and they are a clear majority in many counties; yet Dr. Sanchez could report in 1950 that 'you will not find a single person with a Spanish name employed in the capitol building in Austin.' "[57]

Or exclusion may be far more intangible and subtle yet none-the-less devastating in its effect. Schermerhorn generalizes on the "half-world" of an old culture lost and a new one to which full entry is forbidden:[58]

> Most of the Mexican Americans in the U.S. have reached a cultural plane so different from their way of living in their country of origin that they would find readjustment in Mexico difficult if not impossible. On the other hand, they are kept from cultural participation in American life by invisible barriers that are none the less real in spite of their mysterious submergence in the folkways. Latin Americans have had their web of culture torn in gaping holes and are forced to mend

56 Burma, SSG, 107.

57 Julian Samora and William N. Dean, "Language Usage as a Possible Index to Acculturation" (LU), *Sociology and Social Research*, May-June, 1956, 307-311.

58 R. A. Schermerhorn, *These Our People* (TOP), 193.

them with any materials they can find. For those who are unable to accept new ways or are shut off by the curtain of indifference, there is only a half-world to live in, a Zwischenwelt between the old and the new. The price of failure to assimilate is underprivilege, the price of underprivilege is the ability to assimilate.

For the individual this exclusion can be deeply disturbing. The "Jaun Perez" of Ruth Tuck's study of San Bernadino felt he had gained much by coming to this country but that he had also lost much. "I have exchanged the spiritual for the material . . . I am like the man who went to the *cambiador* but who could not count. I do not precisely know what I got in return. I live better, I have more things, but I do not feel at home in the world."[59]

Another authority comments on this observation as epitomizing a basic truth about Spanish-speaking people within our borders:[60]

> This "not feeling at home in the world" has plagued all immigrants everywhere for a time. It has continued to plague the descendants of Mexican immigrants because even to the fifth and sixth generations these Americans whose parents crossed the Rio Grande River rather than the Atlantic are known as "Mexicans," "foreigners." Economically they have been cut off from all but the barest benefits of our culture. Lacking knowledge of our American life and customs, afraid to relax the only safeguards they know, the Mexican family has held tight those old traditions that have the most significance.

An important part of the pattern of exclusion is the general majority refusal to differentiate between "Mexicans" as indicated in the last statement. McWilliams observes that "While some of the native-born have 'passed' completely into the Anglo-American world, the majority have not been able to do so nor have they always wished to do so. Constant discrimination, which became more pronounced with the arrival of the immigrants, has complicated their existence and stiffened their resistance to absorption. *The Anglo Americans, in fact, have made it impossible for them to dissociate themselves, as a*

---

59 Tuck, NWF, 106.
60 Beatrice Griffith, *American Me* (AM), 93.

group, from the immigrants."[61] The emphasis is ours, and, once again, the responsibility is "ours."

9. Responsibility for group identification

The last two quotations lead into the present point and place the greater part of the responsibility for minority group identification on the dominant majority.

Certainly, for both majority and minority, group identification is an existing "fact of life." Saunders has described the contemporary relation in these terms:[62]

> Subjectively defined, the Spanish-speaking people are those who think of themselves as "we" in response to the labels "Spanish-speaking," "Mexican," "mexicana," "Latin-American," "Spanish-American," and similar terms and are thought of by Anglos in terms of "they" in response to these identifying symbols. The criteria used on both sides in making these subjective identifications are usually multiple rather than single and include such characteristics as physical appearance, name, language, dress, place of residence, and general deportment, most of which convey cultural or subcultural meanings to everybody.

Several authorities have pointed out the large measure of majority responsibility for the appearance of sub-groupings within the Spanish-speaking minority. Acculturation tends to be age-stratified and the borrowings from majority offerings are likely to be those closest at hand. As instance observe juvenile delinquency and juvenile gangs. The California *pachucos* are a case in point. "The roots of *Pachiquismo*," in common with youth gangsterism in the majority culture, "grow in rich but shallow soil. They are nourished by an intense vitality, individualism, frustration and rebellion."[63] But the dimension of minority status multiplies and defines the frustrations:[64]

> Among the California *pochos,* discrimination and segregation, coupled with the large proportion of individuals of Mexican descent within the area, is responsible for the tendency to

61 McWilliams, NFM, 210.
62 Saunders, CDMC, 42-43.
63 Beatrice Griffith, AM, 45.
64 Donovan Senter, "Acculturation Among New Mexican Villagers in Comparison to Adjustment Patterns of Other Spanish-Speaking Americans (ANM), *Rural Sociology,* Vol. X, 1945. Abstracted in *Acculturation, Critical Abstracts, North America,* Bernard J. Siegel, Editor.

place a high value upon their Mexican and racial characteristics. The gang movement is based on psychological problems
and is an attempt to achieve distinction by refusing to copy
the ways of either the Mexican or the English-speaking
groups. . . .

But delinquents and non-delinquents, old and young, newcomers and original settlers are lumped, pushed together,
identified as one stereotyped group by the majority. The present writers tend strongly to share the view of Arnold and
Caroline Rose that it is our insistence on our "we-ness" and
their "they-ness" which is the major influence in creating,
strengthening and perpetuating the group consciousness of the
Spanish-speaking minority. The Roses' position deserves full
statement:[65]

> In terms of biological race or social characteristics most of
> the minority groups of the United States are far from being
> homogeneous groups. There is nothing in their biological make-
> up or their intrinsic social structure which holds the mem-
> bers together or leads them to feel a sense of kinship for one
> another. What makes minorities social groups is pressure from
> the outside and the consequences of that pressure. These create
> "group identification," which is defined as all the ways in
> which members of a group feel a sense a unity with each
> other, and the ways by which they manifest that unity. We use
> the term "group identification" in a positive sense. It involves
> not only a recognition that one is a member of a racial or re-
> ligious group because of one's ancestry, nor only a recognition
> that the majority group defines one as belonging to the racial or
> religious group. It also involves a positive desire to identify one-
> self as a member of the group, and a feeling of pleasure when
> one does so identify himself. Thus an almost equivalent term for
> group identification is "morale," except that it should be under-
> stood that individual members of minority groups can increase
> their personal morale without necessarily increasing their iden-
> tification with their group.
> Some members of the minority groups object to the statement
> that group identification is a consequence of prejudice and dis-
> crimination from the majority. Obviously there are other fac-
> tors, since groups that are equally discriminated against have
> different degrees of group identification. But the proposition is
> nevertheless advance that in the United States minority groups
> develop group identification as an adjustment to, and a way of

---

65 Rose & Rose, AD, 178-79.

opposing, majority prejudice. At first a common tradition may keep the members of an ethnic group united. But without majority prejudice minority groups would gradually merge with the majority in all ways and disappear as separate entities. . . . One of the necessary early stages in the amalgamation of groups is the disappearance of group identification: The loyalty to one's group and the desire to see it remain independent and strong must decline. Some individuals may resist the decline of group identification and participate in movements to "save our unique culture," but unless the group succeeds in separating itself, the absence of barriers to communication and contact will gradually eliminate all differences, biological and cultural, between the groups. Group morale then declines, but the individual members of the group then form new groups—on bases other than those of racial or nationality background—and new group identifications are formed.

10. Responsibility for the Vicious Circle

Prejudice, stereotyping, discrimination and segregation are interlocked and interacting parts of a total pattern and process of majority subordination of a minority. They tend to reenforce, perpetuate and "justify" each other. There is no escape from the circle, no way to get off the merry-go-round. As Simmons, whose entire work is an exceptionally able treatment of dominant and subordinate status in the Anglo-Mexican relation, has observed:[66]

> Looked at from one point of view, the sources of intergroup conflict provide the "need" for subordination of one group by another, the stereotype serves to channel the attempts to satisfy the "need" and discrimination provides the channel through which the "need" can be satisfied.

The special relation of the concept of the vicious circle as advanced by Myrdal, MacIver, Simmons and others to the problems of missionary opportunity among Spanish Americans will receive attention in the final chapter of this report. Here the stress is on majority responsibility for its existence. We, not the Mexicans or Puerto Ricans developed these prejudices, created these stereotypes. It is we who discriminate, we who enforce segregation.

Before turning from this overview of cultural relations to

---

66 Simmons, AAMA, 44.

some particular areas of cultural discrimination of crucial importance, two word pictures are offered. They are cited to illustrate both the complexity and the depth of the cultural chasm that needs to be bridged.

The first is drawn from Schermerhorn's *These Are Our People*, the title is ours:[67]

The Loiterer

A row of parked cars stood by the elementary school in a northern city as the parents came to take their children home. For several days the occupants of the automobiles had noticed a short swarthy man acting queerly as school let out. He seemed to be hiding first behind one car and then another, peering toward the school. If challenged, he would seem confused, and then run behind another car, where he kept his diligent watch on the children with no apparent purpose. Alarmed by his peculiar behavior, the parents finally notified the policeman at the next crossing. Soon an officer arrived to question the stranger; the man's broken English was so unintelligible that he was taken to court, where charges of loitering were made against him. Not until he had lodged in the city jail for two days was his story at all clear; then his wife appeared with a social worker to explain that he meant no harm to anyone. He was only a Mexican industrial worker on a night shift at one of the city's largest factories. Worried by his daughter's sudden adoption of American ways, he had come to the school to spy on her to discover whether she walked home with boys. If she did, he was going to refuse permission to attend school any longer. His objection was based on his own cultural heritage from Mexico, where segregation of the sexes was the rule and coeducation would have been a shocking affront to conventional practices. Only with difficulty had he been persuaded to let his daughter go to an American school at all, and apparently he felt that his traditional male discipline in the home would suffer unless he made certain that she was not taking on "loose" American ways on the way home from school. In old Mexico his word was law; so after his arrival in the American city he became increasingly anxious as his methods of control were challenged. By the time he was noticed, he was too disturbed to care about appearances in his attempt to re-establish restraint over his daughter.

Of course the court records in this case would simply designate a "Mexican arrested for loitering." Multiply this by many more cases in which culture conflict is the basic difficulty and

---

67 Schermerhorn, TOP, 173-4.

it becomes apparent why the Mexican arrest rate is high as compared with the other immigrant and ethnic groups. Although this instance represents only one rather simplified type of cultural conflict, there are many of a more serious sort noted below, all complicated by the general lack of cultural participation in American life, a defect which is perhaps as serious for the Mexican Americans as for any other minority group.

The second is an Arizona incident described and titled by Carey McWilliams:[68]

The Forty Blonde Babies

It was in Clifton, also, that the famous affair of the forty blonde babies occurred. The same year that La Nine de Cabora had built a hospital for the Mexicans of Clifton, a new priest, whose name was Father Mandin, came to the local Catholic church. One day the new priest received a routine letter from a New York foundling home, asking if there were any good Catholics in Clifton who might want to adopt children. New to Clifton and unfamiliar with his Mexican parishioners, Father Mandin naively read the letter at the next Sunday service. When asked if any of them desired to adopt children, almost the entire congregation, with audible enthusiasm, lifted their hands. Greatly pleased by this generous response, Father Mandin immediately wrote the hospital to send the children along but specified that only those of fair complexion should be sent since the Mexicans had insisted that they wanted "blonde babies."

On October first, forty children from eighteen months to five years of age arrived in Clifton accompanied by Sister Anna Michella. Each child carried a tag which gave its name and birthday and the name of the adopting family. The entire Mexican population of Clifton went with Father Mandin to the station to greet Sister Anna Michella and the forty blonde children. Quite unprepared to cope with the situation, Sister Anna Michella vainly protested that the foster homes would first have to be inspected before she would release the children from her care. But the Mexicans, in a passion of enthusiasm, would not be put off with such technicalities and insisted on immediate delivery of their wonderful blonde wards. After a great deal of argument, Father Mandin upheld the position of his parishioners. Before a child was delivered to its foster parents, however, the parents had first to reimburse Sister Anna Michella for the cost of the clothes in which the children had made the journey and for their rail fare to Clifton. The families imme-

---

68 McWilliams, NFM, 200-202.

diately paid over the sums stipulated and great enthusiasm prevailed in South Clifton that night as the Mexican community celebrated the arrival of the children.

When word got around that the Mexicans had "bought forty blonde babies" a mob of three hundred angry Anglo-Americans assembled in downtown Clifton. Everyone agreed that the iniquity of the situation cried for redress and so a posse was formed which made the round of the Mexican homes collecting the children. When one Mexican miner suggested that a court order would be necessary before the custody of the children could be changed, a leader of the posse shoved a gun in his ribs and said: "Here's your court order." Once collected the forty children were taken to the local hotel. "It was raining," writes the historian of Clifton, "and the crowd had swollen and they were in an angry mood. There was even talk of hanging the priest." Some of the children were sick, probably from the excitement and the feasts of chili, beans, and tortillas which had been prepared for them. A few, the irate Anglo-Americans noted, even had the odor of beer on their breath. Before the night was over, the children had been parceled out to various residents of Clifton. Later the New York foundling home, bewildered by this strange mix-up in faraway Arizona, brought suit to recapture possession of the children but, in the meantime, adoption proceedings had been perfected, and the Supreme Court of Arizona upheld the adoptions in a decision which was affirmed by the United States Supreme Court. Great was the sorrow of the Mexican copper miners of Clifton when the beautiful blonde children, in their handsomely embroidered hand-stitched garments, were taken from them.

Chapter V

SOME PARTICULAR AREAS OF
CULTURAL DISCRIMINATION

Out of the interaction which occurs when two cultures such as the Anglo and the Hispano confront one another, five cultural components have been selected for special consideration—attitudes towards race, religion, and class (because they represent especially sensitive areas in majority-minority relations) and language and education (because of their importance in cultural transmission). These cultural components will be seen first through the majority definition of the status-carrying pattern, second through the minority heritage, and last through the cultural interaction which results.

LANGUAGE

Language, as Woods has stated, "is one of the strongest bonds uniting a cultural group" and is its "sign of recognition" and "badge of brotherhood."[1] It serves as an essential key to the implicit and explicit values of a community.[2]

> Language allows the individual to participate symbolically in the life of the group and thereby acquire the meanings and goals that are central to its life. Without knowledge of the language, the individual remains indefinitely outside the meaningful existence of the adopted society. Its standards have no significance, its goals have no relevance, and its values have no importance for the individual if he cannot communicate with the other members of the group.

For such reasons "the retention of traditional tongue is often the principal aim of those who seek to prevent an ethnic group from losing its identity, while the loss of that language is taken as a measure of amalgamation."[3]

---

1 Woods, CVA, 25.
2 Francis E. Merrill and H. Wentworth Eldredge, *Culture & Society* (CS), 509.
3 Caroline F. Ware in Locke & Stern, *When People Meet* (WPM), 478.

Majority Definition

The United States, being an English-speaking country, accords the use of English preferred status. English is required in the schools and only in the state of New Mexico is there any official recognition of a second language (Spanish) having some equality of status with English in the conducting of public affairs.

While it is understandable that English is the preferred language in an English-speaking nation, it is more difficult to understand the lack of concern among Americans to acquaint themselves with additional languages. As Kluckhohn has commented: "Americans have been characteristically inept at foreign languages. Like the British, we have expected everybody else to learn English."[4] Commenting on this as it relates to New Mexico, one writer has observed: "There is no official compulsion or encouragement for the Anglos to learn Spanish, but most of the old-timers know some. . . . But 'educated' Anglos who speak Spanish appear to be proportionately fewer than 'uneducated' ones. With 'education' apparently goes a sort of cultural arrogance. It is especially noticeable in the southeastern sections of the state."[5]

Although North Americans[6] do not learn other languages, they exhibit a strange sensitivity to the use of anything but English in their presence. They often imagine themselves the subject of the conversation carried on in a different tongue and Tuck, in her observations, found that the use of Spanish in public ranked foremost among Anglos as a cause of friction and ill-feeling between the two populations. Saunders has also observed:[7]

> Many Anglos are annoyed and sometimes become suspicious or angry when, in their presence, Spanish-speaking people begin to "jabber" in their own language. The irritation is likely

---

4 Clyde Kluckhohn, *Mirror for Man* (MFM), 145.

5 Adamic, NN, 49-50.

6 The use of the term "American" in this country to designate *only* persons of the United States is often cited by Latin Americans as symbolic of our arrogance and self-centeredness. In Latin America, people of Canada are usually referred to as *canadiense*, people of Mexico as *mejicano* or *mexicano*, and people of the United States, inasmuch as "United Statesian" is awkward in Spanish as well as in English, as *norteamericano*.

7 Saunders, CDMC, 112.

to be particularly strong when there are observable signs of levity in the conversation. At such times the Anglos feel they are being laughed at, or at best, "talked about." Feelings thus engendered occasionally find expression in retaliatory acts against the Spanish-speaking. More often they are worked off in indignant discussions with other Anglos in which the main theme of the conversation is the old familiar one: "If they don't want to learn English, why don't they go back where they came from."

Saunders also has commented on the persistent and largely unfounded notion among Anglos in the Southwest that many Spanish-speaking people pretend not to know English even when they do. This becomes, he says, an easy rationalization for the Anglo in situations where lack of knowledge of Spanish prevents establishing a good relationship and places the blame for the lack of communication on the Spanish-speaking person.

Minority Heritage

Spanish, obviously, is the heritage of the minority. Coming from Spanish-speaking countries, Spanish was the language in the immigrant's early childhood—the period when values and behavior patterns are formed; its use persists in many native-born families. In 1940, by official count, there were 1,861,000 persons who reported Spanish as the principal language spoken in their childhood home and unofficial estimates have run as high as four million.[8]

Bi-lingualism, especially among those who have attended United States schools, is becoming more common but often the acquisition of English is primarily used in situations involving Anglos. A study of Tucson in 1947 revealed that the language used depended largely on the intimacy of the situation and who was involved. In *Anglo-Mexican* relations, English was the standard; in *formal relations in the Spanish community*, English was also widely used; in *informal* relations there was a rapid shifting from one language to the other, especially among younger persons; and in *intimate* relations, Spanish was almost universally dominant.[9]

---

8 Brown & Roucek, *One America* (OA), 343.
9 George C. Barherti, "Social Functions of Language in a Mexican-American Community," (SFL), *Acta Americana*, Vol. 5, 1947, 185-202.

Simmons, too, observed that among "even those who speak unaccented English there is a tendency to lapse into Spanish whenever in company of another Mexican."[10] He further found that "a premium is placed on speaking 'good' unaccented English, but the retention of Spanish is valued just as highly 'as a mark of culture that should not be abandoned.'" He goes on to say that "Mexican Americans who favor full assimilation to the Anglo-American model tend to minimize the use of Spanish among themselves and attempt to eliminate it altogether by speaking only English to their children, a practice condemned by those who hold to the 'best of both ways.'"[11] There is, in this connection, a strong community expectation that all Mexican Americans should maintain identification with *la raza* and exhibit pride in their Mexican descent, and an equally strong condemnation of those who seem overly anxious for Anglo acceptance.

Language differences between generations are in evidence. Saunders illustrates this as he speaks about one of the families on "Felicia Street."[12]

> Virginia and Rafael know quite a bit of English, but never feel at home in the language and prefer to talk in Spanish. The older children are bilingual, and switch from one language to another in their conversation. The young ones know some Spanish but prefer to speak English, the language of the comic strip characters, the movie comedians, and the radio cowboys.

Added to a general deficiency in English, many Spanish Americans have only a limited use of Spanish itself. The high degree of illiteracy among immigrants and among New Mexican Hispanos greatly limits the use of the language, especially in its literary functions. Among second and third generations, too, a great many having had no formal training in it can neither read nor write Spanish, even though they may speak it fluently.

Cultural Integration

The lack of true bilingualism on the part of both Anglos and Spanish Americans limits the amount of communication

10 Simmons, AAMA, 407.
11 Simmons, AAMA, 407.
12 Saunders, CDMC, 112.

between the two groups and makes impossible a wide range of relationships. On the part of the Spanish-speaking, life problems—getting a job, visiting the doctor or staying in a hospital, seeing public officials, or merely traveling from one place to another—are made more difficult by their lack of English. Among Anglos, cultural reciprocity is limited without bilingual exchange and the old pattern of cultural influence (i.e., a one-directional flow toward Anglo ways) rather than cultural interflow continues to predominate.

The dominant group's rejection of the use of Spanish results in several reactive responses among Spanish-Americans. First, there is evidence that Spanish-Americans do not feel free to speak Spanish when Anglos are around.[13] Further, "inability to speak English or to feel at ease with it, is a powerful factor in the tendency of many Spanish-speaking people to avoid any but the most necessary contacts with Anglos. . . . Language difference is both a cause and an effect of isolation, and as such exerts a strong influence in the perpetuation of other cultural traits of Spanish-speaking people and in retarding their integration into the Anglo group."[14] Such isolation is probably one of the most important explanations of the greater persistence of Spanish than languages of other immigrant groups.

Pressure to too quickly conform to the standard of English does not give recognition to the security-providing function of language or to its values in communicating with the traditions of an individual's past. The problem is one of giving an individual "more self-confidence and security, never less." "He needs to add a language, but not to lose the language of his home, family, and childhood" for "the child who lives in a Spanish-speaking home and goes to an English-speaking school moves in two worlds, and needs to be at home in both."[15]

EDUCATION

Education, in its broad meaning, refers to the transmission of the culture to its new members. In primitive societies this

---

13 Barberti, SFL, 185-202.
14 Saunders, CDMC, 111.
15 Fresno County Project, "Teaching Bilingual Children" (TBC), Introduction.

was accomplished mainly through informal means, but as cultures have accumulated and increased in content, the process—requiring an increasing amount of time—becomes formalized into a specialized institution. Thus, when we speak of "education" in the United States it is its institutionalized form, *i.e.*, the school system, that usually comes to mind.

Majority Definition

Formal education—and much of it—is highly valued in the United States. The widespread "faith in education"—noted by observers as characteristic of the American scene*—has led to mass public education and compulsory attendance laws. The school system is not only a compartmentalized institution "removed from kinship and religious groupings" but has largely displaced these in importance in acting as the focus of community life. The school has become, Robin Williams notes, "the knot in the web of community life."[16]

With schools holding such a central role in the development of the community's cohesiveness, the orientation of the instructors becomes highly significant. In the United States this orientation is predominantly middle class. Allison Davis writes: ". . . in each of the regions of this country, more than 95% of all school teachers are from the middle class. . . . Teachers and administrators tend to lay stress on punctuality, responsibility, and ambition to get ahead in this world because such qualities are part of their own basic culture."[17]

This orientation coincides with and reinforces another striking characteristic of the United States educational system. With this society's emphasis on achievement and monetary success, the educational system is valued in how well it pays off in future dollars. It becomes a "ladder or escalator" to white-collar, technical, managerial, and professional occupations, the occupations of status in the society. "During the last generation," Kluckhohn has observed, "education has supplanted the frontier as a favorite means of social mobility,

16 Robin M. Williams, Jr., *American Society* (AS), 285.

17 Allison Davis, "Light from Anthropology on Intercultural Relations," *Cultural Groups and Human Relations* (CGHR), 84.

for we have continued to define success in terms of mobility rather than in terms of stability."[18]

Minority Heritage

The tradition regarding education brought from rural Mexico and which existed in New Mexican Hispano communities contrasts markedly with the norm of the contemporary United States.[19]

> Education was largely a matter of informal indoctrination. There was no emphasized concept of progress and hence no need for the acquisition of new knowledge. All that a person needed to know to live successfully in the village could be acquired through the informal process of socialization. The child listened, observed, and asked questions. . . . There was no literary tradition and virtually no knowledge of reading or writing. Very rarely, and then only in the larger communities, were there schools, and what few existed taught little that was of value to a person living in a village.

The drive for vertical mobility which underlies much of education in the United States was also largely absent from the Mexican and Hispano value system.[20]

> The Anglo American's goal of success, with its achievement and recognition components, is closely integrated with the functioning of the occupational system since it channels motivational forces into performance of an occupational role as the principal means of realizing success. The Mexican American, on the other hand, is oriented to goals which accord major emphasis to the obligations of familism, friendship, hospitality—all the objects of the Mexican's distinctive definition of reciprocal obligation—and for the Mexican worker, access to status in the Mexican American community is based in large part on the degree of fulfillment of these obligations.

The political, social and economic background of the Spanish-speaking agricultural communities, therefore, did not place a high evaluation on formal education. Illiteracy was the rule rather than the exception and the function of education—i.e., the transmission of the community's behavior patterns and values—was carried on largely through informal and intimate contacts.

---

18 Kluckhohn, MFM, 246.
19 Saunders, CDMC, 50.
20 Simmons, AASA, 261.

Cultural Interaction

The acceptance of the American norm of formal education has caught on in most Spanish American communities in the United States, but a carrying through of the norm is often not in evidence. Margaret Mead has noted that in the Hispano communities "Spanish Americans have come to put a great stress on the idea of education, but it is always 'for the children.' . . . Soon these children are old enough to go to work, then to marry and settle down. They want education—for their children. The mañana pattern carries along. And in school the teachers have found it very difficult to motivate these children, as they do the Anglo children, in terms of future benefits—grades or better jobs or high standards of living."[21]

Educational statistics for Spanish American children reveal a low degree of formal school training (See page ▓). A 1942 study in Texas found 43% of the total number of Latin American children of school age not even enrolled in school. Of those who were enrolled, 37,000 were in the first grade, 19,000 in the second and less than 6,000 in the eighth grade—indicating the high proportion of early dropouts.

Kibbe has cited the following as among the main reasons for low attendance in schools by Latin American children: migrancy, illness and general poverty, lack of motivation on the part of Latin American parents to send their children to school, prevailing attitudes on the part of Anglo American children and teachers which make the child feel his presence in class is distasteful, and lack of enforcement of school attendance laws. But she cites residential segregation which leads, in turn, to school segregation and the separation of Spanish-speaking children from contact with English speaking children as an especially important contributing factor.[22] Simmons comments that the handicaps which stem from segregated schools and the inferior facilities which usually are found in them continue to plague the Latin American student if he goes on to higher grades. "Many Mexican Amer-

21 Mead, CPTC, 174.
22 Kibbe, LAT, 82-103.

icans drop out at an early grade in primary school, and of the rest, knowing only the 'Mexican school,' as it is referred to by both Mexicans and Anglos, many cannot face the adjustment required in entering the 'mixed' high school."[23]

The school often represents the first encounter of a Spanish-speakiing child with Anglo ways and this first encounter establishes the dominant-subordinate pattern he will encounter time and again during his life.[24]

> The Mexican American child spends his pre-school years in a community of his own ethnic group, learns Spanish as his primary language, and comes to the school experience with no conception of the Anglo world beyond that imparted at second hand by his socializing agents. The school thus provides the first opportunity . . . for contact with the Anglo group. For the majority of Mexican children this first contact consists not of relationships with other Anglo American children but with an Anglo teacher as the sole representative of an ethnic group other than their own, a relationship which is the prototype of later relationships with Anglos in that the Mexican is subordinate while the Anglo is dominant.

Furthermore this teacher is usually a product of middle-class Anglo culture. Kibbe has written:[25]

> Above and beyond all these reasons for the Spanish-speaking child's failure to make satisfactory progress in school is another consideration of paramount importance. With frequent outstanding exceptions, our elementary teachers have been lacking entirely in a knowledge and understanding of Latin American children; and until the very recent past, the teacher-training institutions in Texas were not actively aware of the fact that the successful instruction of Spanish-speaking children requires special teaching methods and classroom materials, in addition to a general and fairly comprehensive knowledge and understanding of their social characteristics and economic background.

A far earlier writer has vividly illustrated another educational problem which stems from Anglo-American dominance. Writing of education in Taos County, New Mexico, she said:[26]

---

23 Simmons, AASA, 134.
24 Simmons, AASA, 122-3.
25 Kibbe, LAT, 102-103.
26 Mary Austin, "The Indian-Mexican Settlements of San Juan and Chamita," in Park and Miller, *Old World Traits Transplanted* (OWTT), 189.

There is nothing whatever in any textbook which would create in any child's mind the least suspicion that reading is a method of coming into touch with its environment. This country has a beautiful and dramatic mythology, but there is only Greek mythology in the school readers. On his way to school the child is confronted with an abundant and beautiful flora, but the references in the reader are to English daffodils and New England Mayflowers. He reads about Bunker Hill, but nothing about Black Mesa. Fray Marcos and De Vargas are not even names to him.

The lack of enthusiasm among many Spanish-Americans for formal school training beyond the most elementary education is interrelated with the lack of evidence that further education leads to increased opportunities.[27]

The Hispano believes in education but, in view of the Anglo-dominated setup, distrusts its effects. According to Burris, "he has seen . . . children leave the village and come back bitter." What's the use, he thinks, of educating his? Their chances for white-collar jobs are limited. Most Anglo employers don't inquire into their qualification; the fact that they are Hispanos rules them out. What's the use of a schooling which opens their mind and vision to a world of wider horizons, when their opportunities to enter that world remain closed. As things go, it is perhaps better for one's children to stay uneducated workers and peasants.

However, Spanish Americans who have become or who aspire to middle class status adhere more closely to the Anglo pattern. Not only do they emphasize the attendance of their own children, but they view education as the best means of raising the level of the ethnic group as a whole, usually making it one of the major aims of community service organizations.

If one accepts the point of view that a complex society with a democratic form of government such as that of the United States requires a literate citizenship, some formal schooling for each member is essential. Finding the means by which all members have an opportunity for such basic education becomes, therefore, one side of the problem. In the case of Spanish-speaking persons some of the more difficult hurdles are: how to overcome the problems of mi-

---

27 Adamic, NN, 56.

grancy, how to eliminate residential segregation which leads to segregated schools, how to cope with special language problems, how to recruit understanding teachers, how to revise curricula in all schools to develop an appreciation of Spanish-Indian and Southwestern cultural contributions.

But another problem related to motivation is involved. In the educational system of the United States, as we have seen, one of the most effective motivations for obtaining extensive education lies in its utility in achieving upward mobility. The positive and negative sides of such an orientation can and should be discussed, but as long as they continue to act as the primary motivation for formal training its relevance to Spanish Americans requires demonstration. The limits placed by Anglos on occupational and social opportunities suggests that educated Spanish Americans will often experience frustration unless more opportunities are made available to them; others may not attend school any longer than is absolutely required of them. Allison Davis who has made special study of the problems of motivating minority and lower class students writes that it is unrealistic to expect persons to continue in school unless some rewards are in sight. "Our society must convince them of the *reality* of the *rewards* at the end of the anxiety-laden climb. . . . Our society cannot hope, therefore, to educate the great masses of low-class people in any really effective manner until it has *real* rewards to offer them for learning the necessary anxiety."[28]

SOCIAL CLASS

In most societies some form of ranking its members on a vertical basis can be observed but the criteria on which ranking is based differ, depending on the basic values of the community.

The Majority Definition

In the United States which is characteristically an acquisitive society, prestige is expressed predominantly in material or monetary terms. Income and occupation have assumed

---

[28] Allison Davis, "Socialization and Adolescent Personality," in *Readings in Social Psychology* (RSP), Theodore M. Newcomb and Eugene L. Hartley (editors), 150.

special importance in determining status. Furthermore, manual work is looked down upon and persons, in the absence of other traditional values, attempt to demonstrate their importance by moving out of the working class and into white collar or professional employment.

The Minority Heritage

Almost all of the Spanish-speaking population of the Southwest came to the United States as unskilled labor into agricultural or unskilled railroad employment. They were, and many remain, in the working class.

While strict class lines based on land ownership existed in the rural villages of Mexico, the same emphasis on vertical mobility found in the United States was largely missing among the immigrants. They embodied not so much an orientation toward achievement and a success ideal but rather toward family honor, friendship and generosity to the community. (See quotation from Simmons on page ██.) Too, rural Mexico had an almost total lack of a middle class, a person was rich or poor with little chance of changing status.

Cultural Interaction

The Anglo's stereotypic attitude toward Spanish Americans is that they are a one-class, undifferentiated mass. In the minds of many, "Mexican" is synonymous with "low class." In reality, however, many different statuses exist although they are not always based on Anglo criteria.

Simmons[29] found that in the Spanish-American community, two main types of status exist. On the one hand, divisions are based on wealth, income and occupation as in Anglo society. On this basis the Mexican American community is divided between two groups: a large unskilled labor or lower class group and a much smaller middle class of merchants, professionals, etc. The middle class is differentiated from the other not only in their economic level

---

29 Most of this section is based on Ozzie Simmon's excellent analysis (AASA) of the class patterns in a Mexican-American community in South Texas and in the metropolitan area of San Antonio.

but also in their ambition to achieve in Anglo terms and in their adoption of Anglo ways. They feel more in competition with Anglos than lower class persons and try to distinguish themselves as much as possible from the lower class in order to demonstrate to the Anglos the latter's error in assuming that all Spanish-speaking persons are alike. This involves an acceptance of Anglo standards and often leads to middle class Mexican Americans making the same error as Anglos in defining the lower class as an undifferentiated mass. Focussing on the disorganized elements in the community and forgetting the hard-working, orderly, stable lower-class families, stereotypic adjectives of "indolent," "ignorant," etc. are used by them to describe the lower income group as a whole.

But the Spanish-speaking community is ranked on a second set of criteria. This second definition of status arises out of the values which predominate in the *colonia* and in Mexico but which are less important in the dominant society. Here prestige or community recognition depends on the adherence to values of family, friendship and generosity more than wealth and education.[30] Dislike and disapproval is extended to the "lower element," i.e., disorganized persons which exhibit "loose" morality, excessive drinking, and uninhibited aggressions. It is more respectability and non-respectability that matters. However Simmons found that stable lower class Mexican Americans are more accepting of deviant behavior than Anglos or middle class Mexican Americans.[31]

Lower class Mexican Americans are not unaware of Anglo and middle class values of success and achievement but Simmons believes that they are not willing to subscribe to them since they consider their own more attractive and important. "The positive advantages that the lower class Mexican enjoys as recipient of concrete and personal response and recognition from his group far outweight the vague, remote and imper-

---

30 Thurston found the same differentiation in the Los Angeles *colonia* that he studied. "There is considerable prestige differentiation in Pueblo in terms of wealth display, propriety and likable personal qualities. . . . The most prestigeful families are not the very wealthiest but are families which combine wealth with the other two qualities." Richard G. Thurston, *Urbanization and Sociocultural Change in a Mexican American Enclave* (USC), 39.

31 Simmons, AAMA, 394.

sonal benefits he *might* obtain by entering the stressful world of competitive mobility, with the concomitant necessity for self-denial and renunciation."[32]

In contrast to the middle class which feels competitive with and often resentful of Anglos, the lower class Spanish Americans largely handle their conflict with Anglos by staying within the *colonia* and avoiding all but the minimum of contact. While this solves some problems, it contributes to others. It perpetuates the language barrier and eliminates even the rare opportunities for mutual appreciation between the Spanish and the Anglo community that might exist. It also makes it simple for Anglos, unfamiliar with the group, to form their opinions about Spanish Americans from a few conspicuous cases which make the headlines or appear in published crime statistics.

Cutting across both Mexican American groups—the middle class and the working class—flows a characteristic that is demanded by the Spanish-speaking community, *i.e.*, pride and interest in *la raza*. While identification with the group may take different forms of emphasis, the person who wishes to maintain status within the Spanish community must not deny his Spanish heritage. He must honor the *colonia's* values of family loyalty and generosity.

If he wishes to have status in the Anglo community and to escape undifferentiating prejudice, the Spanish American must also achieve in Anglo terms, *i.e.*, he must rise on the vertical mobility scale. But here he faces the barriers to mobility. Jobs are not available, social relations are often restricted, especially for dark-skinned persons, and educational opportunities are limited. Thus the dominant Anglo group itself is responsible for much of the continuation of the conditions that it deplores and the Spanish American finds himself repeatedly relegated to a position of inferior status in the total community.

RACIAL ATTITUDES

In Western culture, physical differences—especially of color —have been used to perpetuate dominance of certain groups

---

32 Idem.

over others. This technique of dominant-subordinate relations, at least some authorities believe, has been built up to its present level as the result of European colonial expansion into areas inhabited by people differing in physical traits. The colonists observing the different physical characteristics of the peoples they encountered and their "primitive" cultures assumed a relationship between the two, and extended an "inferior" value judgment to both, thus paving the way to the most tenacious of the modern fallacies concerning race.[33]

> This contemporary creed, with its double-edged assumption of the innate superiority of the race and culture of those who possess more complex and advanced forms of civilization, and of the inferiority of those who do not, is particularly a product of the modern colonial area, and thus of Occidental origin, at least in its extreme and characteristic form. Particularly in its aspect of associated color prejudice, it seems peculiarly and intimately associated with modern European colonial expansion. On that basis it furnishes the standard ideology and stock rationalization of economic imperialism. . . . Both the race culture and the race superiority aspects of the doctrine are completely invalidated so far as the case rests on grounds of scientific warrant or historical truthfulness.

Majority Definition

The physical form which is accorded preferred status in the United States is a tall, light-skinned "North European" type. The degree of dissimilarity to this type generally holds a corresponding loss of acceptance and, although one can find individual and local deviations from this norm, North European whites find the greatest ease of entry to privileges and opportunities if other things are equal.

This evaluation, transplanted into the early American colonies from Europe, became intensified and solidified during the slavery period and has persisted to such a degree that the United States is known throughout the world as among the most racially intolerant of nations. The internalization of attitudes of white supremacy by most members of the society is indicated by a study by Emory Bogardus.[34] In this study Dr.

---

33 Locke & Stern (WPU), 9. A summary of the views of Frank Boas.

34 Emory S. Bogardus, "The Measurement of Social Distance," in Newcomb & Hartley (RSP), 504.

Bogardus found that the status evaluation given various ethnic groups corresponded to their similarity or divergence from the North European type. "Mexicans" ranked low except in acceptance for employment. Only 3% of the 1,725 respondents indicated they would admit Mexicans to close kinship with their own group through marriage (the most intimate of social relationships) and no more than 12% indicated they were willing to admit them "to my street as neighbors." (In this same study "Spaniards" were rated much higher, 28% approving intergroup marriage and 55% willing to have them as neighbors.)

Although Spanish Americans in this country range from very light to dark skins, in the minds of Anglos they are often thought of as a homogeneous group.[35]

> The Mexican, constituting the second largest minority in this region, while not officially classed as "colored," has generally come to be designated as "non-white." Discuss the component parts of your population, or of a meeting, or audience, and you will find yourself facing three classes in the mind of the average citizen: "White," "Colored," and "Mexican" or "White," "Colored" and "Non-White." Thus the Mexican may not be considered "colored," but he certainly is not "white" either, in the opinion of the man on the street.

Persons that do not fit the stereotype, physically and/or culturally, become "Spanish" to Anglos or are not considered part of the minority.

Minority Inheritance

Spanish Americans of the Southwest are primarily *mestizo* (an Indian-Spanish mixture); they represent considerable heterogeneity with a range from almost "pure" Indian to almost "pure" European. Racial intolerance, at least as it is known in the United States, is not part of the Spanish American heritage.[36]

> The Mexicans, by tradition and custom, are a racially tolerant group. The acute sense of personal dignity, a Spanish legacy, strengthens the notion that no man should be judged accord-

35 Carlos E. Casteñada, "The Second Rate Citizen and Democracy," in *Are We Good Neighbors?* (AWGN), by Alonso S. Perales, 19.
36 Ernesto Galanza, "Program for Action," (PFA), *Common Ground,* Summer, 1949, 27-38.

ing to his color or his race. Normally, Mexican communities in the United States have preserved remarkably well this valuable cultural trait.

A different pattern of interaction with the indigenous Indian populations by Spanish and British colonists has led to more acceptance of non-European physical and cultural types in Mexico than in the United States.[37]

> The Latin regimes—Spanish, Portuguese and French—although quite as ruthless politically and economically as any imperialist colonial system, seem to have exhibited considerable tolerance for cultural difference, and thus to have produced appreciable hybridization of the two cultures. Indeed they are almost everywhere characterized by a considerable degree of interpenetration of the colonizing and the aboriginal culture. The Anglo-Saxon tradition of imperialism, British, that is, with somewhat parallel attitudes on the part of the former German colonial regime, has, on the contrary, the conviction of cultural incompatibility and persistently holds on, often with overt prejudice, to its own cultural tradition.

The synthesis of the native with the invading culture that occurred in the Spanish colonies has resulted in not only less attention being given to physical differences but Indian influences assume more importance in the country's historical and cultural traditions. *The* national hero of Mexico, for example, is Benito Juarez, a full-blooded Indian. The Virgin of Quadalupe, the most honored of religious symbols, is portrayed as an Indian woman. In recent years, there has been a conspicuous and organized effort to bring the Indian heritage of Mexico into even greater prominence through the integration of Indian art and other cultural forms into the total Mexican cultural fabric.

Cultural Interaction

Racial discrimination is experienced by the Mexican immigrant and his native-born children in the United States. The intensity differs from region to region—the northern cities are said to be less hostile and Texas the worst in the Southwest—but Ruth Tuck has said:[38]

---

37 Locke & Stern (WPM), 89.
38 Tuck, NWF, 52.

There are Mexican-Americans who can honestly say that they have never encountered any of the cruder forms of discrimination, although they may have been aware of some of the subtler ones. . . . It is safe to say that the entire population of Mexican descent, including those who have been relatively untouched personally, is aware of barriers against it. Reactions may vary from resentment to defeatism, according to personalities—but I have yet to encounter, from the most successful Monticello Avenue merchant to the humblest old fruit-picker in the *barrio pequeño,* any lack of awareness.

Darker-skinned Spanish Americans are more likely to experience severe discrimination. Describing the situation in 1930, Gamio wrote:[39]

The darkest-skinned Mexican experiences almost the same restrictions as the Negro, while a person of medium-dark skin can enter a second-class lunchroom frequented also by Americans of the poorer class, but will not be admitted to a high-class restaurant. A Mexican of light-brown skin as a rule will not be admitted to a high-class hotel, while a white cultured Mexican will be freely admitted to the same hotel, especially if he speaks English fluently.

Although responsible for discriminatory practices, Anglos try hard to disclaim any hint of racial antagonism. Simmons found that candidates who bring up the issue in political campaigns are criticized in letters to the editor of local newspapers. Tuck said that when "Descanso" tries to build up a case for "its own tolerance and generosity, it falls back on the old theme of assimilation," thus shifting the blame away from themselves. "The Mexicans just won't assimilate, that's the trouble." "They stick together, and won't make outside friendships." "They like to live with their own kind."[40] Simmons sums it up by saying: "Racial beliefs about the Mexican have been predominantly ambiguous."[41]

In order to avoid the stigma attached to color in this country there is a temptation among some Spanish Americans to deny and protest against any designation of "non-white."[42]

The native-born Spanish-speaking elements resent any attempt to designate them in a manner that implies a "non-white"

39 Gamio, MIUS, 53.
40 Tuck, NWF, 93.
41 Simmons, AASA, 406.
42 McWilliams, NFM, 43.

racial origin. Being called "Mexican" is resented, not on the basis of nationality, but on the assumption of racial difference. Because of the Anglo American's attitude toward race, the first reaction of the New Mexican, as Dr. Arthur L. Campa has pointed out, "is to disassociate himself from anything that carries a Mexican implication." To do this, he must insist on his difference in origin. Thus he is of "pure Spanish blood," a direct descendant "of the Spanish conquerors," etc. . . . But the difficulty with "Spanish American," as Dr. Campa adds, is that, while it suits the New Mexican in the abstract, there is little in his appearance and origin that upholds the distinction he is trying so hard to make.

Further repudiation of Mexican and/or Indian heritage is revealed in persons who change their names from Spanish to Anglo-sounding ones, in light-skinned persons who call themselves "Spanish" rather than Mexican, and in families, in the process of acculturation, who move away from the *colonia* and break all group ties.

Another form of reaction to Anglo discrimination can be observed in persons who rarely venture out of the confines of the *colonia*, thus avoiding all but the minimum of contact with non-Spanish people. Some of the strength of the *orgullo racial*, or pride in being Mexican, comes as a reaction to the lack of acceptance by the larger community.

All of these protective devices, of course, are forms of self-denial and reflect some adoption of the Anglo attitudes of Spanish-Mexican inferiority. They are thus exchanging a historical unconcern about race for a pattern of racial discrimination. Adoption of the Anglo pattern of discrimination which Dennis Chavez has defined "as American as the hot-dog" represents an unfortunate backsliding.

RELIGION

All known societies have exhibited some form of religious beliefs and ritual and in a sociological sense it can be said that religion both reinforces the society's norms and values and helps define them to its members. In primitive societies, religion is interwoven into community life in a highly integrated manner; in modern industrialized societies it tends to be more compartmentalized and embodied in the separate formal institution of the church.

[128]

Majority Definition

It is impossible to present here a comprehensive description of religion in the United States but some of its main characteristics, as observed by students of the culture, can be outlined.

1. The United States is in tradition a Protestant country. Although other faiths are represented, Protestantism, introduced through the early colonists, has dominated in cultural influence and in numbers.

2. The Protestant ethic which fitted well into the expanding American economy was and continues to be an important influence in the nation's character. This ethic which emphasized individual initiative and self-denial has been summarized by Saxon Graham as follows:[43]

> . . . The Protestant ethic was that the individual should work in the material world to accumulate goods. His success in this effort would signify his election to heaven. Protestantism further taught that once accumulated, these goods could not be spent on oneself. The ascetism of the religion allowed no fleshly pleasures or ostentatious display. Instead, the profits of work were put back into the operation of business, creating ever improving facilities for trade and production. Thus, Protestantism, as a substitute for Catholicism, gave sacred sanction to the capitalistic values of individualism, competition, and asceticism.

3. The religious pattern in the United States is characterized by denominationalism, i.e., a multiplicity of groups often with only minor differences separating them.

4. Characteristically, Protestantism has had an aversion to traditionalism. From Reformation and Calvinistic influences, austerity in form and a minimum of ritual and pomp has been emphasized.

5. Although freedom of worship has been idealized, there has persisted an undertone of anti-Catholicism within the Protestant community. At times this hostility has broken out into violence (in movements such as the Ku Klux Klan and the Know-Nothing Party) and although such violent and blatant expression is not condoned, the pervasiveness of an

---

[43] Saxon Graham, *American Culture* (AC), 218-219.

anti-Catholic sentiment has been sufficient, as Schermerhorn points out, to prevent a Catholic from being elected President.

6. Although church attendance and participation in public worship is expected, "religiousness" in terms of dependence on "God's judgment" has been cited as not characteristic of the society.[44]

> The anthropologist must also characterize our culture as profoundly irreligious. More than half of our people still occasionally go through the forms, and there are rural and ethnic islands in our population where religion is still a vital force. But very few of our leaders are still religious in the sense that they are convinced that prayer or the observance of church codes will affect the course of human events. Public figures participate in public worship and contribute financially to a church for reasons of expediency or because they know that churches represent one of the few elements of stability and continuity in our society. But belief in God's judgments and punishments as a motive for behavior is limited to a decreasing minority.

7. Science and human effort is emphasized over mysticism and fatalism.[45]

> Mysticism and supernaturalism have been very minor themes in American life. Our glorification of science and our faith in what can be accomplished through education are two striking aspects of our generalized conviction that secular, humanistic effort will improve the world in a series of changes, all or mainly for the better. We further tend to believe that morality and reason must coincide. Fatalism is generally repudiated, and even acceptance seems to be uncongenial—though given lip service in accord with Christian doctrine.

8. Religious organizational life in the United States, especially in the highly urbanized areas, is "extraordinarily segregated from other institutional structures." "The very fact that religion in our culture is so frequently equated with the churches is a telling indication of the compartmentalization of religious norms."[46]

9. There has been a traditional emphasis placed on separation of church and state.

---

44 Kluckhohn, MFM, 248.
45 Kluckhohn, MFM, 232.
46 Williams, AS, 399.

Minority Heritage

The history of religion and the church in Mexico is a fascinating and turbulent one. Catholic priests accompanied the first colonists and proselytizing among the Indians was used as a rationalization of Spanish colonization in the Western Hemisphere. Tannenbaum comments that "The speedy conversion of the Indians seemed like a miracle to the friars and provided the conquerors with a moral justification that salved their consciences."[47] Gruening, however, writes that this justification was made in retrospect and that "no allusion to the faith appears in the articles drawn up between Columbus and the crown. 'Oh, Lord,' prayed Columbus on his first voyage, 'direct me where I may find the gold mine.' "[48]

Historians provide accounts of the extreme pressures by the Catholic Church on the indigeneous populations in the Spanish Colonies, but they also cite it as the only "protector and friend of the Indian, as the only advocate and well-wisher he had to claim upon." "Its defense of the Indians as human beings possessed of souls and capable of redemption saved the Indian from the infamy of being branded a soul-less creature incapable of a life of the spirit, to be identified only with the beast of the field."[49]

Furthermore, Catholicism could be fitted easily into the way of life of the Indians.[50]

> It proved easy for the Indian to keep in the Catholic Church the faith he had had so long and to identify his own deep religious sense with the new forms that adorned the temples, often built upon the places where the older idols had rested. . . . An essential link between the past and the present was preserved and gave life a sense of continuance and a sense of direction. The Indians worked for the Church, built its temples, adorned and embellished its walls, tilled its lands, knelt before the Host, and obeyed the Fathers of the Church, because that was the kind of religious life they had always known.

The tendency of the Indian to adopt the Roman Catholic faith and to fit it into his earlier religious traditions produced

---

47 Tannenbaum, MSPB, 122.
48 Ernest Gruening, *Mexico and Its Heritage* (MIH), 171.
49 Tannenbaum, MSPB, 122-3.
50 Tannenbaum, MSPB, 124.

a Catholicism in Mexico that was far different from that imported from Spain. Gruening goes so far as to say, "The Mexican people are not Catholics,"[51] meaning that, in reality, through the interblending of Indian and Spanish influences, a new religion had emerged.

Within Mexican communities further local peculiarities were produced by isolation and the shortage of priests. Each village adopted its own saint and most of the day-by-day religious affairs were conducted by an important layman. "The parochial village knew the humble church that it adorned and the sacred image of the saint that it guarded and worshipped. The saint was the very particular saint of that particular village, the center of its life."[52] The concept of the Universal Church and devotion to it was "alien, unknown" to the folk who "had retained in their forms of worship many of the older patterns belonging to an older faith."[53] Thus, according to Tannenbaum, anti-clericalism and the ideal of a Universal Church, were, in Mexico, "middle- and upper-class and European" and to a large extent confined to the cities.[54]

How true this was in the states from which most immigrants to the United States originated is unclear in the literature. It seems clear that certain states had a higher proportion of priests to the population than others, giving a stronger European influence to the Catholicism. Certain communities, even rural ones, saw more of and were more directly involved in the church-state conflict than were others. The states which produced most of the immigrants to the United States—Jalisco, Guanajuata, and Michoacan—according to scattered references, were among the states which saw more of both revolutionary-led anti-clerical activity and Catholic-led anti-revolutionary skirmishes but the effect, if any, of this activity on the religious life of the ordinary Mexican villager is not made clear as illustrated by the following comment of Gruening in 1927.[55]

---

51 Gruening, MIH, 229.
52 Tannenbaum, MSPB, 125.
53 *Idem.*
54 Tannenbaum, MSPB, 126.
55 Gruening, MIH, 285.

If the Mexican hierachy misjudged the possibilities of outside aid it misjudged its internal strength in Mexico still more. It expected that the boycott would bring the Mexican Government to its knees. Nothing of the kind happened: indeed the rebellion merely further exposed the character of Mexican Catholicism and the weakness of the clergy's hold on its people. It is idle to say that a popular movement was put down by armed force. On the contrary the army did much to keep alive rebellion. Except in relatively few regions the clergy passed out of the lives of the supposedly Catholic people without a ripple. The reason is simple. As long as the Mexican could go to church and worship his idol in the shape of a saint's image he was content. The loss of his priest meant little to him. Indeed in more than a dozen different villages in the states of Hidalgo, Tlaxcala, and Puebla, villagers expressed to me in the spring of 1927 their preference for the new order of things because, as they said, they could now worship without paying for the privilege. Out of several score with whom I conversed in those three states, one only, an old man, in the village of Ecatepec, Tlaxcala, expressed a regret that a priest was not available for the baptism of new-born children. This of course is not typical of all Mexico. In other sections, particularly in Jalisco, Guanajuato, Queretaro, and Michoacan, unquestionably some villagers miss their priests. There seems to be a definite relation between the peasants' concern in the clerical controversy and the benefit they have derived from agrarian reform. Where they have received land they apparently care little, or less, about the absence of a priest and his services. Land fills their lives.

The church-state conflict, in any case, was a deep and serious one. The Church, rich and influential, identified itself with the Crown and became one of the main targets of the developing political movements. The success of the revolution was to make Mexico the first country in Latin America where the Church was disestablished.[56]

> Juarez, on July 12, 1857, in the midst of a bitter civil war promulgated the laws that have in fact set the pattern for State and Church relations ever since. He confiscated all of the Church's properties, suppressed the religious orders, and empowered the governors to designate the buildings to be used for religious services. . . .
> The position of the Church was further weakened by President Lerdo de Tehada's decrees of September 24, 1873 and De-

---

56 Tannenbaum, MSPB, 130-131.

cember 14, 1874. . . . He made marriage a civil contract, prohibited religious institutions from acquiring real property or lending money on mortgages, replaced the oath by a simple declaration, forbade the establishment of any monastic order, prohibited the teaching of religion in any of the governmental establishments, suppressed religious holidays, stopped any manifestations of religion in public, regulated the ringing of church bells, denied priests the right to be heirs or legatees, prohibited the use of any special religious dress in public, and nullified any special privileges that members of the priesthood might have enjoyed under law.

After the Revolution of 1910, the conflict between Church and State again became a burning issue. A period of violence and highly stringent restrictions on any religious activity lasted until 1935 "when Cardenas quietly used his influence to modify the situation in favor of the Church. . . . The results of this change of policy made it possible for President Avila Camacho to declare that he was a believer and to institute a greater tolerance for the activities of the Church. The recent revision of Article 3, dealing with education, by removing the most objectionable features as seen by the Church, has further improved Church-State relations in Mexico."[57]

The above paragraphs, of course, are only a brief outline of the many-faceted history of the Catholic Church in Mexico. They do, however, provide some background for a discussion of the religious heritage brought by the immigrants as they settled in the predominately Protestant Southwest.

1. While the United States is predominantly Protestant, most Spanish-speaking persons come out of a Catholic background. This Catholicism, however, had strong Indian and "folk" overtones.

2. The Protestant ethic of individual striving and saving which permeates the United States culture, differs from traditional Mexican-Hispano community values. In the Mexican and Hispano villages, familism, generosity, friendship, noncompetitiveness and communalism were important and carried religious sanction; work was seen as the means of attaining these values rather than an end in itself as is common in contemporary life in the United States.

---

57 Tannenbaum, MSPB, 135.

3. In contrast with the Protestant pattern of austerity and anti-traditionalism, Mexican-Indian Catholicism placed high evaluation on ritual, fiestas, visual religious symbols, and tradition.[58]

> In order to show their response to the *santo* for his protection and special favors, the villagers hold an annual fiesta in his honor . . . candles . . . flowers . . . firecrackers . . . Mass . . . dances . . . costumes . . . masks . . . pulque . . .
> The church usually towers far above the rude jacales or the small adobe structures which are grouped around it. . . . In it are found the highest artistic contributions of the community. The decorations of the altars, the drawings, the carvings, and the color all represent the best talent that the local community affords.

4. To be Catholic was taken for granted in Mexico and little knowledge of other religious forms existed. Rather than an anti-Protestant feeling, there was relatively little knowledge of Protestantism.

5. Denominationalism was not familiar but neither was an identification with a Universal Roman Catholic Church common. Mexican Catholicism was village-centered.

6. The Mexican-Indian village life was in marked contrast to Kluckhohn's characterization of the United States culture as "profoundly irreligious." All of life was imbued with religious meaning. Redfield describes the early folk societies and the interdependence of the religious, the moral and the economic in the following paragraph:[59]

> For in these folk societies the sacred quality of life is important, and pervades those activities which in the city world exist merely as instruments to the achievement of practical ends. Piety is stressed, rather than expediency or efficiency. The interdependence of religious experience, moral life, and agriculture just mentioned, is perhaps the most obvious aspect of the pervasiveness of the sacred quality. In measuring off the land to be cleared for a new field of corn, no more must be measured than one is sure to clear and plan, for the bush—say the Maya—belongs to the gods of the bush, and they would be angry should one take more than one needs. And the harvest is not man's to consume until he has, in symbol, given it back to its real owners, the gods (or the saint), in the first-fruit ceremonies.

58 Whetten, RM, 463-67.
59 Redfield, FCW. 39.

7. Fate, rather than science and human effort, was held in reverence. The emphasis on change—through knowledge and effort—did not hold significance in the subsistence economy in which they lived.

8. It has been pointed out that religion in the United States is highly compartmentalized and that stress is placed on worship service attendance and participation in organized church activities. In the Mexican and Hispano community religion permeated all of life. The fiesta, the *santo*, the art forms held community as well as religious significance. "Planting and harvest; birth, death, and marriage; sickness and health; recreation; leadership and authority patterns were all invested with religious significance and associated with religious ritual, so that religion formed the core of all institutional activity."[60]

9. Indian influences were—and remain—prominent in the forms of worship.[61]

> It is said that many an Indian Christ adorns the village church in Mexico today. The most venerated of all figures in the Mexican church is the Indian Madonna, the Virgen of Guadalupe. Her image appears in homes all over Mexico, taxicabs carry it frequently on their dashboards, it even rides on many a crowded urban bus.

10. The history of church and state affairs has been a violent one. Existing laws give the state extensive control over the church although they are not strictly enforced at the present time.

Cultural Interaction

Because the religious life in Mexico was so often deeply inter-woven into other community activities, emigration for the Mexican usually meant a severing of religious as well as other community ties. The new settlements in the United States, on the other hand, except in isolated instances, were not likely to manifest the same type of integration of the religious with the non-religious built up over years of stable community life in the interior of Mexico.[62]

---

60 Saunders, CDMC, 49.
61 John A. Crow, *Mexico Today* (MT), 65.
62 Tuck, NWF, 155.

One of the things which Juan Perez missed when he came to the United States was the community social life which followed the round of the Church calendar. The festal dates, some of them dating from a pre-Conquest religion, were closely tied to the seasonal agricultural cycle and tied yet again to the particular region, in that the special saints of the city, the locality, and the *barrio* were feted. Religious observance was inextricably inter-twined with attachment to the *tierra* and with the rural subsistence economy. Many of these activities could, and did, go on without the assistance of a priest. They were religious in name, but in substance often approached more clearly such secular recreation as community processions. One of the most distinctive and important phases of the life of a small Mexican community, they compensated, in Juan Perez' mind, for many other failures of the Church.

In the small Catholic parish in the United States, the immigrant found nothing to replace the old community life. It would have been impossible to transplant—it was too closely tied to the activities and associations of a region.

Griffith has concluded that "the strong faith that supported them in Mexico was not alone sufficient to give them the strength and wisdom they sought to live at peace in an industrial civilization. Thus it is today that for many Mexican Americans, the acknowledgement of the church is often one of token recognition."[63] Manuel Gamio in 1930 observed that "it is clear that a large part of the Mexican immigrants abandon Catholicism."[64] A vacuum then exists. What is to fill it? What are the alternatives of religious life from which a Spanish American can choose?

Although the Spanish-speaking person usually comes out of a Catholic background, Roman Catholicism in this country is not the same as in Mexico. Sister Murray, noting the small proportion of active Catholics in San Antonio, says, "the Catholic Church in the United States is too cold and formalized; it lacks the emotional appeal it has in Mexico."[65] In connection with her discussion of the absence of substitutes for the community-religious life familiar in Mexico, Ruth Tuck makes this comment about the Catholic parish in the United States:[66]

---

63 Griffith, AM, 181.
64 Gamio, MIUS, 117.
65 Sister M. J. Murray, *A Socio-Cultural Study of 118 Mexican Families Living in a Low-Rent Housing Project in San Antonio, Texas* (SCS), 80.
66 Tuck, NWF, 155.

But, for many years, nothing which even remotely took its place existed in the Mexican American parish. The instruction of the young in catechism, the administration of the sacraments, and the erection of a large fine church structure were the goals of most parish priests. Few attempts were made to provide recreational outlets for the community under the sponsorship of the parish church, or to center the life of a Mexican colony around it. An opportunity for a tremendously effective piece of work certainly existed. That the opportunity was not realized may account for some of the indifference of the *colonias* nominal Catholics.

A Roman Catholic bishop has been quoted as saying that the Catholic Church is reaching effectively only 10% of the Spanish-speaking people of California and other states of the Southwest.[67] Sister Murray, in her study of 118 housing project families of San Antonio, found that although 90% were nominally Catholic, "only 38% attend mass every Sunday and a much smaller percentage frequent the Sacraments regularly, send their children to a Catholic school and actively participate in church organization functions."[68] Reporting on a study of the Mexican American family in Detroit, Humphrey concluded that church attendance was irregular and that children went largely to please their parents.[69] A Los Angeles *colonia* study conducted in 1949 found only about 15 families out of a possible hundred families attended mass regularly and most of these were represented by women and children.[70]

That part of the disinclination for Spanish-speaking Americans to be actively Catholic in this country may be due to the limited effort and leadership of the Catholic Church in the areas of settlement is suggested by the following statement by Taft and Robbins:[71]

> In particular regions, or at particular times, the Catholic Church did not effectively provide leadership, however. For example, among the considerable number of ante-bellum immigrants to the South, and more recently among large numbers

---

67 Rev. José I. Candeleria in an address to a National Council of Churches meeting on Spanish work.
68 Murray, SCS, 64.
69 Norman D. Humphrey, "The Changing Structure of the Detroit Mexican Family: An Index of Acculturation" (CSDM), *American Sociological Review,* Dec., 1944, 622-26.
70 Thurston, USC.
71 D. R. Taft and Richard Robbins, *International Migration* (IM), 457.

coming from Mexico, this leadership has been inadequate from the viewpoint of Catholics.

Although there is some evidence that a larger proportion of Mexican Americans are attracted to Protestant churches in the United States than in Mexico, the total numbers are small. Robert Jones found that in Chicago about one in thirty were Protestant, whereas the estimate for Mexico is one in two hundred.[72] Sister Murray found a handful of Protestant families in the San Antonio housing project which had been converted from Catholicism, observing that they seemed quite sincere in their new beliefs.

For a Spanish American person to become Protestant, it would seem he must feel some discord with the Spanish-speaking community. Simmons found that Protestants in the community he studied were "very puritanically-minded"[74] and that they were the only total abstainers in the *colonia* which generally accepts and expects moderate drinking.[75] He further observed that they seem "to be preoccupied with the 'Protestant ethic' placing emphasis on this-worldly achievement and material success, extolling the virtues of sobriety and thrift."[76] Murray's Protestant respondents seemed to be related to a greater economic "success" and represented a more "progressive," Anglo-oriented group. In the Los Angeles community studied by Thurston, the only Protestant church working in the area was an "allelujah" church and its worship forms represented a sharp deviation from the religious life familiar to the *colonia*. The community referred politely to the members of the Pentecostal Mission as "Protestants" but otherwise as "allelujahs."[77]

> The loud singing and frenzied speech is an item of curiosity, especially for young boys, who like to gather at the always-open door or directly across the street. It also seems to provide a release for aggressions in the form of jokes and, occasionally, in the hurling of stones at the sides of the building.

If Catholic churches in the U. S. can be cited as "cold and too formal," Protestant churches, especially missions, must

---

72 Griffith, AM, 190.   76 Simmons, AAMA, 92.
74 Simmons, AAMA, 92.   77 Thurston, USC, 36.
75 Simmons, AAMA, 105.

seem even more bleak and austere to the Spanish American as he compares it with the church he knew "at home." Northrop has commented:[78]

> A church with the diversity of vivid colors which the Indian aesthetic imagination demands would shock a Protestant congregation. But imagine, conversely, how the Protestant religion must appear to the religious Mexicans. Its exceedingly verbal preaching, its aesthetic color-blindness, and its emotional tepidity and coldness must make it look to them like no religion at all.

Furthermore, Protestants have not always considered Spanish Americans as their area of concern. Griffith says:[79]

> Like Catholicism, organized Protestantism has not taken a definite stand either on the Negro or the Mexican in America. A few church leaders have made their convictions clear by their actions, but their very struggles demonstrate that the Church hasn't done the job it could do, either in sufficiently backing young men and women leaders, or in aligning itself with progressive movements to break down prejudice and discrimination.
>
> The elaborate alibis and pretexts of Protestant churchgoers to avoid responsibility toward the Mexicans take these forms: "They are Catholics and not our concern. They are a subnormal race, mostly Indian; they can't learn our American way of living and don't want to; they are just greasers and could never be anything anyway. The crimes of this town come from these people—we're already paying out more for their health and charity than for any group. They cause all the trouble in our community."

Simmons found that the local Protestant churches in the border area demonstrate little active interest in proselytizing among Mexican Americans in the area, leaving this "missionary work" to groups from the North.

With a weak and nominal Catholicism and little adoption of Protestantism, it is not surprising that a persistence of superstition and "folk" beliefs can be found among the Spanish-speaking. The belief in *mal ojo* (the evil eye) and the survival of *brujas* (women with special powers) is not uncommon in many Spanish-speaking communities. *Los Penitentes*, a flagellistic order disapproved by the Catholic Church, still prac-

---

78 F. S. C. Northrop, in Whetten (RM), 467.
79 Griffith, AM, 191.

tices its worship of pain and death in isolated areas of New Mexico and Colorado.[80] Griffith indicates that the strength and unquestioning acceptance of these old beliefs is not as great among younger persons as among the older but that they have not thrown them off completely.[81]

> How much the children who grow up with these superstitions are affected by them depends of course upon education and other factors. Some will deny "those old superstitions." Then after talking confidentially, they are apt to shrug their shoulders and say "Some believe in them—they say such things aren't possible, but I don't know. . . . " Almost unconsciously they will slip you a folk belief as fact or church dogma.

Saunders has suggested that differences in religious choice are partly related to "class" patterns.[82] He writes that devout Catholicism, with many members among the adult males in the *penitente* order is the pattern among the still-isolated villagers of New Mexico. The lower class of urban and suburban areas remain Catholic, but the church does not occupy the place in their lives that it did in the villages, and the men, although nominally members, frequently do not attend services except on holidays or other special occasions. Membership in the *penitente* organization is not common. The lower middle class or urban or suburban persons differ from the lower class in that they have less close ties with the church and a small proportion show a tendency to accept the Protestant religion. In the urban-suburban upper-middle class "noticeably different in a number of respects from the lower-middle and lower classes" the proportion that are Protestant, although still small, is higher than among either of the other two classes. The small urban upper class which enjoys a status based mainly on old family tradition is likely to be strongly Catholic. The use of Spanish and English follows about the same pattern with the lower classes mainly using Spanish and the middle classes using English more frequently. The exception is the small upper class which knows and uses English but sees that all family members know Spanish well and use it on ceremonial

---

80 John Burma has an interesting summary of this Order in his book, *Spanish-Speaking Groups in the United States*, Appendix.
81 Griffith (AM), 183.
82 Saunders, CDMC, 80-84.

occasions. This last group takes pride and is the most secure in its Spanish background.

If the Spanish-speaking person decides on affiliating with a particular church he is confronted with another set of alternatives from which he must choose—*i.e.*, the "Anglo" or the "Spanish" church. In some areas this choice does not exist —attendance at the Spanish church may be the only alternative because of severe discrimination or residential segregation—or there may be no special church because the small size of the Spanish-speaking population makes it impossible. But where it does, the choice brings into focus dominant-minority conflict. In the "Anglo" church, the Spanish American is likely to come into direct and personal contact with people who do not see him as an individual but as a "Spanish American" or a "Mexican." He may not be entirely acceptable because of his physical appearance, his economic status, or his non-Anglo ways. He may be reminded in many subtle ways that he is not really part of the group and that his attendance and participation is at the sufferance of the Anglo members.

The second choice—the ethnic church—while it may answer problems of language, also perpetuates the isolation between Anglo and Spanish-speaking people and symbolizes the separation that exists between them. It represents the inability of Anglos and Spanish to communicate across their cultural differences.[83]

> The separation between Anglo and Mexican is complete and explicit in the area of religious worship. . . . The fact that the *colonia* Protestant churches consist of all-Mexican congregations is indicated by the names they bear, Mexican-Methodist, Mexican-Baptist, Mexican-Christian, and Spanish Lutheran and by their practice of conducting their service entirely in Spanish. Each of these denominations is represented among the Anglo churches but there is no contact between the two churches of the same denomination. . . . The writer attended many Sunday services of the Anglo Protestant churches and never observed a Mexican American worshipper in any of them.

Simmons observed that in San Antonio when Anglo churches give aid to the Mexican counterpart in the city, Anglo members visit the Mexican church "to assess the progress of the

---

83 Simmons, AAMA, 153.

church" but never "to worship in common with their Mexican brethren." He also noted that the "Mexican" churches were small wooden structures with few facilities while the Anglo churches of the same denomination were large, attractive and well-equipped.

Perhaps the most common pattern among Spanish Americans is little or no involvement in any church life. "The realm of the sacred has diminished," Saunders has written, "the secular has expanded."[84] "If you ask the youngsters why they are not more interested in going to church, you may be told, 'You start forgetting about it. You don't come across it enough in your life, and after awhile it just doesn't mean anything to you.' This fact of whether the church has meaning for them is probably the key to their attitude toward the church."[85]

Simmons did not find, as one might expect, much anti-Catholicism expressed by Anglos in their discussions about Spanish Americans. He interpreted this rather surprising fact to mean that fears were minimal because of the only nominal adherence of Mexican Americans to the Catholic church. He added, however, that although not the cause, the difference in religion between Spanish-speaking and Anglos undoubtedly reinforced the separation of the two groups.

How can the chasm be bridged? Pauline Kibbe, whose book deals primarily with economic and social problems has given attention to what she views as the "task of the churches."[86]

> Reduced to their simplest form, the problems in Texas represent nothing more nor less than the failure to apply Christian principles to our everyday dealings with each other. There is certainly nothing new about the teachings of Christ, but a new day would dawn in Texas if the Christian doctrines in which we profess to believe were actually to become the philosophy by which we live seven days a week instead of one.
>
> Christian neighborliness does not begin across imaginary state or national boundary lines. It begins here and now. . . . It begins with a concerted attack upon discrimination of any kind because of language differences or national origin, wherever and whenever such prejudices may be encountered.

This, she states, "is not charity. It is democratic living."

---

84 Saunders, SSPC, 8.
85 Griffith, AM, 181.
86 Kibbe, LAT, 268.

Chapter VI

PUERTO RICAN BACKGROUND

TODAY as in the past, Spanish Americans have been saying a
great deal about the sense of brotherhood that prevails among
them and about the loyalty they have to many of the values
of their Spanish American culture. They point out the need in
the world today for some of these values as against the more
materialistic values of Western civilization. A recent compila-
tion of articles on the general subject of the "Interrelations of
Cultures" published by UNESCO includes several articles that
express this point of view. Professor Ayala of the University
of Puerto Rico discusses this in considerable detail in the article
entitled "The Place of Spanish Culture."[1]

> In Western Christian civilization a body of culture has ex-
> isted with characteristics of its own, since the period of the
> Spanish Empire's political expansion in the sixteenth century
> and covers still all those territories in which the Spanish
> language is still predominant.
> The living fact of a persisting and clearly-defined cultural
> community, based principally on identity of language, is evi-
> dent wherever the Spaniard—whether from the Peninsula or
> the Americas—carries his language. Just as the North Ameri-
> can refers to us all as "Spanish," so we all, whether we be in
> the United States of America, in France or elsewhere, have a
> sense of brotherhood.
> For us, our language is not only an instrument of sponta-
> neous and immediate communication; it is also the only gen-
> erally recognized symbol of our collective unity, which *ipso*
> *facto* gives it a positive emotional value.
> Even after three—or, more accurately, four—centuries, the
> form impressed on our culture in the sixteenth century has per-
> sisted in its essential character of humanistic Christianity.
> However much it may have deteriorated, this is still a poten-
> tial resource at this critical moment in the history of man-

---

1 UNESCO, *Interrelations of Cultures* (IOC), 237, 238, 241, 242.

kind, when the forces which have brought us through modern times to our present situation are not merely useless, but actually dangerous. The world needs to be given a new spiritual trend in keeping with the new conditions.

What are those conditions? One factor is the really extraordinary efficiency which has enabled the West (directed since the Reformation by nations freed from the narrow dogmatism in which Spain has continued to live) to develop technology and to use it to spread its power. There is no longer any *terra incognita* in our planet, which has been rigorously reduced to a single technical unity, which has in other words been conquered by Western man. The very magnitude of the political forces now dominant makes the possibility of armed conflict between them disastrous—possibly it would mean the end of all our civilization. If we rule out that one disastrous possibility of war, the ambition and competition for power which have hitherto constituted the driving force of technical progress lose all meaning. Technology will then have to be adjusted to a world no longer governed by functionalism under the impulse of the will to power, but directed by spiritual values capable of giving a new meaning to human life. We shall have to renounce that unbridled activism from which both the positive and the negative results of progress derive, that is to say a rise in the general standard of living combined with appalling destruction and oppression.

At the point we have reached—and man's present general bewilderment shows clearly that we stand at the cross-roads—the archaistic Spanish culture offers, in its pure tradition, inestimable resources capable of rendering invaluable services to a world in the throes of spiritual reorganization.

North Americans have been singularly unaware of the flaws in their own culture and insensitive to the values of other cultures, a majority group characteristic that has often been the cause of inter-group tensions. Actually, we North Americans have been so sure of the superiority of our Anglo-Saxon institutions and customs that we have tended to think of the "American way" as the best way of life for the rest of the world. And these illusions about our own culture have kept us from understanding the hold that Spanish American culture has on the people of the Spanish-speaking countries.

Puerto Rico became a part of the United States sixty years ago. For more than fifty years of that time she was in essence a colony of the United States. As such, her Spanish American culture came under attack for she was dominated both economically and politically by the mainland. Administered by people of Anglo-Saxon tradition, the policy was to introduce Anglo-Saxon ideas and values. English was substituted for Spanish as the language of the island in the schools as well as in all branches of public life. But despite these policies of the U.S. Government, Puerto Rico today still is basically Spanish American and Spanish is its principal language.

In a final statement, the UNESCO Committee that had been considering the problems presented by the contacts and relations of cultures in the world today summarized its findings under the heading "Humanism of Tomorrow and the Diversity of Cultures." Part of its summary statement is as follows:[2]

> The cultures of the world have been affected profoundly by technology, war and political change. The customs and beliefs of peoples who had lived as their ancestors lived, are being rapidly transformed by changed material conditions and external influences. The aspirations of peoples who have long sought political independence and autonomy, are being suddenly realized. The ideas and ideals of nations have been affected by contact with those of other nations, with whom they have previously had little or no relation; and from the efforts to treat economic, social and political problems which are recognized as common, there have arisen tensions which threaten the fundamental values of civilization. The crisis of our times is a crisis of cultures as well as of economics and politics; and what happens to the values of art, science, literature, philosophy, and religion affects, and is affected by, what happens to the material conditions of life and the international relations of nations.
>
> The problem of international understanding is a problem of the relations of cultures. From those relations must emerge a new world community of understanding and mutual respect. That community must take the form of a new humanism in which universality is achieved by the recognition of common values in the diversity of cultures.

Puerto Rico and the mainland United States have come a long way toward mutual understanding and appreciation of each other's traditions. The colonial period is over for Puerto Rico and her recently acquired Commonwealth status seems to give her the local self-rule for which she had struggled so long. The economic and social transformation of the Island that

---

2 UNESCO, IOC, 379, 382.

has taken place largely under her own efforts has been described as a transformation "which for a long time will be one of the
wonders of human history."[3]

But, as is true of all of the underdeveloped countries of the
world today, Puerto Rico has a population problem. At her present level of economic development, Puerto Rico cannot support her entire population though her Governor has estimated
that she may be able to do so by 1975. For the present, however, and for the next fifteen or twenty years at least, freedom
of migration will be essential to her well being. It is this situation that is presenting a new challenge to all mainland Americans and in a special way to the churches.

A Colony of Spain

Some knowledge of the early history of Puerto Rico is essential if we are to understand its present society and the values
and customs of those that come to the mainland to live. Many
of its present-day values and customs had their origin during
the long period of Spanish colonial rule.

Dr. Silvio Zavala, in an article in the UNESCO publication
referred to above, points out that the strength and degree of
development of the native peoples of the country to which the
colonizers came had a great deal to do with the type of society
that developed.[4]

> The repercussions of a meeting between different cultures
> naturally depend on the strength and degree of development of
> the peoples who are joining their destinies.
> The European colonizers who settled in uninhabited or
> sparsely populated lands with rudimentary cultures were in a
> different position from those who came into contact with large
> groups of culturally advanced Indians. This is in part the cause
> of the profound difference between the colonization of the
> half-empty territory which now constitutes the United States,
> or the large plain of the Rio de la Plata, and the occupation of
> the well-populated lands of Mexico and Peru. Again, in the
> Antilles and in Brazil respectively, the Spanish and Portuguese
> colonists failed in their attempts at permanent amalgamation
> with the Indians. For once they had broken up the weak or-
> ganizations which they found on arrival, the colonizers drew

3 Rexford G. Tugwell, "What Next for Puerto Rico" (WNPR), *Annals of the
American Academy of Political and Social Science,* Jan., 1953, 145.
4 UNESCO, IOC, 249.

on African labour, and the societies they instituted were therefore ethnically and culturally very different from the Amerindian societies. So that the very nonexistence or weakness, or alternatively, the prevalence in large numbers of a native population, greatly influenced the composition of the new society which grew out of contact with the whites; it was also partly responsible for the differences in the types of cultural exchange.

Puerto Rico is one of the islands of the Greater Antilles where Dr. Zavala says the native Indian tribes were relatively weak and primitive in culture as compared with the Aztecs and Incas of Mexico. There were two Indian tribes on the island when Columbus sighted it in 1493, the Borinquens and the Caribs. Ponce de León established permanent settlement a few years later and then followed a period of conflict between the Indians and the colonizers. Some authorities say that most of the Indians were wiped out by disease or war leaving little trace in the present population; others say that they migrated to other islands in the Caribbean; while others hold that the majority of them took to the mountains in the interior of the island. Professor Earl Parker Hanson in his recent book about modern Puerto Rico takes issue with the prevailing theory of "ruthless extermination" of the Puerto Rican Indian tribes and holds that some elements of the population, if not pure Indian, are unmistakably partially Indian. The indications are, he says, that:[5]

> . . . the majority simply retreated to the island's central mountain range, leaving the coastal strip to the invading whites. For almost three centuries after the first settlement, the mountainous interior remained crown territory, unsought and unused by white settlers. In many places in the interior, today, physiognomies are almost pure Indian. Among the "jibaros" there are obviously more Indian genes than is generally believed or can be accounted for by the prevailing doctrine of ruthless extermination.

Other authorities substantiate Professor Hanson's theory. Discussing "The Puerto Rican Peasant and His Historical Antecedents" in 1930 Professor José C. Rosario described the Puerto Rican peasantry as follows:[6]

---

5 Hanson, TSPR, 52-53.
6 Clark, PRIP, 540.

> . . . It was composed of Spanish individuals who scattered
> throughout the Island to cultivate their farms, and who when
> not married to Spanish women mixed freely at first with the
> Indian women which were mandated to them, and later with
> negro (sic) women slaves. Nevertheless, a great number kept
> their Spanish blood pure, many examples being noticeable
> today in both town and country.

The intermixture of Spanish and Negro elements of the
population dates back to very early Spanish times and assimilation has been going on from the beginning with the result
that the population on the whole has been growing lighter because of the predominance of the white element. But, according
to Professor Rosario, this trend toward light skin did not begin
until the second half of the 19th century. Negro slaves, he says,
were brought to the island early and they constituted a relatively large proportion of the total population. When the first
census was taken in 1531 about twenty years after the original
settlement, the proportion of blacks was so large "that the
king took notice of the small number of whites as compared
with the number of negroes" and issued an "order compelling
slave traders to bring one free white settler for every five
negroes imported. Arrangements were also made to send 50
Spanish peasant families to Porto Rico to help increase the
white population."[7]

The importation of Negro slaves continued but white Spanish
settlers did not come in large numbers during these years because of the unsettled situation caused by the "continuous attacks of the English, the French, and the Caribs of the neighboring islands upon the young colony."[8] As a result, a census
taken in the latter part of the eighteenth century (1776) showed "that there was a great mixture of whites and blacks, the
number of mulattoes being larger than the number of whites."[9]
Although more whites began to migrate to the island in the
1800's, Negroes and mulattoes still represented more than half
of the population in 1846. In 1855, a cholera epidemic took a
heavy toll of the slave population, as a result of which the
ratio appears to have been permanently reduced. In 1899 when

7 Rosario in Clark, PRIP, 539.
8 Clark, PRIP, 539.
9 Clark, PRIP, 541.

the United States Army took its census of the island, Negroes constituted only 38 percent of the population and the proportion they represent has declined ever since.

There seems to be no question that only a small part of the present population of Puerto Rico is of unmixed white ancestry and that much the greater part is a mixture of Indian and white, Negro and white, or a mixture of all three. However, there are no really reliable statistics. Professor Rosario said of the Puerto Rican population in 1930:[10]

> Racial statistics in Porto[11] Rico are only approximations to the truth, as the population is extremely intermixed and there are not only two colors, but an infinity of shades. It is next to impossible, in many cases, to determine whether a person is white or slightly colored. In such cases, of which there are thousands, the strictness or tolerance of the census agent determines how the person is to be classed.

The general opinion seems to be that there are only two classes of the present population of Puerto Rico that are of pure Spanish blood, neither of which comprise a sizeable proportion of the migrants to the mainland. They are the upper class Puerto Ricans who have been the social and political leaders since Spanish colonial times and a portion of *jibaros* or peasants. However, as has been stated, there was considerable intermarriage in the early years between the Spaniards that came to be referred to as *jibaros* with the native Indians and the Negro slaves.

While great economic progress was being made on the mainland in the 400 years after its discovery, the economic situation on the the island of Puerto Rico was very different. There were many reasons for this. The island was small and its natural resources extremely limited. There was no gold as had been found in South and Central America so Spain came to value Puerto Rico principally for its strategic position in the Caribbean, especially while it was at war with the English, the French, and the Dutch.

Throughout the Spanish colonial period, the economy was largely agricultural, for land was the island's principal natural

---

10 Clark, PRIP, 546.
11 "Porto," a common spelling until the later fixing of "Puerto" by law.

resource. There was a small peasantry living chiefly in the mountains and tilling its own land, but most of the land under cultivation was used for the production of cash crops—coffee, sugar cane, and tobacco. The work on these large plantations was done by "a migratory landless group of laborers, including emancipated slaves who moved from district to district in search of work."[12]

With all the land under cultivation, too little was planted in food for home consumption so that very early the population began to show signs of undernourishment and this became worse as the population increased. The Brookings Institution report of the Island's economic condition said:[13]

> Undernourishment among the common people was apparently chronic, and anemia, the result primarily of hookworm, was so common as almost to justify the claim that it was universal. The diet of the *jibaro,* or mountaineer, was criticized by Spanish and Island writers as both inadequate and unbalanced. Writing in 1887 a distinguished local physician declared that the nourishment which the majority of the country people received was so scanty that it scarcely sufficed to replace organic waste, and not infrequently provisions were of such bad quality that their use should have been prohibited.
>
> . . . The area devoted to food crops was apparently declining before 1898 and Porto Rico imported a considerable fraction of the food stuffs consumed. In this the Island resembles our own cotton states and the neighboring West Indian Islands. Over 70 per cent of the customs duties collected by the government were levied upon imported foods, and in addition there were heavy excise taxes on provisions.

There was very little manufacturing during the Spanish period. "Measured by values, fully three-fourths of the domestic produce shipped in 1894 and 1895 left its shores in unmanufactured forms, and practically all the remainder consisted of raw sugar, molasses, and distilled spirits."[14]

Discontent with the economic and political conditions of the island took organized form during the nineteenth century and resulted in important changes in the island's relationship with Spain. Hanson says:[15]

---

12 Clark, PRIP, xvii.
13 Clark, PRIP, xviii.
14 Clark, PRIP, xxiii.
15 Hanson, TSPR, 26, 27.

The nineteenth century saw a marked though erratic movement of liberalization on the island, of preoccupation with political and economic reform, of groping toward civil liberties— which in turn resulted in the emergence of a number of truly Puerto Rican political and cultural leaders. The island's population, which had hitherto been amorphous in the cultural sense, assumed shape and identity in the sense of becoming truly Puerto Rican. It also became specific and vocal about its grievances and began to force sporadic reforms from Spain. The old mercantilistic colonial rule was altered. Commerce with the United States and foreign colonies was authorized and established. Other reforms included freedom of the press, separation of civil and military powers, and the creation of cultural societies.

One of the eventual results was the creation of an important "revolutionary" newspaper, *La Democracia,* which came to be founded by Luis Muñoz Rivera, father of the island's present governor. Founded and used during the Spanish regime for the purpose of arousing the national consciousness of the Puerto Rican . people and espousing their political emancipation, it was later to be used, under American rule, for the same purposes by Muñoz Marín.

An Autonomist party was formed, . . . dedicated to the island's eventual self-government. Spain tried repressive measures, but the voice of the Puerto Ricans was not too clamorous to be stilled. Finally, in 1897, Muñoz Rivera obtained for Puerto Rico the first real constitution, the first real charter of home rule that the island had ever had.

Early American Rule

The granting of that constitution by Spain which gave Puerto Rico local autonomy was received with jubilation. However, it was not put into effect before the United States took over the island from Spain. An account of United States administration of the island from 1898, when it was ceded by Spain to the United States, to 1952 when commonwealth status was acquired is given in an article by Dr. Antonio Fernós-Isern, Resident Commissioner for Puerto Rico in the U. S. House of Representatives, in the January 1953 issue of the *Annals of the American Academy of Political and Social Science.*[16]

For some 375 years, Puerto Rico had been administered by an absolutist regime and it was only at the very end of that regime, which came in 1868, that separation from Spain began

---

16 Antonio Fernos-Isern, "From Colony to Commonwealth" (FCC).

to take hold in the minds of a few Puerto Ricans. But in the last thirty years of Spanish rule, the movement for local autonomy grew so strong that the constitution referred to above was finally obtained in 1897. However, according to Professor Fernós-Isern, the people of Puerto Rico were not at the time unwilling to become part of the United States for "not only did the people of Puerto Rico expect to retain, under the United States sovereignty, all political authority that Spain had relinquished to them as an autonomous state in 1897, but they looked forward to added freedom, if for no other reason than that the change of political allegiance meant a change from a monarchial system to a republican democratic regime."[17] General Miles had brought the following message to the people of Puerto Rico when he took over the island for the United States:[18]

> The people of the United States in the cause of liberty, justice and humanity . . . come bearing the banner of freedom, inspired by a noble purpose . . . (to) bring you the fostering arm of a nation of free people, whose greatest power is in justice and humanity to all those living within its fold . . . not to make war upon the people of a country that for centuries has been oppressed but, on the contrary, to bring you protection, not only to yourselves, but to your property, to promote your prosperity, and to bestow upon you the immunities and blessings of the liberal institutions of our government . . . to give to all within the control of its military and naval forces the advantages and blessings of enlightened civilization.

But whether or not Puerto Rico was enthusiastic about being taken over by the United States, they "expected United States nationality to take the place of Spanish nationality."[19] They expected to be integrated into the United States as were other parts of the Spanish empire when taken over, as for example had been the case with Louisiana. But when Congress finally enacted legislation for the island in 1900, the relationship it established between the United States and Puerto Rico was very different from what the Puerto Ricans had expected. Dr. Fernós-Isern says:[20]

---

17 Fernos-Isern, FCC, 18.
18 Quoted in Bailey W. and Justine Diffie, *Porto Rico: A Broken Pledge* (PRBP), 3.
19 Fernos-Isern, FCC, 19.   20 Fernos-Isern, FCC, 18.

It was a great disappointment for the people of Puerto Rico to see that the United States Congress, in its first legislative act for Puerto Rico, took the position of an absolute sovereign, and that, without consultation with the people of Puerto Rico, it created a governmental structure for the island and established political, economic, and fiscal relationships between Puerto Rico and the United States Government. The people of Puerto Rico were declared to be citizens of Puerto Rico under the protection of the United States.

Among other provisions of the Organic Act of 1900, the Governor of the island and his Cabinet were to be appointed by the President of the United States. As things worked out, of all the governors appointed by the President none were Puerto Ricans except the very last one who was appointed to fill out the unexpired term of Governor Tugwell in 1946 and this came only as a result of the strong political movement on the island led by Muñoz Marín and his Popular Democratic party.

With the passage of the Organic Act of 1900, "separation and independent sovereignty" were talked of in Puerto Rico for many years as the only ultimate solution for the island. Meanwhile, there was "unceasing protest" and some gains were made. The Jones Act of 1917 amended the Organic Act of 1900 by granting United States citizenship to the people of Puerto Rico. "This gave them full standing as such citizens if they became residents of the United States, but of itself United States citizenship brought no changes as to civil or political rights to be enjoyed by the residents of Puerto Rico."[21]

Meanwhile the economic and social conditions of the island had grown worse. The Act of 1900 had restricted land ownership by agricultural corporations to 500 acres but this provision of the law was ignored by the administration in Washington. According to Professor Fernós-Isern:[22]

In a few years more than half of the best agricultural land of the tiny island, with one of the densest populations of the world, was owned or controlled by four sugar absentee corporations, whose local governmental influence kept taxes and wages down and would-be strikers within "law and order." In many ways a big sugar corporation was a state within the

21 Fernos-Isern, FCC, 20.
22 Fernos-Isern, FCC, 19.

state. Thus the benefits of economic union with the United States were largely lost to the people of the island.

Economic conditions continued to grow worse. The great depression caused extreme suffering and there had been little improvement on the island when World War II broke out. Moreover, the island was little affected by the prosperity that developed on the mainland as a result of the war. Enemy submarines were among the obstacles in the earlier years of the war.

Movement for Reform

There had been no progress in self-government after 1917. In fact, there was opposition to it from several sources even on the island. But, in the late 1930's, a movement for economic and political reform led by Muñoz Marín, the present Governor, with the support of the people of the rural areas in particular, got under way. The party's campaign slogan was "Bread, Land, and Liberty" but the emphasis was on bread and land and improved social conditions; independence was not the major issue.

Professor Hanson summarizes the high points of this campaign as follows:[23]

> The platform of the Popular Democratic party was unique in that it said nothing about ultimate political status. Indeed, it was stressed throughout the campaign that status—independence, statehood, or dominion status—was in no way a campaign issue; the Partido Popular bid for the vote entirely on the issues of social-economic reform. Muñoz and his followers campaigned for the enforcement of the Five-Hundred-Acre Law, for legislative steps in making sugar a public utility and so assuring that independent cane growers would receive fair prices for their crops, for effective steps toward the improvement of the banking system toward the end of liberalizing credits to farmers and businessmen, for land to be given free to landless agricultural workers, for the promotion of local industries, for social legislation to protect the island's workers, for slum clearance, for reforms in the school system and the extension of education.

One of Muñoz' first acts after being elected to the island legislature was to help put through a land reform bill for the

---

23 Hanson, TSPR, 175.

island designed to implement the 500 acre provision of the Act of 1900, still on the books. This bill aroused concern in Washington for the sugar interests were a powerful lobby. Washington was undecided as to whether or not to support the bill and recommended the Governor's signature as was then required of all legislation adopted by the island legislature. As a result, Interior Secretary Ickes sent Rexford Tugwell to the Island to investigate the situation. This led to Tugwell's later appointment as Governor of the Island and ushered in a period during which for the first time the island people, the administration in Washington, and the U. S. Congress began to work together to find a solution for the economic and social conditions of the island. The fact that Muñoz Marín and the leaders of his party were now talking of the island's needs in other terms than independence from the United States apparently helped to bring about the administration's change in attitude.

The New Constitution

In 1947, Congress amended the Jones Act of 1917 to make the office of Governor of Puerto Rico elective, and to give the Governor the appointive power over all his Cabinet members with the advice and consent of the Senate of Puerto Rico. Only three years later, Public Law 600 was enacted by Congress which established an entirely new relationship. Discussing this in their article, "The Commonwealth Constitution," the authors say:[24]

> . . . Under the terms of Public Law 600 of the Eighty-first Congress, adopted July 3, 1950, Puerto Rico's status has changed from that of involuntary dependency to that of voluntary association. The federal controls and limitations have been superseded by a fundamental law drafted by the people of Puerto Rico. As a consequence, the Puerto Rican people's right to govern themselves is no longer based upon privileges conferred by Congress but rather upon the principle of the consent of the governed.
> Public Law 600 could work this transformation because it was no ordinary Act of Congress. Rather, it was a compact between Congress and the people of Puerto Rico. Its first sec-

---

24 Victor Gutiérrez-Franqui and Henry Wells (TCC), *Annals of The American Academy*, Jan., 1953, 34.

tion declared the law to be enacted "in the nature of a compact," and its second section provided that the act as a whole could take effect only if approved by the Puerto Rican people.

In a referendum of June 4, 1951, the people of Puerto Rico voted overwhelmingly for Public Law 600, thus making themselves a party to the compact and consenting to its terms. On August 27, 1951 the people of Puerto Rico again went to the polls—this time to select delegates to a Constitutional convention. The 92 elected delegates sat in continuous session and on February 6, 1952 agreed on a constitution which they recommended to the people for approval. On March 3, 1952, the people of Puerto Rico ratified the proposed constitution by a large majority and sent it to the President and Congress for approval. Describing what happened in Washington, Professor Hanson says:[25]

> Congressional approval of the new constitution was not granted without a certain amount of haggling. At one time certain members of Congress tried to stipulate, through an amendment to the new constitution, that Puerto Rico should never be allowed to amend it without specific consent from Congress. That raised a storm of protest. . . .
> Muñoz Marín cabled to Washington: " . . . People here are dismayed with amendment that nullifies the significance of the whole constitutional process. To the limitations rightfully imposed on state constitutions and the Puerto Rican constitution, the amendment adds an obvious colonial touch. The people of Puerto Rico in voting to accept Law 600 in the nature of a compact, in which the principle of government by consent was "fully recognized," certainly had no idea they were consenting to any trace of colonialism. No self-respecting people would. Free men may live under such circumstances but they will certainly not go to the polls and vote that they love and cherish them. I fear that if the matter cannot be remedied in conference, great moral harm will be done to our people and some moral harm to the good name of the United States in the world. You can rely on us to protect the good name of the United States.

The Congressional amendment governing amendments to Puerto Rico's constitution was stricken out, but Congress did remove certain provisions from the Bill of Rights of the pro-

---

25 Hanson, TSPR, 390-391.

posed constitution which Professor Hanson describes as follows:[26]

These were provisions under which the government acknowledged certain responsibilities toward the people and defined eventual goals toward which government and people should strive jointly. They were taken almost verbatim from the Universal Declaration of Human Rights of the United Nations, although they were in no way new in Puerto Rico. For years before the writing of the constitution, the Puerto Rican government had acted in conformance with their terms, had *lived* them without debate, as though they had already been put on paper as the basic law of the land.

. . . The Congressional action of eliminating those sections baffled the Puerto Ricans, since the Universal Declaration of Human Rights had been approved by the General Assembly of the United Nations—and so also by the United States—on December 10, 1948. Puerto Rico's leaders, however, were not too disturbed. Since they are now free to amend their own constitution without interference, they can at any time put the various sections once eliminated by Congress back in again.

Discussing Puerto Rico's constitution in the January 1953 issue of the Annals, Professors Gutiérrez-Franqui and Henry Wells say:[27]

Although squarely within the American constitutional tradition, the Constitution of the Commonwealth is no slavish copy of any American document. It departs from its models in a number of significant details in order to provide a fundamental law that is workable in terms of Puerto Rican traditions and consistent with contemporary Puerto Rican needs. Its bill of rights, for example, is broader in scope than traditional bills of rights, which tend to include only restraints upon governmental action. It not only increases the protections normally afforded to private rights but also goes beyond them to guarantee certain social and economic rights that require positive governmental action for their fulfillment. Similarly the Constitution introduces certain innovations in the structure of the three branches in order to create a government competent to deal with the complex problems of an expanding and increasingly industrialized economy, and yet a government limited in power and responsible to the people.

As a result of this combination of modern and traditional elements, the Commonwealth Constitution is well designed to

---

26 Hanson, TSPR, 391-392.
27 TCC, 35, 36.

protect both individual and social rights, to promote the effective and responsible dispatch of public business, and to permit full local determination of purely local affairs.

It is only fair to state, also, that there still is difference of opinion in Puerto Rico as to what the eventual solution of the island's relation to the United States should be. An article by a priest in Aguadilla, Puerto Rico on the pros and cons of statehood for Puerto Rico reviewed the situation in a recent issue of *Commonweal* and discussed in particular the probable economic effects that would result. He ends his article as follows:[28]

> Thus the local political situation and the local economic situation combine to make statehood or independence equally impossible for the island of Puerto Rico. There is no doubt that at some future date Puerto Rico will indeed become a state. But as for the island's soon becoming a state, the Union's fifty-first, there is no immediate prospect of it.

Operation Bootstrap

As has been indicated, it was their determination to improve the economic and social condition of the island that won the support of the people of Puerto Rico for the leaders of the Popular Democratic party. Professor Harvey S. Perloff describes the condition Puerto Rico was in when they took over:[29]

> The year 1941 marked a turning point in the economic development of Puerto Rico, as in so many other aspects of Puerto Rican life. It was in that year that the people of the island, under a new leadership, undertook the task of transforming their economy and of providing the means for achieving their aspirations for higher levels of living.
>
> By the end of 1940, when the newly formed Popular Democratic party was making its first bid for office, and at a time when most other areas had already achieved substantial recovery from the depth of the depression, the insular economy was still in a seriously depressed state and, more significantly, revealed dangerous imbalance and structural difficulties.
>
> The sugar industry, the backbone of the economy, had stopped growing. Whatever inherent potentials for expansion it might have retained—and at best these were limited because

[28] Edward J. Dunne, "Is Puerto Rico Next?" (IPRN), *Commonweal*, July 3, 1959, 350.

[29] Harvey S. Perloff, "Transforming the Economy," *Annals of the American Academy*, January, 1953, 48, 49 and 50.

most of the best land in the island was already in sugar cultivation—an actual lid on its growth had been imposed by the sugar quota system. Other agricultural industries were also past the peak of their growth for a variety of reasons; the tobacco industry was suffering from the long-term shift to cigarette smoking and was in a disorganized state; fruits had lost out to mainland and offshore competition.

The important sectors of agriculture were subject to land monopoly and absentee ownership. According to the 1940 census, about one-half of 1 per cent of the farms contained one-third of the total arable farm land, and this was the best land in the lowlands. There was little effort at diversification, and when sugar production was limited, much of the land simply lay idle. The small farmer, characteristically owning or renting two or three acres on the side of a hill, found it difficult to make ends meet or to feed his own family. Most of those in agriculture were landless farm laborers dependent on a few months of low-paid work.

With the end of the period of growth of the major agricultural industries, employment in agriculture had leveled off, so that no more persons were employed in farming in 1940 than had been so employed in 1920. The labor force had increased by over 40 per cent between 1920 and 1940, yet no important new processing industries had been developed to help fill the large employment gap. The only significant expansion in manufacturing took place in sugar milling and in home needlework. Manufacturing employment, outside of these two categories, was at the same level in 1940 as it had been twenty years earlier, while total employment in manufactures reported by the census of 1940 was hardly greater than it was at the time of the 1930 census.

As a result of the divergent population and employment trends, some 18 per cent of the labor force was unemployed in 1940, while a large share of those who did find employment were working only a few months of the year or were engaged in peripheral service and trade jobs. Wages were pitifully small. Sugar workers, who averaged fifteen cents an hour, were the highest paid in agriculture. Home needleworkers rarely received more than four or five cents an hour. . . .

Governor Muñoz Marín recently described the situation that had developed under U. S. administration of the island:[30]

Fifteen cents an hour is not much of a wage for a grown man. Not when he has a wife and children to support. It

---

30 Luis Muñoz Marín, "Operation Bootstrap," in *The Day I Was Proudest to be an American* (DIPA), edited by Donald Robinson.

means that his family is hungry most of the time. And ragged. And sick.

It can do bad things to a man's spirit to come home after a hard week's work with only a few dollars' pay and see his famished children cough blood. It can make him give up hope. Tomorrow stands for just another nightmare. The same nightmare that yesterday was and today is.

This was life, not so very long ago, for a special group of Americans—the two million and more people on the island of Puerto Rico. Hundreds of thousands of them were unemployed, and those who had work received only a pitifully few pennies. Starvation and squalor were everywhere. And disease. Tuberculosis, malaria, and dysentery in particular. The death rate for tuberculosis was four and a half times that of the continental United States.

The number of babies who died in infancy was pathetic. Life expectancy for the population at large was a puny forty and a half years.

Do you wonder that the people's mood was one of tragic apathy? That homeless waifs roamed the streets, not knowing and not caring who their parents were? That honest men committed ·crimes—if you can call stealing a loaf of bread a crime—in front of policemen so they could be sent to prison. In prison they could eat.

Under "Operation Bootstrap" things have changed. Much has been written about it of which the following statement is typical:[31]

Looking at Puerto Rico today, it is hard to realize that only seventeen years ago the Island was an underdeveloped area typical of many underdeveloped areas throughout the world. As recently as 1940, Puerto Rico had an agricultural economy dependent almost entirely upon sugar cane. Densely populated and with few natural resources, the Island bore all of the earmarks of underdevelopment: low wages, poverty, mass unemployment, too few schools, poor housing, and poor health conditions. Puerto Rico in 1940 was often referred to as "the stricken land" and "a land without hope."

The following interesting statement on "Operation Bootstrap" appears in *Methodism in Puerto Rico* recently published by the Division of National Missions of the Board of Missions of the Methodist Church.[32]

---

31 *Puerto Rico's Operation Bootstrap* (PROB), published by Commonwealth of Puerto Rico, Department of Labor, Migration Division.

32 Department of Research and Survey, *Methodism in Puerto Rico* (MPR), 4-5.

. . . The program of self-improvement entered into by the present Government of Luis Muñoz Marín is a most ambitious one and achieving amazing success in education, public housing and economic development. "Operation Bootstrap" program is transforming much of the Island's life. This transformation is more far reaching than is generally recognized. Take the field of education, public schools have been established at an amazing rate. A conference with officials in the Board of Education, including the Commissioner, unfolded an amazing success story and what is more significant, plans for the future which, if achieved, will bring within the range of every Puerto Rican youth the possibility of achieving a high school education with the University of Puerto Rico ahead. In spite of the limited number of high schools available the present enrollment at the University is phenomenal. In spite of this great influx of students plans are made to expand its facilities looking confidently toward the day when the University of Puerto Rico will be classed as one of America's greatest universities.

One must not conclude that this quest for education is limited to the youth alone. An equally amazing story of adult education could also be told. Seldom in the annals of mankind is there to be found the story of people whose thirst and pursuit of knowledge equals that of modern day Puerto Rico.

What is true in the field of education is equally true in the housing, health and economic fields. Truly here is a great people on the march. Methodism will need to stretch herself to achieve a spiritual advance paralleling that promised by "Operation Bootstrap."

Recent statistical data published by the Commonwealth of Puerto Rico comparing conditions in Puerto Rico now with those that existed at the beginning of "Operation Bootstrap" show how significant the gains have been. As will be seen in the following table, the general death rate has been greatly reduced as well as the infant mortality rate, and life expectancy increased 22 years between 1940 and 1957.

	1940	1955	1957
Population	1,869,255	2,263,000	2,281,000
Birth rate per 1,000	38.5	35.0	32.6
Death rate per 1,000	18.4	7.2	7.0
Rate of natural increase	20.1	27.8	25.6
Infant mortality per 1,000	113.4	55.1	51.4
Life expectancy at birth	46 yrs.	68 yrs.	68 yrs.

Source: *Facts & Figures,* January 1959 edition, published by Commonwealth of Puerto Rico, Migration Division, Department of Labor, New York.

[162]

The next table shows the changes that have taken place economically. Whereas 30 percent of the national income in the period 1939-40 still was derived from agriculture, including the principal cash crops that the island economy had depended on for so many years, in the period 1957-58 only 14 percent of the national income was derived from that source.

	1939-1940 Amount	%	1957-1958 Amount	%
Total national income	$225,000,000	100.0	$1,079,000,000	100.0
Agriculture	68,500,000	30.4	155,000,000	14.4
Manufacturing	25,700,000	11.4	230,900,000	21.4
Construction	2,500,000	1.1	46,700,000	4.3
Transportation and pub. ut.	15,600,000	6.9	96,100,000	8.9
Trade and services	43,600,000	19.3	226,100,000	24.7
Government	44,800,000	20.0	227,400,000	21.1
Other	24,700,000	11.0	56,600,000	5.2

Source: *Facts & Figures,* January 1959 edition, published by Commonwealth of Puerto Rico, Migration Division, Department of Labor, New York.

According to the publication from which the above data were taken, the number of manufacturing establishments had increased from 798 in 1939-40 to 2,032 in 1957-58. Employment in manufacturing occupations increased from 25,758 to 74,577 in the same time period. Average family income rose from $660 in 1940 to $2,400 in 1956, an increase of 263.6 percent. In family purchasing power there was an increase of 80.2 percent after allowing for the rise in the cost of living in the period 1940-56.

Puerto Rico has become famous for its slum clearance and housing program. For the rural areas it has had a social program for building thousands of new homes of concrete. These are sanitary, hurricane-proof, fireproof, and attractive at a cost of only $300. Discussing what has been done in the urban areas Professor Hanson says:[33]

> In an almighty effort, the government plans and builds low-cost housing projects, decent, sanitary, sturdy, the inhabitants of which are charged rent according to their ability to pay. One such project, within the city limits of San Juan, comprises 7,000 concrete houses and is considered the largest single low-cost housing project to be built anywhere in the Western

33 Hanson, TSPR, 356.

world; it amounts to the building, in one great mass production operation, of a city of between 20,000 and 30,000 people, with stores, schools, movies, roads, bus lines, paved streets, sewer facilities, running water, electric light and power, adequate sanitary and health environment, and all the other things that go into a modern urban settlement. Slum clearance projects, decently designed and priced apartment dwellings, spring up in all the various cities, one by one as plans are completed and money is available with the help of federal aid.

The significance of Puerto Rico's development economically, politically, and socially in the present world situation has been pointed out by many persons. Speaking of the problems of the vast underdeveloped areas of today's world in the Introduction to Professor Hanson's book, Chester Bowles says:[34]

> At a time when we Americans urgently need to burn deeply into our private consciences and public policies a sympathetic grasp of the hopes and strivings of the underdeveloped world, it is both fortunate and arresting that Puerto Rico can teach us so much.
> . . . More than most Americans, those who live in Puerto Rico share the hopes and heartaches of that two thirds of mankind who remain ill clad, ill housed, and ill fed. Yet nowhere, except perhaps in the agricultural settlements of Israel or in some of the industrial and village projects of India, have there been pioneering efforts at economic development which match in promise the techniques recently evolved in Puerto Rico.
> For Puerto Rico has been a microcosm of evils recurring in much of the world. Indeed the same central problems seem inescapably to repeat themselves wherever people are emerging from colonialism. . . .
> For all that it accomplished as the local adjunct of the New Deal in the nineteen thirties, the Puerto Rico Reconstruction Administration early demonstrated the ineffectiveness of a rigid planning, which was benevolently prepared and supervised by a government outside the immediate context of local needs. Thus a decade ago Puerto Ricans learned a lesson which should now be a truism: that if a people are to be saved from whatever danger threatens them, whether it be the militant aggression of communism or the social scourge of poverty and disease, they will in the last analysis save themselves through their own indigenous power, pride, and responsibility. If outsiders are to be helpful, their help must take the form of friendly and unobtrusive support.

---

34 Hanson, TSPR, ix-xii.

Cultural Difference

We have seen that there is a considerable consensus among the authorities as to the distinctiveness of Mexican and Hispano culture, especially in its rural setting. Frequently it is offered as an outstanding contemporary prototype of the folk pole of a folk culture to modern-man continuum. No such degree of consensus exists as to the character, status or the rate of change of Puerto Rican culture. There are wide areas of disagreement and a flourishing debate.

Theodore Brameld's recent study underlines this diversity of opinion at many points. In discussing whether or not the distinctions of Puerto Rican culture are being "assimilated" and replaced by North American traits he summarizes the reactions of his "leader respondents" as follows:[35]

> Several refused to admit that, as defined, this process has thus far actually occurred in important ways. The majority held that assimilation has occurred, but again they disagreed as to where and what kind.

Scholarly opinion ranges widely. At one extreme there is a tendency to stress the likeness of Puerto Rican and mainland U. S. culture and to deny sharp difference almost entirely. Dr. Ayala of the University of Puerto Rico expressed this view and deserves somewhat extended quotation:[36]

> In relative and indefinite terms it is acceptable, no doubt, to refer to a Spanish culture, as well as to a Puerto Rican, Colombian, New England, or California culture. This points out local variations, and there is no harm in it; we all understand each other. But in more precise terms, and taking the word "culture" in a strict sense, the United States and the Spanish American countries, together with England, France, Spain, and others, belong to the same Western culture, internally diversified, of course, until it reaches the social atoms which are human individuals. We may properly speak about impact, collision, overlaping, or assimilation, only when cultures of completely different and independent roots come into contact. This concept of acculturation or transculturation would be valid, for example, to study the relationships of the European conquerors, colonizers, or immigrants with the Indians of the Americas.

---

35 Brameld, ROC, 160.
36 Francisco Ayala, *"The Transformation of the Spanish Heritage"* (TSH), *Annals of the American Academy*, Jan. 1953, 104-105.

The cultural relations between Puerto Rico and the United States are of a very different nature, because when political contact started with the American invasion of the island, Puerto Rico was already a territory perfectly and completely incorporated into the Western culture, within the Spanish branch, just as the United States was, under the Anglo-Saxon branch. The cultural imbalances which the political diminion could have caused . . . would be, rather, maladjustments between two sections of the same culture, and only in these relative terms should they be considered.

Not even in the very fundamental aspect of religion should we speak about an impact of different cultures; for even though in one country the Reformed churches are prevalent while in the other it is the Catholic Church, they are both forms of Christianity, and the prevalence of each church is moderated and balanced by the respective influence of the strong North American Catholic majority and of the Puerto Rican Protestant minorities.

However it should be noted, that this is the same Professor Ayala cited at the beginning of this chapter. At another time and addressing a somewhat different audience, his position comes closer to a middle ground; Spanish culture does have a distinct place. "Even after three—or more accurately, four— centuries, the form impressed on our culture in the sixteenth century has persisted in its essential character of humanistic Christianity . . . the archaistic Spanish culture offers, in its pure tradition, inestimable resources capable of rendering invaluable services to a world in the throes of spiritual reorganization."[37]

The other extreme is expressed by Dr. Reuter of Fisk University in one of the last articles that he wrote.[38] For him, writing in 1946, Puerto Rico's cycle of change is "perhaps a paradigm of folk contacts generally."[39] In his eyes the Spanish culture strain on the island is "medieval" not modern.[40] Moreover:[41]

The masses of the population were little touched even by the culture of Spain. They had no possessions and no economic or

---

37 Ayala, IOC, 237-242.

38 Edward Byron Reuter, "Culture Contacts in Puerto Rico" (CCPR), *American Journal of Sociology,* Sept. 1946, 91-101.

39 Reuter, CCPR, 93.

40 Reuter, CCPR, 94.

41 Reuter, CCPR, 94.

[166]

social opportunities. They were engaged in crude and simple types of agriculture learned from the aborigines; they had few tools or other work equipment. Their habitations were for the most part such as they had learned to construct on the Indian pattern. When slavery was abolished in the nineteenth century, the freedmen, like the other landless persons, had a semi-servile status. They had no chance to advance economically or otherwise in the social scale. They were illiterate and quite unaware of changes in the outside world.

The impact of mainland culture on this society has been rapid and severe, "more happened in the first two decades of American life than in the four centuries of Spanish occupation."[42] The result as Reuter saw it was confusion:[43]

> Much that has come to Puerto Rico from the mainland contacts has been bewildering rather than enlightening. With a four-hundred-year background of primitive, folk, and medieval culture, the people had a slender basis for understanding and adjustment. In consequence, they were brought within the economy without being brought within the culture. The externals of American life were superimposed; the essentials of Western culture have not been assimilated. The medieval values remain. In the present, Puerto Rico is neither Spanish nor American; it is something of both—a mixture in externals of the medieval and the modern, not a fusion and blending of cultural realities.

If change was rapid in the first twenty years of U. S. possession it has been breath-taking in the thirteen years since Reuter wrote. Without minimizing the present differences of "informed" opinion on crucial questions in relation to the Puerto Rican culture, certain points of fairly general agreement seem to have emerged. Among them are:

1. As compared with most of the Spanish areas of settlement in South and Central America the aboriginal Indian influence on Puerto Rican culture is relatively slight. Indeed Brameld goes so far as to say that "little if anything of unique importance from the pre-Spanish epoch of the Island can be singled out as a trait or complex of its living culture."[44]

2. By contrast with the isolation of the Mexican situation,

---

42 Reuter, CCPR, 95.
43 Reuter, CCPR, 98.
44 Brameld, ROC, 150.

[167]

the Puerto Rican experience has been that of multiple influence.[45]

> As "the crossroads of the Caribbean" it has been influenced by four great caravans of culture—the Indian nations, Spanish colonists, African slaves, and North American capitalist-democrats . . . these four caravans . . . have been the most impressive and direct.

Its nature as an island and its location make its history and its present that of a crossroads—and its culture also a crossroads, mixed culture.

3. Again by contrast with Mexico, and however its past may be characterized, it stands now much closer to the modern-industrial pole. The folk culture origins are far more remote, even questionable. The dominant migrant flow to the U. S. mainland—from the Puerto Rican cities and from the Mexican rural villages—reenforces this contrast. As is frequently true the borrowings from the mainland in this area are most quickly and most strongly in the economic fields and in manufacturing as over against agriculture. Brameld's exploration of cultural "assimilation" with "leader respondents" in Puerto Rico provides evidence:[46]

> The largest affirmative consensus was at the point of economic processes—merchandising, banking, and manufacturing all being selected by one or another to exemplify its accomplishment . . . agricultural practices, moreover, are considerably farther away from assimilation than are industrial practices.

4. Puerto Rican culture, again however characterized, is changing and changing very rapidly, both from internal and external—mainland—stimulation. Here Brameld, Ayala and Reuter, together with almost all other commentators would find common ground. Brameld's selection of book title, *The Remaking of a Culture*, and the chapter heading of the sections just quoted, "A Culture in Dynamic Flux," tell the story, just as do the bare statistics of "Operation Bootstrap."

As with the Spanish-speaking people of the Southwest certain special areas of cultural difference, friction and majority

---

45 Brameld, ROC, 150.
46 Brameld, ROC, 160.

discrimination require special attention. The special areas considered in the Puerto Rican case are language, education, racial attitudes and religion.

Language

Even today some Americans think that Puerto Rico is rapidly becoming an English-speaking country and "the picture of a Puerto Rico where the Spanish language is retreatng before the advances of English is widespread also in the Spanish American countries," according to Dr. Ayala. He reports an incident that bears this out.[47]

An example of this wrong idea is the question put recently by Congressman E. H. Hedrick of West Virginia to Mr. Antonio Fernós-Isern, the Resident Commissioner of Puerto Rico, asking if the majority of the Puerto Ricans *still* speak Spanish. Mr. Fernós-Isern answered: "The community language of the island is Spanish. Puerto Rico is a community of Spanish extraction completely. Naturally, the people speak Spanish in the family, from father to child, as English is spoken in the United States." He added that about 3o per cent speak English fluently, and that "most of the population understand English to the extent to which they have been educated.

However, Ayala adds that there has been considerable modification of the language and, in the opinion of many, considerable deterioration as a result of American educational policy as discussed elsewhere.

There seems to be no official tendency to substitute English for Spanish in the printed or spoken language of the island. On the contrary, the Department of Education of Puerto Rico in 1948 decided to go into the publishing business because of the small amount of material available in Spanish and the needs of the educational program for such material. Hanson stresses the value of many of these publications for better inter-American relations, mentioning among others the publication of the first objective and scholarly text on the history of the United States that ever has been available in Spanish.

But the use of English is growing. Professor Hanson adds:[48]

47 Ayala, TSH, 104.
48 Hanson, TSPR, 329-330.

One of the marked features of Puerto Rico's changing culture is the present swelling demand for instruction in English— by taxi drivers and waiters who serve a swelling stream of continental customers, by Puerto Ricans who work in factories managed by continentals, by Puerto Ricans who plan to migrate to the continent either permanently or temporarily as members of harvest gangs, by men and women in all walks of life as well as by their children. Under current systems and orientation, it will not be many years before all Puerto Ricans are bilingual.

Professor Ayala offers this modification:[49]

> We cannot talk of bilingualism (for this consists of the indistinct and alternative use of both languages), and much less of hybridism. The native language of the island is Spanish; and English is learned as a second language. Its knowledge is essential for practical and cultural reasons, so it is a general aspiration that it be spread and perfected as much as possible.

But even though English is being taught in the schools and there is evident desire among the people of the island to learn English, it remains true that Spanish is the language that most migrants will be using on their arrival on the mainland.

On the mainland, there has been some difference of opinion on the use of Spanish in the schools. English, of course, is the language of instruction used and there seems to be no intention of introducing instruction in Spanish. However, some educators have recommended the employment of bilingual teachers wherever possible for at least a period when adjustment is most difficult. Others hold that knowledge of Spanish is useful for teachers of Spanish-speaking children but not essential.

The school system in New York City has operated on the latter basis for the most part with the result that many Puerto Rican children not only have not learned English but have missed a great deal of the content of the school programs. Describing this situation in his recent book about Spanish Harlem, Dan Wakefield gives the following examples:[50]

> . . . The case of "Manny," the father who wants to go to school and study agriculture—but first has to learn to read and

---

49 Ayala, TSH, 108.
50 Dan Wakefield, *Island in the City* (ITC), 158 and 171-172.

write in the evenings after his laboring job because he was
pushed through and out of the neighborhood schools without
those basic skills—is not an unusual or isolated case. The
kids of average intelligence or above average intelligence who
can barely cope with the basic uses of the English language
when they get out of school are not the exceptions but the rule
in this community. The roots of the tragedy reach back hundreds of years.

María Flores, who went through this system, and now is
watching her daughters go through it, explained that in cases
where the family speaks mainly Spanish at home and the teachers speak only English at school, "the first couple of years
are lost on the kids. It takes a couple of years before they
understand English well enough to really know what's going on,
and by then, of course, they've lost all the instruction they
should have been getting in the other subjects in the first two
years. They never really catch up."

Wakefield says that the New York City Board of Education's
first active attempt to cope with the language problem came
in 1948 when the Substitute Auxiliary program was devised.
Under this program, teachers that were bilingual in Spanish
and English were to meet in the morning with small groups
of newly arrived children to help "orient" them to the community and teach them fundamental English and in the afternoon they were to meet with newly arrived parents. Only eight
such teachers were hired in 1948 but by 1957 the number had
increased to 76 for the city. The author's judgment is that this
was obviously a valuable but stopgap program for a school
population including more than 100,000 Puerto Rican students
although it was seldom related to the regular classroom instruction.

"In the classroom itself," he says, "there were few bilingual
teachers, and by 1958 there still were relatively few on a regular basis. The stringent, often criticized requirements of dic-
tion and accent set by the New York City school board for
regular teachers makes it extremely difficult for bilingual
teachers with a Spanish-speaking background to get anything
but a substitute position in the school system."[51]

Wakefield cites a report of the Education Division of the
Commonwealth of Puerto Rico Migration Division in New

---

51 Wakefield, ITC, 172.

York City to the effect that there are a great many qualified teachers of Puerto Rican origin living on the mainland who have not been able to get employment in the city schools. He quotes from the report as follows:[52]

> . . . The study was made on the basis of 155 Puerto Rican teachers whose applications for employment were on file with the Commonwealth of Puerto Rico's New York office. All but three of the applicants held college degrees. There were 132 with Bachelor's degrees and twenty with Master's degrees. Eighty-eight (57 per cent) of the applicants indicated that their English was "fluent"; and fifty-eight (37 per cent) that it was "moderate." Seventy-four of the applicants attended a series of orientation conferences sponsored by the Commonwealth, and twenty-four others completed a fifteen-week English-improvement course. Out of that number a representative of the Education Division of the Commonwealth of Puerto Rico Migration Division said that in 1958 only "several" had been hired as regular teachers in the New York school system.

The recently published report sponsored by the New York City Board of Education called *The Puerto Rican Study, 1953-1957*, is primarily concerned with the teaching of English to Spanish-speaking children particularly the methods that have been found most effective. One of the conclusions reached as a result of the research done was the conclusion that "knowledge of Spanish is useful but is not essential to successful teaching of English to Spanish-speaking children."[53] The weight and interpretation of this particular conclusion in the implementing of the study remains to be seen.

Wakefield cites in the following quotation a very different emphasis by the subcommittee on Education, Recreation, and Parks of the Mayor's Committee on Puerto Rican Affairs on the basis of its study in 1951:[54]

> In the schools whose total school population is over 26% Puerto Rican, only 5% of the teachers claim any skill in the use of Spanish. In districts having 49% and 42% Puerto Ricans, we find that only 7.6% and 6.1% respectively of the teaching body can communicate with the pupils or their parents in a

---

52 Wakefield, ITC, 173.

53 *The Puerto Rican Study, 1953-1957*, sponsored by The Board of Education of the City of New York, under a Grant-in-Aid from the Fund for the Advancement of Education, 1958, 96.

54 Wakefield, ITC, 173-174.

common language . . . If increased proportionately to the
Puerto Rican school population, we should need approximately
1,000 real-Spanish-speaking teachers . . . Almost one third of
the schools reporting have no Spanish-speaking teachers.
We disagree with the viewpoint that the teachers' use of
Spanish in the classroom serves as a crutch. If we accept as
our basic goal the child's adjustment to his new environment,
it is important that he communicate . . . in Spanish until he
is able to express himself somewhat adequately in English.

The program worked out by the Board of Education is based
on English textbooks and guides apparently assuming that
the teacher does not know Spanish. The report itself contains
no explanation of the basis of the findings that knowledge of
Spanish is not essential.

Education

One of the most widely-talked-about aspects of Puerto Rico's
progress since 1940 is the progress that has been made in the
field of education. Under Spanish rule, there was almost no
educational program for the people as shown by the fact that
in 1899 only 8 percent of the children of school age actually
attended school. Under the first thirty years of administration
by the United States, school attendance increased but because
of the educational methods imposed by the administration in
Washington, there was grave dissatisfaction among Puerto
Rican educators and widespread resentment among the people.
Dr. Earl Parker Hanson, Executive Secretary of the Puerto
Rican Planning Division of the Reconstruction Administration
in 1935-36 and in 1952 organizer of an inter-university area
study course on the island conducted jointly by the Universities of Delaware and Puerto Rico, speaks out of extended experience and with real insight. He summarizes U. S. educational policies as follows:[55]

> When we stepped into the Puerto Rican scene in 1898, one
> of our first steps was to enlarge the island's school system con-
> siderably and to reshape it toward the end of accelerated
> Americanization. Continental educators who knew nothing
> about Puerto Rico and its problems went to the island as
> commissioners of education and shaped curricula after conti-
> nental patterns, regardless of whether they were suited to the is-

55 Hanson, TSPR, 52-53.

land's needs. Puerto Rican children early began to learn about the United States; their social studies deal with life in the United States rather than with the Puerto Rican life to which they must adjust themselves; most of the history taught them was the history of the United States; their books were written in English and designed for continental students rather than for Puerto Ricans.

Worse yet, it was decreed early that all the teaching in all the grades had to be done in the English language. That was supposed to be a good way in which to teach English to the Spanish-speaking Puerto Ricans, and to make them truly bilingual. It didn't work. Teachers who knew no English suddenly had to acquire it for fear of losing their jobs; thereafter they had to do their teaching in a language that was poorly mastered and foreign to them. Children who had never in their lives heard any language but Spanish were suddenly expected, on entering the first grade, to master the three R's and other subjects, taught to them in a language they knew nothing about, by teachers who spoke it poorly and had difficulty in expressing themselves in it. The result was not any sudden, miraculous mastery of the English language by the Puerto Ricans; it was confusion mounting toward intellectual chaos and compounded by resentment.

In 1930, the situation improved with the appointment of Dr. José Padín, a Puerto Rican, as Commissioner of Education. Dr. Hanson continues:[56]

> . . . He managed to install important reforms under the so-called Padín plan, in which all the teaching in the primary schools was done in Spanish, but English became a required subject of study. The plan was extremely popular and worked excellently, until the turbulent year of 1936, when the Nationalists embarked on a program of violence and assassination and in some American quarters got all the Puerto Ricans blamed for the acts of a few fanatics. That was the year when tensions began to mount, and relations between Puerto Rico and Washington became badly strained. Senator William H. King of Utah, as head of the Senate Committee on Territories, made a quick trip to Puerto Rico to see what was wrong. As a result of his visit, the English language, instead of remaining a desirable subject of study, again became a political football. The chain reaction set off by King resulted in a situation in which the Americanism and loyalty of many a Puerto Rican came to be judged, not by his knowledge of the English language, but by his attitude toward the fantastic reforms

56 Hanson, TSPR, 53-54.

instigated by Washington; if he deplored those reforms because they were obviously bad pedagogy, he was widely accused of being un-American or anti-American.

Federal officials took King in tow on his arrival in Puerto Rico and organized a motorcade which drove to all parts of the island to show the Senator how the Puerto Ricans lived and what the United States was doing to alleviate their lot. But he seemed in no way interested in slums or in reconstruction projects, or in anything else except the question of whether little boys and girls spoke English. . . .

From 1936 to 1948, the educational system of Puerto Rico was in a turmoil largely over the question of English versus Spanish as the primary language in the schools. "Finally, in 1948," says Professor Hanson, "Congress gave the Puerto Ricans the right to elect their own governor, who could, in turn, appoint his own Commissioner of Education, responsible to the governor and people of Puerto Rico rather than to some accidental, obdurate Senator with fixed ideas but little knowledge of Puerto Rican life and affairs."[57]

Despite the controversy over language that persisted until 1948, considerable progress began to be made in the educational system with the coming into power of the Popular Democratic party in 1941. "Probably no place in the world has made as many gains in such a short time as this Commonwealth of the United States," says a recent publication of the Puerto Rico Department of Public Instruction. The following excerpts from this publication indicates the kind of progress that has been made:[58]

> Puerto Ricans are justifiably proud of the progress they have made in the last few years in many phases of their educational program. Probably no place in the world has made as many gains in such a short time as this Commonwealth of the United States.
>
> Puerto Ricans usually employ the year 1940 as the base for their statistics. That date is considered by them the beginning of their modern era. In that year there were 303,000 children in school. Today there are 533,000. In 1940 only 50% of the children from 6 to 18 years of age ever got to school. Today 72% of the Puerto Rican boys and girls of that age group are in school.

57 Hanson, TSPR, 60.
58 Leonard S. Kenworthy, *Education in Puerto Rico* (EPR), 3, 4 and 5.

Under their Six Year Plan a goal was set for 1960 of 91% of the pupils of elementary school age in school. That goal has already been achieved.

Even more important is the increased "holding power" of the schools. In 1948 about 50% of the children had dropped out by the end of the third grade. Today the majority of pupils stay in school through the sixth grade.

In the last 14 years there has been a phenomenal increase in the number of high school pupils. In that year there were only 10,000 students in high schools. Today there are over 40,000.

Literacy has increased from 69% to 78% in the intervening years since 1940. . . .

Spectacular progress has been made in vocational education, an essential part of the industrialization of the Island.

One of the most notable aspects of the educational program in Puerto Rico is the enthusiasm that has been aroused in the people, according to Professor Hanson, who says that the entire society from the loftiest professor to the lowliest *jibaro* is education-minded as never before. He attributes this largely to the role that the educators of Puerto Rico have defined for public education and uses as one illustration of this a Puerto Rican-prepared article that appeared in the Cuban magazine *Carteles* of April 26, 1953. We read, says Professor Hanson, that the aims of the island's public instruction are:[59]

. . . to improve the pupils' physical, mental, and spiritual health; to raise the living standard of the Puerto Rican people; to educate the people in optimum utilization of available resources, in the improvement of domestic and individual economy, in the frugal life, and in the spirit which shapes and tempers attitudes toward material necessities; to teach that the maximum fruition of man is through creation rather than acquisition; to improve the tone of human relations through instruction as well as practical examples of collaboration in matters of respect and consideration for others; to develop skills for communication and the solution of problems through the wide administration of various curricular materials such as reading and writing, the natural sciences, mathematics, the social sciences, and vocational arts; and finally to develop firm sets of values and respect for the same.

Dr. Theodore Brameld, who very recently published the results of his 3-year study of Puerto Rican education in its rela-

59 Hanson, TSPR, 320.

tion to the changes that are taking place in Puerto Rican culture, expresses the belief that the Puerto Rican experience has great significance for both the so-called underdeveloped countries of Latin America and for the United States in its dealings with these countries. "For, in myriad ways," he says, "Puerto Rico has at least as much to teach as it has to learn. With all its differences, the character of its culture and the effort it exerts to build a strong program of public education are rewarding, even exciting, lessons to countries that in some respects may be richer or more experienced."[60]

The vitality of Puerto Rico's educational program, Dr. Brameld says, is evidenced by the continuous questioning and study that goes on among Puerto Rican educators for the right solution of such basic questions as:[61]

1. What is the purpose of education?
2. What is education's proper role in a period of cultural change such as the island is now experiencing?
3. Should education be "deliberately and consciously concerned to help citizens come to terms with the interactive effects of North American and Puerto Rican cultures upon each other"?
4. Should Puerto Rican education "promote assimilation of North American cultural patterns"?

The question of assimilation of North American culture is a vital one at the present time and one on which there is considerable disagreement. The pamphlet, *Education in Puerto Rico*, referred to above, has the following to say:[62]

> Despite the tremendous progress in Puerto Rican education in the last few years, many problems still remain to plague educators in that island Commonwealth. Some of them are the inevitable problems of a system which is bursting at the seams. Others are more fundamental problems of goals and methods of attaining them.
> One of the most basic problems is the extent to which young Puerto Ricans should be "Americanized." This is a question of long-term goals which will have to be decided by the general populace of the island, but a question on which the educators should have much to say, as it vitally affects every phase of education.

---

60 Brameld, ROC, xvii.
61 Brameld, ROC, 175-178.
62 Kenworthy, EPR, 7-8.

With close economic and political ties with the United States, with rapid industrialization and urbanization, and a growing feeling of kinship to the States, the question of how much of their Spanish background can be retained in the next generation continues to cause controversy. Certainly older and even middle-aged people are proud of their Spanish cultural heritage, but whether this pride can be developed in the oncoming generation is still open to question. Already most of the African and Indian heritage has disappeared; whether the same will eventually happen to the Spanish heritage remains to be seen.

Some educators are concerned on this point, but the role of the schools in helping to determine goals does not seem too clear at the present time. Many people hope that Puerto Rico can develop a rich cross-roads culture, moulded from the best of their European, North and Latin American traditions. But this problem of goals has not really been faced adequately by educators in Puerto Rico so far as the writer can find.

Developments in education on the island have significance for the education of Puerto Ricans who come to the mainland. Fortunately there is more and more collaboration in the working out of methods and policies. Even though there seems to be no prospect for the widespread development of bilingualism on the mainland and this means that Spanish-speaking Puerto Ricans will be handicapped in many ways, many officials, professional workers, and others who have regular contacts with the Puerto Ricans are learning Spanish. As a result of a recent thorough study of the situation in New York City, the Board of Education has developed plans that, despite qualifications made earlier, give substantial consideration to the language problems of the Puerto Rican pupils.

Attitudes on Color and Race

It is undoubtedly true that some prejudice based on skin color as well as race has existed for some time and still exists in Puerto Rico but it is also true that the attitudes there are different from those that have existed on the mainland. On the other hand, some students of island life believe that the tendency in the past to minimize the degree of prejudice on the island and to discount its significance has not been warranted.

Mills and Senior in their *Puerto Rican Journey* pointed out that discriminatory attitudes toward race had existed before the United States took over the island. Carey McWilliams in his revised edition of *Brothers Under the Skin* deals with the matter more sharply saying that "despite many eloquent disclaimers, it is quite clear that racial prejudice does exist in Puerto Rico."[63] Brameld, the most recent source available, corroborates this but says that prejudice is relatively weak though "the correlation between low income and dark pigmentation remains disquietingly high."[64]

Mills and Senior draw comparisons between island and mainland attitudes in the following statement:[65]

> When the Spaniards, who are Caucasians, represented authority on the island, the colonial, in his aspiration to achieve equality with his rulers, began to adopt their attitudes toward race. Thus, even before 1898, while the Negro was not discriminated against, the Caucasian had higher status, and wherever it was possible to do so, Negro blood was denied. But the Spaniard's racial intolerance was more subtle than the rigid distinction made in the United States, and despite the growing infiltration of United States standards, the colored Puerto Rican does possess a feeling of racial security in his own environment. Everyone is first a Puerto Rican and only second a member of a particular racial group. Problems concerning race are status problems for each individual rather than genuine "racial" problems.

McWilliams agrees that the effects of racial prejudice are very different on the island and on the mainland but he believes that a paradoxical situation exists there as the following excerpt indicates:[66]

> The existence of a large "mixed population" is what accounts for the absence of lynchings, riots, and racial violence in Puerto Rico. Cases of rape ascribed to race are almost unknown and there is little overt discrimination. Racial differences are generally ignored in shops, theaters, hotels, and public conveyances. Negroes are numerous in the teaching profession and colored youngsters attend the public schools on a base of equality. Legally sanctioned segregation does not exist in any form and the humiliation of Negroes by statute would be unthinkable. All in all, Mr. Luis Muñoz Marín was

---

63 McWilliams, BUTS, 204.
64 Brameld, ROC, 6.
65 Mills and Senior, PRJ, 7.
66 McWilliams, BUTS, 203-204.

probably correct when he wrote, some years ago, that "the nearest approach to social equality . . . within the supposedly permanent territory of the United States" is to be found in Puerto Rico. In fact Puerto Rico might be cited as a perfect illustration of the fact that social equality can coexist with racial discrimination and prejudice. Indeed this is the real Puerto Rican paradox.

For despite many eloquent disclaimers, it is quite clear that racial prejudice does exist in Puerto Rico. Mr. Muñoz Marín, for example, points out that a few "discreet instances" of intermarriage can even be noted "in the highest social pinnacles." Would these marriages be few in number or discreetly noted if racial prejudice did not exist? In the course of a chapter devoted to the thesis that prejudice is virtually nonexistent in Puerto Rico, Vincenzo Petrullo notes that "as elsewhere, it happens that most Negroes in Puerto Rico are poor and live close to the soil." Others have also noted a preponderance of Negroes in certain sections of the island and have called attention to the fact that most of Puerto Rico's slum dwellers are Negroes. Yet Negroes have lived on the island for centuries with no bars to intermarriage and little overt discrimination. Mr. Petrullo reveals the answer to the riddle—the Puerto Rican paradox—when he casually observes that "the whites being dominant, the colored element is ignored, much as we ignore the colored peoples in the States, except that the Puerto Ricans are considerably less color conscious."

On the basis of the research carried on by several students of the race problem, McWilliams comes to the conclusion that Puerto Ricans actually are very color conscious; that this is reflected in their speech and in the tendency of the Puerto Rican migrant to New York to stress "his Spanish name, his knowledge of Latin-American music and the Spanish language, and his different food habits, all by way of distinguishing himself from the mainland 'colored' (much in the way the New Mexico 'Spanish Colonial' insists that he is different from the Mexican immigrant)." Mr. McWilliams refers to Maxine Gordon's findings to show how this has affected intergroup relationships on the mainland.[67]

As Miss Gordon points out, this racial ambivalence sets up a many-sided pattern of conflict: (1) between colored New

---

[67] McWilliams, BUTS, 205-206 (Quoting "Race Patterns and Prejudices in Puerto Rico," by Maxine W. Gordon, *American Sociological Review*, April, 1949).

Yorkers and colored Puerto Ricans in competition for white social and economic privileges; (2) between Puerto Ricans, white and colored, and white residents of the mainland who are inclined to regard all Puerto Ricans as colored; and (3) between white and colored Puerto Ricans since the former do not relish being identified with the latter. "The white Puerto Rican," writes Miss Gordon, "withdraws discreetly . . . from the Negro islander. . . . When he visits the mainland, the white Puerto Rican avoids the Puerto Rican 'Harlems' in New York or elsewhere. In the relative immunity of an unknown outsider, he may even divorce himself completely from his fellow white Puerto Ricans and identify himself as 'Spanish' or 'Latin,' both terms ambiguous to the average continental. . . . Since the white Puerto Rican is never sure of his status with continentals, he denies relationship to the Negro wherever he finds him: in Puerto Rico, on the continent, in the Caribbean, or elsewhere in Latin-America. More significantly, he denies any tinge of Negro blood he himself may knowingly but secretly possess."

Brameld, whose findings on racial atttitudes in Puerto Rico are based on the opinions of two selected groups of respondents (one group of grass roots representatives and the other made up of national leaders), examined the situation from two viewpoints: 1) class structure; and 2) the island's democratic ideology and the actual practice of racial democracy. As to race and the class structure Brameld says:[68]

Any inspection of "vertical" order in Puerto Rican culture would be incomplete without attention to race relations. If the not quite unanimous judgment of our respondents was correct, attitudes toward people of color (and the infinite shadings of skin range from black through brown to white) are primarily attitudes derived from socio-economic divergences rather than from the kind of race consciousness one finds in South Africa or the Southern region of the United States.

Though one leader was sure that race prejudice is virulent under the surface, the preponderant opinion was otherwise: the average colored person is likely to have lower status and lower class position than the average white person, not because he is considered to belong to an inferior race, but because he is likely to have a poorer job and hence less of the amenities that money affords. . . .

Respondents did not deny that a limited kind of segregation occurs in island restaurants, hotels, swimming pools, and other

---

68 Brameld, ROC, 66, 103.

places where tourists and the well-to-do gather. Segregation, however, does not result from official rules established by the management (such rules would be illegal) but rather from the fact that the average colored citizen cannot afford luxury prices. That he might also feel uncomfortable for fear of being unwelcome in such surroundings may likewise be an intangible factor, as it would be in many northern cities of the Continent. At the same time, a few Negroes do appear in the most expensive establishments. More serious in terms of our problem is the fact that they were reported to be excluded by membership qualifications from most if not all upperclass casinos, from certain businessmen's clubs, and from such religious organizations as the Catholic Daughters of America.

Professor Brameld found what to him seemed to be serious "discrepancies between ideology and configuration" in the feelings of some of the persons interviewed. He says:[69]

As anyone knows who has looked into the matter, one of the most revealing tests of such feelings is that of attitudes toward marriage between races. Only one of the "white" respondents on the subcultural level would have no serious objection to racial inter-marriage for his own children. Three "white" fathers insisted they would do all they could to prevent it. Reasons were diverse: one respondent said that it would "lower the race"; another said that "white is for white" and "black for black"; still another feared that his daughter would be boycotted by her friends and that his grandchildren would suffer if they went to the United States.

Brameld points out that both groups of respondents expressed the opinion that "whatever race prejudice remains tends to intensify with the rising status level" but "that democracy, racially as well as politically, is far from a mere shibboleth to most Puerto Ricans—hence that an impressive compatibility is already revealed between their explicit allegiance to its principles and their implicit acceptance of them. . . ."[70]

Wakefield on the basis of his study of the people of Spanish Harlem also points up the fact that there is a tendency in Puerto Rico to draw distinctions between people of dark and light skins and contends that the situation that Puerto Ricans

69 Brameld, ROC, 103-104.
70 Brameld, ROC, 104-105.

find on the mainland tends to increase this attitude among some of them.[71]

> . . . The darker-skinned migrants did not face the new discrimination of the mainland with all the innocence that often is believed. Because there is no legal discrimination based on color in Puerto Rico, it is commonly simply stated that "there is no discrimination." But the darker-skinned people on the island are seldom found in office or professional positions, or in the top hotels, night clubs, or social activities. When the Puerto Ricans meet discrimination on the mainland, it is not altogether a new experience.
>
> Life on the mainland has, if anything, heightened the Puerto Rican's color consciousness, for they are anxious not to be identified as American Negroes. It doesn't take long to learn that the Negroes are lowest on the scale in American life, and in order not to be like them the darker Puerto Ricans are often the most reluctant to learn English. Speaking only Spanish identifies them as foreign and therefore not just a Negro. . . .

The literature makes it clear, however, that most Puerto Ricans, white and Negro, encounter mainland attitudes on race and color and find them most objectionable. Besides affecting conditions of their everyday lives such as where they can live and where they can work, the attitude of white racial superiority closes the avenues of communication that need to be kept open if genuine cultural exchange is to take place.

A study of *The Puerto Rican in New Jersey* found that Puerto Ricans come up against prejudice in most communities in a variety of ways. In discussing their acceptance in the community, the report says:[72]

> The Puerto Rican, like the American Negro, is a second class citizen in his community. He is discriminated against in churches, schools, homes, places of public accommodation, and employment. A member of the clergy stated that Puerto Ricans seemed to be tolerated in the churches in his community but were not really accepted. A different member of the clergy thought that the Puerto Rican would participate in community programs and activities as soon as he adjusted himself to his new home, increased his standard of living, and as soon as he learned to speak English fluently.

71 Wakefield, ITC, 38, 41.
72 Jones, PRNJ, 39-40 and 44.

Expressions and statements from public and private citizens about Puerto Ricans revealed attitudes of mistrust, misunderstanding, and dislike towards Puerto Ricans by half of the persons interviewed in this survey. One public official immediately exploded when he heard the name Puerto Rican mentioned. He could hardly contain himself. He finally settled down, and invited the writer to sit down with him in his office and review the local situation. Before the writer left him, this official requested that he not be portrayed as being prejudiced against Puerto Ricans. The unfortunate condition here, is that he is in a position to let any Puerto Rican who comes into his community feel his wrath. Another public official immediately went off into a discussion of how the influx of Puerto Ricans into his community would introduce "tropical health diseases and would increase the health problems of the community." He is a health official.

The situation in New Jersey is duplicated wherever Puerto Ricans have settled but there is evidence that some communities have met the situation much more adequately than others.

Religion

There are no adequate statistics either for the island or the mainland on the religious preferences of Puerto Ricans. Rev. David Barry, of the City Mission Society, says that "one out of every 5 or 6 Puerto Ricans coming to the U. S. has a Protestant background."[73] The Roman Catholic estimate is that "Puerto Ricans are Catholic, 90% of them, at least."[74] The variation in these estimates indicates the lack of objective data.

It has been said by a number of commentators that a large number of the island population as well as many of the migrants to the mainland have no church affiliation. It has also been said by students of the matter that many Puerto Ricans are not bound to any one religion, that many have connections with several religious groups. More than one authority has pointed to the fact that many Puerto Ricans attend spiritualist services regularly and also belong to or attend Roman Catholic or Protestant services as well, sometimes both.

---

[73] David Barry, *The Opportunity for Protestant Churches Among Puerto Ricans,* Mimeographed address at April 8, 1959 Conference.

[74] Rev. William Ferree, Rev. Joseph P. Fitzpatrick, S.J., and Rev. John D. Illich, *Spiritual Care of Puerto Rican Migrants,* Report on Conference held in San Juan, Puerto Rico, April 11 to 16, 1955, Office of the Coordinator of Spanish American Catholic Action, Chancery Office of N. Y. Archdiocese (SCPRM), 7.

After spending six months in Spanish Harlem, Wakefield came to the conclusion that "most Puerto Ricans seem to have a marvelous, immense capacity for religion."[75]

> Ramón Diaz, the adult director of a teen-age club in Spanish Harlem, is a whole appendix in himself to William James' Varieties of Religious Experience. Ramón was baptized a Catholic, came from the Island to the mainland on a Bahai pilgrimage, joined the East Harlem Protestant Parish, and attends the private sessions of the spirits. He, like nearly every other Puerto Rican, sees nothing contradictory or strange in devotion to different religions at the same time. Ramón is an honest man, and he is faithful to all. Why shouldn't he be? They all have different functions and serve different purposes. As María Flores explained her view of these functions, "You go to the Catholic church to get baptized and married and have the last rites." For day-to-day hopes and fears, however, the contact with the spirits of the dead and their specific cures and revelations seems more the answer. There are many in the neighborhood who take an active part in the community activities of the Protestant churches, belong to the Catholic church, and attend spiritualist sessions in the homes of friends.

According to a recent study sponsored by the Social Science Research Center of the University of Puerto Rico, *The People of Puerto Rico*, there are three main religious groups in the island—the Roman Catholics, and two groups of Protestant denominations. The study includes in one Protestant group such denominations as Episcopalians, Methodists, and Presbyterians who adhere to the "zoning agreement" that was drawn up at the time of United States occupation of the island. In the other Protestant group, the study includes the Pentecostals and other groups that began work in the island somewhat later than the other denominations. Spiritualism, which finds widespread adherence, the authors believe to be a supplement and not an alternative to Catholicism or Protestantism.

Roman Catholicism

For the most part, in the discussions of Puerto Rican Catholicism there has been little reference to the historical background of the island. The study referred to above discusses

---

75 Wakefield, ITC, 64-65.

the history of Catholicism on the island giving reasons for its strength and weaknesses. The following excerpts pertain to the 400-year period of Spanish rule.[76]

> Neither the governmental patterns nor the nature of religion in Puerto Rico during the four centuries of Spanish control can be understood without full recognition of the role of the Catholic church. Puerto Rico was colonized by Catholics acting under the sovereignty of a Catholic power in which the function of Church and State was closely linked, and it continued to be almost completely Catholic until the American occupation severed this link and permitted the entrance of other creeds.

> A number of factors prevented the integration of the bulk of the people into the institutional framework of the Church. The Church itself was poor, population was quite dispersed, and there were never enough priests on the island.

> In Puerto Rico, the general weakness of the Church in dealing with religious heterodoxy, together with its inadequate personnel and sheer physical inability to reach the people, made its religious ministrations rather ineffective. It succeeded in preventing Moors, Jews, Protestants and other non-Catholics from entering the island, but it could not insure religious orthodoxy among its parishioners. The people frequently did not attend mass, obtain sacraments, confess, pay tithes, marry in church, or baptize, even under the pain of excommunication. Religious heterodoxy in local belief has probably existed since the sixteenth century. The cult of the saints, belief in magic, and perhaps many Indian and African Negro beliefs developed in the context of a nominal Catholic ideology.

> Discredited because of its political subordination to Spain, the Church lost much of its already weakened spiritual power over the island's population. The Church could not exact piety from the people by resorting to use of the State apparatus. Its efforts to enforce Church marriage, for example, merely linked the Church and the repressive labor laws of the State in the minds of the people. . . . In 1861, the mayors of the island were ordered to turn over to the parish priests the names of all people living in common-law union. The priests in turn were to exhort the sinners to marry in church. In case of refusal, such individuals were liable to prosecution under the vagrancy laws. . . .

> As the gap between the people and the Church widened, different groups in the population turned to various religious al-

---

76 Julian H. Steward and associates, *The People of Puerto Rico, A Study in Social Anthropology* (POPR), successively pages 42, 43, 44, 60, 84-85, 86, 87.

ternatives. Some upper-class Puerto Ricans, many of them anti-Spanish in their motivation and attracted by the rationalist trends in European thought which accompanied the political upheavals of the nineteenth century, became skeptics, free-thinkers, or formed lodges of Freemasonry. An illegal group of Protestants was organized near the town of Aguadilla in the 1860's. . . . Other groups of the same kind met in secret, read the Bible in Spanish, and propagated anti-Spanish senti-ment along with Protestant belief. . . .

The Steward study summarizes the developments since the end of Spanish rule and describes some of the changes that seem to be related to the influence of the American branch of the church on the island.[77]

After the United States became sovereign over Puerto Rico, the Catholic church was completely dissociated from govern-ment, and the island opened to missionization of Protestant sects. The weakened and discredited position of the Catholic church during the nineteenth century had permitted consider-able heterogeneity in local belief and practice. The economic and political events of the twentieth century brought further heterogeneity, and the introduction of Protestant churches made it possible for new types of institutionalized religion to sup-plant Catholicism in certain areas while Catholicism itself took on new meanings in others.

During the present century, the total membership of the Catholic church has increased, but so has that of the various Protestant denominations. The relatively weaker position of the Catholic church is best revealed by the attendance figures. A survey of the tobacco, coffee, and fruit regions showed that only 62 per cent of the Catholics attend church, although the frequency rate of attendance is not stated. Data from a sugar plantation showed that only 57.1 per cent attend church.

Certain aspects of Catholicism, however, make for ready ac-ceptance of the Church. For example, the Church continues to attach more importance to salvation through dispensation of the sacraments than to ethical decisions in daily life, which re-sult from a strongly emphasized individual conscience. . . .

Today's religious societies, many of which have American origins and which align members along age, sex, and class status lines—for example, the Holy Name Society, the Daughters of Mary, the Catholic Daughters of America, the Knights of Co-lumbus—may be supplanting the saint cults. These have the form of the urban *cofradias*, or *sodalities*, and appear to be a product of lessening isolation, of a decline of local cultural

---

[77] Julian H. Steward, POPR, 84-87.

differentiation, and of an increase in American cultural influence. How far they manage to integrate the rural areas into their activities is still unknown. . . .

Summarizing the developments in the 20th century, Dr. Steward says:[78]

> While the twentieth century may be regarded as a period of diversified institutionalized religions in Puerto Rico, it is also a period during which the social and political functions of religion were sharply curtailed. The traditional social and political binding force of Catholicism—never too strong—gave place to new binding forces that developed from new patterns of cultural organization. Economic and social sanctions replaced religious ones in large areas of behavior. . . . In so far as religion had a place in the new values, Protestantism, which has always been concerned with individual needs rather than with ritual conformity, exerted a strong appeal. But Protestantism never became as all-pervasive as Catholism had once been, for there are many areas in modern life that have grown away altogether from the sphere of religion. . . .

Brameld in his brief discussion of religion in the island, agrees in general with the Steward study. He finds, as others have, that the "services of the Catholic Church are attended regularly by a much larger proportion of women than men."[79]

Despite the growth of both established and Pentecostal Protestantism, it has been the general assumption that the great majority of Puerto Ricans remained attached to the Catholic Church. This is the view of the Catholic Church itself which still claims most of the population of the island. A recently published report of a conference on the "Spiritual Care of Puerto Rican Migrants," shows that the Church is now giving a great deal of attention to the needs of the people of the island as well as of the mainland. The following quotation indicates the thoroughness with which they are facing the situation on the island.[80]

> Finally, the religious background was placed in a focus that made it very clear. Father Boyd's description of his parish with 92,000 souls and seven priests; Father Gregory's report of 8,000 souls for every priest; impressed upon the participants the over-

---

78 Julian H. Steward, POPR, 29.
79 Theodore Brameld, ROC, 105.
80 Rev. William Ferree and Associates, SCPRM, 17-18.

whelming task of so few trying to develop a strong faith in so many. The immensity of the problem was made doubly clear as the participants visited the parishes on the Island and observed the geographical area, sometimes approaching a hundred square miles, covered by a single parish—so often by a single priest—and the extremely difficult, mountainous terrain which a priest must cover, sometimes on foot or by mule, in visiting his flock and often saying Mass only once a month in each outlying mission.

Still more impressive than the evidence of the difficulties was the evidence of the remarkably vigorous and dynamic Catholic life of the island. A hasty review of the papers read is enough to convince the reader of the increasingly fruitful apostolate of the Church on the Island. Still more convincing to the participants was their own observation of the growing number of churches, chapels and schools, often matching if not surpassing in beauty and functional design some of the finest Catholic buildings of the Mainland. . . .

More important than these external signs was the evidence, sincerely and repeatedly given, of the deeply Catholic spirit of the Puerto Rican people. . . .

The report of the conference referred to above shows that the Catholic Church is studying the situation among Puerto Ricans on the mainland with similar thoroughness.

Protestantism

The Steward study presents its picture of Protestantism as it has developed in Puerto Rico.[81]

After the United States occupation of Puerto Rico, the Protestant churches undertook large-scale proselytization programs in the island. These programs had their greatest impact in the cities and towns, rather than in the rural barrios. . . .
While the organized Protestant churches have made inroads on the religious monopoly previously held by the Catholic church, they have not succeeded in penetrating the rural areas in strength. . . .
In missionizing the island most of the leading denominations agreed to divide Puerto Rico into zones, each to confine its activities to one such division. Towns with a population in excess of 10,000 are open to competition by all groups. The local denominational groups co-operate in an island-wide federation which runs a training seminary. However, the mission boards are in certain other of their activities somewhat more

---

81 Steward, POPR, 408, 87 and 88.

competitive, each trying to assign credit for Protestant achievements to its particular denomination. In contrast, the Seventh Day Adventists and the Pentecostals do not consider themselves bound by the zoning agreements. These denominations show the most clearly demarcated lower-class characteristics, and they have grown more rapidly than any of the other denominations on the island. Their churches are entirely self-supporting and do not in any way depend on the policy of the mission boards in the United States. They thus show greater flexibility in adapting themselves to local conditions, and their preachers are often laymen without any previous training in formal theology. In contrast to the other denominations which try to combine a more staid form of service, on the pattern of American Protestant middle-class behavior, with a combination of social service work and schooling, the Pentecostals permit the individual considerable freedom of expression, including the conversion of religious ecstasy into bodily move-

A number of characteristics tend to emphasize the class character of the Pentecostal type groups. While they share the taboos on drinking, dancing, smoking, and sexual promiscuity with other Protestant denominations, they follow lower-class custom by refusing to make an issue of consensual marriage. They employ secular, lower-class recreational patterns—like beating rhythm and singing to the accompaniment of guitars and other instruments—in the religious service. On the other hand, they de-emphasize the classic Protestant ethic of hard work which is stressed by other Protestant groups who apparently would have the workers adopt middle-class standards. ments.

The study also found the influence of Pentecostal groups very strong in the rural areas. In one barrio on the southern coast which the authors have called Barrio Poyal, the study describes the work of this denomination as follows:[82]

> In Barrio Poyal, the Pentecostals are led by a lay pastor who continually travels (and on foot) throughout the barrio to conduct services regularly in Oriente, at Vieja, at the barrio beach, and in the small, remote colonias in the north of Poyal. . . . This pastor devotes himself with utter selflessness to his faith; he supports himself and his family with a portion of the contributions made by church members plus the money his wife earns as a seamstress. He and his family live in a fashion equal in its humbleness to that of his neighbors. An old building, which once held the barrio's biggest store, has been rented by the faith and is used almost nightly for meetings. Benches have been built, the interior painted, a welcome sign hung out, and

---

82 Steward, POPR, 408-409.

the building thus transformed into an acceptable place of worship. The Pentecostal sect, like many fundamentalist sects, is marked by its uncompromising opposition to such local customs as drinking, dancing, and gambling. . . .

One important feature of the Pentecostal service is its emphasis on participation. Everyone can sing, everyone can undergo the religious experience which involves the taking on of an exalted, translike state (promesa), everyone is made to feel that his participation is an essential of the religious procedure. This participatory character of the Pentecostal church, though it may afford amusement to some, must be seen also as one component of its success.

The majority of both the barrio and the municipio congregations is male, and it is mainly to men that the appeals of the Pentecostals seems directed.

Since each of the three main competing religious groups (Catholic, established Protestant, Pentecostal) has some Poyal adherents, it is difficult at first glance to see how class differences may be operating in terms of religious affiliation. In the town, however, the differences between Catholic and Protstant churches on the one hand, and the Pentecostal church on the other, are quite noticeable. The town Pentecostal church, unlike the other two, lies several blocks away from the central plaza; it is supported by local contributions only, and is a much poorer and more poorly equipped building than are those of its rivals. It has been pointed out, too, that the Catholic and Protestant churches make their appeals particularly to the middle-class people in town; the Pentecostal church concentrates on the poorer people.

It may be said that the only religious spirit that is expressed in Barrio Poyal which may come to mean significant changes in the very immediate future is that in the Pentecostal faith. In broad terms, however, religion is not an important force in the barrio. Attitudes toward the universe and life appear to be markedly secularized. . . .

Spiritualism

The same study has the following evaluation of the impact of spiritualism on the island:[83]

The impact of spiritualist beliefs seems to be greater in communities which are now undergoing comparatively rapid culture change than in those isolated, culturally homogeneous areas of small farms, where the saint cult is strong, or in areas which have been proletarianized for a long time. That is, spiritualism seems to occur primarily among sociocultural groups

---

83 Steward, POPR, 88.

which are losing or have recently lost their traditional way of life. It attracts socially maladjusted individuals—those who are attempting to maintain their traditional social role and status in a changing society and those whose special psychological organization makes it impossible for them to function smoothly in their own sociocultural group and who seek contact with the supernatural to restore or achieve status.

Wakefield finds that Puerto Ricans on the mainland have very much the same religious tendencies as those on the island. He finds effective work being done by both Pentecostal churches and the denominations that have been established longer as well as the Catholic Church. However, he emphasizes the tendency to embrace more than one religion and the strength of Spiritualism.

Padilla also found a tendency to embrace more than one religion in the group she studied. She says:[84]

> In religion members of the same family may hold different views, and small children may be allowed to choose the church they wish to attend, regardless often of their parents' own church membership. So, it was not strange that the grammar school age children of a Pentecostal minister in Eastville were members of the Presbyterian church. In principal, "All religions are good, they all believe in God," and it really does not make much difference which particular church one follows. All that is necessary, it is said, is that "one must believe in something," and to religion appeals are made in crisis and desperation. Children, nonetheless, should go to some church as part of their growing up, for it helps them to be good.

Rand's description of Puerto Rican religious life in New York City is as follows:[85]

> . . . Most Puerto Ricans are Roman Catholics in theory, but they are not too well integrated or disciplined into the Church on their island. Besides, there has long been an anti-clerical tendency there, and it has been strengthened by nearly six decades of mainland American rule. Many Puerto Ricans who come up are inclined away from the Church to start with, and when they settle into a Puerto Rican neighborhood they find no Church structure dominating its social life, as would be the case at home. So they break off and join one of the Protestant store-front congregations—perhaps one to which relatives

---

84 Elena Padilla, *Up From Puerto Rico* (UFPR), 124.
85 Rand, TPR, 20 and 21.

or fellow-townsmen of theirs belong already—and this gives them a new focus for their emotions.

Of course a vast number of the migrants remain true to the Catholic Church, but as a rule these are absorbed into existing parishes; they don't change the facades on the Puerto Rican streets. Many who *don't* remain true to the Church, besides, continue to use Catholic images—most Puerto Ricans, including Protestants, seem to have a general belief in these.

Puerto Ricans on the Mainland

Many characteristics of the Puerto Ricans who have come to the mainland that would be of concern to the churches have not been dealt with thus far. In a sense they cannot be adequately dealt with without original research. There is a serious lack of systematic, penetrating or comprehensive study of the Puerto Ricans on the mainland. This is to be accounted for partially by the comparative newness of the Puerto Rican migration and its fluidity, as well as by a considerable diversity among the Puerto Ricans.

A good many communities have brought together factual reports about the Puerto Ricans in their areas but these reports quite naturally have tended to be confined to the securing of the more obvious types of information such as the numbers of Puerto Ricans coming in, where they concentrate, the jobs they hold and the conditions under which they live.

Some characteristics of the Puerto Rican population on the mainland that would have broader significance would include:

1. The extent to which their purpose in coming to the mainland is economic betterment and whether they will tend to return to the Island when the Island economic conditions reach the point at which the economy can support its population adequately.

2. The extent to which the present Puerto Rican population is a transient population.

3. The extent to which Puerto Ricans have the ability to move into jobs of greater skill than those most of them now hold.

4. Their interest in organizational activities including unions.

5. The extent to which they tend to avoid the ghetto life and move into all areas of the community.

[193]

6. The influence of mainland life on Puerto Rican families. The community studies that have been made for the most part do not cover such points and where they are mentioned there frequently is rather wide difference of opinion, coupled with a lack of decisive data.

Economic Betterment

There is quite general agreement that one important reason for coming to the mainland is the better economic opportunity offered. Mills and Senior emphasize this in *Puerto Rican Journey*. The economic situation in Puerto Rico in relation to the rate of population increase provides the push, and better pay on the mainland when jobs are available provides the pull. Rand found this to be true when he visited the island in 1957 before publishing his recent book. He says:[86]

> Why Puerto Ricans leave home is a question one gets many answers to. A couple of these are definite and incontrovertible: Puerto Ricans leave home because there are too many of them there, and because they can earn more money in New York or its hinterland. Even despite the migration to our mainland, 15 percent of the Puerto Rican labor force is said to be unemployed now, and another 15 percent employed but partially; able-bodied men with any ambition naturally abhor that situation. As for the pay difference, one often hears that Puerto Ricans can earn twice as much in New York as on their island, and that living costs in the two places differ little except for the item of fuel and warm clothes in the New York winter. This is probably an exaggeration, yet by and large more pay can be made in New York (in good times)—and more can be saved, too, or spent on TV sets or washing machines.

Aside from the wages themselves, Elena Padilla in her recent study found that Puerto Ricans like to come to the mainland because of the greater number of things they can buy, though they often find themselves weighed down with debt as a result. She says:[87]

> More things can be bought in New York, and many, such as furniture, clothes, and appliances that ease housework, can be obtained on the installment plan. Not only do such articles become necessities, they are also regarded as symbols of gen-

---

86 Christopher Rand, TPR, 51-52.
87 Padilla, UFPR, 30.

eral welfare and success. In Puerto Rico these were considered to be available only to the rich. In New York lending companies offer loans through circular letters and suggest borrowing a lump sum to pay off small, separate debts. Unexpected layoffs and underemployment point up the ephemeral quality of Puerto Ricans' economic security and well-being, and while the search for another job continues, welfare aid may have to be secured or severe hardships faced.

Mills and Senior as well as others point out that the rate of migration declines in periods of even minor recessions on the mainland. Rand quotes an official of the island as saying:[88]

"We know exactly when there's to be a recession on the mainland," one such official remarked to me. "We have only to watch the Puerto Ricans coming back here. They are the last to be hired and the first to be fired, and if a slump is coming they know it right away."

Transients or Settlers

Miss Padilla would divide Puerto Ricans on the mainland roughly into two categories on the basis of their attitudes toward settling on the mainland or returning to the island at some future time. She states her point of view as follows:[89]

Many Hispanos see their lives and those of their children as unfolding in this country. To them, Puerto Rico is something of the past, and for many of the children who are growing up or have grown up in the United States, Puerto Rico is less than an echo; it is a land they have never visited, a "foreign country." Some migrants consciously decide at some point or other to make their homes here, to stay in this country permanently, never again turning back to look at Puerto Rico. These are to be found even among recent migrants. They are the people who view their future as being tied up with whatever life in New York may offer. We can call these Hispanos settlers, and can distinguish them from transients or those who regard their future life as gravitating toward Puerto Rico and who hope to return to live there later on, after their children have grown up or when they have enough savings to buy a house or start a business.

She describes the settler and the reasons for his tendency to settle as follows:[90]

---

88 Rand, TPR, 52.
89 Padilla, UFPR, 301.
90 Padilla, UFPR, 301-302.

Settlers who have migrated to New York as adults are those who have lost or who give little importance to their relationships with their home towns, their friends and relatives who are still in Puerto Rico or are recent migrants to New York. They have cut off their emotional ties with the homeland, but they may still have significant interpersonal relationships with their kin and within cliques that may consist largely of persons from their own home town who are residents of New York. The settler fulfills or expects to fulfill his social needs in relation to living in New York.

One sort of settler has in his formative years moved away from his home town, rural or urban, in Puerto Rico to another town or city in the island itself. He started to break away from the primary relations and bonds of his home town then. By the time he comes to New York, he has already experienced life situations in which primary groups derived from his home town contexts have no longer operated for him, in which he has developed new social bonds, wherever he may have been. The primary group relationships of this kind of settler lack the continuity and history of those of the settler who, throughout his life, whether in Puerto Rico or New York, has been able to continue depending and relying on persons known for many years.

The transients she characterizes as follows:[91]

> The migrant who is essentially a transient, on the other hand, still maintains ties with the homeland: he has a strong feeling of having a country in Puerto Rico, a national identity there, and there he has friends and relatives whom he writes, visits, and can rely upon. "If things get bad" (si las cosas se ponen malas), he can go back to Puerto Rico and get sympathy and help from those he grew up with. The transient migrants can be expected to feel obligated to their Puerto Rican friends and relatives, should these come to New York. The settler, on the other hand, is likely to say that he will "not return to Puerto Rico even if I have to eat stones in New York," and he will feel less bound to friends and relatives left in the island.

"But becoming a settler," she says, "does not necessarily involve a conscious decision. Transients may change into settlers as life orientations and social relations that are satisfactory and meaningful to them become part of their life in New York. The fundamental difference between settlers and transients is

---

91 Padilla, UFPR, 303.

that the settler's life is organized in New York, while that of the transient is both in New York and in Puerto Rico."[92]

Miss Padilla does not attempt to estimate how many of the mainland Puerto Ricans could be classified as "settlers" and how many as "transients." This would be very important to know especially if the proportion of "transients" tends to be much higher than the rest of the population. Presumably she takes into consideration the economic factors mentioned above that might be responsible for many Puerto Ricans returning to the island who under other conditions would tend to remain here.

Occupational Advancement

Many reports on Puerto Rican migrants explain that they began coming to the mainland in large numbers because of the demand for unskilled and semi-skilled labor resulting from the restrictions in immigration from Europe. It has been said by many that Puerto Ricans, like earlier immigrants, have had to take the lower-grade jobs because that is where the demand was. A study by Rutgers University explains what has happened as follows:[93]

> The expanding economy of the United States, added to the social mobility of older immigrant groups, produced a demand for unskilled and semiskilled labor, and, at the same time a proportionately smaller supply of available manpower in these occupational categories. There were, thus, opportunities available for workers willing to perform jobs that were unappealing—because of the nature of the work and the relatively low wages—to American workingmen. For the Puerto Rican, the opportunities offered were no worse than those open to them at home. Besides, the pay and stability of the jobs were much better than could be expected, generally, in Puerto Rico.

Rand describes the occupational situation of the Puerto Ricans in New York as follows:[94]

> On the job-ladder the Puerto Ricans share the lower rungs with the Negroes, but do not share them equally. The Negroes have a slight advantage in most lines, because of language and because they have been here longer. This does not apply to the

---

92 Padilla, UFPR, 303.
93 Fred O. Golub, *The Puerto Rican Workers in Perth Amboy, New Jersey* (PRPA), 3.
94 Rand, TPR, 9-11.

garment trade, though, where Puerto Rican women are in great demand. Puerto Rico has an old tradition of fine needle-work, and Puerto Ricans are also rated high in both "manual" and "finger" dexterity. . . . The Spanish-speakers make up almost a fifth of the ILGWU's New York City membership, and one hears that the garment industry would be in a bad way without them. . . . You can find Puerto Rican men in those shops too, and in many other of the light New York manu-facturing plants. . . .

Many Puerto Ricans also work at assembling TV and elec-tronic equipment in New York and nearby cities. Many are messenger-boys. And of course many work in hotels and res-taurants, chiefly in the lower jobs like those of busboy, dish-washer, or vegetable man, though they can rise a good deal higher if they learn English and are determined. . . .

There are some two thousand Puerto Rican civil servants in New York, with an association of their own. Many of them are mail-carriers and the most august of them, perhaps, is a ship's architect in the Brooklyn Navy Yard. . . .

Speaking of Puerto Ricans employed in foam rubber manu-facture, the same author says:[95]

The men catering to these demanding tastes included many Puerto Ricans, and I learned from a foreman that in this plant, again, the Puerto Rican's main difficulty was with language. Weakness in English could prevent them from advancing into really skilled jobs, for in these they would have to follow or-ders that came in on paper, as blueprints or as notes with di-mensions written in.

Discussing the capacity of Puerto Ricans for advancement on the occupational ladder, Rand says:[96]

The Puerto Ricans' capacity for further advance into mod-ernism is something I have heard different views on. In labor circles I have heard that they are often not ambitious on a job, and will refuse promotion to some higher stratum—to the op-eration of a more complex machine, for instance—because the pay there is only a dollar more a week, say, and they are happy where they are. I have also heard that many gifted Puerto Rican youths drop out of the educational system in New York be-tween junior and senior high school because they don't know their own potentiality—they can't visualize how much higher they may climb in the end if they keep up their schooling.

---

95 Rand, TPR, 141.
96 Rand, TPR, 145-146.

Rand quotes an informant who had observed Puerto Ricans here and Mexicans in the Southwestern part of the United States as believing that Puerto Ricans are considerably less primitive by our standards than the Mexicans. The reasons for this, Rand's informant said, were as follows:[97]

> The Mexican culture at home has never felt the impact of our own as the Puerto Rican has since 1898. Perhaps as a result the Puerto Ricans are relatively aggressive, in a good sense. They feel they are pioneers when they come to New York, and they look eagerly to whatever is new. They are willing to work well and hard. They have real manual dexterity, as they show in the garment industry and in assembling TV and radio sets. The Mexicans don't get into things like that, though. They are much more tied to a preindustrial culture—they have more identity with older folkways.

More and more Puerto Ricans are getting experience in certain industries on the island so that the general level of experience probably is higher each year among the migrants who come to the mainland.

Interest in Organizations

There has been considerable discussion as to the Puerto Ricans' adaptability to organization. Some say flatly that the Puerto Rican is not organization-minded. This would make him seem very queer to most mainlanders whose affinity for organizations seems to be boundless. There is no evidence, however, to indicate that when an organization seems to have some genuine purpose such as a labor union, political club, or parent teacher association, the Puerto Rican is as willing to support it as any one.

The interest of Puerto Ricans in the labor movement is well known. Though some have had unfortunate experiences with racketeering unions, they seem to be as interested in labor organization as the average worker. The Rutgers University study reporting on the five major manufacturing industry groups in Perth Amboy in which Puerto Ricans are most likely to be employed—food, apparel, leather, stone, and primary metals—discusses union affiliation as follows:[98]

---

97 Rand, TPR, 144-145.
98 Golub, PRPA, 14.

Only a very small number of Puerto Ricans in Perth Amboy had belonged to, or had any experience with unions while in Puerto Rico. However, approximately one-half of the Puerto Ricans employed in Perth Amboy now belong to unions.

In those firms where they are required to join the union, they become union members in much the same way as do other employees. Union officials report that their Puerto Rican members are no better or no worse than other members. They do not present any unusual problems to the unions in the way of grievances or employee relations. Several unions as well as employers stated that there were fewer grievances from Puerto Ricans than from other union members.

They attend union meetings in about the same ratio as non-Puerto Rican members, but generally do not take an active part in the meetings. There is no record as yet of any Puerto Rican being elected to a union office, except for one man who serves on a shop committee.

Discussing the occupations in which Puerto Ricans are employed in New York City, Rand says that "the International Ladies' Garment Workers' Union has about forty thousand 'Spanish-speaking' members in the city—the bulk of these are Puerto Ricans. . . . The Spanish-speakers make up almost a fifth of the ILGWU's New York City membership, and one hears that the garment industry would be in a bad way without them."[99]

When the Puerto Ricans appear disinterested in organizing into groups, the difficulty may well be with the majority approach to them. Rand seems to imply this in the following excerpt from his book:[100]

Time and again, when asking experts about the Puerto Ricans in New York, I have met the complaint that they lack leadership, or lack organizations of their own. It has then come out that this is a necessity in American life now—especially, perhaps, in big cities.

Recently a social worker was telling me about his approach to the Puerto Ricans. "We visit them in the housing projects," he said, "and draw them into activities. They must have a way to express themselves, and we want to develop initiative in their community itself, so they can make a contribution. This initiative unfolds through settlement-house programs, P.T.A.-type activities, and so forth. The Puerto Rican leaders have to rise through their own circles before they can function in the com-

99 Rand, TPR, 10.
100 Rand, TPR, 150-151.

munity leadership. So we feel we must get them in action—in action together as Puerto Ricans, and then also in action with others."

At first I couldn't understand the need for all this stirring-up. But later some Health Department people told me that it was hard to reach individual Puerto Ricans here because they hadn't developed community groups through which this could be done. And other city officials told me that no minority group had grown strong in New York until it had raised up its own leaders. So finally it dawned on me that most individuals can't find a true position in society here nowadays—can't "relate," as the social worker might have put it—unless they are held in place by a tissue of clubs, unions, and other groupings.

The Puerto Ricans, it seems, are not "joiners" by tradition, and so they have a hard time fitting into this pattern of ours. On their island their family and village relationships are enough to give them a sense of "belonging," but in New York these aren't enough. Something else must be found, and that is one of the hardest parts of their adjustment. (I have been assured that the problem will solve itself, however, when New York's present Puerto Rican children grow up, as they are being fully indoctrinated—by the schools, settlement houses, boys' clubs, Scouts, and so forth—in the "joining" idea.)

Dispersion of Puerto Rican Population

In 1952, the Welfare and Health Council of New York City published a report showing the distribution of the Puerto Rican population throughout the city in 1950 by boroughs, health areas, and census tracts.[101] This report supplements the city-wide New York City data published in the Census Bureau report on Puerto Ricans in Continental United States.

The report presents the data separately for persons of Puerto Rican birth and persons of Puerto Rican parentage and also for white and nonwhite within each group. Table 1 shows the numerical distribution of the Puerto Rican population by boroughs and the percentage distribution by boroughs and within boroughs. Tables 2-A to 2-E show the numerical distribution of the Puerto Rican population and the total population and the percent which the total Puerto Rican population constituted of the total population in each health area. Tables 3-A to 3-E report the numerical distribution only, by census tracts.

---

101 Welfare and Health Council of New York City, Research Bureau, *Population of Puerto Rican Birth or Parentage, New York City: 1950* (PPRB).

[201]

Though there is much more to be obtained from the data made available in the report, it is probably sufficient here to mention some of the highlights only. Table 1 shows that more than half of the Puerto Ricans, both mainland-born and island-born, were living in Manhattan in 1950 and still larger proportions of non-white Puerto Ricans. The same table shows that Manhattan had the highest proportion of island-born Puerto Ricans and Queens the largest proportion of those whose parents were born on the island.

In interpreting Tables 2-A to 2-E which present the census data for each of the five boroughs by health areas, the report says:[102]

> Although the health area tables reveal a heavy concentration of the Puerto Rican population in certain neighborhoods, particularly in sections of Manhattan and the Bronx, evidence that the process of dispersion is underway is found in the fact that there is but one of the 352 health areas which does not have at least one resident belonging to this group. This is Health Area 79.20 in the Bay Ridge section of Brooklyn. The borough distribution figures suggest a tendency, followed by other cultural groups in the past, for families of the second generation and for families with children born here to leave the center of the City and the original "colonies." One notes that the second generation constitutes nearly 37 percent of the small Queens population of Puerto Rican background; in Manhattan, this group is less than 22 percent of the total. But, without knowledge of the age distribution of this second generation and in view of the small number in this group—about 58,700, such comments are merely speculations on straws in the wind.

The range in the proportion of Puerto Ricans to total population between health areas in the 5 boroughs was as follows by boroughs:

Borough	Minimum	Maximum	Average
Bronx	Less than one-tenth of one percent	34.2	4.3
Brooklyn	None	21.6	1.5
Manhattan	0.1	68.8	7.1
Queens	Less than one-tenth of one percent	1.6	0.3
Richmond	Less than one-tenth of one percent	1.2	0.4

---

102 Welfare and Health Council of New York City, PPRB, 2.

Almost a third of the health areas had less than 50 Puerto Ricans in 1950 and more than half had less than 100, as shown in the tabulation below:

Borough	Total Health Areas	Less than 100	Less than 50
All boroughs	352	180	106
Bronx	65	32	17
Brooklyn	118	74	52
Manhattan	89	11	5
Queens	69	54	27
Richmond	11	9	5

The 1950 census data used for this study showed only 19,631 "non-white" Puerto Ricans in the city as compared with 226,675 "white" Puerto Ricans. A little over 70 percent of the 19,631 non-whites were concentrated in Manhattan as compared with 55 percent of the others. There were no "non-white" Puerto Ricans whatsoever in 113 health areas and from 1 to 5 only in 83 other health areas.

The Puerto Rican population of New York City now is much more than it was in 1950 and whether the distribution has changed relatively from borough to borough is not known.

No similar studies are known to be available for other cities which have relatively large Puerto Rican populations. The Philadelphia study reported that "at least 50% of the estimated Puerto Rican population lived in one of three areas."[103]

If New York City is at all typical, it appears that Puerto Ricans as a group tend to move out of the more concentrated areas as the housing situation provides openings. Whether this would be true if the proportion of non-white Puerto Ricans in the population were different cannot be predicted.

Family Life

As in many other areas of contemporary life among Puerto Ricans on the mainland, the characteristics of the Puerto Rican family should be examined both in the light of devel-

---

103 Arthur Siegel, Harold Orlans, and Loyal Greer, *Puerto Ricans in Philadelphia, A Study of Their Demographic Characteristics, Problems and Attitudes* (PRP), iv.

opments in the island as well as on the mainland. Steward and his associates present rather extensive data on the subject for each of the subcultures which they examined. Brameld's study also considered the Puerto Rican family in some detail as one of the social institutions with which social scientists and others should be concerned in connection with the remaking of Puerto Rican culture.

Both authorities recognize the impact of modern industrialization on family life in Puerto Rico. Brameld describes his findings as follows:[104]

> The traditional family, which includes the important *compadrazgo* relationship of ceremonial kinship, has been characterized by a powerful cohesiveness. Slowly but steadily since at least 1900, however, the effects of such forces as urbanization, industrialization, and intercultural relations are detected in a diminution of this cohesiveness. Simultaneously, the structure of hierarchical authority, though still very strong, has been modified in the direction of greater participation in family affairs by the wife and mother, by a somewhat diminished authoritarian discipline over children, and by relatively new wage-earning roles on the part of adult female members. The double standard, exemplified by the practice of concubinage, is also diminishing—faster, apparently, than consensual marriage, though this too is less prevalent than earlier as a result of legal obstacles and of such influences as organized religion. At the same time, the habit of protectiveness of children even into young maturity remains pronounced—unmarried females, for example, having considerably less freedom to associate with males than is found in the cultures of North America.

Speaking of the changing family patterns, the same author says:[105]

> Whatever instabilities the family suffers from today are enmeshed with those of the wider culture. The key to these instabilities lies in the conflict between what one respondent called the allegiance to "familialism," on the one hand, and Island-wide tasks and goals, on the other hand. Like other conflicts that we shall have occasion to examine, this one is by no means exclusively Puerto Rican. It is virtually world-wide—indeed, one symptom of the crisis in human affairs to which we have already called attention.

---

104 Brameld, ROC, 56.
105 Brameld, ROC, 57.

Steward finds that the characteristics of the family differ considerably from one subculture to another. He says:[106]

Not all community culture, however, consists of local aspects of formal national institutions. The family, for example, is an entirely local matter. It is true that a type of family may prevail over much or even most of an area and that marriage laws may be established on a national level, but the family is not part of any kind of national structure.

Within the rural neighborhoods of all four communities the family constitutes the household and forms the basic economic and social unit. The subcultural groups, however, differ greatly in the relations of the members of the families to one another and in the relations between families.

The total socioeconomic setting within which the family functions is an important determinant of certain relationships between members of the family. It conditions the relative importance of the husband and the wife and the extent to which individuals may function in independence of the family unit. In addition, consideration of property and inheritance have important bearing on whether a marriage union is consensual, civil, or religions and whether a married couple lives with the parents of one or the other spouse or sets up an independent residence. The combination of the factors has produced patrilineal families in some groups and matrilineal families in others.

Ritual kinship is a device derived from the Hispanic tradition for extending close personal relations to individuals outside the consanguinal and affinal family. *Compadres,* or co-parents, may be relied upon for help as such, and sometimes even more, than members of one's own family. The extension of personal ties through ritual kinship, however, is patterned in quite different ways, which correspond to the socioeconomic structuring of the different communities.

In discussing the future of the Puerto Rican family, Brameld ventures to state what seem to him desirable goals in the following paragraphs:[107]

Yet, even were it possible, we think it undesirable to urge the preservation of the old familial order. Undesirable because, in terms of the values of democratic living, the patriarchal structure permits too little sharing, too much arbitrary power. Undesirable, too, because we are dubious of the effects upon personality development from, say, the overprotection of children or from the circumscribed, inequalitarian privileges accorded the female sex.

---

106 Steward, POPR, 9, 472-473, 474, 475.
107 Brameld, ROC, 57-58.

At the same time, a desirable future for the Puerto Rican family does not lie in repudiation of its historic virtues. Certainly it is not to be found in the anarchic permissiveness that many Continental families have recently substituted for the overstrictness of earlier generations. The solution to the problem of too much discipline is not to discard all discipline. Nor is the solution to the problem of introverted family loyalty no family loyalty at all. Precisely because the typical Puerto Rican family has more firmly retained respect for the importance of both discipline and loyalty, it is in some ways better equipped to achieve an amalgam with the newer, more democratic trends in its culture than is the kind of North American family which too often swings to the other extreme.

Judging from what has been written about Puerto Ricans on the mainland, the tendencies that have been developing in Puerto Rico are reflected among those who migrate to the mainland, except that they seem to be more pronounced. Padilla discusses the family in a New York community as follows:[108]

> In the practice of family living, in the economy of the household, and in the organization of family life, the basic group recognized among Eastville Puerto Ricans is the nuclear family. In New York the nuclear family is more sharply delineated and has greater importance than in Puerto Rico. The extended family group as defined here in terms of a united family is still linked in many important ways to the nuclear family, but in the context of New York the concept of the united family has been and is changing. The independent life careers of nuclear families, the social differentiation in status and achievements, social race, and the different types of life outlooks and values which migrants and their children have developed in New York City have all contributed to the modification of the united family, restricting and changing many of the activities and obligations delegated to it in the context of life in Puerto Rico.

> In Eastville some individuals who considered themselves a part of a united family while their parents were alive now complain about the indifference of their relatives, particularly that of their nephews and nieces. Complaints are also heard about "how much the family members quarrel with each other when they are together." Both of these complaints are characteristic of those individuals whose brothers and sisters migrated years apart from each other and whose children have grown up in New York without much social contact or interaction with their

---

108 Padilla, UFPR, 119-120, 123.

aunts and uncles. Often these children will have felt no ties of affection and no obligations toward their relatives on meeting them in New York. It is not uncommon to hear among adults who have lived in New York all or most of their lives expressions of disapproval of their uncles, aunts, and cousins who have migrated recently. They do not see much mutual ground on which to meet, given their understandings versus those of these relatives, and they refuse to be bound in family obligations or ties or friendship with them. Young adults who have grown up in New York do, however, seem to be friendlier and more accepting of the uncles, aunts, and cousins whom they have known since early childhood. With these they maintain sustained interpersonal relationships, and may continue to do so throughout most of their lives.

The problems of family living and the decisions that affect family size, the training of children, and the behavior of family members are affected by the norms, ethical values, and religious ideas of the Hispano sociocultural group. These cannot be explained in terms of religious orthodoxies, nor in terms of the social ethics of either Puerto Rico or the United States. The norms and ethics and religion of Hispano migrants make sense only in terms of their specific Puerto Rican backgrounds and their specific life experiences in the United States.

Beatrice Bishop Berle in her study of *80 Puerto Rican Families in New York City* found that four types of family organization prevail among the 80 Puerto Rican families in her study. She describes them as follows:[109]

1. The nuclear family, a stable couple with their own child or children;
2. A stable couple with their own child or children and also a child or children of a previous union of one or both parents;
3. A woman with a child or children and without a stable male partner; and
4. The extended family, which may involve any of the above three types, plus a grandmother and married or unmarried brothers and sisters living in the same apartment, in the same building, or in the immediate neighborhood.

Though material is very scant, what there is would seem to indicate that the "extended family" which some have believed to be the typical Puerto Rican family unit has become less prevalent both in Puerto Rico and on the mainland.

---

[109] Beatrice Bishop Berle, *80 Puerto Rican Families in New York City:* Health and Disease Studied in Context, (PRF), 91.

Chapter VII

SUMMARY AND CONCLUSIONS

WHAT remains to be done is to state as concisely and explicitly as possible some major emergent issues posed by the facts and considerations dealt with in the chapters preceding this one. What does this survey of Spanish-speaking Americans, of Mexicans and Puerto Ricans in the continental United States, have to say to us?

A. Two Distinct Groups

Although both these groups have Spanish as their background tongue and both are "out groups" in the eyes of the overwhelming portion of the American majority, their differences outweigh their similarities. There are many reasons for this conclusion, some major ones follow:

1. There is very little geographic overlap in the areas of Mexican[1] and of Puerto Rican settlement. They have followed largely separate paths.

2. The migration from Mexico was and is overwhelmingly rural-agrarian; the migration from Puerto Rico was and is as overwhelmingly urban-industrial.

3. The folk-culture background of a great many Mexican Americans is relatively close and still operative, the extent of transition to modern industrial man very limited. For most Puerto Ricans who have come to the mainland this folk tradition appears to be relatively remote and vestigial, the transition has largely been made before they left Puerto Rico.

4. The typical labor pattern of the Mexican here is crude, hard, common labor, whether rural or urban. The typical labor

---

[1] "Mexican" in this section is used as an inclusive term to cover all Spanish Americans who have come "North from Mexico."

pattern of Puerto Ricans here ranges from semi-skilled to craft skilled for women and men alike.

5. Although far mlabor for both groups is still largely migratory and seasonal, this involves a far smaller proportion of Puerto Ricans than it does of Mexicans. The contrast in relative stability is an important one.

6. The residential pattern for various reasons, some of them accidental, is probably less segregated for most Puerto Ricans than for most Mexicans.

7. While direct evidence is scanty, the indirect evidence of many of the factors listed above, plus the fact of an English requirement in Puerto Rican schools, tend to indicate a substantially greater bilingual ability or at least readiness upon arrival in the Continental United States for the Puerto Ricans. This hypothesis needs and deserves further testing.

8. All Puerto Ricans are citizens, many Mexicans are not.

9. The area of greatest Puerto Rican settlement is New York City. While falling far short of perfection, both the legal protections and the "climate" against discrimination are comparatively higher than in many other sections of the country, including the Southwest (exceptions in the Southwest would be overwhelmingly Spanish background communities).

10. These and other corollary factors probably combine to indicate a somewhat lower intensity of discrimination and a somewhat greater ability to combat discrimination for the Puerto Ricans as a group.

11. While proof calls for much further study, the hypothesis is advanced that Puerto Rican readiness, willingness and actual desire for extensive cultural merger is substantially higher than that of Mexicans.

B. Yet One Problem

Although, as we have just seen, the divergences probably outweigh the similarities between Puerto Ricans and Mexicans, they are both part of one problem. This is a problem for which neither group is responsible and which affects many more Americans than the total number of both groups combined. The problem is majority exclusion, discrimination and prejudice. The fact that this is a problem created and perpetuated by the majority, defined as a "problem" by the "majority mind," makes it no less a hard fact of contemporary American life.

Historically and at present the dominant American majority has seized on observable differences as rationalization for economic exploitation and social discrimination. Five outstanding tests may be listed in approximate rank order of their use and importance for the dominant group:

1. Skin color
2. Language other than English
3. Other cultural differences
4. Economic and social class status
5. Religion other than "regular" Protestant.

On every one of these counts most Puerto Ricans and Mexicans stand indicted in the typical majority judgment. The skin color test tends to be far more exacting than that of the U. S. Census taker, and even will infer non-existent difference of skin color from the Puerto Rican or Mexican label. Actually this process of often unjustified inference tends to flow freely from any one of the points listed to any or all of the others. Under the "rules of the game" established by the majority, Puerto Ricans and Mexicans begin with five strikes against them. They are quite literally out before they have had a chance to get in the game.

This is the problem. It is very real and very deeply rooted in the habits of thought and action of "majority" Americans. The existent barriers are no less real and stubborn because they violate true Christian conscience, elementary logic or that rarity—common sense. The mission of the Christian Church is unequivocally clear. It is the breaking down of all barriers between man and man, between God's children. But the mission will not be advanced by sentimental evasions of the hard realities and the tremendous difficulties of accomplishment.

Nor will the traditional conscience salvers of seeking out a tiny token number of "nice" Puerto Ricans, Mexicans or Negroes suffice. In a very real sense the positive discrimination in favor of majority selected individuals (or of one

[210]

minority group by itself) serves to strengthen and perpetuate rather than to reduce the basic pattern of majority discrimination. As Jackie Robinson has said no Negro "has it made" until all Negroes have genuinely equal opportunity. No man, majority or minority, is free until all are free.

It is in this essential frame of reference that we turn now to a plus and minus summary of the findings of this study as they relate to Protestant missionary opportunity among Spanish Americans.

Some Plus Factors

What are some major considerations that indicate real Protestant "opportunity" in serving Americans of Spanish-speaking origin? Among them might be the following:

1. Their numbers are great and are steadily increasing. There are over 3,000,000 who have come north from Mexico, at last estimate 849,000 here from Puerto Rico. The inclusive total is probably near or over 4 million persons.

2. Both continued immigration and natural increase which outstrips the "Anglo" rate means the proportion of the total population will increase in the years ahead, barring severe depression.

3. There is a widening geographic dispersion both of Mexicans and Puerto Ricans. Accessibility (and inferentially opportunity) will become increasingly general rather than limitedly regional.

4. For the Puerto Ricans there has been another kind of dispersion. Especially in New York but also in some other cities the housing situation at the time of their arrival precluded the ghetto type segregation inflicted on previous immigrants. Their housing while usually poor is scattered throughout the city. They are "available" to many more churches.

5. Bi-lingualism, knowledge of English as well as Spanish, is bound to increase. This trend is reenforced at many points but especially by the impact of the U.S. continental schools where English is invariably the language of instruction on the children. Puerto Rican emphasis on increasing education and on English as a required subject also plays a role. Preliminary analysis of questionnaires from churches in this field indicates

[211]

the Sunday School is rare that does not employ some English.

6. While exact proportions are not known, the proportion of persons without active church affiliation is even higher than that in the general population, and higher than the homeland patterns.

7. Institutional Roman Catholicism, for many Puerto Ricans and Mexicans has had an historic identification with imperialism, exploitation and autocratic power in the homelands. It has had relatively even less success in retaining active contact in this country. For many their "church" was local, an inseparable part of the whole community; the break from the latter carried with it a loosening of the hold of all its ways. Even for many of the more broadly faithful the churches here are "different, cold, not for us." Genuine effort to improve service and relations have had only limited success.

8. Both population groups are relatively young and vigorous. The proportions of the young married, of youth and children are relatively high. This youth and vigor is a great potential asset.

9. The proportion of families and the solidarity of family ties tends to be high. Converts can be won not "one by one" but family by family.

Some Minus Factors

This having been said, what are some major considerations that pose real difficulties and barriers for Protestant work with Spanish Americans here? Among these are the following:

1. The magnet that draws these people to our shores is economic. They come for a job. Clarence Senior has said that this consideration outweighs all others, even those of extreme discrimination. Equally, they return home in large numbers when jobs become scarce. Whatever is not related to the securing and holding of a job at higher pay than at home is peripheral to their focus of concern.

2. Many think in temporary terms. A return to Puerto Rico or Mexico is a live option, both actually and psychologically. For many, especially of the first generation, the continental United States never becomes "home." The difficuities for the

established local church of the transient mentality are well known.

3. Temporariness has another dimension. With the job not the place paramount both groups are probably more mobile within the United States than is the highly mobile general population. The same problem is posed for the churches.

4. Even for those who have severed all ties to Mexico and Puerto Rico, for the very many who have no prior experience and would find themselves less at home there than here, there remain the stark facts of majority exclusion. Desire to overcome these barriers may have withered away after repeated rebuff, or perhaps the desire itself may never have found soil in which to grow.

5. The listing above suggests another hypothesis for which there is much evidence but not enough to consitute definitive proof: except in the economic—the job—sphere there is probably relatively little felt need for cultural assimilation. For many, even most, this may not be a high priority goal or even a goal at all.

6. There has been a long history of Anglo-Spanish American group conflict and mutual hostility. The authorities concur in labeling this as the major tie that binds Spanish-Americans together and makes them in any sense a common group. All institutions ascribed to the Anglos including the churches are "on the other side."

7. Our churches (and the phrase grows out of the very majority-minority dichotomy being stressed), most of them and the largest of them, tend to be located elsewhere than where Mexicans and Puerto Ricans are congregated. It must be added that many of our people—and our ministers—have little or no desire to bring the two closer together.

8. The perpetual confusion of our own contemporary and particular culture with Christianity, and the frequent substitution of the former for the latter, are far more obvious and offensive to all those on the outside than to those on the inside who often scarcely notice the substitution.

9. The present trend of "regular Protestantism" is away from rather than toward the nation's minorities. We are increasingly middle class, increasingly "status seekers," to use the

current phrase for a long-time component of our society. The success ladder we have borrowed from the culture (certainly not from the Gospel) climbs steadily away from the disadvantaged minorities. It is no wonder that the more proletarian, less inhibited "sects" have had greater success.

10. The considerations above and others contribute to a situation in which for many Mexicans and Puerto Ricans becoming Protestant is to be a renegade, a traitor. It is to betray and desert *la raza*, to be unfaithful to a vague, non-institutional Catholicism; to be, in short, a renegade from the highest group values and a deserter to Anglo ways and Anglo social climbing.

11. Some studies have offered evidence of a widespread image of Protestantism among Spanish Americans. For them the symbols invoked are strictness, pietistic negatives, coldness and colorlessness, fundamentalism, smallness and isolation. The symbols are, of course, not inaccurate for many churches working with these people in the name of Protestantism. They apply also to much of our mission work in both countries—it is a curious and significant fact that even liberal Protestants have frequently exported a brand of Protestantism very different than that believed and practiced in the sponsoring churches. With Puerto Ricans especially we are now reaping what we sowed. Our own home missions have sometimes followed the same tendency.

Need it be said, against the background of what is known of Puerto Rican and Mexican culture, that this set of images is bound to result in a highly selective appeal to relatively few and strongly deviant Spanish Americans?

Strategy of Action

Clearly there is both opportunity and need for "mission" among Spanish-speaking Americans. Equally clearly effective mission cannot be accomplished easily or without a drastic revision of past and present tactics and strategy. A new and comprehensive total strategy is required. What are some of the essential principles of such a basic strategy? These propositions are advanced:

1. There must be real comprehension and adjustment to diversity. Puerto Ricans and Mexicans are not the same. Within

[214]

each group there are sub-groups, generations at odds, and a wide range of individual variation. The situational settings vary just as widely. Response must be multiple, flexible, adaptable. The English-Spanish language question, as an important example, is not capable of an either-or answer. The pattern of offering in any large center of concentration should probably run the gamut of possible choices and combinations. This will not be accomplished without cooperative planning.

2. While effective strategy should comprehend diversity, it should also give opportunity for moving toward unity. This does not mean that the nature of that unity can or should be prejudged, but the process should encourage a continual and progressive seeking by *all* concerned.

3. It is essential that the opinions and wishes of the people most directly concerned be encouraged, respected and accorded real power in decision making. It is the last that is most crucial and least often fulfilled in our almost incorrigible tendency to paternalism. The key decisions should be theirs not ours.[2]

4. Intelligent strategy must recognize the probability of a continuing stream of arrival of both Puerto Ricans and Mexicans. Past migrations have had a relatively short history and then the streams have dried up. Strategies of step by step "assimilation" have been applicable. There is strong likelihood that the streams studied here will flow for some time. An overall strategy geared simply to the early arrivals will neglect yesterday's and tomorrow's newcomers.

5. A strategy of service rather than one of institutional aggrandizement must recognize the urgent need for church to serve as a social force active and effective in the areas of the needs of Spanish Americans. These we have seen are first of all economic—jobs, wages, opportunities for training and advancement, decent housing, the whole gamut of real economic security—and secondarily but still importantly, the combatting of all forms of group discrimination.

6. The "integrated approach" of contemporary social science

_____

2 See Appendix 1 for extended discussion of "Cultural Democracy" as it relates directly to this principle.

[215]

is necessary also for the churches. There must be recognition that economic and social discrimination is a single problem for which the majority is responsible and which affects all minorities. If the historic succession of exploited and excluded minorities is not to be perpetuated, solutions for Spanish Americans are dependent on an effective attack on the whole pattern of majority group discrimination and on all aspects of majority controlled institutions, including the church, which support the pattern.

7. Strategic attack on this great problem calls for our best efforts, our greatest skills and training in new skills, for multiple ministry and large investment.

8. Success will not be won by a sub-section of a sub-section within each denomination. It will require not only the backing but the active participation of whole denominations and the whole church. It is in our pews that an immensely powerful portion of the "majority" sits. It is we, our minds and our actions, that must be changed if this mission is to be accomplished. The real strategic target is not Puerto Ricans or any other minority or all of them together, it is ourselves and our church. We and it must be drastically reconstituted—in the Gospel terms: reborn. It is appropriate that this should be so. The issues involved are not minor, isolated, peripheral; they lie at the core of the central Christian mission. They are at least as old as Jesus and the Samaritans, as Paul and Peter at Antioch. Failure on these issues comes close to being total failure. At no point is the gap between our belief and our practice wider; at no point is it more crucial.

9. Even the whole church cannot alone and unaided expect to change our whole society. The churches' independent thrust, its clear vision of the need and program of action, its own restructuring of itself, requires supplement through alliance and coordination with all other forces working toward the same goals, particularly those organizations created and supported by the minorities themselves.

Social Science on Tactics

How then can we begin to approach such a tremendous task? Obviously victory cannot be won at one stroke or overnight. Perhaps the most helpful guidance along this line comes from the social scientific conceptions of the vicious circle and the ascending spiral as they operate in just this area of majority discrimination against minorities. Robert MacIver has said that "a thorough understanding of the vicious circle argument is an essential objective of any educational campaign against inter-group prejudice."[3] We have illustrated and discussed the vicious circle in what has gone before. It is a process in which "undesirable results become the justification of the undesirable conditions."[4]

> Its peculiar property is that it takes the existence of one link in the circle as independently given, as a fact of nature or even as ordained by God, and concludes from that premise that the next link, the behavior predicated on the earlier link, is not prejudiced or discriminatory but a rational and proper response to the inferior capacities or qualities of the group subjected to it.

One simple illustration is drawn from the writer's own experience. The scene was an Imperial Valley, California town. Majority premise: "all Mexicans are dirty." Consequence: "running water (and street paving) are unnecessary in Mex-town." Next step: cleanliness in these circumstances is extremely difficult. Majority conclusion: "You see all Mexicans *are* dirty, why waste water and paving on them."

The circle is "vicious" not only in that it allows for no prerequisites for improvement but in that it becomes a progressive justification for still further lowering of standards. A setback at any point in the circle worsens the whole situation. A decline in living standards increases majority prejudice; an increase in majority prejudice worsens living standards. So is goes.

Credit belongs to Gunnar Myrdal for stressing that the circle can work both ways. The downward spiral can become an upward spiral. Improvement at one point in the circle can start a chain reaction upward. An essential point is that some points

---

3 Robert MacIver, *More Perfect Union* (MPU), 66.

4 MacIver, MPU, 66 and for second quotation, 65. For excellent discussion of these concepts and resulting tactical suggestions see Myrdal, AAD, especially Appendix 3, 1065-1070, Goodwin Watson, *Action for Unity* and MacIver, MPU. Simmons, AAMA, uses the concept in an especially systematic way, but unfortunately in an unpublished Ph.D. dissertation.

of improvement are both more possible and more effective than others in launching a "benign" circle.

The strategic objective "must be to move through the points of least resistance to new positions, from which again it must seek out new points of least resistance."[5] Serious and highly fruitful study has been made in this area. There are many practical leads as to how best to conduct such a campaign. Such propositions as Watson's that an attack on segregation is more effective than an attack on prejudice, or McIver's priority for economic objectives, analyses such as Myrdal's rank order of prejudice and a genuine host of others can be of immense tactical help.

Rome was not built in a day, but Rome was built. The ways of building toward a society governed by "the love of God and neighbors" are difficult but passable. Do we have the will?

---

5 MacIver, MPU, 136.

Appendix I

CULTURAL DEMOCRACY

In the field of culture contact, as in intergroup relations, there has been a considerable shift of emphasis as knowledge and experience has increased. Out of a point of view that it is most desirable to have a single, *homogeneous* culture to which all newcomers must adjust, there has, in recent years, emerged a new ideal which stresses cultural diversity and cultural *heterogeneity*. It has also become increasingly recognized that the attainment of this ideal is deeply and inextricably interwoven with a second ideal: democratic intergroup relations.

Although the problem of incorporating new members into the society is and continues to be a universal problem, probably no other nation has been faced with it on such a continuing basis as the United States. From the very first contacts of the European colonies with each other and with the Indian communities which were located on the borders of the white settlements the problem has existed. The colonial period, however, was not characterized by any particular ideal or model of how different groups should meet and unite and the pattern which developed might best be described as haphazard—sometimes involving coercion, sometimes involving real cooperation, and, in other instances, simply "trial and error."

In the 1800's, increased immigration and a growing sense of nationalism led to the gradual articulation of an ideal for the incorporation of newcomers into American society. This concept—the vague but familiar "melting pot"—held that each of the cultural groups coming into the country had something valuable to contribute to the whole. From each the best should be selected; the separate strands to be woven together into a single, unique and superior "American" culture. The concept stressed cultural homogeneity or "oneness" as a way to avoid conflict and looked upon the developing cultural enclaves with suspicion.

This dream of a new American culture to which all migrant groups would contribute their best, to which all would abandon their peculiarities in haste, and which held that no one group would consider itself superior did not materialize.

The envisioned ideal had a central requirement that no one culture would dominate; all groups held an equal chance to contribute. In reality, however, a dominant cultural pattern, largely rooted in the early English settlements, was already fixed in American society. This dominant culture did not leave the way open to free exchange of ideas and behavior patterns. Attitudes of racial and cultural superiority already dominated the scene, and, as a result, the dream evolved in practice as forced adjustment to an already established culture. In its later stages it took the form of frenzied pressure to "Americanize" and nativist groups were formed which spread fear and distrust of late-coming immigrant groups.

Furthermore, the success of the melting pot also depended on a rapid surrender of traditional habits and attitudes by immigrants to those of their adopted country. But the newcomers did not automatically give up their former ways; instead, cultural enclaves, both rural and urban, sprouted. While some of the persistence of "Old World" ways could be explained as a defense against discrimination and severe pressures to "Americanize," groups less discriminated against also retained certain cultural peculiarities. What the proponents of cultural homogeneity had not adequately recognized was that cultural traits, learned over many years and integrated into the individual personality, are not dropped overnight and that to be pressured to do so will lead to defensive responses or to "cultural deterioration, disintegration of family life and maladjustments in our social life."[1]

It is largely through the increased knowledge of cultural anthropologists that a new ideal of how groups should "meet and unite" has emerged. This ideal—cultural democracy[2]—does not

---

1 E. George Payne in Cole and Cole, MAP, 147.

2 This concept also appears in the literature as "cultural pluralism," "cultural diversity," "integration," etc.

define a specific end-goal but emphasizes the *atmosphere* in which acculturation takes place.

A report submitted to the National Resources Committee of the Federal Government in 1938 discussed the inadequacies of the earlier viewpoint and emphasized the need for respect of all cultures:[3]

"The existence of diverse cultural heritages in American society has often been regarded as an evil, to be overcome as rapidly as possible. Movements initiated for the purpose of promoting harmony have sometimes tended, through excess or zeal, toward enforced assimilation or regimentation. They have tended toward the suppression of initiative, the destruction of traditional moral and artistic values, the fostering of feelings of inferiority and confusion, and toward personal and social conflict. "Assimilation, if it takes places at all must be," as Fairchild has observed, "unenforced, primarily the product of natural spontaneous associations with those who embody the assimilating nationality. It was and is a great injustice to the immigrant to assume that he might assimilate himself by an act of the will. The first step in assimilation is the cultivation by native Americans of the greatest possible sympathy toward immigrant life and culture. The first step for the immigrant is that he must have an opportunity to 'live in America.' " Blame of the immigrant for his lack of assimilation, probably the greatest hindrance to the old Americanization movement, completely prevents this sort of sympathy.

. . . the waning enthusiasm for Americanization programs and the much-advertised failure of the melting-pot are to be accepted not as failure, but as a change in emphasis—a change away from attempts to enforce conformity and toward an understanding of the fundamental conditions and character of cultural processes.

In true cultural democracy, cultural variation is not only accepted but welcomed, and cultural reciprocity or exchange between groups is viewed as a natural outcome because no group plays a completely dominating role. It provides an atmosphere in which the migrant can make adjustment to a new environment with a minimum of personal shock and loss of security.

But not only the migrant benefits from an atmosphere which encourages and appreciates cultural exchange: the larger so-

---

3 *The Problems of a Changing Population*, Report of the Committee on Population Problems to the National Resources Committee, 234.

ciety also gains by being able to learn and take from the cultural patterns of the newcomers. The end result is an enrichment of the total culture.[4]

> Cultures may develop complexity through certain internal development and variation, but by far the main source of cultural growth and development seems always to have been through the forces of external contact. Even in relatively early historic periods culture was already composite in many areas, due largely to group contact and cultural interchange. Many internal spurts of cultural development have also been the result of the stimulating "cross-fertilizing" effects of culture contact. Civilization is largely the accumulative product and residue of this ever-widening process of culture contact, interchange and fusion.

Locke and Stern also point out that the degree to which a culture continues to be dynamic may depend on its ability to permit cultural exchange. "Progress, indeed, in many instances seems proportional to the degree to which a society has a many-sided cultural exposure. Provided it can integrate them, a variety of culture contacts is a favorable situation for any culture. Groups do, of course, differ widely in their susceptibility to cultural change, but none are so conservative as to be completely resistant. Progressive societies, on the other hand, maintain and extend their formal agencies of contact, and thereby both share and contribute to the sum total of civilization."[5] Bogardus, too, states: "Cultural pluralism implies that any culture needs to make culture additions and resultant integration lest it become weak through inbreeding."[6]

Cultural diversity—if adequately understood and practiced—does not negate the central unity that each society must have to function as a whole. In fact, it has been suggested that freedom for cultural variation is the only manner in which divergent cultures can be truly incorporated into the fabric of a unified society.[7]

> Is it possible to maintain the unity necessary to a society while permitting a wide range of cultural values and group allegi-

---

4 Alain Locke and Bernhard J. Stern, *When Peoples Meet* (WPM), 7.
5 Locke and Stern, WPM, 10.
6 Emory S. Bogardus, "Cultural Pluralism and Acculturation," (CPA), *Sociology and Social Research,* Vol. 34, #2, 1949, 128.
7 Edward P. Dozier, George E. Simpson, and J. Milton Yinger, "The Integration of Americans of Indian Descent," (IAID), *The Annals,* May, 1957, 158.

ances? Most social scientists are convinced that it is possible. Indeed, they are likely to declare that only by maintenance of freedom for cultural variation can a heterogeneous society keep conflict at a minimum, preserve the flexibility necessary in a time of rapid change, and support the cultural value, so widely shared, of individual freedom.

Neither does cultural diversity serve as a means of isolating certain minority groups from the opportunities obtained by the larger society. It means, rather, that cultural groups proceed in acculturation at the speed and in the direction which is constructive rather than destructive to the groups' members. "Freedom to be completely assimilated as individuals would be a live option; but freedom to be related to the total society as culturally differentiated groups would be equally possible. . . . This interpretation implies, moreover, full equality in health services, in educational, political, and economic opportunity among all groups."[8]

While cultural democracy is undoubtedly based upon more sound sociological and anthropological knowledge than the earlier concept of the melting pot, its workability depends largely on the existence of an atmosphere in which cultural variation can exist without discrimination. "The prime obstacle in the path of the actual realization of cultural democracy is an unfortunate tradition of majority-prescribed and dominated culture,"[9] was the viewpoint of Randolph Bourne in 1920, a viewpoint which continues to hold validity into the present.

If the current barriers to it are not effectively attacked, cultural democracy will remain an unrealized and far-distant goal. Ruth Tuck has observed that in Descanso, a fictituous but yet real California town, "intercultural harmony" is often talked about but not internalized by the dominant society. The inability to give up dominance precludes a realization of the goal of intercultural harmony and exchange and reduces it to a "fad" or "fashion" rather than a workable approach to minority problems.[10]

---

8 Dozier, Simpson and Yinger, IAID, 159.
9 Locke and Stern, WPM, 689.
10 Tuck, NWF, 96.

As the new concept of culture as a way of living spreads across Descano's better educated persons, a whole train of assorted ideas is growing up in its wake. One can hear a great deal about cultural conflict and intercultural problems or, occasionally, intercultural harmony.

(but)

When Descanso talks about intercultural harmony, it still means harmony in which it carries the dominant part. We can appreciate other ways of life, it feels, but only as a preliminary to converting their ways to our ways, down to the last detail of speech and mannerism.

But even as the United States has adopted and maintains attitudes of white and Anglo-Saxon cultural superiority as part of its culture, there is some room for optimism. The attitudes of racial and cultural superiority are "culturally formed" and subject to change like any other culture trait. In this regard, Ruth Benedict has stated: "The recognition of the cultural basis of race prejudice is a desperate need in present Western civilization. . . . Traditional Anglo-Saxon intolerance is a local and temporal culture-trait like any other. Even people as nearly the same blood and culture as the Spanish have not had it, and race prejudice in the Spanish-settled countries is a thoroughly different thing from that in countries dominated by England and the United States."[11]

Thus it emerges that the barriers to cultural democracy are the same factors as those which underlie racial discrimination. Cultural democracy is not something which we now have but it is an attainable *goal* which is dependent on discovering the means to an inclusive and democratic society.

---

11 Ruth Benedict, *Patterns of Culture* (PC) in Locke and Stern, WPM, 15.

Appendix II

THE SPANISH-SPEAKING WORK
OF THE
NEW YORK CITY MISSION SOCIETY

By David W. Barry

THE NEW YORK CITY Mission Society started the first Spanish-speaking Protestant mission in New York City in 1912. It followed the pattern of work among immigrants that the Society had been engaged in since the mid-nineteenth century: a non-denominational church working in the vernacular, headed by a clergyman indigenous to the culture being served, staffed by missionaries and Christian educators, and emphasizing both education and social service in addition to a vigorously evangelical program. This church, the First Spanish Evangelical Church (now called the Church of the Good Neighbor), became the mother church for numerous other Spanish-speaking churches of various denominational affiliations, some starting as branches or off-shoots and others representing splits.

Today the New York City Mission Society is responsible for six centers of Spanish-speaking Protestant work. One, the Church of the Open Door, has so small a Spanish program that it can scarcely be counted. The others are as follows, with statistics:

| Church | Denom. | Members | S.S. | Finances | | |
				Raised Locally	Denom. Support	NYCMS Support
Good Neighbor	Non-denom.	374	597	$24,900	—	$ 54,710
Bronx Spanish	Cong.	404	474	21,448	$ 2,100	5,740
Crossroads	Presb.	425	552	24,300	16,660	24,970
DeWitt	Reformed	187	681	15,600	12,000	15,626
All Nations*	Methodist	41	55	—	2,400	840
		1,431	2,359	$86,248	$33,160	$101,886

* Financial statistics are for salary of pastor only.

[225]

About one-fifth of the Crossroads constituency and over half of the DeWitt is not of Spanish-speaking origin. The Good Neighbor budget includes the operation of a sizeable neighborhood house program.

Out of over a century of work with language groups, City Mission has evolved a framework of policy, flexible and subject to continuous refinement, but fairly clear in its outlines. The remainder of this memorandum deals with these policies.

1. City Mission makes every effort to utilize indigenous leadership. In four of the five churches, the senior minister has Spanish as his native tongue; in the fifth, a strong Puerto Rican is associate minister with freedom to develop his Spanish-speaking program along whatever lines are most effective. Thus our faith in indigenous Christian leadership is visibly symbolized in top, not secondary, positions. In two churches, the minister has an associate whose native tongue is English. The remaining staff positions are fairly evenly divided between English and Spanish.

2. The problem of securing educationally qualified indigenous personnel is usually solved by employing staff with ability, but inadequate education, and then making it possible through financial assistance and scheduling of time for them to complete their education on a part-time basis. We also have provision for educational leaves.

3. City Mission pushes its Spanish churches to assume as much financial responsibility as they can, and the annual per capita giving of $62 is evidence of our considerable success here. At the same time, we recognize that effective work in low-income, bi-lingual communities is a complex job requiring special resources, and we do not hesitate to provide substantial subsidy beyond what the members can do for themselves, in order to give the program of the church the dimensions it needs.

4. We believe that good work can be done best when housed in adequate and appropriate buildings. In the last seven years we have invested about $750,000 in new or renovated facilities for Spanish work.

5. If missions is defined as Christian outreach to groups who are economically underprivileged and/or culturally alien,

we believe both aspects should be kept in balance. Even though many Puerto Ricans are poor and uneducated, we do not make the mistake of identifying "Puerto Rican" with "poor and ignorant." We believe in maintaining a mission to a *cultural group* as well as to the deprived, and we express in our work a genuine respect for the Spanish culture and what it has to contribute to American society. It is this attitude more than anything else, I believe, that has won for City Mission the confidence of the Puerto Rican community.

6. Our basic approach to cultural assimilation is to train the younger generation to become the nucleus of the English-speaking congregations of the future. In two of the four churches, growing English-speaking congregations are being built around young adults of Puerto Rican ancestry, who are reaching out to include other ethnic elements from the community.

7. We try to maintain an educational program of the highest calibre at all age levels, under the supervision of a trained director of Christian education. We maintain a central resources office constantly screening educational materials to find those appropriate to this work; we have also actually written curricula. It will be noted that our church school enrollment is two-thirds again larger than church membership, and we assume the training we give these youngsters will determine the quality of the future church. Along with this goes a strong emphasis on leadership training, which expresses our hope that these young people will be tomorrow's church and civic leaders.

8. Our social service and group work program is as strong as we can afford to make it, in response to the immediate and urgent needs of the communities in which Puerto Ricans are required to live. As much as possible, this program too is manned by volunteers indigenous to the community rather than professionals or volunteers from outside, so that this service is seen as the church in action. An example would be our bilingual housing clinics, staffed by volunteers who have taken training in the technicalities of registering tenant complaints, applying for housing projects, etc.

9. The Society has auxiliary resources which are available

to the Spanish churches, adapted to their needs, and very much used. These include a children's camp, a family camp, a scholarship program, purchasing services, youth conferences, a bi-lingual casework and referral service, a public relations office and general supervisory and administrative assistance. Resources of this kind interwoven into the programs of the Spanish-speaking churches can give them a richness and a variety which the isolated church cannot provide.

10. Evangelism in our Spanish work takes many forms, most of them fairly conventional: the door-to-door canvass, recruitment through church members of friends and acquaintances, cottage meetings, training of children for membership Close to one-half of our members had Roman Catholic backgrounds when they came to New York City. In most of these cases, our first contact was through some program of service to specific needs, such as the housing clinic or the summer camp. At Good Neighbor, nearly half of the children in Sunday school were first contacted through the community center program.

11. We have many unresolved problems. The rigid moralism of Puerto Rican Protestantism concerning such activities as dancing is a constant source of friction not only in youth programs, but in any attempt to relate Spanish work to English-speaking constituencies. Resources in the Spanish language for Christian education at all age levels are very limited. Our Protestant work is always at a disadvantage vis-a-vis Roman Catholic work when it comes to social service resources available directly to the clergy. Trained leadership is extremely scarce, largely because the churches have not provided varied vocational opportunities for Spanish-speaking youth to train for. Our denominational and interdenominational agencies have not been very imaginative in devising ways for the Puerto Rican to feel wanted and at home in our ecclesiastical structure. Despite all this, the Puerto Rican has probably been more responsive to Protestant evangelism than any previous newcomer group from a dominantly Roman Catholic culture, with the possible exception of the earlier Italian immigrants.

March 25, 1959

BIBLIOGRAPHY

General

Adamic, Louis. *Nation of Nations* (NN). New York: Harper and Bros., 1945. Quoted by permission.

Allport, Gordon W. *The Nature of Prejudice.* Garden City, N. Y.: Doubleday & Co., 1958.

American Academy of Political and Social Science, *The Annals*, "Controlling Group Prejudice." March, 1946.

Ashley-Montagu, M. F. *Statement on Race: An Extended Discussion in Plain Language of the UNESCO Statement by Experts on Race Problems.* New York: Henry Schuman, 1951.

Ashworth, Mae Hurley, Editor. *Who?—Spanish-Speaking Americans in the U.S.A.* New York: Friendship Press, 1953. Quoted by permission.

Barron, Milton L., Editor. *American Minorities.* New York: Alfred A. Knopf, 1957.

Beals, Ralph. "Acculturation" in *Anthropology Today: An Encyclopediac Inventory*, A. L. Kroeber, Chmn. Chicago: University of Chicago Press, 1953.

Beard, Charles A. and Mary R. *The Rise of American Civilization.* New York: The MacMillan Co., 1930.

Benedict, Ruth. *Patterns of Culture* (PC). Boston: Houghton-Mifflin Co., 1934. Quoted by permission.

Berle, Beatrice Bishop. "80 Puerto Rican Families in New York City" (PRF) Health and Disease Studies in Context. New York: Columbia University Press, 1958.

Bernard, William Spencer. *American Immigration Policy—A Reappraisal.* Published under Sponsorship of the National Committee on Immigration Policy. New York: Harper & Bros., 1950. Quoted by permission.

Berry, Brewton. *Race Relations: The Interaction of Ethnic & Racial Groups.* Boston: Houghton-Mifflin Co., 1951.

Bogardus, Emory S. "Cultural Pluralism and Acculturation" (CPA). *Sociology and Social Research,* Vol. 34, #2, 1949.

————. "The Measurement of Social Distance," in *Readings in Social Psychology* (RSP). Theodore M. Newcomb and Eugene L. Hartley (Editors).

Brooks, Charles Alvin. *Christian Americanization.* Council of Women for Home Missions and Missionary Education, Movement of the U.S. and Canada, 1919.

Broom, Leonard and Kitsure, John I. "The Validation of Acculturation: A Condition to Ethnic Assimilation," *American Anthropologist*, February, 1955.

[229]

Brown, Francis J. and Roucek, J. S. (Editors). *One America* (OA). Englewood Cliffs, N. J.: Prentice-Hall, 1945. Revised Edition of *Our Racial & National Minorities*.

————. *Our Racial and National Minorities* (ORNM). Englewood Cliffs, N.J.: Prentice-Hall, 1939. Quoted by permission.

Brown, Ina C. *Race Relations in a Democracy*. New York: Harper & Bros., 1949. Quoted by permission.

Bruner, Edward M. "Cultural Transmission and Cultural Change," *Southwestern Journal of Anthropology*, Vol. 12, #2, 1956.

Burma, John H. *Spanish-Speaking Groups in the United States* (SSG). Durham, N. C.: Duke University Press, 1955. Quoted by permission.

Cole, Stewart G. and Mildred W. *Minorities and the American Promise* (MAP). New York: Harper & Bros., 1954. Quoted by permission.

Commager, Henry Steele. *Living Ideas in America*. New York: Harper & Bros., 1951. Quoted by permission.

Cultural Groups and Human Relations (CGHR). 12 Lectures before the Conference on Educational Problems of Special Cultural Groups. New York: Bureau of Publication, Teachers College, Columbia University, 1951.

Davis, Allison. "Light from Anthropology on Intercultural Relations." (See *Culture Groups and Human Relations*.) Quoted by permission.

————. "Socialization and Adolescent Personality," in *Reading in Social Psychology* (RSP). Theodore M. Newcomb and Eugene L. Hartley (editors).

Dodson, Dan W., Editor. "Racial Integration," *The Journal of Educational Sociology*, the Payne Educational Sociology Foundation, Inc., October, 1954.

Dozier, Edward P.; Simpson, George E.; and Yinger, J. Milton. "The Integration of Americans of Indian Descent," *The Annals of the American Academy of Political and Social Science*, May, 1957.

Fitzpatrick, J. P. "Mexicans and Puerto Ricans Build a Bridge: Role of the Spanish-Speaking Catholic Church," *America*, Dec. 31, 1955.

Forster, Arnold. *A Measure of Freedom*. Garden City, N. Y.: Doubleday & Co., 1950.

Gallagher, Buell Gordon. *Color and Conscience: the Irrepressible Conflict*. New York & London: Harper & Bros., 1946. Quoted by permission.

Giles, H. H., Editor. "Human Relations Education for Democracy," *The Journal of Educational Sociology*, February, 1950.

————. "Human Relations Practices," *The Journal of Educational Sociology*, February, 1951.

Gillin, John Lewis and Gillin, John Philip, *Cultural Sociology*. New York: The MacMillan Co., 1948.

Gittler, Joseph B., Editor. *Understanding Minority Groups*. New York: John Wiley & Sons, 1956.

Graham, Saxon. *American Culture* (AC). New York: Harper & Bros., 1957. Quoted by permission.

Handlin, Oscar. *The American People in the Twentieth Century* (ATC). Cambridge: Harvard University Press, 1954. Quoted by permission.

————. *Race and Nationality in American Life* (RNAL). Garden City, N. Y.: Doubleday & Co., 1957. Reprint by arrangement with Little, Brown and Co. and Atlantic Monthly Press. Quoted by permission.

Higham, John. *Strangers in the Land; Patterns of American Nativism* (SIL). New Brunswick, N. J.: Rutgers University Press, 1955. Quoted by permission.

Hirsh, Selma. *The Fears Men Live By*. New York: Harper & Bros., 1955. Quoted by permission.

Information Please Almanac. New York: The MacMillan Co., 1958.

Johnson, Charles S. (Editor). "Education and the Cultural Process," *The American Journal of Sociology*, Vol. XLVIII, #6, May, 1943.

Kahl, Joseph A. *The American Class Structure*. New York: Rinehart & Co., 1953.

Klineberg, Otto (Editor). *Characteristics of the American Negro*. New York: Harper & Bros., 1944. Quoted by permission.

Kluckhohn, Clyde. *Mirror For Man* (MFM). New York: McGraw-Hill Co., 1949. Quoted by permission.

Lewin, Kurt. *Resolving Social Conflicts: Selected Papers on Group Dynamics*. New York: Harper & Bros., 1948. Quoted by permission.

Linton, Ralph (Editor). *The Science of Man in the World Crisis*. New York: Columbia University Press, 1945.

————. *The Study of Man, An Introduction*. New York: Appleton-Century-Crofts, Inc., 1936.

Locke, Alain and Stern, Bernhard J. (Editors). *When Peoples Meet* (WPM). New York: Progressive Education Association, 1942.

MacIver, R. M. *Group Relations and Group Antagonisms*. New York: Harper & Bros., 1944. Quoted by permission.

————. *The More Perfect Union: A Program for the Control of Inter-Group Discrimination in the United States*. New York: The MacMillan Co., 1948.

McWilliams, Carey. *Brothers Under the Skin* (BUS). Boston: Little, Brown & Co., 1951.

Maisel, Albert Q. *They All Chose America* (TCA). New York: Thomas Nelson & Sons, 1957. Quoted by permission.

Marden, Charles F. *Minorities in American Society*. New York: American Book Co., 1952.

Mead, Margaret (Editor). *Cultural Patterns & Technical Change* (CPTC). The New American Library, 1955.

Merrill, Francis E. and Eldredge, H. Wentworth. *Culture and Society* (CS). New York: Prentice-Hall, Inc., 1952. Quoted by permission.

Myrdal, Gunner. *An American Dilemma: the Negro Problem & Modern Democracy* (AAD). New York: Harper & Bros., 1944. Quoted by permission.

National Resourcs Committee. *The Problems of a Changing Population*, May, 1938.

Newcomb, Theodore M. and Hartley, Eugene L. (Editors). *Readings in Social Psychology* (RSP). New York: Henry Holt & Co., 1947.

[231]

Nida, Eugene A. *Customs and Culture.* New York: Harper & Bros., 1954. Quoted by permission.

Oldham, J. H. *Christianity and the Race Problem.* New York: George H. Doran & Co., 1924.

Park, Robert E. and Miller, Herbert A. *Old World Traits Transplanted* (OWTT). New York: Harper and Bros., 1921. Quoted by permission.

Powdermaker, Hortense. *Probing our Prejudices.* New York: Harper & Bros., 1944. Quoted by permission.

President's Committee on Civil Rights. *To Secure These Rights* (TSTR). New York: Simon & Schuster, 1947.

Redfield, Robert. "Folkways and City Ways" (FCW) in Herring, Hubert and Weinstock, Herbert (Editors). *Renascent Mexico.* New York: Crown Publishers (Covici-Friede), 1935.

Rose, Arnold and Caroline. *America Divided* (AD). New York: Alfred A. Knopf, 1950.

Saenger, Gerhart. *The Social Psychology of Prejudice, Achieving Intercultural Understanding and Cooperation in a Democracy.* New York: Harper & Bros., 1953. Quoted by permission.

Sanders, Irwin T. (Editor). *Societies Around the World.* New York: The Dryden Press, 1953.

Schermerhorn, R. A. *These Our People* (TOP). Boston: D. C. Heath & Co., 1949.

Service, Elman R. "Indian-European Relations in Colonial Latin America," *American Anthropologist,* June, 1955.

Siegel, Bernard J. (Editor). *Acculturation, Cultural Abstracts, North America.* Stanford: Stanford University Press, 1955. Quoted by permission.

Simpson, George E. and Yinger, J. Milton. *Racial and Cultural Minorities: an Analysis of Prejudice and Discrimination.* New York: Harper & Bros., 1953. Quoted by permission.

Solomon, Barbara Miller. *Ancestors and Immigrants, A Changing New England Tradition.* Cambridge: Harvard University Press, 1956. Quoted by permission.

"Study of Democratic Development," in *The Annals of the American Academy of Political and Social Science,* January, 1953.

Taft, D. R. and Robbins, Richard. *International Migrations* (IM). New York: Ronald Press Co., 1955. Copyright 1955. Quoted by permission.

Tenenbaum, Samuel. *Why Men Hate.* New York: The Beechhurst Press, 1947.

Van den Berghe, Pierre L. "The Dynamics of Racial Prejudice: An Ideal-Type Dichotomy," in *Social Forces,* December, 1958.

Walter, Paul A., Jr. *Race and Cultural Relations.* New York: McGraw-Hill Co., 1952. Quoted by permission.

Warner, W. Lloyd, and Srole, Les. "Differential Assimilation of American Ethnic Groups," in Barron, Milton L. *American Minorities.* New York: Alfred A. Knopf, 1957.

Weaver, Galen R. "Toward Racially Inclusive Churches," *Social Action,* Jan., 1959.

Williams, Robin M. *American Society* (AS). New York: Alfred A. Knopf, Inc., 1952.

———. *The Reduction of Intergroup Tensions:* A Survey of Research on Problems of Ethnic, Racial and Religious Group Relations. New York: Social Science Research Council, 1947.

———. "Unity and Diversity in Modern America," *Social Forces,* Oct., 1957.

Woods, Sister Frances Jerome. *Cultural Values of American Ethnic Groups* (CVA). New York: Harper & Bros., 1956. Quoted by permission.

Yinger, J. Milton and Simpson, George E. "The Integration of Americans of Mexican, Puerto Rican, and Oriental Descent," in *The Annals of the American Academy of Political and Social Science,* March, 1956.

Young, Donald. *American Minority Peoples,* A Study in Racial and Cultural Conflicts in the U.S. New York: Harper & Bros., 1932. Quoted by permission.

Mexicans

Barherti, George C. "Social Functions of Language in a Mexican American Community" (SFL). *Acta Americana,* Vol. 5, 1947.

Beals, Ralph and Humphrey, Norman. *No Frontier to Learning: The Mexican Student in the United States.* Minneapolis: University of Minnesota Press, 1957.

Biesan, John. "Cultural and Economic Factors in Panamanian Race Relations," *American Sociological Review,* December, 1949.

Blair, William. "Spanish-Speaking Minorities in a Utah Mining Town," *Journal of Social Issues,* No. 1, 1952.

Bogardus, E. S. *The Mexican in the U.S.* Los Angeles: University of Southern California Press, 1934.

Broom, Leonard and Shevky, Eshref. "Mexicans in the United States: a Problem in Differentiation" (MUS). *Sociology and Social Research,* Jan.-Feb., 1952.

Burma, John. "The Present Status of Spanish Americans in New Mexico," *Social Forces,* December, 1949.

Common Ground, "The Mexican American: A National Concern." Summer, 1949.

Crow, John A. *Mexico Today* (MT). New York: Harper & Bros., 1957. Quoted by permission.

Encyclopedia Britannica. Vol. 15. Quoted by permission.

Fresno County Project. "Teaching Bilingual Children" (TBC). 1954 (Mimeographed booklet).

Galarza, Ernesto. "Program for Action" (PFA). *Common Ground,* Summer, 1949.

Gamio, Manuel. "Cultural Patterns in Modern Mexico," *The Quarterly Journal of Inter-American Relations,* Vol. I, No. 2. Cambridge, Mass.: 1939.

———. *The Mexican Immigrant.* Chicago: University of Chicago Press, 1931.

[233]

————. *Mexican Immigration to the United States* (MIUS). Chicago: University of Chicago Press, 1930. Copyright 1950 by the Univ. of Chicago. Quoted by permission.

Goldstein, Marcus S. *Demographic and Bodily Changes in Descendants of Mexican Immigrants.* University of Texas, Institute of Latin American Studies, Austin, 1943.

Griffith, Beatrice. *American Me* (AM). Cambridge, Mass.: Houghton-Mifflin Co., 1948. Quoted by permission.

Gruening, Ernest. *Mexico and Its Heritage* (MIH). New York: The Century Co., 1928.

Haynes, Roy L. and Johnson, Charles E. "Helping Hands Across the Border," in *Employment Security Review*, March, 1958.

Herring, Hubert C. and Terrill, Katherine. *The Genius of Mexico* (GOM). New York: The Committee on Cultural Relations with Latin America, 1931.

Herring, Hubert C. and Weinstock, Herbert (Editors). *Renascent Mexico.* New York: Crown Publishers (Covici-Friede), 1935.

Howard, George P. *We Americans North and South.* New York: Friendship Press, 1951.

Hulbert, Winifred. *Latin American Backgrounds.* New York: Friendship Press, 1935.

Humphrey, Norman D. "The Changing Structure of the Detroit Mexican Family: An Index of Acculturation," *American Sociological Review*, December, 1944.

Immigration and Naturalization Service, *Annual Report* (AR57). Washington, D. C., 1957.

————. *Annual Report* (AR58). Washington, D. C., 1958.

————. *I and N Reporter* (IN58). July, 1958.

Infield, Henrick. *People in Ejidos.* New York: Frederick A. Praeger, Inc., 1954.

Jacobs, Paul. "The Forgotten People," *The Reporter*, January, 1959.

Jones, Robert. "Ethnic Family Patterns: The Mexican Family in the United States," *American Journal of Sociology*, May, 1948.

————. "Mexican American Youth," *Sociology and Social Research*, Vol. 32, No. 4, March-April, 1948.

Kibbe, Pauline R. *Latin Americans in Texas* (LAT). Albuquerque: University of New Mexico Press, 1946. Quoted by permission.

Kingrea, Nellie W. *History of the First Ten Years of the Texas Good Neighbor Commission.* Ft. Worth: Texas Christian University Press, 1954.

Kluckhohn, Frank L. *The Mexican Challenge.* New York: Doubleday, Doran & Co., Inc., 1939.

Lewis, Oscar. "Mexico Since Cardenas," *Social Research*, Spring, 1959.

Little, Wilson. *Spanish-Speaking Children in Texas.* University of Texas Press, Austin, 1944.

Mackay, John A. *That Other America.* New York: Friendship Press, 1935.

Mann, Albert Z. "These Are Our Migrants." Minnesota Council of Churches: Minneapolis, Minnesota, 1955. (Mimeographed report).

[234]

McDonagh, E. C. "Attitudes Toward Ethnic Farm Workers in the Coachella Valley," *Sociology and Social Research*, September, 1955.

McWilliams, Carey. *North From Mexico: The Spanish-Speaking People of the United States* (NFM). Philadelphia: J. B. Lippincott Co., 1949. Quoted by permission.

————. "America's Disadvantaged Minorities," *Journal of Negro Education*, Vol. 20, Summer, 1951.

Murray, Sister M. J. *A Socio-Cultural Study of 118 Mexican Families living in a Low-Rent Housing Project in San Antonio, Texas* (SCS). Washington, D. C.: Catholic University of America, 1954. Quoted by permission.

New York Times, July 6, 1958, July 26, 1958, August 29, 1958. Quoted by permission.

Perales, Alonso S. *Are We Good Neighbors?* San Antonio: Artes Graficas, 1948.

Perry, Everett L. *Presbyterian U.S.A. Educational Work in New Mexico.* New York: Office for Field Survey, Board of National Missions of the Presbyterian Church in the U.S.A., November, 1957.

President's Commission on Migratory Labor. *Migratory Labor in American Agriculture* (MLAA). 1951.

Redfield, Robert. *The Folk Culture of Yucatan* (FCY). Chicago: University of Chicago Press, 1941. Copyright 1941 by the Univ. of Chicago. Quoted by permission.

Rivera, Julius. "Selected Characteristics of Two Migrant Groups Visiting Colorado in 1957," Colorado State Department of Public Health, Denver, Colorado, March, 1958. (Mimeographed report)

Rosenfeld, Albert. "New Mexico's Fading Color Line: Albuquerque Leads the Way," *Commentary*, September, 1955.

Samora, Julian and Deane, Wm. N. "Language Usage as a Possible Index to Acculturation" (LU). *Sociology and Social Research*, May-June, 1956, Vol. 40.

Sanchez, George. *Forgotten People*. Albuquerque: University of New Mexico Press, 1940.

Saunders, Lyle. *Cultural Difference and Medical Care: The Case of the Spanish-Speaking People of the Southwest* (CDMC). New York: Russell Sage Foundation, 1954. Quoted by permission.

————. "The Spanish-Speaking People in Cultural Transition" (SSPC). Mimeographed paper prepared for Council on Spanish American Work (Protestant) of the Southwest, Phoenix, January 21-23, 1958.

————. *A Guide to Materials Bearing on Cultural Relations in New Mexico*. Albuquerque: University of New Mexico Press, 1944.

———— and Leonard, Olen E. *The Wetback in the Lower Rio Grande Valley of Texas* (WLRG). Austin: University of Texas Press, 1951.

Sayres, William C. "Disorientation and Status Change," *Southwestern Journal of Anthropology*, Vol. 12, No. 1, 1956.

Senter, Donovan. "Acculturation Among New Mexican Villagers in Comparison to Adjustment Patterns of Other Spanish-Speaking Americans" (ANM), *Rural Sociology*, Vol. X, 1945.

Sherman, G. W. "Around the U.S.A.: A People Comes of Age," *The Nation*, March 28, 1953.

Simmons, Ozzie G. *Anglo-Americans and Mexican Americans in South Texas: A Study in Dominant Subordinate Group Relations* (AAMA). Ph.D. Thesis, Harvard University, 1952. (Unpublished).

Southwest Journal of Anthropology, Vol. 13, #1, Spring, 1957; Vol. 12, #1, 1956; Vol. 12, #2, 1956. Albuquerque: University of New Mexico.

Steinberg, S. H. (Editor). *The Statesman's Year Book*, 1952. New York: MacMillan, 1952.

Spicer, Edward H.; Dozier, Edward P.; and Barker, George C. "Social Structure and the Acculturation Process," *American Anthropologist*, June, 1958.

Stilwell, Hart. "The Wetback Tide" (WT). *Common Ground*, Vol. IX, #4.

Sturm, Roy A. *Methodism in the Rio Grande Conference*. New York: Dept. of Research and Survey, Board of Missions of the Methodist Church, 1958.

Talbert, Robert H. *Spanish-Name People in the Southwest and the West* (SNP). Fort Worth: Texas Christian University, 1955.

Tannenbaum, Frank. *Mexico, The Struggle for Peace and Bread* (MSPS). New York: Alfred A. Knopf & Co., 1950.

Tuck, Ruth. *Not With the Fist* (NWF). New York: Harcourt, Brace & Co., 1949. Copyright, 1946, by Ruth Tuck. Reprinted by permission of Harcourt, Brace and Co., Inc.

Thurston, Richard G. *Urbanization and Sociocultural Change in a Mexican American Enclave* (USC). Ph.D. Thesis. Los Angeles: University of California, 1957. (Unpublished).

U. S. Census of Population 1950: *Persons of Spanish Surname*, Special Report, P-E, #3C.

————. *Nativity and Parentage*, Special Report P-E, #3E.

————. *U. S. Summary, General*, Characteristics, P-B1.

U. S. Department of Labor. "Proceedings of Consultation on Migratory Farm Labor," 1957.

Whetten, Nathan L. *Rural Mexico* (RM). Chicago: The University of Chicago Press, 1948. Copyright 1948 by Univ. of Chicago. Quoted by permission.

Puerto Ricans

Abrams, Charles. *Forbidden Neighbors*. New York: Harper & Bros., 1955. Quoted by permission.

Anastasi, Anne and de Cruz, Jesus. "Language Development and Non-Verbal IQ of Puerto Rican Preschool Children in New York City," *Journal of Abnormal and Social Psychology*. July, 1953.

Arter, Rhetta M. *Between Two Bridges*. A Study of Human Relations in the Lower East side of Manhattan, the Area Served by the Educational Alliance, Center for Human Relations. New York: New York University Press, 1956.

―――――. *Living in Chelsea.* The Center for Human Relations Studies. New York University, 1954.

Ayala, Francisco. "The Transformation of the Spanish Heritage" (TSH). *The Annals of the American Academy of Political Science and Social Science,* January, 1953.

Barry, David W. "The Spanish-Speaking Work of the New York City Mission Society." March 25, 1959. (Mimeographed report)

Beauchamp, Mary and Associates. *Building Neighborliness* . . . in a Community on the Lower East Side of New York City, Center for Human Relations and Community Studies, New York University in cooperation with the National Conference of Christians and Jews and the University Settlement. September, 1957.

Biaggi, Jose Pedro. *The Puerto Rican Tragedy.* New York: Editorial Cronistas Ibero-Americanas, 1933.

Board of Education, City of New York. *The Puerto Rican Study,* 1953-1957. 1958.

Brameld, Theodore. *The Remaking of a Culture* (ROC). New York: Harper & Bros., 1959. Quoted by permission.

Bureau of the Census, U. S. Department of Commerce, 1950 Population. *Puerto Ricans in Continental United States.* Special Report, P-E No. 3D.

Bureau of the Census, U. S. Department of Commerce, 1950 Population. "Puerto Rico, General Characteristics." P-B53.

Bureau of the Census, U. S. Department of Commerce, 1950 Population. *Puerto Rico, Number of Inhabitants.* P-A53.

Bureau of Employment Security, U. S. Department of Labor. "Puerto Rican Farm Workers in the Middle Atlantic States." November, 1954.

Bureau of Employment Security, U. S. Department of Labor. "The Puerto Rican Migratory Program." In *Employment Security Review,* March, 1958.

Chenault, Laurence R. *The Puerto Rican Migrant in New York City.* New York: Columbia University Press, 1938. Quoted by permission.

Clark, Victor S. and others. *Porto Rico and Its Problems* (PRIP). Washington, D. C.: The Brookings Institution, 1930. Quoted by permission.

Commission on Race and Housing. *Where Shall We Live?* Berkeley and Los Angeles: University of California Press, 1958.

Commonwealth of Puerto Rico, Department of Labor. *Conclusions of Migration Conference.* San Juan, Puerto Rico: March 1-7, 1953 (Mimeographed)

Commonwealth of Puerto Rico. "Constitution of the Commonwealth of Puerto Rico," *The Annals of the American Academy of Political and Social Science.* January, 1953.

Commonwealth of Puerto Rico, Migration Division, Department of Labor. *The Jobs We Do.* 1956.

Commonwealth of Puerto Rico, Department of Labor, Migration Division. *A Summary in Facts and Figures.* New York: January, 1959 edition.

Commonwealth of Puerto Rico, Department of Labor, Migration Division. *Puerto Rico's Operation Bootstrap* (PROB).

Community Council of Greater New York, Research Department. *Fact Book on Children in New York City*. New York: April, 1957.

Davis, Kingsley. "Puerto Rico: A Crowded Island," *The Annals of the American Academy of Political and Social Science*, January, 1953.

Diffie, Bailey W. and Whitfield, Justine. *Porto Rico: A Broken Pledge* (PRBP). New York: The Vanguard Press, 1931. Quoted by permission.

Division of National Missions of the Board of Missions of the Methodist Church, Department of Research and Survey. *Methodism in Puerto Rico* (MPR). 1958. (Mimeographed)

Dodson, Dan W. *Between Hell's Kitchen and San Juan Hill*, Human Relations Studies, Inc., Center for Human Relations Studies. New York: 1952.

Dunne, Edward J. "Is Puerto Rico Next?" *Commonweal*, July 3, 1954.

Emerson, Rupert. "Puerto Rico and American Policy Toward Dependent Areas," *The Annals of the American Academy of Political and Social Science*, January, 1953.

Feldman, Arnold S. and Hatt, Paul K. "Social Structures as Affecting Fertility in Puerto Rico," *The Annals of the American Academy of Political and Social Science*, January, 1953.

Fernos-Isérn, Antonio. "From Colony to Commonwealth" (FCC). *The Annals of the American Academy of Political and Social Science*, January, 1953.

Ferre, Luis A. "The Plea of Puerto Rico," a statement read at the public hearing held at Ponce, P.R. on the 23rd of November, 1949, by a subcommittee of the Committee of Labor and Education of the House of Representatives of the United States.

Ferree, Rev. William; Fitzpatrick, Rev. Joseph P.; and Illich, Rev. John D. *Spiritual Care of Puerto Rican Migrants*, a Report on the First Conference on the Spiritual Care of Puerto Rican Migrants, held in San Juan, P.R., April 11-16, 1955.

Friedrich, Carl J. "The World Significance of the New Constitution," *The Annals of the American Academy of Political and Social Science*, January, 1953.

Galbraith, J. K. and Solo, Carolyn Shaw. "Puerto Rican Lessons in Economic Development," *The Annals of the American Academy of Political and Social Science*, January, 1953.

Gallart-Mendia, Joaquin. "Puerto Rico: Labor Laws and Their Enforcement," *Monthly Labor Review*, December, 1955.

Garden State Service Cooperative Association, Inc. "Labor Management on the Farm." Trenton, New Jersey.

Gary Post Tribune (Six Articles). "The Lorain and Gary Experience with Puerto Rican Workers." Washington, D. C.: Office of Puerto Rico, 1948.

Glazer, Nathan. "New York's Puerto Ricans," *Commentary*, December, 1958.

Golub, Fred T. "The Puerto Rican Worker in Perth Amboy, N. J.," The Institute of Management and Labor Relations, Rutgers University. New Brunswick, New Jersey, March, 1956.

[238]

Gordon, Maxine W. "Cultural Aspects of Puerto Rico's Race Problem," *American Sociological Review*, June, 1950.

Gutierrez-Franqui, Victor and Wells, Henry. "The Commonwealth Constitution," *The Annals of the American Academy of Political and Social Science*, January, 1953.

Hamilton, Walton. "The Puerto Rican Economy Linked With the Mainland," *The Annals of the American Academy of Political and Social Science*, January, 1953.

Handlin, Oscar. *The Newcomers: Negroes and Puerto Ricans in a Changing Metropolis*. Cambridge, Mass.: Harvard University Press (to be published in fall of 1959).

Handsaker, Morrison. "Seasonal Farm Labor in Pennsylvania." A Study Prepared by Lafayette College for the Pennsylvania State Department of Labor and Industry. Easton, Pennsylvania, 1953.

Hanson, Earl Parker. *Transformation, the Story of Modern Puerto Rico* (TSPR). New York: Simon and Schuster, 1955. Quoted by permission. Revised Edition to be published by Alfred A. Knopf, Inc. in 1966.

Hastings, William F. and Ruth A. *Puerto Rico Today and Tomorrow*. New York: Friendship Press, 1948.

Head, Edward D. "The Change Created by the Influx of New Racial Groups,"*Catholic Charities Review*, October, 1957.

Herberg, Will. "The Old-Timers' and the Newcomers: Ethnic Group Relations in a Needle Trades Union," *Journal of Social Issues*, Vol. 9, No. 1, 1953.

Jaffe, A. J., Editor. "Puerto Rican Population of New York City, Demographic and Labor Force Characteristics, Vital Statistics and Social and Welfare Statistics," Bureau of Applied Social Research, Columbia University. New York: January, 1954.

Jones, Isham B. "The Puerto Rican in New Jersey: His Present Status," N. J. State Department of Education, Division Against Discrimination. Newark: July, 1955.

Kenworthy, Leonard S. "Education in Puerto Rico," Department of Education Press, Commonwealth of Puerto Rico, December, 1955.

Main, Willett S. "In-Migration of Puerto Rican Workers, September 3, 1952," Wisconsin State Employment Service. (Mimeographed memorandum)

Manners, Robert A. and Steward, Julian H. "The Cultural Study of Contemporary Societies: Puerto Rico," *The American Journal of Sociology*, September, 1953.

Massimine, E. Virginia. "Challenges of a Changing Population," Center for Human Relations Studies, New York University. New York, 1954.

Migration Division, Department of Labor, Commonwealth of Puerto Rico in cooperation with Farm Placement Service, United States Employment Service, Bureau of Employment Security, U. S. Department of Labor. "How to Hire Agricultural Workers from Puerto Rico." 1953.

Mills, C. Wright; Senior, Clarence; and Goldsen, Rose Kohn. *The Puerto Rican Journey*. New York: Harper & Bros., 1950. Quoted by permission.

Monserrat, Joseph. "Background and General Information on Puerto Rico

[239]

and the Puerto Rican Migrant," Department of Labor, Commonwealth of Puerto Rico. (Paper read at 79th Conference of the National Conference of Social Workers. Chicago, May 25-30, 1952).

Moscoso, Teodoro. "Industrial Development in Puerto Rico," *The Annals of the American Academy of Political and Social Science,* January, 1953.

Muñoz, Amato, Pedro. "Congressional Conservatism and the Commonwealth Relationship," *The Annals of the American Academy of Political and Social Science,* January, 1953.

Muñoz Marín, Luis. "An American to Serve the World," a speech delivered on April 7, 1956, before the Annual Convention of the Associated Harvard Clubs held at Coral Gables, Florida. Department of Education Press, Commonwealth of Puerto Rico, 1956.

Muñoz Marín, Luis. "Development Through Democracy," *The Annals of the American Academy of Political and Social Science,* January, 1953.

O'brien, Robert W. "A Survey of the Puerto Ricans in Lorain, Ohio." Neighborhood House Association of Lorain, 1954. (Mimeographed)

Padilla, Elena. *Up From Puerto Rico* (UFPR). New York: Columbia University Press, 1958. Quoted by permission.

Perloff, Harvey S. "Transforming the Economy," *The Annals of the American Academy of Political and Social Science,* January, 1953.

Rand, Christopher. *The Puerto Ricans* (PR). New York: Oxford University Press, 1958. Quoted by permission.

Reuter, Edward Byron. "Culture Contacts in Puerto Rico." *The American Journal of Sociology,* September, 1946. Quoted by permission.

Roberts, Lydia J. and Stefani, Rosa Luisa. "Patterns of Living in Puerto Rican Families," Department of Home Economics, University of Puerto Rico, 1949.

Robinson, Donald, Editor. *The Day I Was Proudest to be an American* (DIPA). New York: Doubleday, 1958. Copyright © 1958 by Donald Robinson. Reprinted by permission of Doubleday and Co., Inc.

Rottenberg, Simon. "Labor's Role in Industrialization," *The Annals of the American Academy of Political and Social Science,* January, 1953.

Ruoss, Meryl. "Midcentury Pioneers and Protestants. A Survey Report of the Puerto Rican Migration to the U. S. Mainland and in particular a Study of the Protestant Expression Among Puerto Ricans of New York City." The Pathfinder Service for the Churches, November 14, 1953.

Senior, Clarence. "Bibliography on Puerto Ricans in the United States," Migration Division, Department of Labor, Commonwealth of Puerto Rico. New York: April, 1959.

————. "Implications of Population Redistribution," Address before the Eleventh Annual Conference of the National Association of Intergroup Relations Officials, Kansas City, Missouri, Nov. 20, 1957. Published by N.A. of Intergroup Relations Officials, New York. (Mimeographed)

————. "Migration and Puerto Rico's Population Problem," *The Annals of the American Academy of Political and Social Science,* January, 1953.

————. "Puerto Rican Dispersion in the United States," *Social Problems,* October, 1954.

————. "Puerto Rican Migration, Spontaneous and Organized," *Monthly Labor Review*, December, 1955.

————. "Puerto Rico: Migration to the Mainland," *Monthly Labor Review*, December, 1955.

————. "Strangers and Neighbors, The Story of our Puerto Rican Citizens," Anti-Defamation League, Freedom Pamphlet Series. New York, 1952.

Siegel, Arthur; Orlans, Harold; and Greer, Loyal. "Puerto Ricans in Philadelphia," A Study of Their Demographic Characteristics, Problems and Attitudes, published by the Commission on Human Relations, Philadelphia, April, 1954. (Mimeographed)

Sierra-Berdecia, Fernando. "Puerto Rico: Labor Unions and Labor Relations," *Monthly Labor Review*, December, 1955.

Sternau, Herbert. *Puerto Rico and the Puerto Ricans.* Published by the Council of Spanish American Organizations and the American Jewish Committee, April, 1958.

Steward, Julian H. "Culture Patterns of Puerto Rico," *The Annals of the American Academy of Political and Social Science*, January, 1953.

———— (and Associates). *The People of Puerto Rico* (POPR). A Social Science Research Center Study, College of Social Sciences, University of Puerto Rico. University of Illinois Press, 1956. Quoted by permission.

Stycos, J. Mayone. *Family and Fertility in Puerto Rico, A Study of the Lower Income Group.* New York: Columbia University Press, 1955.

Stycos, J. Mayone and Hill, Reuben. "The Prospects of Birth Control in Puerto Rico," *The Annals of the American Academy of Political and Social Science*, January, 1953.

Tugwell, R. G. "What Next for Puerto Rico?" (WNPR). *The Annals of the American Academy of Political and Social Science*, January, 1953.

UNESCO. *Interrelations of Cultures, Their Contribution to International Understanding* (IOC). UNESCO, Paris, 1953.

Wakefield, Dan. *Island in the City, The World of Spanish Harlem* (ITC). Boston: Houghton-Mifflin Company, 1959. Quoted by permission.

Weiss, Samuel and Jaffe, A. J. "Puerto Rico: The Labor Force and Level of Living," *Monthly Labor Review*, December, 1955.

Welfare and Health Council of New York City, "Population of Puerto Rican Birth and Parentage, New York City," published by Research Bureau, Welfare and Health Council of New York City. New York: September, 1952.

Welfare and Health Council of New York City, "Puerto Ricans in New York City," Report of the Committee on Puerto Ricans in New York City, February, 1948.

Wertham, Fredric. *The Circle of Guilt.* New York: Rinehart & Co., Inc., May, 1955.

Wickenden, Elizabeth. "Puerto Rico's Contribution to Public Welfare," The Journal of the American Public Welfare Association.

Zorrilla, Frank. "Puerto Rico: Wage Structure and Minimum Wages," *Monthly Labor Review*, December, 1955.

[241]

Published for Department of The Urban Church
Division of Home Missions

by the Office of Publication & Distribution
475 Riverside Drive, New York 27, N. Y.

NATIONAL COUNCIL OF THE CHURCHES OF CHRIST
IN THE U.S.A.

Price ■

EO6-10   Printed in U.S.A.

The Mexican American

An Arno Press Collection

Castañeda, Alfredo, et al, eds. **Mexican Americans and Educational Change.** 1974
Church Views of the Mexican American. 1974
Clinchy, Everett Ross, Jr. **Equality of Opportunity for Latin-Americans in Texas.** 1974
Crichton, Kyle S. **Law and Order Ltd.** 1928
Education and the Mexican American. 1974
Fincher, E. B. **Spanish-Americans as a Political Factor in New Mexico, 1912-1950.** 1974
Greenwood, Robert. **The California Outlaw:** Tiburcio Vasquez. 1960
Juan N. Cortina: Two Interpretations. 1974
Kibbe, Pauline R. **Latin Americans in Texas.** 1946
The Mexican American and the Law. 1974
Mexican American Bibliographies. 1974
Mexican Labor in the United States. 1974
The New Mexican Hispano. 1974
Otero, Miguel Antonio. **Otero:** An Autobiographical Trilogy. 1935/39/40
The Penitentes of New Mexico. 1974
Perales, Alonso S. **Are We Good Neighbors?** 1948
Perspectives on Mexican-American Life. 1974
Simmons, Ozzie G. **Anglo-Americans and Mexican Americans in South Texas.** 1974
Spanish and Mexican Land Grants. 1974
Tuck, Ruth D. **Not With the Fist.** 1946
Zeleny, Carolyn. **Relations Between the Spanish-Americans and Anglo-Americans in New Mexico.** 1974